THE ATTORNEY'S HANDBOOK
on
CONSUMER BANKRUPTCY
and
CHAPTER 13

JOHN H. WILLIAMSON
Attorney at Law

ARGYLE PUBLISHING COMPANY
Lakewood, Colorado

Other law books by John H. Williamson:

The Attorney's Handbook on Small Business Reorganization Under Chapter 11

The Attorney's Handbook on Drinking Driving Defense

Handbook on The Law of Small Business Enterprises

Seventeenth Edition, 1993

**Supplements updating this handbook are published
periodically, and a new edition is published annually.**

ISBN 1-880730-04-9

Published and Distributed by
ARGYLE PUBLISHING COMPANY

10395 West Colfax Avenue
Lakewood, Colorado 80215
(Telephone: 1-800-955-4569)
(Fax: 303-237-2617)

Printed in the United States of America

CONTENTS

CHAPTER ONE

ADVISING A CONSUMER DEBTOR

CHAPTER TWO

LIQUIDATION UNDER CHAPTER 7

EXHIBITS FOR CHAPTER TWO

CHAPTER THREE

ADJUSTMENT OF DEBTS UNDER CHAPTER 13

CHAPTER FOUR

FAMILY FARMER BANKRUPTCIES UNDER CHAPTER 12

EXHIBITS FOR CHAPTER FOUR

APPENDIXES

INTRODUCTION

The Attorney's Handbook on Consumer Bankruptcy and Chapter 13 is designed to serve as a ready reference to attorneys and legal assistants in the handling of chapter 7 consumer cases, chapter 13 cases, and chapter 12 cases. The handbook contains all resource materials needed to handle typical cases of this sort except the local rules, copies of which may be obtained from the local bankruptcy court.

The text and supplemental materials contained in this edition of the handbook incorporate all changes in the Bankruptcy Code and the Federal Rules of Bankruptcy Procedure through January 1, 1993. All changes in practice and procedure have also been incorporated into the handbook, as have the new and revised Official Bankruptcy Forms and other documents.

The supplemental materials contained in the handbook include the following:

1. Completed samples of official petitions, schedules, and statements.
2. Bankruptcy Work Sheets designed for use in gathering data for the filing of any type of bankruptcy case. The work sheets may be photocopied from the handbook for noncommercial purposes, if desired.
3. Samples of frequently-used motions, documents and pleadings.
4. The text of all relevant chapters of the Bankruptcy Code, current through January 1, 1993.
5. The complete text of the Federal Rules of Bankruptcy Procedure, current through January 1, 1993.
6. Complete lists of property exempt under the laws of each state, under the federal bankruptcy laws, and under federal nonbankruptcy law. Each list is current through January 1, 1993, unless otherwise noted.

Chapter one of the handbook contains a brief discussion on advising financially troubled consumer debtors. Included here are discussions of the appropriateness of nonbankruptcy remedies, chapter 7, and chapter 13 for a typical consumer debtor.

Chapters two and three deal, respectively, with the handling of chapter 7 and chapter 13 cases. Part A of each chapter contains a series of questions and answers designed to explain chapter 7 and chapter 13 to persons (including debtor-clients) who are not familiar with bankruptcy law or proceedings. Part B of each chapter deals with the preparation of chapter 7 and chapter 13 cases and Part C of each chapter deals with the filing and handling of such cases. Chapter four deals with the preparation, filing, and handling of family farmer bankruptcy cases under chapter 12 of the Bankruptcy Code.

The handbook is designed to serve as a ready reference in the day-to-day representation of individual debtors in chapter 7, chapter 12, and chapter 13 cases. It is not necessarily designed for in-depth legal research associated with such functions as brief writing. However, the author has attempted to support each legal proposition with a citation of authority that will usually lead the reader to more extensive authority on the subject.

In using this handbook, the reader is encouraged to use the subject indexes appearing on the last six pages of the handbook. Separate subject indexes are provided for chapter 7, chapter 13, and chapter 12 matters. The subject index refers the reader to the appropriate page of test, and the paragraph notes appearing on each page of text refer the reader to the location of the desired item in the test.

CHAPTER ONE

ADVISING A CONSUMER DEBTOR

1.01 Analyzing a Debtor's Financial Problem

Before an attorney can advise a debtor on how best to resolve his or her financial difficulties, the debtor must truthfully and fully disclose his or her financial situation to the attorney. Unaided, most consumer debtors are unable or unwilling to recite every relevant detail of their financial situation to an attorney. It is the attorney's task, then, to ask the appropriate questions necessary to obtain the information from the debtor. The preliminary information needed to intelligently analyze a typical debtor's financial problem includes the following:

(1) The number of debts owed by the debtor.

(2) The approximate total dollar amount of all debts owed by the debtor.

(3) A brief description of each significant debt sufficient to determine whether it is dischargeable, whether it is secured, and whether there are codebtors.

(4) The debtor's attitude toward each significant debt (i.e., whether the debtor wishes to repay it, discharge it, etc.).

(5) A brief description of the debtor's significant assets and the extent to which each constitutes security for a debt.

(6) Whether foreclosures, repossessions, garnishments, attachments, or other actions that may require immediate bankruptcy relief have been initiated or threatened against the debtor or the debtor's property, and if so, by whom.

(7) The debtor's periodic income from all sources.

In most cases the above information should enable the attorney to propose an appropriate remedy for a typical consumer debtor. The remedies available to most consumer debtors include: (1) determining the debtor's liability for a significant debt, (2) an out-of-court agreement with the debtor's creditors, (3) filing a proceeding under chapter 7 of the Bankruptcy Code, and (4) filing a proceeding under chapter 13 of the Bankruptcy Code, or, if the debtor is a farmer, under chapter 12 of the Bankruptcy Code.

For some consumer debtors, refinancing may also be an alternative. However, for most consumer debtors who have reached the point of consulting an attorney regarding their financial problem, refinancing is not a viable alternative.

1

1.02 The Nonbankruptcy Alternatives

For most financially-troubled consumer debtors the only nonbankruptcy alternatives are: (1) determining the debtor's liability for a significant debt, and (2) a formal or informal out-of-court agreement with creditors for the repayment of all or a portion of the debtor's debts. Determining the debtor's liability for a significant debt may be necessary if the debtor's financial crisis is caused by one or two large debts, such as a substantial child support obligation, an unliquidated claim for personal injury or breach of contract, or a large medical bill. In such instances the debtor is likely to need independent representation or advisement on the claim giving rise to the debt, rather than debt relief in general.

For a debtor who needs general debt relief, an out-of-court agreement with creditors offers the great advantage of avoiding the stigma of bankruptcy. If such an agreement is simple and easy to negotiate, it may also be less expensive to the debtor than a bankruptcy proceeding. The principal disadvantage of such an agreement is that dissenting creditors cannot be bound thereunder and a single hostile creditor can often scuttle an otherwise workable agreement. Also, if the creditors are too numerous or geographically widespread, it may be logistically difficult to consummate an agreement. Finally, there is no way to prevent adverse creditor action while such an agreement is being negotiated.

An agreement with creditors is most likely to be feasible when there are only a few creditors, when most major creditors are unsecured and located in the same geographical area, when the debtor has sufficient income or assets with which to make realistic payments to creditors, and when the debtor does not need the emergency relief provided by the automatic stay in bankruptcy proceedings.

The best method of notifying creditors of a debtor's desire to negotiate an out-of-court agreement is by telephone. If the creditors are so numerous that telephoning is not practicable, an agreement with creditors is probably not practicable either. The agreement should be negotiated quickly because it is usually necessary to disclose the debtor's nonexempt assets to creditors, and delays may give hostile or aggressive creditors an opportunity or excuse to proceed against the assets.

When negotiating with creditors it is important to understand that it is not legally necessary to treat all creditors alike. Even creditors with identical claims can be treated differently. Some creditors may prefer to take substantially less than 100 cents on the dollar in return for early payment, while others may prefer to collect all or most of their claims over an extended period. However, the agreement will disclose each creditor's terms, and large discrepancies in creditor treatment may cause negotiation difficulties. A useful negotiating device is to compute the chapter 7 liquidation value of the debtor's estate and prorate it among the creditors so that each unsecured creditor will know what it would receive should the debtor file under chapter 7.

An agreement with creditors may be drafted so that the debtor makes payments directly to each creditor, or so that the debtor makes payments to a disbursing agent, who, in turn, makes the disbursements to creditors. Much depends upon the number of creditors and the preferences of the parties. If a disbursing agent is appointed, it is a better practice to appoint someone other than the debtor's attorney to perform this task: a major creditor or a bank are likely candidates. A sample Agreement With Creditors is set forth in Exhibit 1-A at the end of this chapter.

1.03 Chapter 7 vs. Chapter 13

If the nonbankruptcy alternatives are not feasible, most consumer debtors must choose between a liquidation proceeding under chapter 7 of the Bankruptcy Code and a debt adjustment proceeding under chapter 13 of the Bankruptcy Code. A brief description of a chapter 7 case is set forth in section 2.01, infra, and a brief description of a chapter 13 case is set forth in section 3.01, infra. These sections should be consulted if the reader is unfamiliar with such proceedings.

The following factors should be considered in determining whether chapter 7 or chapter 13 is more appropriate for a consumer debtor:

(1) **The dischargeability of the debtor's debts.** There are ten classes of debts that are not dischargeable under chapter 7 (see section 2.17, infra, for a list). Under chapter 13 debts for alimony, maintenance or support, debts for death or personal injury related to drunk driving, debts for criminal restitution, most debts for student loans, debts not covered by the plan, and installment debts maturing after the close of the plan are not dischargeable. If a debtor has substantial debts that are dischargeable under chapter 13 and nondischargeable under chapter 7, chapter 13 is likely to be preferable to chapter 7 for the debtor. The eligibility of the debtor for a discharge may also be a factor to consider. A person who has received a discharge in the last six years is not eligible for a chapter 7 discharge, but is eligible for a chapter 13 discharge.

(2) **Retaining the debtor's secured property.** A debtor who is in default on an important secured obligation, such as a home mortgage or an automobile loan, is usually permitted to cure the default within a reasonable period under chapter 13 and thereby retain the secured property. The curing of defaults in secured obligations is not normally permitted in a chapter 7 case. However, under chapter 7 the debtor is permitted to redeem or set aside liens against certain exempt personal property (see section 2.12, infra).

(3) **Retaining the debtor's nonexempt assets.** Under chapter 7 a debtor must turn all nonexempt property (or its cash equivalent) over to the trustee. Under chapter 13 a debtor is usually permitted to retain his or her nonexempt property, provided that meaningful payments are made to unsecured creditors. Thus, if a debtor has a large equity in his or her home or other important or substantial nonexempt assets, chapter 13 may be preferable.

(4) **The debtor's income.** In order to qualify under chapter 13, a debtor must have "regular income," which is defined as income sufficiently stable and regular to enable a debtor to make payments under a chapter 13 plan. If a debtor is unemployed or otherwise devoid of regular income, a chapter 13 case may not be feasible. On the other hand, chapter 7 may not be feasible for a consumer debtor who has sufficient income with which to repay a significant portion of his or her debts within a reasonable period because the chapter 7 case of such a debtor may be dismissed by the court as an abuse of chapter 7 (see section 2.04, infra).

(5) **The debtor's attitude toward his or her debts.** If a debtor has a sincere and realistic desire to repay all or most of his or her unsecured debts, chapter 13 is usually preferable. If a debtor desires to repay only one or two debts, the best practice may be to file under chapter 7 and later reaffirm the debts that the debtor wishes to repay. Finally, chapter 7 is preferable for the debtor who simply wishes to obtain a fresh financial start by discharging all debts as quickly and inexpensively as possible.

(6) **The time and expense factor.** Chapter 13 cases normally last from three to five years, with a discharge granted at the close of the case. Chapter 7 cases of typical consumer debtors last about six months, and a discharge is normally granted about four months after the case is filed. In chapter 13 cases, the attorney's fees and administration expenses are considerably more than in chapter 7 cases. If a debtor is unable or unwilling to make meaningful payments and otherwise comply with a chapter 13 plan during the entire duration of the plan and to bear the additional expenses involved, a chapter 13 case may not be in the debtor's best interest. Also, if anything is likely to occur during the duration of the case that would diminish or eliminate the debtor's ability to make payments under a plan, then a chapter 13 case may not be advisable.

AGREEMENT FOR PAYMENT OF DEBTS

WHEREAS, _____, the debtor, is indebted to _____, the creditors, for the debts shown on Schedule A attached hereto; and

WHEREAS, the debtor is unable to pay the debts described in Schedule A as they become due and is eligible for relief under the Bankruptcy Code; and

WHEREAS, the parties desire to provide for the payment of the debts shown in Schedule A upon the terms and within the periods set forth in Schedule A for each debt without the filing of an action under any chapter of the Bankruptcy Code.

THEREFORE, the parties agree as follows:

1. The debtor agrees to pay the total sum of $ _____ on the _____ day(s) of every month as provided in paragraph 2 of this Agreement, commencing on _____ and continuing until all sums required to pay the debts described in Schedule A upon the terms set forth in Schedule A have been paid.

2. The debtor shall transmit the payments described in paragraph 1 of this Agreement to _____, the disbursing agent. The disbursing agent shall promptly forward the funds paid by the debtor under this Agreement to the creditors described in Schedule A in the following manner: The funds shall be prorated among the creditors in accordance with the ratio that the amount owed by the debtor to each creditor under the terms of this Agreement bears to the total amount owed to all creditors under the terms of this Agreement, except that if the amount owed to a creditor is or becomes less than $20.00, the balance of the amount owed to that creditor shall be paid in full. If no disbursing agent is provided for in this Agreement, or if the disbursing agent shall fail or refuse to perform the duties described in this paragraph, the debtor shall make payments directly to the creditors in the manner set forth in this paragraph.

3. The creditors agree to forbear from the filing or enforcement of any actions, liens, or security devices on the account of any debt covered in this Agreement, and further agree to take no action to collect any portion of any debt covered in this Agreement from the debtor or from any other person, for so long as the obligations required of the debtor hereunder are fulfilled, either by the debtor or the guarantor.

4. This Agreement shall become null and void in the event that the obligations required of the debtor hereunder are not fulfilled, or in the event that a proceeding under the Bankruptcy Code is lawfully commenced by or against the debtor. In either event, the parties shall not be deemed to have waived or forfeited any rights that would have existed had this Agreement not been entered into.

5. The debtor's obligations under this Agreement are guaranteed (or secured) by _____.

6. The terms of this Agreement shall be binding upon the parties, their legal representatives, successors, and assigns.

Dated: _____

_____   _____
Debtor   Creditor

_____   _____
Disbursing Agent   Creditor

_____   _____
Guarantor   Creditor

CHAPTER TWO
LIQUIDATION UNDER CHAPTER 7

PART A *
QUESTIONS AND ANSWERS ABOUT CHAPTER 7

1. What is chapter 7 and how does it work?

Chapter 7 is that part (or chapter) of the Bankruptcy Code that deals with liquidation. The Bankruptcy Code is that part of the federal laws that deal with bankruptcy. A person who files under chapter 7 is called a debtor. In a chapter 7 case, the debtor must turn his or her nonexempt property over to a trustee, who then converts the property to cash and pays the debtor's creditors. In return, the debtor receives a chapter 7 discharge, if he or she pays the filing fee, is eligible for such a discharge, and obeys the orders and rules of the court.

2. What is a chapter 7 discharge?

It is a court order releasing a debtor from all of his or her dischargeable debts and ordering the creditors not to attempt to collect them from the debtor. A debt that is discharged is one that the debtor is released from and does not have to pay. Some debts, however, are not dischargeable under chapter 7, and some persons are not eligible for a chapter 7 discharge.

3. What debts are not dischargeable under chapter 7?

All debts of any kind or amount, including out-of-state debts, are dischargeable under chapter 7 except those listed below. The following types of debts are not dischargeable under chapter 7:

(1) Debts for certain taxes, including taxes that became due within the last three years.

(2) If the creditor files a complaint and if the court so rules, debts for obtaining money, property, services, or credit by means of false pretenses, fraud, or a false financial statement (included here are certain debts for luxury goods or services and for certain cash advances made within 20 days before the case is filed).

(3) Debts not listed on the debtor's chapter 7 papers, unless the creditor knew of the case in time to file a claim.

(4) If the creditor files a complaint and if the court so rules, debts for fraud, embezzlement, or larceny.

(5) Debts for alimony, maintenance, or support, with certain very limited exceptions.

(6) If the creditor files a complaint and if the court so rules, debts for intentional or malicious injury to the person or property of another.

(7) Debts for certain fines or penalties.

(8) Debts for educational benefits and student loans that became due within the last seven years, unless a court finds that not discharging the debt would impose an undue hardship on the debtor and his or her dependents.

(9) Debts for death or personal injury caused by the debtor's operation of a motor vehicle while unlawfully intoxicated.

(10) Debts that were or could have been listed in a previous bankruptcy case of the debtor in which the debtor did not receive a discharge.

5

4. What persons are not eligible for a chapter 7 discharge?

The following persons are not eligible for a chapter 7 discharge:

(1)   A person who has been granted a discharge in a chapter 7 case filed within the last six years.

(2)   A person who has been granted a discharge in a chapter 13 case filed within the last six years, unless 70 percent or more of the unsecured claims were paid off in the chapter 13 case.

(3)   A person who files a waiver of discharge that is approved by the court in the chapter 7 case.

(4)   A person who conceals, transfers, or destroys his or her property with the intent to defraud his or her creditors or the trustee in the chapter 7 case.

(5)   A person who conceals, destroys, or falsifies records of his or her financial condition or business transactions.

(6)   A person who makes false statements or claims in the chapter 7 case, or who withholds recorded information from the trustee.

(7)   A person who fails to satisfactorily explain any loss or deficiency of his or her assets.

(8)   A person who refuses to answer questions or obey orders of the bankruptcy court, either in his or her bankruptcy case or in the bankruptcy case of a relative, business associate, or corporation with which he or she is associated.

5. What persons are eligible to file under chapter 7?

Any person who resides in, does business in, or has property in the United States may file under chapter 7, except a person who has been involved in another bankruptcy case that was dismissed within the last 180 days on certain grounds.

6. What persons should not file under Chapter 7?

A person who is not eligible for a chapter 7 discharge should not file under chapter 7. Also, a person who has substantial debts that are not dischargeable under chapter 7 should not file under chapter 7. In addition, it may not be wise for a person with current income sufficient to repay a substantial portion of his or her debts within a reasonable period to file under chapter 7, because the court may dismiss the case as constituting an abuse of chapter 7. Although it is not a legal requirement, some experts say that a person's dischargeable debts should exceed the value of his or her nonexempt assets by at least a thousand dollars before it is wise to file under chapter 7.

7. How much is the chapter 7 filing fee and when must it be paid?

The filing fee is $120 for either a single or a joint case. If a debtor is unable to pay the filing fee when the case is filed, it may be paid in installments, with the final installment due within 120 days. The period for payment may later be extended to 180 days by the court, if there is a valid reason for doing so. The entire filing fee must ultimately be paid, however, or the case will be dismissed and the debtor will not receive a discharge. The fee charged by the debtor's attorney for handling the chapter 7 case is in addition to the filing fee.

8. Where is a chapter 7 case filed?

In the office of the clerk of the bankruptcy court in the district where the debtor has resided or maintained a principal place of business for the greatest portion of the last 180 days. The bankruptcy court is a federal court and is a unit of the United States district court.

9. May a husband and wife file jointly under chapter 7?

Yes. A husband and wife may file a joint petition under chapter 7. If a joint petition is filed, only one set of bankruptcy forms is needed and only one filing fee is charged.

10. Under what conditions should both spouses file under chapter 7?

Both husband and wife should file if one or more substantial dischargeable debts are owed by both spouses. If both spouses are liable for a substantial debt and only one spouse files under chapter 7, the creditor may later attempt to collect the debt from the nonfiling spouse, even if he or she has no income or assets. In community property states it may not be necessary for both spouses to file if all substantial dischargeable debts are community debts. The community property states are Arizona, California, Idaho, Louisiana, Nevada, New Mexico, Texas, and Washington.

11. When should a chapter 7 case be filed?

The answer depends on the status of the debtor's dischargeable debts, the nature and status of the debtor's nonexempt assets, and the actions taken or threatened to be taken by the debtor's creditors. The following rules should be followed:

(1) Don't file under chapter 7 until all anticipated debts have been incurred, because it will be another six years before the debtor is again eligible for a chapter 7 discharge. For example, a debtor who has incurred substantial medical expenses should not file under chapter 7 until the illness or injury has either been cured or covered by insurance, as it will do little good to discharge, say, $50,000 of medical debts now and then incur another $50,000 in medical debts in the next few months.

(2) Don't file under chapter 7 until the debtor has received all nonexempt assets to which he or she may be entitled. If the debtor is entitled to receive an income tax refund or a similar nonexempt asset in the near future, he or she should not file under chapter 7 until after the refund or asset has been received and disposed of. Otherwise, the refund or asset will become the property of the trustee.

(3) Don't file under chapter 7 if the debtor expects to acquire property through inheritance, life insurance or divorce in the next 180 days, because unless such property is exempt, it will become the property of the trustee.

(4) If hostile creditor action threatens a debtor's exempt assets or future income, the case should be filed immediately to take advantage of the automatic stay that accompanies the filing of a chapter 7 case (see Question 12, below). If a creditor has threatened to attach or garnishee the debtor's wages or if a foreclosure action has been instituted against the debtor's residence, it may be necessary to file a chapter 7 case immediately in order to protect the debtor's interest in the property.

12. How does the filing of a chapter 7 case affect collection and other legal proceedings that have been filed against the debtor in other courts?

The filing of a chapter 7 case automatically stays (or stops) virtually all collection and other legal proceedings pending against the debtor. A few days after a chapter 7 case is filed, the court mails a notice to all creditors ordering them to refrain from any further action against the debtor. If necessary, this notice may be served earlier by the debtor or the debtor's attorney. Any creditor who intentionally violates the automatic stay may be held in contempt of court and may be liable to the debtor in damages. Criminal proceedings and actions to collect alimony, maintenance, or support from exempt property or property acquired by the debtor after the chapter 7 case was filed are not affected by the automatic stay.

13. May a person file under chapter 7 if his or her debts are being administered by a financial counselor?

Yes. A financial counselor has no legal right to prevent anyone from filing under chapter 7.

14. How does filing under chapter 7 affect a person's credit rating?

It will usually worsen it, if that is possible. However, some financial institutions openly solicit business from persons who have recently filed under chapter 7, apparently because it will be at least six years before they can again file under chapter 7. If there are compelling reasons for filing under chapter 7 that are not within the debtor's control (such as an illness or an injury), some credit rating agencies may take that into account in rating the debtor's credit after filing.

15. Are the names of persons who file under chapter 7 published?

When a chapter 7 case is filed, it becomes a public record and the name of the debtor may be published by some credit-reporting agencies. However, newspapers do not usually report or publish the names of consumers who file under chapter 7.

16. Are employers notified of chapter 7 cases?

Employers are not usually notified when a chapter 7 case is filed. However, the trustee in a chapter 7 case often contacts an employer seeking information as to the status of the debtor's wages or salary at the time the case was filed. If there are compelling reasons for not informing an employer in a particular case, the trustee should be so informed and he or she may be willing to make other arrangements to obtain the necessary information.

17. Does a person lose any legal or civil rights by filing under chapter 7?

No. Filing under chapter 7 is not a criminal proceeding, and a person does not lose any civil or constitutional rights by filing.

18. May employers or governmental agencies discriminate against persons who file under chapter 7?

No. It is illegal for either private or governmental employers to discriminate against a person as to employment because that person has filed under chapter 7. It is also illegal for local, state, or federal governmental units to discriminate against a person as to the granting of licenses (including a driver's license), permits, and similar grants because that person has filed under chapter 7.

19. Does a person lose all of his or her property by filing under chapter 7?

Usually not. Certain property is exempt and cannot be taken by creditors, unless it is encumbered by a valid mortgage or lien. A debtor is usually allowed to retain his or her unencumbered (or unsecured) exempt property in a chapter 7 case. A debtor may also be allowed to retain certain encumbered (or secured) exempt property (see Question 28, below). Depending on the law of the local state, property that is exempt in a chapter 7 case may be either property that is exempt from creditors under state law or property that is declared exempt in the Bankruptcy Code.

20. When must a debtor appear in court in a chapter 7 case and what happens there?

The first court appearance is for a hearing called the "meeting of creditors." This hearing usually takes place about a month after the case is filed. At this hearing the debtor is put under oath and questioned about his or her debts and assets by the hearing officer or trustee. In most chapter 7 consumer cases no creditors appear in court; but any creditor that does appear is usually allowed to question the debtor. There may be another hearing scheduled about three months later called the "discharge and reaffirmation hearing," which the debtor may have to attend if he or she is reaffirming a dischargeable debt (see Question 33, below).

21. What happens after the meeting of creditors?

After the meeting of creditors, the trustee may contact the debtor regarding the debtor's property, and the court may issue certain orders to the debtor. These orders are sent by mail and may require the debtor to turn certain property over to the trustee, or provide the trustee with certain information. If the debtor fails to comply with these orders, the case may be dismissed and the debtor may be denied a discharge.

22. What is a trustee in a chapter 7 case, and what does he or she do?

The trustee is an officer of the court, appointed to gather the debtor's nonexempt property, convert it to cash, and pay what are called dividends to creditors. In addition, the trustee has certain administrative duties in a chapter 7 case, and is the officer in charge of seeing to it that the debtor performs the required duties in the case. A trustee is appointed in a chapter 7 case, even if the debtor has no nonexempt property.

23. What are the debtor's responsibilities to the trustee?

The law requires the debtor to cooperate with the trustee in the administration of a chapter 7 case, including the collection by the trustee of the debtor's nonexempt property. If the debtor does not cooperate with the trustee, the chapter 7 case may be dismissed and the debtor may be denied a discharge.

24. What happens to the property that the debtor turns over to the trustee?

It is usually converted to cash, which is used to pay the fees and expenses of the trustee and to pay dividends to creditors. The trustee's fee is usually $45 plus a percentage of the amount collected from the debtor.

25. What if the debtor has no nonexempt property for the trustee to collect?

If, from the debtor's chapter 7 forms, it appears that the debtor has no nonexempt property, a notice will be sent to the creditors advising them that there appears to be no assets from which to pay creditors, that it is unnecessary for them to file claims, and that if assets are later discovered they will then be given an opportunity to file claims.

26. How are secured creditors dealt with in a chapter 7 case?

Secured creditors are creditors with valid mortgages or liens against property of the debtor. Property of the debtor that is encumbered by a valid mortgage or lien is called secured property. A secured creditor is usually permitted to repossess or foreclose its secured property, unless the value of the secured property exceeds the amount owed to the creditor. A secured creditor must prove the validity of its mortgage or lien and obtain a court order before repossessing or foreclosing on secured property. The debtor should not turn any property over to a secured creditor until a court order has been obtained. The debtor may be permitted to retain or redeem certain secured personal property (see Question 28, below).

27. How are unsecured creditors dealt with in a chapter 7 case?

An unsecured creditor is a creditor without a valid lien or mortgage against property of the debtor. If the debtor has nonexempt assets, unsecured creditors may file claims with the court within 90 days after the first date set for the meeting of creditors. The trustee will examine these claims and file objections to those deemed improper. When the trustee has collected all of the debtor's nonexempt property and converted it to cash, and when the court has ruled on the trustee's objections, the trustee will distribute the funds (i.e., pay dividends) to the unsecured creditors according to the priorities set forth in the Bankruptcy Code. Administrative expenses, claims for wages, salaries, and contributions to employee benefit plans, claims for the refund of certain deposits, and tax claims, are given priority, in that order, in the payment of dividends by the trustee. If there are funds remaining after the payment of these priority claims, they are distributed pro rata to the remaining unsecured creditors.

28. What secured property may a debtor retain or redeem in a chapter 7 case?

A debtor may retain and redeem certain secured personal and household property, such as household furniture, appliances and goods, wearing apparel, and tools of trade, without payment to the secured creditor, if the property is exempt and if the mortgage or lien against the property was not incurred for the purpose of financing the purchase of the property. A debtor may also retain and redeem without payment to the secured creditor any secured property that is both exempt and subject only to a judgment lien. Finally, a debtor may redeem certain exempt personal, family, or household property by paying to the secured creditor an amount equal to the value of the property, regardless of how much is owed to the creditor. Certain deadlines are imposed on the enforcement of these rights by the debtor.

29. How can a debtor minimize the amount of money or property that must be turned over to the trustee in a chapter 7 case?

In a chapter 7 case the debtor is required to turn over to the trustee only the nonexempt money or property that he or she possessed at the time the case was filed. Many nonexempt assets of consumer debtors are liquid in nature and tend to vary in size or amount from day to day. It is wise, therefore, for the debtor to engage in some negative estate planning so as to minimize the value or amount of these liquid assets on the day and hour that the chapter 7 case is filed. The most common nonexempt liquid assets, and the assets that the trustee will be most likely to look for, include the following:

(1) cash,
(2) bank accounts,
(3) prepaid rent,
(4) landlord and utility deposits,
(5) accrued earnings and benefits,
(6) tax refunds, and
(7) sporting goods.

It is usually advantageous for the debtor to take steps to insure that the value of each of these assets is as low as possible on the day and hour that the chapter 7 case is filed. By doing this the debtor will not be cheating or acting illegally; the debtor will simply be using the law to his or her advantage, much the same as a person who takes advantage of loopholes in the tax laws.

Cash. If possible, the debtor should have no cash on hand when the chapter 7 case is filed. Further, if the debtor has received cash or the equivalent of cash in the form of a paycheck or the closing of a bank account shortly before the filing of the case, the debtor should obtain receipts when disposing of the funds in order to prove to the trustee and the court that the funds were disposed of prior to the filing of the case. Money possessed by the debtor shortly before the filing of a chapter 7 case may be spent on such items as food and groceries, the chapter 7 filing fee, the attorney's fee in the chapter 7 case, and the payment of up to $600 to creditors whom the debtor intends to continue paying after the filing of the chapter 7 case. Payments should not be made to friends or relatives, however, as the trustee may later recover these payments.

Bank Accounts. The best practice is to close out all bank accounts before filing under chapter 7. If a bank account is not closed, the balance of the account should be as close to zero as the bank will allow and all outstanding checks must clear the account before the case is filed. If the debtor has written a check to someone for, say, $50 and if the check has not cleared the account when the case is filed, the $50 in the account to cover the outstanding check will be deemed an asset of the debtor and will have to be paid to the trustee.

Prepaid Rent. If the debtor's rent is paid on the first day of the month and if the debtor's chapter 7 case is filed on the tenth day of the month, the portion of the rent covering the last 20 days of the month, if not exempt, will be deemed an asset of the debtor and will later have to be paid to the trustee. If possible, the debtor should make arrangements with the landlord to pay rent only through the date that the case is to be filed and to pay the balance of the rent from funds acquired after the case is filed. If this is not possible, the case should be filed near the end of the rent period.

Landlord and Utility Deposits. Unless they are exempt, the debtor should attempt to obtain the refund of all landlord and utility deposits before filing a chapter 7 case. Otherwise, the deposits, or their cash equivalents, will have to be paid to the trustee.

Accrued Earnings and Benefits. In most states, and under the federal law, only a certain percentage (usually 75%) of a debtor's earnings are exempt. Therefore, the trustee may be allowed to take the nonexempt portion (usually 25%) of any accrued and unpaid wages, salary, commissions, vacation pay, sick leave pay, and other accrued and nonexempt employee benefits. Normally, then, the best time to file a chapter 7 case is the morning after payday. Even then, if the pay period does not end on payday, the debtor may have accrued earnings unless special arrangements are made with the employer. If annual leave or vacation pay is convertible to cash, it should be collected by the debtor before the chapter 7 case is filed, as should any other nonexempt employee benefits that are convertible to cash.

Tax Refunds. In most states, a tax refund is not exempt and becomes the property of the trustee if it has not been received by the debtor prior to the filing of a chapter 7 case. Therefore, if the debtor is scheduled to receive a tax refund, a chapter 7 case should not be filed until after the refund has been received and disposed of. Even if the case is filed before the end of the tax year, if the debtor later receives a refund, the trustee may be entitled to the portion of the refund earned prior to the filing of the case. The best practice, then, is to either file the chapter 7 case early in the tax year (but after the refund from the previous year has been received) or make arrangements to insure that there will be no tax refund for that year.

Sporting Goods. If the debtor owns guns, fishing gear, skis, cameras, or similar items of value that are not exempt, he or she will later have to turn them, or their cash equivalent, over to the trustee. Such items should be disposed of prior to the filing of the case, especially if they are of considerable value.

30. May a utility company refuse to provide service to a debtor if the company's utility bill is discharged under chapter 7?

If, within 20 days after a chapter 7 case is filed, the debtor furnishes a utility company with a deposit or other security to insure the payment of future utility services, it is illegal for a utility company to refuse to provide future utility service to the debtor, or to otherwise discriminate against the debtor, if its bill for past utility services is discharged in the chapter 7 case.

31. What should the debtor do if he or she moves before the chapter 7 case is closed?

The debtor should immediately notify the bankruptcy court in writing of the new address. Because most communications between a debtor and the bankruptcy court are by mail, it is important that the bankruptcy court always have the debtor's current address. Otherwise, the debtor may fail to receive important notices and the chapter 7 case may be dismissed. Many courts have change-of-address forms for debtors to use when they move, and the debtor should obtain one if a move is planned.

32. How is a debtor notified when his or her discharge has been granted?

Usually by mail. Most courts send a form called "Discharge of Debtor" to the debtor and to all creditors. This form is a copy of the court order discharging the debtor from his or her dischargeable debts, and it serves as notice that the debtor's discharge has been granted. It is usually mailed about four months after a chapter 7 case is filed.

33. What if a debtor wishes to repay a dischargeable debt?

A debtor may repay as many dischargeable debts as desired after filing under chapter 7. By repaying one creditor, a debtor does not become legally obligated to repay any other creditor. The only dischargeable debt that a debtor is legally obligated to repay is one for which the debtor and the creditor have signed what is called a "reaffirmation agreement." If the debtor was not represented by an attorney in negotiating the reaffirmation agreement with the creditor, the reaffirmation agreement must be approved by the court to be valid. If the debtor was represented by an attorney in negotiating the reaffirmation agreement, the attorney must file the agreement and the attorney's statement with the court in order for the agreement to be valid. If a dischargeable debt is not covered by a reaffirmation agreement, a debtor is not legally obligated to repay the debt, even if the debtor has made a payment on the debt since filing under chapter 7, has agreed in writing to repay the debt, or has waived the discharge of the debt.

34. How long does a chapter 7 case last?

A chapter 7 case begins with the filing of the case and ends with the closing of the case by the court. If the debtor has no nonexempt assets for the trustee to collect, the case will most likely be closed shortly after the debtor receives his or her discharge, which is usually about four months after the case is filed. If the debtor has nonexempt assets for the trustee to collect, the length of the case will depend on how long it takes the trustee to collect the assets and perform his or her other duties in the case. Most consumer cases with assets last about six months, but some last considerably longer.

35. What should a person do if a creditor later attempts to collect a debt that was discharged under chapter 7?

When a chapter 7 discharge is granted, the court enters an order prohibiting the debtor's creditors from later attempting to collect any discharged debt from the debtor. Any creditor who violates this court order may be held in contempt of court and may be liable to the debtor in damages. If a creditor later attempts to collect a discharged debt from the debtor, the debtor should give the creditor a copy of the order of discharge and inform the creditor in writing that the debt has been discharged under chapter 7. If the creditor persists, the debtor should contact an attorney. If a creditor files a lawsuit against the debtor on a discharged debt, it is important not to ignore the matter, because even though a judgment entered against the debtor on a discharged debt can later be voided, voiding the judgment may require the services of an attorney, which could be costly to the debtor.

36. How does a chapter 7 discharge affect the liability of cosigners and other parties who may be liable to a creditor on a discharged debt?

A chapter 7 discharge releases only the debtor. The liability of any other party on a debt is not affected by a chapter 7 discharge. The only exception to this rule is in community property states where the spouse of a debtor may also be released from certain community debts.

37. What is the role of the attorney for a consumer debtor in a chapter 7 case?

The debtor's attorney performs the following functions in the chapter 7 case of a typical consumer debtor:

(1) Analyze the amount and nature of the debts owed by the debtor and determine the best remedy for the debtor's financial problems.

(2) Advise the debtor of the relief available under both chapter 7 and chapter 13 of the Bankruptcy Code, and of the advisability of proceeding under each chapter.

(3) Assemble the information and data necessary to prepare the chapter 7 forms for filing.

(4) Prepare the petitions, schedules, statements and other chapter 7 forms for filing with the bankruptcy court.

(5) Assist the debtor in arranging his or her assets so as to enable the debtor to retain as many of the assets as possible after the chapter 7 case.

(6) Filing the chapter 7 petitions, schedules, statements and other forms with the bankruptcy court, and, if necessary, notifying certain creditors of the commencement of the case.

(7) If necessary, assisting the debtor in the redemption of personal property, the setting aside of mortgages or liens against exempt property, and otherwise carrying out the matters set forth in the debtor's statement of intention.

(8) Attending the meeting of creditors with the debtor.

(9) If necessary, preparing and filing amended schedules, statements, and other documents with the bankruptcy court in order to protect the rights of the debtor.

(10) If necessary, attending the discharge and reaffirmation hearing with the debtor and assisting the debtor in reaffirming certain debts and in overcoming obstacles to the granting of a chapter 7 discharge.

The fee paid, or agreed to be paid, to an attorney representing a debtor in a chapter 7 case must be disclosed to and approved by the bankruptcy court. The court will allow the attorney to charge and collect only a reasonable fee. Many attorneys collect all or most of their fee before the case is filed.

CHAPTER TWO

PART B

PREPARING A CHAPTER 7 CASE

2.01 Chapter 7 - A General Description

Original jurisdiction for a chapter 7 case lies in the federal district court. In most districts, all voluntary chapter 7 cases are referred by the district court to the bankruptcy court, which is a unit or subdivision of the federal district court. A voluntary chapter 7 case for a consumer debtor is initiated by the filing of a voluntary petition seeking relief under chapter 7 of the Bankruptcy Code with the clerk of the bankruptcy court in the proper district. The debtor must also prepare and file, usually with the petition, statements and schedules showing the debtor's assets and liabilities, current income and expenditures, and financial affairs at the time of filing. The filing of a voluntary petition constitutes an order for relief under chapter 7, and an interim trustee is appointed to examine the debtor, collect the debtor's nonexempt property and assets, and administer the debtor's bankruptcy estate. In chapter 7 consumer cases, the interim trustee normally serves throughout the case.

filing of chapter 7 case, general aspects

While the debtor's interest in his or her nonexempt property must be turned over to the trustee, the debtor may retain his or her interest in any property that is exempt under applicable state or federal law. Mortgaged or secured property of the debtor, the debt for which the debtor is in default, is usually turned over to the secured creditor. However, if the debtor has an equity in secured property, the debtor's equity in the property is treated as unsecured property.

chapter 7 case, effect of on debtor's property

If the debtor pays the filing fee in the chapter 7 case and otherwise qualifies for a chapter 7 discharge, the debtor will be discharged from all dischargeable debts. In addition, the filing of a chapter 7 petition automatically stays all actions and proceedings against the debtor and his or her property, except criminal proceedings, certain governmental proceedings, and certain actions for the collection of alimony, mainte-nance or support.

chapter 7 case, relief accorded debtor

The trustee or a creditor may file an objection to the granting of the debtor's chapter 7 discharge within the time set by the court. The most common grounds for denying a chapter 7 discharge are the fail-ure of the debtor to pay the filing fee in the chapter 7 case, the failure of the debtor to obey an order of the court, and where it is shown that the debtor received a discharge in another bankruptcy case filed within the last six years. Also, in order to obtain (and retain) a chapter 7 discharge, the debtor must cooperate with the trustee in the administration of the case, including the collection of the debtor's nonexempt property.

chapter 7 discharge, general aspects

Certain types of debts are not dischargeable under chapter 7, even if the debtor receives a discharge. The most common types of debts that are not dischargeable under chapter 7 are debts for taxes, debts for alimony, maintenance or support, and most student loan debts. Other debts, such as debts for money or credit obtained through the use of false financial statements, are nondischargeable only if the creditor files a complaint to determine their dischargeability within the required time and proves their nondischargeability.

chapter 7 case, dischargeable debts

Unsecured creditors must file their claims within 90 days after the first date set for the meeting of creditors, unless it appears that the debtor has no nonexempt assets, in which case creditors are notified not to file claims. Except for certain personal property that the debtor may redeem or set aside liens against, secured creditors may reclaim or repossess the property upon which they have valid liens, after obtaining relief from the automatic stay and establishing the validity of their liens.

chapter 7 case, rights of creditors

15

chapter 7 case,
court
appearances

       The debtor must appear in court for a hearing called the meeting of creditors, which is normally held about a month after the case is filed. The debtor's chapter 7 discharge is usually granted three or four months after the case is filed. If the debtor is reaffirming dischargeable debts, he or she may have to appear in court for the discharge and reaffirmation hearing, which is held when the discharge is granted or shortly thereafter. The chapter 7 case of a typical consumer debtor is closed about six months after the case is filed, or earlier if the debtor has no nonexempt assets.

title 11 cases,
procedure and
jurisdiction

core
proceedings,
what
constitutes

       As indicated above, the bankruptcy court is a unit of the federal district court. Each district court may provide that any or all title 11 cases and any or all proceedings arising under title 11 or in title 11 cases shall be referred to the bankruptcy judges in the district. See 28 U.S.C. 157(a). In most districts, all voluntary chapter 7 cases are referred to the bankruptcy judges by the district court. Thereafter, the bankruptcy judges may hear and determine the referred title 11 cases and all core proceedings arising in such cases, and may enter final judgments and orders in such matters. See 28 U.S.C. 157(b)(1). Core proceedings are those proceedings necessarily involved in the administration of a title 11 case, and include practically all matters arising in a typical chapter 7 consumer case. See 28 U.S.C. 157(b)(2) for a list of proceedings included as core proceedings. It is left to the bankruptcy judge to determine, either on its own motion or on the motion of a party, whether a proceeding is core or non-core. Unless the parties agree otherwise, only the district court may issue a final order or judgment in a non-core proceeding. See 28 U.S.C. 157(b)(3). The district court may, for cause, withdraw any case or proceeding previously referred to the bankruptcy court. See 28 U.S.C. 157(d). The provisions of 28 U.S.C. 157 are set forth in Appendix I of this handbook.

2.02 The Local Bankruptcy Rules and Forms

Bankruptcy Rule 9029 permits a local court to adopt rules governing the practice and procedure in bankruptcy cases, provided that such rules are consistent with the Rules of Bankruptcy Procedure and do not prohibit or limit the use of the Official Forms. Copies of the local rules are normally provided to attorneys practicing in the district at little or no charge. Both the Bankruptcy Code and the Rules of Bankruptcy Procedure leave many administrative and procedural aspects of chapter 7 cases to the discretion of the local courts, and most bankruptcy courts have adopted local rules governing certain aspects of bankruptcy practice and procedure. For example, the number of copies of any document required to be filed in a bankruptcy case is left to local rule. Some courts have only limited local rules, and few, if any, local forms. Others have adopted extensive local rules and forms dealing with many aspects of chapter 7 cases, including the initial filing requirements. In any event, it is important to obtain a copy of the local rules prior to the commencement of a chapter 7 case. The local rules will be referred to frequently throughout this handbook. A telephone call, letter, or trip to the clerk's office is all that is normally required to obtain a copy of them.

local rules,
importance of

local rules, how
to obtain

2.03 The Debtor's Transactions With His or Her Attorney

The fees charged by the debtor's attorney in a chapter 7 case, whether paid or agreed to be paid before or after the filing of the case, are subject to the review and approval of the bankruptcy court. See 11 U.S.C. 329 and Bankruptcy Rule 2017. On the motion of a party in interest or on the court's own initiative, the court, after notice and a hearing, may determine whether any direct or indirect payment of money or transfer of property by the debtor to an attorney for services rendered or to be rendered in contemplation of the filing of a chapter 7 case by the debtor is excessive. See Bankruptcy Rule 2017(a).

attorney's fee,
review of by
court

On the motion of the debtor or the United States trustee, or on the court's own initiative, the court may, after notice and a hearing, determine whether any direct or indirect payment of money or transfer of property, or any agreement therefor, by the debtor to an attorney after the order for relief is excessive, if the payment or transfer, or agreement therefor, is for services in any way related to the case. See Bankruptcy Rule 2017(b). If the attorney's compensation is found by the court to exceed the reasonable value of any such services, the court may cancel the fee agreement or order that any payments received by the attorney, to the extent excessive, be returned to the entity that made the payments, or, if the funds or property would have been property of the debtor's estate, turned over to the trustee. See 11 U.S.C. 329(b).

attorney's fee,
excessive amount
disposition of

In practice, the debtor's attorney is required to file with the court (and transmit to the United States trustee) within 15 days after the order for relief, or as otherwise directed by the court, a statement disclosing the compensation paid or agreed to be paid to the attorney in the case. See Bankruptcy Rule 2016(b) and 11 U.S.C. 329(a). While the form of this statement may be dealt with by local rule, it must substantially conform to Bankruptcy Form B 203, which is entitled Disclosure of Compensation of Attorney for Debtor. A sample of this form is set forth in Exhibit 2-A, at the end of this chapter.

attorney's dis-
closure state-
ment, form and
contents

In the disclosure statement, the attorney must disclose his or her entire compensation arrangement with the debtor and indicate the amount paid and the amount to be paid. It should be noted that an attorney's compensation includes not only the direct payment of money, but any direct or indirect payment of money or transfer of property, or agreement therefor, as long as the payment, transfer, or agreement is for services in any way related to the chapter 7 case. See Bankruptcy Rule 2017(b). Any agreement to share fees with other persons or attorneys, except members or regular associates of the attorney's law firm, must also be disclosed. See Bankruptcy Rule 2016(b). If a local form is not provided, Exhibit 2-A may be used as a guide in preparing the disclosure statement, but the local rules should be checked for additional requirements.

attorney's
compensation,
what
constitutes

The amount of compensation approved by bankruptcy courts for attorneys representing consumer debtors in chapter 7 cases varies considerably from district to district and from case to case. Generally, the amount ranges from $200 to $800 for representing a single debtor through the discharge and reaffirmation hearing, although much depends upon the complexity of the particular case. A slightly higher fee is normally allowed for the representation of both debtors in a joint case. While the debtor's attorney in a chapter 7 case is not entitled to a priority claim against the bankruptcy estate for services rendered in representing the debtor, if the attorney performs services of value to the estate, he or she may be entitled to compensation from the estate under 11 U.S.C. 331 and Bankruptcy Rule 2016(a).

It is usually in the interest of the debtor's attorney in a chapter 7 case to collect all, or as much as possible, of his or her compensation prior to the filing of the case because the attorney's claim for the balance of his or her compensation might be held to be a dischargeable debt in the case. The Bankruptcy Code is not clear on the issue of the dischargeability of the fees of the debtor's attorney in a chapter 7 case and there appear to be no reported cases on the issue. However, the discharge of unpaid attorney fees would appear to be unjust in light of the provisions 28 U.S.C. 1930(a) and Bankruptcy Rule 1006(b) permitting the payment of the filing fee in installments after the filing of the case and prohibiting the payment of any attorney fees until after the filing fee has been paid in full. In any event, if all or a portion of the attorney's compensation is unpaid when the case is filed, the safest practice is to have the compensation agreement guaranteed or secured by a nonfiling third party. A reaffirmation agreement reaffirming the balance of the attorney's compensation should not be used because of the obvious conflict of interest that such an agreement would present to the attorney.

The functions performed by an attorney representing a typical consumer debtor in a chapter 7 case are set forth in the answer to Question 37 in Part A of this chapter, supra.

2.04 Interviewing the Debtor - Matters to Cover

It is important that the information collected from the debtor be both accurate and complete. Otherwise, the chapter 7 forms cannot be properly completed and the interests of the debtor will not be adequately served. To this end, it is usually better to interview both the debtor and his or her spouse, if one exists, even if only one of them is contemplating filing. Many times it becomes evident during the interview that both spouses are liable for several of the debts and that a joint petition should be filed (see section 2.05, infra). If the local state has community property laws, it is especially important to confer with both spouses because of the liability of the spouses' community property for the debts of either spouse and because of the effect of the discharge of one spouse on the community creditors of the nonfiling spouse (see section 2.17, infra). Also, it often happens that the nonfiling spouse is more familiar with the family financial situation that the filing spouse.

accurate data, how to obtain

The only proven method of gathering all of the needed information without repeated interviews and telephone calls is to use work sheets, or similar documents, that call for all of the required information without repetition and leave nothing to memory or chance. Some attorneys use an extra copy of the chapter 7 forms for this purpose; others have devised work sheets of their own. The attorney without work sheets will find the Bankruptcy Work Sheets appearing in Exhibit 2-B at the end of this chapter useful. Simply photocopy these work sheets and follow the instructions contained therein, and all of the required information will have been assembled in the order appearing on the chapter 7 forms. It is often helpful to give a copy of the work sheets to the debtor to take home and fill out. Once assembled, the information can easily be transferred from the work sheets to the appropriate schedules and statements by a typist or secretary, using the completed forms found in the exhibits at the end of this chapter as guides.

bankruptcy work sheets, use of

When interviewing the debtor, or the debtors in a joint case, the following matters should be addressed:

(1) **Informing the debtor of the relief available under chapters 7, 11, 12 and 13.** The debtor should be informed of the relief available under chapters 7, 11, 12 and 13 of the Bankruptcy Code because the debtor's attorney must sign a declaration that he or she has informed the debtor of such relief, and the voluntary petition contains a statement for the debtor to sign stating that the debtor is aware of chapters 7, 11, 12 and 13, understands the relief available under each chapter, and chooses to proceed under chapter 7. See Exhibit 2-C at the end of this chapter for the applicable provisions of the voluntary petition and the attorney's declaration, which is in Exhibit B to the petition. The Notice to Individual Consumer Debtor, which may be found in Exhibit 2-S at the end of this chapter, summarizes the relief available under each chapter of the Bankruptcy Code.

other chapters, advising debtor

(2) **The debtor's eligibility for chapter 7 relief.** An individual may not be a debtor under chapter 7 (or under any other chapter of title 11) if he or she has been a debtor in a title 11 case that was pending at any time during the preceding 180 days if - (1) the case was dismissed by the court for the willful failure of the debtor to abide by the orders of the court or to appear before the court in the proper prosecution of the case, or (2) the debtor requested and obtained the voluntary dismissal of the case following the filing of a request for relief from the automatic stay. See 11 U.S.C. 109(g). If the debtor has been involved in a previous bankruptcy case that was terminated during the last 180 days, the circumstances of the termination of the previous case should be examined to insure that the debtor qualifies as a debtor under title 11. If the debts of the debtor are primarily consumer debts (i.e., debts incurred by an individual primarily for a personal, family, or household purpose), the court may dismiss a chapter 7 case filed by an individual debtor if it finds that the granting of relief would be a substantial abuse of the provisions of chapter 7. See 11 U.S.C. 707(b). Cases filed by consumer debtors who appear to have sufficient income to repay a significant portion of their dischargeable debts within a reasonable period, whether in a chapter 13 case or otherwise, are likely to be dismissed under 11 U.S.C. 707(b). See In re Keniston, 60 B.R. 742, and section 2.20, infra. Such debtors should consider filing under chapter 13. See section 1.03, supra, for a discussion of the relative advantages of chapters 7 and 13 for consumer debtors.

dismissal of previous bankruptcy case, eligibility of debtor

abuse of chapter 7, dismissal of case for

(3) **The eligibility of the debtor for a chapter 7 discharge.** The conditions under which a chapter 7 discharge will not be granted are listed in section 2.17, infra. The debtor should be questioned as to each applicable condition to insure that he or she is eligible for a chapter 7 discharge. Receiving a discharge in a chapter 7 case filed within the last six years is the most common cause of debtor ineligibility. If the debtor is not eligible for a chapter 7 discharge, his or her eligibility for a chapter 13 discharge should be investigated (see section 3.18, infra).

(4) **The dischargeability of the debtor's debts under chapter 7.** Even if a debtor is eligible for a chapter 7 discharge, the debtor may have debts that are nondischargeable under chapter 7. The classes of debts that are not dischargeable under chapter 7 are listed in section 2.17, infra, and the debtor's debts should be checked against this list. In consumer cases, the most common classes of nondischargeable debts are debts for alimony, maintenance or support, debts for certain taxes, debts for certain student loans, certain debts for "luxury goods or services" or cash advances, and debts for damages resulting from the operation of a motor vehicle while intoxicated. It is also important to ascertain whether any of the debtor's debts have been dealt with in a previous bankruptcy case. If so, it is important to determine how the prior case was concluded and the status of the debts in the prior case. Unless the court, for cause, ordered otherwise in the prior case, the dismissal of the prior case does not bar the discharge of the debts in a later case if the debts were dischargeable in the prior case. See 11 U.S.C. 349(a). If the debts were nondischargeable in the prior case, they may or may not be dischargeable in a later case depending on the reasons for their nondischargeability in the prior case. See section 2.17, infra, for further reading.

(5) **Obtaining the names and addresses of all potential creditors.** In any bankruptcy case it is obviously important to obtain the names and correct addresses of all of the debtor's creditors, because the claims of unlisted or incorrectly listed creditors are likely not to be discharged in the case. See 11 U.S.C. 523(a)(3) and section 2.07 infra. If a claim is unliquidated, if the debtor does not feel morally or legally obligated to a particular creditor, or if the debtor intends to repay a certain creditor (usually a friend, relative, or important business creditor), the debtor will often fail to identify or list that party as a creditor. The debtor should be questioned to ascertain the existence of such creditors. It is also important to discover and list all nondischargeable claims. This is especially true of tax claims, because if the debtor has nonexempt assets such a claim may be paid by the trustee and the debtor relieved of a post-bankruptcy obligation.

(6) **Introducing the debtor to the concept of negative estate planning.** The purpose of negative estate planning is to reduce the amount of liquid assets that the debtor must turn over to the trustee. It is usually necessary for the debtor to take steps prior to the filing of the chapter 7 case in order to avoid the subsequent loss of these assets or their cash equivalent. The concept of negative estate planning is discussed at length in the answer to Question 29 in Part A of this chapter, supra.

(7) **Informing the debtor of the chapter 7 process and of the rights and duties of debtors under chapter 7.** A chapter 7 case will proceed more smoothly if the debtor understands the concepts and procedures involved in the case, as well as the rights, duties and responsibilities of debtors in chapter 7 cases. Otherwise, if the debtor later becomes dissatisfied with the case, he or she will be likely to blame the attorney for any shortcomings. It is suggested that the debtor's attorney reproduce the questions and answers set forth in Part A of this chapter, supra, and give a copy of them to the debtor prior to the filing of the case. The questions and answers contained in Part A, supra, will answer most questions raised by consumer debtors. The duties and rights of debtors in chapter 7 cases are discussed in sections 2.11 and 2.12, infra.

(8) **Making arrangements for the payment of the filing fee and the attorney's fee.** The debtor should be advised that the entire $120 filing fee must be paid, either when the case is filed or within the period set by the court (see section 2.09, infra), or the case will be dismissed and a discharge will not be granted. For the protection of both the attorney and the debtor, there should be no misunderstanding as to either the amount or the terms of the fee to be charged by the attorney for handling the case. If the attorney's fee is to be guaranteed or secured by a third party, or if the fee arrangement is at all complicated, the fee agreement should be reduced to writing and signed by all parties.

(9) **Ascertaining the debtor's need for immediate bankruptcy relief.** Consumer debtors frequently delay consulting with an attorney until one or more creditors have taken steps to repossess, foreclose upon, or garnishee the debtor's property or earnings. If creditor action of this nature has been taken, or if such action is imminent, immediate steps to invoke the relief provided by the automatic stay should be taken. The relief provided by the automatic stay may be obtained by filing the bankruptcy petition and serving notice of such filing and of the automatic stay upon the appropriate creditors and other responsible parties (see section 2.09 and 2.10, infra). The need for immediate bankruptcy relief often depends upon the status of threatened creditor action under local law. For example, if under local law a debtor can redeem repossessed property until such time as the property has been lawfully sold by the creditor, it may be necessary to file a chapter 7 case and obtain the benefit of the automatic stay before the repossessed property is sold by the creditor. If a foreclosure action has been commenced against property in which the debtor has an equity, it may be necessary to implement the relief provided by the automatic stay before the debtor's right to cure the default or redeem the property under local law has expired. In any event, it is important to ascertain the exact status of any actual or threatened creditor action against the debtor or the debtor's property.

emergency bankruptcy relief, necessity of

(10) **Discovering avoidable preferential or fraudulent transfers.** Because the trustee is empowered to recover avoidable preferential or fraudulent transfers made by the debtor, it is important to ascertain whether the debtor has made such transfers. Preferential and fraudulent transfers are defined and discussed in section 2.16, infra. If the debtor has made significant transfers of property or funds to family members, friends, or business associates within the last 12 months that may be recoverable by the trustee, filing under chapter 7 may not be advisable, at least at this time. The existence and avoidability of such transfers should be checked.

avoidable transfers, discovery of

2.05 A Joint Chapter 7 Case

joint petition,
filing fee

An individual and his or her spouse may file a joint petition under chapter 7. See 11 U.S.C. 302(a). Only a husband and wife may file a joint petition under chapter 7, however, and an unmarried couple may not file a joint petition even if they are jointly liable for all or most of the debts, own property together, and live as husband and wife in every respect other than being lawfully married. See In re Malone, 50 B.R. 2.

joint case, how
administered

The filing fee for a joint petition is the same as for a single petition, and normally only one set of statements and schedules need be prepared and filed in a joint case. In most instances, the cases of both parties in a joint petition will be consolidated and administered jointly under Bankruptcy Rule 1015(b), which means that both parties will have their court appearances scheduled for the same time and the same trustee will be appointed for both estates. The local rules should be checked for provisions dealing with joint petitions.

joint petition,
when advisable

Generally speaking, if both spouses are liable for one or more significant dischargeable debts, they should file a joint petition. If only one spouse files, at least one creditor will usually try to collect its claims from the nonfiling spouse, even if he or she is unemployed and has no nonexempt assets. If only one spouse files in such a situation, the other spouse often winds up filing a few months later, thereby incurring additional legal and filing fees. In instances where it is difficult to determine whether one or both spouses are liable for a significant dischargeable debt, the best practice is to file a joint petition if there is any chance that both spouses may be liable for the debt. However, if it is clear that only one spouse is liable for all significant dischargeable debts, a joint petition is not usually necessary. In community property

joint petition,
community
property

states, if all of the debts of one spouse are community debts, a joint filing may not be necessary (see section 2.17, infra). Finally, if one spouse has strong personal or moral reasons for not filing, a joint petition should not be filed.

joint petition,
use of federal
bankruptcy
exemptions

If the laws of the local state permit (i.e., do not preclude) the use of the federal bankruptcy exemptions, both parties in a joint case must use either the federal bankruptcy exemptions or the state and non-bankruptcy federal exemptions. See 11 U.S.C. 522(b), and section 2.08, infra. If one spouse in a jointly-administered case elects the federal bankruptcy exemptions and the other spouse elects the state exemptions, the order of the court directing joint administration of the cases must fix a reasonable time within which either spouse may amend his or her election so that both claim under the same exemption laws. The order must also notify the debtors that unless they elect to claim their exemptions under the same exemption laws within the time fixed by the court, they will both be deemed to have elected under the federal bankruptcy exemptions. See Bankruptcy Rule 1015(b).

joint petition,
when not
advisable

If the above exemption election requirement will impose a hardship on one spouse, a joint filing may not be desirable, although if the parties choose to file separately, they must do so in such a manner that their cases will not be jointly administered under Bankruptcy Rule 1015(b). Also, in certain situations where the debtors' equity in their jointly-owned residence or homestead exceeds the amount of the state homestead exemption, a joint filing may not be desirable. See section 2.08, infra, for further reading on this matter.

2.06 The Chapter 7 Forms

Bankruptcy Rule 1001 provides that the Bankruptcy Rules and Official Forms shall govern the procedure in bankruptcy cases. Bankruptcy Rule 9009 provides that the Official Forms may be used with such alterations as may be appropriate and that the Official Forms may be combined and their contents rearranged to permit economies in their use. Bankruptcy Rule 9029 provides that the local bankruptcy rules may not prohibit or limit the use of the Official Forms.

official forms. use of

11 U.S.C. 521(1) requires a debtor to file a list of creditors, and, unless the court orders otherwise, a schedule of assets and liabilities, a schedule of current income and current expenditures, and a statement of the debtor's financial affairs. A list of creditors is contained in the debtor's schedules of liabilities and need not be filed separately unless the schedules of liabilities are not filed with the petition.

list of creditors. filing requirements

Bankruptcy Rule 1007(b)(1) requires the debtor to file schedules of assets and liabilities, a schedule of current income and expenditures, a schedule of executory contracts and unexpired leases, and a statement of financial affairs, each prepared as prescribed by the appropriate Official Form. Bankruptcy Rule 1007(b)(2) requires an individual debtor in a chapter 7 case to file a statement of intention as required by 11 U.S.C. 521(2) prepared as prescribed by the appropriate Official Form.

schedules and statements. filing requirements

The following forms may be needed in a chapter 7 case for a typical consumer debtor:

forms needed. typical case

Voluntary Petition (Official Form 1)

Schedules A through J (Official Form 6)

Statement of Financial Affairs (Official Form 7)

Application and Order to Pay Filing Fee in Installments, (Official Form 3, if needed)

Disclosure of Compensation of Attorney for Debtor (Bankruptcy Form B 203 or a local form)

Chapter 7 Individual Debtor's Statement of Intention (Official Form 8).

Notice to Individual Consumer Debtor (Bankruptcy Form B 201)

Address Cards or Address Matrix (a local form, if required)

Many districts require additional local forms (such as an informational summary sheet) to be completed and filed in chapter 7 cases, and the local rules should be checked for such requirements. The required local forms are usually supplied by the clerk of the bankruptcy court or the United States trustee, and the local rules often contain copies of them. The official forms must be purchased, usually in prepackaged sets, from a supplier of legal forms at a cost of about $10 per set.

chapter 7 forms. where to find

2.07 Preparing Chapter 7 Forms for Filing

When the proper forms have been obtained and the necessary information assembled, the next task is that of preparing the chapter 7 forms for filing. The forms will be similar to those appearing in the exhibits at the end of this chapter, and it is suggested that the exhibits be used as guides in preparing the forms for filing. If the Bankruptcy Work Sheets appearing in Exhibit 2-B at the end of this chapter were used to assemble the information, the assembled data will be in the order required by the chapter 7 forms, beginning with Schedules A through J and continuing through the Statement of Financial Affairs.

It is important that the chapter 7 forms be properly and completely prepared, both substantively and technically. If the forms are technically incomplete or incorrect, the clerk is likely to refuse to process them and return them to the debtor's attorney for corrections. It should be noted here that Bankruptcy Rule 1008 requires that all petitions, lists, schedules, statements, and amendments thereto be verified or contain an unsworn declaration as provided in 28 U.S.C. 1746. This rule applies only to the original copy of each document. See Bankruptcy Rule 9011(c). Other documents need not contain an unsworn declaration or be verified unless specifically required by a particular Bankruptcy Rule. See Bankruptcy Rule 9011(b).

Bankruptcy Rule 9011(a) requires every petition, pleading, motion, and other paper filed in a chapter 7 case by a party represented by an attorney, other than a list, schedule, statement, or amendments thereto, to be signed by at least one attorney of record in the attorney's individual name, with the attorney's office address and telephone number stated. The signature of an attorney constitutes a certificate that the attorney has read the document, that to the best of the attorney's knowledge it is well grounded in fact, is warranted in law, and is not interposed for an improper purpose. An unsigned document may be stricken unless it is signed promptly after the omission is called to the attention of the person whose signature is required. If a document is signed in violation of this rule, the court may impose sanctions on the signer, including an order to pay the legal and other expenses incurred by any party as a result of the improper signature. See Bankruptcy Rule 9011(a).

Not only should the information on the forms be accurate and complete, but the forms should be consistent with one another. For example, if Schedule F shows a recent automobile repair bill, the automobile should appear in Schedule B, or its transfer reflected in the Statement of Financial Affairs. If a large debt for furniture, say, appears in Schedule F, the furniture should appear in Schedule B.

If a debtor's chapter 7 forms are incomplete or incorrect, the debtor may be deprived of rights or property to which he or she would otherwise be entitled, or the debtor's attorney may later find it necessary to file motions or prepare amended schedules and statements. Also, a $20 fee may be charged for amending the schedules. It obviously makes sense, both professionally and economically, to prepare the forms correctly the first time.

The preparation of each document normally required in a chapter 7 case for a typical consumer debtor is discussed separately below.

Voluntary Petition. Use Exhibit 2-C at the end of this chapter as a guide in preparing this document. The Voluntary Petition, as set forth in Official Form 1, is largely self-explanatory and simple to complete. Each of the rectangular boxes appearing on the petition should contain a response. If the answer to a particular question or request for information is "none," or if the debtor has no information to provide for a particular box, the word "none" should be typed in the box. For example, if a joint case is not being filed, the word "none" should be typed in boxes wherein the name and other information related to the joint debtor is requested. The petition is required to contain a full caption. See Bankruptcy Rule 1005 and Official Form 16A. The information required in a full caption is set forth in block style in Official Form 1 and the form therefore complies with the caption requirements. See Committee Notes to Official Form 1.

voluntary
petition,
preparation of

Special rules are applicable to the preparation of a computer-generated petition. If a box in the petition contains multiple choices, a computer-generated petition that shows only the choice made is acceptable for filing. All sections of the petition must be shown and completed, however, unless the instructions on the official form of the petition state that the box is applicable only to cases filed under a chapter other than the one selected by the debtor. If the debtor has no information to provide for a particular box, a computer-generated petition should so indicate by inserting the word "none" in the box. For example, if the debtor has no prior bankruptcies to report, the word "none" should appear in the appropriate location on the petition. See Introduction and General Instructions to Official Forms.

computer-
generated
petition,
special rules

The completed petition must be signed by the debtor's attorney and by the debtor, or by both debtors if a joint petition is being filed. Exhibit A is not needed in chapter 7 cases for either individual or corporate debtors. If the debtor (or either debtor in a joint case) is an individual with primarily consumer debts, the debtor (or both debtors in a joint case) must sign in the box indicating that he or she is aware of chapters 7, 11, 12 and 13 of the Bankruptcy Code and chooses to proceed under chapter 7. If the debtor (or either debtor in a joint case) is an individual with primarily consumer debts, the debtor's attorney must sign Exhibit B at the bottom of the petition indicating that the attorney has advised the debtor of chapters 7, 11, 12 and 13 of the Bankruptcy Code and of the relief available under each chapter.

voluntary
petition,
exhibits and
signatures

In addition to the Voluntary Petition, a chapter 7 debtor must file some 10 separate schedules (denoted as Schedules A through J), a statement of financial affairs, and in most cases a statement of intention. Schedules A through J are contained in Official Form 6, which must be used in all chapter 7 cases. Schedules A, B, C, D, E and F in Official Form 6 are the debtor's schedules of assets and liabilities. Schedule G is a list of the debtor's executory contracts and unexpired leases. Schedule H is a list of codebtors (i.e., those liable with the debtor on one or more claims). Schedules I and J are schedules of the debtor's current income and current expenditures.

chapter 7
debtor, required
schedules and
statements

The schedules in Official Form 6 should be filed alphabetically and should be preceded by a Summary of Schedules and followed by an Unsworn Declaration under Penalty of Perjury. The order of the schedules (i.e., A through J alphabetically) corresponds to the customary pattern by which trustees review such documents and to the standard format of the accounting profession for balance sheets. The Summary of Schedules must contain a short title caption containing the name of the court, the debtor's name, and the case number and chapter, if known (see Official Form 16B). The individual schedules need only contain the debtor's name and the case number, if one exists. The Summary of Schedules must necessarily be prepared last because it contains information from the other schedules.

official Form 6,
general
requirements

Special requirements are also applicable to the preparation of computer-generated schedules. In a computerized law office the organizational structure of the schedules can be built into the computer program, and the rigid columnar format contained in the printed schedules need not be strictly adhered to. Schedules generated by computer which provide all of the information requested by the prescribed form are fully acceptable, regardless of the format of the printed page. The information must be appropriately labelled, however. In Schedule B, for example, all of the categories of personal property must be printed on the filed document together with the debtor's response to each category. The space occupied by each category may be expanded if necessary so that attachments are not needed. Instructions provided on the printed forms can simply be built into the computer program; they need not be reprinted on the filed document. See Introduction and General Instructions to Official Forms.

computer-
generated
schedules,
special
requirements

Schedule A - Real Property. Use Exhibit 2-D at the end of this chapter as a guide in preparing Schedule A. All real property in which the debtor has a legal, equitable or future interest should be listed in Schedule A. Included here should be real property owned as a co-tenant or under community property laws, and real property in which the debtor has a life estate or a right or power excisable for the debtor's own benefit. However, real property interests resulting solely from executory contracts or unexpired leases should be listed in Schedule G and not on Schedule A. If the debtor owns no interest in any real property, the word "none" should be typed under "Description and Location of Property." If a joint petition is being filed or if the debtor is married, indicate by the appropriate letter in the third column of the official form for Schedule A whether the property is owned by the husband, wife, jointly or, in community property states, as community property. The value of the property appearing in the fourth column of the official form for Schedule A should be the estimated current market value of the property without regards to any encumbrances or exemptions. Only the amount of any claim secured by the property should appear in the fifth (or far right) column of the official form for Schedule A. The creditor's name need not be listed on this schedule. If the property is free and clear and is not security for a claim, the word "none" should be typed in the fifth column under "Amount of Secured Claim."

Schedule B - Personal Property. Use Exhibit 2-E at the end of this chapter as a guide in preparing Schedule B. All interests of the debtor in personal property should be listed on this schedule except interests resulting solely from executory contracts or unexpired leases, which should be listed on Schedule G. When completing Schedule B, it may be advisable to inform the debtor that an intentional failure to disclose assets in a bankruptcy case is grounds for the denial or revocation of a chapter 7 discharge and is a federal criminal offense (bankruptcy fraud) punishable by 5 years imprisonment and a $5,000 fine. See 18 U.S.C. § 152.

Schedule B should reflect the personal property of the debtor as of the time (i.e., the day and hour) that the case is filed, not necessarily as of the time of the debtor's interview with the attorney. If at all possible, the debtor should have no nonexempt cash, bank deposits, household or sporting goods, prepaid rent, accrued earnings, or tax refunds at the time of filing, because such items, or their cash equivalent, will be deemed property of the estate and must later be turned over to the trustee. The results of any negative estate planning required to reduce or eliminate nonexempt liquid assets of this type should be reflected in this schedule. Negative estate planning is discussed in the answer to Question 29 in Part A of this chapter, supra.

In completing Schedule B, something should be denoted for each category of property listed on the schedule. If the debtor has no property of a particular category, an "X" should be typed in the appropriate location in the column entitled "None." Property such as household goods and furnishings, wearing apparel, and sporting goods should be itemized with reasonable particularity (see Exhibit 2-E at the end of this chapter). If property of the debtor is being held by a creditor or other person, the person's name and address should be listed in the column entitled "Description and Location of Property."

If additional space is needed to list or describe a particular category of property appearing on the schedule, a separate sheet should be used. The sheet should be identified with the case name, case number (if known), and the schedule and category number and attached to the last page of the Schedule B. If a joint petition is being filed or if the debtor is married, the appropriate letter should be typed in the fourth column from the left indicating whether the property is owned by the husband, wife, jointly, or, in community property states, as community property.

The value to be shown in the right-hand column in Schedule B is the estimated current market value of the property without regards to any encumbrances or exemptions. The market value of such items as annuities or life insurance policies is normally the refund or cash surrender value of the policy or contract. It may be necessary to contact the debtor's insurance agent or company to determine the exact refund or cash surrender value of a policy or contract. When completing item 11 in Schedule B, it should be noted that the Supreme Court has ruled that the debtor's interest in a ERISA-qualified retirement plan does not constitute property of the estate. See Patterson v. Shumate __ U.S.__, 112 S. Ct. 2242, 119 L.ed. 2d 519 (1992), and section 2.15, infra.

schedule A.
preparation
requirements

schedule B.
property listed
on

bankruptcy
fraud, what
constitutes

schedule B.
negative estate
planning

schedule B.
preparation
requirements

schedule B.
attachments to

schedule B.
preparation
requirements

Schedule C - Property Claimed as Exempt. Use Exhibit 2-F at the end of this chapter as a guide in preparing Schedule C. Before completing this schedule the debtor must elect the exemptions to which he or she is entitled (i.e., the federal bankruptcy exemptions or the applicable state and federal nonbankruptcy exemptions) by checking the appropriate box at the top of the schedule. In a joint case, both debtors must make the same election. See section 2.08, infra, for further reading on the claiming of exemptions.

schedule C, election of exemptions

In completing Schedule C, each item of property claimed as exempt should be described sufficiently to insure the applicability of the exemption law to the property. If the property claimed as exempt is described in particularity in Schedule A or B, it is usually permissible to refer to that schedule for a full description of the property rather than duplicating the description. If a joint petition is being filed, the exemptions claimed by each debtor should be separately shown (see Exhibit 2-F).

schedule C, description of property

Complete lists of all property exempt under the federal bankruptcy exemptions (11 U.S.C. 522(d)), under federal nonbankruptcy law, and under the law of each state are set forth in Appendix III in the back of this book. The property of the debtor as set forth in Schedules A and B should be checked against the applicable lists of exempt property to determine the debtor's exempt property. The value of the exemption claimed in the third column on Schedule C should be the amount allowed by the applicable exemption law or the current market value of the debtor's interest in the property, whichever is less. For example, if the debtor's equity in an automobile is $1,000 (e.g., a $4,000 vehicle that is subject to a $3,000 mortgage) and if the applicable exemption law permits a $1,500 motor vehicle exemption, the claimed exemption should be $1,000. The value shown in the right-hand column of Schedule C should be the estimated current market value of the debtor's interest or equity in the property (i.e., the estimated current market value of the property regardless of the exemption, but less any valid encumbrances against the property).

schedule C, valuation of property, amount of exemption

Schedule D - Creditors Holding Secured Claims. Use Exhibit 2-G at the end of this chapter as a guide in preparing Schedule D. All of the debtor's secured or partially-secured creditors should be listed on this schedule, including those whose claims may result from an executory contract or unexpired lease. Included here should be creditors holding mortgages, deeds of trust, statutory or judicial liens, and other lawful forms of security interests in real or personal property of the debtor. In community property states, secured community creditors should be included if the debtor is married, whether or not a joint petition is being filed. See section 2.17, infra, for a list of community property states. If the debtor has no secured debts, the box appearing near the top of Schedule D should be checked.

schedule D, creditors to be listed on

In completing Schedule D, the creditors should be listed in alphabetical order. If a party other than a spouse in a joint case is or may be liable with the debtor for the payment of a secured claim, an "X" should be typed in the appropriate location in the column marked "Codebtor." If a joint petition is being filed, indicate whether the husband, wife, both of them jointly, or, in community property states, their community property is liable for the claim by typing the appropriate letter in the column marked "Husband, Wife, Joint, or Community." If a claim is contingent, unliquidated, or disputed, an "X" should be typed in the appropriate column. If a claim is only partially secured (i.e., if the amount of the claim exceeds the estimated value of the collateral), the estimated amount of the unsecured portion of the claim should appear in the column marked "Unsecured Portion, If Any."

schedule D, preparation requirements

Schedule E - Creditors Holding Unsecured Priority Claims. Use Exhibit 2-H at the end of this chapter as a guide in preparing Schedule E. All unsecured claims that are or may be entitled to priority of payment must be listed on this schedule. Tax claims are the most common type of unsecured priority claim. The claims must be listed separately by type of priority, and the types of priority claims listed on the schedule must be indicated by checking the appropriate boxes at the beginning of the schedule. Schedule E should be completed in substantially the same manner as that described above for Schedule D, except that the amount of the claim entitled to priority should be shown in the specified column. The type of priority for each claim should also be indicated. If the debtor has no unsecured priority debts of any type, the appropriate box at the beginning of the schedule should be checked. It is especially important to list every qualifying tax claim on Schedule E because most tax claims are nondischargeable (see section 2.17, infra) and it will be to the debtor's advantage if such claims are paid by the trustee.

schedule E, preparation requirements

tax claims, importance of listing

Schedule F - Creditors Holding Unsecured Nonpriority Claims. Use Exhibit 2-I at the end of this chapter as a guide in preparing Schedule F. All general unsecured claims should be listed on this schedule, including unsecured nonpriority claims resulting solely from executory contracts or unexpired leases (which should also be listed on Schedule G) and unsecured claims of codebtors and persons who have cosigned or guaranteed debts of the debtor. However, claims listed on Schedule D or Schedule E that are partially unsecured or partially without priority should not be repeated or duplicated on Schedule F. Accordingly, the unsecured portion of the claim of a partially-secured creditor should not be listed on Schedule F if the claim is listed on Schedule D.

schedule F, creditors to be listed on

The creditors on Schedule F should be listed alphabetically by surname or firm name to the extent feasible. If the claim has been assigned, the name and address of the assignee should also be listed (see Exhibit 2-I). If a person other than a spouse in a joint case is or may also be liable for a particular debt, an "X" should be typed next to the creditor's name in the column marked "Codebtor." If a joint petition is being filed, the appropriate letter should be typed in the column marked "Husband, Wife, or Joint" to indicate which of the debtors is liable for each claim. If a particular claim is contingent, unliquidated, or disputed, an "X" should be typed in the appropriate column. Only genuine or real disputes should be indicated, however, because a disputed claim may necessitate an additional court appearance for the debtor. If the debtor has no unsecured nonpriority debts, the box near the top of Schedule F should be checked.

schedule F, preparation requirements

The exact amount of each creditor's claim should be shown, if possible, so as to avoid the necessity of later responding to the trustee's inquiry should the creditor file a claim for a substantially different amount. It may be necessary to contact certain creditors to ascertain the exact amount of their claims. If the exact amount cannot be ascertained and an estimated amount is shown, an appropriate notation should be made on the schedule. In showing when the claim was incurred, the month and year is normally sufficient. If the claim has been assigned, the name and address of the assignee should be listed in the middle column of Schedule F, unless a local rule provides otherwise. See Exhibit 2-I, infra.

schedule F, amount of claim

assigned claim, how to list

For many consumer debtors Schedule F is the most important document filed because it contains most of the debts that the debtor wishes to discharge. It is important, therefore, that all unsecured creditors, including unsecured community creditors in community property states, be listed on this schedule and that their addresses be complete and accurate. The claim of any creditor omitted from the schedule will not be discharged unless the creditor had notice or actual knowledge of the case in time to file a claim or, if necessary, a complaint to determine the dischargeability of the debt. See 11 U.S.C. 523(a)(3). The debtor is required to make a good faith attempt to obtain the correct address of all creditors, and the claim of any incorrectly-listed creditor who fails to receive notice of the proceeding in time to file a claim may not be discharged. See Ward v. Meyers, 265 Ark. 448, 578 S.W. 2nd 570, and Matter of Robertson, 13 B.R. 726. However, if a debt is duly scheduled and the proper address of the creditor given, the creditor will be deemed to have received notice of the case and its claim will be discharged, even if the creditor failed to receive actual notice of the case. See Jones v. Martin, 23 Ariz. App. 182, 531 P. 2nd 559, and In Re Vega, 15 B.R. 174. If a significant creditor cannot be located, the feasibility of serving notice by publication under Bankruptcy Rule 2002(l) should be considered.

unlisted or incorrectly listed creditor, dischargeability of debt

Schedule G - Executory Contracts and Unexpired Leases. Use Exhibit 2-J at the end of this chapter as a guide in preparing Schedule G. All executory contracts and unexpired leases of real or personal property to which the debtor is a party should be listed on this schedule, regardless of whether the debtor intends to continue performing his or her obligations under the contract or lease after the case is filed. Any timeshare interests to which the debtor is a party should also be included on this schedule.

schedule G, parties to be listed on

If the debtor is or will upon rejection of the contract or lease become obligated to a party to an executory contract or unexpired lease, it is important that the party be listed as a creditor on the appropriate schedule (D, E, or F depending on the status of the creditor under the contract or lease), because otherwise the creditor may not receive notice of the case and the debt might not be discharged. All contracts or leases should be described with particularity. In the case of a lease, it should be specified whether the lease is for nonresidential real property because such leases must be assumed by the trustee within 60 days of the order for relief or the lease will be deemed rejected under 11 U.S.C. 365(d).

parties to contracts, listing as creditors

If the debtor has no executory contracts or unexpired leases, the appropriate box near the top of Schedule G should be checked. In determining whether the debtor is a party to an executory contract, it is important to understand the definition of an executory contract. An executory contract is a contract under which the obligations of both parties to the contract are unperformed to the extent that a failure of either party to complete its obligations under the contract would constitute a breach of contract sufficient to excuse performance by the other party. See In re Adolphsen, 38 B.R. 776. In other words, an executory contract is a contract under which performance remains due by both parties.

executory contract, definition of

Schedule H - Codebtors.
Use Exhibit 2-K at the end of this chapter as a guide in preparing Schedule H. Listed on this schedule should be the name and address of every person or entity, other than a spouse in a joint case, that is or may be liable with the debtor on any debt listed by the debtor in Schedules D, E or F, including all guarantors or co-signers. In community property states, a married debtor filing a single petition should include the name and address of the nondebtor spouse on this schedule (all names used by the nondebtor spouse during the last six years should be listed). If the debtor has no codebtors, the appropriate box should be checked.

schedule H, preparation requirements

Schedule I - Current Income of Individual Debtor(s).
Use Exhibit 2-L at the end of this chapter as a guide in preparing Schedule I. The information listed on this schedule should be complete and accurate because it may be used by the court in deciding whether the case should be dismissed under 11 U.S.C. 707(b) as an abuse of chapter 7 (see section 2.20 infra). In any event, the debtor is likely to be questioned on the information appearing in Schedule I, so it is important that the information be complete and accurate. The column labeled "Spouse" should be completed only if a joint petition is being filed. If the debtor has regular income from a business, profession or farm, a detailed statement describing the income should be attached to Schedule I.

schedule I, preparation requirements

Schedule J - Current Expenditures of Individual Debtor.
Use Exhibit 2-M at the end of this chapter as a guide in preparing Schedule J. Because the debtor may be questioned on the information appearing in this schedule and because the information may be used by the court in conjunction with the information in the debtor's schedule of current income in deciding whether to dismiss the case under 11 U.S.C. 707(b) as an abuse of chapter 7, care should be taken to assure that the information listed on this schedule is accurate. If a joint petition is being filed and if the spouses maintain separate households, the appropriate box at the top of Schedule J should be checked and a separate Schedule J should be completed for each spouse. If the debtor has regular expenses from the operation of a business, profession or farm, a separate statement describing such expenses should be prepared and attached to Schedule J.

schedule J, preparation requirements

Declaration Concerning Debtor's Schedules.
Use Exhibit 2-N at the end of this chapter as a guide in preparing this document. This declaration must be signed by the debtor and by both debtors if a joint petition is being filed. The signatures need not be notarized, verified, or attested, however, and original signatures are needed only on the original document. See Bankruptcy Rule 9011(c).

Declaration to schedules, signatures required

Summary of Schedules.
Use Exhibit 2-O at the end of this chapter as a guide in preparing this document. This document must contain what is called a "short title caption," which means that the name of the court, the name of the debtor (or the names of the debtors in a joint case), and the case number, if one exists. See Official Form 16B. The information required in the body of the document is self-explanatory and should be obtained from the appropriate schedules. Even though this document is completed last, it should appear as the first sheet of the schedules when filed with the court.

summary of schedules, preparation requirements

Statement of Financial Affairs.
Use Exhibit 2-P at the end of this chapter as a guide in preparing the statement of financial affairs. Unless the court orders otherwise, every chapter 7 debtor must file a statement of his or her financial affairs. See Bankruptcy Rule 1007(b)(1). However, in a joint case a joint statement of financial affairs may be filed showing the combined financial affairs of both debtors.

statement of financial affairs, filing requirement

Official Form 7 must be used as the debtor's statement of financial affairs, whether or not the debtor is or has been engaged in business. Questions 1 through 15 in the statement of financial affairs must be completed by all debtors. If the debtor (or one of the debtors in a joint case) has been "engaged in business," questions 16 through 21 must also be answered. An individual debtor is "engaged in business" for purposes of the statement of financial affairs if the debtor is, or has been within the past two years, any of the following: an officer, director, managing executive, or person in control of a corporation; a general partner of a partnership; or a sole proprietor or self-employed person. See instructions on Official Form 7.

The questions appearing in the statement of financial affairs are generally self-explanatory and each question should be answered completely. If the answer to a particular question is "none" or if the question is not applicable, the box marked "none" should be checked. If additional space is needed to fully answer a question, a separate sheet should be used. The separate sheet should be attached to the statement and identified with the name of the case, the case number (if one exists), and the number of the question being answered. If the debtor (or neither debtor in a joint case) has not been "engaged in business," as defined above, questions 16 through 21 need not be answered. If computer-generated forms are used for the statement of financial affairs, it should be noted that if the answer to a question is "none" or "not applicable," an affirmative statement to that effect must appear on the form, and the complete text of each question must be printed on the filed document. Also, if computer-generated forms are used, the amount of space allocated to a particular question may be expanded so that attachments are not needed.

The debtor, or both debtors in a joint case, must sign the declaration on the last page of the statement of financial affairs. The signatures need not be notarized, verified or attested, and original signatures are needed only on the original copy of the statement. See Bankruptcy Rule 9011(c).

Application and Order to Pay Filing Fee in Installments. Use Exhibit 2-Q at the end of this chapter as a guide in preparing this document. Official Form 3 should be used for this document. Both the application and the order are simple to complete. In completing the application, it should be remembered that the filing fee may be paid in up to four installments with the final installment payable not later than 120 days after the date of filing. See Bankruptcy Rule 1006(b)(2). For cause shown, the court may extend the time for any installment, provided that the last installment must be paid within 180 days after the date of filing. The local rules may require the filing of a pauper's oath, or similar document, with the application, and they should be checked for these and other requirements pertaining to the application and order.

Disclosure of Compensation of Attorney for Debtor. If a local form is not provided for this statement, use Bankruptcy Form B 203, a completed copy of which is set forth in Exhibit 2-A at the end of this chapter. See section 2.03, supra, for the preparation requirements of this statement. Unless otherwise directed by the court, this statement is not required to be filed until 15 days after the date of filing in a voluntary case, but to avoid oversight it is a good practice to file the statement when the case is filed. A copy of this statement should be retained by the attorney.

Chapter 7 Individual Debtor's Statement of Intention. Use Exhibit 2-R at the end of this chapter as a guide in preparing this statement. Official Form 8 should be used for this statement. This statement is required by 11 U.S.C. 521(2)(A) and Bankruptcy Rule 1007(b)(2). A copy of the statement must be served on each creditor named in the statement and on the trustee. A certificate of service should be filed with the statement. The statement of intention need not be filed until the earlier of 30 days after the date of the filing of the petition or the date of the meeting of creditors, but it is often more convenient to file the statement with the petition. See section 2.11, infra, for further reading on the preparation, service, and filing requirements of this statement.

Notice to Individual Consumer Debtor. Use Exhibit 2-S at the end of this chapter as a guide in preparing this form, if any preparation is required. Prior to the commencement of a chapter 7 case by an individual whose debts are primarily consumer debts, the clerk is required to give written notice to the individual indicating each chapter of title 11 under which the individual may file. See 11 U.S.C. 342(b). This form is used to fulfill the clerk's statutory function. A local version of this form may be required, and the local rules should be checked in this regard.

clerk's notice to consumer debtor, requirement of

Address Cards or Address Matrix. These documents are required in some districts to assist the clerk or the United States trustee in sending the required notices. The documents should contain the names and addresses of all creditors, the debtor, the debtor's attorney, and all other parties entitled to receive notices from the court. The local rules should be checked for additional requirements related to these documents. The local rules should also be checked for additional documents or forms required to be filed in chapter 7 cases.

address label sheet, preparation of

2.08 Claiming Exemptions

11 U.S.C. 522(b) provides that a debtor may exempt from property of the estate either of the following: (1) the property specified in 11 U.S.C. 522(d) (i.e., the federal bankruptcy exemptions), unless precluded from doing so by state law, or (2) property that is exempt under federal law other than Section 522(d) or under applicable state or local law, and interests in property held by the debtor as a tenant by the entirety or as a joint tenant, to the extent exempt under nonbankruptcy law. Thus, if state law precludes a debtor from using the federal bankruptcy exemptions, as is now the case in most states, then the debtor is limited to the exemptions described in (2) above.

If state law permits (i.e., does not preclude) the use of the federal bankruptcy exemptions, then the debtor may use either the federal bankruptcy exemptions or the nonbankruptcy federal and state exemptions, whichever are more favorable. The debtor must choose between the federal bankruptcy exemptions and the other exemptions, however, and may not use parts of each. If state law permits the use of the federal bankruptcy exemptions, the exemptions may be applied separately to each debtor in a joint case. See 11 U.S.C. 522(m). In deciding whether to use the federal bankruptcy exemptions or the state exemption laws, it should be noted that the federal bankruptcy exemptions apply to any debtor and are not limited, as many state exemption laws are, to certain classes of debtors (such as heads of households).

In joint cases and in individual cases filed by debtors whose estates are administered jointly, both debtors must elect to exempt property either under the federal bankruptcy exemptions or under the state and nonbankruptcy federal exemption laws. The debtors must be given a reasonable period within which to choose the exemption laws to be used, but if they fail to choose the same laws, the federal bankruptcy exemptions will be applied to both debtors. See 11 U.S.C. 522(b), Bankruptcy Rule 1015(b), and section 2.05, supra.

A debtor is required to list all property claimed as exempt in Schedule C. If a debtor fails to file a Schedule C or otherwise claim exemptions within the required period, a dependent of the debtor may file a list of exempt property within 30 days thereafter. See Bankruptcy Rule 4003(a) and 11 U.S.C. 522(l), and see section 2.09, infra, for the Schedule C filing requirements. Because any exemptions not timely claimed by the debtor or dependent of the debtor may be deemed waived (see Matter of Blue, 5 B.R. 723), it is important to list all exempt property on the Schedule C.

If a debtor employs the state and federal nonbankruptcy exemption laws, it should be noted that federal income tax refunds due the debtor are deemed property of the estate and are not exempt under the federal earnings exemption law (nor, presumably, under similar state earnings exemption laws). See Kokoszka v. Belford, 417 U.S. 642, 41 L.Ed. 2nd 374, 94 S.Ct. 2431.

If an exemption is allowed for "household goods" or a similar vaguely defined term, the term should be construed as broadly as reasonably possible so that as many items as possible may be claimed thereunder. For example, the term "household goods" has been construed to include such items as lawnmowers, garden tractors, and power tools used in the home, as well as television recording and stereo systems. See Matter of Beard, 5 B.R. 429. Conversely, the term has also been construed to exclude such items as motor vehicles, bottle collections, and guns. See In Re Norman, 32 B.R. 562, and Matter of Noggle, 30 B.R. 303. The term "tools of trade" has been construed to include a specially equipped motor vehicle. See In Re Seacord, 7 B.R. 121. However, the term "tools of trade" must be construed based on the trade or occupation of the debtor on the date of filing and not at an earlier time. See In Re Rule, 38 B.R. 37.

If a homestead or similar exemption is being claimed under state law, and if the law requires the exemption to be filed or recorded to be valid, the filing or recording requirements should be complied with before the chapter 7 petition is filed. The homestead filing requirements, if any, of each state are noted with the applicable exemption law in Appendix III in the back of this book. The recorded or filed declaration of homestead, or other evidence of exemption, should be properly identified (by recording number and date) on Schedule C. The local rules should be checked for additional filing requirements, especially in connection with the claiming of homestead exemptions.

homestead
exemption,
recording
requirements

If joint debtors must claim under a state homestead exemption law, if the homestead is owned jointly by the debtors, if their combined equity in the homestead exceeds the amount of the allowed exemption, and if local law permits the exemption to be claimed but once in joint case, it may be advantageous for only one spouse to file under chapter 7. Depending on the language of the state exemption statute, such a procedure may enable the filing spouse to report only one-half of the equity in the homestead as an asset in the case and still claim the full homestead exemption. It may then be possible for the other spouse to file under chapter 7 a few months later and again claim the full homestead exemption. The allowability of such a procedure under local law should be thoroughly checked before proceeding, however.

homestead
exemption,
jointly owned
property

11 U.S.C. 522(b) provides that for purposes of determining exemptions, the applicable state law is that of the state in which the debtor's domicile has been located for 180 days immediately preceding the filing of the petition, or for a longer portion of the 180-day period than in any other place. Because the venue provisions permit the filing of the petition in districts other than where the debtor is domiciled (see section 2.09, infra), the situation may arise where the exemption laws of a foreign state are applicable to the case.

exemption laws
of foreign
state, when
applicable

It is common for a debtor to have waived one or more exemptions during the course of his or her financial transactions. Any waiver of exemptions should be checked, however, because the waivers described below in this paragraph are unenforceable in chapter 7 cases. A waiver of exemptions executed in favor of an unsecured creditor is unenforceable in a chapter 7 case with respect to the creditor's claim against exempt property. See 11 U.S.C. 522(e). The debtor's right to set aside judicial liens and certain other security interests against exempt property under 11 U.S.C. 522(f) is not affected by a waiver of exemptions (see section 2.12, infra). A waiver by the debtor of the right to set aside transfers of exempt property or to recover exempt property is unenforceable in a chapter 7 case. See 11 U.S.C. 522(e).

waiver of
exemptions,
enforceability
of

A debtor may claim exemptions against previously transferred property that is recovered by the trustee, to the extent that the debtor could have exempted the property had it not been transferred, if the transfer of the property by the debtor was not voluntary and the debtor did not conceal the property, or if the debtor could have avoided the transfer under 11 U.S.C. 522(f). See 11 U.S.C. 522(g). If the trustee fails to act to recover property that the debtor could claim as exempt, the debtor may act to recover it. See 11 U.S.C. 522(h),(i). The debtor is also entitled to file a supplemental schedule claiming exemptions against property acquired within 180 days after the commencement of the case that is includible in the bankruptcy estate. See Bankruptcy Rule 1007(h), and section 2.11, infra. Finally, it should be noted that if a debtor intends to redeem exempt property under Section 722, the intention must be disclosed in the debtor's Statement of Intention. See section 2.11, infra, for further reading on statements of intention.

transferred
property,
claiming
exemptions on

after-acquired
property,
claiming
exemptions on

Property claimed by the debtor as exempt is deemed exempt unless a timely objection is filed.   See 11 U.S.C. 522(l). The trustee or a creditor may object to the debtor's list of exempt property, but the objection must be filed within 30 days after the conclusion of the meeting of creditors or the filing of any amendments to the list, unless, within such period, further time is granted by the court. The Supreme Court has ruled that the 30-day period for filing objections to the debtor's list of exempt property is mandatory and that the exemptions claimed by the debtor must be granted if an objection or a request for an extension of time is not filed during that period, even if the claimed exemptions are clearly improper. See Taylor v. Freeland & Kronz, ___ U.S. ___, 112 S. Ct. 1644, 118 L.Ed. 2d 280 (1992).

Copies of the objection to the list of exempt property must be mailed to the trustee and to the person claiming the exemption (usually the debtor) and to the person's attorney. See Bankruptcy Rule 4003(b). A notice of the time for filing objections to the debtor's list of exempt property is often contained in the notice of commencement of case (see Exhibit 2-V). The objecting party has the burden of proving that the exemptions were not properly claimed, and the court, after a hearing on notice, must determine the issues presented by the objections. See Bankruptcy Rule 4003(c).

Unless the case is dismissed, the property claimed as exempt by the debtor is not liable, either during or after the case, for any debt of the debtor that arose, or is treated as having arisen, before the commencement of the case, except for nondischargeable debts for taxes, alimony, maintenance or support, debts secured by properly filed tax liens and liens that are not avoided during the bankruptcy case, and certain debts owed to a federal depository institutions regulatory agency. See 11 U.S.C. 522(c).

CHAPTER TWO

PART C

FILING AND HANDLING A CHAPTER 7 CASE

2.09 Filing a Chapter 7 Case

A chapter 7 case should be filed in a district in which the domicile, residence, principal place of business, or principal assets of the debtor have been located for 180 days immediately preceding the commencement of the case, or for a longer portion of such 180-day period than the domicile, residence, principal place of business, or principal assets were located in any other district. See 28 U.S.C. 1408. Thus, a debtor who has resided in two districts during the previous 180 days, must have resided (or have had a principal place of business, etc.) in the local district for 91 days in order to satisfy the venue requirements for filing in that district.

venue requirements, chapter 7 case

If a chapter 7 case is commenced in an improper district, on the timely motion of a party in interest and after a hearing on notice to the debtor and other entities as directed by the court, the case may be dismissed or, if the court determines such to be in the interest of justice or for the convenience of the parties, transferred to another district. See 28 U.S.C. 1406, 1412, and Bankruptcy Rule 1014(a)(2). If a chapter 7 case is filed in a proper district, the court may nevertheless order the case transferred to another district upon a finding that such a transfer is in the interest of justice or for the convenience of the parties. See 28 U.S.C. 1412, and Bankruptcy Rule 1014(a)(1). If a timely motion is not filed, the right to object to venue may be deemed waived, as venue is not jurisdictional in bankruptcy cases. See In Re Potts, 724 F. 2nd 47, and Advisory Committee's Notes to Bankruptcy Rule 1014. Motions relating to venue are core proceedings and may be heard and determined by a bankruptcy judge. See In Re Thomasson, 60 B.R. 629.

procedures when case filed in wrong district

If two or more cases by or against the same debtor are filed in different districts, the court in which the earlier case was commenced shall, upon the timely filing of a motion and after a hearing on notice, determine which case or cases shall proceed. Unless otherwise ordered by the court in which the earlier case was commenced, the proceedings in the other courts are stayed until the determination is made. See Bankruptcy Rule 1014(b).

two or more cases, same debtor, procedures

The number of copies of any form or document to be filed in a bankruptcy case is left to local rule. See Advisory Committee Notes to Bankruptcy Rules 1002 and 1007. It should be noted that a copy of most documents filed with the clerk must be transmitted by the clerk to the United States trustee. See Bankruptcy Rules 1002(b) and 1007(l). If the local rules do not include copies for the United States trustee, an additional copy may have to be filed. If the local rules are silent on the number of copies of a particular document to be filed, the original and two copies of the document will usually suffice.

chapter 7 forms, number of copies to file

The filing fee is $120 for both single and joint cases. The Supreme Court has ruled that it is not unconstitutional to deny a debtor a discharge solely because the debtor is financially unable to pay the filing fee. See United States v. Kras, 409 U.S. 434, 34 L.Ed. 2nd 626, 93 S.Ct. 631. Therefore, even if the debtor is indigent, arrangements must be made for the eventual payment of the filing fee within the time limits set forth in Bankruptcy Rule 1006 (120 days extendable to 180 days), because 28 U.S.C. 1930(a) requires a person commencing a chapter 7 case to pay a $120 filing fee, either at the time of filing or in installments.

filing fee, amount, necessity of payment

voluntary
petition, where
filed
A voluntary chapter 7 case is commenced by filing a voluntary petition with the clerk of the bankruptcy court in the proper district and division. If a bankruptcy clerk has not been appointed in the district, the petition (and all other documents in the case) should be filed with the clerk of the district court. If the case is not being filed on an emergency basis, the schedules, statements, and other documents described in section 2.07, supra, should be filed with the petition.

emergency
filing,
procedure
If the debtor is in need of emergency bankruptcy relief and the case must be commenced before the schedules, statements, and other documents can be prepared, the case may be commenced by filing the petition accompanied by a list containing the names and addresses of all of the debtor's creditors. See Bankruptcy Rule 1007(a)(1). If the filing fee is not paid in full when the petition is filed, an Application to Pay Filing Fee in Installments and Order must also be prepared and filed with the petition. The local rules may also require the Notice to Individual Consumer Debtor to be filed with the petition.

schedules and
statements, when
filed
If not filed with the petition, the schedules and statements, other than the statement of intention, must be filed within 15 days after the petition is filed. Any extension of the time for filing the schedules and statements may be granted by the court only on motion for cause shown and on notice to the United States trustee, the trustee, or other party as the court may direct. See Bankruptcy Rule 1007(c). A failure to file the schedules and statements within the required time constitutes grounds for dismissal of the case. See 11 U.S.C. 707(a)(3). The filing requirements for the statement of intention are set forth in sections 2.07, supra, and 2.11, infra.

notice of
commencement of
case
If it is important to deliver notice of the commencement of the case and of the automatic stay to certain creditors in advance of the mailing of the notice of commencement of case by the clerk, either a certified copy of the filed petition or a certificate of commencement of case signed by clerk (if available locally) may be used for this purpose.

2.10 The Automatic Stay

11 U.S.C. 362(a) provides that the filing of a petition operates as a stay, applicable to all entities, of the following:

automatic stay, proceedings affected by

(1) the commencement or continuation, including the issuance or employment of process, of a judicial, administrative, or other proceeding against the debtor that was or could have been commenced before the filing of the petition, or to recover a claim against the debtor that arose before the commencement of the case;

(2) the enforcement against the debtor or the debtor's property of a judgment obtained before the commencement of the case;

(3) any act to obtain possession of property of or from the debtor's bankruptcy estate, or to exercise control over property of the estate;

(4) any act to create, perfect, or enforce any lien against property of the debtor's bankruptcy estate;

(5) any act to create, perfect, or enforce against property of the debtor, any lien to the extent that such lien secures a claim that arose before the commencement of the case;

(6) any act to collect, assess, or recover a claim against the debtor that arose before the commencement of the case;

(7) the setoff of any debt owing to the debtor that arose before the commencement of the case against any claim against the debtor; and

(8) the commencement or continuation of a proceeding before the United States Tax Court concerning the debtor.

11 U.S.C. 362(b) provides that the filing of a petition does not operate as a stay of the following:

automatic stay, proceedings not affected by

(1) criminal proceedings against the debtor;

(2) the collection of alimony, maintenance or support from property that is not property of the debtor's bankruptcy estate;

(3) acts taken to perfect interests in property to the extent that the trustee's rights and powers are subject to such perfection;

(4) the commencement or continuation of actions or proceedings of governmental units to enforce police or regulatory powers;

(5) the enforcement of a non-money judgment obtained by a governmental unit to enforce police or regulatory powers;

(6) the setoff of certain debts and claims related to dealings in commodity contracts, forward contracts, or securities contracts;

(7) the setoff by a repo participant of certain debts and claims in connection with repurchase agreements;

(8) actions taken by the Secretary of H.U.D. to foreclose certain mortgages;

(9) the issuance to the debtor of tax deficiency notices by governmental units;

(10) any act by a lessor under an expired lease of nonresidential real property to obtain possession of such property from the debtor; and

(11) the presentment of a negotiable instrument and the giving of notice of and protesting dishonor of such an instrument.

automatic stay,
duration of

Unless earlier terminated by the court, the automatic stay brought about by the filing of a chapter 7 petition continues as against property of the debtor's bankruptcy estate as long as the property remains in the estate. See 11 U.S.C. 362(c)(1). Unless earlier terminated by the court, the stay of all other acts continues until the case is dismissed or closed, or until a discharge is granted or denied, whichever occurs first. See 11 U.S.C. 362(c)(2). It should be noted that if a discharge is granted, it operates as an injunction against the commission of certain acts against the debtor and the debtor's property. See 11 U.S.C. 524(a), and section 2.17, infra.

automatic stay,
relief from

Relief from the automatic stay may be granted by the court for cause upon the motion of an aggrieved party, after notice and a hearing. See 11 U.S.C. 362(d), Bankruptcy Rule 4001(a)(1), and section 4.06, infra. Motions for relief from the stay filed by secured creditors seeking to reclaim or foreclose on their collateral is the most common type of relief from the stay sought in chapter 7 consumer cases. Ex parte relief from the automatic stay may also be granted upon a showing of immediate and irreparable damage to the moving party. See Bankruptcy Rule 4001(a)(2) and 11 U.S.C. 362(f).

relief from
stay, right of
debtor

In chapter 7 consumer cases, secured creditors often seek to reclaim or foreclose on their collateral. To do this, they must file a motion for relief from the automatic stay under Bankruptcy Rules 4001(a) and 9014 and pay a $60 filing fee. If the secured property is exempt or abandoned property which the debtor has a right to redeem under 11 U.S.C. 722, exempt property against which the debtor may set aside a lien or security interest under 11 U.S.C. 522(f), or exempt property in which the creditor's security interest has not been perfected, the debtor should oppose the motion for relief from stay. See section 2.12, infra, for further reading on the Section 722 and Section 522(f) rights of the debtor. Especially if the secured property has little market value, it may be possible to negotiate such matters with the creditor, even if the creditor's security interest in the property is valid.

secured
property, duties
of debtor

If the debtor has an interest (i.e., an equity) in the property sought to be reclaimed or foreclosed on by the creditor, notice of the motion for relief from the stay must be served on the debtor and the debtor's attorney. See Bankruptcy Rule 9014. However, if the property sought to be reclaimed is nonexempt property and has not been abandoned by the trustee, the motion for relief will normally involve the debtor only to the extent that the debtor must be advised of the outcome of the motion so as to know whether to turn the property over to the trustee or the creditor. Secured property should not be turned over to a creditor unless and until an order to that effect has been issued.

violation of
automatic stay,
damages for

Any creditor action in violation of the automatic stay is voidable at the request of the trustee or the debtor. See Matter of Lee, 35 B.R. 452. An individual debtor injured by a willful violation of the automatic stay may recover actual damages, including costs and attorney's fees, from the party violating the stay, and, under appropriate circumstances, punitive damages may also be recovered. See 11 U.S.C. 362(h).

2.11 Duties of the Debtor

The duties of the debtor in a typical chapter 7 case are set forth below:

duties of debtor
in chapter 7
case

(1) The debtor must file, unless the court orders otherwise, schedules of assets and liabilities, a schedule of current income and current expenditures, a schedule of executory contracts and unexpired leases, and a statement of financial affairs. See Bankruptcy Rule 1007(b) and 11 U.S.C. 521(1). These documents are usually filed with the petition in consumer cases. If not, they must be filed within 15 days thereafter. See Bankruptcy Rule 1007(c).

(2) If the debtor has consumer debts secured by nonexempt property, the debtor must file within the prescribed period a statement of the debtor's intention with respect to such property and carry out the specified intentions within 45 days thereafter. See 11 U.S.C. 521(2). This duty is discussed below in this section.

(3) The debtor must attend the meeting of creditors and must submit to an examination under oath at the times ordered by the court. See Bankruptcy Rule 4002 and 11 U.S.C. 343.

(4) The debtor must attend the hearing on any complaint filed objecting to the debtor's discharge and must testify if called as a witness. See Bankruptcy Rule 4002.

(5) If a schedule of property has not been filed, the debtor must immediately inform the trustee in writing of the location of any real property in which the debtor has an interest and of the name and address of every person holding money or property subject to the debtor's withdrawal or order. See Bankruptcy Rule 4002.

(6) The debtor must surrender to the trustee all property of the bankruptcy estate and any recorded information, including books, documents, records, and papers, relating to such property. See 11 U.S.C. 521(4).

(7) The debtor must cooperate with the trustee to the extent necessary to enable the trustee to perform his or her duties. See 11 U.S.C. 521(3) and Bankruptcy Rule 4002.

(8) The debtor must appear at the discharge and reaffirmation hearing, if one is held. See 11 U.S.C. 521(5), 524(d), Bankruptcy Rule 4008, and section 2.18, infra.

(9) Within the prescribed period, the debtor must file a supplemental schedule with respect to any property that the debtor acquires or becomes entitled to acquire, within 180 days after the filing of the petition, by bequest, devise or inheritance, as a result of a divorce or property settlement agreement with the debtor's spouse, or as a beneficiary of a life insurance policy or death benefit plan. This duty continues even if the case is closed. See Bankruptcy Rule 1007(h), 11 U.S.C. 541(a)(5), and section 2.15, infra.

(10) The debtor must pay the balance of the filing fee, if any, that was not paid when the petition was filed. See 28 U.S.C. 1930(a) and Bankruptcy Rule 1017(b). Otherwise the case will be dismissed (see section 2.20, infra).

(11) The debtor must file a statement with the court showing any change of the debtor's address. See Bankruptcy Rule 4002.

(12) The debtor must comply with all lawful orders of the bankruptcy court. See 11 U.S.C. 727(a)(6),(d)(3).

The debtor should be advised of these duties, which, of course, do not end with the filing of the statements and schedules, nor with the meeting of creditors, nor even with the issuance of a chapter 7 discharge. A failure of the debtor to perform the required duties may result in the dismissal of the case or a denial or revocation of the debtor's discharge. See Bankruptcy Rule 1017 and 11 U.S.C. 707, 727(a),(d). While a failure to keep the court advised of the debtor's current mailing address may not in itself constitute sufficient grounds for dismissal of the case or a denial or revocation of the debtor's discharge, it may result in the failure of the debtor to obey a court order or cooperate with the trustee, because communications with the debtor are normally carried out by mail. The local rules may contain additional duties for a chapter 7 debtor, and they should be checked in this regard.

duties of debtor
effect of
failure to
perform

incorrect
address of
debtor,
effect of

If the debtor's schedules of assets and liabilities include consumer debts secured by property of the bankruptcy estate, the debtor must file with the clerk a written statement of the debtor's intention with respect to the retention or surrender of the secured property, specifying whether the debtor intends to redeem the property from the lien, reaffirm the debt secured by the property, claim the property as exempt, or surrender the property. See 11 U.S.C. 521(2)(A). Property of the bankruptcy estate is generally nonexempt property owned by the debtor in which the debtor has an equity. See 11 U.S.C.
541(a) and section 2.15, infra. A consumer debt is a debt incurred primarily for a personal, family, or household purpose. See 11 U.S.C. 101(8).

The debtor must file a statement of intention using Official Form 8 within 30 days after the date of filing of the chapter 7 petition or by the date of the meeting of creditors, whichever is earlier, unless the court, for cause and within such period, grants additional time within which to file the statement. See 11 U.S.C. 521(2)(A). A copy of the statement of intention must be served on the trustee and on the creditors named in the statement on or before the date when the statement is filed with the clerk. See Bankruptcy Rule 1007(b)(2). Unless the local rules provided otherwise, the statement of intention may be served on the trustee and creditors by mail, in which event an appropriate certificate of service by mail should be filed with the statement. A sample Statement of Intention is set forth in Exhibit 2-R, at the end of this chapter.

The debtor is required to perform the intentions with respect to secured property as specified in the statement of intention within 45 days after the statement is filed, unless the court, for cause and within the 45 day period, grants additional time. See 11 U.S.C. 521(2)(B). Amendments to the statement of intention are governed by Bankruptcy Rule 1009(b), which provides that the statement may be amended by the debtor at any time before the expiration of the time for performing the intentions and that notice of any amendment must be given to the trustee and any entity affected thereby.

For debtors with consumer debts secured by property of the bankruptcy estate, the filing of a statement of intention, as well as the carrying out of such intentions, constitutes an important aspect of a chapter 7 case. If the statement is not properly filed, the debtor may lose property that he or she would otherwise be entitled to retain, or the case may be dismissed for cause, because the duty to file such a statement is mandatory if the debtor's schedules of assets and liabilities reflect the presence of consumer debts secured by property of the bankruptcy estate. See 11 U.S.C. 521(2), 707(a). Thus, a statement of intention must be filed even if the debtor intends merely to surrender the property to a creditor or the trustee. A failure to carry out the intentions specified in the statement of intention may result in either the loss of the property or the dismissal of the case for cause, as one of the duties of the trustee is to ensure that the debtor performs the intentions specified in the statement. See 11 U.S.C. 704(3), 707(a).

The debtor's conduct should be appropriate during any court appearance, as bankruptcy judges have contempt powers. Contempt committed in the presence of a bankruptcy judge may be determined summarily by the bankruptcy judge, and the order of contempt must recite the facts, be signed by the bankruptcy judge, and be entered of record. See Bankruptcy Rule 9020(a). Other contempt committed in the case may be determined by the bankruptcy judge only after a hearing on notice. See Bankruptcy Rule 9020(b). An order of contempt entered by a bankruptcy judge is effective 10 days after a copy thereof is served on the person named in the order unless an objection is filed, in which case the order must be reviewed by the district court under Bankruptcy Rule 9033. See Bankruptcy Rule 9020(c).

2.12 Rights of the Debtor

The rights of a debtor in a chapter 7 case include the following:

rights of debtor in chapter 7 case

(1) The right to redeem certain exempt or abandoned property from liens. See 11 U.S.C. 722 and 11 U.S.C. 506(d). This right is discussed below in this section.

(2) The right to set aside judicial liens against exempt property, nonpossessory, nonpurchase-money security interests against certain exempt personal property, and unsecured liens. See 11 U.S.C. 522(f) and 11 U.S.C. 506(d). This right is discussed below in this section.

(3) The right to continued service from a utility company if a debt owed by the debtor to the utility for service rendered before the commencement of a chapter 7 case is not paid when due (i.e., is discharged). To retain this right, however, the debtor must, within 20 days of the date of the filing of the case, furnish adequate assurance of payment for future services in the form of a deposit or other security, the amount of which may be modified by the court if so requested. See 11 U.S.C. 366.

utility service, debtor's rights to

(4) The right to protection against discriminatory treatment as to employment by both private employers and governmental units, and as to the granting of licenses, permits, and similar grants by governmental units, solely on account of the filing of a chapter 7 case and certain matters related thereto. See 11 U.S.C. 525. This right is discussed below in this section.

(5) The right to the protection provided by the automatic stay, unless relief from the stay is granted by the court. See 11 U.S.C. 362, Bankruptcy Rule 4001, and section 2.10, supra.

(6) The right to exclude from the bankruptcy estate property claimed as exempt under the applicable exemption laws, unless the exemption is lawfully waived. See 11 U.S.C. 522(b), Bankruptcy Rule 4003, and section 2.08, supra.

(7) The right to a chapter 7 discharge, unless that right is lawfully waived or is denied or revoked by the court for cause after a hearing on notice. See 11 U.S.C. 727, Bankruptcy Rule 4004, and section 2.17, infra.

(8) The right to the discharge of certain debts unless a complaint to determine their dischargeability is timely filed. See 11 U.S.C. 523(c), Bankruptcy Rule 4007(c), and section 2.17, infra.

(9) The right to file a complaint to determine the dischargeability of any debt at any time, even after the case has been closed. See Bankruptcy Rule 4007(b) and section 2.17, infra.

(10) The right to certain advisements by the court regarding the reaffirmation of dischargeable debts. See 11 U.S.C. 524(d), and section 2.18, infra.

It has been held that a debtor's right to protection against discriminatory treatment under 11 U.S.C. 525 prevents a state from revoking or refusing to grant the debtor a driver's license, under its financial responsibility laws, solely because a judgment for damages against the debtor was discharged in a bankruptcy proceeding. See In Re Hinders, 22 B.R. 810, and In Re Arminio, 38 B.R. 472.

refusal to grant driver's license as discriminatory treatment

The debtor may redeem tangible personal property intended primarily for personal, family, or household use from liens securing dischargeable consumer debts, if such property is exempt to the debtor or has been abandoned by the trustee, by paying to the lien holder the amount of the allowed secured claim secured by such lien. Further, any waiver by the debtor of this redemption right is void. See 11 U.S.C. 722. A consumer debt is defined as a debt incurred by an individual primarily for a personal, family, or household purpose. See 11 U.S.C. 101(8). A claim is deemed secured only to the extent of the value of the claimant's interest in the secured property (the amount of which cannot exceed the value of the property), and the balance of the claim, if any, is deemed unsecured. See 11 U.S.C. 506(a). In most cases, therefore, the debtor may redeem the property by paying to the creditor an amount equal to the value of the secured property as agreed upon or determined by the court, regardless of the amount purportedly secured by the lien.

redemption of personal property under section 722

consumer debt, definition of

section 722 redemption, necessity of filing statement of intention

In order to redeem property under Section 722, the debtor must, within the required period, file and serve on the appropriate parties a statement of intention stating that the debtor intends to redeem the specified property under Section 722. Otherwise, the debtor may be precluded from redeeming the property. Further, it will be necessary for the debtor to carry out the redemption within 45 days after the filing of the statement, unless the court grants additional time. See 11 U.S.C. 521(2). See section 2.11, supra, for further reading on the statement of intention.

section 722 redemption, when useful

section 722 redemption, method of payment

Section 722 may be useful to the debtor in situations where the amount of the indebtedness greatly exceeds the market value of the secured property. The redemption of the debtor's furniture, appliances, and automobile can often be implemented under Section 722, frequently at a fraction of the outstanding indebtedness. The redemption of property under Section 722 may, at times, be achieved through negotiations with the creditor, often pursuant to an agreement by the debtor to reaffirm a portion of the debt. If court approval is required to enforce a Section 722 redemption, a lump sum payment by the debtor will be required. Installment payments are generally not permitted under Section 722 unless the creditor so agrees. See In Re Bell, 700 F. 2d 1053.

section 722 redemption, motions, procedure

If a negotiated redemption is not feasible, a motion to redeem tangible personal property under Section 722 must be filed pursuant to Bankruptcy Rule 6008. The motion should request the court to authorize the redemption of the property and, if not previously determined, to determine the value of the creditor's allowed secured claim secured by such property. A sample of such a motion is set forth in Exhibit 2-T at the end of this chapter. At a hearing on a Rule 6008 motion, the debtor, as the owner of the property, is normally permitted to testify as to the value of the property. See Rule 701 of the Federal Rules of Evidence and the cases cited thereunder. In order to lend credibility to the debtor's testimony, he or she should be prepared to state the price paid for the property, its present condition, and when and from whom it was purchased or otherwise acquired. Recent photographs of the property may also be helpful.

proof of claim, when to object

If, prior to the hearing, the creditor files a proof of claim alleging an excessive value for the secured property, it may be necessary to file an objection to the allowance of the claim in order to preserve the debtor's right to dispute the amount of the claim. See 11 U.S.C. 502(a) and Bankruptcy Rules 3001(f) and 3007. An objection to the allowance of the claim may be incorporated in the Rule 6008 motion, unless the local rules provide otherwise. In any event, the local rules should be checked for additional procedural requirements applicable to motions under Bankruptcy Rule 6008.

section 722 redemption, abandoned property

It should be remembered that property does not necessarily have to be exempt to be redeemable under Section 722. Qualifying property may also be redeemed if it has been abandoned by the trustee. If the property has little market value but is of value to the debtor, the trustee may be persuaded to abandon it by the payment of a token amount. If the trustee unreasonably refuses to abandon such property, a motion to compel its abandonment may be filed under Bankruptcy Rule 6007(b). See 11 U.S.C. 554(b). A $60 fee is charged for filing such a motion.

redeeming exempt property under Section 506(d)

In addition to the Section 722 redemption rights, it has been held that a debtor may redeem exempt property, including the debtor's residence, from a partially-secured creditor by paying the secured portion of the creditor's claim and avoiding the balance of the creditor's lien under 11 U.S.C. 506(d). See Gaglia v. First Federal S. & L., 889 F.2d 1304. Such a redemption can be accomplished by filing a motion under Bankruptcy Rule 3012 to value the secured portion of the creditor's claim and avoid the unsecured balance of the lien under Section 506(d). Then, by paying the secured claim, which will be equal to the value of the property less the amount of the senior encumbrances against it, the debtor will completely extinguish the creditor's lien on the property. This is a useful procedure for redeeming exempt property from second or third mortgage holders who have little security for their claims. See section 2.17, infra, for further reading on the avoidance of liens under Section 506(d).

11 U.S.C. 522(f) provides that notwithstanding any waiver of exemptions, the debtor may avoid (i.e., set aside) the fixing of a lien on an interest of the debtor in property, to the extent that the lien impairs an exemption to which the debtor would have been entitled, if the lien is a judicial lien or a nonpossessory, nonpurchase-money security interest in any of the following property: (1) household furnishings, household goods, wearing apparel, appliances, books, animals, crops, musical instruments, or jewelry, held primarily for the personal, family, or household use of the debtor or a dependent of the debtor, (2) implements, professional books, or tools of the trade of the debtor or a dependent of the debtor, or (3) professionally prescribed health aids of the debtor or a dependent of the debtor. Thus, under Section 522(f) the debtor may set aside judicial liens against exempt property, and nonpurchase-money liens against the three classes of property described above if the property is exempt and not in the possession of the secured creditor.

avoiding liens
under section
522 (f), general
aspects

If the debtor wishes to avoid a lien against property that is exempt under the state exemption laws, the wording of the applicable exemption statute should be checked. If the exemption law exempts only "the debtor's interest" in certain property (usually household goods, wearing apparel, etc.), a few courts have held that a lien that has existed against the property since the inception of the debtor's ownership is not avoidable under Section 522(f) under the theory that "the debtor's interest" in the property does not include the lienholder's interest and renders the lienholder's interest in the property nonexempt and, therefore, not avoidable under Section 522(f). See In Re Pine, 717 F. 2d 281, and In Re Mc Manus, 681 F. 2d 353 (these cases deal with the exemption laws of Tennessee, Georgia, and Louisiana).

section 522(f),
exempt property,
what constitutes

It should be noted that the line of reasoning followed in the above cases was expressly disapproved by the Supreme Court in Owen v. Owen, 500 U.S. ___, 114 L.Ed. 2d 350, 111 S.Ct. ___ (1991), where the court held that a husband could avoid under Section 522(f) his ex-wife's lien on a homestead that the husband purchased after the divorce, even though the lien existed prior to the date when the property qualified as a homestead under state (Florida) law and even though the wife's lien was recognized as being enforceable against the homestead under state law. In Farrey v. Sanderfoot, 500 U.S. ___, 114 L.Ed. 2d 337, 111 S.Ct. ___ (1991), the Supreme Court held that a husband could not avoid his ex-wife's lien on his homestead under Section 522(f) where the ex-wife's lien was created by the same divorce decree that transferred the ex-wife's interest in the homestead to the husband. It would appear, then, that a lien on exempt property created by a divorce decree may be avoided under Section 522(f) as long as the lien sought to be avoided is not on property that was transferred from the lien-holder spouse to the debtor in the divorce settlement.

section 522(f),
construction of
by supreme court

A principal duty of the attorney for a consumer debtor in a chapter 7 case is to investigate the possibility or necessity of avoiding liens under Section 522(f). If the debtor has property subject to liens that are avoidable under Section 522(f), it may be possible to resolve the matter by agreement with the creditor. If not, it will be necessary to file a motion to avoid the lien under Bankruptcy Rule 4003(d). A sample of such a motion may be found in Exhibit 2-U at the end of this chapter. Proceedings under such motions are governed by Bankruptcy Rule 9014, which requires reasonable notice and a hearing. Some courts have local rules governing motions of this type, and they should be checked before proceeding.

avoiding liens
under section
522 (f),
procedure

If the lien being avoided secures a consumer debt, as it usually does, the debtor must also file and serve on the appropriate parties a statement of intention in order to preserve his or her rights against the property in question. See section 2.11, supra, for further reading on the filing of a statement of intention.

avoiding liens,
necessity of
filing statement
of intention

As noted above, the debtor may also avoid liens, to the extent that they are unsecured, under 11 U.S.C. 506(d). The avoidance of such liens may be necessary to prevent a lien from surviving the bankruptcy case and encumbering the debtor's postbankruptcy property. The avoidance of liens under Section 506(d) is discussed in section 2.17, infra.

avoiding
unsecured liens
under section
506(d)

2.13 The Meeting of Creditors

The United States trustee must call a meeting of creditors to be held not less than 20 nor more than 40 days after the filing of a voluntary chapter 7 case. The meeting may be held at a regular place for holding court or at any other convenient place within the district designated by the United States trustee. If the place designated for the meeting is not regularly staffed by the United States trustee, the meeting may be held not more than 60 days after the filing of the case. See Bankruptcy Rule 2003(a).

In practice, a few days after the commencement of a chapter 7 case, a document entitled Notice of Commencement of Case Under Chapter 7 of the Bankruptcy Code, Meeting of Creditors, and Fixing of Dates is sent to the debtor and all creditors and other parties in interest. This document will be referred to as the notice of commencement of case. The exact content of the notice varies with the type and status of the debtor. If the debtor is an individual or joint debtor with no assets, Official Form 9A will be sent by the clerk. If the debtor is an individual or joint debtor with assets, Official Form 9C will be sent. If the debtor is a corporation or partnership, Official Form 9B must be used in a no-asset case and Official Form 9D in an asset case. A sample of Official Form 9A is set forth in Exhibit 2-V at the end of this chapter. The notices contained in the notice of commencement of case include the following:

(1) Notice of the name and address of the debtor, the debtor's attorney, and the trustee.

(2) Notice of the date the case was filed, the case number, and whether the case was converted to chapter 7 from another chapter.

(3) In an asset case, notice of the deadline for filing proofs of claim. In a no-asset case, notice that there appear to be no assets and that unsecured creditors should not file claims until they are notified to do so.

(4) Notice of the date, time, and location of the meeting of creditors.

(5) Notice of the deadline for filing complaints objecting to the debtor's discharge or to determine the dischargeability of certain types of debts.

(6) Notice that a petition under chapter 7 has been filed, that an order for relief has been entered, and that all documents filed with the court by the debtor are available for inspection.

(7) Notice of the automatic stay and the effect thereof on creditors.

(8) Notice of the conduct and procedure of the meeting of creditors.

(9) Notice of the function of the trustee in collecting and liquidating the debtor's nonexempt property.

(10) Notice of the debtor's right to keep exempt property and of the creditors' right to object to the exemptions claimed by the debtor.

(11) Notice that the debtor is seeking to discharge certain debts and of the creditors' right to object to the debtor's discharge or to the dischargeability of certain debts.

(12) In an asset case, notice of the necessity of filing a proof of claim in order to share in any payment from the estate and of the place to file a proof of claim.

(13) Notice of the address of the Clerk of the Bankruptcy Court.

In a voluntary case commenced by an individual debtor whose debts are primarily consumer debts, the clerk, or some other person as the court may direct, must give the trustee and all creditors notice by mail of the order for relief not more than 20 days after the date of the order. See Bankruptcy Rule 2002(o). The clerk, or such other person as the court may direct, must also give the debtor, the trustee, and all creditors not less than 20 days notice of the meeting of creditors. See Bankruptcy Rule 2002(a). The meeting of creditors is often referred to as the Section 341(a) meeting.

The United States trustee or a designee thereof must preside at the meeting of creditors. The business of the meeting includes an examination of the debtor under oath and may include the election of a trustee or a creditors' committee. The presiding officer must have the authority to administer oaths. See Bankruptcy Rule 2003(b)(1). The examination of the debtor may relate only to the acts, conduct, or property of the debtor, to the liabilities and financial condition of the debtor, or to matters which may affect the administration of the debtor's estate or the debtor's right to a discharge. See Bankruptcy Rule 2004(b). The court may neither preside at nor attend the meeting of creditors. See 11 U.S.C. 341(c). It should be noted that trustees and creditors' committees are seldom elected in consumer cases, and the interim trustee appointed when the case is filed usually serves throughout the case.

meeting of creditors. general requirements

While creditors seldom attend meetings of creditors in consumer cases, any creditor that does appear is normally permitted to examine the debtor, provided that the person appearing is qualified to do so under any applicable local rule. Any examination under oath at the meeting of creditors must be recorded verbatim by the United States trustee using electronic sound recording equipment or other means of recording. Such record must be preserved by the United States trustee and made available for public access for two years thereafter. Upon request, the United States trustee must provide a certified copy or transcript of the recording at the expense of the person making the request. See Bankruptcy Rule 2003(c). The meeting of creditors may be adjourned from time to time by announcement at the meeting of the adjourned date and time, without further written notice. See Bankruptcy Rule 2003(e). If not previously filed, the debtor's statement of intention must be filed at the meeting of creditors. See 11 U.S.C. 521(2)(A), and section 2.11, supra.

meeting of creditors. examination and recording requirements

In many districts written instructions are sent to the debtor, and often to the debtor's attorney, usually with the notice of commencement of case. These instructions often require the debtor to bring certain documents to the meeting. The debtor should, of course, bring the required documents to the meeting, otherwise the meeting may be postponed to a later date, and necessitate another court appearance. Even if they are not called for in the instructions issued by the court or United States trustee, the case is likely to proceed more smoothly if the debtor is instructed to bring certain important documents to the meeting of creditors. These documents may include the following:

meeting of creditors. documents required

(1) Deeds or other instruments of title to any real estate in which the debtor has an interest.

(2) The recorded evidence of the debtor's homestead exemption, if recording is required under state law to perfect the exemption.

(3) If necessary in the case, receipts showing how and where the debtor spent any money received just prior to the filing of the petition (see section 2.07, supra).

In most chapter 7 consumer cases, the meeting of creditors lasts only a few minutes and is quite informal, although the actual amount of time spent at the hearing will often depend on when a particular case is called, because several consumer cases are often scheduled for the same time. After the meeting of creditors, the matters remaining for the debtor's attorney in a typical consumer case may include filing amended schedules or statements, opposing objections to the debtor's discharge, reaffirming dischargeable debts, and carrying out the intentions specified in the statement of intention, including the redemption of personal property under Section 722 and the avoidance of liens against exempt property under Section 522(f).

meeting of creditors. length of hearing, matters remaining after

2.14 Filing Amended Schedules and Statements

If any of the schedules or statements filed in the case are incomplete or in an improper form, the clerk may refuse to process the case until amendments or corrected documents are filed curing the defects. A failure to comply with requirements of the local rules is another common reason for the rejection of filed chapter 7 documents. When filed documents are rejected by the clerk, a notice or form letter is often sent to the debtor's attorney indicating the corrections that must be made before the case can be processed. A failure to file the required amended or corrected documents within the time stated in the notice or set forth in the local rules may result in the dismissal of the case. See 11 U.S.C. 707(a).

Once the schedules and statements have been accepted by the clerk, the need to file amendments will not arise again in a typical consumer case until the meeting of creditors. If the addresses listed on the schedules for any of the creditors were incorrect, the notices mailed to those creditors by the clerk will have been returned to the court by the Postal Service by the time of the meeting of creditors, in which event the hearing officer may advise the debtor's attorney of their return. However, because the claims of creditors who do not receive notice of the case may not be discharged (see section 2.07, supra), it is important that the court file be checked for returned notices, and the debtor's attorney should specifically

inquire or personally check the file in this regard. It should be noted that unless otherwise ordered by the court in a case, the papers filed in a chapter 7 case and the dockets of the bankruptcy court are public records, open to examination by any entity at reasonable times without charge. See 11 U.S.C. 107.

If a notice sent to a creditor has been returned, an amendment to the appropriate schedule should be promptly filed. The fee for amending a schedule of liabilities or list of creditors after the notice to creditors has been sent is $20; provided that the court may, for good cause, waive the charge. No fee is charged for amendments to other documents. In addition to amending the schedules, it is a good practice for the debtor's attorney to send written notice of the chapter 7 case to any incorrectly-listed creditor at the corrected address. The notice should identify the case and indicate the last day for filing claims in the case. A copy of the notice of commencement of the case (Exhibit 2-V) will usually suffice as the notice. The notice should be sent even if the time for filing claims has expired, especially if no dividend will be paid in the case. The local rules should be checked for additional requirements in this regard. If a correct address for an incorrectly-listed creditor cannot be found, service of notice by publication under Bankruptcy Rule 2002(l) should be considered.

It occasionally happens that the testimony of the debtor at the meeting of creditors reveals an obvious error or omission in either the schedules or the statement of financial affairs. The need to file an amended Schedule C, showing revised or additional exemptions is not uncommon, and the need for such an amendment should always be checked whenever an amendment is made to a schedule of assets. In this regard it should be noted that leave of court to file amendments is not required because Bankruptcy Rule 1009(a) provides that a voluntary petition, list, schedule, or statement may be amended by the debtor as a matter of course at any time before the case is closed. However, notice of the amendment must be given to the trustee and any entity affected thereby. See Bankruptcy Rule 1009(a). It should be noted that the statement of intention may be amended by the debtor at any time before the expiration of the period in which the intentions are to be performed and that the debtor must give notice of the amendment to the trustee and any entity affected thereby. See Bankruptcy Rule 1009(b).

When preparing amendments to schedules or statements, only the corrected information need be shown, and it is not necessary to repeat the unamended information contained in the original document unless the local rules provide otherwise. Use Exhibit 2-W at the end of this chapter as a guide in preparing amended documents. The amended documents must be verified and filed in the same number of copies as required of the original documents and a copy of the amendment should be given to the trustee and any entity affected thereby. See Bankruptcy Rules 1008 and 1009(a).

A party in interest other than the debtor may seek to amend a petition, schedule, or statement by filing a motion to amend. After notice and a hearing, the court may order the amendment sought in the motion, and the clerk must give notice of the amendment to the entities designated by the court. See Bankruptcy Rule 1009(a).

2.15 The Debtor's Bankruptcy Estate

Under 11 U.S.C. 541(a), the commencement of a chapter 7 case creates an estate comprised of the following property, wherever located: debtor's estate,
property
included

(1) All legal or equitable interests of the debtor in property as of the commencement of the case, except powers that the debtor may exercise only for the benefit of another and otherwise-enforceable restrictions on the transfer of a beneficial interest of the debtor in a trust.

(2) All interests of the debtor and the debtor's spouse in community property as of the commencement of the case that is either under the sole, equal, or joint management and control of the debtor or is liable for an allowable claim against the debtor or the debtor and the debtor's spouse, to the extent that such interest is so liable.

(3) Any interest in property that the trustee recovers or preserves by avoiding transfers or otherwise.

(4) An interest in property that would have been property of the estate if such interest had been an interest of the debtor on the date the petition was filed, if the debtor acquires or becomes entitled to acquire the property within 180 days after such date - (a) by bequest, devise, or inheritance, (b) as a result of a property settlement agreement with the debtor's spouse or an interlocutory or final divorce decree, or (c) as a beneficiary of a life insurance policy or death benefit plan.

(5) Proceeds, product, offspring, rents, and profits of or from property of the estate, except earnings from services performed by an individual debtor after the commencement of the case.

(6) Any interest in property that the estate acquires after the commencement of the case.

Property of the bankruptcy estate does not include any power that the debtor may exercise solely for the benefit of another entity or any interest of the debtor under a lease of nonresidential real property that has expired before the commencement of the case or that expires by its own terms during the case. See 11 U.S.C. 541(b). However, an interest of the debtor in property becomes property of the estate notwithstanding any provision that restricts or conditions the transfer of such interest by the debtor, or that is conditioned on the insolvency or financial condition of the debtor, on the commencement of a case under the bankruptcy laws, or on the appointment of or the taking of possession by a trustee in a bankruptcy case, and that creates an option to effect a forfeiture, modification, or termination of the debtor's interest in property. See 11 U.S.C. 541(c)(1). 11 U.S.C. 541(c)(2) provides that a restriction on the transfer of a beneficial interest of the debtor in a trust that is enforceable under applicable nonbankruptcy law is enforceable in a bankruptcy case. This provision has been construed by the Supreme Court to exclude from the bankruptcy estate the debtor's interest in a ERISA-qualified retirement plan containing anti-alienation provisions. See Patterson v. Shumate, ___ U.S. ___, 112 S. Ct. 2242, 119 L.Ed. 2d 519 (1992). Property in which the debtor holds only legal title and not an equitable interest becomes property of the estate only to the extent of the debtor's legal title to the property. See 11 U.S.C. 541(d). The estate has the benefit of any defense available to the debtor as against any entity other than the estate, including statutes of limitation, statutes of fraud, usury, and other personal defenses, and a waiver of any such defense by the debtor after the commencement of the case does not bind the estate. See 11 U.S.C. 558. debtor's estate,
property not
includeddebtor's estate,
defenses of

Of special concern to consumer debtors is the provision in subparagraph (4) above dealing with after-acquired property. Within 10 days after the information comes to the debtor's knowledge, or within such further time as the court may allow, the debtor is required to file a supplemental schedule with respect to any property that the debtor acquires, or becomes entitled to acquire, within 180 days after the date of filing of the petition - (1) by bequest, devise, or inheritance, (2) as a result of a property settlement agreement with the debtor's spouse or a divorce decree, or (3) as a beneficiary of a life insurance policy or death benefit plan. See Bankruptcy Rule 1007(h). The duty to file such a schedule continues notwithstanding the closing of the case before the schedule is or can be filed. However, if any of the property so acquired by the debtor is exempt, the debtor may claim the exemptions on the supplemental schedule. See Bankruptcy Rule 1007(h) and section 2.08, supra. A failure to file such a supplemental schedule may result in the denial or revocation of the debtor's chapter 7 discharge. See 11 U.S.C. 727(a)(2)(B),(d)(2) and section 2.17, infra. after-acquired
property,
reporting
requirements

2.16 Duties and Powers of the United States Trustee and the Bankruptcy Trustee

The Attorney General must appoint a United States trustee for each region, and one or more assistant United States trustees in regions where the public interest so requires. See 28 U.S.C. 581(a), 582. There are 21 such regions in the United States, each of which is composed of two or more districts. Generally, a United States trustee is responsible for appointing (or serving as) trustees in bankruptcy cases, monitoring the administration of bankruptcy cases, and generally relieving bankruptcy judges of administrative responsibilities and of the burden of appointing persons who may later litigate before them. See 28 U.S.C. 586.

The duties and responsibilities of the United States trustee in chapter 7 cases are set forth in 28 U.S.C. 586 and 11 U.S.C. 307, 341, 343, 701(a). In chapter 7 consumer cases, the duties and responsibilities of the United States trustee include the following:

(1) Appointing, from the panel of private trustees, a disinterested person to serve as interim trustee in the chapter 7 case, or serving as interim trustee in the case if no member of the panel is willing to serve.

(2) Convening and presiding at the meeting of creditors.

(3) Taking appropriate action to insure that all reports, schedules, and fees are promptly filed and paid.

(4) Monitoring the progress of the case and taking appropriate action to prevent undue delay.

(5) Raising and being heard on any issue in the case.

(6) Notifying the United States Attorney of matters relating to acts that may constitute a federal crime and assisting in the prosecution of such crimes.

To enable the United States trustee to carry out its duty of monitoring bankruptcy cases, the clerk of the bankruptcy court is required to transmit to the United States trustee copies of all petitions, schedules, statements, and amendments thereto filed in the case. See Bankruptcy Rules 1002(b), 1007(l), 1009(c), and 5005(b). The clerk is also required to transmit to the United States trustee most notices that are issued in bankruptcy cases. See Bankruptcy Rule 2002(k). In addition, any person or party who files a pleading, motion, objection or similar paper relating to the approval of a compromise or settlement, the dismissal or conversion of a case, the employment of a professional person, an objection to or waiver or revocation of a discharge, or certain other enumerated matters must transmit a copy thereof to the United States trustee. See Bankruptcy Rule 9034.

Promptly after the order for relief in a chapter 7 case, the United States trustee must appoint an interim trustee to serve in the case. The trustee must be a disinterested person who is a member of the panel of private trustees created under 28 U.S.C. 586(a)(1), or who was serving as trustee in the case before it was converted to chapter 7. See 11 U.S.C. 701(a). The interim trustee serves as trustee in a chapter 7 case unless the creditors elect a trustee, an event that seldom happens in chapter 7 consumer cases. See 11 U.S.C. 702(d).

The duties of a bankruptcy trustee are set forth in 11 U.S.C. 704, Bankruptcy Rule 2015, and Part VI of the Rules of Bankruptcy Procedure. The trustee's duties in a chapter 7 consumer case include the following:

(1) Collecting and liquidating the property of the debtor's bankruptcy estate, and closing the estate as expeditiously as is compatible with the best interests of the parties in interest.

(2) Accounting for all property received and keeping a record of the receipt and disposition of all property and money received.

(3) Insuring that the debtor timely performs the intentions specified in the statement of intention.

(4) Investigating the financial affairs of the debtor.

(5) Examining proofs of claim and objecting to the allowance of any claim that is improper, if a purpose would be served.

(6) Opposing the discharge of the debtor, if advisable.

(7) Furnishing such information concerning the estate and its administration as is requested by the parties in interest, unless the court orders otherwise.

(8) Filing and transmitting to the United States trustee an inventory of the debtor's property, if such an inventory was not previously filed in the case.

(9) Giving notice of the case to every person known to be holding money or property subject to the withdrawal or order of the debtor.

(10) Giving notice of any proposed abandonment of property of the estate.

(11) Making a final report and filing a final account of the administration of the estate with the court.

If a joint petition is filed, the debtors' estates are usually consolidated and administered jointly by a single trustee. See 11 U.S.C. 302(b) and Bankruptcy Rules 1015(b) and 2009(c)(1). The trustee must attend the meeting of creditors and examine the debtor (or debtors in a joint case) as to his or her assets. Unless there is an applicable exemption, the trustee is likely to question the debtor closely as to any liquid assets possessed by the debtor at the time of filing. If it is determined at the hearing that the debtor possessed nonexempt assets at the time of filing, the trustee may request that the assets, or their cash equivalent, be turned over to the trustee by a specified date. After the hearing, the trustee may correspond with the debtor's employer to determine the status of the debtor's earnings at the time of filing. If nonexempt property is subsequently located, the trustee normally advises the debtor as to when and where to turn the property over. If the debtor disputes either the existence or the amount or value of any alleged nonexempt property claimed by the trustee, the request to turn over the property should be contested and the matter either negotiated with the trustee or litigated under Bankruptcy Rule 9014 or otherwise.

joint case, appointment of trustee

trustee, collection of nonexempt assets, procedure

The trustee may not always insist that nonexempt assets be turned over. It is often possible for the debtor to purchase the trustee's interest in such assets at a negotiated price. In such cases the trustee may permit the debtor to pay the agreed price in reasonable installments. Such a procedure may be convenient for a debtor whose homestead or other exemption doesn't quite cover the equity in the debtor's home or other property, and for a debtor with nonexempt personal property that is of value to the debtor but which has little market value. The trustee may also sell the estate's equity or interest in secured property to a creditor with a security interest in the property.

purchase of trustee's interest in nonexempt property

If the trustee has a substantial interest in property, a portion of which is exempt, and if the debtor is unable to purchase the trustee's interest in the property, the trustee may sell the property and reimburse the debtor for the exempt portion of the property from the proceeds of the sale. If the estate's interest in otherwise exempt property is nominal, the trustee may abandon the property upon proper notice. See Bankruptcy Rule 6007(a). A trustee who unreasonably refuses to abandon the estate's interest in property may be compelled to do so by the filing of a motion under Bankruptcy Rule 6007(b). See 11 U.S.C. 554(b).

sale of exempt property by trustee, procedure

The trustee's fee in a chapter 7 case is $45, which comes from the filing fee, plus, if allowed by the court, a percentage of all monies disbursed by the trustee in the case. The percentage portion of the trustee's fee may not exceed fifteen percent of the first $1,000, six percent of the next $2,000, and three percent of the balance of all monies disbursed. See 11 U.S.C. 326(a), 330(b).

trustee's fee, amount of

Insofar as they pertain to typical consumer cases, the powers of the trustee to set aside liens and transfers of property may be summarized as follows:

preferential
transfers.
avoidance of by
trustee

(1) Under 11 U.S.C. 547(b), the trustee may avoid (i.e., set aside) as a preference any transfer of property of the debtor to or for the benefit of a creditor that - (a) was made for or on account of an antecedent debt owed by the debtor before the transfer, (b) was made while the debtor was insolvent, (c) was made on or within 90 days before the date of the filing of the petition or within one year before the date of filing if the creditor was an insider who had reasonable cause to believe that the debtor was insolvent at the time of the transfer, and (d) that enabled the creditor to receive more than it would have received as a creditor in the case if the transfer had not occurred. There are seven types of transfers, however, that may not be avoided as a preference. See 11 U.S.C. 547(c). Included here are contemporaneous transfers for new value given to the debtor, most transfers made in the ordinary course of business, and, in the case of an individual debtor whose debts are primarily consumer debts, transfers wherein the aggregate value of all property constituting or affected by the transfer is less than $600. See 11 U.S.C. 547(c).

fraudulent
transfers.
avoidance of by
trustee

(2) Under 11 U.S.C. 548(a), the trustee may avoid as fraudulent any transfer of an interest of the debtor in property, or any obligation incurred by the debtor, that was made or incurred within one year prior to the date of the filing of the petition, if the debtor - (a) made the transfer or incurred the obligation with actual intent to hinder, delay, or defraud any entity to which the debtor was or became indebted, or (b) received less than a reasonably equivalent value in exchange for the transfer or obligation and was insolvent at the time or became insolvent, undercapitalized, or unable to pay his or her debts as a result of the transaction.

unauthorized
transfers.
avoidance of by
trustee

(3) Under 11 U.S.C. 549(a), the trustee may avoid any unauthorized transfer of property of the bankruptcy estate that occurs after the commencement of the case, except - (a) a transfer to a good faith purchaser without knowledge of the commencement of the case and for present fair equivalent value, and (b) a transfer to a purchaser at a judicial sale of real property located in a county other than the county in which the case is commenced, unless a copy of the petition was recorded in such county prior to the transfer.

trustee's
avoidance powers
under local law

(4) Under 11 U.S.C. 544(a) the trustee may avoid or set aside any lien, transfer of property or obligation incurred by the debtor that could be avoided or set aside under local law by - (a) a creditor that extended credit to the debtor at the time the bankruptcy case was commenced and obtained, with respect to such credit, a judicial lien against the debtor's property, (b) a creditor that extended credit to the debtor at the time the bankruptcy case was commenced and obtained, with respect to such credit, an execution that was returned unsatisfied or (c) a bona fide purchaser of real property from the debtor at the time the case was commenced who is permitted under local law to perfect the transfer. Section 544(a) gives the trustee the avoidance powers of a judgment creditor or bona fide purchaser of real estate under local law, whether or not such a creditor or purchaser actually exists. The specific powers of the trustee under this section depend largely on the law of the local state. Section 544(b) permits the trustee to set aside transfers that are avoidable by unsecured creditors under local law, such as transfers made by the debtor in violation of state fraudulent conveyance or bulk sales laws. See In re Landbank Equity Corp., 83 B.R. 362, and In re Express Liquors, Inc., 65 B.R. 952.

actions by
trustee. venue
restrictions

In regards to the above powers of the trustee, it should be noted that the trustee is subject to certain venue restrictions in commencing actions to recover money or property. See 28 U.S.C. 1409. Of interest in consumer cases is the provision stating that the trustee may commence a proceeding to recover money or property worth less than $1,000 or a consumer debt of less than $5,000 only in the district in which the defendant resides. See 28 U.S.C. 1409(b).

The trustee has extensive powers to assume or reject executory contracts and unexpired leases of the debtor. Generally, the trustee, with the approval of the court, may assume or reject any executory contract or unexpired lease of the debtor. See 11 U.S.C. 365(a). However, if there has been a default in an executory contract or unexpired lease of the debtor, the trustee may not assume such contract or lease unless, at the time of the assumption, the trustee - (1) cures, or provides adequate assurance that he or she will promptly cure, such default, (2) provides compensation to the injured party, other than the debtor, for any actual losses resulting from the default, and (3) provides adequate assurance of future performance under the contract or lease. See 11 U.S.C. 365(b). A proceeding to assume, reject, or assign an executory contract or unexpired lease is governed by Bankruptcy Rule 9014, which requires a motion, with notice and a hearing. See Bankruptcy Rule 6006(a). The powers and duties of the trustee with respect to executory contracts and unexpired leases are set forth in 11 U.S.C. 365 and Bankruptcy Rule 6006. See section 2.07, supra, for a definition of the term "executory contract."

executory contracts, assumption or rejection by trustee

The trustee and any other party in interest, including the United States trustee, and any attorney, accountant, or employee of a party in interest, may not conduct or take part in ex parte contacts, meetings, or communications with a bankruptcy judge concerning matters affecting a particular case or proceeding. See Bankruptcy Rule 9003.

prohibition of ex parte contacts with bankruptcy judge

2.17 The Chapter 7 Discharge

In a chapter 7 case, the court must grant the debtor a discharge unless:

chapter 7
discharge,
eligibility
requirements

(1) the debtor is not an individual;

(2) the debtor, with intent to hinder, delay, or defraud a creditor or the trustee, has transferred, removed, destroyed, mutilated, or concealed - (a) property of the debtor, within one year before the date of filing, or (b) property of the bankruptcy estate, after the date of filing;

(3) the debtor has, without justification, concealed, destroyed, mutilated, falsified, or failed to keep or preserve recorded information from which the debtor's financial condition or business transactions may be ascertained;

(4) the debtor knowingly and fraudulently and in connection with the case - (a) made a false oath or account, (b) presented or used a false claim, (c) gave, offered, received, or attempted to obtain money, property, or advantage, or a promise of same, for acting or forbearing to act in the case, or (d) withheld from the trustee recorded information relating to the debtor's property or financial affairs;

(5) the debtor has failed to satisfactorily explain, prior to the determination of the denial of discharge, any loss or deficiency of assets;

(6) the debtor has refused in the case - (a) to obey a lawful order of the court, other than an order to respond to a material question or to testify, (b) on the ground of privilege against self-incrimination, to respond to a material question approved by the court or to testify, after having been granted immunity with respect to same, or (c) on a ground other than privilege against self-incrimination, to respond to a material question or to testify;

(7) the debtor has committed any act specified in (2) through (6) above, within one year before the date of filing, or during the case, in connection with another title 11 case concerning an insider (i.e., a relative, partner, partnership, or corporation of the debtor);

(8) the debtor has been granted a discharge in a chapter 7 or chapter 11 case that was commenced within six years before the date of filing of the present case;

(9) the debtor has been granted a discharge in a chapter 12 or chapter 13 case that was commenced within six years before the date of filing of the present case, unless payments under the plan in the prior case totalled at least - (a) 100 percent of the allowed unsecured claims in such case, or (b) 70 percent of such claims and the plan was proposed by the debtor in good faith and was the debtor's best effort; or

(10) the court approves a written waiver of discharge executed by the debtor after the order for relief under chapter 7. See 11 U.S.C. 727(a).

chapter 7
discharge, when
granted

complaints
objecting to
discharge,
motions to
dismiss, filing
requirements

In the chapter 7 case of an individual debtor, the court must forthwith grant the debtor a discharge upon the expiration of the time fixed for the filing of complaints objecting to the discharge of the debtor and the time fixed for filing a motion to dismiss the case as a substantial abuse of chapter 7 under Bankruptcy Rule 1017(e), unless a complaint objecting to the discharge of the debtor has been filed, a motion to dismiss under Bankruptcy Rule 1017(e) is pending, or the debtor has filed a waiver of discharge or requested that the granting of the discharge be delayed. See Bankruptcy Rule 4004(c). A complaint objecting to the discharge of the debtor under 11 U.S.C. 727(a) and a motion to dismiss under Bankruptcy Rule 1017(e) must be filed not later than 60 days following the first date set for the meeting of creditors, unless, on the motion of a party in interest made within the 60-day period and after a hearing on notice, the court, for cause, extends the time for filing. See Bankruptcy Rules 1017(e) and 4004(a),(b). Not less than 25 days notice of the time fixed for the filing of complaints objecting to the discharge of the debtor must be given to the United States trustee, all creditors, and the trustee. See Bankruptcy Rule 4004(a). This notice is usually contained in the notice of commencement of case (Exhibit 2-V).

The trustee, a creditor, or the United States trustee may file complaints objecting to the discharge of the debtor. See 11 U.S.C. 727(c)(1). At the request of a party in interest, the court may order the trustee to examine the acts and conduct of the debtor to determine whether grounds exist for a denial of discharge. See 11 U.S.C. 727(c)(2). If a complaint objecting to the discharge of the debtor is filed, the proceeding commenced by the complaint is an adversary proceeding governed by Part VII of the Rules of Bankruptcy Procedure. See Bankruptcy Rule 4004(d). That such a proceeding is a core proceeding, see 28 U.S.C. 157(b)(2)(J). At the trial on such a complaint, the party filing the complaint has the burden of proving the objection. See Bankruptcy Rule 4005. The applicability of any local rules to such proceedings should also be checked.

complaints objecting to discharge, procedure under

Notwithstanding the duty of the court to forthwith grant the debtor a chapter 7 discharge upon the expiration of the time for filing complaints or motions, on the motion of the debtor the court may defer the granting of the discharge for a period of 30 days and, on motion within such 30-day period, may defer the granting thereof to a date certain. See Bankruptcy Rule 4004(c) and any applicable local rules. This provision is useful if the debtor is attempting to negotiate a reaffirmation agreement with a creditor, because such agreements must be made prior to the granting of the discharge to be enforceable. See 11 U.S.C. 524(c), and section 2.18, infra.

granting of discharge, motion to defer

Not more than 30 days following the entry of an order granting or denying a discharge, and on not less than 10 days notice to the debtor and the trustee, the court may hold a discharge and reaffirmation hearing, which, if held, the debtor must attend. See 11 U.S.C. 524(d) and Bankruptcy Rule 4008. Such a hearing is usually held only if the debtor's discharge has been denied or if the debtor wishes to enter into a reaffirmation agreement with a creditor under 11 U.S.C. 524(c). Motions by the debtor for the approval of reaffirmation agreements must be filed at or before this hearing, and the court is required to perform certain functions in regard to such agreements. See Bankruptcy Rule 4008, and section 2.18, infra. Many courts have local rules dealing with discharge and reaffirmation hearings, which should be checked and complied with.

discharge and reaffirmation hearing, when held, procedure

The debtor may waive the right to a chapter 7 discharge by filing and obtaining court approval of a written waiver of discharge executed by the debtor after the order for relief under chapter 7. See 11 U.S.C. 727(a)(10), Bankruptcy Rule 4004(c), and any applicable local rules.

waiver of discharge

The order of discharge must conform substantially to Official Form 18. See Bankruptcy Rule 4004(e). A sample order of discharge is contained in Exhibit 2-X at the end of this chapter. The clerk is required to promptly mail a copy of the final order of discharge to all creditors, the United States trustee, and the trustee. See Bankruptcy Rule 4004(g). If so desired, a final order of discharge may be registered in another district by filing a certified copy of the order with the clerk of the bankruptcy court in the other district. When so registered, the order of discharge has the same effect as an order of the court of the district where it is registered. See Bankruptcy Rule 4004(f). If an order is entered denying or revoking a discharge, or if a waiver of discharge is filed and approved by the court, the clerk must promptly mail a notice of no discharge to all creditors. See Bankruptcy Rule 4006.

order of discharge, requirements, notice

On the request of the trustee, a creditor, or the United States trustee, and after notice and a hearing, the court, under 11 U.S.C. 727(d), may revoke the chapter 7 discharge of a debtor if:

revocation of discharge, grounds for

(1) the discharge was obtained through the fraud of the debtor, and the requesting party did not know of such fraud until after the granting of the discharge;

(2) the debtor acquired property that is property of the bankruptcy estate, or became entitled to acquire property that would be property of the estate, and knowingly and fraudulently failed to deliver or report such property to the trustee; or

(3) the debtor refused in the case - (a) to obey a lawful order of the court, other than an order to respond to a material question or to testify, (b) on the ground of privilege against self-incrimination, to respond to a material question approved by the court or to testify, after having been granted immunity with respect to the matter for which the privilege was invoked, or (c) on a ground other than privilege against self-incrimination, to respond to a material question approved by the court or to testify.

revocation of discharge, procedure

A proceeding to revoke a chapter 7 discharge is an adversary proceeding governed by Part VII of the Bankruptcy Rules, and the party seeking revocation of must file a complaint. See Bankruptcy Rule 7001. Complaints seeking the revocation of a discharge on the grounds stated in subparagraph (1) above must be filed within one year after the granting of the discharge. Complaints seeking revocation on the grounds stated in subparagraphs (2) and (3) above must be filed within one year after the granting of the discharge or before the closing of the case, whichever is later. See 11 U.S.C. 727(e). The local rules should also be checked for requirements dealing with revocation proceedings.

chapter 7 discharge, debts not discharged

A chapter 7 discharge in a voluntary case discharges an individual debtor from all debts that arose (or are deemed to have arisen) prior to the filing of the petition except the debts listed below. See 11 U.S.C. 727(b). Under 11 U.S.C. 523(a), a chapter 7 discharge does not discharge an individual debtor from the following debts:

(1) Debts for the following taxes and customs duties -

dischargeability of tax debts

    (a) income taxes and gross receipts taxes - (i) for tax years ending on or before the date of filing of the case for which returns, if required, were last due within three years before such date, (ii) assessed within 240 days before the date of filing of the case, plus additional periods if offers to compromise such taxes were made, or (iii) not assessed before, but assessable after the commencement of the case, excluding the taxes specified in (b) and (c) of this subparagraph;

    (b) taxes with respect to which a return, if required, was either not filed or filed late, but within two years before the date of filing of the case;

    (c) taxes with respect to which the debtor made a fraudulent return or willfully attempted to evade or defeat.

dischargeability of debts procured by fraud or false financial statements

(2) If the court so rules under a complaint to determine dischargeability, debts for obtaining money, property, services, or an extension, renewal, or refinance of credit by - (a) false pretenses, false representation, or actual fraud, other than a statement with respect to the debtor's financial condition or that of an insider (included here are certain debts for "luxury goods or services" and debts for certain cash advances, which are discussed below), or (b) the use of a written statement with respect to the financial condition of the debtor or an insider that is materially false, on which the creditor reasonably relied, and that the debtor caused to be made or published with intent to deceive.

dischargeability of unlisted debts

(3) Debts that were neither listed nor scheduled in the case with the name of the creditor, if known, in time to permit the timely filing of a proof of claim, or, with respect to the debts described in paragraphs (2), (4), or (6) herein, the timely filing of a complaint to determine dischargeability, unless the creditor had notice or actual knowledge of the case in time for such filing.

dischargeability of debts for larceny or embezzlement

(4) If the court so rules under a complaint to determine dischargeability, debts for embezzlement, larceny, or fraud or defalcation while acting in a fiduciary capacity.

dischargeability of debts for alimony, maintenance or support

(5) Debts to a spouse, former spouse, or child of the debtor for alimony, maintenance or support in connection with a separation agreement, a divorce decree or other court order, or a property settlement agreement, but not to the extent that - (a) such debt is assigned to another entity, voluntarily, by operation of law, or otherwise (other than debts assigned for collection under section 402(a)(26) of the Social Security Act or assigned to the Federal Government or to a state or political subdivision thereof), or (b) such debt is not in the nature of alimony, maintenance or support.

(6) If the court so rules under a complaint to determine dischargeability, debts for willful and malicious injury by the debtor to another entity or to the property of another entity.

dischargeability of debts for willful or malicious injury

(7) Debts for fines, penalties, or forfeitures payable to and for the benefit of a governmental unit, except tax penalties and penalties imposed for transactions or events that occurred more than three years before the date of filing of the petition.

dischargeability of debts for fines or penalties

(8) Debts for an education benefit overpayment or loan made, insured, or guaranteed by a governmental unit or made under a program funded in whole or in part by a governmental unit or non-profit institution, or for an obligation to repay funds received as an educational benefit, scholarship or stipend, unless the loan, benefit, scholarship or stipend overpayment first became due more than seven years (excluding any applicable suspension of the repayment period) before the date of filing of the petition, or unless the nondischarge of the debt will impose an undue hardship on the debtor and the debtor's dependents. The dischargeability of debts for student loans or educational obligations is discussed below in this section.

dischargeability of debts for student loans or educational obligations

(9) Debts for death or personal injury caused by the debtor's operation of a motor vehicle if such operation was unlawful because the debtor was intoxicated from using alcohol, a drug, or another substance.

dischargeability of debts caused by drunk driving

(10) Debts that were or could have been scheduled by the debtor in a prior bankruptcy case in which the debtor waived or was denied a discharge on any grounds other than having been granted a discharge in a prior bankruptcy case filed within the previous six years.

dischargeability of debts listed in prior bankruptcy case where discharge was denied

Notwithstanding subparagraph (10) above, a debt that was excepted from discharge in a prior bankruptcy case of the debtor under subparagraphs (1), (3), or (8) above, is dischargeable in a later case, unless the debt is otherwise nondischargeable in the later case. See 11 U.S.C. 523(b). Also, unless the court, for cause, ordered otherwise in the prior case, the dismissal of a prior bankruptcy case does not bar the discharge in a later case of the debts listed in the prior case if the debts were dischargeable in the prior case. See 11 U.S.C. 349(a).

dischargeability in present case of debts not discharged in prior case

In applying the above-listed exceptions to discharge, the general rule is that when a debt is determined to be nondischargeable, the attendant attorney fees, interest, and costs associated with the debt are also nondischargeable. See In Re Fitzgerald, 109 B.R. 893. Thus, attorney fees awarded in a divorce decree wherein alimony, maintenance, or support was awarded are generally held to be in the nature of alimony, maintenance or support and therefore nondischargeable. See In Re Williams, 703 F. 2d 1055 and DuPhily v. DuPhily, 52 B.R. 971. However, if the attorneys fees are found to be in the nature of a property settlement, they are dischargeable. See In Re Harke, 24 B.R. 645.

nondischargeable debts, dischargeability of related fees and costs

Debts for obtaining money, property, services or credit by actual fraud, if proven by a creditor filing a complaint to determine dischargeability, are nondischargeable under 11 U.S.C. 523(a)(2) (i.e., paragraph (2)(a) above). Under this section, a mere failure of a debtor to fulfill a promise to pay for goods or services is not fraudulent. However, if a debtor purchases or obtains goods, services or money on credit with no intention of paying the debt or with knowledge that it will be financially impossible to pay the debt, the debt may be deemed fraudulent and nondischargeable under Section 523(a)(2). See In Re Schmidt, 70 B.R. 634. Credit purchases made by a debtor on the eve of bankruptcy are likely to be deemed fraudulent under this section, especially if the financial condition of the debtor at the time was such that repayment was virtually impossible. See In Re Schrader, 55 B.R. 608. The standard of proof required of a creditor seeking to establish the nondischargeability of a debt under 11 U.S.C. 523(a) is that of a "preponderance of the evidence". "Clear and convincing evidence" is not required to establish any of the exceptions to discharge, including fraud. See Grogan V. Garner, 498 U.S. ____, 112 L. Ed. 2d 755, 111 S. Ct. 654 (1991).

debts procured by fraud, dis-chargeability, burden of proof

debts for luxury
goods or
services or cash
advances,
dischargeability
It should be noted that the following debts of an individual debtor are presumed to be nondischargeable: (1) consumer debts aggregating $500 or more owed to a single creditor for "luxury goods or services" incurred on or within 40 days before the order for relief, and (2) cash advances aggregating more than $1,000 that are extensions of consumer credit under an open end credit plan obtained on or within 20 days before the order for relief. See 11 U.S.C. 523(a)(2)(C). "Luxury goods or services" do not include goods or services reasonably acquired for the support or maintenance of the debtor or a dependent of the debtor, and "extensions of consumer credit under an open end credit plan" means cash advances under a plan wherein the creditor reasonably contemplates repeated transactions, which prescribes the terms of such transactions, and which provides for a finance charge on the unpaid balance. See 11 U.S.C. 523(a)(2)(C) and 15 U.S.C. 1602(i). The issue of whether particular goods purchased by the debtor constitute "luxury goods" must be determined in light of the debtor's personal circumstances. See In Re Herran, 66 B.R. 323.

luxury goods or
services, what
constitutes

luxury goods,
effect of
presumption
The statutory presumption of nondischargeability has the effect of imposing on the debtor the burden of coming forward with evidence sufficient to rebut the presumption. If such evidence is produced, however, the burden of establishing the nondischargeability of the debt reverts to the creditor. See In Re Faulk, 69 B.R. 743, and In Re Koch, 83 B.R. 898.

debts for
student loans or
educational
obligations,
nondis-
chargeability of
The issue of the nondischargeability of debts for student loans or educational obligations under 11 U.S.C. 523(a)(8) frequently arises in chapter 7 cases. It should be noted initially that the nondischargeability of debts for qualifying student loans or educational obligations is self executing, which means that it is not necessary for the creditor to file an objection or complaint, or even to appear in the chapter 7 case, in order for the debt to be nondischargeable. Accordingly, a post-discharge attempt to collect a qualifying student loan does not violate the discharge injunction issued by the bankruptcy court. See In Re Barth, 86 B.R. 146. Further, the nondischargeability of a student loan debt in a chapter 7 case can be determined in a state court, because the issue is not within the exclusive jurisdiction of the bankruptcy court. See In Re Craig, 56 B.R. 479.

debts for
student loans or
educational
obligations,
dischargeability
For a student loan or educational obligation to be nondischargeable, the loan or obligation must have been made, insured or guaranteed by a qualifying governmental or nonprofit institution or must constitute an obligation to repay funds received by the debtor as an educational benefit or scholarship, and must first have become due within seven years prior to the date of filing of the chapter 7 case, excluding any periods during which payment of the loan was suspended or deferred. See 11 U.S.C. 523(a)(8). For a student loan to be nondischargeable, it must be shown that the proceeds of the loan were used by the debtor for educational purposes. See In Re Ealy, 78 B.R. 897.

debts for
student loans or
educational
obligations,
undue hardship,
what constitutes
The debtor may establish that a qualifying student loan or educational obligation is dischargeable by proving that the nondischarge of the loan or obligation will impose an undue hardship on the debtor and his or her dependents. Undue hardship may be proven by showing that, based on the debtor's current income and expenses, the debtor and his or her dependents cannot maintain a minimal standard of living if forced to repay the loan, that such circumstances are likely to continue for a significant portion of the repayment period, and that the debtor has made a good faith effort to repay the loan. See Brunner v. New York State Higher Educational Services Corp., 831 F. 2d 395.

debts for
student loans,
dischargeability
of guarantor or
co-maker
Are the nondischargeability provisions of 11 U.S.C. 523(a)(8) also applicable to parents or other nonstudents who sign as guarantors or co-makers of student loan obligations? While several courts have ruled that student loans are equally nondischargeable as to guarantors (see In Re Behr, 80 B.R. 124), other, more recent, cases have held that debts for student loans may be discharged by nonstudent guarantors and co-makers without a showing of undue hardship. See In Re Wilcon, 135 B.R. 709, and In Re Pelkowski, 135 B.R. 254.

The debtor is discharged from the debts specified in paragraphs (2), (4), and (6) above unless the creditor to whom the debt is owed timely files a complaint to determine the dischargeability of the debt and the court, after a hearing on notice, determines that the debt shall not be discharged. See 11 U.S.C. 523(c) and Bankruptcy Rule 4007(c). It should be noted that if a creditor files a complaint to determine the dischargeability of a consumer debt under paragraph (2) above, and if the debt is found by the court to be dischargeable, the court may enter judgment against the creditor and in favor of the debtor in the amount of the debtor's costs plus a reasonable attorney's fee for the proceeding if the court finds that the position of the creditor was not substantially justified, except that such costs and fees shall not be awarded if special circumstances would make such an award unjust. See 11 U.S.C. 523(d).

complaint to
determine
dischargeability
of debt, when
required

same, when
debtor may
recover costs

The court is required to fix a time for the filing of complaints to determine the dischargeability of debts under 11 U.S.C. 523(c), which time shall be not later than 60 days after the first date set for the meeting of creditors. The creditors must be given at least 30 days notice of the time fixed for the filing of such complaints, which notice is customarily contained in the notice of commencement of case (Exhibit 2-V). Upon motion made before the time for filing has expired, the court may, for cause and after a hearing on notice, extend the time for the filing of such complaints. See Bankruptcy Rule 4007(c).

same, filing and
notice
requirements

A proceeding commenced by the filing of a complaint to determine the dischargeability of a debt is an adversary proceeding governed by Part VII of the Rules of Bankruptcy Procedure. See Bankruptcy Rule 4007(e). However, the court need not determine the issues raised by such a complaint until after it has ruled on any complaints filed objecting to the discharge of the debtor under 11 U.S.C. 727(a). See Advisory Committee's Notes to Bankruptcy Rule 4007. Some districts have local rules governing the procedures under complaints to determine the dischargeability of debts under 11 U.S.C. 523(c).

same, procedure
under

It is important to understand that complaints may be filed to determine the dischargeability of any debt, not just those that are discharged if a complaint is not filed. A complaint to determine the dischargeability of a debt other than the debts described in the second paragraph above may be filed by the debtor or a creditor at any time, either during the case or after the case has been closed. See Bankruptcy Rule 4007(a),(b). This is a useful procedure for determining the dischargeability of debts whose dischargeability may be questionable. The filing fee for such a complaint is $120.

complaint to
determine the
dischargeability
of any debt,
filing
requirements

Except for the 10 classes of debts that are nondischargeable under 11 U.S.C. 523 (see the list above in this section), a chapter 7 discharge discharges the debtor from all debts that arose before the date the petition was filed or that are deemed to have arisen before such date, regardless of whether a proof of claim is filed or allowed. See 11 U.S.C. 727(b). Except with respect to certain community debts and property (see below, this section), the discharge of a debt does not affect the liability of another entity on, or the property of another entity for, such debt. See 11 U.S.C. 524(e).

chapter 7
discharge,
effect of on
discharged debts

An order of discharge in a chapter 7 case has the following effect on the discharged debts and liabilities of the debtor:

order of
discharge,
effect of

(1) It voids any judgment at any time obtained, to the extent that such judgment is a determination of the personal liability of the debtor with respect to a discharged debt, whether or not discharge of the debt is waived.

(2) It operates as an injunction against the commencement or continuation of an action, the employment of process, or any act, to collect, recover, or offset a discharged debt as a personal liability of the debtor, whether or not discharge of the debt is waived.

(3) It operates as an injunction against the commencement or continuation of an action, the employment of process, or an act, to collect or recover from, or offset against, certain community property of the debtor acquired after the commencement of the case, on account of an allowable community claim, except such claims that are not dischargeable against the debtor or that would not be dischargeable against the debtor's spouse in a similar case concerning the spouse, whether or not discharge of the debt based on the community claim is waived. See 11 U.S.C. 524(a).

chapter 7
discharge,
effect of in
community
property states

In community property states, all of the community property of the debtor and the debtor's spouse, with some minor exceptions, becomes property of the debtor's bankruptcy estate, whether or not the debtor's spouse files under chapter 7. See 11 U.S.C. 541(a)(2). The community creditors of the debtor and the debtor's spouse are permitted to share in the distribution of the community property. See 11 U.S.C. 726(c). The community creditors of the nonfiling spouse, with only limited exceptions, are then enjoined and precluded from later moving against community property of the nonfiling spouse acquired after the commencement of the debtor's case. See 11 U.S.C. 524(a)(3). Thus, in community property states the nonfiling spouse of the debtor may receive a discharge of community debts without filing under chapter 7. The states with community property laws are Arizona, California, Idaho, Louisiana, Nevada, New Mexico, Texas, and Washington.

community
property states,
list of

attempt to
collect
discharged debt,
debtor's
obligation

Occasionally a creditor will seek to collect a claim against the debtor that was discharged in a chapter 7 case. If the debtor does not wish to pay the claim, the creditor should be advised, preferably in writing, that the debt has been discharged and of the effect of the order of discharge. A copy of the debtor's order of discharge (Exhibit 2-X), which sets forth the injunctive relief granted by the court in connection with the discharge, will provide the creditor with the required notice. It should be noted that except for debts covered by enforceable reaffirmation agreements (see section 2.18, infra), the debtor is not legally obligated to pay any portion of a discharged debt under any circumstances. See 11 U.S.C. 524(a).

attempt to
collect
discharged debt,
creditor's
liability

If a creditor pursues a discharged claim against the debtor, the creditor may be held in contempt of court and may be liable to the debtor for damages. See Hix v. Avco Financial Services, 13 B.R. 752, and In Re Myers, 18 B.R. 362. If a dispute later arises as to whether a debt was discharged in the chapter 7 case, the case may be reopened without the payment of an additional filing fee for the purpose of filing a complaint to determine the dischargeability of the debt. See 11 U.S.C. 350(b) and Bankruptcy Rule 4007(b).

chapter 7
discharge,
effect of liens
and sureties

It should be understood that a chapter 7 discharge relates only to the personal liability of the debtor for the discharged debts. The liability of sureties and guarantors of the debtor is not affected by the discharge, and creditors with valid liens that were not avoided during the case may proceed against property of the debtor that is subject to such liens, including exempt property. See 11 U.S.C. 522 (c)(2) and In Re Schroff, 94 B.R. 279. Because the unchallenged lien of a creditor who does not file a proof of claim survives the bankruptcy case (see In Re Tarnow, 749 F.2d 464), the debtor's attorney should insure that the liens of all such creditors are avoided during the case. General liens of judgment and tax creditors and mortgage liens of creditors with little or no security (i.e., second or third mortgage holders) are often not asserted by the creditor during the case. Such liens should be avoided during the case, however, so that they will not survive the case and encumber the debtor's postbankruptcy property.

avoiding
unsecured liens,
necessity of

avoiding
unsecured liens
under section
506(d),
procedure

Judgment liens against exempt property of the debtor may be avoided under 11 U.S.C. 522(f). This matter is discussed in section 2.12, supra. To the extent that they are unsecured, liens may also be avoided under 11 U.S.C. 506(d), which provides that a lien is void to the extent that it does not secure an allowed secured claim unless proof of the claim was not filed in the case. That the debtor may avoid liens under Section 506(d), including liens against exempt property, see In Re Folendore, 862 F.2d 1537 and Gaglia v. First Federal S. & L., 889 F.2d 1304. The debtor should seek to avoid the lien of any under-secured creditor who does not file a proof of claim or otherwise seek to enforce its lien during the case. If necessary, the debtor should obtain a written order identifying and avoiding the lien. The order can then be recorded or otherwise used to expunge the lien of record. Such a lien may be challenged by filing an adversary proceeding under Part VII of the Bankruptcy Rules or, less expensively, by filing a proof of the claim on the creditor's behalf under Bankruptcy Rule 3004 and then filing a motion under Bankruptcy Rule 3012 to value the secured claim and avoid the unsecured portion of the lien under Section 506(d). If the existence of such a lien is discovered after the case has been closed, it has been held that in the absence of prejudicial delay, the court will reopen a case for the purpose of avoiding a lien. See In Re Ricks, 62 B.R. 681.

2.18   Reaffirming Dischargeable Debts

Under 11 U.S.C. 524(c), an agreement between a holder of a claim and the debtor, the consideration for which is wholly or partially based on a dischargeable debt, is enforceable, to the extent that it is otherwise enforceable under nonbankruptcy law, whether or not discharge of the debt is waived, only if:

(1) the agreement was made before the granting of the chapter 7 discharge;

(2) the agreement contains a clear and conspicuous statement advising the debtor that the agreement may be rescinded at any time prior to discharge or within 60 days after the agreement has been filed with the court, whichever occurs later, by giving notice of rescission to the holder of the claim;

(3) the agreement is filed with the court, accompanied by a declaration or affidavit by the attorney that represented the debtor in negotiating the agreement with the creditor stating that the agreement represents a fully informed and voluntary agreement by the debtor and does not impose an undue hardship on the debtor or a dependent of the debtor;

(4) the debtor does not rescind the agreement at any time prior to discharge or within 60 days after the agreement has been filed with the court, whichever occurs later, by giving notice of rescission to the holder of the claim;

(5) the court, at the discharge and reaffirmation hearing, informs the debtor that he or she is not legally required to enter into the agreement, and of the legal effects and consequences of the agreement and of a default thereunder; and

(6) if the debtor was not represented by an attorney in negotiating the agreement and if the debt is not a consumer debt secured by real property, the court approves the agreement as not imposing an undue hardship on the debtor or a dependent of the debtor and as being in the best interest of the debtor.

reaffirmation agreement, when enforceable

As indicated above, if the debtor was represented by an attorney in negotiating the reaffirmation agreement with the creditor, court approval of the agreement is not required. Also, whether or not the debtor was represented by an attorney during the negotiations, if the debt being reaffirmed is a consumer debt secured by real property of the debtor (such as a home mortgage), court approval of the agreement is not required. See 11 U.S.C. 524(c)(6). In summary, court approval of a reaffirmation agreement is required only if the debtor was not represented by an attorney in negotiating the agreement and the debt being reaffirmed is not a consumer debt secured by real property of the debtor.

reaffirmation agreement, when court approval required

In most cases, then, court approval of a reaffirmation agreement will not be required, and it will only be necessary for the debtor's attorney to file the reaffirmation agreement and the attorney's declaration or affidavit with the court. Bankruptcy Form B 240, it should be noted, contains both a simplified reaffirmation agreement and an attorney's declaration. See Exhibit 2-Y, at the end of this chapter. The agreement portion of Form B 240 is incomplete and should not be used if the debtor's arrangement with the creditor is at all complicated. If the agreement with the creditor is not a simple one, a separate reaffirmation agreement should be drafted, using the sample reaffirmation agreement appearing in Exhibit 2-Z at the end of this chapter as a guide. A summary of the separate agreement should then be shown on Form B 240. If the debt being reaffirmed is a consumer debt secured by property of the bankruptcy estate (as is usually the case), it will also be necessary to file a statement of intention and serve it upon the appropriate parties within the required period (see section 2.11, supra).

reaffirmation agreement, filing requirements

statement of intention, necessity of filing

The Rules of Bankruptcy Procedure do not specify a time requirement for the filing of attorney's declarations and reaffirmation agreements not requiring court approval. However, the requirement in Bankruptcy Rule 4008 that a motion by the debtor for approval of a reaffirmation agreement be filed prior to or at the discharge and reaffirmation hearing at least implies that attorney's declarations and reaffirmation agreements should be filed prior to or at the discharge and reaffirmation hearing. It should be noted that many districts have local rules dealing with these matters.

reaffirmation agreement, when to file

If the local rules are silent on the matter, the agreement and the attorney's declaration (i.e., Bankruptcy Form B 240) should be filed prior to or at the discharge and reaffirmation hearing so as to enable the court to perform its statutory function of advising the debtor. It should be remembered that even though court approval of a reaffirmation agreement may not required, the debtor must still attend the reaffirmation hearing for two reasons: (1) the debtor is required by statute to attend the hearing in person, and (2) for the agreement to be valid, the court must advise the debtor as provided in subparagraph (5) above. See 11 U.S.C. 524(c),(d).

It is important to note that Bankruptcy Rule 4004(c) permits the court, upon the motion of the debtor, to defer the entry of an order granting a discharge for 30 days, and, upon a further motion made within such 30-day period, to a date certain. This provision may be useful in the negotiation of a reaffirmation agreement because of the requirement that such agreements be made prior to the granting of the discharge.

If court approval of a reaffirmation agreement is required, Bankruptcy Form B 240, appropriately completed, together with any separate agreement, must be filed with the court at or before the discharge and reaffirmation hearing. See Bankruptcy Rule 4008. A debtor seeking court approval of a reaffirmation agreement must present grounds for its approval, and the debtor should be prepared to show at the hearing that the agreement will not impose an undue hardship and is in his or her best interests. Many districts have local rules governing procedures for obtaining court approval of reaffirmation agreements, and they should be checked in this regard. A sample Bankruptcy Form B 240 is set forth in Exhibit 2-Y at the end of this chapter.

It should be noted that nothing contained in 11 U.S.C. 524(c) or (d) prevents a debtor from voluntarily paying a discharged or dischargeable debt. See 11 U.S.C. 524(f). The debtor should be advised, however, that he or she is not legally obligated to pay (or continue paying) a creditor with whom he or she does not have an valid reaffirmation agreement, even if the debtor has waived the discharge of the debt in writing, agreed in writing to repay the debt, or made one or more payments on the debt after the commencement of the chapter 7 case. See 11 U.S.C. 524(a), 727(b). Further, any judgment entered against the debtor based on a discharged debt is voidable at the request of the debtor. See In Re Levy, 87 B.R. 107.

2.19 Creditors - Claims, Setoffs, and Dividends

An unsecured creditor must file a proof of claim with the clerk of the bankruptcy court within 90 days after the first date set for the meeting of creditors for the claim to be allowed, unless the claim is filed on the creditor's behalf by the trustee, the debtor or a codebtor, or a guarantor. See Bankruptcy Rule 3002(a),(b),(c). There are six exceptions to the 90-day requirement for filing proofs of unsecured claims. The exceptions deal with claims by the governmental units, claims for infants or incompetents, claims which become allowable as a result of judgments, claims arising from the rejection of executory contracts or unexpired leases, and claims in chapter 7 no-asset cases where a notice of no dividend is given and nonexempt assets are later discovered. See Bankruptcy Rule 3002(c). The clerk, or some other person as the court may direct, must give each creditor notice of the time allowed for the filing of claims. See Bankruptcy Rule 2002(f). This notice is normally contained in the notice of commencement of case (see Exhibit 2-V).

proof of claim, filing and notice requirements

If notice of insufficient assets to pay a dividend (i.e., a notice of no dividend) is given in the notice of commencement of case, and if the trustee subsequently notifies the court that payment of a dividend appears possible, the clerk must notify the creditors of that fact and that proofs of claim may be filed within 90 days after the mailing of the notice. See Bankruptcy Rule 3002(c)(5).

notice of no dividend

Secured creditors are not specifically dealt with in the Rules of Bankruptcy Procedure, although it is clear that they may file claims. Many districts have adopted local rules dealing with the filing of claims and evidences of security interests by secured creditors. In some districts they are required to file proofs of claim within a certain period if they are claiming a security interest in property of the estate. In other districts they are required to file evidences of their lien or security interest with the trustee within a certain period. The local rules should be checked in this regard.

secured claims, filing requirements

If a security interest in property of the debtor is claimed, a proof of claim must be accompanied by evidence that the security interest has been perfected. See Bankruptcy Rule 3001(d). In most consumer cases, secured creditors proceed against their security instead of filing a claim, unless the local rules require such a filing. However, if the debtor or another entity contests the creditor's right to proceed against the secured property, the creditor may have to file a claim in order to assert or prove its standing as the holder of an allowed secured claim. In any event, before proceeding against its security, a secured creditor must file a motion for relief from the automatic stay under Bankruptcy Rule 4001 and any applicable local rules. The debtor's rights and duties with respect to such proceedings are discussed in section 2.10, supra.

secured claims, procedure for reclaiming security

An allowed secured claim of a creditor that is secured by a lien on property of the bankruptcy estate, or that is subject to a setoff, is a secured claim only to the extent of the value of the creditor's interest in the property, or to the extent of the amount subject to setoff, as the case may be. See 11 U.S.C. 506(a). The balance of the claim is deemed unsecured. The value of a partially-secured creditor's interest in the property is determined in light of the purpose of the valuation and of any proposed disposition or use of the property. The valuation may be made in conjunction with any hearing on the disposition of the property or on the motion of any party in interest. See 11 U.S.C. 506(a) and Bankruptcy Rule 3012.

secured claim, extent of allowance

Under 11 U.S.C. 506(d), the lien of an under-secured creditor who files a proof of claim is deemed void to the extent that it does not secure an allowed secured claim. However, if such a creditor does not file a proof of claim, the creditor's lien survives the bankruptcy proceeding unless it is challenged by the debtor. See In Re Tarnow, 749 F.2d 464. Therefore, a creditor with little security may be well advised not to file a proof of claim on the chance that the debtor will not avoid the lien and thereby permit it to survive the case.

under-secured creditor, survival of lien

If the value of the secured property exceeds the amount of the allowed secured claim (i.e., if the creditor is over secured), the creditor may also be allowed interest on the claim and any reasonable fees, costs, and charges provided for in the agreement under which the claim arose. See 11 U.S.C. 506(b). The trustee may recover from the property the expenses of preserving or disposing of the property. See 11 U.S.C. 506(c).

secured claim, inclusion of costs and fees

proof of claim,
general
requirements

A proof of claim, including a claim for wages, salary, or commissions, must conform to Official Form 10. See Bankruptcy Rule 3001(a). In some districts a proof of claim form is contained on the reverse side of the notice of commencement of case. A proof of claim must be executed by the creditor or the creditor's authorized agent, except for claims filed on the creditor's behalf by the trustee, the debtor, a codebtor, or a person who has secured the creditor. See Bankruptcy Rules 3001(b), 3004, and 3005. When a claim, or an interest in property of the debtor securing the claim, is based on a writing, the original or a duplicate of the writing must be filed with the proof of claim. If the writing has been lost or destroyed, a statement of the circumstances of its loss or destruction must be filed with the claim. See Bankruptcy Rule 3001(c). A sample proof of claim is set forth in Exhibit 3-G, at the end of chapter three, infra.

proof of claim,
filing of by
debtor or
trustee

If a creditor fails to file a claim on or before the first date set for the meeting of creditors, the debtor or the trustee may file a claim in the name of the creditor, a notice of which the clerk must forthwith mail to the creditor, the debtor, and the trustee. See Bankruptcy Rule 3004 and 11 U.S.C. 501(c). This is a useful procedure for the debtor in respect to claims for nondischargeable debts, especially priority taxes claims (see section 2.04, supra). If the creditor thereafter files a proof of claim, it supersedes the claim filed by the trustee or debtor on the creditor's behalf. See Bankruptcy Rule 3004.

proof of claim,
filing of by
codebtor or
guarantor

If a creditor does not file a proof of claim, one who is or may be liable with the debtor to the creditor (i.e., a codebtor), or one who has secured the creditor, may, within 30 days after the expiration of the 90-day period for filing claims, execute and file a proof of claim in the name of the creditor, if known, or if unknown, in the person's own name. However, no distribution may be made on the claim except on satisfactory proof that the original debt will be diminished by the amount distributed. The creditor may thereafter file a proof of claim, which shall supersede the proof of claim filed on its behalf. See Bankruptcy Rule 3005(a) and 11 U.S.C. 501(b).

subrogated
claims,
allowance of

An entity that is liable with the debtor on a claim of a creditor, or that has secured a claim of a creditor, and that pays such claim, is subrogated to the rights of the creditor to the extent of such payment. See 11 U.S.C. 509(a). However, the entity is not subrogated to the rights of the creditor to the extent that (1) its claim for reimbursement is allowed as a separate claim, disallowed as a claim, or subordinated by agreement or otherwise, or (2) as between the debtor and the entity, the entity received consideration for the debt. See 11 U.S.C. 509(b). Certain priority claims (i.e., unsecured claims for wages, salaries, commissions, contributions to employee benefit plans, the return of certain deposits, etc.) lose their priority if they are subrogated. See 11 U.S.C. 507(d). It should be noted that subordination agreements are enforceable in chapter 7 cases to the same extent that they are enforceable under nonbankruptcy law. See 11 U.S.C. 510(a).

transferred
claims, proof
of, filing
requirements

If a claim has been transferred other than for purposes of security before proof of the claim is filed, the proof of claim may be filed only by the transferee or an indenture trustee. See Bankruptcy Rule 3001(e)(1). If a claim other than one based on a publicly traded note, bond or debenture, is transferred other than for purposes of security after the filing of a proof of claim, evidence of the transfer must be filed by the transferee and the clerk must notify the alleged transferor of the filing and of the time for filing objections. See Bankruptcy Rule 3001(e)(2).

claims
transferred for
security, filing
requirements

objection to
transfer of
claim, procedure

If a claim, other than one based on a publicly traded note, bond or debenture, has been transferred for security before the filing of the proof of claim, either the transferor or the transferee, or both, may file a proof of claim in the full amount. See Bankruptcy Rule 3001(e)(3) for additional requirements. If a claim, other than one based on a publicly traded note, bond or debenture, is transferred for security after the filing of a proof of claim, evidence of the terms of the transfer must be filed by the transferee and the clerk must notify the alleged transferor of the filing and of the time for filing objections. See Bankruptcy Rule 3001(e)(4) for additional requirements. If an objection or motion is filed objecting to the transfer of a filed claim, a copy of the objection or motion, together with notice of the hearing, must be mailed or otherwise delivered to the transferor or transferee at least 30 days prior to the hearing. See Bankruptcy Rule 3001(e)(5).

A creditor may withdraw a claim as of right by filing a notice of withdrawal, except that if an objection to the claim or a complaint against the creditor in an adversary proceeding has been filed, the creditor may not withdraw the claim except on order of the court after a hearing on notice. See Bankruptcy Rule 3006.

An objection to the allowance of a claim must be in writing and filed with the clerk of the bankruptcy court. A copy of the objection and a notice of the hearing thereon must be mailed or otherwise delivered to the claimant, the debtor, and the trustee at least 30 days prior to the hearing. If an objection is joined with a demand for relief of the kind specified in Bankruptcy Rule 7001 (i.e., to determine the validity or priority of a lien, etc.), it becomes an adversary proceeding. See Bankruptcy Rule 3007. The local rules may contain provisions dealing with objections to claims, and they should be checked in this regard.

A properly executed and filed proof of claim constitutes prima facie evidence of the validity and amount of the claim. See Bankruptcy Rule 3001(f). Unless a party in interest files an objection to a properly filed claim, it is deemed allowed. See 11 U.S.C. 502(a). If an objection to a claim is properly made, the court, after a hearing on notice, must determine the amount of the claim as of the date of filing of the petition and allow the claim in that amount, unless the claim is not allowable under the Bankruptcy Code. See 11 U.S.C. 502(b).

In determining the allowability of claims, it should be noted that the following claims are not allowable under the Bankruptcy Code:

(1) Claims that are unenforceable against the debtor or property of the debtor by reason of an agreement or applicable law for any reason other than because a claim is contingent or unliquidated, are not allowable. See 11 U.S.C. 502(b)(1). This provision has the effect of giving the estate the benefit of any defenses to a claim that the debtor may possess. See 11 U.S.C. 558.

(2) Claims for unmatured interest are not allowable. See 11 U.S.C. 502(b)(2). This provision has the effect of denying unsecured creditors postpetition interest on their claims.

(3) Claims for taxes assessed against property of the estate are not allowable to the extent that the claim exceeds the value of the estate's interest in the property. See 11 U.S.C. 502(b)(3).

(4) Claims of insiders or attorneys of the debtor are not allowable to the extent that the claim exceeds the reasonable value of such services. See 11 U.S.C. 502(b)(4).

(5) Claims for unmatured alimony, maintenance, or support are not allowable to the extent that the claim is nondischargeable. See 11 U.S.C. 502(b)(5). This provision essentially bars claims for postpetition alimony, maintenance, or support.

(6) Claims of lessors for damages resulting from the termination of leases of real property are not allowable to the extent that the claim exceeds certain limits. See 11 U.S.C. 502(b)(6) for the specific limits.

(7) Claims of employees for damages resulting from the termination of employment contracts are not allowable to the extent that the claim exceeds certain limits. See 11 U.S.C. 502(b)(7) for the specific limits.

(8) Claims resulting from a reduction, due to late payment, in the amount of an otherwise applicable credit available to the debtor in connection with an employment tax on wages, salaries, or commissions earned from the debtor are not allowable. See 11 U.S.C. 502(b)(8). This provision applies mainly to claims of governmental units for unemployment taxes.

In addition, the claim of an entity from which property is recoverable by the trustee and the claim of an entity that is a transferee of a voidable transfer are not allowable, unless the entity has paid the amount or turned over the property for which it is liable. See 11 U.S.C. 502(d). Certain claims for reimbursement
or contribution are not allowable. See 11 U.S.C. 502(e). Contingent or unliquidated claims, the liquidation of which would unduly delay the closing of the case, must be estimated by the court for purposes of allowance. See 11 U.S.C. 502(c). It should be noted that proceedings to liquidate or estimate personal injury or wrongful death claims against the bankruptcy estate for purposes of distribution are not core proceedings. See 28 U.S.C. 157(b)(2)(B). See 11 U.S.C. 508 for the effect on a creditor's claim of payments or transfers received in another proceeding.

A party in interest may move for the reconsideration of an order allowing or disallowing a claim, whereupon the court, after a hearing on notice, must enter an appropriate order. See Bankruptcy Rule 3008. See 11 U.S.C. 502(j) for the effect of an order of reconsideration on the payment of claims.

A creditor with a right of setoff is treated as a secured creditor to the extent of the amount of the setoff. See 11 U.S.C. 506(a). A setoff is a right under nonbankruptcy law that exists between two parties to net (or setoff) their respective ascertainable debts that arose out of unrelated transactions. See In re IML Freight, Inc., 65 B.R. 788. The general rule is that a creditor may offset a mutual debt owed by the creditor to the debtor that arose before the commencement of the case against a claim of the creditor against the debtor that arose before the commencement of the case, except to the extent that:

(1) the creditor's claim against the debtor is disallowed,

(2) the creditor's claim was transferred to the creditor by a person other than the debtor after the commencement of the case or within 90 days prior to the date of filing of the petition and while the debtor was insolvent, or

(3) the debt owed to the debtor by the creditor was incurred by the creditor within 90 days before the date of filing, while the debtor was insolvent, and for the purpose of obtaining a right of setoff against the debtor. See 11 U.S.C. 553(a).

In addition, the trustee is permitted to recover all or part of most setoffs that occur within 90 days prior to the filing of the petition. See 11 U.S.C. 553(b). A debtor is presumed to have been insolvent during the 90 day-period preceding the filing of the petition. See 11 U.S.C. 553(c). Creditors are precluded by the automatic stay from exercising a right of setoff after the commencement of the case. See 11 U.S.C. 362(a)(7).

Subject to the provisions of 11 U.S.C. 553 described above, a creditor may validly exercise a right of setoff prior to the commencement of the case, provided that the setoff is completed and that a verifiable record, such as a bookkeeping entry or letter, exists to indicate a completion of the setoff. See In re Mc Cormick, 5 B.R. 726. After the commencement of the case, a creditor with an unexercised right of setoff should file a proof of claim showing the setoff as its security and file a motion for relief from the automatic stay for the purpose of exercising its right of setoff. A creditor who does nothing to enforce or protect its unexercised right of setoff may lose the right of setoff and be required to pay over to the trustee the full amount of the debt that it owes to the debtor.

It should be noted that if the debtor is denied a discharge, the statute of limitations will not have expired on claims against the debtor. 11 U.S.C. 108(c) provides that if applicable law, an order entered in a proceeding, or an agreement fixes a period for commencing a civil action in a court other than a bankruptcy court on a claim against the debtor, and if such period has not expired before the filing of the petition, then such period shall not expire until the later of - (a) the end of such period, including any suspensions of such period occurring on or after the commencement of the case, or (b) 30 days after notice of the termination or expiration of the automatic stay with respect to such claim. Thus, the statute of limitations on claims against the debtor will expire either at the time it would have otherwise expired or 30 days after receipt of the order of discharge, the notice of no discharge, or the notice of dismissal of the case, whichever is later.

Dividends to creditors must be paid as promptly as practicable in the amounts and at the times ordered by the court. Dividend checks shall be made payable and mailed to each creditor whose claim has been allowed, unless a power of attorney authorizing another person to receive dividends has been executed and filed in accordance with Bankruptcy Rule 9010. In that event, dividend checks shall be made payable to the creditor and to the other person and shall be mailed to the other person. See Bankruptcy Rule 3009. However, no dividend in an amount of less than five dollars shall be distributed by the trustee to any creditor unless authorized by local rule or by order of the court. See Bankruptcy Rule 3010(a).

dividends to
creditors.
procedure

Dividends are not paid to general unsecured creditors until all priority expenses and claims have been paid. See 11 U.S.C. 726(a). Under 11 U.S.C. 507(a), expenses and claims have priority in the following order:

priority claims
and expenses.
order of
priority

(1) Allowed administrative expenses (e.g., trustee's fees, etc.), and filing fees assessed against the bankruptcy estate.

(2) Certain unsecured claims arising before the appointment of a trustee in an involuntary case.

(3) Allowed unsecured claims for wages, salaries or commissions, including vacation, severance, and sick leave pay, earned by an individual within 90 days before either the date of filing of the petition or the date of the cessation of the debtor's business, whichever occurred first, but only to the extent of $2,000 for each individual.

(4) Allowed unsecured claims for contributions to employee benefit plans, within certain limits.

(5) Certain allowed unsecured claims (up to a limit of $2,000 for each individual) of fishermen and persons engaged in the production or raising of grain.

(6) Allowed unsecured claims of individuals, to the extent of $900 each, arising from the deposit of money for the purchase, lease, or rental of property, or the purchase of services, for the personal, family, or household use of such individuals, that were not delivered or provided.

(7) Allowed unsecured claims of governmental units for certain taxes.

2.20 The Dismissal, Conversion, or Closing of a Chapter 7 Case

chapter 7 case, methods of termination

A chapter 7 case may terminate in any of the following manners: (1) by the dismissal of the case under 11 U.S.C. 707(a) or 707(b); (2) by the conversion of the case to a case under chapter 11, 12, or 13 of title 11; or (3) by the closing of the case, with or without the granting of a discharge.

dismissal for abuse of chapter 7, requirements

After notice and a hearing, the court, on its own motion or on the motion of the United States trustee, but not at the request or suggestion of any party in interest, may dismiss the chapter 7 case of an individual debtor whose debts are primarily consumer debts if it finds that the granting of relief would be a substantial abuse of the provisions of chapter 7. See 11 U.S.C. 707(b). While a statutory presumption exists in favor of granting the relief requested by the debtor, the presumption may be rebutted by competent evidence. See In Re Strong, 84 B.R. 541. Dismissal under this section may not be sought by a creditor. See In Re Young, 92 B.R. 782.

substantial abuse of chapter 7, what constitutes

In determining what constitutes a substantial abuse of chapter 7, the courts have generally held that if it appears that a qualifying debtor will have sufficient income with which to repay a meaningful portion of his or her debts, either in a case under chapter 11, 12, or 13, or otherwise, then the case may be dismissed as a substantial abuse of chapter 7. See In re Bell, 56 B.R. 637. It should be noted that Section 707(b) applies only to debtors whose debts are primarily consumer debts, which are debts incurred primarily for a personal, family, or household purpose. Business debts are not consumer debts, and Section 707(b) has been held not to apply to a debtor whose business debts constituted more than one-half of the total amount of debts, even though the number of consumer debts was substantially greater than the number of business debts. See In Re Kelly, 841 F. 2d 908.

dismissal for abuse of chapter 7, procedure

A chapter 7 case may be dismissed for substantial abuse under Section 707(b) only on the motion of the United States trustee or on the court's own motion and after a hearing on notice to the debtor, the trustee, the United States trustee, and such other parties in interest as the court directs. The motion by the United States trustee must be filed not later than 60 days after the first date set for the meeting of creditors, unless within such period the court for cause extends the time. If the hearing is on the court's own motion, notice of the motion must be served on the debtor not later than 60 days after the first date set for the meeting of creditors. The motion or notice, as the case may be, must advise the debtor of all matters that will be submitted to or considered by the court at the hearing. See Bankruptcy Rule 1017(e).

dismissal of chapter 7 case for cause, procedure

The court may dismiss a chapter 7 case under 11 U.S.C. 707(a) only after notice and a hearing, and only for cause, including nonpayment of the filing fee, unreasonable delay by the debtor that is prejudicial to creditors, and, on the motion of the United States trustee only, the failure of the debtor to timely file the required schedules and statements. A proceeding to dismiss a chapter 7 case under 11 U.S.C. 707(a) is a contested matter governed by Bankruptcy Rule 9014. See Bankruptcy Rule 1017(d).

dismissal for failure to pay filing fee, procedure

After a hearing on notice to the debtor and the trustee, the court may dismiss a chapter 7 case for failure to pay any installment of the filing fee. See Bankruptcy Rule 1017(b)(1). Within 30 days after a dismissal for failure to pay the filing fee, notice of the dismissal must be mailed by the clerk to all creditors appearing on the list of creditors and to those who have filed claims. See Bankruptcy Rule 1017(b)(3).

dismissal of case, general requirements

dismissal of case by debtor, requirements

Except for dismissals for substantial abuse under 11 U.S.C. 707(b), a chapter 7 case may not be dismissed, whether on the motion of the debtor, for want of prosecution, by the consent of the parties, or for any other cause, prior to a hearing on not less than 20 days notice by mail to the debtor, the trustee, and all creditors, a list of which, if not previously filed, must be provided by the debtor within the time fixed by the court. See Bankruptcy Rules 1017(a), 2002(a). If dismissal is sought by the debtor, the debtor, too, must show cause, as a chapter 7 case may be dismissed only for cause and may not be dismissed solely because of a change of heart by the debtor. See In Re Pagnotta, 22 B.R. 521.

The debtor may, without cause, convert a chapter 7 case to a case under chapter 11, 12, or 13 at any time, provided that the case has not been previously converted to chapter 7 from chapter 11, 12 or 13, and provided that the debtor qualifies as a debtor under the chapter to which conversion is sought. See 11 U.S.C. 706(a),(d). Any waiver of this right of conversion by the debtor is unenforceable. See 11 U.S.C. 706(a). The voluntary conversion of a chapter 7 case under 11 U.S.C. 706(a) is implemented by the filing and service of a motion under Bankruptcy Rule 9013. See Bankruptcy Rule 1017(d). A hearing is not required on such a motion unless the court so directs. See Advisory Committee's Notes to Bankruptcy Rule 1017(d). A debtor who converts a chapter 7 to a case under chapter 11 must pay a $400 filing fee.

conversion of case by debtor. procedure

On the motion of a party in interest, and after notice and a hearing, the court may convert a chapter 7 case to a case under chapter 11 at any time. See 11 U.S.C. 706(b). However, the court may not convert a chapter 7 case to a case under chapter 12 or chapter 13 unless the debtor requests such conversion. See 11 U.S.C. 706(c). Thus, a chapter 7 case may be converted to chapter 11 over the objection of the debtor, but not to chapter 12 or 13.

involuntary conversion of case. general requirements

Except for voluntary conversions under 11 U.S.C. 706(a) and dismissals for substantial abuse under 11 U.S.C. 707(b), proceedings to dismiss a chapter 7 case or to convert a chapter 7 case to another chapter are governed by Bankruptcy Rule 9014. See Bankruptcy Rule 1017(d). Under Bankruptcy Rule 9014, the desired relief must be requested by motion and there must be reasonable notice and an opportunity for a hearing afforded the party against whom relief is sought. Reasonable notice in dismissal proceedings means not less than 20 days notice by mail to the debtor, the trustee, and all creditors, except that after 90 days following the first date set for the meeting of creditors, the court may direct that notices be mailed only to those creditors who have filed claims in the case or who may still legally do so. See Bankruptcy Rules 2002(a)(5), 2002(h). The motion must be in writing and must state with particularity the grounds therefor and set forth the relief or order sought. It must be served on the United States trustee, the trustee, and the persons specified in any applicable Bankruptcy Rule or by the court. See Bankruptcy Rules 9013 and 9034.

proceedings to dismiss or convert case. procedure

The conversion of a chapter 7 case to a case under another chapter constitutes an order for relief under the new chapter, but, with minor exceptions, does not change the date of the filing of the petition, the date of the commencement of the case, or the date of the order for relief. See 11 U.S.C. 348(a). Notice of conversion of the case must be given by the clerk or such other person as the court may direct to the debtor, all creditors, and the United States trustee. See 11 U.S.C. 348(c) and Bankruptcy Rules 2002(f), (k). The conversion of a chapter 7 case to another chapter terminates the services of the trustee serving in the chapter 7 case.

conversion of case to another chapter. effect of

Unless the court, for cause, orders otherwise, the dismissal of a chapter 7 case - (1) reinstates any proceeding superseded by the case, reinstates certain transfers voided or preserved in the case, and reinstates certain liens voided in the case, (2) vacates certain orders, judgments, or transfers ordered in the case, and (3) revests the property of the bankruptcy estate in the entity in which such property was vested immediately before the commencement of the case. See 11 U.S.C. 349(b). The dismissal of a case also causes the debtor to lose the postcase benefit of any exemptions claimed in the case, including the federal bankruptcy exemptions. See 11 U.S.C. 522(c). Unless the court, for cause, orders otherwise, the dismissal of a chapter 7 case does not bar the discharge, in a later case under title 11, of debts that were dischargeable in the case dismissed. See 11 U.S.C. 349(a). Finally, the dismissal of a case terminates the automatic stay. See 11 U.S.C. 362(c)(2).

dismissal of case. effect of

Appeals from final orders, judgments, and decrees (and, with leave of the appellate court, of interlocutory orders and decrees) of bankruptcy judges must be taken to the United States district court in the district in which the bankruptcy court is located. See 28 U.S.C. 158(a). However, if the circuit in which the district court sits has established a bankruptcy appellate panel, appeals from final orders, etc. of bankruptcy judges may, with the consent of all parties, be taken to the appellate panel, provided that the local district judges, by majority vote, have authorized the referral of such appeals to the appellate panel. See 28 U.S.C. 158(b). The provisions of 28 U.S.C. 158 are set forth in Appendix I, infra. Appellate procedures are contained in Part VIII of the Rules of Bankruptcy Procedure, which are set forth in Appendix II, infra.

appeals. procedures

closing case.
procedure

     The trustee must close the estate as expeditiously as is compatible with the best interests of the parties in interest. See 11 U.S.C. 704(1). The trustee must also make a final report and file a final account of the administration of the estate, if any, with the court. See 11 U.S.C. 704(9). If the net proceeds of the case exceed $1,500, the clerk, or such other person as the court may direct, must give the debtor and all creditors notice by mail of a summary of the trustee's final report and account. See Bankruptcy Rule 2002(f)(8). Otherwise, a chapter 7 case may be closed without notice to the debtor or the creditors, unless the local rules provide otherwise.

final decree.
contents

     After the estate, if any, has been fully administered, the court must enter a final decree - (1) discharging the trustee, (2) making such provisions by way of injunction or otherwise as may be equitable, and (3) closing the case. See 11 U.S.C. 350(a). If no objection is filed to the trustee's final report and account within 30 days after the filing thereof, it may be presumed that the estate has been fully administered. See Bankruptcy Rule 5009. The closing of a case terminates the automatic stay to the extent that it was not earlier terminated. See 11 U.S.C. 362(c)(2).

reopening case.
rules governing

     Upon the motion of the debtor or other party in interest, a chapter 7 case may be reopened in the court in which the case was closed to administer assets, to accord relief to the debtor, or for other cause. See 11 U.S.C. 350(b). The reopening of a chapter 7 case lies in the discretion of the bankruptcy court. See In Re Smith, 68 B.R. 897. While the court will normally reopen a case if good cause is shown, if the debtor has been guilty of laches or if other equitable grounds exist for not reopening a case, the court may properly refuse to do so. See In Re Carilli, 65 B.R. 280. If a chapter 7 case is reopened, a trustee may not be appointed by the United States trustee unless the court determines that a trustee is necessary to protect the interests of creditors and the debtor or to insure the efficient administration of the case. See Bankruptcy Rule 5010.

EXHIBIT 2-A   69

UNITED STATES BANKRUPTCY COURT

__SOUTHERN__   **DISTRICT OF** ___OHIO___

IN RE Sidney Samuel Smith
and Sarah Arlene Smith,   Case No. _____
                                                              (If known)

                              Debtors   Chapter ____7_____

DISCLOSURE OF COMPENSATION OF ATTORNEY FOR DEBTOR

1. Pursuant to 11 U.S.C. § 329(a) and Bankruptcy Rule 2016(b), I certify that I am the attorney for the above-named debtor(s) and that the compensation paid to me within one year before the filing of the petition in bankruptcy, or agreed to be paid to me, for services rendered or to be rendered on behalf of the debtor(s) in contemplation of or in connection with this bankruptcy case is as follows:

For legal services, I have agreed to accept .... $ _600.00_____

Prior to the filing of this statement I have received .... $ _None_____

Balance Due .... $ _600.00_____

2. The source of the compensation paid to me was:

    ☒ Debtor s   ☐ Other (specify)

3. The source of the compensation to be paid to me is:

    ☒ Debtor s   ☐ Other (specify)

4. ☒ I have not agreed to share the above-disclosed compensation with any other person unless they are members or associates of my law firm.

    ☐ I have agreed to share the above-disclosed compensation with a person or persons who are not members or associates of my law firm. A copy of the agreement, together with a list of the names of the people sharing in the compensation, is attached.

5. In return for the above-disclosed fee, I have agreed to render legal service for all aspects of the bankruptcy case, including:

    a. Analysis of the debtor's financial situation, and rendering advice to the debtor in determining whether to file a petition in bankruptcy;

    b. Preparation and filing of any petition, schedules, statements, and plan which may be required.

    c. Representation of the debtor at the meeting of creditors and confirmation hearing, and any adjourned hearings thereof;

    d. Representation of the debtor in adversary proceedings and other contested bankruptcy matters;

    e. (other provisions as needed) __Assisting the debtors in carrying out their Statement of__
        __Intention._____

6. By agreement with the debtor(s), the above-disclosed fee does not include the following services: __Appeals from__
    ____rulings of bankruptcy court._____

CERTIFICATION

    I certify that the foregoing is a complete statement of any agreement or arrangement for payment to me for representation of the debtor(s) in this bankruptcy proceeding.

Date: __January 15, 1992_____   _Alice B. Chase_____
                                            Alice B. Chase
                                            Attorney for Debtor(s)
                          Name of Law firm Chase and Chase
                                   Address 2000 Market Street
                                            Columbus, OH 43222
                                            Telephone: 614-333-3300

BANKRUPTCY FORM B 203 – Argyle Publishing Co., 10395 West Colfax Ave., Lakewood, CO 80215

EXHIBIT 2-B

(These work sheets may be reproduced for use by an attorney in the practice of law)

BANKRUPTCY WORK SHEETS

GENERAL INFORMATION: The questions in these work sheets should be answered by or on behalf of the debtor if a single case is to be filed or by or on behalf of both spouses if a joint case is to be filed. In these work sheets, a debtor is a person for whom a bankruptcy case is filed under chapter 7, chapter 12, or chapter 13 of the Bankruptcy Code. The DEBT FORM referred to below is located on the last page of these work sheets.

INSTRUCTIONS TO DEBTOR: Answer each question completely and truthfully. If more space is needed to completely answer a question, complete the answer on a separate sheet of paper or on the back of the work sheet. If you do not understand a question write "Don't Understand" after the question. Do not guess at the answer to any question. Except as otherwise directed below in these work sheets, the questions that are marked with an * should be answered only if a joint case is being filed, and the requested information related to your spouse in the other questions should be given only if a joint case is being filed. When indicating ownership of property or liability for a debt, use "H" for husband, "W" for wife, and "J" for joint ownership or liability by both husband and wife. The value listed for any item should be the estimated present market value of the item without regard to any lien, mortgage or exemption.

ADVISEMENT TO DEBTOR: Official Bankruptcy Forms will be completed using the information that you give in these work sheets and you will be required to sign a declaration stating under penalty of perjury that the information is true and correct. **A failure to disclose assets in a bankruptcy case is a federal crime punishable by imprisonment for up to five years and by a fine of up to $5,000.** In addition, a failure to provide complete and accurate information on your bankruptcy forms may result in the dismissal of your bankruptcy case or in a denial of your bankruptcy discharge, which means that your debts will not be discharged. Also, a debt owed to a creditor who is not listed on your bankruptcy forms, or whose address on the forms is incorrect, will probably not be discharged, in which case you will remain liable to that creditor after the bankruptcy case.

Preliminary Information

1. List the name of the debtor, or the primary debtor if a joint case is to be filed. _____

2. List the name of the spouse of the person listed above. _____

3. List the date or dates upon which these work sheets were completed. _____

Petition Information

4. What is your full name? _____

*5. What is your spouse's full name? _____

6. What other names have you used in the last 6 years (include married or maiden names and names under which you have conducted business)? _____
_____

*7. What other names has your spouse used in the last 6 years (include married or maiden names and names under which he or she has conducted business)? _____
_____

8. What is your social security or tax identification number? _____

*9. What is your spouse's social security or tax identification number? _____

10. What is your street address? _____
                      no. & street   city   state   zip code

11. In what county is your residence or principal place of business located? _____

*12. What is your spouse's street address? _____
                      no. & street   city   state   zip code

*13. In what county is your spouse's residence or principal place of business located? _____

* Answer question only if a joint case is being filed.

EXHIBIT 2-B   Bankruptcy Work Sheets - page 2   71

14. What is your mailing address? _____

*15. What is your spouse's mailing address? _____

16. Where are your principal business assets, if any, located? _____

17. Where have you resided for the last 180 days? _____

18. Are you engaged in a business other than as an employee? _____ If so, state the type or field of business that you are engaged in and briefly describe the nature of the business. _____

_____

19. Has a bankruptcy case been filed by or against you within the last 6 years? _____ If so, when and where was the case filed and what was the case number? _____

20. Is there a bankruptcy case now pending against your spouse or against a business partner or associate of yours? _____ If so, attach papers showing the particulars of the case.

Schedule A Information - Your Real Estate

21. Do you or your spouse own or have an interest in any real estate? _____

22. If the answer to question 21 is yes, complete the following showing each parcel of real estate that you or your spouse own or have an interest in:

Address of property	Legal description of property	Nature of your interest in the property	Nature of your spouse's interest in the property	Date property acquired	Estimated market value of property	Amount of each mortgage or lien against property

Schedule B Information - Your Personal Property

23. How much cash do you now have? $_____

*24. How much cash does your spouse now have? $_____

25. When do you next get paid? _____ How much do you expect to receive? $_____ To what date will you then be paid? _____

*26. When does your spouse next get paid? _____ How much will he or she receive? $_____ To what date will he or she then be paid ? _____

27. Are you owed any accrued and unpaid vacation, sick leave, or similar pay? _____ If so, how much is owed and who owes it? $_____ _____

*28. Is your spouse owed any accrued and unpaid vacation, sick leave, or similar pay? _____ If so, how much is owed and who owes it? $_____ _____

29. Do you or your spouse have any accounts, deposits, or shares in any bank or financial institution? _____ If so, complete the following showing each account, deposit or share:

Name and address of financial institution	Name or names under which the account, deposit or shares are registered	Amount of deposit or account, or value of shares

* Answer question only if a joint case is being filed.

30. Do you or your spouse have any security deposits with a landlord, telephone company, utility company, or anyone else? _____ If so, state who made each deposit and list the amount of each deposit and the name and address of the holder of each deposit. _____

_____

31. Do you or your spouse own any household goods or furnishings, including audio, video, or computer equipment? _____ If so, using a separate sheet of paper or the back of this sheet, list each item, or group of items and show the location and estimated market value of each without regard to any mortgage or lien, and state whether the items are owned by you, your spouse, or jointly. State the total market value of all of these items without regard to any mortgages or liens. $_____

32. Do you or your spouse own any books, pictures, art objects, antiques, stamp, coin, record, tape, compact disc, or other collections or collectibles? _____ If so, describe them, list their location and estimated market value, and state whether they are owned by you, your spouse, or jointly. _____

_____

33. What is the total market value of all of your wearing apparel? $_____ Using a separate sheet of paper or the back of this sheet, list each item of wearing apparel that has a market value of $20 or more. Include such items as watches and similar articles that are not made of gold or silver or set with gems.

*34. What is the total market value of all of your spouse's wearing apparel? $_____ Using a separate sheet of paper or the back of this sheet, list each item of wearing apparel that has a market value of $20 or more. Include such items as watches and similar articles that are not made of gold or silver or set with gems.

35. Do you or your spouse own any furs or jewelry? _____ If so, identify each item, list its location and market value, and identify its owner. _____

_____

36. Do you or your spouse own any firearms, sports equipment, photographic equipment, or other hobby equipment? _____ If so, identify each item, list its location and estimated market value, and identify its owner. _____

_____

37. Do you or your spouse own an interest in a life insurance policy? _____ If so, identify each policy by policy number, owner, name of insurance company, amount of death benefit, and name of beneficiaries, and list the cash surrender or refund value of each policy. _____

_____

38. Do you or your spouse own or have an interest in an annuity? _____ If so, identify each annuity by number, owner, and issuer and list the value and terms of each annuity. _____

_____

39. Do you or your spouse have an interest in an IRA, ERISA, Keogh, or other retirement, pension, or profit-sharing plan? _____ If so, identify each plan and list the present value of the interest of you or your spouse in each plan. _____

_____

40. Do you or your spouse own any stock in a corporation or an interest in any partnership, joint venture, or other business? _____ If so, describe the stock or interest and list its owner and estimated market value.

_____

41. Do you or your spouse own any government or corporate bonds or similar instruments? _____ If so, describe each instrument and list its owner, location, and market value. _____

42. Do you or your spouse own any accounts receivable? _____ If so, describe them and list their owner and estimated value. _____

* Answer question only if a joint case is being filed.

EXHIBIT 2-B   Bankruptcy Work Sheets - page 4   73

43. Are you or your spouse owed any accrued and unpaid alimony, maintenance, support, or property settlement payments? _____ If so, how much is owed, by and to whom is it owed, and what is the nature of the obligation? $_____ _____

44. Are you or your spouse entitled to any tax refunds or other money, the amount of which has been determined? _____ If so, state the amount owed and identify the person to whom it is owed and the entity that owes it. $_____ _____

45. Do you or your spouse own or have an equitable or future interest in any property? _____ If so, describe each interest and list its owner and present market value. _____

_____

46. Do you or your spouse own or have an interest of any kind in the estate of a deceased person, in a death benefit plan, in the death benefits in a life insurance policy, or in a trust? _____ If so, describe each interest and list its owner and present market value. _____

_____

47. Are you or your spouse entitled to any tax refunds or do you have any counterclaims or rights of setoff against other persons, the existence or amount of which is presently unclear or undetermined? _____ If so, describe each one, identify its owners, and estimate its present value. _____

_____

48. Do you or your spouse own or have an ownership interest in any patents, copyrights, or other intellectual property? _____ If so, describe each interest, list its value, and identify the owners. _____

_____

49. Do you or your spouse own or have an ownership interest in any license, franchise, or similar property? _____ If so, describe each interest and list its estimated market value, and identify the owners. _____

_____

50. Do you or your spouse own or have an ownership interest in any automobiles, trucks, trailers, or other vehicles or accessories? _____ If so, describe each vehicle or accessory, identify the owners, and list its location, vehicle identification number, if any, and estimated market value. _____

_____

_____

51. Do you or your spouse own or have an ownership interest in any boats, motors, or accessories? _____ If so, describe each item, list its location and market value, and identify the owners. _____

_____

52. Do you or your spouse own or have an ownership interest in any aircraft or accessories? _____ If so, identify each item, list its location and market value, and identify the owners. _____

_____

53. Do you or your spouse own any office equipment, office furnishings, or office supplies? _____ If so, using a separate sheet of paper or the back of this sheet, list each item or group of items, show the location and market value of each, and identify the owners.

54. Do you or your spouse own or have an ownership interest in any machinery, fixtures, equipment, or supplies used in business? _____ If so, identify each item or group of items, list their location and market value, and identify the owners. _____

_____

55. Do you or your spouse own or have an ownership interest in any commercial inventory? _____ If so, describe the inventory, list its location and market value, and identify the owners. _____

_____

56. Do you or your spouse own or have an ownership interest in any animals? _____ If so, describe each animal or group of animals, list their location and market value, and identify the owners. _____

_____

57. Do you or your spouse own or have an ownership interest in any growing or harvested crops? _____ If so, describe the crops, list their market value, and identify the owners. _____

_____

58. Do you or your spouse own or have an ownership interest in any farming equipment or implements? _____ If so, using a separate sheet of paper or the back of this work sheet, describe each item, list its location and market value.

59. Do you or your spouse own any farm supplies, chemicals, or feed? _____ If so, describe each item or group of items, list their market value and identify the owners. _____

_____

60. Do you or your spouse own or have an ownership interest in any other personal property of any kind that has not been listed above in these work sheets? _____ If so, describe the property, list its location and market value, and identify the owners. _____

_____

Schedule D Information - Your Secured Debts

61. Do any of your creditors have liens, mortgages, or other encumbrances against any of your property? _____ If so, how many debts are owed to those creditors? _____. Fill out a separate DEBT FORM for each debt owed to those creditors and write the word "secured" at the top of each completed form.

*62. Do any of your spouse's creditors have liens, mortgages, or other encumbrances against any of his or her property other than those creditors for whom a form was filled out in response to question 61? _____ If so, how may debts are owed to those creditors? _____ Fill out a separate DEBT FORM for each debt owed to those creditors and write the word "secured" at the top of each completed form.

Schedule E Information - Your Priority Unsecured Debts

63. Do you or your spouse owe any debts to employees for wages, salaries, or commissions, including vacation, severance, or sick leave pay? _____ If so, identify the employees and the persons liable for the debt, and list the amount owed to each employee and the dates that the wages, etc. were earned. _____

_____

64. Do you or your spouse owe any debts for unpaid employer's contributions to employee benefit plans? _____ If so, identify the employees, the plan, and the person liable for the debt, and list the amount owed and the dates that the services were rendered for the unpaid contributions. _____

_____

65. Do you or your spouse operate a grain storage facility or a fish produce storage or processing facility? _____

66. Do you or your spouse owe any debts for the return of deposits made for the purchase, lease, or rental of property or services that were not provided? _____ If so, describe each debt, list the amount owed for each, and identify the persons liable for the debt. _____

_____

67. Do you or your spouse owe any debts to any local, state, or federal government for taxes, customs, duties, or penalties? _____ If so, describe each debt, list the name and address of the governmental department to whom it is owed, list the amount owed and the date that it first became due and identify the persons liable for the debt. _____

_____

* Answer question only if a joint case is being filed.

EXHIBIT 2-B   Bankruptcy Work Sheets - page 6   75

Schedule E Information - Your General Unsecured Debts

68. Fill out a separate DEBT FORM for each general unsecured debt that you owe (that is, for each debt that was not listed or described in response to questions 61-67). How many of these debts are there? _____

*69. Fill out a separate DEBT FORM for each general unsecured debt that your spouse owes that has not been listed or described in response to questions 61-68. How many of these debts are there? _____

Schedule G Information - Your Existing Contracts and Leases

70. Are you or your spouse a party to any contracts or leases that are still in effect? _____ If so, describe each contract or lease and list the name and address of all parties to each contract or lease. _____

_____

_____

Schedule H Information - Codebtors

71. Is anyone beside yourself liable for any of your debts? _____ If so, the name and address of each person that is liable with you for a particular debt should appear in items 4 and 5 of the DEBT FORM filled out for that debt. List the name and address of each of these persons. _____

_____

_____

*72. Is anyone beside you and your spouse liable for any of your spouse's debts? _____ If so, the name and address of each person that is liable with your spouse for a particular debt should appear in item 4 of the DEBT FORM filled out for that debt. List the name and address of each of these persons other than those listed in response to question 72. _____

_____

_____

Schedule I Information - Your Current Income

73. What is your marital status? _____

74. List the name, age, and relationship of each of your dependents. _____

_____

_____

75. What is your occupation? _____

76. List the name and address of your employer. _____

_____

77. How long have you been employed by this employer? _____

78. What is your spouse's occupation? _____

79. List the name and address of your spouse's employer. _____

_____

80. How long has your spouse been employed by this employer? _____

* Answer question only if a joint case is being filed.

81. Complete the following showing your current monthly income. If you are not paid on a monthly basis, either pro-rate your income to a monthly amount or enter the periodic amount and make an appropriate notation. The column labeled "Your Spouse's Income" must be completed if a joint case is being filed or if you are married and filing a single chapter 12 or 13 case, unless you and your spouse are separated.

	YOUR INCOME	YOUR SPOUSE'S INCOME
Current monthly gross wages, salary, and commissions	$_____	$_____
Estimated monthly overtime	$_____	$_____
SUBTOTAL	$_____	$_____
LESS PAYROLL DEDUCTIONS		
a. Payroll taxes and social security	$_____	$_____
b. Insurance	$_____	$_____
c. Union dues	$_____	$_____
d. Other (Specify: _____)	$_____	$_____
SUBTOTAL OF PAYROLL DEDUCTIONS	$_____	$_____
TOTAL NET MONTHLY TAKE HOME PAY	$_____	$_____
Regular income from operation of business or profession or farm (attach detailed statement)	$_____	$_____
Income from real property	$_____	$_____
Interest and dividends	$_____	$_____
Alimony, maintenance or support payments payable to the debtor for the debtor's use or that of dependents listed above.	$_____	$_____
Social security or other government assistance (Specify) _____	$_____	$_____
Pension or retirement income	$_____	$_____
Other monthly income (Specify) _____	$_____	$_____
TOTAL MONTHLY INCOME	$_____	$_____

TOTAL COMBINED MONTHLY INCOME $ _____

Describe any increase or decrease of more than 10% in any of the above categories anticipated to occur within the year following the filing of this document:

EXHIBIT 2-B   Bankruptcy Work Sheets - page 8   77

Schedule J Information - Your Current Expenditures

82. Complete the following by estimating the average monthly expenses of yourself and your family. Payments that are made other than monthly should be pro-rated to a monthly amount, if possible. Otherwise make an appropriate notation. If a joint petition is being filed and if your spouse maintains a separate household, make a separate list of expenditures for your spouse to the right of your list.

YOUR
EXPENDITURES

Rent or home mortgage payment (include lot rented for mobile home) .... $_____

Are real estate taxes included?   Yes_____   No _____

Is property insurance included?   Yes_____   No _____

Utilities: Electricity and heating fuel .... $_____

             Water and sewer .... $_____

             Telephone .... $_____

             Other _____   ...... $_____

Home maintenance (repairs and upkeep) .... $_____

Food .... $_____

Clothing .... $_____

Laundry and dry cleaning .... $_____

Medical and dental expenses .... $_____

Transportation (not including car payments) .... $_____

Recreation, clubs and entertainment, newspapers, magazines, etc. .... $_____

Charitable contributions .... $_____

Insurance (not deducted from wages or included in home mortgage payments)

             Homeowner's or renter's .... $_____

             Life .... $_____

             Health .... $_____

             Auto .... $_____

             Other _____   ...... $_____

Taxes (not deducted from wages or included in home mortgage payments)

(Specify) _____   ...... $_____

Installment payments: (In chapter 12 and 13 cases, do not list payments to be included in the plan)

             Auto .... $_____

             Other _____

                                                      ...... $_____

             Other _____   ...... $_____

             Other _____   ...... $_____

Alimony, maintenance, and support paid to others .... $_____

Payments for support of additional dependents not living at your home .... $_____

Regular expenses from operation of business, profession, or farm (attach detailed statement)......... $_____

Other _____   ...... $_____

Other _____   ...... $_____

TOTAL MONTHLY EXPENSES .... $_____

Statement of Financial Affairs Information

NOTE – If you are filing a chapter 12 or chapter 13 case and if you are married and living with your spouse, then the questions below pertaining to your spouse must be answered, and the requested information related to your spouse must be given, even if you are not filing a joint case.

83. How much gross income have you received from your employment or business in this calendar ** year? $_____

84. How much gross income have you received from your employment or business during each of the last two calendar ** years? Last year: $_____   Year before: $_____

*85. How much gross income has your spouse received from his or her employment or business in this calendar ** year? $_____

*86. How much gross income has your spouse received from his or her employment during each of the last two calendar ** years? Last year: $_____   Year before: $_____

87. How much income have you received other than from your employment or business during the last two years? $_____ What was the source of this income? _____

*88. How much income has your spouse received other than from his or her employment or business during the last two years? $_____ What was the source of this income? _____

89. Complete the following showing each creditor to whom you or your spouse have paid more than $600 in the last 90 days.

Name and address of creditor	Date of payment	Maker of payment	Amount paid	Amount still owing

90. Complete the following showing each payment that you or your spouse have made within the last 365 days to (or for the benefit of) a relative or business associate of any kind.

Name and address of creditor	Relationship of creditor to you	Date of payment	Maker of payment	Amount paid	Amount still owing

91. Complete the following showing all lawsuits in which you or your spouse have been involved as a party during the last 365 days.

Name of case and case number	Nature of case	Court	Status or disposition of case

* Answer question only if a joint case is being filed, except as directed in the note at the top of this page.

** If you operate your business on a fiscal year other than the calendar year, substitute fiscal year for calendar year and identify your fiscal year.

EXHIBIT 2-B   Bankruptcy Work Sheets - page 10   79

92. Complete the following showing all money or property of yourself or your spouse that has been attached, garnished or seized in a court proceeding within the last 365 days.

Name and address of creditor	Date of seizure	Owner of property seized	Description and value of property seized

93. Complete the following showing all property owned by yourself or your spouse that within the last 365 days has been repossessed by a creditor, foreclosed upon, or otherwise returned to the seller.

Name and address of creditor or seller	Date of repossession, foreclosure or return	Description and value of property	Owner of property

94. Have your or your spouse made an assignment for the benefit of creditors within the last 120 days? _____ If so, attach copies of all papers relating to the assignment.

95. Has any of your property or your spouse's property been held by a custodian, receiver, or other court-appointed official during the last 365 days? _____ If so, attach copies of all papers relating to the proceeding.

96. Complete the following showing all gifts or charitable contributions made by you or your spouse within the last 365 days, except ordinary gifts to family members totalling less than $200 per recipient and charitable contributions of less than $100 per recipient.

Name and address of recipient	Relationship of recipient to you	Date of gift	Description and value of gift	Person who made the gift

97. Complete the following showing any losses from fire, theft, or other casualty, or from gambling, that you or your spouse have incurred during the last 365 days.

Type of loss	Property lost	Date of loss	Amount of loss	Covered by insurance?	Person who incurred the loss

98. Complete the following showing all transfers of money or property within the last 365 days by or on behalf of you or your spouse to attorneys or other persons for debt consolidation or the filing of a bankruptcy case.

Name and address of person paid	Date of payment	Name of person who made payment	Amount paid or value and description of property transferred

99. Complete the following showing all transfers of money or property made by you or your spouse within the last 365 days, other than property or money transferred in the ordinary course of your business or financial affairs and the transfers listed in response to question 98.

Name and address of transferee	Relationship of transferee to you	Date of transfer	Description and value of property transferred	Owner of property transferred

100. Complete the following showing all checking, savings, or other financial accounts, certificates of deposits, and shares in banks, credit unions or other financial institutions that you or your spouse have closed, transferred, or sold during the last 365 days.

Name and address of financial institution	Name of account, account number and type of account	Amount of final balance of account	Date of any sale and amount received

101. Complete the following showing all safety deposit boxes or other boxes or depositories in which you or your spouse have kept cash, securities, or other valuables within the last 365 days.

Name and address of bank or depository	Names and address of all persons with access to box or depository	Description of contents	Date of transfer or surrender, if any

102. Has any creditor, including a bank, made a setoff against a debt or deposit of you or your spouse within the last 90 days? _____ If so, list the name and address of the creditor and the date and amount of the setoff. _____

_____

103. Do you or your spouse hold or control any property owned by another person? _____ If so, list the name and address of the owner, describe the property, and list its value and location. _____

_____

104. Have you or your spouse moved during the last 24 months? _____ If so, give the address of each place where either of you lived during that period, the name or names used at that address, and the dates of occupancy. _____

_____

EXHIBIT 2-B   Bankruptcy Work Sheets - page 12   81

105. Have you or your spouse, within the last two years, been any of the following: (a) an officer, director, managing executive, or the owner of more than 5% of the voting stock of a corporation; (b) a general partner of a partnership; or (c) a sole proprietor or self-employed person? Yourself _____ Your spouse _____
If both answers are "no" or if your spouse is not filing and the answer for yourself is "no," then questions 106-111 need not be answered. Otherwise, each of the questions below must be answered.

106. Complete the following showing all business with which you or your spouse have been involved in the manner described in question 105 during the last two years.

Name and address of business	Nature of business	Dates of beginning and ending of business operation	Owner of business

Note: The following questions should be answered for any business listed in the answer to question 106.

107. List the names and addresses of, and the dates services were rendered by, any bookkeepers or accountants who kept or supervised the keeping of the books and records of your business within the last six years.

_____

_____

108. List the names and addresses of, and the dates services were rendered by, any firms or persons who, within the last two years, have audited the books and records of your business or prepared a financial statement for you or your business. _____

_____

109. List the names and addresses of all firms or persons who now have possession of your business books and records, and if any of your business books and records are not available, explain why. _____

_____

110. List the name and address of all banks, creditors, trade agencies, and other parties to whom you have issued a financial statement within the last two years and the date the statement was issued. _____

_____

111. Complete the following showing the last two inventories taken of your business property.

Date of inventory	Inventory supervisor	Amount of inventory in dollars	Basis of inventory (cost, market value, etc.)	Name and address of person having custody of inventory records

DEBT FORM

Instructions to Debtor: Complete one of these forms for each debt of any kind. If possible, attach a copy of the creditor's most recent statement or bill to the completed form. Respond to every question on this form. Write "N/A" in the blank after each question that does not apply to a particular debt. If more space is needed to answer a question, use the back of the form.

1. List the complete name and address of the party to whom this debt is owed. _____
   name

   _____ _____ _____ _____
   address   city   state   zipcode

2. What is the creditor's account number for this debt? _____

3. Is this debt covered or secured by a mortgage, lien, pledge, or other security interest on any property? _____
   If so, is this property listed elsewhere in these Work Sheets? _____ In what question? _____
   If it is not listed in these Work Sheets, describe the property and list its owner, value and location. _____

   _____

4. Which of the spouses is liable for this debt (check one)? Husband _____ Wife _____ Both _____

5. Is anyone beside you or your spouse liable for this debt? _____ If so, list the person's name and address. _____

6. Has this debt been turned over to someone for collection? _____ If so, to whom? _____
   name

   _____ _____ _____ _____
   address   city   state   zipcode

7. When did you incur this debt? Month _____ Year _____

8. What did you receive in consideration for this debt? _____

9. Does this creditor owe you a debt? _____ If so, can the creditor's debt be setoff against your debt? _____

10. Is this debt contingent upon anything? _____ If so, explain _____

11. Has the final amount of this debt been determined? _____

12. Do you admit that you are liable for the full amount of this debt? _____ If not, explain. _____

    _____

13. Do you and the creditor agree on the amount of this debt? _____ If not, explain. _____

    _____

14. What is the total amount of this debt? $_____

15. Have you given a written financial statement in connection with this debt? _____ If so, attach a copy of the statement to this form and state to whom and when the statement was given. _____

    _____

16. Do you wish to reaffirm (i.e., remain liable for after bankruptcy) all or any part of this debt? _____

17. If this debt is secured by any of your property, state your intention with regard to this debt (check one):
    (a) I wish to turn the property over to the creditor. _____
    (b) I wish to reaffirm this debt and retain the property. _____
    (c) I wish to claim the property as exempt and redeem it from the creditor. _____
    (d) I wish to claim the property as exempt and contest the lien against it. _____

18. Are the payments on this debt current or delinquent? _____ If delinquent, how many payments are you behind? _____ What is the total amount of the arrearage? $_____

19. Is this a debt of someone else that you have cosigned, guaranteed, secured, or otherwise became liable for? _____ If so, list the other person's name, address and relationship to you. _____

    _____

EXHIBIT 2-C 83

United States Bankruptcy Court	VOLUNTARY PETITION

Southern _____ District of ___ Ohio _____

IN RE (Name of debtor – If Individual, enter Last, First, Middle)	NAME OF JOINT DEBTOR (Spouse) (Last, First, Middle)
Smith, Sidney Samuel	Smith, Sarah Arlene

ALL OTHER NAMES used by the debtor in the last 6 years (include married, maiden and trade names)	ALL OTHER NAMES used by the joint debtor in the last 6 years (include married, maiden and trade names)
Sidney S. Smith Sid Smith Enterprises	Sarah A. Smith Sarah A. Jones

SOC SEC/TAX I.D. NO. (If more than one, state all)	SOC SEC/TAX I.D. NO. (If more than one, state all)
544-78-8246	337-91-5432

STREET ADDRESS OF DEBTOR (No. and street, city, state, and zip code)	STREET ADDRESS OF JOINT DEBTOR (No. and street, city, state, and zip code)
2200 South Elm Street Columbus, OH 43211 — COUNTY OF RESIDENCE OR PRINCIPAL PLACE OF BUSINESS: Franklin	2200 South Elm Street Columbus, OH 43211 — COUNTY OF RESIDENCE OR PRINCIPAL PLACE OF BUSINESS: Franklin

MAILING ADDRESS OF DEBTOR (If different from street address)	MAILING ADDRESS OF JOINT DEBTOR (If different from street address)
Same	Same

LOCATION OF PRINCIPAL ASSETS OF BUSINESS DEBTOR (If different from addresses shown above)	VENUE (Check one box)
Same	☒ Debtor has been domiciled or has had a residence, principal place of business, or principal assets in this District for 180 days immediately preceding the date of the petition or for a longer part of such 180 days than in any other District ☐ There is a bankruptcy case concerning debtor's general partner or partnership pending in this District

INFORMATION REGARDING DEBTOR (Check applicable boxes)

TYPE OF DEBTOR

☐ Individual   ☐ Corporation Publicly Held
☒ Joint (Husband & Wife)   ☐ Corporation Not Publicly Held
☐ Partnership   ☐ Municipality
☐ Other _____

NATURE OF DEBT
☒ Non-Business/Consumer   ☒ Business - Complete A & B below
80 percent   20 percent

CHAPTER OR SECTION OF BANKRUPTCY CODE UNDER WHICH THE PETITION IS FILED (Check one box)

☒ Chapter 7   ☐ Chapter 11   ☐ Chapter 13
☐ Chapter 9   ☐ Chapter 12   ☐ Sec. 304 – Case Ancillary to Foreign Proceeding

FILING FEE (Check one box)

☐ Filing fee attached

☒ Filing fee to be paid in installments (Applicable to individuals only) Must attach signed application for the court's consideration certifying that the debtor is unable to pay the fee except on installments under Rule 1006(b). See Official Form 3.

A. TYPE OF BUSINESS (Check one box)

☐ Farming   ☐ Transportation   ☐ Commodity Broker
☐ Professional   ☐ Manufacturing/   ☐ Construction
☐ Retail/Wholesale   Mining   ☒ Real Estate
☐ Railroad   ☐ Stockbroker   ☐ Other Business

B. BRIEFLY DESCRIBE NATURE OF BUSINESS

Real estate sales business, part time.

NAME AND ADDRESS OF LAW FIRM OR ATTORNEY

Chase and Chase
Attorneys at Law
2000 Market Street
Columbus, OH 43222
Telephone No. 614-333-3300

NAME(S) OF ATTORNEY(S) DESIGNATED TO REPRESENT THE DEBTOR (Print or Type Names)

Alice B. Chase
☐ Debtor is not represented by an attorney

STATISTICAL ADMINISTRATIVE INFORMATION (28 U.S.C. § 604)
(Estimates only) (Check applicable boxes)

THIS SPACE FOR COURT USE ONLY

☐ Debtor estimates that funds will be available for distribution to unsecured creditors.
☒ Debtor estimates that after any exempt property is excluded and administrative expenses paid, there will be no funds available for distribution to unsecured creditors.

ESTIMATED NUMBER OF CREDITORS

1-15	16-49	50-99	100-199	200-999	1000-OVER
☐	☒	☐	☐	☐	☐

ESTIMATED ASSETS (In thousands of dollars)

Under 50	50-99	100-499	500-999	1000-9999	10,000-99,000	100,000-over
☒	☐	☐	☐	☐	☐	☐

ESTIMATED LIABILITIES (In thousands of dollars)

Under 50	50-99	100-499	500-999	1000-9999	10,000-99,000	100,000-over
☐	☐	☒	☐	☐	☐	☐

ESTIMATED NO. OF EMPLOYEES – CHAPTER 11 & 12 ONLY

0	1-19	20-99	100-999	1000-over
☐	☐	☐	☐	☐

ESTIMATED NO. OF EQUITY SECURITY HOLDERS –CHAPTER 11 & 12 ONLY

0	1-19	20-99	100-499	500-over
☐	☐	☐	☐	☐

Name of Debtor _____

Case No. _____

(Court use only)

FILING OF PLAN

For Chapter 9, 11, 12 and 13 cases only. Check appropriate box.

☐ A copy of debtor's proposed plan dated_____ is attached.

☐ Debtor intends to file a plan within the time allowed by statute, rule, or order of the court.

PRIOR BANKRUPTCY CASE FILED WITHIN LAST 6 YEARS (If more than one, attach additional sheet)

Location Where Filed	Case Number	Date Filed
None		

PENDING BANKRUPTCY CASE FILED BY ANY SPOUSE, PARTNER, OR AFFILIATE OF THIS DEBTOR (If more than one, attach additional sheet)

Name of Debtor	Case Number	Date
None		

Relationship	District	Judge

REQUEST FOR RELIEF

Debtor requests relief in accordance with the chapter of title 11, United States Code, specified in this petition.

SIGNATURES

ATTORNEY

x _Alice B. Chase_   January 15, 1992
Signature of Attorney   Date

INDIVIDUAL/JOINT DEBTOR(S)	CORPORATE OR PARTNERSHIP DEBTOR
I declare under penalty of perjury that the information provided in this petition is true and correct.	I declare under penalty of perjury that the information provided in this petition is true and correct, and that the filing of this petition on behalf of the debtor has been authorized.
x _Sidney Samuel Smith_ Signature of Debtor	x _____ Signature of Authorized Individual
January 15, 1992 Date	_____ Print or Type Name of Authorized Individual
x _Sarah Arlene Smith_ Signature of Joint Debtor	_____ Title of Individual Authorized by Debtor to file this Petition
January 15, 1992 Date	_____ Date

EXHIBIT "A" (To be completed if debtor is a corporation requesting relief under chapter 11.)

☐ Exhibit "A" is attached and made a part of this petition.

TO BE COMPLETED BY INDIVIDUAL CHAPTER 7 DEBTOR WITH PRIMARILY CONSUMER DEBTS (See P.L. 98–353 § 322)

I am aware that I may proceed under chapter 7, 11, 12 or 13 of title 11, United States Code, I understand the relief available under each such chapter, and I choose to proceed under chapter 7 of such title.

If I am represented by an attorney, Exhibit "B" has been completed.

x _Sidney Samuel Smith_   January 15, 1992
Signature of Debtor   Date

x _Sarah Arlene Smith_   January 15, 1992
Signature of Joint Debtor   Date

EXHIBIT "B" (To be completed by attorney for individual chapter 7 debtor(s) with primarily consumer debts.)

I, the attorney for the debtor(s) named in the foregoing petition, declare that I have informed the debtor(s) that (he, she, or they) may proceed under chapter 7, 11, 12 or 13 of title 11, United States Code, and have explained the relief available under each such chapter.

x _Alice B. Chase_   January 15, 1992
Signature of Attorney   Date

EXHIBIT 2-D   85

In re Sidney Samuel Smith, et al   Case No. _____
_____
              Debtor   (If known)

SCHEDULE A - REAL PROPERTY

Except as directed below, list all real property in which the debtor has any legal, equitable, or future interest, including all property owned as a cotenant, community property, or in which the debtor has a life estate. Include any property in which the debtor holds rights and powers exercisable for the debtor's own benefit. If the debtor is married, state whether husband, wife, or both own the property by placing an "H," "W," "J," or "C" in the column labeled "Husband, Wife, Joint, or Community." If the debtor holds no interest in real property, write "None" under "Description and Location of Property."

Do not include interests in executory contracts and unexpired leases on this schedule. List them in Schedule G – Executory Contracts and Unexpired Leases.

If an entity claims to have a lien or hold a secured interest in any property, state the amount of the secured claim. See Schedule D. If no entity claims to hold a secured interest in the property, write "None" in the column labeled "Amount of Secured Claim."

If the debtor is an individual or if a joint petition is filed, state the amount of any exemption claimed in the property only in Schedule C – Property Claimed as Exempt.

DESCRIPTION AND LOCATION OF PROPERTY	NATURE OF DEBTOR'S INTEREST IN PROPERTY	HUSBAND, WIFE, JOINT, OR COMMUNITY	CURRENT MARKET VALUE OF DEBTOR'S INTEREST IN PROPERTY, WITHOUT DEDUCTING ANY SECURED CLAIM OR EXEMPTION	AMOUNT OF SECURED CLAIM
House and lot located at 2200 South Elm Street, Columbus, Ohio Legal description: Lot 34, Block 12, Abner's Subdivision, Franklin County, Ohio	Ownership in fee simple	J	$90,000.00	$85,320
Vacant lot located at 700 Fox Street, Elyria, Ohio Legal description: Lots 17 and 18, Block 4, Adams Addition, Lorain County, Ohio	Contract purchaser	H	$8,000.00	$12,220

Total > $ 98,000.00

(Report also on Summary of Schedules.)

OFFICIAL FORM 6, Schedule A – Argyle Publishing Co., 10395 West Colfax Ave., Lakewood, CO 80215

In re _Sidney Samuel Smith, et al_   Case No. _____

Debtor   (If known)

SCHEDULE B - PERSONAL PROPERTY

Except as directed below, list all personal property of the debtor of whatever kind. If the debtor has no property in one or more of the categories, place an "x" in the appropriate position in the column labeled "None." If additional space is needed in any category, attach a separate sheet properly identified with the case name, case number, and the number of the category. If the debtor is married, state whether husband, wife, or both own the property by placing an "H," "W," "J," or "C" in the column labeled "Husband, Wife, Joint or Community." If the debtor is an individual or a joint petition is filed, state the amount of any exemptions claimed only in Schedule C – Property Claimed as Exempt.

Do not list interests in executory contracts and unexpired leases on this schedule. List them in Schedule G – Executory Contracts and Unexpired Leases.

If the property is being held for the debtor by someone else, state that person's name and address under "Description and Location of Property."

TYPE OF PROPERTY	N O N E	DESCRIPTION AND LOCATION OF PROPERTY	HUSBAND, WIFE, JOINT, OR COMMUNITY	CURRENT MARKET VALUE OF DEBTOR'S INTEREST IN PROPERTY, WITHOUT DEDUCTING ANY SECURED CLAIM OR EXEMPTION
1. Cash on hand.		Cash	H	$5.00
2. Checking, savings or other financial accounts, certificates of deposit, or shares in banks, savings and loan, thrift, building and loan, and homestead associations, or credit unions, brokerage houses, or cooperatives.	X			
3. Security deposits with public utilities, telephone companies, landlords, and others.		Deposit with Ohio Telephone Company	J	$20.00
4. Household goods and furnishings, including audio, video, and computer equipment.		Sharp television set (color) Kenmore washer & dryer G.E. Refrigerator 2 Tables + 12 chairs Microwave oven Electric range Misc. cooking and eating utinsels 4 beds and bedding	J J J J J J J J	$100.00 $200.00 $ 50.00 $100.00 $ 50.00 $ 40.00 $ 50.00 $400.00
5. Books, pictures and other art objects, antiques, stamp, coin, record, tape, compact disc, and other collections or collectibles.		Compact disk & tape player Misc. books Stamp collection	J J W	$200.00 $100.00 $ 50.00
6. Wearing apparel.		Rolex wrist watch Personal clothing Personal clothing	H H W	$200.00 $200.00 $200.00
7. Furs and jewelry.		Gold ring Wedding ring	H W	$200.00 $400.00
8. Firearms and sports, photographic, and other hobby equipment.		Fishing rod and gear Nikon camera	H J	$ 50.00 $ 50.00
9. Interests in insurance policies. Name insurance company of each policy and itemize surrender or refund value of each.		Prudential Insurance Co. policy no. 778947 – surrender value	H	$2,767.00
10. Annuities. Itemize and name each issuer.	X			

EXHIBIT 2-E   87

In re ___Sidney Samuel Smith, et al___   Case No. _____
                    Debtor   (If known)

SCHEDULE B - PERSONAL PROPERTY
(Continuation Sheet)

TYPE OF PROPERTY	NONE	DESCRIPTION AND LOCATION OF PROPERTY	HUSBAND, WIFE, JOINT, OR COMMUNITY	CURRENT MARKET VALUE OF DEBTOR'S INTEREST IN PROPERTY, WITHOUT DEDUCTING ANY SECURED CLAIM OR EXEMPTION
11. Interests in IRA, ERISA, Keogh, or other pension or profit sharing plans. Itemize.		IRA account of Sarah A. Smith in Big State Bank, Columbus, OH (Acct. No. 77-473-12)	W	$4,790.00
12. Stock and interests in incorporated and unincorporated businesses. Itemize.	X			
13. Interests in partnerships or joint ventures. Itemize.	X			
14. Government and corporate bonds and other negotiable and nonnegotiable instruments.	X			
15. Accounts receivable.		Account of James J. Wood, 4702 Back Street, Columbus, OH 43224, for commission rebate	H	$150.00
16. Alimony, maintenance, support, and property settlements to which the debtor is or may be entitled. Give particulars.		Property settlement payment owed by James J. Jones in Divorce Action No. 27284, Franklin County District Court	W	$1,250.00
17. Other liquidated debts owing debtor including tax refunds. Give particulars.		Federal income tax refund	J	$377.24
		Accrued salary owed by Jackson Enterprises, Inc.	H	$220.00
18. Equitable or future interests, life estates, and rights or powers exercisable for the benefit of the debtor other than those listed in Schedule of Real Property.	X			
19. Contingent and noncontingent interests in estate of a decedent, death benefit plan, life insurance policy, or trust.	X			
20. Other contingent and unliquidated claims of every nature, including tax refunds, counterclaims of the debtor, and rights to setoff claims. Give estimated value of each.	X			
21. Patents, copyrights, and other intellectual property. Give particulars.	X			
22. Licenses, franchises, and other general intangibles. Give particulars.	X			

In re   Sidney Samuel Smith, et al   Case No. _____

          Debtor   (If known)

SCHEDULE B - PERSONAL PROPERTY
(Continuation Sheet)

TYPE OF PROPERTY	N O N E	DESCRIPTION AND LOCATION OF PROPERTY	HUSBAND, WIFE, JOINT, OR COMMUNITY	CURRENT MARKET VALUE OF DEBTOR'S INTEREST IN PROPERTY, WITHOUT DEDUCTING ANY SECURED CLAIM OR EXEMPTION

23. Automobiles, trucks, trailers and other vehicles and accessories.		1988 Honda Civic
		    I.D. # 77546219
		1986 Ford Pickup Truck
		    I.D. D 7H9654321
			W
			
			H
				$4,000.00
				
				$3,000.00

24. Boats, motors, and accessories.	X			
25. Aircraft and accessories.	X			
26. Office equipment, furnishings and supplies.		Desk and chair File cabinet	H H	$ 50.00 $ 20.00
27. Machinery, fixtures, equipment, and supplies used in business.		IBM Typewriter	H	$ 50.00
28. Inventory.	X			
29. Animals.	X			
30. Crops - growing or harvested. Give particulars.	X			
31. Farming equipment and implements.	X			
32. Farm supplies, chemicals, and feed.	X			
33. Other personal property of any kind not already listed. Itemize.	X			

_2_ continuation sheets attached

                                                Total > $19,339.24

(Include amounts from any continuation sheets attached. Report total also on Summary of Schedules.)

OFFICIAL FORM 6, Schedule B (page 3) – Argyle Publishing Co., 10395 West Colfax Ave., Lakewood, CO 80215

EXHIBIT 2-F   89

In re <u>Sidney Samuel Smith, et al</u>   Case No. _____
            Debtor   (If known)

SCHEDULE C - PROPERTY CLAIMED AS EXEMPT

Debtor elects the exemptions to which debtor is entitled under:

(Check one box)

☐ 11 U.S.C. § 522(b)(1): Exemptions provided in 11 U.S.C. § 522(d). Note: These exemptions are available only in certain states.

☒ 11 U.S.C. § 522 (b)(2): Exemptions available under applicable nonbankruptcy federal laws, state or local law where the debtor's domicile has been located for the 180 days immediately preceding the filing of the petition, or for a longer portion of the 180-day period than in any other place, and the debtor's interest as a tenant by the entirety or joint tenant to the extent the interest is exempt from process under applicable nonbankruptcy law.

DESCRIPTION OF PROPERTY	SPECIFY LAW PROVIDING EACH EXEMPTION	VALUE OF CLAIMED EXEMPTION	CURRENT MARKET VALUE OF PROPERTY WITHOUT DEDUCTION EXEMPTION
PROPERTY CLAIMED AS EXEMPT BY SIDNEY SAMUEL SMITH			
House and lot located at 2200 South Elm Street, Columbus, Ohio (homestead)	R.C. § 2329.66(A)(1)	$5,000.00	$4,680.00 (equity)
1986 Ford Pickup Truck	R.C. § 2329.66(A)(2)	$1,000.00	$ none (no equity)
Personal clothing & watch	R.C. § 2329.66(A)(3)	$400.00	$400.00
4 Beds & bedding	R.C. § 2329.66(A)(3)	$200.00	$200.00
Electric range & refrigerator	R.C. § 2329.66(A)(3)	$100.00	$ 90.00
Account due from J. Wood, ½ of federal income tax refund, 25% of disposable earnings	R.C. § 2329.66(A)(4)(a)	$400.00	$398.62
Television set, washer and dryer, 2 tables & 12 chairs, microwave oven, cooking and eating utensils, compact disk & tape player, misc. books, fishing rod & gear, camera	R.C. § 2329.66(A)(4)(b)	$900.00	$900.00
Gold ring	R.C. § 2329.66(A)(4)(c)	$200.00	$200.00
Avails of life insurance policy	R.C. § 2329.66(A)(6)(b)	$2,767.00	$2,767.00
75% of disposable earnings	R.C. § 2329.66(A)(13)	$165.00	$165.00
Telephone deposit, desk, chair, file cabinet	R.C. § 2329.66(A)(17)	$ 90.00	$ 90.00
PROPERTY CLAIMED AS EXEMPT BY SARAH ARLENE SMITH			
Stamp collection, ½ of federal income tax refund	R.C. § 2329.66(A)(17)	$250.00	$238.62
1988 Honda Civic	R.C. § 2329.66(A)(2)	$1,000.00	$1,000.00 (equity)
Wedding ring	R.C. § 2329.66(A)(4)(c)	$400.00	$400.00
Personal clothing	R.C. § 2329.66(A)(3)	$200.00	$200.00
IRA account	R.C. § 2329.66(A)(10)(c)	$4,790.00	$4,790.00

OFFICIAL FORM 6, Schedule C – Argyle Publishing Co., 10395 West Colfax Ave., Lakewood, CO 80215

EXHIBIT 2-G

In re <u>Sidney Samuel Smith, et al</u>   Case No. _____
           Debtor   (If known)

SCHEDULE D - CREDITORS HOLDING SECURED CLAIMS

State the name, mailing address, including zip code, and account number, if any, of all entities holding claims secured by property of the debtor as of the date of filing of the petition. List creditors holding all types of secured interests such as judgment liens, garnishments, statutory liens, mortgages, deeds of trust, and other security interests. List creditors in alphabetical order to the extent practicable. If all secured creditors will not fit on this page, use the continuation sheet provided.

If any entity other than a spouse in a joint case may be jointly liable on a claim, place an "X" in the column labeled "Codebtor," include the entity on the appropriate schedule of creditors, and complete Schedule H – Codebtors. If a joint petition is filed, state whether husband, wife, both of them, or the marital community may be liable on each claim by placing an "H," "W," "J," or "C" in the column labeled "Husband, Wife, Joint, or Community."

If the claim is contingent, place an "X" in the column labeled "Contingent." If the claim is unliquidated, place an "X" in the column labeled "Unliquidated." If the claim is disputed, place an "X" in the column labeled "Disputed." (You may need to place an "X" in more than one of these three columns.)

Report the total of all claims listed on this schedule in the box labeled "Total" on the last sheet of the completed schedule. Report this total also on the Summary of Schedules.

☐ Check this box if debtor has no creditors holding secured claims to report on this Schedule D.

CREDITOR'S NAME AND MAILING ADDRESS INCLUDING ZIP CODE	CODEBTOR	HUSBAND, WIFE, JOINT, OR COMMUNITY	DATE CLAIM WAS INCURRED, NATURE OF LIEN, AND DESCRIPTION AND MARKET VALUE OF PROPERTY SUBJECT TO LIEN	CONTINGENT	UNLIQUIDATED	DISPUTED	AMOUNT OF CLAIM WITHOUT DEDUCTING VALUE OF COLLATERAL	UNSECURED PORTION, IF ANY
ACCOUNT NO. 4719224 Big Bank of Columbus 200 Main Street Columbus, OH 43215		J	May, 1987 First mortgage on family home located at 2200 South Elm St. VALUE $ 90,000				$85,320	none
ACCOUNT NO. 47-12-1147 Easy Loans, Inc. 4000 East 10th Ave. Cleveland, OH 44111		W	August, 1988 First mortgage on 1988 Honda Civic VALUE $ 4,000				$3,070	none
ACCOUNT NO. 572-12-14 Fast Finance Company 937 Market Street Columbus, OH 43212		H	July, 1991 First mortgage on 1986 Ford Pickup and lot at 700 Fox Street VALUE $ 11,000				$12,220	$1,220
ACCOUNT NO. VALUE $								
ACCOUNT NO. VALUE $								
ACCOUNT NO. VALUE $								

_____ continuation sheets attached

                                   Subtotal > $ 100,610
                    (Total of this page)

                                    Total > $ 100,610
           (Complete only on last page of Schedule D)

(Report total also on Summary of Schedules)

EXHIBIT 2-H   91

In re   Sidney Samuel Smith, et al   Case No. _____
              Debtor   (If known)

SCHEDULE E - CREDITORS HOLDING UNSECURED PRIORITY CLAIMS

A complete list of claims entitled to priority, listed separately by type of priority, is to be set forth on the sheets provided. Only holders of unsecured claims entitled to priority should be listed in this schedule. In the boxes provided on the attached sheets, state the name and mailing address, including zip code, and account number, if any, of all entities holding priority claims against the debtor or the property of the debtor, as of the date of the filing of the petition.

If any entity other than a spouse in a joint case may be jointly liable on a claim, place an "X" in the column labeled "Codebtor," include the entity on the appropriate schedule of creditors, and complete Schedule H – Codebtors. If a joint petition is filed, state whether husband, wife, both of them, or the marital community may be liable on each claim by placing an "H," "W," "J," or "C," in the column labeled "Husband, Wife, Joint, or Community."

If the claim is contingent, place an "X" in the column labeled "Contingent." If the claim is unliquidated, place an "X" in the column labeled "Unliquidated." If the claim is disputed, place an "X" in the column labeled "Disputed." (You may need to place an "X" in more than one of these three columns.)

Report the total of claims listed on each sheet in the box labeled "Subtotal" on each sheet. Report the total of all claims listed on this Schedule E in the box labeled "Total" on the last sheet of the completed schedule. Repeat this total also on the Summary of Schedules.

☐ Check this box if debtor has no creditors holding unsecured priority claims to report on this Schedule E.

TYPES OF PRIORITY CLAIMS (Check the appropriate box(es) below if claims in that category are listed on the attached sheets)

☐ Extensions of credit in an involuntary case

Claims arising in the ordinary course of the debtor's business or financial affairs after the commencement of the case but before the earlier of the appointment of a trustee or the order for relief. 11 U.S.C. § 507(a)(2).

☐ Wages, salaries, and commissions

Wages, salaries, and commissions, including vacation, severance, and sick leave pay owing to employees, up to a maximum of $2000 per employee, earned within 90 days immediately preceding the filing of the original petition, or the cessation of business, whichever occurred first, to the extent provided in 11 U.S.C. § 507(a)(3).

☐ Contributions to employee benefit plans

Money owed to employee benefit plans for services rendered within 180 days immediately preceding the filing of the original petition, or the cessation of business, whichever occurred first, to the extent provided in 11 U.S.C. § 507(a)(4).

☐ Certain farmers and fishermen

Claims of certain farmers and fishermen, up to a maximum of $2000 per farmer or fisherman, against the debtor, as provided in 11 U.S.C. § 507(a)(5).

☐ Deposits by individuals

Claims of individuals up to a maximum of $900 for deposits for the purchase, lease, or rental of property or services for personal, family, or household use, that were not delivered or provided. 11 U.S.C. § 507(a)(6).

☒ Taxes and certain other debts owed to governmental units

Taxes, customs duties, and penalties owing to federal, state, and local governmental units as set forth in 11 U.S.C. § 507(a)(7).

SCHEDULE E - CREDITORS HOLDING UNSECURED PRIORITY CLAIMS
(Continuation Sheet)

Taxes
TYPE OF PRIORITY

CREDITOR'S NAME AND MAILING ADDRESS INCLUDING ZIP CODE	CODEBTOR	HUSBAND, WIFE, JOINT, OR COMMUNITY	DATE CLAIM WAS INCURRED AND CONSIDERATION FOR CLAIM	CONTINGENT	UNLIQUIDATED	DISPUTED	TOTAL AMOUNT OF CLAIM	AMOUNT ENTITLED TO PRIORITY
ACCOUNT NO. 544-78-8246 Internal Revenue Service P.O. Box 197760 Bloomington, IL 61799		J	December, 1989 1989 Income Taxes owed by Sidney S. and Sarah A. Smith			X	$5,427	$5,427

Sheet no. __1__ of __1__ sheets attached to Schedule of Creditors Holding Priority Claims

Note to Reader: In practice, a separate continuation sheet should be used for each type of priority claim. The sheets were combined here to conserve space.

Subtotal (Total of this page) ➤ $ 5,427

Total (Complete only on last page of Schedule E) ➤ $ 5,427

(Report total also on Summary of Schedules)

In re <u>Sidney Samuel Smith, et al</u>   Case No. _____
              Debtor   (If known)

SCHEDULE F - CREDITORS HOLDING UNSECURED NONPRIORITY CLAIMS

State the name, mailing address, including zip code, and account number, if any, of all entities holding unsecured claims without priority against the debtor or the property of the debtor, as of the date of filing of the petition. Do not include claims listed in Schedules D and E. If all creditors will not fit on this page, use the continuation sheet provided.

If any entity other than a spouse in a joint case may be jointly liable on a claim, place an "X" in the column labeled "Codebtor," include the entity on the appropriate schedule of creditors, and complete Schedule H – Codebtors. If a joint petition is filed, state whether husband, wife, both of them, or the marital community may be liable on each claim by placing an "H," "W," "J," or "C" in the column labeled "Husband, Wife, Joint, or Community."

If the claim is contingent, place an "X" in the column labeled "Contingent." If the claim is unliquidated, place an "X" in the column labeled "Unliquidated." If the claim is disputed, place an "X" in the column labeled "Disputed." (You may need to place an "X" in more than one of these three column.)

Report the total of all claims listed on this schedule in the box labeled "Total" on the last sheet of the completed schedule. Report this total also on the Summary of Schedules.

☐ Check this box if debtor has no creditors holding unsecured nonpriority claims to report on this Schedule F.

CREDITOR'S NAME AND MAILING ADDRESS INCLUDING ZIP CODE	CODEBTOR	HUSBAND, WIFE, JOINT OR COMMUNITY	DATE CLAIM WAS INCURRED AND CONSIDERATION FOR CLAIM. IF CLAIM IS SUBJECT TO SETOFF, SO STATE.	CONTINGENT	UNLIQUIDATED	DISPUTED	AMOUNT OF CLAIM
ACCOUNT NO. 77-14-01 Ace Drug Store 900 Maple Street Columbus, OH 43210		J	May – August, 1991 Purchase of merchandise and medical supplies				$872.12
ACCOUNT NO. 987654 Bobbit Lumber Co. 1427 North Oak Street Newark, OH 43055		H	June, 1987 Purchase of building supplies Acct. assigned to: ABC Collectors 700 Main Street Columbus, OH 43204				$2,540.00
ACCOUNT NO. none Charles C. Chase 11277 West Smith Road Cleveland, OH 44119	X	J	December, 1990 Personal loan				$4,227.00
ACCOUNT NO. 4516-17-11176 Davidson's Department Store P.O. Box 9976 Houston, TX 77002		W	April – Sept. 1991 Purchase of merchandise by creditcard				$237.22
ACCOUNT NO. none Eddy's Garage 1222 Kipling Blvd. Columbus, OH 43217		H	November, 1990 Repair of Ford Pickup Truck				$727.12
ACCOUNT NO. 7217-512-7764 First Bank Master Charge P.O. Box 22000 Columbus, OH 43202		J	May – October, 1991 Creditcard charges				$2,727.96

<u> 2 </u>   continuation sheets attached   Subtotal ➤ | $ 11,331.42
                                                                                       (Total of this page)

<u>Note to Reader</u>: The continuation sheets
              have been omitted to   Total ➤ | $ 147,227.11
              conserve space.   (Complete only on last page of Schedule F)

                                                    (Report total also on Summary of Schedules)

OFFICIAL FORM 6, Schedule F (page 1) – Argyle Publishing Co., 10395 West Colfax Ave., Lakewood, CO 80215

EXHIBIT 2-J   93

In re <u>Sidney Samuel Smith, et al</u>   Case No. _____
                    Debtor   (If known)

SCHEDULE G - EXECUTORY CONTRACTS AND UNEXPIRED LEASES

Describe all executory contracts of any nature and all unexpired leases of real or personal property. Include any timeshare interests.

State nature of debtor's interest in contract, i.e., "Purchaser," "Agent," etc. State whether debtor is the lessor or lessee of a lease.

Provide the names and complete mailing addresses of all other parties to each lease or contract described.

NOTE: A party listed on this schedule will not receive notice of the filing of this case unless the party is also scheduled in the appropriate schedule of creditors.

☐ Check this box if debtor has no executory contracts or unexpired leases.

NAME AND MAILING ADDRESS, INCLUDING ZIP CODE, OF OTHER PARTIES TO LEASE OR CONTRACT.	DESCRIPTION OF CONTRACT OR LEASE AND NATURE OF DEBTOR'S INTEREST. STATE WHETHER LEASE IS FOR NONRESIDENTIAL REAL PROPERTY. STATE CONTRACT NUMBER OF ANY GOVERNMENT CONTRACT.
Morton Leasing Company 2000 East Pine Avenue Columbus, OH 43206	Lease of 1991 Buick automobile dated October 12, 1991. Lease No. 77612761
Leo's Lawn Care Service 14760 West 19th Ave. Columbus, OH 43229	Contract to mow lawn for 1992. Contract dated January 2, 1992.

OFFICIAL FORM 6, Schedule G – Argyle Publishing Co., 10395 West Colfax Ave., Lakewood, CO 80215

EXHIBIT 2-K

In re   <u>Sidney Samuel Smith, et al</u>   Case No. _____
        Debtor   (If known)

SCHEDULE H - CODEBTORS

Provide the information requested concerning any person or entity, other than a spouse in a joint case, that is also liable on any debts listed by debtor in the schedules of creditors. Include all guarantors and co-signers. In community property states, a married debtor not filing a joint case should report the name and address of the nondebtor spouse on this schedule. Include all names used by the nondebtor spouse during the six years immediately preceding the commencement of this case.

☐ Check this box if debtor has no codebtors.

NAME AND ADDRESS OF CODEBTOR	NAME AND ADDRESS OF CREDITOR
Arnold A. Smith 2127 Garrison Street Toledo, OH 43614	Charles C. Chase 11277 West Smith Road Cleveland, OH 44119
Margaret M. Maples 900 North Avenue Chicago, IL 60622	Last National Bank 211 Main Street Cincinnati, OH 45222

OFFICIAL FORM 6, Schedule H – Argyle Publishing Co., 10395 West Colfax Ave., Lakewood, CO 80215

EXHIBIT 2-L   95

In re Sidney Samuel Smith, et al   Case No. _____
          Debtor   (If known)

SCHEDULE I - CURRENT INCOME OF INDIVIDUAL DEBTOR(S)

The column labeled "Spouse" must be completed in all cases filed by joint debtors and by a married debtor in a chapter 12 or 13 case whether or not a joint petition is filed, unless the spouses are separated and a joint petition is not filed.

Debtor's Marital Status:	DEPENDENTS OF DEBTOR AND SPOUSE		
Married	NAMES	AGE	RELATIONSHIP
	Nancy Ann Smith	7	Daughter
	Robert John Smith	3	Son

Employment:	DEBTOR	SPOUSE
Occupation	Salesman	Receptionist (part time)
Name of Employer	Jackson Enterprises, Inc.	Wilson Land Company
How long employed	7 years	2 years
Address of Employer	4700 Federal Blvd. Columbus, OH 43227	2177 North 17th Street Columbus, OH 43207

INCOME: (Estimate of average monthly income)

	DEBTOR	SPOUSE
Current monthly gross wages, salary, and commissions (pro rate if not paid monthly.)	$ 1150.00	$ 320.00
Estimated monthly overtime	$ 50.00	$ 0.00
SUBTOTAL	$ 1200.00	$ 320.00
LESS PAYROLL DEDUCTIONS		
a. Payroll taxes and social security	$ 180.00	$ 38.00
b. Insurance	$ 90.00	$ 0.00
c. Union dues	$ 0.00	$ 4.00
d. Other (Specify: _____)	$ 0.00	$ 0.00
SUBTOTAL OF PAYROLL DEDUCTIONS	$ 270.00	$ 42.00
TOTAL NET MONTHLY TAKE HOME PAY	$ 930.00	$ 278.00
Regular income from operation of business or profession or farm (attach detailed statement)	$ 0.00	$ 0.00
Income from real property	$ 0.00	$ 0.00
Interest and dividends	$ 0.00	$ 0.00
Alimony, maintenance or support payments payable to the debtor for the debtor's use or that of dependents listed above.	$ 0.00	$ 0.00
Social security or other government assistance (Specify) _____	$ 0.00	$ 0.00
Pension or retirement income	$ 0.00	$ 0.00
Other monthly income (Specify) _____	$ 0.00	$ 0.00
TOTAL MONTHLY INCOME	$ 930.00	$ 278.00

TOTAL COMBINED MONTHLY INCOME $ 1208.00 _____   (Report also on Summary of Schedules)

Describe any increase or decrease of more than 10% in any of the above categories anticipated to occur within the year following the filing of this document:
          None

In re <u>Sidney Samuel Smith, et al</u>   Case No. _____

Debtor   (If known)

SCHEDULE J - CURRENT EXPENDITURES OF INDIVIDUAL DEBTOR(S)

Complete this schedule by estimating the average monthly expenses of the debtor and the debtor's family. Pro rate any payments made bi-weekly, quarterly, semi-annually, or annually to show monthly rate.

☐   Check this box if a joint petition is filed and debtor's spouse maintains a separate household. If box is checked, complete a separate schedule of expenditures labeled "Spouse."

Rent or home mortgage payment (include lot rented for mobile home)	$	420.00

Are real estate taxes included?   Yes __X__   No _____

Is property insurance included?   Yes __X__   No _____

Utilities: Electricity and heating fuel	$	90.00
Water and sewer	$	20.00
Telephone	$	30.00
Other <u>Property Owners' Association dues</u>	$	5.00
Home maintenance (repairs and upkeep)	$	50.00
Food	$	200.00
Clothing	$	50.00
Laundry and dry cleaning	$	30.00
Medical and dental expenses	$	10.00
Transportation (not including car payments)	$	40.00
Recreation, clubs and entertainment, newspapers, magazines, etc.	$	10.00
Charitable contributions	$	10.00

Insurance (not deducted from wages or included in home mortgage payments)

Homeowner's or renter's	$	0.00
Life	$	40.00
Health	$	0.00
Auto	$	200.00
Other _____	$	

Taxes (not deducted from wages or included in home mortgage payments)

(Specify) _____ $ _____

Installment payments: (In chapter 12 and 13 cases, do not list payments to be included in the plan)

Auto	$	150.00
Other <u>Furniture payments</u>	$	40.00
Other _____	$	
Other _____	$	
Alimony, maintenance, and support paid to others	$	0.00
Payments for support of additional dependents not living at your home	$	0.00
Regular expenses from operation of business, profession, or farm (attach detailed statement)	$	0.00
Other _____	$	
Other _____	$	
TOTAL MONTHLY EXPENSES (Report also on Summary of Schedules)	$	1395.00

[FOR CHAPTER 12 AND 13 DEBTORS ONLY]

Provide the information requested below, including whether plan payments are to be made bi-weekly, monthly, annually, or at some other regular interval.

A. Total projected monthly income .... $ _____

B. Total projected monthly expenses .... $ _____

C. Excess income (A minus B) .... $ _____

D. Total amount to be paid into plan each _____ $ _____
                                          (interval)

OFFICIAL FORM 6, Schedule J - Argyle Publishing Co., 10395 West Colfax Ave., Lakewood, CO 80215

EXHIBIT 2-N _____ 97

In re   Sidney Samuel Smith, et al   Case No. _____
           Debtor   **(If known)**

DECLARATION CONCERNING DEBTOR'S SCHEDULES

DECLARATION UNDER PENALTY OF PERJURY BY INDIVIDUAL DEBTOR

I declare under penalty of perjury that I have read the foregoing summary and schedules, consisting of _____16_____
sheets, and that they are true and correct to the best of my knowledge, information, and belief.   (Total shown on summary page plus 1.)

Date   January 15, 1991 _____   Signature: _~~Sidney Samuel Smith~~_
                                                        Debtor

Date   January 15, 1991 _____   Signature: _~~Sarah Arlene Smith~~_
                                                   Joint Debtor, if any

                         (If joint case, both spouses must sign.)

DECLARATION UNDER PENALTY OF PERJURY ON BEHALF OF CORPORATION OR PARTNERSHIP

I, the _____ (the president or other officer or an authorized agent of the corporation or a member
or an authorized agent of the partnership) of the _____ (corporation or partnership) named
as debtor in this case, declare under penalty of perjury that I have read the foregoing summary and schedules, consisting of _____
sheets, and that they are true and correct to the best of my knowledge, information, and belief.   (Total shown on summary page plus 1.)

Date _____   Signature: _____

                                      _____
                                 (Print or type name and title of individual signing on behalf of debtor.)

                   (An individual signing of behalf of a partnership or corporation must indicate position or relationship to debtor.)

Penalty for making a false statement or concealing property: Fine of up to $500,000 or imprisonment for up to 5 years or both. 18 U.S.C.
§§ 152 and 3571.

OFFICIAL FORM 6, Declaration – Argyle Publishing Co., 10395 West Colfax Ave., Lakewood, CO 80215

EXHIBIT 2-O

UNITED STATES BANKRUPTCY COURT

_____SOUTHERN_____ DISTRICT OF ___OHIO___

IN RE Sidney Samuel Smith
and Sarah Arlene Smith

Case No. _____
(If known)

Debtor Chapter ___7___

SUMMARY OF SCHEDULES

Indicate as to each schedule whether that schedule is attached and state the number of pages in each. Report the totals from Schedules A, B, D, E, F, I, and J in the boxes provided. Add the amounts from schedules A and B to determine the total amount of the debtor's assets. Add the amounts from Schedules D, E, and F to determine the total amount of the debtor's liabilities.

AMOUNTS SCHEDULED

NAME OF SCHEDULE	ATTACHED (YES/NO)	NO. OF SHEETS	ASSETS	LIABILITIES	OTHER
A – Real Property	Yes	1	$98,000.00		
B – Personal Property	Yes	3	$19,339.24		
C – Property Claimed as Exempt	Yes	1			
D – Creditors Holding Secured Claims	Yes	1		$100,610.00	
E – Creditors Holding Unsecured Priority Claims	Yes	2		$ 5,427.00	
F – Creditors Holding Unsecured Nonpriority Claims	Yes	3		$147,227.11	
G – Executory Contracts and Unexpired Leases	Yes	1			
H – Codebtors	Yes	1			
I – Current Income of Individual Debtor(s)	Yes	1			$ 1,208.00
J – Current Expenditures of Individual Debtor(s)	Yes	1			$ 1,395.00
Total Number of Sheets of ALL Schedules >		15			
Total Assets >			$117,339.24		
Total Liabilities >				$253,264.11	

GENERAL INSTRUCTIONS: The first page of the debtor's schedules (the Summary of Schedules) and the first page of any amendments thereto must contain a caption as in Form 16B. Subsequent pages should be identified with the debtor's name and case number. If the schedules are filed with the petition, the case number should be left blank.

Schedules D, E, and F have been designed for the listing of each claim only once. Even when a claim is secured only in part or entitled to priority only in part, it still should be listed only once. A claim which is secured in whole or in part should be listed on Schedule D only, and a claim which is entitled to priority in whole or in part should be listed on Schedule E only. Do not list the same claim twice. If a creditor has more than one claim, such as claims arising from separate transactions, each claim should be scheduled separately.

Review the specific instructions for each schedule before completing the schedule. The following schedules and documents should be completed:

Summary of Schedules (above)
Schedule A - Real Property
Schedule B - Personal Property
Schedule C - Property Claimed as Exempt
Schedule D - Creditors Holding Secured Claims
Schedule E - Creditors Holding Unsecured Priority Claims

Schedule F - Creditors Holding Unsecured Nonpriority Claims
Schedule G - Executory Contracts and Unexpired Leases
Schedule H - Codebtors
Schedule I - Current Income of Individual Debtor(s)
Schedule J - Current Expenditures of Individual Debtor(s)
Unsworn Declaration under Penalty of Perjury

EXHIBIT 2-P   99

UNITED STATES BANKRUPTCY COURT

SOUTHERN _____ DISTRICT OF _____OHIO_____

IN RE Sidney Samuel Smith
and Sarah Arlene Smith

Case No. _____
                    (If known)

                        Debtor   Chapter _____7_____

STATEMENT OF FINANCIAL AFFAIRS

This statement is to be completed by every debtor. Spouses filing a joint petition may file a single statement on which the information for both spouses is combined. If the case is filed under chapter 12 or chapter 13, a married debtor must furnish information for both spouses whether or not a joint petition is filed, unless the spouses are separated and a joint petition is not filed. An individual debtor engaged in business as a sole proprietor, partner, family farmer, or self-employed professional, should provide the information requested on this statement concerning all such activities as well as the individual's personal affairs.

Questions 1 – 15 are to be completed by all debtors. Debtors that are or have been in business, as defined below, also must complete Questions 16 – 21. Each question must be answered. If the answer to any question is "None," or the question is not applicable, mark the box labeled "None." If additional space is needed for the answer to any question, use and attach a separate sheet properly identified with the case name, case number (if known), and the number of the question.

DEFINITIONS

"In business." A debtor is "in business" for the purpose of this form if the debtor is a corporation or partnership. An individual debtor is "in business" for the purpose of this form if the debtor is or has been, within the two years immediately preceding the filing of this bankruptcy case, any of the following: an officer, director, managing executive, or person in control of a corporation; a partner, other than a limited partner, of a partnership; a sole proprietor or self-employed person.

"Insider." The term "insider" includes but is not limited to: relatives of the debtor; general partners of the debtor and their relatives; corporations of which the debtor is an officer, director, or person in control; officers, directors, and any person in control of a corporate debtor and their relatives; affiliates of the debtor and insiders of such affiliates; any managing agent of the debtor. 11 U.S.C. § 101(31).

---

1. Income from employment or operation of business

None

☐ State the gross amount of income the debtor has received from employment, trade, or profession, or from operation of the debtor's business from the beginning of this calendar year to the date this case was commenced. State also the gross amounts received during the two years immediately preceding this calendar year. (A debtor that maintains, or has maintained, financial records on the basis of a fiscal rather than a calendar year may report fiscal year income. Identify the beginning and ending dates of the debtor's fiscal year.) If a joint petition is filed, state income for each spouse separately. (Married debtors filing under chapter 12 or chapter 13 must state income of both spouses whether or not a joint petition is filed, unless the spouses are separated and a joint petition is not filed.)

	AMOUNT	SOURCE (if more than one)	YEAR
H	$575	Jackson Enterprises, Inc.	1992
H	$31,210	Jackson Enterprises, Inc.	1990-1991
H	$9,780	Sid Smith Enterprises	1990-1991
W	$160	Wilson Land Company	1992
W	$4,740	Wilson Land Company	1990-1991

---

2. Income other than from employment or operation of business

None

☐ State the amount of income received by the debtor other than from employment, trade, profession, or operation of debtor's business during the two years immediately preceding the commencement of this case. Give particulars. If a joint petition is filed, state income for each spouse separately. (Married debtors filing under chapter 12 or chapter 13 must state income for each spouse whether or not a joint petition is filed, unless the spouses are separated and a joint petition is not filed.)

	AMOUNT	SOURCE (if more than one)	YEAR
H	$4,475.00	Sale of IBM stock	1991
W	$3,400.00	Property settlement from ex-husband	1990

3. Payments to creditors

None

☐ a. List all payments on loans, installment purchases of goods or services, and other debts, aggregating more than $600 to any creditor, made within 90 days immediately preceding the commencement of this case. (Married debtors filing under chapter 12 or chapter 13 must include payments by either or both spouses whether or not a joint petition is filed, unless the spouses are separated and a joint petition is not filed.)

NAME AND ADDRESS OF CREDITOR	DATES OF PAYMENTS	AMOUNT PAID	AMOUNT STILL OWING
Big Bank of Columbus 200 Main Street Columbus, OH 43215	11-30-91 12-30-91	$420.00 $420.00	$85,405.00 $85,320.00
Easy Loans, Inc. 4000 East 10th Ave. Cleveland, OH 44111	12-20-91	$890.00	$3,070.00

None

☒ b. List all payments made within one year immediately preceding the commencement of this case to or for the benefit of creditors who are or were insiders. (Married debtors filing under chapter 12 or chapter 13 must include payments by either or both spouses whether or not a joint petition is filed, unless the spouses are separated and a joint petition is not filed.)

NAME AND ADDRESS OF CREDITOR AND RELATIONSHIP TO DEBTOR	DATE OF PAYMENT	AMOUNT PAID	AMOUNT STILL OWING

4. Suits, executions, garnishments and attachments

None

☐ a. List all suits to which the debtor is or was a party within one year immediately preceding the filing of this bankruptcy case. (Married debtors filing under chapter 12 or chapter 13 must include information concerning either or both spouses whether or not a joint petition is filed, unless the spouses are separated and a joint petition is not filed.)

CAPTION OF SUIT AND CASE NUMBER	NATURE OF PROCEEDING	COURT AND LOCATION	STATUS OR DISPOSITION
Bill Collectors, Inc. v. Sidney S. Smith and Sarah A. Smith. Case No. 47653	Collection of account of Mercy Hospital	Franklin County District Court, Columbus, OH	Default judgment entered on 12-1-91

EXHIBIT 2-P

None

b. Describe all property that has been attached, garnished or seized under any legal or equitable process within one year immediately preceding the commencement of this case. (Married debtors filing under chapter 12 or chapter 13 must include information concerning property of either or both spouses whether or not a joint petition is filed, unless the spouses are separated and a joint petition is not filed.)

NAME AN ADDRESS OF PERSON FOR WHOSE BENEFIT PROPERTY WAS SEIZED	DATE OF SEIZURE	DESCRIPTION AND VALUE OF PROPERTY
Luxury Living, Inc. 2700 Easy Street Columbus, OH 43211	June 3, 1991	Home entertainment center $2,500.00

5. Repossessions, foreclosures and returns

None

List all property that has been repossessed by a creditor, sold at a foreclosure sale, transferred through a deed in lieu of foreclosure or returned to the seller, within one year immediately preceding the commencement of this case. (Married debtors filing under chapter 12 or chapter 13 must include information concerning property of either or both spouses whether or not a joint petition is filed, unless the spouses are separated and a joint petition is not filed.)

NAME AND ADDRESS OF CREDITOR OR SELLER	DATE OF REPOSSESSION, FORECLOSURE SALE, TRANSFER OR RETURN	DESCRIPTION AND VALUE OF PROPERTY
Sample's Auto Sales 1200 North Elm Street Columbus, OH 43202	May 9, 1991	1990 Buick Regal automobile $15,000.00

6. Assignments and receiverships

None

a. Describe any assignment of property for the benefit of creditors made within 120 days immediately preceding the commencement of this case. (Married debtors filing under chapter 12 or chapter 13 must include any assignment by either or both spouses whether or not a joint petition is filed, unless the spouses are separated and a joint petition is not filed.)

NAME AND ADDRESS OF ASSIGNEE	DATE OF ASSIGNMENT	TERMS OF ASSIGNMENT OR SETTLEMENT

101
OFFICIAL FORM 7 (page 3) – Argyle Publishing Co., 10395 West Colfax Ave., Lakewood, CO 80215

None
☒ b. List all property which has been in the hands of a custodian, receiver, or court-appointed official within one year immediately preceding the commencement of this case. (Married debtors filing under chapter 12 or chapter 13 must include information concerning property of either or both spouses whether or not a joint petition is filed, unless the spouses are separated and a joint petition is not filed.)

NAME AND ADDRESS OF CUSTODIAN	NAME AND LOCATION OF COURT CASE TITLE & NUMBER	DATE OF ORDER	DESCRIPTION AND VALUE OF PROPERTY

---

7. Gifts

None
☐ List all gifts or charitable contributions made within one year immediately preceding the commencement of this case except ordinary and usual gifts to family members aggregating less than $200 in value per individual family member and charitable contributions aggregating less than $100 per recipient. (Married debtors filing under chapter 12 or chapter 13 must include gifts or contributions by either or both spouses whether or not a joint petition is filed, unless the spouses are separated and a joint petition is not filed.)

NAME AND ADDRESS OF PERSON OR ORGANIZATION	RELATIONSHIP TO DEBTOR, IF ANY	DATE OF GIFT	DESCRIPTION AND VALUE OF GIFT
Manhood College 40 Main Street Smithville, AR 72110	None	March 3, 1991	Cash $300.00

---

8. Losses

None
☐ List all losses from fire, theft, other casualty, or gambling within one year immediately preceding the commencement of this case or since the commencement of this case. (Married debtors filing under chapter 12 or chapter 13 must include losses by either or both spouses whether or not a joint petition is filed, unless the spouses are separated and a joint petition is not filed.)

DESCRIPTION AND VALUE OF PROPERTY	DESCRIPTION OF CIRCUMSTANCES AND, IF LOSS WAS COVERED IN WHOLE OR IN PART BY INSURANCE, GIVE PARTICULARS	DATE OF LOSS
Car radio $200.00	Radio stolen from parked car. Insurance paid $100.00	June 1, 1991

EXHIBIT 2-P   103

9. Payments related to debt counseling or bankruptcy

None
☐   List all payments made or property transferred by or on behalf of the debtor to any persons, including attorneys, for consultation concerning debt consolidation, relief under the bankruptcy law, or preparation of a petition in bankruptcy within one year immediately preceding the commencement of this case.

NAME AND ADDRESS OF PAYEE	DATE OF PAYMENT, NAME OF PAYOR IF OTHER THAN DEBTOR	AMOUNT OF MONEY OR DESCRIPTION AND VALUE OF PROPERTY
Credit Consultants 427 Market Street Columbus, OH 43220	October 12, 1991	$200.00
Alice B. Chase Attorney at Law 2000 Market Street Columbus, OH 43222	January 10, 1991	$300.00

10. Other transfers

None
☐   List all other property, other than property transferred in the ordinary course of the business or financial affairs of the debtor, transferred either absolutely or as security within one year immediately preceding the commencement of this case. (Married debtors filing under chapter 12 or chapter 13 must include transfers by either or both spouses whether or not a joint petition is filed, unless the spouses are separated and a joint petition is not filed.)

NAME AND ADDRESS OF TRANSFEREE, RELATIONSHIP TO DEBTOR	DATE	DESCRIBE PROPERTY TRANSFERRED AND VALUE RECEIVED
Best Stock Brokers 8400 East Pine Ave. Columbus, OH 43217 (no relationship with either debtor)	May 10, 1991	40 shares of IBM stock Received $4,475.00

11. Closed financial accounts

None
☐   List all financial accounts and instruments held in the name of the debtor or for the benefit of the debtor which were closed, sold, or otherwise transferred within one year immediately preceding the commencement of this case. Include checking, savings, or other financial accounts, certificates of deposit, or other instruments; shares and share accounts held in banks, credit unions, pension funds, cooperatives, associations, brokerage houses and other financial institutions. (Married debtors filing under chapter 12 or chapter 13 must include information concerning accounts or instruments held by or for either or both spouses whether or not a joint petition is filed, unless the spouses are separated and a joint petition is not filed.)

NAME AND ADDRESS OF INSTITUTION	TYPE AND NUMBER OF ACCOUNT AND AMOUNT OF FINAL BALANCE	AMOUNT AND DATE OF SALE OR CLOSING
Second National Bank 1000 Main Street Columbus, OH 43203	Checking account no. 87-117-415 Final balance - $21.00	January 12, 1992

12. Safe deposit boxes

None
☐ List each safe deposit or other box or depository in which the debtor has or had securities, cash, or other valuables within one year immediately preceding the commencement of this case. (Married debtors filing under chapter 12 or chapter 13 must include boxes or depositories of either or both spouses whether or not a joint petition is filed, unless the spouses are separated and a joint petition is not filed.)

NAME AND ADDRESS OF BANK OR OTHER DEPOSITORY	NAMES AND ADDRESSES OF THOSE WITH ACCESS TO BOX OR DEPOSITORY	DESCRIPTION OF CONTENTS	DATE OF TRANSFER OR SURRENDER, IF ANY
Big State Bank 2000 Westland Plaza Columbus, OH 43227	Sidney S. Smith Sarah A. Smith 2200 South Elm St. Columbus, OH 43211	Wills, legal papers, and family heirlooms of little or no market value.	None

13. Setoffs

None
☐ List all setoffs made by any creditor, including a bank, against a debt or deposit of the debtor within 90 days preceding the commencement of this case. (Married debtors filing under chapter 12 or chapter 13 must include information concerning either or both spouses whether or not a joint petition is filed, unless the spouses are separated and a joint petition is not filed.)

NAME AND ADDRESS OF CREDITOR	DATE OF SETOFF	AMOUNT OF SETOFF
Last National Bank 2100 Columbus Ave. Cleveland, OH 44112	December 2, 1991	$1,757.00

14. Property held for another person

None
☐ List all property owned by another person that the debtor holds or controls.

NAME AND ADDRESS OF OWNER	DESCRIPTION AND VALUE OF PROPERTY	LOCATION OF PROPERTY
Nancy Ann Smith 2200 South Elm St. Columbus, OH 43211 (daughter of debtors)	Savings Certificate in Third National Bank of Akron, OH Value = $279.45 (Funds contributed by grandparents)	Third National Bank 120 Main Avenue Akron, OH 44301

15. Prior address of debtor

None
☐ If the debtor has moved within the two years immediately preceding the commencement of this case, list all premises which the debtor occupied during that period and vacated prior to the commencement of this case. If a joint petition is filed, report also any separate address of either spouse.

ADDRESS	NAME USED	DATES OF OCCUPANCY
2737 Easy Street Columbus, OH 43220	Sidney S. Smith Sarah A. Smith	November 1984 to June 1990

EXHIBIT 2-P   105

The following questions are to be completed by every debtor that is a corporation or partnership and by any individual debtor who is or has been, within the two years immediately preceding the commencement of this case, any of the following: an officer, director, managing executive, or owner of more than 5 percent of the voting securities of a corporation; a partner, other than a limited partner, of a partnership; a sole proprietor or otherwise self–employed person.

An individual or joint debtor should complete this portion of the statement only if the debtor is or has been in business, as defined on page 1 of this statement, within the two years immediately preceding the commencement of this case.

16. Nature, location and name of business

None

☐ a. If the debtor is an individual, list the names and addresses of all businesses in which the debtor was an officer, director, partner, or managing executive of a corporation, partnership, sole proprietorship, or was a self-employed professional within the two years immediately preceding the commencement of this case, or in which the debtor owned 5 percent or more of the voting or equity securities within the two years immediately preceding the commencement of this case.

b. If the debtor is a partnership, list the names and addresses of all businesses in which the debtor was a partner, or owned 5 percent or more of the voting securities, within the two years immediately preceding the commencement of this case.

c. If the debtor is a corporation, list the names and addresses of all businesses in which the debtor was a partner, or owned 5 percent or more of the voting securities, within the two years immediately preceding the commencement of this case.

NAME AND ADDRESS	NATURE OF BUSINESS	BEGINNING AND ENDING DATES OF OPERATION
Sid Smith Enterprises 427 Parkway Blvd. Columbus, OH 43218	Real estate sales	June 1985 to June 1991

17. Books, records and financial statements

None

☐ a. List all bookkeepers and accountants who within the six years immediately preceding the filing of this bankruptcy case kept or supervised the keeping of books of account and records of the debtor.

NAME AND ADDRESS	DATES SERVICES RENDERED
Edith E. Eyestrain, CPA 4201 South Ohio Blvd. Columbus, OH 43223	November, 1987 to June, 1991

None

☐ b. List all firms or individuals who within the two years immediately preceding the filing of this bankruptcy case have audited the books of account and records, or prepared a financial statement, of the debtor.

NAME	ADDRESS	DATES SERVICES RENDERED
Fast Finance Company	937 Market Street Columbus, OH 43212	May, 1991

None
☐ c. List all firms or individuals who at the time of the commencement of this case were in possession of the books of account and records of the debtor. If any of the books of account and records are not available, explain.

NAME	ADDRESS
Edith E. Eyestrain, CPA	4201 South Ohio Blvd. Columbus. OH 43223
Lawrence L. Lawnoer, Attorney at law	2700 Standard Building Columbus, OH 43215

None
☐ d. List all financial institutions, creditors and other parties, including mercantile and trade agencies, to whom a financial statement was issued within the two years immediately preceding the commencement of this case by the debtor.

NAME AND ADDRESS	DATE ISSUED
Fast Finance Company 937 Market Street Columbus. OH 43212	June 7, 1991

18. Inventories

None
☐ a. List the dates of the last two inventories taken of the debtor's property, the name of the person who supervised the taking of each inventory, and the dollar amount and basis of each inventory.

DATE OF INVENTORY	INVENTORY SUPERVISOR	DOLLAR AMOUNT OF INVENTORY (Specify cost, market or other basis)
May 20, 1991	John J. Wood, Account Representative, Fast Finance Company	$2,225.00 (market value)

None
☐ b. List the name and address of the person having possession of the records of each of the two inventories reported in a, above.

DATE OF INVENTORY	NAME AND ADDRESSES OF CUSTODIAN OF INVENTORY RECORDS
May 20, 1991	John J. Wood Account Representative, Fast Finance Company 937 Market Street Columbus, OH 43212

OFFICIAL FORM 7 (page 8) – Argyle Publishing Co., 10395 West Colfax Ave., Lakewood, CO 80215

EXHIBIT 2-P   107

19. Current Partners, Officers, Directors and Shareholders

None

☒ a. If the debtor is a partnership, list the nature and percentage of partnership interest of each member of the partnership.

NAME AND ADDRESS	NATURE OF INTEREST	PERCENTAGE OF INTEREST

None

☒ b. If the debtor is a corporation, list all officers and directors of the corporation, and each stockholder who directly or indirectly owns, controls, or holds 5 percent or more of the voting securities of the corporation.

NAME AND ADDRESS	TITLE	NATURE AND PERCENTAGE OF STOCK OWNERSHIP

20. Former partners, officers, directors and shareholders

None

☒ a. If the debtor is a partnership, list each member who withdrew from the partnership within one year immediately preceding the commencement of this case.

NAME	ADDRESS	DATE OF WITHDRAWAL

None

☒ b. If the debtor is a corporation, list all officers or directors whose relationship with the corporation terminated within one year immediately preceding the commencement of this case.

NAME AND ADDRESS	TITLE	DATE OF TERMINATION

21. Withdrawals from a partnership or distributions by a corporation

None

☒ If the debtor is a partnership or corporation, list all withdrawals or distributions credited or given to an insider, including compensation in any form, bonuses, loans, stock redemptions, options exercised and any other perquisite during one year immediately preceding the commencement of this case.

NAME & ADDRESS OF RECIPIENT	RELATIONSHIP TO DEBTOR	DATE AND PURPOSE WITHDRAWAL	AMOUNT OF MONEY OR DESCRIPTION AND VALUE OF PROPERTY

DECLARATION CONCERNING DEBTOR'S STATEMENT OF FINANCIAL AFFAIRS

(If completed by an individual or individual and spouse)

I declare under penalty of perjury that I have read the answers contained in the foregoing statement of financial affairs and any attachments thereto, consisting of a total of ___10___ sheets, and that they are true and correct.

Date ___January 15, 1992___   Signature: _~Sidney Samuel Smith~_
                                                                            Debtor

Date ___January 15, 1992___   Signature: _~Sarah Arlene Smith~_
                                                                      Joint Debtor, if any

(If joint case, both spouses must sign)

◆ ◆ ◆ ◆ ◆ ◆ ◆ ◆ ◆ ◆ ◆ ◆ ◆ ◆ ◆

(If completed on behalf of a partnership or corporation)

I declare under penalty of perjury that I have read the answers contained in the foregoing statement of financial affairs and any attachments thereto, consisting of a total of _____ sheets, and that they are true and correct to the best of my knowledge, information and belief.

Date _____   Signature: _____

_____
(Print or type name and title of individual signing on behalf of debtor.)

(An individual signing of behalf of a partnership or corporation must indicate position or relationship to debtor.)

Penalty for making a false statement or concealing property: Fine of up to $500,000 or imprisonment for up to 5 years or both. 18 U.S.C. §§ 152 and 3571.

EXHIBIT 2-Q   109

UNITED STATES BANKRUPTCY COURT

<u>SOUTHERN</u>   **DISTRICT OF** <u>OHIO</u>

IN RE Sidney Samuel Smith
and Sarah Arlene Smith   Case No. _____
                                                        (If known)
                                    Debtor   Chapter _____7_____

APPLICATION TO PAY FILING FEE IN INSTALLMENTS

In accordance with Federal Rule of Bankruptcy Procedure 1006, application is made for permission to pay the filing fee on the following terms:

$ <u>None</u>   with the filing of the petition, and the balance of

$ <u>120.00</u>   in <u>4</u>   installments, as follows:

$ <u>30.00</u>   on or before <u>February 3, 1992</u>

$ <u>30.00</u>   on or before <u>March 3, 1992</u>

$ <u>30.00</u>   on or before <u>April 3, 1992</u>

$ <u>30.00</u>   on or before <u>May 3, 1992</u>

I certify that I am unable to pay the filing fee except in installments. I further certify that I have not paid any money or transferred any property to an attorney or any other person for services in connection with this case or in connection with any other pending bankruptcy case and that I will not make any payment or transfer any property for services in connection with the case until the filing fee is paid in full.

Date: <u>January 15, 1992</u>

x *Sarah Arlene Smith*   x *Sidney Samuel Smith*
Signature of Joint Applicant   Signature of Applicant

Sarah Arlene Smith   Sidney Samuel Smith
Name and Address of Joint Applicant   Name and Address of Applicant
  2200 South Elm Street   2200 South Elm Street
  Columbus, OH 43211   Columbus, OH 43211

ORDER

IT IS ORDERED that the debtor pay the filing fee in installments on the terms set forth in the foregoing application.

IT IS FURTHER ORDERED that until the filing fee is paid in full the debtor shall not pay, and no person shall accept, any money for services in connection with this case, and the debtor shall not relinquish, and no person shall accept, any property as payment for services in connection with this case.

BY THE COURT

Date: _____   _____

OFFICIAL FORM 3 – Argyle Publishing Co., 10395 West Colfax Ave., Lakewood, CO 80215

EXHIBIT 2-R

UNITED STATES BANKRUPTCY COURT

__SOUTHERN__ **DISTRICT OF** __OHIO__

IN RE Sidney Samuel Smith
and Sarah Arlene Smith

Case No. _____
(If known)

Debtor

Chapter ____7____

CHAPTER 7 INDIVIDUAL DEBTOR'S STATEMENT OF INTENTION

1. I, the debtor, have filed a schedule of assets and liabilities which includes consumer debts secured by property of the estate.

2. My intention with respect to the property of the estate which secures those consumer debts is as follows:

a. Property to Be Surrendered.

Description of Property	Creditor's Name
1. 1986 Ford Pickup Truck	Fast Finance Company
2. Lot at 700 Fox Street, Columbus, Ohio	Fast Finance Company
3.	
4.	
5.	

b. Property to Be Retained (Check applicable statement of debtor's intention concerning reaffirmation, redemption, or lien avoidance.)

Description of property	Creditor's name	Debt will be reaffirmed pursuant to § 524(c)	Property is claimed as exempt and will be redeemed pursuant to § 722	Lien will be avoided pursuant to § 522(f) and property will be claimed as exempt
1. Family home	Big Bank of Columbus	X		
2. Household furniture	Easy Loans, Inc.		X	
3. Wearing apparel and jewelry	Fast Finance Company			X
4. 1988 Honda Civic	Easy Loans, Inc.	X		
5.				
6.				

3. I understand that § 521(2)(B) of the Bankruptcy Code requires that I perform the above stated intention within 45 days of the date of the filing of this statement with the court, or within such additional time as the court, for cause, within such 45-day period fixes.

Date: __January 15, 1992__

Sidney Samuel Smith
Signature of Debtor

Date: __January 15, 1992__

Sarah Arlene Smith
Signature of Codebtor, if any

OFFICIAL FORM 8 – Argyle Publishing Co., 10395 West Colfax Ave., Lakewood, CO 80215

EXHIBIT 2-S   111

UNITED STATES BANKRUPTCY COURT
SOUTHERN   **DISTRICT OF**   OHIO

NOTICE TO INDIVIDUAL CONSUMER DEBTOR(S)

The purpose of this notice is to acquaint you with the four chapters of the federal Bankruptcy Code under which you may file a bankruptcy petition. The bankruptcy law is complicated and not easily described. Therefore, you should seek the advice of an attorney to learn of your rights and responsibilities under the law should you decide to file a petition with the court. Neither the judge nor the court's employees may provide you with legal advice.

Chapter 7: Liquidation ($120 filing fee)

1. Chapter 7 is designed for debtors in financial difficulty who do not have the ability to pay their existing debts.

2. Under Chapter 7 a trustee takes possession of all your property. You may claim certain of your property as exempt under governing law. The trustee then liquidates the property and uses the proceeds to pay your creditors according to priorities of the Bankruptcy Code.

3. The purpose of filing a Chapter 7 case is to obtain a discharge of your existing debts. If, however, you are found to have committed certain kinds of improper conduct described in the Bankruptcy Code, your discharge may be denied by the court, and the purpose for which you filed the bankruptcy petition will be defeated.

4. Even if you receive a discharge, there are some debts that are not discharged under the law. Therefore, you may still be responsible for such debts as certain taxes and student loans, alimony and support payments, debts fraudulently incurred, debts for willful and malicious injury to a person or property, and debts arising from a drunk driving judgment.

5. Under certain circumstances you may keep property that you have purchased subject to a valid security interest. Your attorney can explain the options that are available to you.

Chapter 13: Repayment of All or Part of the Debts of an Individual with Regular Income ($120 filing fee)

1. Chapter 13 is designed for individuals with regular income who are temporarily unable to pay their debts but would like to pay them in installments over a period of time. You are only eligible for Chapter 13 if your debts do not exceed certain dollar amounts set forth in the Bankruptcy Code.

2. Under Chapter 13 you must file a plan with the court to repay your creditors all or part of the money that you owe them, using your future earnings. Usually the period allowed by the court to repay your debts is three years, but not more than five years. Your plan must be approved by the court before it can take effect.

3. Under Chapter 13, unlike Chapter 7, you may keep all of your property, both exempt and non-exempt, as long as you continue to make payments under the plan.

4. After completion of payments under your plan, your debts are discharged except for alimony and support payments, certain kinds of taxes owed for less than three years, certain student loans, court-ordered restitution in a criminal case, debts arising from a drunk driving judgement, and long term secured obligations.

Chapter 11: Reorganization ($500 filing fee)

Chapter 11 is designed primarily for the reorganization of a business but is also available to consumer debtors. Its provisions are quite complicated, and any decision for an individual to file a Chapter 11 petition should be reviewed with an attorney.

Chapter 12: Family Farmer ($200 filing fee)

Chapter 12 is designed to permit family farmers to repay their debts over a period of time from future earnings and is in many ways similar to Chapter 13. The eligibility requirements are restrictive, limiting its use to those whose income arises primarily from a family-owned farm.

ACKNOWLEDGEMENT

I hereby certify that I have read this notice on this _____15th_____ day of ____January____ , 19 _92_ .

Sidney Samuel Smith
Debtor

Sarah Arlene Smith
Joint Debtor, if any

INSTRUCTIONS: A copy of this notice personally signed by the debtor, or by both debtors in a joint case, must accompany any bankruptcy petition filed with the Clerk. Failure to comply may result in the petition not being accepted for filing.

BANKRUPTCY FORM B 201 – Argyle Publishing Co., 10395 West Colfax Ave., Lakewood, CO 80215

EXHIBIT 2-T

UNITED STATES BANKRUPTCY COURT
FOR THE NORTHERN DISTRICT OF OHIO
EASTERN DIVISION

IN RE   Sidney Samuel Smith and   )
          Sarah Arlene Smith   )   Case No. 92-00117
)
                   Debtors   )   Chapter 7

MOTION TO REDEEM PERSONAL PROPERTY UNDER SECTION 722

The debtors, by their attorney, state and represent as follows:

1. That the property described in paragraph 4 below is tangible personal property intended primarily for the personal, family and household use of the debtors and the debtors' family and such property is exempt to the debtors under the laws of the state of Ohio, to wit: Ohio Revised Code section 2329(A)(3), (4)(b).

2. That the lien of the creditor, Easy Loans, Inc., on such property secures a dischargeable debt that was incurred by the debtors primarily for a personal, family or household purpose, to wit: the purchase of food, supplies, and clothing used by the debtors and the debtors' family.

3. That pursuant to 11 U.S.C. 722, the debtors desire to redeem such property from the lien of the creditor by paying to the creditor the amount of the creditor's allowed secured claim secured by the lien on such property.

4. That the property to be redeemed by the debtors and the alleged value of such property is as follows:

Sharp Television Set #B444564	$ 100.00
General Electric Refrigerator #F3452	$ 50.00
Westinghouse Electric Range #R-44589	$ 40.00
Beds, tables, and chairs described in item	
4 of the debtors' Schedule B	$ 500.00

5. That the amount of the secured claim of the creditor, Easy Loans, Inc., secured by its lien on such property is $690.00, which amount the debtors propose to pay to the creditor in redemption of such property.

WHEREFORE, the debtors move this honorable court to schedule a hearing on notice as provided in Bankruptcy Rule 6008 and thereafter enter an order fixing the amount of the allowed secured claim of the creditor, Easy Loans, Inc., secured by its lien on the property described in paragraph 4 above as $690.00, and permit the debtors to redeem the above-described property by paying to the said creditor the sum of $690.00 within a reasonable period.

Dated: January 30, 1992

                                  Alice B. Chase
                                  Attorney for Debtor
                                  2000 Market Street
                                  Columbus, OH 43222
                                  Telephone: 614-333-3300

CERTIFICATE OF SERVICE BY MAIL

The undersigned certifies under penalty of perjury that he or she has on the date shown below, by first class mail addressed to their respective addresses of record in this case, served a true copy of this document on the trustee and the creditor described in the above document.

Date: _____   _____

EXHIBIT 2-U   113

UNITED STATES BANKRUPTCY COURT
FOR THE NORTHERN DISTRICT OF OHIO
EASTERN DIVISION

IN RE   Sidney Samuel Smith and   )
           Sarah Arlene Smith   )   Case No. 92-00117
)
                    Debtors   )   Chapter 7

MOTION TO AVOID SECURITY INTEREST IN EXEMPT PROPERTY UNDER SECTION 522(f)

The debtors, by their attorney, state and represent as follows:

1. That the creditor, Fast Finance Company, has a nonpossessory, nonpurchase-money security interest in the following described property of the debtors, which property is held primarily for the personal, family, and household use of the debtors and their dependents:

> 1 diamond wedding ring
> 1 gold wedding ring
> 1 Rolex wrist watch
> personal clothing and wearing apparel of debtors

2. That the security interest of the creditor, Fast Finance Company, impairs an exemption to which the debtors would have been entitled under the laws of the State of Ohio, which exemptions have been claimed by the debtors in this case and have been allowed.

3. That the debtors are entitled to avoid the security interest of the creditor, Fast Finance Company, in the above-described property under the provisions of 11 U.S.C. 522(f).

WHEREFORE, the debtors move this honorable court to schedule a hearing on notice as provided in Bankruptcy Rules 4003(d) and 9014 and to thereafter enter an order avoiding the lien of the creditor, Fast Finance Company, in the property described in paragraph 1 above.

Dated: January 30, 1992

                                   Alice B. Chase
                                   Attorney for Debtor
                                   2000 Market Street
                                   Columbus, OH 43222
                                   Telephone: 614-333-3300

CERTIFICATE OF SERVICE BY MAIL

The undersigned certifies under penalty of perjury that he or she has on the date shown below, by first class mail addressed to their respective addresses of record in this case, served a true copy of this document on the trustee and the creditor described in the above document.

Date: _January 30, 1992_

UNITED STATES BANKRUPTCY COURT
District of Kansas

280 U. S. Courthouse
444 S. E. Quincy Street
Topeka, KS 66683

NOTICE OF COMMENCEMENT OF CASE UNDER CHAPTER 7
OF THE BANKRUPTCY CODE,
MEETING OF CREDITORS, AND FIXING OF DATES
(Individual or Joint Debtor No Asset Case)

Case Number: 91-42522
Date Filed (or Converted) :   11/26/91

IN RE(NAME OF DEBTOR)   ADDRESS OF DEBTOR
   Samuel F. Malone, Jr., aka   11260 West 120th Street
   Sam Malone,   805-61-5866   Overland Park, KS 66210

NAME/ADDRESS OF ATTORNEY FOR DEBTOR   NAME/ADDRESS OF TRUSTEE
   Walter F. Smith   Robert L. Baer
   11101 Main Avenue   P.O. Box 2546
   Overland Park, KS 66210   Topeka, KS 66601

DATE/TIME/LOCATION OF MEETING OF CREDITORS   DATE/TIME/LOCATION OF DISCHARGE HEARING
January 13, 1992 at 10:00 am   April 30, 1992 at 1:30 pm
U.S. Post Office Building   Federal Building Room 492
Room 303   444 S.E. Quincy
5th & Kansas   Topeka, KS 66683
Topeka, KS 66603

         Discharge of Debts: Deadline to File a Complaint Objecting to Discharge of the Debtor or to
                    Determine Dischargeability of Certain Types of Debts: 03/13/92

AT THIS TIME THERE APPEAR TO BE NO ASSETS AVAILABLE FROM WHICH PAYMENT MAY BE MADE TO UNSECURED CREDITORS.
DO NOT FILE A PROOF OF CLAIM UNTIL YOU RECEIVE NOTICE TO DO SO.

COMMENCEMENT OF CASE. A petition for liquidation under chapter 7 of the Bankruptcy Code has been filed in this court
by or against the person or persons named above as the debtor, and an order for relief has been entered. You will not
receive notice of all documents filed in this case. All documents filed with the court, including lists of the
debtor's property, debts, and property claimed as exempt are available for inspection at the office of the clerk
of the bankruptcy court.

CREDITORS MAY NOT TAKE CERTAIN ACTIONS. A creditor is anyone to whom the debtor owes money or property. Under the
Bankruptcy Code, the debtor is granted certain protection against creditors. Common examples of prohibited actions by
creditors are contacting the debtor to demand repayment, taking action against the debtor to collect money owed to
creditors or to take property of the debtor, and starting or continuing foreclosure actions, repossessions, or wage
deductions. If unauthorized actions are taken by a creditor against a debtor, the court may penalize that creditor. A
creditor who is considering taking action against the debtor or the property of the debtor should review Sec. 362
of the Bankruptcy Code and may wish to seek legal advice. The staff of the clerk of the bankruptcy court is not
permitted to give legal advice.

MEETING OF CREDITORS. The debtor (both husband and wife in a joint case) is required to appear at the meeting of
creditors on the date and at the place set forth above for the purpose of being examined under oath. Attendance by
creditors at the meeting is welcomed, but not required. At the meeting, the creditors may elect a trustee other than
the one named above, elect a committee of creditors, examine the debtor, and transact such other business as may
properly come before the meeting. The meeting may be continued or adjourned from time to time by notice at the
meeting, without further written notice to creditors.

LIQUIDATION OF THE DEBTOR'S PROPERTY. The trustee will collect the debtor's property and turn any that is not exempt
into money. At this time, however, it appears from the schedules of the debtor that there are no assets from
which any distribution can be paid to creditors. If at a later date it appears that there are assets from which a
distribution may be paid, the creditors will be notified and given an opportunity to file claims.

EXEMPT PROPERTY. Under state and federal law, the debtor is permitted to keep certain money or property as exempt.
If a creditor believes that an exemption of money or property is not authorized by law, the creditor may file an
objection. An objection must be filed not later than 30 days after the conclusion of the meeting of creditors.

DISCHARGE OF DEBTS. The debtor is seeking a discharge of debts. A discharge means that certain debts are made
unenforceable against the debtor personally. Creditors whose claims against the debtor are discharged may never take
action against the debtor to collect the discharged debts. If a creditor believes that the debtor should not receive
any discharge of debts under Sec. 727 of the Bankruptcy Code or that a debt owed to the creditor is not dischargeable
under Sec. 523(a)(2),(4), or (6) of the Bankruptcy Code, timely action must be taken in the bankruptcy court by the
deadline set forth above labeled "Discharge of Debts." Creditors considering taking such action may wish to seek
legal advice.

PURSUANT TO STANDING ORDER of the Court, the trustee may abandon property of the estate under 11 U.S.C. Sec. 554
without further notice within sixty (60) days from the Sec. 341 Meeting of Creditors.

                    DO NOT FILE A PROOF OF CLAIM UNLESS YOU RECEIVE A COURT NOTICE TO DO SO

For the Court: Russell L. Brenner   11/27/91
                       Clerk of the Bankruptcy Court   Date   FORM B9A 0001

EXHIBIT 2-W   115

In re Sidney Samuel Smith, et al   Case No. 92-00177
        Debtor   (If known)

AMENDED SCHEDULE F - CREDITORS HOLDING UNSECURED NONPRIORITY CLAIMS

State the name, mailing address, including zip code, and account number, if any, of all entities holding unsecured claims without priority against the debtor or the property of the debtor, as of the date of filing of the petition. Do not include claims listed in Schedules D and E. If all creditors will not fit on this page, use the continuation sheet provided.

If any entity other than a spouse in a joint case may be jointly liable on a claim, place an "X" in the column labeled "Codebtor," include the entity on the appropriate schedule of creditors, and complete Schedule H – Codebtors. If a joint petition is filed, state whether husband, wife, both of them, or the marital community may be liable on each claim by placing an "H," "W," "J," or "C" in the column labeled "Husband, Wife, Joint, or Community."

If the claim is contingent, place an "X" in the column labeled "Contingent." If the claim is unliquidated, place an "X" in the column labeled "Unliquidated." If the claim is disputed, place an "X" in the column labeled "Disputed." (You may need to place an "X" in more than one of these three column.)

Report the total of all claims listed on this schedule in the box labeled "Total" on the last sheet of the completed schedule. Report this total also on the Summary of Schedules.

☐ Check this box if debtor has no creditors holding unsecured nonpriority claims to report on this Schedule F.

CREDITOR'S NAME AND MAILING ADDRESS INCLUDING ZIP CODE	CODEBTOR	HUSBAND, WIFE, JOINT, OR COMMUNITY	DATE CLAIM WAS INCURRED AND CONSIDERATION FOR CLAIM. IF CLAIM IS SUBJECT TO SETOFF, SO STATE.	CONTINGENT	UNLIQUIDATED	DISPUTED	AMOUNT OF CLAIM
ACCOUNT NO. None Glen's Garage 201 Side Street Columbus, OH 43209 (address change only)		H	April, 1990 Automobile repair				$295.00
ACCOUNT NO. 27-1907 XYZ Medical Services 9777 Rolling Hills Ave. Cincinnati, OH 45227 (additional creditor)		W	January – June, 1988 Medical services provided to brother of Sarah Arlene Smith, the payment of which were guaranteed by Sarah Arlene Smith.				$27,980.00
ACCOUNT NO.							

DECLARATION CONCERNING DEBTOR'S SCHEDULES

DECLARATION UNDER PENALTY OF PERJURY BY INDIVIDUAL DEBTOR

I declare under penalty of perjury that I have read the foregoing summary and schedules, consisting of ___one___ sheets, and that they are true and correct to the best of my knowledge, information, and belief.   (Total shown on summary page plus 1.)

Date February 10, 1992   Signature: _Sidney Samuel Smith_
                                                              Debtor

Date February 10, 1992   Signature: _Sarah Arlene Smith_
                                                              Joint Debtor, if any
                                        (If joint case, both spouses must sign.)

Note to Reader: In practice a separate declaration sheet should be used. They were combined here to save space.

UNITED STATES BANKRUPTCY COURT
DISTRICT OF DELAWARE

IN RE   FREDERICK F. FRESHSTART,   )
         aka FRED FRESHSTART   )   Case No. 92-0176200
)
                        Debtor   )   Chapter 7
)
         Social Security No. 667-87-1717   )

DISCHARGE OF DEBTOR

It appearing that a petition commencing a case under title 11, United States Code, was filed by or against the person named above on _____January 10, 1992_____, and that an order for relief was entered under chapter 7, and that no complaint objecting to the discharge of the debtor was filed within the time fixed by the court [*or* that a complaint objecting to discharge of the debtor was filed and, after due notice and hearing, was not sustained];

IT IS ORDERED that

1. The above-named debtor is released from all dischargeable debts.

2. Any judgment heretofore or hereafter obtained in any court other than this court is null and void as a determination of the personal liability of the debtor with respect to any of the following:

   (a) debts dischargeable under 11 U.S.C. § 523;

   (b) unless heretofore or hereafter determined by order of this court to be nondischargeable, debts alleged to be excepted from discharge under clauses (2), (4) and (6) of 11 U.S.C. § 523(a);

   (c) debts determined by this court to be discharged.

3. All creditors whose debts are discharged by this order and all creditors whose judgments are declared null and void by paragraph 2 above are enjoined from instituting or continuing any action or employing any process or engaging in any act to collect such debts as personal liabilities of the above-named debtor.

Dated: _____July 18, 1992_____

                                        BY THE COURT

                                        _____
                                        United States Bankruptcy Judge

EXHIBIT 2-Y   117

REAFFIRMATION AGREEMENT

Debtor's Name Sidney Samuel Smith and Sarah Arlene Smith	Bankruptcy Case no. 92-00177

INSTRUCTIONS

1) Write debtor's name and bankruptcy case number above.
2) Part A - Must be signed by both the debtor and the creditor.
3) Part B - Must be signed by the attorney who represents the debtor in this bankruptcy case.
4) Part C - Must be completed by the debtor if the debtor is not represented by an attorney in this bankruptcy case.
5) File the completed form by mailing or delivering to the Bankruptcy Clerk.
6) Attach written agreement, if any.

COURT USE ONLY

PART A - AGREEMENT

Creditor's Name and Address

Easy Loans, Inc.
4000 East 10th Avenue
Cleveland, OH 44111

Date Set for Discharge Hearing (if any)

March 1, 1992

Summary of Terms of the New Agreement

a) Principal Amount $ 3,070.00

   Interest Rate (APR) 10.5%

   Monthly Payments $ 188.00

b) Description of Security 1988 Honda
   Civic I.D.# 77HP27491

   Present Market Value $ 4,000.00

The parties understand that this agreement is purely voluntary and that the debtor may rescind the agreement at any time prior to discharge or within 60 days after such agreement is filed with the court, whichever occurs later, by giving notice of recission to the creditor.

Date: January 30, 1992

_____
Debtor's signature

_____
Creditor's signature

_____
Joint Debtor's signature

PART B - ATTORNEY'S DECLARATION

This agreement represents a fully informed and voluntary agreement that does not impose an undue hardship on the debtor or any dependent of the debtor.

Date: January 30, 1992

_____
Attorney for Debtor

PART C - MOTION FOR COURT APPROVAL OF AGREEMENT
(Complete only when the debtor is not represented by an attorney)

I (We), the debtor(s), affirm the following to be true and correct:

1) I am (We are) not represented by an attorney in connection with this bankruptcy case.
2) My (Our) current monthly net income is $ _____ .
3) My (Our) current monthly expenses total $ _____ , including any payment due under this agreement.
4) I (We) believe that this agreement is in my (our) best interest because_____
_____

Therefore, I (we) ask the court for an order approving this reaffirmation agreement.

Date: _____   _____   _____
                            Debtor's signature   Joint Debtor's signature

PART D - COURT ORDER

The court grants the debtor's motion and approves the voluntary agreement upon the terms specified above.

Date: _____   _____
                                     Bankruptcy Judge

BANKRUPTCY FORM B 240 – Argyle Publishing Co., 10395 West Colfax Ave., Lakewood, CO 80215

REAFFIRMATION AGREEMENT

WHEREAS, _____ , the debtor has filed a voluntary petition under Chapter 7 of the United States Bankruptcy Code, in case no. _____ in the United States Bankruptcy Court for the _____ District of _____ ; and

WHEREAS, the debtor has not been granted a discharge in the above-described bankruptcy case; and

WHEREAS, in such bankruptcy case the debt described below constitutes a dischargeable consumer debt not secured by real property of the debtor; and

WHEREAS, the debtor was (was not) represented by an attorney during the course of negotiating this agreement with _____ , the creditor; and

WHEREAS, the debtor has, within the required period, filed a Statement of Intention with the bankruptcy court stating the debtor's intention to reaffirm the debt described below; and

WHEREAS, it is the desire and intention of the debtor, in consideration of the promises and representations herein made by the creditor, to reaffirm the debt described below in the amount shown below.

NOW THEREFORE, the debtor and the creditor agree as follows:

1. The debtor agrees to reaffirm the debt described in this paragraph in the amount of $ _____ only, which amount includes all accrued interest and other charges. The balance of the original debt, if any, is expressly not reaffirmed by the debtor. The debt reaffirmed by this agreement was incurred by the debtor on _____ for _____. The debt reaffirmed by this agreement shall be paid by the debtor to the creditor in the following manner:_____ _____

2. The debt reaffirmed by this agreement is secured by the following property: _____ _____ , which property is now in the possession of the debtor. The debtor may retain possession of such property, provided that the payments described in paragraph 1 above are timely made. The creditor has a valid and enforceable security interest in such property to the extent of the amount of the debt reaffirmed by this agreement, which security interest the creditor agrees to release at its sole expense upon the completion of the payments described in paragraph 1 above.

3. The debtor may rescind this agreement at any time prior to discharge or within 60 days after the agreement is filed with the court, whichever occurs later, by giving notice of rescission to the creditor in writing at the office of the creditor.

* 4. The debtor agrees, as a condition of this agreement, to cause, through the debtor's attorney, a copy of this agreement to be filed with the bankruptcy court on or before _____ , and to cause the said attorney to file with the bankruptcy court an affidavit or declaration in accordance with the provisions of 11 U.S.C. 524(c)(3).

** 5. The debtor agrees, as a condition of this agreement, to file a motion with the bankruptcy court seeking court approval of this reaffirmation agreement in its present form and to diligently seek the entry of an order by the court approving this agreement. Should the bankruptcy court refuse to approve this agreement in its present form, this agreement shall be null and void and shall have no effect on the rights of any party.

6. This agreement constitutes the entire agreement between the parties, and any verbal agreements or representations made by or between the parties are hereby declared void and unenforceable. A signed copy of this agreement shall be given to each party.

Dated: _____   _____   _____
                                                    Creditor   Debtor

* Approved as being a fully informed and voluntary agreement by the debtor and as not imposing an undue hardship on the debtor or a dependent of the debtor:

_____
Attorney for Debtor

* needed if the debtor was represented by an attorney during the course of negotiating the agreement with the creditor

** needed if the debtor was not represented by an attorney during the course of negotiating the agreement with the creditor

CHAPTER THREE

ADJUSTMENT OF DEBTS UNDER CHAPTER 13

PART A *

QUESTIONS AND ANSWERS ABOUT CHAPTER 13

1. What is chapter 13 and how does it work?

Chapter 13 is that part (or chapter) of the Bankruptcy Code under which a person may repay all or a portion of his or her debts under the supervision and protection of the bankruptcy court. The Bankruptcy Code is that portion of the federal laws that deal with bankruptcy. A person who files under chapter 13 is called a debtor. In a chapter 13 case, the debtor must submit to the court a plan for the repayment of all or a portion of his or her debts. The plan must be approved by the court to become effective. If the court approves the debtor's plan, most creditors will be prohibited from collecting their claims from the debtor during the course of the case. The debtor must make regular payments to a person called the chapter 13 trustee, who collects the money paid by the debtor and disburses it to creditors in the manner called for in the plan. Upon completion of the payments called for in the plan, the debtor is released from liability for the remainder of his or her dischargeable debts.

2. How does chapter 13 differ from chapter 7 for a debtor?

The basic difference between chapter 7 and chapter 13 is that under chapter 7 the debtor's nonexempt property (if any exists) is liquidated to pay as much as possible of the debtor's debts, while under chapter 13 a portion of the debtor's future income is used to pay as much of the debtor's debts as is feasible considering the debtor's circumstances. As a practical matter, under chapter 7 the debtor loses all or most of his or her nonexempt property and receives a chapter 7 discharge, which releases the debtor from liability for most debts. Under chapter 13, the debtor usually retains his or her nonexempt property, must pay off as much of his or her debts as the court deems feasible, and receives a chapter 13 discharge, which is broader than a chapter 7 discharge and releases the debtor from liability for some debts that are not dischargeable under chapter 7. However, a chapter 13 case normally lasts much longer than a chapter 7 case and is usually more expensive for the debtor.

3. When is chapter 13 preferable to chapter 7 for a debtor?

Chapter 13 is usually preferable for a person who - (1) wishes to repay all or most of his or her unsecured debts and has the income with which to do so within a reasonable time, (2) has valuable nonexempt property or has valuable exempt property securing debts, either of which would be lost in a chapter 7 case, (3) is not eligible for a discharge under chapter 7, (4) has one or more substantial debts that are dischargeable under chapter 13 but not under chapter 7, or (5) has sufficient assets with which to repay most debts, but needs temporary relief from creditors in order to do so.

4. How does chapter 13 differ from a private debt consolidation service?

In a chapter 13 case, the bankruptcy court can provide aid to the debtor that private debt consolidation services cannot provide. For example, the court has the authority to prohibit creditors from attaching or foreclosing on the debtor's property, to force unsecured creditors to accept a chapter 13 plan that pays only a portion of their claims, and to discharge a debtor from unpaid portions of debts. Private debt consolidation services have none of these powers.

121

5. What is a chapter 13 discharge?

It is a court order releasing a debtor from all dischargeable debts and ordering creditors not to collect them from the debtor. A debt that is discharged is one that the debtor is released from and does not have to pay. There are two types of chapter 13 discharges: (1) a full or successful plan discharge, which is granted to a debtor who completes all payments called for in the plan, and (2) a partial or unsuccessful plan discharge, which is granted to a debtor who is unable to complete the payments called for in the plan due to circumstances for which the debtor should not be held accountable. A full chapter 13 discharge is broader and discharges more debts than a chapter 7 discharge, while a partial chapter 13 discharge is similar to a chapter 7 discharge.

6. What types of debts are dischargeable under chapter 13?

A full chapter 13 discharge granted upon the completion of all payments required in the plan discharges a debtor from all debts except:

(1) debts that were paid outside of the plan and not covered in the plan,

(2) debts for alimony, maintenance, or support,

(3) debts for death or personal injury caused by the debtor's operation of a motor vehicle while unlawfully intoxicated,

(4) debts for restitution included in a criminal sentence imposed on the debtor,

(5) debts for most student loans or educational obligations that first became less than 7 years before the case was filed,

(6) installment debts whose last payment is due after the completion of the plan, and

(7) debts incurred while the plan was in effect that were not paid under the plan.

A partial chapter 13 discharge granted when a debtor is unable to complete the payments under a plan due to circumstances for which the debtor should not be held accountable, discharges the debtor from all debts except:

(1) secured debts (i.e., debts secured by mortgages or liens),

(2) debts that were paid outside of the plan and not covered in the plan,

(3) installment debts whose last payment is due after the completion of the plan,

(4) debts incurred while the plan was in effect that were not paid under the plan, and

(5) debts that are not dischargeable under chapter 7.

7. What is a chapter 13 plan?

It is a written plan presented to the bankruptcy court by a debtor that states how much money or other property the debtor will pay to the chapter 13 trustee, how long the debtor's payments to the chapter 13 trustee will continue, how much will be paid to each of the debtor's creditors, which creditors will be paid outside of the plan, and certain other technical matters.

8. What is a chapter 13 trustee?

A chapter 13 trustee is a person appointed by the United States trustee to collect payments from the debtor, make payments to creditors in the manner set forth in the debtor's plan, and administer the debtor's chapter 13 case until it is closed. In some cases the chapter 13 trustee is required to perform certain other duties, and the debtor is always required to cooperate with the chapter 13 trustee.

9.   What debts may be paid under a chapter 13 plan?

Any debts whatsoever, whether they are secured or unsecured. Even debts that are nondischargeable, such as debts for student loans, alimony or child support, may be paid under a chapter 13 plan.

10.   Must all debts be paid in full under a chapter 13 plan?

No. While certain debts, such as debts for taxes and fully secured debts, must be paid in full under a chapter 13 plan, only an amount that the debtor can reasonably afford must be paid on most debts. The unpaid balance of most debts that are not paid in full under a chapter 13 plan is discharged upon completion of the plan.

11.   Must all unsecured creditors be treated alike under a chapter 13 plan?

No. If there is a reasonable basis for doing so, unsecured debts can be divided into separate classes and treated differently. It may be possible, therefore, to pay certain unsecured creditors in full, while paying little or nothing to others.

12.   How much of a debtor's income must be paid to the chapter 13 trustee under a chapter 13 plan?

Usually all of the disposable income of the debtor and the debtor's spouse for a three-year period must be paid to the chapter 13 trustee. Disposable income is income received by the debtor and his or her spouse that is not reasonably necessary for the support of the debtor and the debtor's dependents.

13.   When must the debtor begin making payments to the chapter 13 trustee and how must they be made?

The debtor must begin making payments to the chapter 13 trustee within 30 days after the debtor's plan is filed with the court, and the plan must be filed with the court within 15 days after the case is filed. The payments must be made regularly, usually on a weekly, bi-weekly, or monthly basis. If the debtor is employed, some courts require the payments to be made by the debtor's employer; otherwise, the payments can be made by either the debtor or the debtor's employer.

14.   How long does a chapter 13 plan last?

A chapter 13 plan must last for three years, unless all debts can be paid off in full in less time. However, a chapter 13 plan can last for as long as five years, if necessary.

15.   Is it necessary for all creditors to approve a chapter 13 plan?

No. To become effective, a chapter 13 plan must be approved by the court, not by the creditors. The court, however, cannot approve a plan unless secured creditors are dealt with in the manner described in the answer to Question 16. Also, unsecured creditors are permitted to file objections to the debtor's plan, and these objections must be ruled on by the court before it can approve the debtor's chapter 13 plan.

16.   How are secured creditors dealt with under chapter 13?

There are four methods of dealing with secured creditors under chapter 13: (1) the creditor may accept the debtor's proposed plan, (2) the creditor may retain its lien and be paid the full amount of its secured claim under the plan, (3) the debtor may surrender the collateral to the creditor, or (4) the creditor may be paid or dealt with outside the plan. It is important to understand that a creditor has a secured claim only to the extent of the value of its security, which cannot exceed the value of the property securing the claim. Thus, a creditor with a mortgage on, say, a $1500 automobile cannot have a secured claim for more than $1500, regardless of how much is owed to the creditor. If the debtor is in default to a secured creditor, the default must be cured (made current) within a reasonable time. Also, interest must be paid on secured claims.

17. How are cosigned or guaranteed debts handled under chapter 13?

If a cosigned or guaranteed consumer debt is being paid in full under a chapter 13 plan, the creditor may not collect the debt from the cosigner or guarantor. However, if a consumer debt is not being paid in full under the plan, the creditor may collect the unpaid portion of the debt from the cosigner or guarantor. A consumer debt is a nonbusiness debt. Creditors may collect business debts from cosigners or guarantors even if the debts are to be paid in full under the debtor's plan.

18. Who is eligible to file under chapter 13?

Any natural person may file under chapter 13 if the person - (1) resides in, does business in, or owns property in the United States, (2) has regular income, (3) has unsecured debts of less than $100,000, (4) has secured debts of less than $350,000, (5) is not a stockbroker or a commodity broker, and (6) has not been a debtor in another bankruptcy case that was dismissed within the last 180 days on certain technical grounds. A person meeting the above requirements may file under chapter 13 regardless of when he or she last filed a bankruptcy case or received a bankruptcy discharge.

19. May a husband and wife file jointly under chapter 13?

A husband and wife may file jointly under chapter 13 if each of them meets the requirements listed in the answer to Question 18 above, except that only one of them need have regular income and their combined debts must meet the debt limitations.

20. When should a husband and wife file jointly under chapter 13?

If both spouses are liable for any significant debts, they should file jointly under chapter 13, even if only one of them has income. Also, if both of them have regular income, they should file jointly.

21. May a self-employed person file under chapter 13?

Yes. A self-employed person meeting the eligibility requirements listed in the answer to Question 18 above may file under chapter 13. A debtor engaged in business may continue to operate the business during the chapter 13 case.

22. May a chapter 7 case be converted to chapter 13?

A pending chapter 7 case may be converted to chapter 13 at any time at the request of the debtor, if the case has not been previously converted to chapter 7 from chapter 13.

23. Where is a chapter 13 case filed?

A chapter 13 case is filed in the bankruptcy court in the district where the debtor has lived or maintained a principal place of business for the greatest portion of the last 180 days. The bankruptcy court is a unit of the federal district court.

24. What fees are charged in a chapter 13 case?

There is a $120 filing fee charged when the case is filed, which may be paid in installments if necessary. In addition, the chapter 13 trustee assesses a fee of 10 percent on all payments made under the plan. Thus, if a debtor pays a total of $5,000 under a chapter 13 plan, the total amount of fees charged in the case will be $620 (a $500 trustee's fee, plus the $120 filing fee). These fees are in addition to the fee charged by the debtor's attorney.

25. Will a person lose any property if he or she files under chapter 13?

Usually not. Under chapter 13, creditors are usually paid out of the debtor's income and not from the debtor's property. However, if a debtor has valuable nonexempt property and has insufficient income to pay enough to creditors to satisfy the court, some of the debtor's property may have to be used to pay creditors.

26. How does filing under chapter 13 affect collection proceedings and foreclosures previously filed against the debtor?

The filing of a chapter 13 case automatically stays (stops) all lawsuits, attachments, garnishments, foreclosures, and other actions by creditors against the debtor or the debtor's property. A few days after the case is filed, the court will mail a notice to all creditors advising them of the automatic stay. Certain creditors may be notified sooner, if necessary. Most creditors are prohibited from proceeding against the debtor during the entire course of the chapter 13 case. If the debtor is later granted a chapter 13 discharge, the creditors will then be prohibited from collecting the discharged debts from the debtor after the case is closed.

27. May a person whose debts are being administered by a financial counselor file under chapter 13?

Yes. A financial counselor has no legal right to prevent a person from filing any type of bankruptcy case, including a chapter 13 case.

28. How does filing under chapter 13 affect a person's credit rating?

It may worsen it, at least temporarily. However, if most of a person's debts are ultimately paid off under a chapter 13 plan, that fact may be taken into account by credit reporting agencies. If very little is paid on most debts, the credit-rating effect of a chapter 13 case may be similar to that of a chapter 7 case.

29. Are the names of persons who file under chapter 13 published?

When a chapter 13 case is filed, it becomes a public record and the name of the debtor may be published by some credit reporting agencies. However, newspapers do not usually publish the names of persons who file under chapter 13.

30. Is a person's employer notified when he or she files under chapter 13?

In most cases, yes. Many courts require a debtor's employer to make payments to the chapter 13 trustee on the debtor's behalf. Also, the chapter 13 trustee may contact an employer to verify the debtor's income. However, if there are compelling reasons for not informing an employer in a particular case, it may be possible to make other arrangements for the required information and payments.

31. Does a person lose any legal rights by filing under chapter 13?

No. Filing under chapter 13 is a civil proceeding and not a criminal proceeding. Therefore, a person does not lose any legal or constitutional rights by filing a chapter 13 case.

32. May employers or government agencies discriminate against persons who file under chapter 13?

No. It is illegal for either private or governmental employers to discriminate against a person as to employment because that person has filed under chapter 13. It is also illegal for local, state, or federal governmental agencies to discriminate against a person as to the granting of licenses, permits, and similar grants because that person has filed under chapter 13.

33. What is required for court approval of a chapter 13 plan?

The court may confirm a chapter 13 plan if: (1) the plan complies with the legal requirements of chapter 13, (2) all required fees, charges and deposits have been paid, (3) the plan was proposed in good faith, (4) each unsecured creditor will receive under the plan at least as much as it would have received had the debtor filed under chapter 7, (5) it appears that the debtor will be able to make the required payments and comply with the plan, and (6) each secured creditor has been dealt with in the manner described in the answer to Question 16 above.

34. When does a debtor have to appear in court in a chapter 13 case?

Most debtors have to appear in court at least twice: once for a hearing called the meeting of creditors, and once for a hearing on the confirmation of the debtor's chapter 13 plan. The meeting of creditors is usually held about a month after the case is filed. The confirmation hearing may be held on the same day as the meeting of creditors or at a later date. The debtor's testimony should not be lengthy at either hearing, however. If difficulties or unusual circumstances arise during the course of a case, additional court appearances may be necessary.

35. What if the court does not approve a debtor's chapter 13 plan?

If the court will not approve the plan proposed by a debtor, the debtor may modify the plan and seek court approval of the modified plan. If the court does not approve a plan, it will usually give its reasons for refusing to do so, and the plan may then be appropriately modified so as become acceptable to the court. A debtor who does not wish to modify a proposed plan may either convert the case to chapter 7 or dismiss the case.

36. How are the claims of unsecured creditors handled under chapter 13?

Unsecured creditors must file their claims with the bankruptcy court within 90 days after the first date set for the meeting of creditors in order for their claims to be allowed. Unsecured creditors who fail to file claims within that period are barred from doing so, and upon completion of the plan their claims will be discharged. The debtor may file a claim on behalf of a creditor, if desired. After the claims have been filed, the debtor may file objections to any claims that he or she disputes. When the claims have been approved by the court, the chapter 13 trustee begins paying unsecured creditors as provided for in the chapter 13 plan. Payments to secured creditors and to special classes of unsecured creditors may begin earlier, if desired.

37. What if the debtor is temporarily unable to make the chapter 13 payments?

If the debtor is temporarily out of work, injured, or otherwise unable to make the payments required under a chapter 13 plan, the plan can usually be modified so as to enable the debtor to resume the payments when he or she is able to do so. If it appears that the debtor's inability to make the required payments will continue indefinitely or for an extended period, the case may be dismissed or converted to chapter 7.

38. What if the debtor incurs new debts or needs credit during a chapter 13 case?

Only two types of credit obligations or debts incurred after the filing of the case may be included in a chapter 13 plan. These are: (1) debts for taxes that become payable while the case is pending, and (2) consumer debts arising after the filing of the case that are for property or services necessary for the debtor's performance under the plan and that are approved in advance by the chapter 13 trustee. All other debts or credit obligations incurred after the case is filed must be paid by the debtor outside the plan. Some courts issue an order prohibiting the debtor from incurring new debts during the case unless they are approved in advance by the chapter 13 trustee. Therefore, the approval of the chapter 13 trustee should be obtained before incurring credit or new debts after the case has been filed. The incurrence of regular debts, such as debts for telephone service and utilities, do not require the trustee's approval.

39. What should the debtor do if he or she moves while the case is pending?

The debtor should immediately notify the bankruptcy court and the chapter 13 trustee in writing of the new address. Most communications in a chapter 13 case are by mail, and if the debtor fails to receive an order of the court or a notice from the chapter 13 trustee because of an incorrect address, the case may be dismissed. Many courts have change-of-address forms that may be used if the debtor moves.

40. What if the debtor later decides to discontinue the chapter 13 case?

The debtor has the right to either dismiss a chapter 13 case or convert it to chapter 7 at any time for any reason. However, if the debtor simply stops making the required chapter 13 payments, the court may compel the debtor or the debtor's employer to make the payments and to comply with the orders of the court. Therefore, the debtor who wishes to discontinue a chapter 13 case should do so through his or her attorney.

41. What happens if a debtor is unable to complete the chapter 13 payments?

A debtor who is unable to complete the chapter 13 payments has three options: (1) dismiss the chapter 13 case, (2) convert the chapter 13 case to chapter 7, or (3) if the debtor is unable to complete the payments due to circumstances for which he or she should not be held accountable, close the case and obtain a partial chapter 13 discharge as described in the answer to Question 6 above.

42. What is the role of the debtor's attorney in a chapter 13 case?

The debtor's attorney performs the following functions in a typical chapter 13 case:

(1) Examining the debtor's financial situation and determining whether chapter 13 is a feasible alternative for the debtor, and if so, whether a single or a joint case should be filed.

(2) Assisting the debtor in the preparation of a budget.

(3) Examining the liens or security interests of secured creditors to ascertain their validity or avoidability, and taking the legal steps necessary to protect the debtor's interest in such matters.

(4) Devising and implementing methods of dealing with secured creditors.

(5) Assisting the debtor in devising a chapter 13 plan that meets the needs of the debtor and is acceptable to the court.

(6) Preparing the necessary pleadings and chapter 13 forms.

(7) Filing the chapter 13 forms and pleadings with the court and paying, or providing for the payment of, the filing fee.

(8) Attending the meeting of creditors, the confirmation hearing, and any other court hearings required in the case.

(9) Assisting the debtor in obtaining court approval of a chapter 13 plan.

(10) Checking the claims filed in the case, filing objections to improper claims, and attending court hearings thereon.

(11) Assisting the debtor in overcoming any legal obstacles that may arise during the course of the case.

(12) Assisting the debtor in obtaining a discharge upon the completion or termination of the plan.

The fee charged by an attorney for representing a debtor in a chapter 13 case must be reviewed and approved by the bankruptcy court. This rule is followed whether the fee is paid to the attorney prior to or after the filing of the case, and whether it is paid to the attorney directly by the debtor or by the chapter 13 trustee. The court will approve only a fee that it finds to be reasonable.

CHAPTER THREE

PART B

PREPARING A CHAPTER 13 CASE

3.01 Chapter 13 - A General Description

A chapter 13 case is initiated by the filing of a petition seeking relief under chapter 13 of the Bankruptcy Code with the clerk of the bankruptcy court in the proper district. The debtor must also file schedules and statements that contain the names and addresses of all creditors, a list of the debtor's assets and liabilities, and other financial information about the debtor. In addition, a debtor must, within 15 days after the petition is filed, file a plan for the adjustment or repayment of his or her debts over a three-to-five year period. Debts of any kind may be dealt with in a chapter 13 plan, including nondischargeable debts. The debtor must usually apply all of his or her disposable income for the period of the plan toward the making of payments under the plan. During the pendency of the case, most creditor actions against the debtor and the debtor's property are stayed.

chapter 13 case, general aspects

Unsecured creditors may file objections to the debtor's plan, but they must accept the plan if it is approved by the court. A secured creditor, however, cannot be forced to accept a chapter 13 plan unless its secured claim is to be paid in full under the plan or its collateral is surrendered. A secured creditor may be paid outside the plan if desired. Unsecured creditors may be paid all or a portion of their claims under the plan, but each unsecured creditor must receive at least as much as it would have received had the debtor filed under chapter 7. All creditors are notified of the filing of the case, and unsecured creditors must file their claims within 90 days of the first date set for the meeting of creditors or their claims will be barred.

creditors in chapter 13 cases, general aspects

If the court finds that a debtor's proposed plan satisfies the legal requirements as to the payment of both secured and unsecured creditors, that the plan has been proposed in good faith, that the debtor will be able to comply with the plan, and that all required fees and charges have been paid or provided for, it may confirm the plan, at which time the plan becomes effective. The debtor, who must appear in court for hearings called the meeting of creditors and the confirmation hearing, must begin making regular payments to the chapter 13 trustee in the amount called for in the plan within 30 days after the plan is filed. The chapter 13 trustee collects the debtor's payments and pays the expenses of administering the plan (usually 10 percent of the amount collected), any unpaid portion of the fee allowed to the debtor's attorney, and the creditors as provided in the plan.

chapter 13 plan, general aspects

Upon the successful completion of a chapter 13 plan, the debtor is granted a full chapter 13 discharge, which is broader than a chapter 7 discharge. A debtor who is unable to complete the payments called for in the plan due to circumstances for which the debtor should not justly be held accountable, may be granted a partial chapter 13 discharge, which is similar to a chapter 7 discharge. Otherwise, an unsuccessful chapter 13 case may be either dismissed or converted to chapter 7.

chapter 13 discharge, general aspects

It should be noted that a bankruptcy court is a unit of the federal district court, and that limitations are imposed on the type and nature of proceedings and cases that a bankruptcy judge may hear. See section 2.01, supra, for a discussion of core vs. non-core proceedings. Generally, however, all proceedings arising in a chapter 13 case may be heard and ruled upon by the bankruptcy judge.

bankruptcy court, general aspects

3.02 The Local Rules and Forms

local rules,
importance of

Bankruptcy Rule 9029 permits a local court to adopt rules governing the practice and procedure in bankruptcy cases, provided that such rules are consistent with the Rules of Bankruptcy Procedure and do not prohibit or limit the use of the Official Forms. Copies of the local rules are normally provided to attorneys practicing in the district at little or no charge. Both the Bankruptcy Code and the Rules of Bankruptcy Procedure leave many administrative and procedural aspects of chapter 13 cases to the discretion of the local courts, and most bankruptcy courts have adopted local rules governing certain aspects of bankruptcy practice and procedure. For example, the number of copies of any document required to be filed in a bankruptcy case is left to local rule. Some courts have adopted only limited local rules, and few, if any, local forms. Others have adopted extensive local rules and forms dealing with many aspects of chapter 13 cases, including the initial filing requirements. In any event, it is important to obtain

local rules, how
to obtain

a copy of the local rules prior to the commencement of a chapter 13 case. The local rules will be referred to frequently throughout this handbook. A telephone call, letter, or visit to the clerk's office is all that is normally required to obtain a copy of them.

3.03 The Debtor's Transactions With The Debtor's Attorney

attorney's fee,
review of by
court

The fees charged by the debtor's attorney in a chapter 13 case, whether paid or agreed to be paid before or after the filing of the case, are subject to the review and approval of the bankruptcy court. See 11 U.S.C. 329 and Bankruptcy Rule 2017. On the motion of a party in interest or on the court's own initiative, the court, after notice and a hearing, may determine whether any direct or indirect payment of money or transfer of property by the debtor to an attorney for services rendered or to be rendered in contemplation of the filing of a chapter 13 case by the debtor is excessive. See Bankruptcy Rule 2017(a).

attorney's fee,
excessive
amount,
disposition of

On the motion of the debtor or the United States trustee, or on the court's own initiative, the court may, after notice and a hearing, determine whether any direct or indirect payment of money or transfer of property, or any agreement therefor, by the debtor to an attorney after the order for relief is excessive, if the payment or transfer, or agreement therefor, is for services in any way related to the case. See Bankruptcy Rule 2017(b). If the attorney's compensation exceeds the reasonable value of any such services, the court may cancel the fee agreement, or order that any payments received by the attorney, to the extent excessive, be returned to the entity that made the payments, or, if the payments were made under the chapter 13 plan or if the funds or property would otherwise have been property of the debtor's estate, order them turned over to the chapter 13 trustee. See 11 U.S.C. 329(b).

attorney's
disclosure
statement

Within 15 days after the date of the order for relief, or as otherwise directed by the court, the debtor's attorney must file with the court and transmit to the United States trustee a statement disclosing the compensation paid or to be paid to the attorney in the case. See Bankruptcy Rule 2016(b) and 11 U.S.C. 329(a). Unless the local rules provide otherwise, Bankruptcy Form B 203, entitled Disclosure of Compensation of Attorney for Debtor, should be used for this statement. A sample of this statement may be found in Exhibit 2-A at the end of chapter 2, supra.

attorney's
compensation,
what constitutes

In the disclosure statement, the attorney must disclose the entire compensation arrangement with the debtor, indicating the amount paid, the amount to be paid, and the source of the funds. The particulars of any agreement to share fees with other persons or attorneys, except members or regular associates of the attorney's law firm, must also be disclosed. See Bankruptcy Rule 2016(b). It should be remembered that an attorney's compensation may include not only the direct payment of money, but any direct or indirect payment of money or transfer of property, or agreement therefor, as long as the payment, transfer, or agreement is for services in any way related to the case. See Bankruptcy Rule 2017(b).

This does not mean that a reasonable fee cannot be charged and collected by an attorney representing a debtor in a chapter 13 case. To the contrary, unless the debtor makes no payments under the plan, the attorney is virtually assured of collecting a reasonable fee in the case because the fee is considered an administrative expense of the case and is treated as a priority claim, entitled to payment before the payment of other claims in the case. See 11 U.S.C. 1326(a). All or a portion of the attorney's compensation may be paid in advance of filing, if the debtor is financially able to do so. However, the main portion of the attorney's fee is customarily paid by the chapter 13 trustee out of the first moneys paid by the debtor under the plan. If the debtor is unable to pay the filing fee when the case is filed and files an application to pay the filing fee in installments, no payments may be made to the debtor's attorney by either the debtor or the chapter 13 trustee until the entire filing fee has been paid. See Bankruptcy Rule 1006(b)(3). *attorney's fee, when collected*

While the amount of compensation approved for attorneys representing debtors in chapter 13 cases varies from district to district and from case to case, the amount generally runs from $500 to $1,500 in non-business cases, depending on the district and the complexity of the case. Slightly higher fees are generally approved for attorneys representing debtors engaged in business. *attorney's fee, amount allowed*

In some districts it may be necessary for the debtor's attorney to prepare, file, and transmit to the United States trustee an Application For Allowance of Compensation, a sample of which is set forth in Exhibit 3-A at the end of this chapter. A local form may be provided for this application in some districts. The local rules should be checked for the requirement of filing this application and for the time within which the application should be filed. *application for allowance of attorney's fee*

The functions performed by the debtor's attorney in a typical chapter 13 case are set forth in the answer to Question 42 in Part A of this chapter, supra. In some districts the local rules specify the functions to be performed by the debtor's attorney in order to obtain court approval of his or her compensation. It should be noted that Bankruptcy Form B 203 (Exhibit 2-A, supra) also specifies certain functions to be performed by the debtor's attorney. *functions of attorney in chapter 13 case*

3.04 The Chapter 13 Eligibility Requirements

Only an individual (i.e., a natural person), or an individual and his or her spouse, may be a debtor under chapter 13. See 11 U.S.C. 109(e). In addition, the debtor must:

(1) reside in the United States, or have a domicile, place of business or property in the United States (see 11 U.S.C. 109(a));

(2) not have been a debtor in a prior title 11 case that was dismissed within the preceding 180 days on certain grounds (see below, this section);

(3) have regular income;

(4) have, on the date of filing, noncontingent, liquidated, unsecured debts of less than $100,000;

(5) have, on the date of filing, noncontingent, liquidated, secured debts of less than $350,000; and

(6) not be a stockbroker or a commodity broker.

An individual with regular income is defined as an individual whose income is sufficiently stable and regular to enable the individual to make payments under a chapter 13 plan. See 11 U.S.C. 101(30). There is no requirement of regular employment, which means that self-employed persons, pensioners, farmers, and other persons with regular income may be debtors under chapter 13. Any individual meeting the above requirements, and his or her spouse (if the spouse meets the requirements of (1), (2), and (6) above), may file under chapter 13. Thus, a husband and wife may file a joint petition under chapter 13 even if only one of them has regular income, provided that their combined debts meet the requirements listed in (4) and (5) above. Stockbrokers and commodity brokers may not file under chapter 13. See 11 U.S.C. 109(e).

An individual may not be a debtor under any chapter of title 11, including chapter 13, if he or she has been a debtor in another title 11 case pending at any time during the preceding 180 days, if the prior case was - (1) dismissed by the court on account of the willful failure of the debtor to abide by orders of the court or to appear in court in the proper prosecution of the case, or (2) dismissed by the court at the request of the debtor following the filing of a request for relief from the automatic stay. See 11 U.S.C. 109(g). The debtor must, of course, meet this title 11 eligibility requirement, as well as the above-listed chapter 13 eligibility requirements, in order to file under chapter 13.

An individual is eligible to file and receive a discharge under chapter 13 regardless of when he or she last received a discharge in either a chapter 7 or a chapter 13 case. See 11 U.S.C. 1328. Debts dealt with in a prior bankruptcy proceeding may be dealt with in a chapter 13 case, and, unless the court in the prior proceeding ordered otherwise, may be discharged. See 11 U.S.C. 349(a). See section 3.18, infra, for further reading on chapter 13 discharges.

3.05 Interviewing the Debtor - Matters to Cover

Even if a joint filing is not initially contemplated, the best practice is to interview both the debtor and the debtor's spouse, if one exists. In most cases, one of the matters to be resolved during the interview is whether the spouses should file jointly under chapter 13, and both spouses should have a voice in the resolution of this issue. Even if a joint filing is not warranted, the nonfiling spouse may be more familiar with the family financial situation than the filing spouse. Also, even in a single filing some of the information required in the chapter 13 forms involves the debtor's spouse. In any event, the debtor should be advised in advance of the nature of the information needed and of the documents and papers to bring to the interview. *chapter 13 case, who to interview*

In order to properly prepare the chapter 13 forms and devise a chapter 13 plan, the information collected from the debtor must be both accurate and complete. The only proven method of gathering all of the needed information without repeated interviews and telephone calls is to use some form of work sheets that call for all of the required information and leave nothing to memory or chance. Some attorneys use an extra copy of the chapter 13 forms for this purpose; others have devised work sheets of their own. *accurate data, how to obtain*

An attorney without work sheets will find the Bankruptcy Work Sheets appearing in Exhibit 2-B at the end of chapter 2, supra, useful. Simply photocopy the work sheets and follow the simple instructions contained therein, and all of the required information will be assembled in the order appearing in the chapter 13 schedules and statements beginning with the voluntary petition and continuing through the schedules and the statement of financial affairs. It may be helpful to give a copy of the work sheets to the debtor prior to the interview. Once assembled, the information can be easily transferred from the work sheets to the appropriate schedules and statements by a typist or secretary, using the completed forms appearing in the exhibits at the end of chapter 2, supra, as guides. *bankruptcy work sheets, use of in chapter 13 case*

To enable an attorney to properly plan and prepare a chapter 13 case, certain other important matters should be covered during the interview with the debtor. In addition to the gathering of data, the following matters should be covered when interviewing the debtor:

(1) The eligibility of the debtor for relief under chapter 13. It should be ascertained whether the debtor is eligible to file under chapter 13, and whether the debtor's debts are dischargeable under chapter 13. See section 3.04, supra, for the chapter 13 eligibility requirements, and see section 3.18, infra, for a list of the debts that are not dischargeable under chapter 13. It should be remembered, however, that even if a debt is nondischargeable under chapter 13, it may still be dealt with in a chapter 13 plan. This aspect of chapter 13 can be helpful to debtors with nondischargeable debts who are threatened with wage garnishments, property seizures, or contempt of court citations. *debtor's eligibility under chapter 13*

(2) Whether a joint or single petition should be filed. The general rule is that if both spouses are liable for significant unsecured or partially secured debts, a joint petition should be filed. Also, a joint petition should be filed if both spouses have significant regular income, unless there is a strong reason for not filing jointly. Finally, if both spouses are liable on a secured debt that is significantly in default, a joint petition should be filed. When it is not clear whether both spouses are liable on an unsecured debt, the safest practice is to file jointly. The local rules may set forth instances when a joint filing is required, and they should be checked in this regard. Filing a joint petition normally entails no more legal or clerical work than a single filing, and the filing fee is the same. In practice, most chapter 13 cases of consumer debtors are joint filings. However, if the spouses are separated or involved in divorce proceedings, or if one spouse is engaged in business without the involvement of the other spouse, a joint filing may not be advisable. *joint vs. single petition*

(3) The debtor's primary reason for filing under chapter 13. Chapter 13 debtors can be divided into three general categories: (1) those who file under chapter 13 primarily to repay unsecured debts, (2) those who file primarily for the chapter 13 discharge, and (3) those who file under chapter 13 primarily for temporary injunctive relief. The three classes of debtors have substantially different attitudes toward chapter 13. Debtors in the first category usually want to repay as much of their unsecured debts as possible, while debtors in the second category invariably want to repay as little of their unsecured debts as possible. Debtors in the third category are usually seeking temporary relief from aggressive creditors until their financial prospects improve. The debtor's attitude should be taken into account in the handling of a case and the devising of a plan.

Debtors in the first category often want to adopt a plan that is too ambitious; that is, they want to pay more into the plan than they can reasonably afford. Such debtors often want to repay every dollar to every creditor, and if this appears impossible they tend to become discouraged and begin to think in terms of chapter 7. In such cases every attempt should be made to accommodate the repayment wishes of the debtor, but if it is obvious that a feasible plan calling for the repayment of all debts is impossible, they should be so advised. It will serve no purpose for such debtors to sink a thousand dollars or more into a plan, and then wind up converting to chapter 7. Such debtors should be advised that it is better to pay their creditors a portion of what is owed to them rather than to pay them nothing, which is what creditors normally receive under chapter 7.

Debtors in the second category usually file under chapter 13 either because they are ineligible for a chapter 7 discharge or because they have debts that are dischargeable under chapter 13 but not under chapter 7. Occasionally such debtors file under chapter 13 because they have valuable nonexempt property that would be lost if they filed under chapter 7, but which they hope to retain under chapter 13. Debtors in this category should be advised that enough of their income must be paid into the plan, and sufficient payments made to unsecured creditors, to satisfy the court that the plan is being proposed in good faith. Also, such debtors should be advised that all of their projected disposable income for a three-year period must be applied to the plan. Debtors with a heavy debt load who are ineligible for a chapter 7 discharge should be advised that their motives in filing under chapter 13 may be closely scrutinized by the court, because many times such debtors are merely seeking a year or two of chapter 13 relief until they are again eligible for a chapter 7 discharge.

Debtors in the third category are likely to be business debtors seeking temporary relief from a few creditors until funds can be obtained to repay their debts. Such debtors should be advised of the good faith requirements of filing under chapter 13, and of the necessity of filing a plan within 15 days after the petition is filed. Also included in this category are debtors seeking injunctive relief from nondischargeable debts for accumulated alimony or child support obligations. Such debtors should be advised that while debts of this nature can be repaid in an equitable manner under chapter 13, the bankruptcy court has no authority to change the amount of alimony or support that must ultimately be paid by the debtor, and that debts of this nature are seldom dischargeable.

(4) The necessity of avoiding liens and security interests. Under 11 U.S.C. 522(f), the debtor may avoid (i.e., set aside) judicial liens against exempt property and nonpurchase-money, nonpossessory security interests in certain exempt personal property. See section 2.12, supra, for further reading and for a full description of the type of property covered. If the debtor has property that is subject to a lien or security interest that may be avoidable under Section 522(f), the avoidability of such a lien or security interest could turn a secured creditor into an unsecured creditor and substantially affect the type of plan adopted by the debtor. It may be necessary, therefore, to determine the avoidability of such liens and security interests prior to the adoption of a plan. The procedure for avoiding such liens in chapter 13 cases is the same as in chapter 7 cases, and the reader is referred to section 2.12, supra, for further reading. The local rules may require motions to avoid liens under Section 522(f) to be filed with the petition or shortly thereafter. It should also be noted that if a lien or security interest of a creditor is avoidable by the trustee as a preferential or fraudulent transfer, it may be avoided in a chapter 13 case as well as in a chapter 7 case. See 11 U.S.C. 103(a), 547-549. See sections 2.16, supra, and 3.08, infra, for further reading on the avoidance of such liens.

[margin note: categories of chapter 13 debtors]

[margin note: advising category 1 debtor]

[margin note: advising category 2 debtor]

[margin note: chapter 13 plan, good faith requirement]

[margin note: advising category 3 debtor]

[margin note: liens and security interests, necessity of avoiding]

(5) **Explaining the chapter 13 process to the debtor.** A chapter 13 case will proceed more smoothly if the debtor understands the concepts and procedures involved. It is suggested that the debtor's attorney reproduce the questions and answers set forth in Part A of this chapter, supra, and give a copy of them to the debtor at the outset of the case. These questions and answers will answer most questions raised by chapter 13 debtors.

chapter 13 process, explaining to debtor

(6) **Advising the debtor of the rights and duties of debtors under chapter 13.** The principal right of a debtor under chapter 13 is the right to propose a plan for the repayment or adjustment of his or her debts under the supervision and protection of the court. Upon the successful completion of a confirmed chapter 13 plan, a debtor has the right to a full chapter 13 discharge under 11 U.S.C. 1328(a) (see section 3.18, infra). A chapter 13 debtor has many of the rights, powers, and duties of a trustee in regards to the possession of property and the running of a business during the case. See 11 U.S.C. 1303. With only limited exceptions, the debtor has the right to dismiss a chapter 13 case or convert it to chapter 7 at any time (see section 3.17, infra). A debtor has the right to modify a chapter 13 plan at any time prior to confirmation and under certain conditions after confirmation (see sections 3.13 and 3.15, infra). See section 2.12, supra, for a list of the rights of debtors under title 11. (All 10 of the rights listed in section 2.12 apply to debtors in chapter 13 cases except right number 7.)

rights of debtor under chapter 13

The primary duties of a debtor in a chapter 13 case are to file the appropriate schedules and statements, file and obtain confirmation of a chapter 13 plan, and make the payments and perform the acts required by the confirmed plan. The debtor must also cooperate with the chapter 13 trustee and comply with the orders and rules of the bankruptcy court. See section 2.11, supra, for a list of the duties of debtors in bankruptcy cases generally. (All of the 11 duties listed in section 2.11 apply to debtors in chapter 13 cases except duty number 2.)

duties of debtor under chapter 13

(7) **Drafting a budget and devising a chapter 13 plan.** These matters are dealt with at length in sections 3.07 and 3.08, infra. While it is usually impossible to devise a final chapter 13 plan at the time of the interview, a preliminary plan should be devised so that the debtor will know what to expect in the case. If the debtor's income and expenses are known, it should be possible to draft a preliminary budget during the interview.

preliminary plan, use of

(8) **Making arrangements for the payment of the filing fee, the attorney's fee, and any required deposit.** The debtor should be advised that the entire $120 filing fee must be paid, either when the case is filed or within the required period (see section 3.10, infra), or the case will be dismissed and a discharge will not be granted. For the protection of both the attorney and the debtor, there should be no misunderstanding as to either the amount or the terms of the fee to be charged by the attorney for handling the case, even if the fee is to be disbursed later by the chapter 13 trustee. If necessary, the fee agreement should be reduced to writing.

payment of costs and fees, arrangements for

(9) **Making arrangements for the commencement of payments under the plan.** Unless the court orders otherwise, a debtor must begin making the payments proposed in the plan within 30 days after the plan is filed with the court. See 11 U.S.C. 1326(a)(1). A plan must be filed with the court within 15 days after the case is filed. Therefore, the debtor must begin making payments within 45 days after the case is filed, or within 30 days of filing if the plan is filed with the petition. In most cases, then, payments to the chapter 13 trustee must begin before the plan is confirmed by the court. If confirmation of the plan is later denied by the court, the payments made by the debtor must be returned to the debtor by the chapter 13 trustee, except for certain administrative expenses (usually the balance of the filing fee, if any, and the compensation, if any, allowed to the debtor's attorney). See 11 U.S.C. 1326(a)(2). Should the debtor fail to commence making timely payments under a proposed plan, the case may be dismissed by the court. See 11 U.S.C. 1307(c)(4). It is important, then, that arrangements be made for the commencement of payments within the required time. By whom the debtor's chapter 13 payments shall be made should also be discussed during the interview. Some courts have a rule or policy that if a debtor is employed, the chapter 13 payments must be forwarded by the debtor's employer directly to the chapter 13 trustee, a procedure enforceable by the court after confirmation under 11 U.S.C. 1325(c). However, until a plan has been confirmed by the court and the final amount of the periodic payment determined, it is usually preferable for the debtor, rather than the employer, to make the payments.

commencement of payments under plan, arrangements for

3.06 Debtors Engaged in Business

A debtor engaged in business may file under chapter 13 if he or she is otherwise eligible (see section 3.04, supra).   A self-employed debtor who incurs trade credit in the production of income from such employment is deemed to be engaged in business. See 11 U.S.C. 1304(a). Unless the court orders other-
wise, a debtor engaged in business may continue to operate the business during the case, and has many of the rights and powers of a trustee in so doing, subject to the limitations applicable to trustees generally and to any special limitations or conditions imposed by the court in a particular case. See 11 U.S.C. 1304(b). However, the debtor may not, without court approval, use, sell, or lease cash collateral or obtain credit, other than unsecured credit in the ordinary course of business. See 11 U.S.C. 1303. This means that the debtor must segregate and account for any cash collateral that may be in the debtor's possession or control at any time during the case. See section 4.07, infra, for the definition of cash collateral and for further reading on the use or sale of cash collateral and the obtaining of credit by the debtor during the case.

A debtor engaged in business must file with the court, with the United States trustee, and with any governmental unit responsible for the collection or determination of any tax arising out of the operation of the debtor's business, periodic reports and summaries of the operation of the business, including a statement of receipts and disbursements, and such other information as the United States trustee or the court may require. See 11 U.S.C. 1304(c). If the reports reflect payments to employees, the amount and location of any funds deducted or withheld for taxes must also be reported. See Bankruptcy Rule 2015(a)(3),(c)(1).

A chapter 13 debtor engaged in business is also required to file a complete inventory of the debtor's property within 30 days after the case is filed (unless an inventory was previously filed or contained in the debtor's bankruptcy schedules), keep a record of the receipt and disposition of any money or property received during the case, and give notice of the case to every entity known to be holding money or property subject to the withdrawal or order of the debtor, including banks, insurance companies, and holders of deposits previously made by the debtor. See Bankruptcy Rule 2015(c)(1). Unless the court orders otherwise, the chapter 13 trustee is required to investigate and file a report on the acts, conduct, assets, liabilities, and financial condition of a debtor engaged in business, on the operation of the debtor's business, and on the desirability of continuing the business. See 11 U.S.C. 1302(c). Many courts and United States trustees have local rules and forms pertaining to chapter 13 debtors that are engaged in business.

The preparation of a budget and a feasible chapter 13 plan is usually more complicated for a debtor engaged in business than for a consumer debtor. For example, a debtor engaged in business has to justify the expenditures necessary for the continuation, preservation, and operation of the business, which expen-ditures often include the debtor's personal compensation, which, in turn, may have to be separately justi-fied. The same general rules apply, however, and the principles and procedures set forth in sections 3.07 and 3.08, infra, should be followed.

The official schedules and statements, and any applicable local forms, should be appropriately modified and supplemented, if necessary, so as to give an accurate financial account of both the debtor and the debtor's business. A debtor engaged in business is required to attach detailed statements to Schedules I and J showing the debtor's income and expenses from the business.

On the request of a party in interest or the United States trustee, the court, after notice and a hearing, may convert the chapter 13 case of a debtor engaged in business to chapter 11 or chapter 12 at any time before confirmation of the plan, except that the chapter 13 case of a farmer may not be so converted without the consent of the debtor. See 11 U.S.C. 1307(d),(e).

3.07 Drafting a Workable Budget

The principal purpose of preparing a budget in a chapter 13 case is to determine the amount of the debtor's projected disposable income, all of which must usually be paid to the chapter 13 trustee. See 11 U.S.C. 1325(b)(1). It is the debtor's budget, more than any other factor, that determines the important matter of the amount of money that the debtor can or must pay into a chapter 13 plan. Further, no chapter 13 plan can succeed unless the debtor is faithful to the budget upon which the plan is based. It is important, therefore, that the debtor understand both the importance of the budget and the restrictions that it may impose on his or her life style.

budget, importance of

A workable budget must meet two requirements: it must be realistic for the debtor, and it must be justifiable to the court. If a budget is not realistic and workable for the debtor for the entire period of the plan, the plan is probably doomed to failure because sooner or later the debtor will be unable to make the payments required under the plan. If the budget, as it appears in the Schedules of Current Income and Current Expenditures, is not justifiable to the court, either because it is too restrictive on the debtor or because it is too generous to the debtor, the court will probably refuse to confirm the debtor's plan.

budget, general requirements

To draft a realistic budget for a debtor, accurate information as to exactly how much money the debtor is taking in and spending each month must be obtained. The data gathered in completing the required schedules and statements will supply most of the needed information. However, the surest method of ascertaining exactly what a debtor spends each month is to examine the entries in his or her checkbook, or other record of expenditures, for the previous several months. An effort should be made to look for quarterly, semiannual, or annual expenses for such items as insurance premiums and taxes. The expenses currently being deducted from the debtor's wages or salary should also be accounted for.

budget, data needed

The Schedules of Current Income and Current Expenditures (Schedules I and J in Official Form 6) may be used in preparing the debtor's budget. However, because each debtor's situation is unique and because it is important that the debtor understand the budget, labels and terms familiar to the debtor should be used, and the terms appearing on the schedules should be appropriately modified. The budget should show average figures for expenses that vary from month to month, such as water, telephone, or utility bills. If the debtor's income varies seasonally, a realistic average should be used if feasible, or separate budgets should be prepared for each season. Income from all sources should be included, including alimony or support payments and food stamps, if received regularly. The impact of inflation on the items appearing in the budget should also be considered, if appropriate.

budget, method of preparation

It is important to include as expenses in the budget the payments to be made on claims that the debtor intends to pay outside of the chapter 13 plan. It is usually preferable to pay fully secured claims upon which the debtor is not in default outside the plan, because by so doing the debtor will avoid the chapter 13 trustee's ten-percent fee, which is assessed on all payments made under the plan. Even if the debtor is in default on a fully secured claim (such as a home mortgage), it may be possible for the debtor to make the regular payments on the claim outside the plan and make only the payments necessary to cure the default under the plan. See section 3.08, infra, for further reading. Unless the debtor is in default on such a claim, it is also preferable for the debtor to pay nondischargeable claims outside the plan. See section 3.18, infra, for a list of debts (or claims) that are nondischargeable under chapter 13. Payments on executory contracts or unexpired leases that the debtor intends to assume should also be paid outside the plan, if the debtor is not in default.

secured or nondischargeable claims, payment outside of plan

As indicated above, it is important that the income and expense figures appearing in the Schedules of Current Income and Current Expenditures be justifiable because of the requirement that all of the debtor's projected disposable income for a three-year period be applied to the plan. See 11 U.S.C. 1325(b)(1). The debtor's budget figures are likely to be closely scrutinized by the court, by the chapter 13 trustee, and perhaps by a disgruntled unsecured creditor or two, to insure that the debtor is in fact complying with this requirement. Disposable income is defined as income received by the debtor which is not reasonably necessary to be expended - (1) for the maintenance or support of the debtor and his or her dependents, or, (2) if the debtor is engaged in business, for the payment of expenditures necessary for the continuation, preservation, and operation of the business. See 11 U.S.C. 1325(b)(2).

debtor's projected disposable income

3.08 Devising an Acceptable Chapter 13 Plan

chapter 13 plan,
mandatory
provisions

The statutory authority for the required and permissible provisions of chapter 13 plans is 11 U.S.C. 1322. The confirmation requirements, which must also be complied with in the preparation of a plan, are found in 11 U.S.C. 1325. Under 11 U.S.C. 1322(a), a chapter 13 plan must:

(1) provide for the submission of all or such portion of the future earnings or income of the debtor to the supervision and control of the chapter 13 trustee as is necessary for the execution of the plan;

(2) provide for the full payment, in deferred cash, of all priority claims, unless the holder of such a claim agrees otherwise; and

(3) if the plan classifies claims, provide the same treatment for each claim within a particular class.

priority claims,
definition

Priority claims are defined in 11 U.S.C. 507(a) and are set forth in section 2.19, supra. The unpaid balance of the filing fee and the compensation allowed to the debtor's attorney are the most common priority claims in chapter 13 cases. Other priority claims include claims for unpaid wages, salaries and employee benefits, and tax claims.

Under 11 U.S.C. 1322(b), a chapter 13 plan may:

chapter 13 plan,
permissive
provisions

(1) designate one or more classes of unsecured claims, provided that if more than one class is designated, all claims within a particular class must be substantially similar and no class of claims may be unfairly discriminated against, except that a plan may treat claims for a consumer debt of the debtor for which another individual is also liable differently than other unsecured claims;

(2) modify the rights of holders of unsecured and secured claims, other than a claim secured only by a security interest in real property that is the debtor's principal residence;

(3) provide for the curing or waiving of any default;

(4) provide for the concurrent payment of secured and unsecured claims;

(5) provide for the curing of any default within a reasonable time and the maintenance of payments while the case is pending on any claim on which the last payment is due after the proposed date of the final payment under the plan;

(6) provide for the payment of postpetition claims;

(7) provide for the assumption or rejection of executory contracts or unexpired leases not previously rejected in the case;

(8) provide for the payment of claims from property of the debtor or the debtor's estate;

(9) provide for the vesting of property of the estate, on or after confirmation of the plan, in the debtor or in another entity; and

(10) include any other appropriate provision not inconsistent with title 11.

chapter 13 plan,
maximum length

11 U.S.C. 1322(c) specifies that a chapter 13 plan may not provide for payments over a period that is longer than three years, unless the court, for cause, approves a longer period, which may not exceed five years. It should be noted that even if a plan is later modified so as to extend the period for making payments, the period may not be extended to a date more than five years after the date when the first payment under the original plan was due. See 11 U.S.C. 1329(c).

Under 11 U.S.C. 1325(a), the following requirements must be satisfied before a chapter 13 plan can be confirmed by the court:

(1) the plan must comply with the provisions of chapter 13 and with any other applicable provisions of title 11;

(2) any fee, charge, or other amount required in the case or under the plan to be paid prior to confirmation must be paid;

(3) the plan must have been proposed in good faith and not by any means forbidden by law;

(4) the value, as of the effective date of the plan, of property to be distributed under the plan on the account of each allowed unsecured claim must be not less than the amount that would be paid on such claim if the estate of the debtor was liquidated under chapter 7 on the same date;

(5) with respect to each allowed secured claim dealt with under the plan - (a) the holder of the claim accepts the plan, or (b) the plan provides that the holder of the claim retains the lien securing its claim and that the value of the property to be distributed under the plan to the holder on the account of the claim is not less than the amount of the claim, or (c) the debtor surrenders the property securing the claim to the holder of the claim; and

(6) it must appear that the debtor will be able to make all payments called for under the plan and to otherwise comply with the plan.

In devising a chapter 13 plan, the following matters should be determined, preferably in the following order: (1) the debtor's primary reason for filing under chapter 13, (2) the length of the plan, (3) the total amount that can be paid on all claims under the plan, (4) the total amount, including interest, that must be paid to the holders of secured claims under the plan, (5) the total amount to be paid to the holders of special classes of unsecured claims under the plan, and (6) the total amount that can be paid to the holders of all other unsecured claims under the plan. While some of the above matters may be interdependent in many cases, each matter should be determined separately in the preparation of a plan. Accordingly, each matter is discussed separately below.

It is important to determine the debtor's reason for filing under chapter 13 when preparing a plan because it is likely to affect every important aspect of the plan. For example, a debtor whose primary reason for filing under chapter 13 is to obtain a discharge will normally want to pay as little to creditors as possible for the shortest allowable period, while a debtor who is filing primarily to repay his or her debts will usually want to pay as much to creditors as possible for the longest allowable period. A debtor whose primary purpose in filing is to pay off a nondischargeable or priority debt will usually want to pay as much as possible on the nondischargeable or priority debt and as little as possible to other creditors. It is important, therefore, to clearly define the debtor's primary reason for filing under chapter 13 before preparing a plan. See section 3.05, supra, for a discussion of the various categories of chapter 13 debtors and their reasons for filing under chapter 13.

The general rule is that the length of a chapter 13 plan must be three years unless the debtor can justify a different period. If the chapter 13 trustee or an unsecured creditor objects to confirmation of a plan, the plan must be for a period of at least three years, unless the objecting creditor is paid in full on the claim. See 11 U.S.C. 1325(b)(1). Even in the absence of such an objection, many courts construe the good faith requirement in 11 U.S.C. 1325(a)(3) as requiring at least a three-year effort by a debtor who does not make significant payments to unsecured creditors. See In Re Davidson, 10 B.R. 374. This means that the length of a chapter 13 plan must be at least three years, unless the debtor can pay off all debts in a shorter period or can otherwise justify a shorter period. A debtor with compelling reasons for implementing a shorter plan may be able to convince the court to confirm such a plan, because the court, at least in the absence of an objection to confirmation, has discretion on the issue. See In Re Harper, 11 B.R. 395.

extending plan. requirements

A chapter 13 plan may not provide for payments over a period longer than three years unless the court, for cause, approves a longer period, which period may not exceed five years. See 11 U.S.C. 1322(c). Thus, a debtor who wishes to extend a plan beyond three years must have a valid reason for doing so. See In Re Price, 20 B.R. 253. Most courts require significant payments to unsecured creditors in order to justify extending a plan beyond three years. See In Re Powell, 15 B.R. 465. The preservation of the debtor's right to a chapter 7 discharge by paying at least 70 percent to all unsecured creditors has been held sufficient to justify extending a plan beyond three years. See In Re Karayan, 82 B.R. 541. The court has considerable discretion in the matter, however, and much depends on the circumstances and attitude of the debtor. Generally, if additional time is needed to pay off nondischargeable or priority claims while making meaningful payments to unsecured creditors, the court is likely to permit, or on occasion require, the debtor to extend the plan to a period of up to five years. See In Re Blackwell, 5 B.R. 748, and In Re Chase, 28 B.R. 814.

determining total amount to be paid on all claims

Once the length of the plan has been determined, the total amount to be paid on all claims under the plan can usually be calculated by simply multiplying the number of periodic payments to be made by the debtor under the plan by the amount of the periodic payment, and subtracting the projected expenses of administration. The calculation may be more difficult if the plan does not call for the debtor to make uniform payments. The amount of the debtor's periodic payment to the chapter 13 trustee is determined primarily from the debtor's budget, which is discussed in section 3.07, supra. The projected expenses of administration are usually the chapter 13 trustee's fee, which is ten percent of all payments made by the debtor under the plan, and any unpaid portions of the filing fee and the fee allowed to the debtor's attorney. If tax or other priority claims are to be paid under the plan, they must be paid in full (unless the creditor agrees otherwise) and should be counted as an administrative expense and deducted from the amount to be paid into the plan by the debtor. The total amount to be paid on all claims under the plan must be calculated in order to determine the feasibility of the plan, both to the court and to the debtor.

contributing assets to plan

If, after calculating the total amount to be paid on all claims under the plan from the debtor's periodic payments, it appears that the amount will be insufficient to either obtain confirmation of the plan or satisfy the debtor's primary purpose in proposing the plan, it may be necessary for the debtor to contribute assets (or the proceeds therefrom) to the plan. This practice is permitted under 11 U.S.C. 1322(b)(8). If the debtor wishes to proceed in this manner, the estimated amount to be realized from the contributed assets should be included in the total amount to be paid on all claims under the plan.

paying secured claims outside of plan

Before the amount that must be paid to the holders of secured claims under the plan can be calculated, it must be determined which of the secured claims are to be paid or dealt with under the plan and the manner in which such claims are to be paid or dealt with under the plan must be resolved. It is generally preferable to pay fully secured claims upon which the debtor is not in default outside the plan, because by so doing the debtor will avoid paying the trustee's fee on the claim. Even if the debtor is in default on a fully secured claim, it may be possible to pay the claim outside the plan and make only the payments necessary to cure the default under the plan. Partially secured creditors must usually be paid under the plan, unless there is no dispute as to the amount of the secured portion of a particular creditor's claim. Fully secured creditors whose claims have accelerated or who have commenced foreclosure or repossession proceedings must also be paid and dealt with under the plan in most instances.

secured claims. plan requirements

Once the secured claims that are to be paid or dealt with under the plan have been ascertained, the difficult task of deciding how to deal with the holders of such claims must be undertaken. Secured creditors have considerable leverage under chapter 13, at least to the extent of their secured interest. To permit confirmation of a chapter 13 plan, the holder of each secured claim dealt with in the plan must either - (1) accept the plan, (2) retain its lien and be paid the full amount of its allowed secured claim, or (3) be given the property securing its claim. Thus, while a chapter 13 plan may modify the rights of secured creditors, such creditors cannot be forced to accept the plan and, unless the proposed plan satisfies one of the three alternatives described above, can either prevent confirmation of the plan or force the debtor to pay the claim outside the plan.

In addition, interest must be paid on all secured claims, either at the rate called for in the agreement giving rise to the claim or, if no rate is specified, at a rate justifiable under the circumstances. See 11 U.S.C. 502(b). Some courts have established interest rates or capitalization tables that must be used in cases where an interest rate is not otherwise specified or agreed upon, and the local rules should be checked in this regard.

secured claims,
interest rate

The two principal functions that should be performed by the debtor's attorney in connection with secured claims are - (1) ascertaining the validity and extent of a creditor's lien or security interest, and (2) providing for the curing of any defaults. In ascertaining the validity and extent of a creditor's lien or security interest, the following aspects of the lien or security should be checked:

secured claims,
matters to check

(1) The validity of the lien or security interest under state law. It should be ascertained whether the recording and other acts required under state law to perfect the lien or security interest have been performed. While this can sometimes be accomplished by examining the proof of claim filed by the secured creditor (Bankruptcy Rule 3001(d) requires a proof of claim claiming a security interest in property of the debtor to be accompanied by evidence that the security interest has been perfected), the best practice is to check directly with the local recording office or official.

secured claim,
validity of lien

(2) The avoidability of the lien or security interest by the debtor under 11 U.S.C. 522(f). Under Section 522(f), the debtor may set aside judicial liens on exempt property and nonpurchase-money security interests in certain exempt personal property that is not in the possession of the creditor. That the Section 522(f) lien avoidance powers apply to chapter 13 debtors, see In Re Hall, 752 F. 2d 582. The procedure for avoiding such liens is the same under chapter 13 as under chapter 7, and the reader is referred to section 2.12, supra, for further reading. If a lien or security interest is avoidable under Section 522(f), the local rules should be checked for special provisions applicable to motions to avoid such liens in chapter 13 cases.

secured claim,
avoidability of
lien under
section 522(f)

(3) The avoidability of the lien or security interest by the trustee. Even if a lien or security interest is valid under local law and is not avoidable by the debtor under Section 522(f), it may be avoidable by the trustee as a preference under 11 U.S.C. 547(b), or as a fraudulent transfer under 11 U.S.C. 548(a). It may be possible to set aside recently created liens and recent repossessions of property by a secured creditor in this manner. See section 2.16, supra, for further reading. The chapter 13 trustee has lien avoidance powers, and if the trustee refuses to act, the debtor may act to avoid a preferential lien. See 11 U.S.C. 103(a), and In Re Saberman, 3 B.R. 316.

secured claim,
avoidability of
lien by trustee

(4) The extent to which the claim is secured. Determining the extent to which a claim is secured is usually necessary in dealing with partially-secured creditors. Under 11 U.S.C. 506(a), an allowed claim secured by a lien on property of the debtor's estate is a secured claim only to the extent of the value of the creditor's interest in such property, and is an unsecured claim to the extent of the excess of the amount of the allowed claim over the value of the creditor's interest in the property. Of course, the value of a creditor's interest in property cannot exceed the value of the property. The valuation of the secured property is usually the main issue in such disputes because the secured portion of the creditor's claim is usually equal to the value of the property. Not surprisingly, the creditor will often assign a higher value to the secured property than the debtor. If a partially secured creditor files a proof of claim claiming a security interest in property of the debtor that exceeds the debtor's estimate of the value of the secured property, an objection to the allowance of the claim should be filed in order to preserve the debtor's right to contest the amount of the secured claim. The local rules and forms often contain provisions dealing with the valuation of secured or partially-secured claims and the bifurcation of partially-secured claims under 11 U.S.C. 506(a), and they should be checked in this regard. See section 3.13, infra, for further reading.

secured claim,
determining
extent of

The curing of defaults can be a troublesome aspect of dealing with fully secured creditors in chapter 13 cases. If the debtor is in default on a secured claim dealt with under the plan, it will be necessary to provide a method in the plan for curing the default within a reasonable time in order to obtain confirmation of the plan. If the underlying agreement requires periodic payments, it may be necessary to make double payments to the creditor (one on the underlying obligation and one curing the default) until the default is cured. Interest must also be paid on the sum necessary to cure the default, either at the rate set forth in the underlying agreement or at a justifiable or court-established rate.

The handling of defaulted home mortgages under a chapter 13 plan can be difficult because of the provision in 11 U.S.C. 1322(b)(2) prohibiting a plan from modifying the rights of creditors secured only by a security interest in real property that is the debtor's principal residence. It should be noted initially that this prohibition is not applicable if the creditor's claim is also secured by a lien on other collateral, such as fixtures, household goods, a farm, or a life insurance policy. See In re Reeves, 65 B.R. 898, and In re Johnson-Allen, 67 B.R. 968. Even if the prohibition is applicable, it is clear that a defaulted home mortgage may be cured under a chapter 13 plan. See 11 U.S.C. 1322(b)(5) and In Re Terry, 780 F. 2d 894. A default on a home mortgage can usually be cured even if a foreclosure judgment has been entered against the debtor in a state court. See In Re Larkin, 50 B.R. 984, and In Re Brunson, 87 B.R. 304. Much depends, however, on the status of the particular foreclosure action and the debtor's redemption and other rights under state law. See Annotation, 67 A.L.R. Fed. 217.

An additional question is whether the claim of the holder of an under-secured home mortgage can be bifurcated under 11 U.S.C. 506(a) (see above) and treated as two claims, one secured and one unsecured. The majority rule is that the holder of an under-secured home mortgage, like any other partially-secured creditor, may be treated in this manner under a chapter 13 plan. See In re Hart, 923 F. 2d 1410. Therefore, in most jurisdictions the partially-secured claim of a creditor secured only by a mortgage on the debtor's principal residence may be divided into secured and unsecured portions, with the unsecured portion treated as a general unsecured claim, while the secured portion is cured under 11 U.S.C. 1322(b)(5). See Wilson v. Commonwealth Mortgage Co., 895 F. 2d 123. It should be noted, however, that this rule is not followed in some jurisdictions, so the rule followed in the local jurisdiction should be ascertained before incorporating such a provision in a chapter 13 plan.

Acceleration clauses in installment obligations are a continual problem in chapter 13 cases. It is generally held that a prepetition acceleration may be "deaccelerated" and cured in a chapter 13 case as though the acceleration clause did not exist. See In Re Taddeo, 685 F. 2d 24, and Grubbs v. Houston First Am. Sav. Assoc., 730 F. 2d 236. Other appellate courts have expressed a contrary view, however. See In Re Glenn, 760 F. 2d 1428. The status of the law on this issue in the local district should be ascertained before attempting to cure an accelerated obligation in a chapter 13 plan.

Once it is determined how each secured claim dealt with under the plan is to be paid, it should be possible to calculate the total amount, including interest, that must be paid to the holders of secured claims under the plan. If this amount exceeds the total amount that can be paid on all claims under the plan, the plan is not feasible and must be changed.

The next matter to determine is the total amount to be paid to the holders of special classes of unsecured claims under the plan. Whether special classes of unsecured claims are to be created under a plan is likely to depend on the debtor's reason for filing under chapter 13. If the debtor's reason for filing is to deal with a specific unsecured debt, such as an accrued alimony or child support obligation or a student loan, it may be necessary to create a special class for the claim in order to carry out the debtor's purpose. Even debtors whose reason for filing under chapter 13 is to repay as many of their debts as possible often have valid reasons for paying more to certain creditors than others. In many cases, then, it will be necessary to establish special classes of unsecured claims in order to comply with the wishes of the debtor.

Under 11 U.S.C. 1322(b)(1), a chapter 13 plan may designate one or more classes of unsecured claims, but may not discriminate unfairly against any class of claims. A plan may place a claim in a particular class only if the claim is substantially similar to the other claims in the class. See 11 U.S.C. 1322(b)(1), 1122(a). Further, if the plan classifies such claims, the same treatment must be provided for each claim within a particular class. See 11 U.S.C. 1322(a)(3). In construing these statutes, the courts invoke a basic fairness test, wherein all similarly-situated claims must be given equal treatment. See In Re Blevins, 1 B.R. 422, and In Re Cooper, 3 B.R. 246.

same, legal requirement

Common sense should be used in deciding whether it is feasible to create a separate class for certain unsecured claims. There must be a justifiable, if not always substantial, difference in the type or nature of a claim to warrant the creation of a separate class for the claim. Unsecured claims for consumer debts of the debtor for which another individual is also liable may, by statute, be treated differently than other unsecured claims, and may therefore constitute a separate class of claims. See 11 U.S.C. 1322(b)(1). Claims for which the debtor received no consideration, such as those in which the debtor was a cosigner or guarantor, may qualify as a separate class of claims, especially if the creditor has a reasonable chance of collecting from the primary obligor. See In Re Gay, 3 B.R. 336. Claims for services or supplies needed by the debtor to remain in business may justify the creation of a separate class, as may claims for the services of a physician or hospital whose future services are needed by the debtor. See In Re Sutherland, 3 B.R. 240. A separate class can usually be justified for nondischargeable claims, such as claims for student loans, child support, or alimony. See In Re Davidson, 72 B.R. 384. A separate class may be created for claims that are dischargeable under chapter 13 but nondischargeable under chapter 7, if a valid reason exists for doing so. See In Re Furlow, 70 B.R. 973. Unsecured priority claims, it should be noted, are required by statute to be paid in full under the plan, so it is not necessary to create a special class for such claims. See 11 U.S.C. 1322(a)(2).

same, practical considerations

A separate class may not be established for the claims of friends, relatives, or other favorites of the debtor. See In Re Stanley, 82 B.R. 858. Further, the payment of an unsecured claim outside the plan constitutes the creation of a separate class of claims, and payments to such a creditor in excess of payments to other unsecured creditors is prohibited. See In Re Green, 70 B.R. 164.

same, prohibited classes

When the special classes of unsecured claims have been determined, the amount to be paid to the holders of such claims must be determined. The amount to be paid on such claims is usually determined by the type of claim and by the availability of funds under the plan. Certain claims, such as important business claims, claims which have been guaranteed by another person, and nondischargeable claims, must usually be paid in full in order to accomplish the purpose of the plan. Other claims need not be paid in full in order to accomplish the purpose of the plan. Much depends on the type of claim, the purpose of the plan, and the availability of funds. Regardless of the purpose of the plan, if insufficient funds are available, after the payment of secured and priority claims, with which to pay a special class of claims in full, then the claims obviously cannot be paid in full. Further, in the absence of a justifiable reason for doing so, most courts will not permit significant payments to be made to special classes of unsecured creditors if little or nothing is paid to general unsecured creditors.

same, determining amount to pay

When the special classes of unsecured claims and the amount to be paid to the holders of such claims have been determined, the total amount to be paid to the holders of special classes of unsecured claims can be calculated. If this amount exceeds the amount remaining after the payment of secured claims, the plan is not feasible and must be changed.

same, total amount paid to

The amount remaining after the payment of special classes of unsecured claims is the total amount that can be paid to the holders of all other (i.e., general) unsecured claims under the plan. It is necessary to ascertain the total amount to be paid to the holders of general unsecured claims for two reasons: (1) to determine whether each unsecured creditor will receive not less than what the creditor would have received had the debtor filed under chapter 7, and (2) to determine the acceptability of the plan to the court.

general unsecured claims, amount paid to

determining
total amount of
general
unsecured claims
To determine the dividend payable to the holders of general unsecured claims under the plan, the total dollar amount of all such claims must be determined. For purposes of preparing the plan, the total dollar amount of such claims must usually be estimated, because the exact amount of each such claim is not usually known until later in the case. In making such an estimate, the unsecured portions of partially secured claims should be counted as unsecured claims.

executory
contracts,
damage claims
from
Executory contracts and unexpired leases rejected in the debtor's plan under 11 U.S.C. 1322(b)(7) are possible sources of unsecured claims. If such a contract or lease is rejected by the debtor, the contracting party becomes either a secured or an unsecured creditor, depending on the terms of the contract or lease, to the extent of any damages incurred as a result of the rejection, and such a claim is determined and allowed or disallowed as though the claim had arisen prior to the date of filing. See 11 U.S.C. 502(g). Unless the amount of the contracting party's damages can be agreed to, the extent and allowability of such damages must be determined by the court, and the total amount of unsecured claims to be dealt with under the plan will not be known until after the court rules on the matter.

general
unsecured
claims,
categories of
plans
In their treatment of general unsecured claims, chapter 13 plans may be categorized as follows: (1) 100-percent plans, where all general unsecured claims are paid in full; (2) 70-percent plans, where the debtor pays general unsecured claims enough (70 percent) to preserve the debtor's right to a chapter 7 discharge (see 11 U.S.C. 727(a)(9) and section 2.17, supra); and (3) minimum payment plans, where the debtor pays as little as the court will allow to the holders of general unsecured claims.

treatment of
unsecured
claims, good
faith
requirements
While the courts vary in their approval of plans that pay as little as possible to unsecured creditors, most courts will confirm a chapter 13 plan that pays little or nothing to unsecured creditors if it is shown that the debtor is acting in good faith and that the plan constitutes the debtor's best effort. See In Re Davis, 68 B.R. 205, and In Re Holiday, 75 B.R. 265. However, if the debtor has valuable non-exempt assets or if substantial payments are being made to special classes of creditors, "good faith" may require that significant payments be made to general unsecured creditors. See In Re Terrill, 68 B.R. 441. Some courts have established fixed percentages that must be paid to unsecured creditors in order to satisfy the good faith requirement. It is important to know the policy of the local court on this matter before devising a plan that proposes to pay as little as possible to any substantial class of unsecured creditors. The chapter 13 trustee in the local district is usually a reliable source of knowledge on the subject, and the local rules should also be checked in this regard.

unsecured
claims,
confirmation
requirements
For a plan to be confirmed, the holder of each unsecured claim in every class must receive not less than what the holder would have received had the debtor been liquidated under chapter 7 on the same date. See 11 U.S.C. 1325(a)(4). Therefore, if a debtor has significant nonexempt assets that would be used to pay dividends to creditors in a chapter 7 case, substantial payments to all unsecured creditors may be required under the plan.

general
unsecured
claims, payment
of
If it appears that the amount payable to general unsecured creditors is sufficient to satisfy both the court and the debtor, the plan should be prepared accordingly. In many cases the best and simplest practice is for the debtor to propose to pay a specified amount (usually the balance left after the payment of priority claims, secured claims, and special classes of unsecured claims) ratably to the holders of general unsecured claims (see Exhibit 3-B, at the end of this chapter).

3.09 Preparing the Chapter 13 Forms

Bankruptcy Rule 1001 provides that the Bankruptcy Rules and Forms shall govern the procedure in chapter 13 cases. Bankruptcy Rule 9009 provides that the Official Forms shall be observed and used with alterations as may be appropriate. Bankruptcy Rule 1007(b)(1) requires the debtor in a chapter 13 case, unless the court orders otherwise, to file schedules of assets and liabilities, a schedule of current income and current expenditures, a schedule of executory contracts and unexpired leases, and a statement of financial affairs prepared as prescribed by the appropriate Official Forms. Bankruptcy Rule 3015(b) provides that the debtor may file a chapter 13 plan with the petition and that if the plan is not filed with the petition it must be filed within 15 days thereafter. There is no official form for a chapter 13 plan, but many districts have adopted local forms for the plan.

official forms, use of

The following forms are needed in the preparation of a typical chapter 13 case:

chapter 13 forms needed, typical case

Voluntary Petition (Official Form 1)

Schedules A through J (Official Form 6)

Chapter 13 Plan and related documents (local forms may be provided, otherwise they must be devised)

Statement of Financial Affairs (Official Form 7)

Application and Order to Pay Filing Fee in Installments (Official Form 3)

Disclosure of Compensation of Attorney for Debtor (Bankruptcy Form B 203)

Application For Allowance of Compensation (a local or devised form, if required)

Address cards or address matrix (a local form, if required)

Notice to Individual Consumer Debtor (Bankruptcy Form B 201 or a local form)

Many districts require additional local forms to be completed and filed in chapter 13 cases, and the local rules should be checked for such requirements. The required local forms are often supplied by the clerk of the bankruptcy court or the United States trustee, and the local rules may contain copies of them. The other forms must be purchased from a supplier of legal forms, usually in prepackaged sets at a cost of about $10 per set. The official forms are most likely to be found in legal and office supply stores. They should be similar to the forms appearing in the exhibits at the end of chapter two, supra.

chapter 13 forms, where to obtain

It is important that the chapter 13 forms be properly and completely prepared, both substantively and technically. If the forms are technically incomplete or improper, the clerk is likely to refuse to process them and may return them to the debtor's attorney for corrections. In this regard it should be noted that Bankruptcy Rule 1008 requires that all petitions, lists, schedules, statements, and amendments thereto to be verified or contain an unsworn declaration as provided in 28 U.S.C. 1746. An original signature is needed only on the original copy of each document, however, if the copies are conformed to the original. See Bankruptcy Rule 9011(c). Other documents need not contain an unsworn declaration or be verified unless specifically required by a particular Bankruptcy Rule. See Bankruptcy Rule 9011(b).

chapter 13 forms, verification requirements

Bankruptcy Rule 9011(a) requires every petition, pleading, motion, and other paper filed in a chapter 13 case by a party represented by an attorney, other than a list, schedule, or statement, or amendments thereto, to be signed by at least one attorney of record in the attorney's individual name, with the attorney's office address and telephone number stated. The signature of an attorney constitutes a certificate that the attorney has read the document, that to the best of the attorney's knowledge it is well grounded in fact, is warranted in law, and is not interposed for an improper purpose. An unsigned document may be stricken unless it is signed promptly after the omission is called to the attention of the person whose signature is required. If a document is signed in violation of this rule, the court may impose sanctions on the signer, including an order to pay the legal and other expenses incurred by any party as a result of the improper signature. See Bankruptcy Rule 9011(a).

signature of attorney, requirement, effect of

The preparation of each document normally required in a chapter 13 case is discussed separately below.

Voluntary Petition. Use Exhibit 2-C at the end of chapter two as a guide in preparing this document. The Voluntary Petition, as set forth in Official Form 1, is self-explanatory and relatively simple to complete. The instructions for completing the petition set forth in section 2.07, supra, should be followed when preparing a chapter 13 petition, except that Exhibit B to the petition and the debtor's acknowledgement of chapters 7, 11, 12 and 13 of the bankruptcy need not be completed in a chapter 13 case. Exhibit A to the petition is also not needed in a chapter 13 case.

Schedules A through J. Use Exhibits 2-D through 2-O at the end of chapter two, supra, as a guide in preparing these schedules. These schedules are prepared in substantially the same manner in a chapter 13 case as in a chapter 7 case and the instructions on their preparation set forth in section 2.07, supra, are equally applicable to chapter 13 cases and should be reviewed if necessary. When completing Schedule I (Current Income of Individual Debtor), the requested information pertaining to the debtor's spouse should be completed even if a joint petition is not being filed, unless the spouses are separated and maintain separate households. If the debtor is engaged in business, a detailed statement of the debtor's income and expenses from the business should be attached to Schedules I and J, respectively. The debtor's total projected monthly income and expenses and the total amount of the debtor's periodic payment under the plan should be calculated and inserted in the appropriate blanks at the bottom of Schedule J. The Declaration Concerning Debtor's Schedules and the Summary of Schedules should be completed in the manner described in section 2.07, supra.

Schedule I and J (the schedules of current income and expenditures) are likely to be closely scrutinized by the chapter 13 trustee and the court in determining whether the debtor's projected disposable income is justifiable. Each item of expense should be checked for reasonableness, and should be verifiable. The amount of excess (or disposable) income shown on Schedule J should be consistent with the amount employed in the debtor's chapter 13 plan. When completing these schedules, expenses that are not incurred on a monthly basis and income that is not received on a monthly basis should be prorated to or estimated on a monthly basis.

It is important to list the debtor's exemptions correctly on Schedule C because to confirm a chapter 13 plan the court must find that each unsecured creditor will receive under the plan not less than what it would have received had the debtor filed under chapter 7, and such a finding requires the court to consider the exemptions claimed by the debtor. Also, if the case is later converted to chapter 7, the exemptions may become important to the debtor. Complete lists of exempt property (both state and federal) may be found in Appendix III, infra. See section 2.08, supra, for further reading on the claiming of exemptions.

Statement of Financial Affairs. Use Exhibit 2-P at the end of chapter two, supra, as a guide in preparing this statement. Official Form 7 must be used for the debtor's statement of financial affairs. Unless the court orders otherwise, every chapter 13 debtor must file a statement of his or her financial affairs. See Bankruptcy Rule 1007(b)(1). In a joint case, however, a joint statement of financial affairs may be filed showing the combined financial affairs of both debtors. The questions appearing in the statement of financial affairs are generally self-explanatory and a response should be made to each question. The instructions for completing the statement of financial affairs set forth in section 2.07, supra, are equally applicable to chapter 13 cases and should be reviewed if necessary.

Chapter 13 Plan and related documents. In many districts a local form is provided for the chapter 13 plan. If no form is provided, use Exhibit 3-B at the end of this chapter as a guide in preparing the plan. The local rules often contain extensive requirements related to the preparation of chapter 13 plans and documents. A summary of the plan, a statement by the debtor, an analysis of the plan, and similar documents are often required. Under Bankruptcy Rule 3015, every plan, or modification thereof, must be dated, and a copy of the plan, or a summary thereof, must be sent to each creditor with notice of the confirmation hearing. See section 3.08, supra, for further reading on the preparation of a chapter 13 plan. The plan must be filed either with the petition or within 15 days thereafter. See Bankruptcy Rule 3015(b).

Disclosure of Compensation of Attorney for Debtor. Use Exhibit 2-A at the end of chapter 2, supra, as a guide in preparing this document. See section 3.03, supra, for the preparation requirements of this document. This document must be filed within 15 days after the order for relief.

attorney's disclosure statement, preparation of

Application For Allowance of Compensation. Use Exhibit 3-A at the end of this chapter as a guide in preparing this document. See section 3.03, supra, for a discussion of the necessity for and the preparation of this document.

See section 2.07, supra, for instructions on the preparation of the Application and Order to Pay Filing Fee in Installments, the Notice to Individual Consumer Debtor, and the address cards or matrix. The local rules should be checked for additional documents or pleadings required to be filed with a chapter 13 petition. Motions to avoid liens under 11 U.S.C. 522(f) and notices disputing the value of secured claims are often required to be filed with the petition or shortly thereafter.

miscellaneous documents, preparation of

CHAPTER THREE

PART C

FILING AND HANDLING A CHAPTER 13 CASE

3.10 Filing a Chapter 13 Case

A chapter 13 case should be filed in a district in which the domicile, residence, principal place of business, or principal assets of the debtor have been located for 180 days immediately preceding the commencement of the case, or for a longer portion of such 180-day period than the domicile, residence, principal place of business, or principal assets were located in any other district. See 28 U.S.C. 1408. Thus, a debtor who has resided in two districts during the previous 180 days must reside (or maintain a principal place of business, etc.) in a particular district for a minimum of 91 days in order to satisfy the venue requirements for filing in that district.

venue requirements, chapter 13 case

The change of venue requirements in chapter 13 cases are the same as those in chapter 7 cases, and the reader is referred to section 2.09, supra, for further reading. If two or more cases by or against the same debtor are filed in different districts, the court in which the earlier case was commenced shall, upon the timely filing of a motion and after a hearing on notice, determine which case or cases shall proceed. Unless otherwise ordered by the court in which the earlier case was commenced, the proceedings in the other courts are stayed until the determination is made. See Bankruptcy Rule 1014(b).

change of venue, requirements

two or more cases, same debtor, procedure

The number of copies of any form or document to be filed in a bankruptcy case is left to local rule. See Advisory Committee Notes to Bankruptcy Rules 1002 and 1007. It should be noted that a copy of most documents filed with the clerk must be transmitted by the clerk to the United States trustee. See Bankruptcy Rules 1002(b) and 1007(l). If the local rules do not include copies for the United States trustee, an additional copy may have to be filed. If the local rules are silent on the number of copies of a particular document to be filed, the original and two copies of the document will usually suffice.

chapter 13 forms, number of copies to file

Bankruptcy Rule 3015(d) requires the clerk to send a copy or summary of the chapter 13 plan with each notice of the confirmation hearing. The rule further states that if required by the court, the debtor shall furnish a sufficient number of copies of the plan to enable the clerk to include a copy with each such notice. Accordingly, many districts require the filing of a sufficient number of copies of the plan (or summaries of the plan in some districts) to permit the clerk to comply with Bankruptcy Rule 3015(d). The local rules should be checked for the specific filing requirements of not only the chapter 13 plan, but any related documents, such as summaries of the plan, statements of the debtor, or similar documents. If the local rules are silent on the subject, the safest practice is to contact the clerk's office in this regard.

chapter 13 plan, number of copies to file

The filing fee is $120 for both single and joint chapter 13 cases. If an Application to Pay Filing Fee in Installments is filed, the filing fee may be paid in up to four installments, with the final installment payable not later than 120 days from the date of filing. For cause, however, the court may extend the time for any installment, provided that the last installment must be paid within 180 days of the date of filing. See Bankruptcy Rule 1006(b)(2). In chapter 13 cases the filing fee must normally be paid prior to confirmation of the plan, and any unpaid portion of the filing fee is usually paid out of the first payments made under the plan by the debtor, which payments must begin within 30 days after the plan is filed, unless the court orders otherwise. See 11 U.S.C. 1326(a)(1).

filing fee, amount, necessity of payment

A chapter 13 case is commenced by filing a voluntary petition seeking relief under chapter 13 of the Bankruptcy Code with the clerk of the bankruptcy court in the proper district and division. If a bankruptcy clerk has not been appointed in the district, the petition (and all other documents in the case) should be filed with the clerk of the district court. If the case is not being filed on an emergency basis, the schedules, statements, plan, and other documents described in section 3.09, supra, should be filed with the petition.

If the debtor is in need of emergency bankruptcy relief and the case must be commenced before the schedules, statements and other documents can be prepared, the case may be commenced by filing the petition accompanied by a list containing the names and addresses of all of the debtor's creditors. See Bankruptcy Rule 1007(a)(1). If the filing fee is not paid in full when the petition is filed, an Application and Order to Pay Filing Fee in Installments must also be prepared and filed with the petition. The Notice to Individual Consumer Debtor should also be filed with the petition.

If not filed with the petition, the schedules and statements must be filed within 15 days after the petition is filed. Any extension of the time for the filing of such statements and schedules may be granted by the court only on motion for cause shown and on notice to the United States trustee, the trustee or other party as the court may direct. See Bankruptcy Rule 1007(c). If not filed with the petition, the chapter 13 plan must also be filed within 15 days thereafter, and the time for filing may not be further extended except for cause and on such notice as the court may direct. See Bankruptcy Rule 3015(b).

If it is important to deliver notice of the commencement of the case and of the automatic stay to certain creditors or other parties in advance of the mailing of the notice of commencement of case by the clerk, either a certified copy of the filed petition or a certificate of commencement of case signed by clerk (if available locally) may be used for this purpose and served upon the appropriate parties.

3.11 The Automatic Stay

The filing of a petition under chapter 13 operates as an automatic stay of acts, claims, and proceedings against the debtor and the debtor's property to the same extent as the filing of a petition under chapter 7. See 11 U.S.C. 362(a),(b). The provisions for obtaining relief from the stay are also the same under chapter 13 as under chapter 7. See 11 U.S.C. 362(d). See section 2.10, supra, for further reading on the automatic stay.

automatic stay, effect of

Chapter 13 contains a special provision dealing with stays of actions against codebtors. See 11 U.S.C. 1301. After an order for relief under chapter 13, which occurs with the filing of a chapter 13 petition, a creditor may not act or commence or continue a civil action to collect all or any part of a consumer debt of the debtor from any individual that is liable on the debt with the debtor, or that has secured the debt, unless the codebtor became liable on or secured the debt in the ordinary course of the codebtor's business, or unless the chapter 13 case is dismissed or converted to another chapter. See 11 U.S.C. 1301(a). However, a creditor may present or give notice of dishonor of a negotiable instrument. See 11 U.S.C. 1301(b).

automatic stay, codebtor

The court, after notice and hearing, may grant relief from the Section 1301 stay to a creditor to the extent that: (1) as between the debtor and the codebtor, the codebtor received the consideration for the creditor's claim, (2) the plan filed by the debtor proposes not to pay the claim, or (3) the creditor's interest would be irreparably harmed by the stay. See 11 U.S.C. 1301(c). Twenty days after the filing of a request for relief from the stay on the grounds that the debtor's plan proposes not to pay the creditor's claim, the stay is terminated with respect to the requesting party unless the debtor or an individual liable on the debt with the debtor files and serves upon the requesting party a written objection to the proposed relief. See 11 U.S.C. 1301(d).

automatic stay, relief from

A secured creditor whose claim is not dealt with in the plan must obtain relief from the automatic stay in order to reclaim or foreclose on its security. See sections 2.10 and 2.19, supra, for further reading on this subject. Motions by such creditors for relief from the stay are normally granted if the debtor is in default on the creditor's claim. The court has discretion in the granting of such relief, however, and a debtor who disputes the alleged default or who can show extenuating circumstances should contest the motion for relief from stay. See In Re Rosenow, 22 B.R. 99.

secured creditors, obtaining relief from stay

Of concern to secured creditors in chapter 13 cases is the problem posed by the debtor who files under chapter 13, obtains the benefit of the automatic stay, and then abandons the plan after making few, if any, payments thereunder. In such instances the creditor may either seek relief from the automatic stay under 11 U.S.C. 362(d) (see section 2.10, supra), or file a motion to dismiss the case under 11 U.S.C. 1307(c) and Bankruptcy Rule 9014 (see section 3.17, infra). The dismissal of the case terminates the automatic stay and permits the creditor to proceed against its security. See 11 U.S.C. 362(c)(1).

defaulting debtor, creditors' remedies

3.12 The Meeting of Creditors

The United States trustee must call a meeting of creditors to be held not less than 20 nor more than 40 days after the filing of a chapter 13 case. The meeting may be held at a regular place for holding court or at any other convenient place within the district designated by the United States trustee. If the place designated for the meeting is not regularly staffed by the United States trustee, the meeting may be held not more than 60 days after the filing of the case. See Bankruptcy Rule 2003.

In practice, a few days after the commencement of a chapter 13 case, a document entitled "Notice of Commencement of Case Under Chapter 13 of the Bankruptcy Code, Meeting of Creditors, and Fixing of Dates" is sent to the debtor and all creditors and other parties in interest. A sample of this document, which is Official Form 9I, may be found in Exhibit 3-C at the end of this chapter. The notices contained in this document include the following:

(1) Notice of the name and address of the debtor, the debtor's attorney, and the trustee.

(2) Notice of the date the case was filed, the case number, and whether the case was converted to chapter 13 from another chapter.

(3) Notice of the deadline for filing proofs of claim.

(4) Notice of the date, time, and location of the meeting of creditors.

(5) Notice as to whether the debtor has filed a plan and either notice of the date, time and location of the confirmation hearing or notice that creditors will be given separate notice of the confirmation hearing.

(6) Notice that a chapter 13 case has been filed, that an order for relief has been entered, and that all documents filed with the court are available for inspection.

(7) Notice of the automatic stay and the effect thereof on creditors.

(8) Notice that the debtor must appear and testify at the meeting of creditors and that creditors may examine the debtor at the meeting of creditors.

(9) Notice that a creditor must file a proof of claim in order to receive payment in the case.

(10) Notice of the purpose of a chapter 13 case.

(11) Notice of the address of the Clerk of the Bankruptcy Court.

The clerk, or such other person as the court may direct, must give the debtor, the trustee, and all creditors not less than 20 days notice of the meeting of creditors. See Bankruptcy Rule 2002(a). If the debtor's debts are primarily consumer debts, notice of the order for relief must be given to the trustee and all creditors within 20 days after the date of the order for relief. See Bankruptcy Rule 2002(o). The clerk, or such other person as the court may direct, must give the debtor, the trustee, and all creditors at least 25 days notice of the confirmation hearing and of the time fixed for filing objections to confirmation of the plan, and the notice must be accompanied by a copy or summary of the debtor's chapter 13 plan. See Bankruptcy Rules 2002(b) and 3015(d), and section 3.13, infra.

The United States trustee or a designee thereof must preside at the meeting of creditors. See Bankruptcy Rule 2003(b)(1). In most chapter 13 cases the United States trustee designates the standing chapter 13 trustee to preside over the meeting of creditors. The court may neither preside at nor attend the meeting of creditors. See 11 U.S.C. 341(c). The meeting of creditors is often referred to as the Section 341(a) meeting.

The order of business at the meeting of creditors includes an examination of the debtor under oath. See Bankruptcy Rule 2003(b)(1). Unsecured creditors who have filed objections to the debtor's plan are likely to attend the meeting, as are secured creditors who have not accepted the plan. Such creditors, as well as the trustee, may examine the debtor under oath if they so desire. See 11 U.S.C. 343. However, any examination of the debtor may relate only to the acts, conduct, property, liabilities or financial condition of the debtor, any matter that may affect the administration of the debtor's estate or the debtor's right to a discharge, or to the operation of the debtor's business and the desirability of its continuance, the source of any money or property acquired or to be acquired by the debtor for the purpose of consummating a plan and the consideration given or offered therefor, and any other matter relevant to the case or to the formulation of a plan. See Bankruptcy Rule 2004(b).

meeting of creditors, order of business

Any examination under oath at the meeting of creditors must be recorded verbatim by the United States trustee using electronic sound recording equipment or other means of recording. Such record must be preserved by the United States trustee and made available for public access for two years thereafter. Upon request, the United States trustee must provide a certified copy or transcript of the recording at the expense of the person making the request. See Bankruptcy Rule 2003(c). The meeting may be adjourned from time to time by announcement at the meeting of the adjourned date and time, without further written notice. See Bankruptcy Rule 2003(e).

meeting of creditors, recording requirements, adjournment

In some districts written instructions are sent to the debtor, and often to the debtor's attorney, usually with the notice of commencement of case. These instructions often require the debtor to bring certain documents to the meeting. The debtor should, of course, bring the required documents to the meeting; otherwise the meeting may be postponed to a later date, necessitating another court appearance. The attorney's application for approval of compensation, if not combined with the attorney's disclosure statement, must be filed at or before this meeting in some districts.

meeting of creditors, required documents

In most districts the standing chapter 13 trustee presides at meetings of creditors in chapter 13 cases. Generally, meetings of creditors are informal and not lengthy, although the actual amount of time spent at a hearing may depend on when a particular case is called, as several cases are often scheduled for the same time period. Also, in many instances the confirmation hearing is held immediately after the meeting of creditors, in which case the amount of time spent at the hearings will depend on the dockets of both the chapter 13 trustee and the court. Disputes arising at the creditors' meeting may have to be taken before the court for resolution, either in conjunction with the confirmation hearing or separately.

meeting of creditors, procedure

If the addresses listed in the schedules for any of the creditors were incorrect, the notices mailed to those creditors will have been returned to the clerk's office by the Postal Service by the time of the meeting of creditors. If the matter is not brought to the attorney's attention by the hearing officer, the attorney should inquire or check the case file to insure that none have been returned. If one or more notices have been returned, it is important that a correct address be obtained for each creditor because the debt owed to a creditor who does not receive notice of the case may be nondischargeable. See 11 U.S.C. 523(a)(3), and Matter of Robertson, 13 B.R. 726. Unless the court directs otherwise, an amended schedule should be filed listing the correct address for any such creditor. Notice of the case should be immediately mailed to any such creditors by the debtor's attorney. A copy of the notice of commencement of case (Exhibit 3-C) will usually suffice as notice of the case.

incorrectly listed creditor, procedure

If an amended schedule is filed, only the corrected information need be shown, unless the local rules provide otherwise. It should be noted that a voluntary petition, list, schedule or statement may be amended by the debtor as a matter of course at any time before the case is closed. See Bankruptcy Rule 1009(a). If a creditor cannot be located, notice of the case may be served by publication under Bankruptcy Rule 2002(l). There is a $20 fee charged for amending a schedule of liabilities or a list of creditors after the notice to creditors has been sent, provided that the court, for good cause, may waive the charge.

filing amended statement, procedure, fee

3.13 Obtaining Confirmation of a Chapter 13 Plan

The clerk of the bankruptcy court, or such other person as the court may direct, must give the debtor, the chapter 13 trustee, and all creditors not less than 25 days notice by mail of the time and place of the hearing on the confirmation of the debtor's plan and of the time fixed by the court for the filing of objections to confirmation of the plan. See Bankruptcy Rule 2002(b). A copy of the debtor's plan, or a summary thereof, must be included with this notice. See Bankruptcy Rule 3015(d).

Objections to confirmation of the debtor's plan must be filed in writing with the court within the time fixed by the court, and served on the debtor, the chapter 13 trustee, and the United States trustee within the time so fixed. Objections to confirmation are contested matters governed by Bankruptcy Rule 9014, which requires a hearing on reasonable notice and does not require the debtor to file a written response to the objection unless the court so orders. See Bankruptcy Rule 3020(b)(1) and 11 U.S.C. 1324.

If the debtor filed a chapter 13 plan with the petition, notice of date, time and place of the confirmation hearing and of the time fixed for the filing of objections to confirmation may be contained in the notice of commencement of case. Otherwise, a separate notice must be sent, often by the debtor under a local rule. This notice is especially important to unsecured creditors because the filing of objections to confirmation is their only method of opposing the debtor's plan. The local rules often contain extensive provisions dealing with the confirmation of chapter 13 plans. They may require the filing of a motion for confirmation and related documents using specified forms, as well as the mailing of notices to creditors by the debtor.

The court must hold a hearing and rule on confirmation of a chapter 13 plan after the giving of appropriate notice. See 11 U.S.C. 1324 and Bankruptcy Rule 3020(b)(2). At the hearing the court will consider the plan proposed by the debtor, together with any accompanying documents and any proposed modifications, as well as any timely-filed objections to confirmation. Matters that must be resolved in order to finalize the plan, such as motions to avoid liens and the valuation of contested security interests, if not previously ruled on by the court, may also be ruled on at the confirmation hearing. Objections or disputes relating to the classification of claims in the plan may also be ruled on by the court at the confirmation hearing, although a separate hearing may be held under Bankruptcy Rule 3013, if desired.

It should be noted that the debtor may modify a chapter 13 plan at any time prior to confirmation as long as the plan, as modified, continues to meet the requirements of 11 U.S.C. 1322, which are listed in section 3.08, supra. See 11 U.S.C. 1323(a). If the debtor files a modified plan, the plan as modified becomes the chapter 13 plan. See 11 U.S.C. 1323(b). However, every modification of a plan must be separately dated. See Bankruptcy Rule 3015(c). If a secured creditor has previously accepted or rejected the plan, the creditor will be deemed to have accepted or rejected the modified plan unless the modification changes the creditor's rights under the plan and the creditor changes its previous acceptance or rejection. See 11 U.S.C. 1323(c). The court, upon notice to the chapter 13 trustee and the creditor, may find that a proposed modification does not change the treatment of a creditor's claim. See Bankruptcy Rule 3019. The local rules should be checked for notice and other requirements relating to the modification of chapter 13 plans prior to confirmation.

An important aspect of many chapter 13 cases is the valuation of contested security interests. Such a valuation is often necessary in order to determine the amount of the allowed secured claim of a partially-secured creditor. In many districts the local rules govern the procedural aspects of valuation proceedings. Under such rules, the debtor may be required to list a value for the security interest of each secured claim (an amount that should appear on the debtor's Schedule D), with the creditor then required to file an objection to the value listed by the debtor within a specified period. If the local rules contain no such provisions, it may be necessary for the debtor to either file an objection to an excessive claim of a partially-secured creditor or file a motion under Bankruptcy Rule 3012 to determine the secured portion of a partially secured claim.

The value of a security interest must be determined in light of the purpose of the valuation and of any proposed use or disposition of the property. See 11 U.S.C. 506(a). It is normally in the debtor's interest to value secured property as low as possible. At the valuation hearing, whether held in conjunction with the confirmation hearing, under Bankruptcy Rule 3012, or otherwise, the debtor should be prepared to present evidence as to the value of the property in question. Usually the debtor is competent to testify as to the value of his or her property. See Federal Rule of Evidence No. 701 and the cases cited thereunder. Therefore, the debtor should be prepared to testify as to the purchase price, date of acquisition, and present condition of the property, and to state his or her opinion as to the value of the property. It may be advisable to employ an appraiser or other expert, especially if the property is valuable and the discrepancy in asserted values is great. Recent photographs of the property may also be helpful.

valuation of security interest, hearing

By seeking a judicial determination of the value of the security interest of a partially-secured creditor, the debtor can often prevent the creditor from blocking confirmation of the plan. This may be accomplished by proposing in the plan that the creditor retain its lien and be paid the secured portion of its claim, with interest, in an equitable manner under the plan. If the court accepts the debtor's proposal and confirms the plan, the creditor will be forced to accept the plan under 11 U.S.C. 1325(a)(5)(B), and the unsecured balance of its claim will be treated under the plan as an unsecured claim. This is the so-called "cramdown" feature of chapter 13. It can be a useful tool for the debtor in dealing with partially secured creditors. It should be noted that in most districts a "cramdown" may be imposed on a partially-secured creditor secured only by a mortgage on the debtor's residence. See section 3.08, supra.

partially-secured creditor, cram-down

To confirm a chapter 13 plan, the court must find that the plan meets the confirmation requirements of 11 U.S.C. 1325(a), which are described in section 3.08, supra. However, in the absence of a timely filed objection to confirmation, the court may find, without receiving evidence, that the plan has been proposed in good faith and not by any means forbidden by law. See Bankruptcy Rule 3020(b)(2). On most other matters, however, the burden rests with the debtor, who should be prepared to show that the remaining provisions of 11 U.S.C. 1325(a) have been complied with in the case. See In Re Crago, 4 B.R. 483. Much of the required information will be contained in the court records and in the schedules, statements and other documents filed by the debtor. However, the court may require additional documentation or testimony from the debtor, especially if the plan appears to be difficult for the debtor to comply with or pays little or nothing to unsecured creditors.

confirmation hearing, procedure

The debtor should be prepared to justify the income and expense figures appearing in the schedules of current income and current expenditures, and to show that all of the debtor's projected disposable income for the period of the plan will be applied to the plan. If the plan establishes special classes of unsecured claims, the debtor should be prepared to justify the classification and treatment of such claims. If assets are to be contributed to the plan by the debtor, the manner in which the assets are to be contributed and the amount to be realized from such assets should be established.

confirmation hearing, debtor's responsibilities

The order of confirmation must conform to Official Form 15, and notice of the entry of the order must be promptly mailed or transmitted by the clerk to the debtor, the creditors, the trustee, the United States trustee, and other parties in interest. See Bankruptcy Rule 3020(c). Notwithstanding the entry of the order of confirmation, however, the court may continue to enter all orders necessary to administer the estate. See Bankruptcy Rule 3020(d). After confirmation, the court may compel any entity from whom the debtor receives income to pay all or any part of such income to the chapter 13 trustee. See 11 U.S.C. 1325(c). A sample Order Confirming Chapter 13 Plan is set forth in Exhibit 3-D at the end of this chapter.

order of confirmation, form, notice

The provisions of a confirmed plan bind the debtor and each creditor, whether or not the claim of the creditor is dealt with under the plan and whether or not the creditor has objected to, accepted, or rejected the plan. See 11 U.S.C. 1327(a). Except as otherwise provided in the plan or in the order confirming the plan, the confirmation of a plan vests the property of the estate in the debtor. See 11 U.S.C. 1327(b). And, except as otherwise provided in the plan or in the order confirming the plan, the property vested in the debtor is free and clear of any claim or interest of any creditor dealt with under the plan. See 11 U.S.C. 1327(c).

chapter 13 plan, effect of

Upon a complaint filed by a party in interest within 180 days after the order of confirmation, and after notice and a hearing, the court may revoke an order of confirmation if the order was procured by fraud. See 11 U.S.C. 1330(a). A proceeding to revoke an order of confirmation is an adversary proceeding governed by Part VII of the Rules of Bankruptcy Procedure. See Bankruptcy Rule 7001. If an order of confirmation is revoked, the court may dismiss the case or convert it to chapter 7, unless the debtor modifies the plan and the modified plan is confirmed by the court. See 11 U.S.C. 1330(b).

3.14 The Chapter 13 Trustee

If a sufficient number of chapter 13 cases are filed in a district, a standing trustee may be appointed to serve in chapter 13 cases filed in the district. See 28 U.S.C. 586(b). If the standing trustee qualifies under 11 U.S.C. 322, he or she will normally be appointed to serve as trustee in a chapter 13 case. Otherwise, a disinterested person must be appointed to serve as the trustee in the case. See 11 U.S.C. 1302(a). The chapter 13 trustee is appointed by the United States trustee. See section 2.16, supra, for further reading on the powers and duties of the United States trustee.

The principal function of the chapter 13 trustee is to collect the payments made by the debtor and disburse the funds as provided in the plan, in the order confirming the plan, and by applicable law. Before making payments under the plan, the chapter 13 trustee must pay any unpaid administrative expenses and fees assessed against the debtor's estate. Such fees and expenses normally include the unpaid portions of the filing fee and the fee allowed the debtor's attorney, and the chapter 13 trustee's, which is ten percent of the amount received by the trustee under the plan. See 11 U.S.C. 1326(b). Except as otherwise provided in the plan or in the order confirming the plan, the trustee must make all payments to creditors under the plan. See 11 U.S.C. 1326(c).

The duties of the chapter 13 trustee are set forth in 11 U.S.C. 1302(b),(c) and Bankruptcy Rule 2015(c). In nonbusiness chapter 13 cases, the duties of the chapter 13 trustee include the following:

(1) Ensure that the debtor commences making timely payments under the plan or proposed plan.

(2) Account for all property received.

(3) Keep a record of receipts and the disposition of money and property received.

(4) Investigate the financial affairs of the debtor.

(5) Examine proofs of claims and object to the allowance of any improper claim, if a purpose would be served.

(6) Oppose the discharge of the debtor, if advisable.

(7) Furnish information concerning the estate and its administration to parties in interest, unless the court orders otherwise.

(8) Appear and be heard at any hearing concerning the value of property subject to a lien, the confirmation of a plan, or the modification of a plan after confirmation.

(9) Advise (except on legal matters) and assist the debtor in performance under the plan.

(10) Approve or disapprove postpetition consumer debts to be incurred by the debtor, if so requested under 11 U.S.C. 1305(c).

(11) Make a final report and file a final account of the administration of the estate with the court.

If the debtor is engaged in business, the duties of the chapter 13 trustee, in addition to the duties listed above, include the following:

(1) Unless ordered otherwise by the court, investigate the acts, conduct, assets, liabilities, and financial condition of the debtor, the operation of the debtor's business, and any other matter relevant to the case or to the formulation of a plan.

(2) File a statement of such investigation as soon as practicable.

(3) File a complete inventory of the property of the debtor within 30 days after being appointed, unless such an inventory has been filed.

(4) File certain periodic reports related to the collection and assessment of certain taxes.

(5) Give notice of the case to every person known to be holding money or property subject to the withdrawal or order of the debtor.

A chapter 13 trustee has the avoidance and other powers of a trustee under any other chapter of title 11. See 11 U.S.C. 103(a). See section 2.16, supra, for a discussion of these powers. While a chapter 13 trustee seldom takes possession of the debtor's estate (see 11 U.S.C. 1306(b)), the trustee is charged with the duty of preserving the estate for the benefit of creditors should the chapter 13 plan fail. See City National Bank & Trust Co. v. Oliver, 230 F. 2nd 686. Under chapter 13, the debtor's estate includes, in addition to the estate that would have existed under chapter 7 (which is described in section 2.15, supra), property of the kind included under chapter 7 that is acquired by the debtor during the pendency of the chapter 13 case, and earnings from services performed by the debtor during the pendency of the chapter 13 case. See 11 U.S.C. 1306(a).

All parties in interest, including the chapter 13 trustee and the United States trustee, and any attorney, accountant, or employee of a party in interest, must refrain from ex parte contacts, meetings, or communications with the bankruptcy judge concerning matters affecting a particular case or proceeding. See Bankruptcy Rule 9003.

3.15 Modifying a Chapter 13 Plan After Confirmation - Postpetition Debts

It often happens that at some point during the course of a chapter 13 case the debtor becomes unable to make the payments required under the plan. Unemployment, illness, injury, a divorce, a business setback, and the failure of the debtor to control his or her spending are the most common causes of a debtor's inability to comply with the plan. Other reasons for modifying a confirmed plan include the making of an outside payment on a claim dealt with under the plan, the incurrence by the debtor of an allowable postpetition debt, and a significant change in the debtor's income or expenses. For a variety of reasons, then, it often becomes necessary for a debtor to modify his or her plan after confirmation. Usually the alternative is dismissal or conversion to chapter 7.

Modification of a chapter 13 plan after confirmation is governed by 11 U.S.C. 1329(a), which provides that at any time after confirmation of a plan, but before the completion of payments under the plan, the plan may be modified, upon the request of the debtor, the trustee, or the holder of an allowed unsecured claim, so as to:

(1) increase or reduce the amount of payments on claims of a particular class provided under the plan,

(2) extend or reduce the time for such payments, or

(3) alter the amount of the distribution to a creditor whose claim is provided for by the plan, to the extent necessary to take account of any payment of such claim other than under the plan.

A showing of good cause is required of any party seeking modification of a chapter 13 plan after confirmation. For the debtor to modify a confirmed plan under 11 U.S.C. 1329(a), a change in the debtor's circumstances must be shown, but the change does not have to be grievous. See In Re Davis, 34 B.R. 319. Many courts, it should be noted, are reluctant to permit the debtor to modify a confirmed plan so as to include one or more additional unsecured creditors if the modification will prejudice the rights of existing

creditors under the plan. See In Re Smura, 84 B.R. 327. Because of the limited instances under which a confirmed chapter 13 plan may be modified, it may be more practicable to amend the order of confirmation than to modify the plan, if the proposed change is not substantial. See In Re Hartford, 7 B.R. 914.

It should be understood that if the debtor's circumstances change so as to increase the amount of the debtor's disposable income, the chapter 13 trustee or an unsecured creditor may request modification of a confirmed plan under 11 U.S.C. 1329(a). See In Re Owens, 82 B.R. 960. Minor changes in the debtor's income or expenses, however, do not warrant modification of a confirmed plan. See In Re Gronski, 86 B.R. 428.

The plan contents requirements of 11 U.S.C. 1322(a),(b) apply to the modification of a plan after confirmation. See 11 U.S.C. 1329(b)(1), and section 3.08, supra. The confirmation requirements of 11 U.S.C. 1325(a) also apply to the modification of a plan after confirmation. See 11 U.S.C. 1329(b)(1). These requirements are also set forth in section 3.08, supra. The plan as modified becomes the debtor's chapter 13 plan unless, after notice and hearing, the proposed modification is disapproved by the court. See 11 U.S.C. 1329(b)(2). Bankruptcy Rule 3015(c) requires any modification to be dated.

If a proposed modification seeks to extend the duration of a chapter 13 plan, it should be noted that a plan modified after confirmation may not provide for payments over a period that expires more than three years after the date that the first payment under the originally-confirmed plan was due, unless the court, for cause, approves a longer period, but the court may not approve a period that expires more than five years after such date. See 11 U.S.C. 1329(c). Thus, a modified plan may not provide for payments by the debtor beyond five years after the date upon which the first payment was due under the originally-confirmed plan.

A secured creditor who has accepted or rejected the originally-confirmed plan will be deemed to have accepted or rejected the modified plan unless the modification changes the rights of the creditor under the plan and the creditor changes its previous acceptance or rejection. See 11 U.S.C. 1329(b)(1), 1323(c). If the rights of a secured creditor are found by the court to be changed by a proposed modification, the clerk or some other party as the court may direct must give the creditor at least 20 days notice of the time fixed by court for accepting or rejecting the proposed modification. See Bankruptcy Rule 2002(a)(6). If the rights of a class of unsecured creditors are found by the court to be changed by the proposed modification, the affected creditors must be given notice and an opportunity to file objections to the confirmation of the modified plan. See 11 U.S.C. 1323(c) and Bankruptcy Rule 3020(b)(1). modified plan,
rights of
creditors

The procedure for modifying a plan after confirmation is a contested matter governed by Bankruptcy Rule 9014, which means that a proceeding to modify a confirmed plan is initiated by the filing of a motion, with reasonable notice and an opportunity for hearing afforded the parties against whom relief is sought. The local rules should be checked for notice and other requirements applicable to motions to modify a plan after confirmation. A sample Motion to Modify Chapter 13 Plan After Confirmation is set forth in Exhibit 3-E at the end of this chapter. modifying plan,
procedure

Chapter 13 debtors frequently encounter a need for credit during the course of the case. The need of money for medical, business, or other emergency purposes, and the need for a new or different automobile or household appliance are common causes of the need for such credit. Postpetition claims may be filed only for - (1) taxes that become payable to a governmental unit while the case is pending, and (2) consumer debts arising after the date of the order for relief under chapter 13 that are for property or services necessary for the debtor's performance under the plan. See 11 U.S.C. 1305(a). However, claims for consumer debts are not allowable if the holder of the claim knew, or should have known, that the prior approval by the trustee of the incurrence of the obligation by the debtor was practicable and was not obtained. See 11 U.S.C. 1305(c). A consumer debt is a debt incurred primarily for a personal, family, or household purpose. See 11 U.S.C. 101(8). Qualifying postpetition claims are allowed or disallowed on the same basis as any other claims, but are determined as of the date the claim arose. See 11 U.S.C. 1305(b). postpetition
claims,
allowance of

Even if a postpetition claim for a consumer debt is allowed by the court, the debt upon which the claim is based is not dischargeable in the case if the prior approval of the chapter 13 trustee was practicable and was not obtained. See 11 U.S.C. 1328(d). It is important to the debtor, therefore, that the trustee's prior approval of such debts be obtained, and the burden of obtaining such approval usually rests with the debtor. A sample of a written request for the trustee's prior approval of a postpetition consumer debt may be found in Exhibit 3-F at the end of this chapter. In some districts the chapter 13 trustee may have forms for such requests. postpetition
claims,
trustee's
approval of

3.16 Creditors - Claims and Payments

roofs of claims, filing and notice requirements

A creditor must file a proof of claim with the clerk of the bankruptcy court within 90 days after the first date set for the meeting of creditors for the claim to be allowed, unless the claim is filed on behalf of the creditor by the trustee, the debtor or a codebtor, or a guarantor. See Bankruptcy Rule 3002(a),(b),(c). There are four exceptions to the 90-day requirement for filing proofs of claims. These exceptions deal with claims by the governmental units, claims for infants or incompetents, claims that become allowable as a result of judgments, and claims arising from the rejection of executory contracts. See Bankruptcy Rule 3002(c). The clerk, or some other person as the court may direct, must give each creditor notice by mail of the time allowed for the filing of claims. See Bankruptcy Rule 2002(f)(3). This notice is normally contained in the notice of commencement of case (see Exhibit 3-C).

proof of claim, by debtor or trustee

If a creditor fails to file a claim on or before the first date set for the meeting of creditors, the debtor or the trustee may file a claim in the name of the creditor, a notice of which the clerk must forthwith mail to the creditor, the debtor, and the trustee. See Bankruptcy Rule 3004 and 11 U.S.C. 501(c). This can be a useful provision for the debtor with respect to claims for nondischargeable debts and claims of partially-secured creditors which the debtor wishes to pay under the plan. If the creditor thereafter files a proof of claim, it supersedes the claim filed by the trustee or debtor on the creditor's behalf. See Bankruptcy Rule 3004. It should be noted that if no claim is filed on behalf of a secured creditor and if the creditor is not dealt with in the plan, the creditor's lien survives the chapter 13 case. See 11 U.S.C. 506(d)(1).

lien of creditor not dealt with in plan

proof of claim, by codebtor or guarantor

If a creditor fails to file a proof of claim, one who is liable with the debtor to the creditor, or one who has secured the creditor, may, within 30 days after the expiration of the 90-day period for filing claims, execute and file a proof of claim in the name of the creditor, if known, or if unknown, in the person's own name. However, no distribution can be made on the claim except on satisfactory proof that the original debt will be diminished by the amount distributed. The creditor may thereafter file a proof of claim, which shall supersede the proof of claim filed on its behalf. See Bankruptcy Rule 3005(a) and 11 U.S.C. 501(b).

subrogated, transferred, offsetting, or improperly filed claims

See section 2.19, supra, for a discussion of subrogated claims, transferred claims, and offsetting claims. See section 3.15, supra, for a discussion of postpetition claims. See Bankruptcy Rule 5005(c) for the procedures when a claim is filed with the wrong official.

proof of claim, where filed, form and content

A proof of claim must be filed with the clerk of the bankruptcy court in the district where the case is pending. See Bankruptcy Rule 5005(a). The local rules often require a proof of claim to be filed in duplicate. A proof of claim is a written statement setting forth a creditor's claim. It must conform substantially to Official Form 10. See Bankruptcy Rule 3001(a). A proof of claim must be executed by the creditor or the creditor's authorized agent, unless it is filed on the creditor's behalf by the debtor, the trustee, a codebtor, or a guarantor. See Bankruptcy Rule 3001(b). If a claim, or an interest in property of the debtor securing a claim, is based on a writing, the original or a duplicate of the writing must be filed with the proof of claim, or its loss or destruction explained in a statement filed with the claim. See Bankruptcy Rule 3001(c). If a security interest in property of the debtor is claimed, the proof of claim must be accompanied by evidence that the security interest has been perfected. See Bankruptcy Rule 3001(d). A sample Proof of Claim is set forth in Exhibit 3-G at the end of this chapter.

withdrawal of claim

A creditor may withdraw a claim as of right by filing a notice of withdrawal, unless an objection to the claim or a complaint against the creditor in an adversary proceeding has been filed. Also, if a creditor has accepted the plan or otherwise participated significantly in the case, the creditor may not withdraw its claim except on order of the court after a hearing on notice. See Bankruptcy Rule 3006.

objections to allowance of claims

An objection to the allowance of a claim must be in writing and filed with the clerk of the bankruptcy court. A copy of the objection and a notice of the hearing thereon must be mailed or otherwise delivered to the claimant, the debtor, and the trustee at least 30 days prior to the hearing. If an objection is joined with a demand for relief of the kind specified in Bankruptcy Rule 7001 (i.e., to determine the validity or priority of a lien, etc.), it becomes an adversary proceeding. See Bankruptcy Rule 3007. The local rules often contain provisions dealing with the filing of objections to claims in chapter 13 cases.

A properly executed and filed proof of claim constitutes prima facie evidence of the validity and amount of the claim. See Bankruptcy Rule 3001(f). Unless a party in interest files an objection to a properly filed claim, it is deemed allowed. See 11 U.S.C. 502(a). If an objection to a claim is timely filed, the court, after a hearing on notice, must determine the amount of the claim as of the date of filing of the petition, and must allow the claim in that amount, except to the extent that:

(1) the claim is unenforceable against the debtor and the debtor's property under any agreement or applicable law for a reason other than because such claim is contingent or unmatured;

(2) the claim is for unmatured interest;

(3) if the claim is for taxes assessed against property of the debtor's estate, the claim exceeds the reasonable value of the estate's interest in the property;

(4) if the claim is for services of an insider or attorney of the debtor, the claim exceeds the reasonable value of such services;

(5) the claim is for a debt for nondischargeable postpetition alimony, maintenance or support;

(6) if the claim is for damages to a lessor for the termination of a lease of real property, the claim exceeds certain specified amounts (see 11 U.S.C. 502(b)(7));

(7) if the claim is for damages for the termination of an employment contract, the claim exceeds certain specified amounts (see 11 U.S.C. 502(b)(8)); or

(8) the claim results from a reduction, due to late payment, in the amount of an otherwise applicable credit available to the debtor in connection with an employment tax on wages, salaries or commissions earned from the debtor. See 11 U.S.C. 502(b).

In addition, the claim of an entity from which property is recoverable by the trustee or that is a transferee of a voidable transfer must be disallowed, unless the entity has paid the amount or turned over the property for which it is liable. See 11 U.S.C. 502(d). Certain claims for reimbursement or contribution are also not allowable. See 11 U.S.C. 502(e). Contingent or unliquidated claims, the liquidation of which would unduly delay the closing of the case, must be estimated by the court for purposes of allowance. See 11 U.S.C. 502(c). It should be noted that proceedings to liquidate or estimate personal injury or wrongful death claims against the estate for purposes of distribution are not core proceedings. See 28 U.S.C. 152(b)(2)(B). Core proceedings are discussed in section 2.01, supra.

A party in interest may move for the reconsideration of an order allowing or disallowing a claim, whereupon the court, after a hearing on notice, must enter an appropriate order. See Bankruptcy Rule 3008. See 11 U.S.C. 502(j) for the effect of an order of reconsideration on the payment of a claim.

An allowed claim of a creditor that is secured by a lien on property of the debtor's estate is a secured claim only to the extent of the value of the creditor's interest in the property. An allowed claim that is subject to a setoff is a secured claim only to the extent of the amount subject to setoff. See 11 U.S.C. 506(a). The balance of such claims are deemed unsecured. Thus, the amount of a creditor's secured claim may not exceed the value of the property securing the claim. The value of a creditor's interest in the property must be determined in light of the purpose of the valuation and of any proposed disposition or use of the property, and such a valuation may be made in conjunction with any hearing on the disposition of the property or on the motion of a party in interest. See 11 U.S.C. 506(a) and Bankruptcy Rule 3012. See section 3.13, supra, for further reading.

The local rules in many districts contain special provisions dealing with the filing and allowance of both secured and unsecured claims in chapter 13 cases. In some districts a proof of claim form is printed on the reverse side of the notice of commencement of case. In some districts the claim form contains a ballot upon which a secured creditor can indicate its acceptance or rejection of the debtor's proposed plan.

claims, examination by debtor

The local rules may also contain provisions dealing with the debtor's rights and obligations with respect to claims and the filing of objections thereto. A procedure is often provided whereby either the clerk or the chapter 13 trustee sends the debtor a list of claims filed and the debtor is given a specific period within which to object to any disputed claims. It is important for the debtor's attorney to be aware of any such local rules.

secured claims, payment of

If a secured claim dealt with under a chapter 13 plan has been allowed, and if it so provided in the plan or in the order confirming the plan, payments on the claim may begin immediately upon confirmation, provided that the priority administrative expenses have been paid or the right to priority of payment waived. See 11 U.S.C. 1326(b)(1). Priority administrative claims usually include the unpaid portions of the filing fee and the fee allowed to the debtor's attorney in the case. The chapter 13 trustee's fee is also collected prior to the payment of claims. See 11 U.S.C. 1326(b)(2).

unsecured claims, payment of

Normally, payments to unsecured creditors may not begin until the period for filing claims has expired, the debtor and the chapter 13 trustee have had an opportunity to examine and file objections to the claims, and the court has entered an order allowing the claims. Many districts have local rules and procedures dealing with this aspect of chapter 13 cases. Payments to the holders of special classes of unsecured claims may begin earlier, however, if the plan so provides and if all claims in the class have been allowed. See Bankruptcy Rule 3021. It should be noted that payments of $15 or less may not be distributed by the chapter 13 trustee unless authorized by local rule or an order of the court. See Bankruptcy Rule 3010(b).

statute of limitations, effect of chapter 13 case

If a chapter 13 case is dismissed or if the debtor does not receive a discharge, the statute of limitations will not have expired on claims against the debtor or against codebtors protected under 11 U.S.C. 1301. 11 U.S.C. 108(c) provides that if applicable law, an order entered in a proceeding, or an agreement fixes a period for commencing a civil action in a court other than a bankruptcy court on a claim against the debtor, or against an individual with respect to which the individual is protected under 11 U.S.C 1301, and if such period has not expired before the filing of the petition, then such period does not expire until the later of - (1) the end of such period, including any suspensions of such period occurring on or after the commencement of the case, or (2) 30 days after notice of the termination or expiration of the automatic stay in the bankruptcy case with respect to such claim. Thus, the statute of limitations on claims against the debtor or a protected codebtor will expire either at the time it would have otherwise expired or 30 days after the order of discharge, the notice of no discharge, or the notice of dismissal of the case, whichever is later.

3.17 An Unsuccessful Chapter 13 Case - Dismissal or Conversion to Chapter 7

An unsuccessful chapter 13 case may either be dismissed or converted to a case under chapter 7, and such dismissal or conversion may be at the request of the debtor or upon the motion of a party in interest or the United States trustee. The debtor may, without cause, convert a chapter 13 case to a case under chapter 7 at any time, and any waiver of this right of conversion is unenforceable. See 11 U.S.C. 1307(a). If the case has not been converted to chapter 13 from another chapter, the court must dismiss a chapter 13 case at any time upon the request of the debtor, and any waiver of this right of dismissal by the debtor is unenforceable. See 11 U.S.C. 1307(b).
voluntary dismissal or conversion of case

Upon the motion of a party in interest or the United States trustee, and upon notice and a hearing, the court may, for cause, dismiss a chapter 13 case or convert it to a case under chapter 7, whichever is in the best interests of the creditors and the estate, except that the chapter 13 case of a farmer may not be converted to chapter 7 unless the debtor requests such conversion. See 11 U.S.C. 1307(c). Under 11 U.S.C. 1307(c), cause for involuntary dismissal or conversion may include:
involuntary dismissal or conversion of case, causes for

(1) unreasonable delay by the debtor that is prejudicial to the creditors;

(2) nonpayment of the filing fee;

(3) failure to timely file a plan;

(4) failure to commence making timely payments under the plan or proposed plan;

(5) denial of confirmation of a plan and denial of time for filing another plan or modifying the proposed plan;

(6) material default by the debtor with respect to a term of a confirmed plan;

(7) revocation of the order of confirmation and denial of confirmation of a modified plan;

(8) termination of a confirmed plan by reason of the occurrence of a condition specified in the plan, other than the completion of payments under the plan; or

(9) only on the motion of the United States trustee, failure to timely file the schedules and other information required by 11 U.S.C. 521(1).

If the debtor dies or becomes incompetent during the pendency of a chapter 13 case, the case may be dismissed. However, if further administration is possible and in the best interest of the parties, the case may proceed in rem and be concluded in the same manner, so far as possible, as though the death or incompetency had not occurred. See Bankruptcy Rule 1016.
death or incompetency of debtor, procedure

At any time before confirmation of a plan, on the motion of a party in interest, and after notice and a hearing, the court may convert a chapter 13 case to a case under chapter 11 or chapter 12, if the debtor qualifies as a debtor under such chapter, except that the chapter 13 case of a farmer may be converted only on the request of the debtor. See 11 U.S.C. 1307(d),(e),(f). A farmer is defined as a person who received more than 80 percent of his or her gross income during the tax year preceding the year in which the case was filed from a farming operation that was owned or operated by such person. See 11 U.S.C. 101(19). A debtor who converts a chapter 13 case to a case under chapter 11 must pay a $400 filing fee. See 28 U.S.C. 1930(a).
conversion of case to chapter 11 or 12

Except for the above-described right of the debtor to dismiss a chapter 13 case without cause under 11 U.S.C. 1307(b), a chapter 13 case may not be dismissed on the motion of the debtor, for want of prosecution, by consent of the parties, or for any other cause, prior to a hearing on notice to all creditors, a list of which, if not previously filed, must be provided by the debtor within the time fixed by the court. See Bankruptcy Rule 1017(a).
dismissal of case, notice and hearing requirements

dismissal for nonpayment of filing fee, procedure

After a hearing on notice to the debtor and the chapter 13 trustee, the court may dismiss a chapter 13 case for failure to pay any installment of the filing fee. See Bankruptcy Rule 1017(b)(1). Within 30 days after a dismissal for failure to pay the filing fee, notice of the dismissal must be mailed by the clerk to all creditors appearing on the list of creditors and to those who have filed claims. See Bankruptcy Rule 1017(b)(3).

involuntary dismissal or conversion, procedure

The procedure for the involuntary dismissal or conversion of a chapter 13 case is governed by Bankruptcy Rule 9014. See Bankruptcy Rule 1017(d). The party seeking dismissal or conversion must file a motion and give the debtor reasonable notice and an opportunity for a hearing. See Bankruptcy Rule 9014. The motion must set forth the relief or order sought and must state with particularity the grounds therefor. The motion should be served by the moving party on the chapter 13 trustee, the debtor, the United States trustee, and such other persons as the court may direct. See Bankruptcy Rules 9013, 9034, and 5005(b), which requires verification of transmittal to the United States trustee. A written response to the motion is not required unless ordered by the court. See Bankruptcy Rule 9014.

voluntary conversion to chapter 7, procedure

To voluntarily convert a chapter 13 case to a case under chapter 7, the debtor need only file a notice of conversion under 11 U.S.C. 1307(a) with the court. A court order is not required because the conversion occurs upon the filing of the notice. See Bankruptcy Rule 1017(d). A sample Notice of Conversion of Case to Chapter 7 Under Section 1307(a) is set forth in Exhibit 3-H at the end of this chapter.

voluntary dismissal, procedure

The voluntary dismissal of a chapter 13 case by the debtor under 11 U.S.C. 1307(b) is effected by the filing and service of a motion under Bankruptcy Rule 9013. See Bankruptcy Rule 1017(d). A copy of the motion should be served on the chapter 13 trustee, the United States trustee, and on such other entities as the court may direct. See Bankruptcy Rules 9013 and 9034. A hearing on the motion is not required unless the court so directs. See Advisory Committee's Notes to Bankruptcy Rule 1017(d). A sample Motion to Dismiss Case Under Section 1307(b) is set forth in Exhibit 3-I at the end of this chapter.

dismissal of case, effect of

Unless the court, for cause, orders otherwise, the dismissal of a chapter 13 case does not bar the discharge in a later title 11 case of debts that were dischargeable in the case dismissed. See 11 U.S.C. 349(a). Unless the court, for cause, orders otherwise, the dismissal of a chapter 13 case: (1) reinstates any proceeding superseded by the case, reinstates certain transfers avoided or preserved in the case, and reinstates certain liens avoided in the case, (2) vacates certain orders, judgments, or transfers ordered in the case, and (3) revests the property of the estate in the entity in which such property was vested immediately before the commencement of the case. See 11 U.S.C. 349(b). The dismissal of the case also causes the debtor to lose the postcase benefit of any exemptions claimed in the case, including the federal bankruptcy exemptions. See 11 U.S.C. 522(c). The dismissal of the case also terminates the automatic stay. See 11 U.S.C. 362(c)(2), 1301(a)(2).

conversion to chapter 7, effect of

The procedure for converting a chapter 13 case to chapter 7 is governed by 11 U.S.C. 348 and Bankruptcy Rule 1019, together with any applicable local rules. The conversion of a chapter 13 case to a case under chapter 7 constitutes an order for relief under chapter 7, but, with only limited exceptions, does not change the dates of the filing of the petition, the commencement of the case, or the order for relief. See 11 U.S.C. 348(a). Within 20 days after the entry of such an order, the clerk or some other person as the court may direct must mail notice of the order converting a chapter 13 case to chapter 7 to the debtor, the United States trustee, and all creditors. See Bankruptcy Rules 2002(f) and 9022.

conversion to chapter 7, procedure

All lists, inventories, schedules, and statements of financial affairs filed in the chapter 13 case shall be deemed filed in the chapter 7 case, unless the court directs otherwise. If such documents have not been previously filed, they must be filed by the debtor within 15 days after entry of the order converting the case to chapter 7. See Bankruptcy Rule 1019(1)(A). A statement of intention, if required, must be filed within 30 days after the entry of the order for relief under chapter 7 or before the first date set for the meeting of creditors, whichever is earlier. See Bankruptcy Rule 1019(1)(B).

All claims filed in the chapter 13 case shall be deemed filed in the chapter 7 case. See Bankruptcy Rule 1019(3). New time periods are commenced for the filing of claims, complaints objecting to discharge, and complaints to determine the dischargeability of debts, except that if a chapter 7 case has been converted to chapter 13 and is thereafter reconverted to chapter 7, and if the time for filing claims or such complaints had expired in the original chapter 7 case, the time for filing is not revived or extended unless the court, for cause, had extended the time on a motion filed before the original time had expired. See Bankruptcy Rule 1019(2).

The conversion of a chapter 13 case to chapter 7 terminates the services of the chapter 13 trustee. See 11 U.S.C. 348(e). After the qualification of, or the assumption of duties by, the trustee in the chapter 7 case, the chapter 13 trustee must forthwith turn over to the chapter 7 trustee all records and property of the estate in the possession and control of the chapter 13 trustee, unless the court orders otherwise. See Bankruptcy Rule 1019(4). Unless the court directs otherwise, the chapter 13 trustee must file with the clerk and transmit to the United States trustee a final report and account within 30 days after the entry of the order of conversion. Within 15 days after the order of conversion, the debtor must file a schedule of unpaid debts incurred after the commencement of the chapter 13 case. If the conversion to chapter 7 occurred after confirmation of the chapter 13 plan, the debtor must file with the court a schedule of property acquired after the filing of the original petition and before the order of conversion, a schedule of postpetition debts that were not included in the final report and account, and a schedule of executory contracts and unexpired leases entered into or assumed after the filing of the original petition and before the entry of the conversion order. See Bankruptcy Rule 1019(5).

A claim against the debtor or the estate that arises after the order for relief in the chapter 13 case and prior to the conversion of the case, other than certain claims for administrative expenses, is treated as if the claim has arisen immediately before the filing of the petition. See 11 U.S.C. 348(d). Upon the filing of a schedule of postpetition debts, written notice must be given to the holders of such claims that their claims may be filed within 60 days. The court must also fix the time, if any, for filing claims arising from other debts or from the rejection of executory contracts or unexpired leases. See Bankruptcy Rule 1019(6).

3.18 The Chapter 13 Discharges

As soon as practicable after the completion by the debtor of all payments under the plan, the court must grant the debtor a discharge under 11 U.S.C. 1328(a), unless the court approves a written waiver of discharge executed by the debtor after the order for relief under chapter 13. A Section 1328(a) discharge is granted by the court as a matter of course without application upon the completion of all payments under the plan. A Section 1328(a) discharge is considerably broader than either a chapter 7 discharge or a Section 1328(b) discharge. A Section 1328(a) discharge, which is a full chapter 13 discharge, discharges a debtor from all debts except:

(1) debts not provided for by the plan, other than debts for disallowed claims;

(2) debts for alimony, maintenance or support as provided in 11 U.S.C. 523(a)(5);

(3) debts for student loans or educational benefits unless the loan or benefit first became due more than 7 years (exclusive of any applicable suspension of the repayment period) before the date the petition was filed or unless excepting the debt from discharge will impose an undue hardship on the debtor and the debtor's dependents;

(4) debts for death or personal injury caused by the debtor's operation of a motor vehicle while unlawfully intoxicated;

(5) debts for restitution included in a criminal sentence imposed on the debtor;

(6) debts whose last payment is due after the date of the final payment under the plan; and

(7) postpetition debts not allowed under 11 U.S.C. 1305, and allowed postpetition consumer debts, the prior approval of which by the trustee was practicable and was not obtained.

It should be noted that while debts for priority claims are dischargeable under Section 1328(a), the discharge of such debts is largely illusory because priority claims must be paid in full under a chapter 13 plan, unless the creditor agrees otherwise. See 11 U.S.C. 1322(a)(2). Priority claims include most tax claims, claims for certain refunds, and, within certain limits, claims for wages, salaries, commissions, and employee benefits. See 11 U.S.C. 507(a). Debts for student loans and educational benefits are dischargeable under chapter 13 to the same extent that they are dischargeable under chapter 7. See section 2.17, supra, for a discussion of the dischargeability of such debts.

A narrower (or partial) discharge may be granted under 11 U.S.C. 1328(b) to a debtor who is unable to complete the payments required under the plan. At any time after confirmation of the plan, and after notice and a hearing, the court may grant a discharge under Section 1328(b) to a debtor who has not completed payments under the plan if - (1) the debtor's failure to complete such payments is due to circumstances for which the debtor should not justly be held accountable, (2) the value of the property actually distributed under the plan on the account of each allowed unsecured claim is not less than the amount that would have been paid on such claim had the debtor filed under chapter 7, and (3) modification of the plan is not practicable.

A Section 1328(b) discharge discharges a debtor from all debts except:

(1) secured debts;

(2) unsecured debts not provided for in the plan, other than debts for disallowed unsecured claims;

(3) unsecured debts whose last payment is due after the date of the final payment under the plan;

(4) postpetition debts not allowed under 11 U.S.C. 1305, and allowed postpetition consumer debts, the prior approval of which by the trustee was practicable and was not obtained.

(5) debts specified in 11 U.S.C. 523(a) (i.e., those not dischargeable under chapter 7 - see section 2.17, supra, for a list).

It is apparent that a Section 1328(b) discharge is not as broad as a chapter 7 discharge. Therefore, if a debtor has debts that are not dischargeable under Section 1328(b), but which are dischargeable under chapter 7, it may be advisable to convert the chapter 13 case to chapter 7 rather than obtaining a discharge under Section 1328(b). Before converting a chapter 13 case to chapter 7, however, it should be ascertained whether the debtor has any valuable nonexempt property that would be lost if the case was converted to chapter 7. It should be noted that the debtor may file a complaint at any time to determine the dischargeability of any debt, including a postpetition debt, under either chapter 13 or chapter 7. See Bankruptcy Rule 4007(b). The conversion of a chapter 13 case to chapter 7 is discussed in section 3.17, supra.

section 1328(b) discharge vs. chapter 7 discharge

To obtain a Section 1328(b) discharge, the debtor must file a motion requesting that the discharge be granted. A sample of such a motion is set forth in Exhibit 3-J at the end of this chapter. Upon the filing of a motion by the debtor for a discharge under Section 1328(b), the court must enter an order fixing a time for the filing of complaints to determine the dischargeability of debts pursuant to 11 U.S.C. 523(c) and giving not less than 30 days notice of the time so fixed to all creditors. See Bankruptcy Rule 4007(d). Notice of the filing of the debtor's motion for a Section 1328(b) discharge must also be given. The local rules may also contain provisions dealing with the filing of such motions. If a complaint is filed either objecting to the discharge of the debtor or to determine the dischargeability of a debt, the proceeding thereunder is governed by Part VII of the Rules of Bankruptcy Procedure. See Bankruptcy Rules 4004(d), 4007(e), and 7001. See section 2.17, supra, for further reading.

section 1328(b) discharge, procedure

Regardless of whether a chapter 13 discharge is granted under Section 1328(a) or Section 1328(b), within 30 days following the grant or denial of a discharge and on not less than 10 days notice to the debtor and the trustee, the court may hold a discharge and reaffirmation hearing, which the debtor must attend if a discharge is denied or if a dischargeable debt is being reaffirmed under 11 U.S.C. 524(c). See 11 U.S.C. 524(d) and Bankruptcy Rule 4008. The local rules may also contain provisions dealing with discharge and reaffirmation hearings. See section 2.18, supra, for further reading on the reaffirmation of dischargeable debts.

discharge and reaffirmation hearing

The order of discharge must conform substantially to Official Form 18. See Bankruptcy Rule 4004(e). It will be similar to Exhibit 2-X at the end of chapter 2, supra, appropriately modified in accordance with the type of discharge granted. The clerk must promptly mail a copy of the final order of discharge to all creditors, the United States trustee, and the trustee. See Bankruptcy Rule 4004(g). If so desired, a final order of discharge may be registered in another district by filing a certified copy of the order with the clerk of the bankruptcy court in the other district. When so registered, the order of discharge has the same effect as an order of the court in the district where it is registered. See Bankruptcy Rule 4004(f).

order of discharge, form, notice

On the request of a party in interest made within one year after a chapter 13 discharge is granted, and after notice and a hearing, the court may revoke a chapter 13 discharge if the discharge was obtained by the debtor through fraud and the requesting party did not know of the fraud until after the discharge was granted. See 11 U.S.C. 1328(e). A proceeding to revoke a chapter 13 discharge must be initiated by the filing of a complaint and the proceedings thereunder are governed by Part VII of the Rules of Bankruptcy Procedure. See Bankruptcy Rule 7001. If an order is entered denying or revoking a discharge, or if a waiver of discharge is filed and approved by the court, the clerk must promptly mail a notice of no discharge to all creditors. See Bankruptcy Rule 4006.

revocation of discharge, grounds, procedure

notice of denial or revocation of discharge

Regardless of whether a chapter 13 discharge is granted under Section 1328(a) or Section 1328(b), the debtor will not be eligible for a chapter 7 discharge for six years from the date of filing of the chapter 13 case unless the payments made under the plan totalled at least - (1) 100 percent of the allowed unsecured claims, or (2) 70 percent of such claims and the plan was proposed by the debtor in good faith and was the debtor's best effort. See 11 U.S.C. 727(a)(9). See section 2.17, supra, for a discussion of the effect of a discharge on the debts and liabilities of the debtor and of the debtor's responsibilities should a creditor later attempt to collect a discharged debt. The effect of a discharge on community debts in community property states is discussed in section 2.17, supra.

eligibility of debtor for chapter 7 discharge

effect of discharge

Appeals in chapter 13 cases, as in all title 11 cases, are governed by 28 U.S.C. 158 and Part VIII of the Rules of Bankruptcy Procedure. Final judgments, orders, and decrees of bankruptcy judges may be appealed as of right, while interlocutory orders may be appealed only with leave of the appellate court. Appeals from orders, judgments, and decrees of bankruptcy judges must be taken to the district court unless a bankruptcy appellate panel has been established in the local circuit and appeals thereto have been authorized in the local district. Even if appeals to the bankruptcy appellate panel have been authorized locally, an appeal to the panel may be taken only with the consent of all parties to the appeal. See 11 U.S.C. 158.

3.19 Closing a Chapter 13 Case

Ninety days after the final distribution under a chapter 13 plan, the chapter 13 trustee must stop payment on any check remaining unpaid, and any remaining property of the estate must be paid into the court and disposed of under chapter 129 of title 28. See 11 U.S.C. 347(a). The chapter 13 trustee must file with the clerk a list of the names and addresses of all known persons entitled to be paid under chapter 129 of title 28, together with the amounts that they are entitled to be paid from the remaining property of the estate that is paid into the court under 11 U.S.C. 347(a). See Bankruptcy Rule 3011.

When the administration of the estate has been completed, the chapter 13 trustee must make a final report and file a final account of the administration of the estate with the court. See 11 U.S.C. 1302(b)(1), 704(9). If the trustee files a final report and final account and certifies that the estate has been fully administered, and if no objection thereto is filed within 30 days by the United States trustee or a party in interest, it is presumed that the estate has been fully administered. See Bankruptcy Rule 5009. The local rules often contain procedures governing the closing of chapter 13 cases. Normally, a chapter 13 case is closed as a matter of course without the assistance of the debtor or the debtor's attorney. A copy or summary of the trustee's final report or final accounting is customarily sent to the debtor and the debtor's attorney.

After the estate has been fully administered, including the return or distribution of any deposit required by the plan, the court must enter a final decree discharging the chapter 13 trustee and closing the case. See 11 U.S.C. 350(a). The closing of the case terminates the automatic stay to the extent that it was not earlier terminated. See 11 U.S.C. 362(c)(2), 1301(a)(2).

Upon the motion of the debtor or other party in interest, a chapter 13 case may be reopened in the court in which the case was closed to administer assets, to accord relief to the debtor, or for other cause. See 11 U.S.C. 350(b). If a chapter 13 case is reopened, a trustee shall not be appointed by the United States trustee unless the court determines that a trustee is necessary to protect the interests of creditors and the debtor or to insure an efficient administration of the case. See Bankruptcy Rule 5010.

EXHIBIT 3-A   169

UNITED STATES BANKRUPTCY COURT
CENTRAL DISTRICT OF CALIFORNIA

IN RE   John Paul Jones and   )
        Shirley Ann Jones   )   Case No. 92B-13-0066
)
                          Debtors   )   Chapter 13

APPLICATION FOR ALLOWANCE OF COMPENSATION

The undersigned attorney for the debtors states and represents as follows:

1. The total fee to be charged by the attorney for legal services rendered or to be rendered for the debtors in this bankruptcy case, exclusive of costs, is $800.00, of which none has been paid, leaving a balance of $800.00.

2. The source of the compensation paid or to be paid is the debtors, which compensation shall, by agreement with the debtors, be paid by the Chapter 13 trustee as a priority administrative claim in the bankruptcy case, upon approval thereof by the court.

3. The attorney has filed a document entitled Disclosure of Compensation of Attorney for Debtor with the court, the provisions of which are incorporated by reference in this application.

4. The legal services rendered or to be rendered by the attorney in connection with this bankruptcy case include the following:

Examining and analyzing the debtor's financial situation and advising the debtors thereon.

Preparing and filing the petition, schedules, statements, plan and other necessary documents and pleadings in the case.

Representing the debtors at the meeting of creditors, the confirmation hearing, and all other court hearings in the case.

Assisting the debtors in obtaining confirmation of the debtors' plan and in carrying out and consummating the plan.

5. The undersigned attorney is admitted to practice before this court and in the state of California, maintains a law practice at the address shown below on this application, is a disinterested person with respect to this bankruptcy case and does not hold or represent an interest adverse to the estate with respect to the matter for which the attorney has been employed, and is competent and experienced in the handling of Chapter 13 bankruptcy cases.

WHEREFORE, the undersigned attorney respectfully applies for allowance of the compensation described above in this application and requests that the unpaid balance of such compensation be approved by the court as a priority administrative claim in the case, to be paid by the Chapter 13 trustee out of the funds deposited with the trustee by the debtor.

Dated: January 5, 1992

_____
John T. Smith
Attorney for Debtors
6200 Wilshire Blvd.   Suite 3333
Los Angeles, CA 90012
Telephone: 213-344-7666

CERTIFICATE OF TRANSMITTAL BY MAIL

The undersigned certifies under penalty of perjury that he or she has on the date shown below, by first class mail addressed to their respective addresses of record, transmitted a true copy of this document to the United States trustee and the Chapter 13 trustee.

Date: _____   _____

UNITED STATES BANKRUPTCY COURT
CENTRAL DISTRICT OF CALIFORNIA

IN RE   John Paul Jones and   )
         Shirley Ann Jones   )   Case No. 92B-13-0066
)
                         Debtors   )   Chapter 13

CHAPTER 13 PLAN

I. PROPERTY AND FUTURE EARNINGS.

1. The debtors submit the following property and future earnings to the supervision and control of the trustee:

Future earnings: $520.00 per month for the duration of the plan.
Other property: federal income tax refund in the amount of $650.00.

II. DURATION OF PLAN.

1. The payments shall be made by or on behalf of the debtors to the trustee for a period of 36 months.

III. CLASSIFICATION AND TREATMENT OF CLAIMS.

1. Priority claims. The following claims are entitled to priority under section 507 of the Bankruptcy Code in the following amounts:

Trustee's compensation	$ 1,433.00
Attorney's Fees, debtors' attorney	800.00
Tax claim, City of Los Angeles	555.00
	$ 3,292.00

2. Claims dealt with in the plan that are secured only by real estate constituting the debtors' principal residence: None.

3. Secured or unsecured claims dealt with in the plan on which the last payment is due after the date on which the final payment under the plan is due: None.

4. Other allowed secured claims dealt with in the plan:

Big Bank of Santa Monica   base amount $205.00 per mo. for 36 mos.
                                default amount $61.00 per mo. for 9 mos.
                        (includes interest at 10% per annum on default)

Last Mortgage Company   base amount $110.50 per mo. for 36 months
                        (includes interest at 12% per annum)

EXHIBIT 3-B   171

5. Other allowed unsecured claims dealt with in the plan. The other allowed unsecured claims will be divided into two classes: Class A and Class B.

Class A claims will consist of the following claim -

Veronica L. Jones, support arrearage claim - $52.00 per mo. for 16 mos.
(this claim will be paid in full, with no interest)

Class B claims will consist of all other unsecured claims, which shall share pro rata the sum of $3,339.00, which will constitute the payment of approximately 32% of the anticipated total of such claims.

IV. OTHER PROVISIONS.

1. The monthly support claim of Veronica L. Jones, and the claim of Federal Mortgage Company, which is secured by the debtors' residence, shall be paid outside the plan.

2. Insurance to protect the liens of creditors holding secured claims will not be provided under the plan.

3. The effective date of this plan will be the date of the order confirming the plan.

4. Property of the estate will vest in the debtors at the time of confirmation of the plan, unless otherwise stated in the order confirming the plan.

5. The payments by the debtors will be made directly to the trustee by the husband's employer, Royal Sales Company, beginning with the first pay period following the issuance of the order confirming the plan. The federal income tax refund will be deposited with the trustee immediately upon the receipt thereof by the debtors.

6. Payments on the secured claims and the Class A unsecured claim shall begin as soon as funds therefor are received by the trustee. The priority claims shall be paid as soon as funds are available therefor, after the payment of secured and Class A unsecured claims.

Dated: January 20, 1992

_____
John Paul Jones, debtor

_____
Shirley Ann Jones, debtor

_____
John T. Smith
Attorney for Debtors
6200 Wilshire Blvd.   Suite 3333
Los Angeles, CA 90012
Telephone: 213-344-7666

FORM B91 6/90 United States Bankruptcy Court NORTHERN DISTRICT OF FLORIDA Case Number: 91-0241	NOTICE OF COMMENCEMENT OF CASE UNDER CHAPTER 13 OF THE BANKRUPTCY CODE, MEETING OF CREDITORS, AND FIXING OF DATES

In re (Name of Debtor)
 	
COGBURN, ROOSTER D.
 	
COGBURN, DIXIE M.
  AKA COGBURN, DIXIE MAY
  AKA COGBURN, DIXIE SMITH
	Address of Debtor
	1720 W. 18TH STREET
	PANAMA CITY, FL 32405
	
	Date Filed
	November 19, 1991
		Soc. Sec./Tax ID Nos.
		612-32-3985
		
		277-90-1234

Addressee:	Address of the Clerk of the Bankruptcy Court 227 N. Bronough St, Room 3120, Tallahassee, FL 32301

Name and Address of Attorney for Debtor William B. Jones 700 Magnolia Avenue Panama City, FL 32401	Telephone Number (904) 773-5368	Name and Address of Trustee David Rogers 100 Peachtree St., #850 Atlanta, GA 30303	Telephone Number (800) 825-1973

FILING CLAIMS
Deadline to file a proof of claim: April 6, 1992

DATE, TIME, AND LOCATION OF MEETING OF CREDITORS
January 6, 1992, 1:00 P.M., 30 W. Government St., Panama City, FL

FILING OF PLAN AND DATE, TIME, AND LOCATION OF HEARING ON CONFIRMATION OF PLAN
A plan has not been filed as of this date. Creditors will be given separate notice of the hearing on confirmation of the plan.

COMMENCEMENT OF CASE. An individual's debt adjustment case under chapter 13 of the Bankruptcy Code has been filed in this court by the debtor or debtors named above, and an order for relief has been entered. You will not receive notice of all documents filed in this case. All documents filed with the court, including lists of the debtor's property and debts, are available for inspection at the office of the clerk of the bankruptcy court.

CREDITORS MAY NOT TAKE CERTAIN ACTIONS. A creditor is anyone to whom the debtor owes money. Under the Bankruptcy Code, the debtor is granted certain protection against creditors. Common examples of prohibited actions by creditors are contacting the debtor to demand repayment, taking action against the debtor to collect money owed to creditors or to take property of the debtor, and starting or continuing foreclosure actions, repossessions, or wage deductions. Some protection is also given to certain codebtors of consumer debts. If unauthorized actions are taken by a creditor against a debtor, or a protected codebtor, the court may penalize that creditor. A creditor who is considering taking action against the debtor or the property of the debtor, or any codebtor, should review §§ 362 and 1301 of the Bankruptcy Code and may wish to seek legal advice. The staff of the clerk of the bankruptcy court is not permitted to give legal advice.

MEETING OF CREDITORS. The debtor (both husband and wife in a joint case) is required to appear at the meeting of creditors on the date and at the place set forth above in the box labeled "Date, Time, and Location of Meeting of Creditors" for the purpose of being examined under oath. Attendance by creditors at the meeting is welcomed, but not required. At the meeting, the creditors may examine the debtor and transact such other business as may properly come before the meeting. The meeting may be continued or adjourned from time to time by notice at the meeting, without further written notice to the creditors.

PROOF OF CLAIM. Except as otherwise provided by law, in order to share in any payment from the estate, a creditor must file a proof of claim by the date set forth above in the box labeled "Filing Claims." The place to file the proof of claim, either in person or by mail, is the office of the clerk of the bankruptcy court. Proof of claim forms are available in the clerk's office of any bankruptcy court.

PURPOSE OF A CHAPTER 13 FILING. Chapter 13 of the Bankruptcy Code is designed to enable a debtor to pay debts in full or in part over a period of time pursuant to a plan. A plan is not effective unless approved by the bankruptcy court at a confirmation hearing. Creditors will be given notice in the event the case is dismissed or converted to another chapter of the Bankruptcy Code.

Pursuant to 11 U.S.C. Sec. 554(a) the Trustee will abandon at Sec. 341 meeting of creditors all property determined to be burdensome or of inconsequential value to the estate. Any objections to the above abandonments shall be filed within fifteen (15) days after the conclusion of the meeting. (Secured property will not be abandoned at the meeting absent proof of perfection provided to the trustee prior to the meeting.)

CLERK
BANKRUPTCY COURT
NORTH/DIST-FLA

For the Court: LARRY A. PACE Clerk of the Bankruptcy Court	November 21, 1991 Date

91 NOV 21 PM 2:37

CREDITORS FILING CLAIMS MUST FILE THE ORIGINAL CLAIM WITH THE CLERK, BANKRUPTCY COURT; A COPY MUST THEN BE SERVED ON THE TRUSTEE AT THE ADDRESS LISTED ABOVE.

FILED

EXHIBIT 3-D   173

UNITED STATES BANKRUPTCY COURT
CENTRAL DISTRICT OF CALIFORNIA

IN RE   John Paul Jones and   )
           Shirley Ann Jones   )   Case No. 92B-13-0066
)
                   Debtors   )   Chapter 13

ORDER CONFIRMING CHAPTER 13 PLAN

The court finds that the debtors' plan was timely filed on January 20, 1992 and was modified on January 30, 1992; that a summary of the plan, or a summary of the final modification of the plan, was transmitted to the creditors as provided in Bankruptcy Rule 3015; and that the plan as modified satisfied the requirements of section 1325 of the Bankruptcy Code;

IT IS ORDERED THAT:

The debtors' plan be and hereby is confirmed, with the following provisions:

1. Payments:

    Amount of each periodic payment: $520.00

    Due date of each periodic payment: The 5th day of each month.

    Period of periodic payments: 36 months.

Payable to:

Joseph F. Smith
Standing Trustee
1233 East Fifth Avenue
Los Angeles, CA 90027

Payroll Deduction:

☒ Unless previously ordered, the debtor's employer is ordered to deduct payments from the debtor's earnings, draw checks in the name of the standing trustee, and deliver or mail the same to the standing trustee on or before each due date until further order of this court.

☐ No payroll deduction is ordered.

2. Attorney's Fees:

    The debtors' attorney is awarded a fee in the amount of $800.00, of which $800.00 is due and payable from the estate.

3. Miscellaneous Provisions:

    The debtors shall transmit the entire amount of their 1991 federal income tax refund to the standing trustee, pursuant to the confirmed plan.

Date: February 20, 1992

                                      _____
                                      United States Bankruptcy Judge

UNITED STATES BANKRUPTCY COURT
CENTRAL DISTRICT OF CALIFORNIA

IN RE   John Paul Jones and   )
            Shirley Ann Jones   )   Case No. 92B-13-0066
)
                    Debtors   )   Chapter 13

MOTION TO MODIFY CHAPTER 13 PLAN AFTER CONFIRMATION

The debtors by their attorney, state and represent as follows:

1. That since confirmation of their Chapter 13 plan on February 20, 1992, the debtor John Paul Jones has suffered a loss of income in the average monthly amount of $100.00 as a result of a decrease in sales by The Royal Sales Company, the company by whom the debtor is employed as a commission salesman.

2. That because of the reduction in the amount of income, the debtors are no longer able to pay the sum of $520.00 per month as required in the present Chapter 13 plan, but are able to pay the sum of $450.00 per month and propose, in the modified Chapter 13 plan, to extend the time for payments under the plan from 36 months to 40 months in order to compensate for the reduction in the amount of the monthly payment.

3. That the modification proposed by the debtor will not modify the rights of the holder of any secured claim being dealt with under the plan, and will modify the rights of only the holders of allowed Class B unsecured claims to the extent that the time of payment of their respective claims will be extended.

4. That a copy of the debtor's modified Chapter 13 plan dated May 11, 1992 is attached to this motion and that a copy of same, together with a copy of this motion, has been sent to the Chapter 13 trustee, the United States trustee and the holders of all allowed Class B unsecured claims.

WHEREFORE, the debtor moves this honorable court, to enter an order confirming the debtor's modified Chapter 13 plan dated May 11, 1992.

Date: May 11, 1992.

                                          _____
                                          John T. Smith
                                          Attorney for Debtors
                                          6200 Wilshire Blvd.   Suite 3333
                                          Los Angeles, CA 90012
                                          Telephone: 213-344-7666

CERTIFICATE OF TRANSMITTAL AND SERVICE BY MAIL

The undersigned certifies under penalty of perjury that he or she has, on the date shown below, by first class mail addressed to their respective addresses of record in this case, transmitted and served a true copy of this document to the United States trustee, the Chapter 13 trustee, and the holder of each allowed Class B unsecured claim.

Date: _____   _____

EXHIBIT 3-F   175

UNITED STATES BANKRUPTCY COURT
CENTRAL DISTRICT OF CALIFORNIA

IN RE   John Paul Jones and   )
        Shirley Ann Jones   )   Case No. 92B-13-0066
)
                                Debtors   )   Chapter 13

REQUEST FOR TRUSTEE'S PRIOR APPROVAL OF CONSUMER DEBT

The debtors, by their attorney, hereby request the Chapter 13 trustee's prior approval of the following consumer debt for the reasons set forth below:

1.   The debt for which the Chapter 13 trustee's prior approval is sought is a proposed debt to the Friendly Finance Company for funds with which to purchase a used 1990 Buick Regal automobile.

2.   The debtors' previous automobile was recently damaged in an accident and the cost of repairing the automobile would far exceed its value.

3.   The debtors have made arrangements for the purchase of a 1990 Buick Regal automobile I.D. No. 333935JK33P884 from Better Buy Used Cars, 3333 Broadway, Inglewood, California for the price of $10,700.00. $2,000.00 of the purchase price will be paid from the proceeds of the insurance on the debtor's previous automobile, and the debtors propose to borrow $8,700.00 from the Friendly Finance Company to pay the balance of the purchase price of the automobile.

4.   The proposed loan from Friendly Finance Company will be payable at the rate of $100.00 per month for the duration of the plan and at the rate of $350.00 per month thereafter. The annual interest rate on the loan shall be 18 percent, and the debtors propose to pay the debt as a secured claim under the modified Chapter 13 plan and to reaffirm the unpaid balance of the claim upon completion of the plan.

5.   The debtors need the automobile that is proposed to be purchased in order to maintain employment and continue performance under the Chapter 13 plan. The debtors will be able to maintain the Chapter 13 payments after the incurrence of the debt to Friendly Finance Company.

Dated: April 1, 1992   _____
                                             John Paul Jones, debtor

_____
John T. Smith   _____
Attorney for Debtors   Shirley Ann Jones, debtor
6200 Wilshire Blvd.   Suite 3333
Los Angeles, CA 90012
Telephone: 213-344-7666

Debt approved: _____
                        Chapter 13 Trustee   Date

Debt disapproved: _____
                        Chapter 13 Trustee   Date

United States Bankruptcy Court	PROOF OF CLAIM
Central _____ District of California	

In re (Name of Debtor)	Case Number
	92B-13-0066

NOTE: This form should not be used to make a claim for an administrative expense arising after the commencement of the case. A request for payment of an administrative expense may be filed pursuant to 11 U.S.C. § 503.

Name of Creditor (The person or other entity to whom the debtor owes money or property)	☐ Check box if you are aware that anyone else has filed a proof of claim relating to your claim. Attach copy or statement giving particulars.
Western Supply Company	
Name and Address Where Notices Should Be Sent	☐ Check box if you never received any notices from the bankruptcy court in the case.
Western Supply Company 2070 Garrison Street Columbus, OH 43218	☐ Check box if this address differs from the address on the envelope sent to you by the court.
Telephone No. 614-319-7722	THIS SPACE IS FOR COURT USE ONLY

ACCOUNT OR OTHER NUMBER BY WHICH CREDITOR IDENTIFIES DEBTOR. 89-713972	Check here if the claim ☐ replaces ☐ amends } a previously filed claim dated _____

1. BASIS FOR CLAIM

☒ Goods sold
☐ Services performed
☐ Money loaned
☐ Personal injury/wrongful death
☐ Taxes
☐ Other (Describe briefly)

☐ Retiree benefits as defined in 11 U.S.C. § 1114(a)
☐ Wage, salaries, and commissions (Fill out below)
Your social security number_____
Unpaid compensation for services performed
from _____ to _____
(date)   (date)

2. DATE DEBT WAS INCURRED May 24, 1990	3. IF COURT JUDGEMENT, DATE OBTAINED: None

4. CLASSIFICATION OF CLAIM. Under the Bankruptcy Code all claims are classified as one or more of the following: (1) Unsecured nonpriority, (2) Unsecured Priority, (3) Secured. It is possible for part of a claim to be in one category and part in another.

CHECK THE APPROPRIATE BOX OR BOXES that best describe your claim and STATE THE AMOUNT OF THE CLAIM.

☐ SECURED CLAIM $ _____

Attach evidence of perfection of security interest

Brief Description of Collateral

☐ Real Estate   ☐ Motor Vehicle   ☐ Other (Describe briefly)

Amount of arrearage and other charges included in secured claim above, if any

$ _____

☒ UNSECURED NONPRIORITY CLAIM $ _772.00_____

A claim is unsecured if there is no collateral or lien on property of the debtor securing the claim or to the extent that the value of such property is less than the amount of the claim.)

☐ UNSECURED PRIORITY CLAIM $ _____

Specify the priority of the claim.

☐ Wages, salaries, or commissions (up to $2000, earned not more than 90 days before filing of the bankruptcy petition or cessation of the debtor's business, whichever is earlier) - 11 U.S.C. § 507(a)(3)

☐ Contributions to an employee benefit plan - 11 U.S.C. § 507(a)(4)

☐ Up to $900 of deposits toward purchase, lease or rental of property, or purchase of services, for personal, family, or household use - 11 U.S.C. § 507(a)(6)

☐ Taxes or penalties of governmental units - 11 U.S.C. § 507(a)(7)

☐ Other - 11 U.S.C. §§ 507(a)(5) - (Describe briefly)

5. TOTAL AMOUNT OF CLAIM AT TIME CASE FILED:	$772.00 (Unsecured)	$_____ (Secured)	$_____ (Priority)	$772.00 (Total)

☐ Check this box if claim includes prepetition charges in addition to the principal amount of the claim. Attach itemized statement of all additional charges.

6. CREDITS AND SETOFFS: The amount of all payments on this claim has been credited and deducted for the purpose of making this proof of claim. In filing this claim, claimant has deducted all amounts that claimant owes to debtor.

THIS SPACE IS FOR
COURT USE ONLY

7. SUPPORTING DOCUMENTS: Attach copies of supporting documents, such as promissory notes, purchase orders, invoices, itemized statements of running accounts, contracts, court judgments, or evidence of security interests. If the documents are not available, explain. If the documents are voluminous, attach a summary.

8. TIME-STAMPED COPY: To receive an acknowledgment of the filing of your claim, enclose a stamped, self-addressed envelope and copy of this proof of claim.

Date January 30, 1992	Sign and print the name and title, if any, of the creditor or other person authorized to file this claim (attach copy of power of attorney, if any) *James F. Stone* James F. Stone, Credit Manager

Penalty for Presenting Fraudulent Claim: Fine of up to $500,000 or imprisonment for up to 5 years, or both. 18 U.S.C. §§ 152 and 3571.

EXHIBIT 3-H   177

UNITED STATES BANKRUPTCY COURT
CENTRAL DISTRICT OF CALIFORNIA

IN RE   John Paul Jones and   )
Shirley Ann Jones   )   Case No. 92B-13-0066
)
Debtors   )   Chapter 13

NOTICE OF CONVERSION OF CASE TO CHAPTER 7 UNDER SECTION 1307(a)

The debtors, by their attorney, represent and state as follows:

1. The debtors are no longer able to comply with their Chapter 13 plan and do not desire to modify the plan.

2. The debtors qualify as debtors under Chapter 7 of the Bankruptcy Code.

3. Under section 1307(a) of the Bankruptcy Code, the debtors are entitled to convert their Chapter 13 case to a case under Chapter 7 at any time, and the debtors now wish to convert this Chapter 13 case to a case under Chapter 7.

WHEREFORE, the debtors, pursuant to Rule 1017(d) of the Rules of Bankruptcy Procedure, hereby give notice of the conversion of this Chapter 13 case to a case under Chapter 7 of the Bankruptcy Code.

Dated: March 3, 1992

Approved:

_____   _____
John T. Smith
John Paul Jones, debtor   Attorney for Debtors
6200 Wilshire Blvd.   Suite 3333
_____   Los Angeles, CA 90012
Shirley Ann Jones, debtor   Telephone: 213-344-7666

CERTIFICATE OF TRANSMITTAL BY MAIL

The undersigned certifies under penalty of perjury that he or she has on the date shown below, by first class mail addressed to their respective addresses of record, transmitted a true copy of this document to the United States trustee and the Chapter 13 trustee.

Date: _____   _____

UNITED STATES BANKRUPTCY COURT
CENTRAL DISTRICT OF CALIFORNIA

IN RE   John Paul Jones and   )
         Shirley Ann Jones   )   Case No. 92B-13-0066
)
                        Debtors   )   Chapter 13

MOTION TO DISMISS CASE UNDER SECTION 1307(b)

The debtors, by their attorney, represent and state as follows:

1. The debtors are no longer able to comply with their Chapter 13 plan and do not desire to modify the plan.

2. This Chapter 13 case has not been converted to Chapter 13 from another chapter of the Bankruptcy Code.

3. Under section 1307(b) of the Bankruptcy Code, the debtors are entitled to have this Chapter 13 case dismissed at any time, and the debtors, by this motion, respectfully request that such case be dismissed and the estate closed as soon as practicable.

WHEREFORE, the debtors, pursuant to Rule 1017(d) of the Rules of Bankruptcy Procedure, move this honorable court to enter an order dismissing this case and closing the estate as soon as practicable.

Dated: March 3, 1992

Approved:

_____   _____
                                          John T. Smith
John Paul Jones, debtor   Attorney for Debtors
                                          6200 Wilshire Blvd.   Suite 3333
                                          Los Angeles, CA 90012
_____   Telephone: 213-344-7666
Shirley Ann Jones, debtor

CERTIFICATE OF TRANSMITTAL BY MAIL

The undersigned certifies under penalty of perjury that he or she has on the date shown below, by first class mail addressed to their respective addresses of record, transmitted a true copy of this document to the United States trustee and the Chapter 13 trustee.

Date: _____   _____

EXHIBIT 3-J   179

UNITED STATES BANKRUPTCY COURT
CENTRAL DISTRICT OF CALIFORNIA

IN RE   John Paul Jones and   )
         Shirley Ann Jones   )   Case No. 92B-13-0066
)
                  Debtors   )   Chapter 13

MOTION FOR DISCHARGE OF DEBTORS UNDER SECTION 1328(b)

The debtors, by their attorney, represent and state as follows:

1. That the debtors will be unable to complete the payments required of them under the Chapter 13 plan due to circumstances for which they should not justly be held accountable; to wit: the debtor, John Paul Jones, has been discharged by his employer, The Royal Sales Company, and has been unable to find other employment despite diligent efforts on his part to do so, and the debtor, Shirley Ann Jones, is employed only part time, thus rendering the debtors unable to maintain the payments required of them under their Chapter 13 plan.

2. That because of the uncertainty as to when the debtor, John Paul Jones will find employment sufficient to permit the debtors to resume the Chapter 13 payments, a modification of the Chapter 13 plan is not practicable.

3. That the value of the property actually distributed under the debtors' Chapter 13 plan on the account of each allowed unsecured claim is greater than the amount that would have been distributed to the holders of such claims had the estates of the debtors been liquidated under Chapter 7 of the Bankruptcy Code.

WHEREFORE, the debtors move this honorable Court to enter an order granting the debtors a discharge under section 1328(b) of the Bankruptcy Code.

Dated: March 16, 1992

                                        _____
                                        John T. Smith
                                        Attorney for Debtors
                                        6200 Wilshire Blvd.   Suite 3333
                                        Los Angeles, CA 90012
                                        Telephone: 213-344-7666

CERTIFICATE OF TRANSMITTAL BY MAIL

The undersigned certifies under penalty of perjury that he or she has on the date shown below, by first class mail addressed to their respective addresses of record, transmitted a true copy of this document to the United States trustee and the Chapter 13 trustee.

Date: _____   _____

CHAPTER FOUR

FAMILY FARMER BANKRUPTCIES UNDER CHAPTER 12

4.01 Chapter 12 - A General Description

Chapter 12 of the Bankruptcy Code is modeled after chapter 13. Like chapter 13, chapter 12 debtors and certain codebtors receive the protection of the automatic stay. Under chapter 12, like chapter 13, only the debtor may file a plan, the plan may be confirmed without creditor approval, the debtor must make periodic payments to a trustee who makes payments to creditors as specified in the plan, and the debtor receives a discharge at the close of the case.

chapter 12, similarity to chapter 13

Chapter 12 differs from chapter 13 in several important particulars, however. First of all, the filing fee for a chapter 12 case is $200, as opposed to $120 for a chapter 13 case. Secondly, only a "family farmer" with regular annual income may be a debtor under chapter 12. A "family farmer" may be an individual, an individual and spouse, a corporation, or a partnership. To qualify as a family farmer, a debtor's aggregate debts must not exceed $1,500,000, and 80 percent of the debtor's aggregate noncontingent, liquidated debts must arise out of a farming operation. Certain other income and ownership requirements must also be met. See section 4.02, infra, for further reading.

chapter 12, eligibility requirements

With court approval, farmland and farm equipment may be sold under chapter 12 free and clear of the interest of any secured creditor. The proceeds of the sale, however, are subject to the creditor's interest. A chapter 12 debtor is permitted to continue to operate the debtor's farming operation during the course of the case unless the debtor is removed by the court as a debtor in possession for cause, which includes fraud, dishonesty, incompetence, or gross mismanagement. If the debtor is removed as a debtor in possession, the chapter 12 trustee is empowered to run the debtor's farm.

chapter 12, general aspects

Under chapter 12, a debtor must file a plan within 90 days after the filing of the petition, unless the court extends the period. The hearing on confirmation of the plan must be concluded within 45 days after the plan is filed, unless the court extends the period. The maximum length of a chapter 12 plan may not exceed three years, unless the court, for cause, approves a longer period of up to five years. In most cases all of the debtor's disposable income must be applied to the plan during the period of the plan.

chapter 12 plan, general requirements

At the close of a chapter 12 case, the debtor receives a discharge in the same manner as in a chapter 13 case, except that a chapter 12 debtor who has completed the plan payments receives a discharge similar to a chapter 7 discharge instead of the broad discharge granted to a debtor under chapter 13.

chapter 12 discharge

A seven year sunset is provided for chapter 12. Section 302(f) of the Bankruptcy Judges, United States Trustees, and Family Farmer Bankruptcy Act of 1986 (H.R. 5316) provides as follows:

chapter 12, when repealed

"Chapter 12 of title 11 of the United States Code is repealed on October 1, 1993. All cases commenced or pending under chapter 12 of title 11, United States Code, and all matters and proceedings in or relating to such cases, shall be conducted and determined under such chapter as if such chapter had not been repealed. The substantive rights of parties in connection with such cases, matters, and proceedings shall continue to be governed under the laws applicable to such cases, matters, and proceedings as if such chapter had not been repealed."

Procedurally and substantively, a chapter 12 case is prepared, filed, and handled very much like a chapter 13 case. With the exceptions noted above in this section and a few other minor differences, chapter 12 is substantially the same as chapter 13. The reader is referred to section 3.01, supra, for a general description of a chapter 13 case.

4.02 The Chapter 12 Eligibility Requirements

regular annual income. definition

Only a family farmer with regular annual income may be a debtor under chapter 12. See 11 U.S.C. 109(f). The term "family farmer with regular annual income" means a family farmer whose annual income is sufficiently stable and regular to enable the family farmer to make payments under a chapter 12 plan. See 11 U.S.C. 101(19). A "family farmer" includes:

(1) an individual -

chapter 12 eligibility requirements. individual

    (a) who is engaged in a farming operation,

    (b) whose aggregate debts do not exceed $1,500,000,

    (c) not less that 80 percent of whose aggregate noncontingent, liquidated debts, on the date the case is filed, arose out of a farming operation that the individual owns or operates, except that a debt for such individual's principal residence may be excluded unless the debt arose out of the farming operation, and

    (d) who received from the farming operation more than 50 percent of such individual's gross income for the taxable year preceding the year in which the case is filed;

(2) an individual and his or her spouse who jointly meet the requirements set forth in (1) above; and

(3) a corporation or partnership -

chapter 12 eligibility requirements. corporation or partnership

    (a) more than 50 percent of the outstanding stock or equity of which is held by one family, or by one family and the relatives of the family members, and the family or relatives conduct the farming operation,

    (b) more than 80 percent of the value of the assets of which consist of assets related to the farming operation,

    (c) the aggregate debts of which do not exceed $1,500,000,

    (d) not less than 80 percent of the aggregate noncontingent, liquidated debts of which, on the date the case is filed, arose out of a farming operation owned or operated by the corporation or partnership, except that a debt for one dwelling maintained by a shareholder or partner as a principal residence may be excluded, unless the debt arose out of the farming operation, and

    (e) the stock of which is not publicly traded. See 11 U.S.C. 101(18).

farming operation. definition

A "farming operation" includes farming, tillage of the soil, dairy farming, ranching, the production or raising of crops, poultry, or livestock, and the production of poultry or livestock products in an unmanufactured state. See 11 U.S.C. 101(20).

title 11 eligibility requirements. individual

It should be noted that an individual may not be a debtor under any chapter of title 11, including chapter 12, if he or she has been a debtor in another bankruptcy case pending during the preceding 180 days if the prior case was dismissed on certain grounds. See 11 U.S.C. 109(g) and handbook section 3.04, supra. A debtor is eligible to file and receive a discharge under chapter 12 regardless of when the debtor last received a discharge under any chapter of the Bankruptcy Code. See 11 U.S.C. 1228. Debts dealt with in a prior bankruptcy case may be dealt with in a chapter 12 case, and, unless the court in the prior case ordered otherwise, may be discharged in the chapter 12 case. See 11 U.S.C. 349(a).

4.03 Miscellaneous Chapter 12 Matters

Many aspects of chapter 12 cases are patterned after chapter 13. The chapter 12 matters discussed in this section are closely related to the same matters in a chapter 13 case. Rather than duplicate the materials appearing in chapter three of this handbook, the reader is referred to the appropriate section in chapter three, with any significant differences in chapter 12 cases noted.

The local bankruptcy rules and forms. See section 3.02, supra, for a discussion of the local bankruptcy rules and forms. In some districts there may be special rules or forms applicable only to chapter 12 cases. The local rules should be checked for the existence of such rules or forms.

local bankruptcy rules and forms

The debtor's transactions with the debtor's attorney. The same statutes and rules govern the debtor's transactions with the debtor's attorney in a chapter 12 case as in a chapter 13 case. See section 3.03, supra, for further reading. As in a chapter 13 case, the debtor's attorney in a chapter 12 case is required to file Bankruptcy Form B 203, entitled Disclosure of Compensation of Attorney for Debtor, or a local substitute, with the court within 15 days after entry of the order for relief and obtain court approval of all compensation. See Exhibit 2-A at the end of chapter 2, supra, for a sample Bankruptcy Form B 203.

attorney's disclosure statement

Chapter 12 cases differ from chapter 13 cases in that the amount of an attorney's compensation is usually more in a chapter 12 case, because of the greater complexity of the case, and the debtor's attorney may have to prepare and file on behalf of the debtor in possession an application to employ the attorney.

11 U.S.C. 327(a), which is made applicable to a chapter 12 debtor in possession by 11 U.S.C. 1203, requires court approval of an attorney employed by the debtor in possession. Therefore, it may be necessary to file and transmit to the United States trustee an Application to Employ Attorney in order to comply with this requirement. It should be noted that the court may not approve the payment of compensation to an attorney from funds of the estate if prior approval of the attorney's employment was not obtained. See 11 U.S.C. 328(a) and In re Johnson, 21 B.R. 217. It is also important to note that the court may deny compensation to an attorney who is not a disinterested person or who holds or represents an interest adverse to the interest of the estate. See 11 U.S.C. 328(c), and see 11 U.S.C. 101(14) for the definition of a "disinterested person." The matters to be covered in an application to employ an attorney are set forth in Bankruptcy Rule 2014(a). A sample Application to Employ Attorney is set forth in Exhibit 4-A at the end of this chapter.

application to employ attorney, when needed

debtor's attorney, legal requirements

If, prior to filing, the attorney was paid in full for all services to be rendered in the case, or if the attorney's entire fee is to be paid by the chapter 12 trustee under the debtor's plan, then the filing of an application to employ the attorney may not be required. The local rules and practices should be checked in this regard.

The chapter 12 trustee. The chapter 12 trustee is appointed in the same manner and under the same authority as a chapter 13 trustee. In many districts the chapter 12 trustee and the chapter 13 trustee are the same person. The duties and functions of a chapter 12 trustee are set forth in 11 U.S.C. 1202, and are essentially the same as those of a chapter 13 trustee in cases where the debtor is engaged in business. See section 3.14, supra, for further reading. The significant differences in the duties and functions of a chapter 12 trustee are:

chapter 12 trustee, appointment of

chapter 12 trustee, duties of

(1) the chapter 12 trustee is not required to investigate the financial affairs of the debtor;

(2) the chapter 12 trustee must appear and be heard at any hearing concerning the sale of property of the estate (see 11 U.S.C. 1202(b)(3)(D);

(3) the chapter 12 trustee has additional duties and functions if the debtor ceases to be a debtor in possession (see 11 U.S.C. 1202(b)(5);

(4) the chapter 12 trustee may, with court approval, sell farmland and farm equipment of the estate free and clear of any interest in such property of any entity other than the estate; and

(5) the fee charged by a chapter 12 trustee is 10 percent of the first $450,000 paid under the plan, and 3 percent of the balance of such payments (see 28 U.S.C. 586(e)(1)(B)(ii)).

The meeting of creditors. The meeting of creditors in a chapter 12 case is the same as the meeting of creditors in a chapter 13 case in all important respects. See section 3.12, supra, for further reading. It should be noted that in chapter 12 cases it is unlikely that the confirmation hearing will be held in conjunction with the meeting of creditors because the debtor is not required to file a plan until 90 days after the order for relief under chapter 12. In a chapter 12 case, the notice of commencement of case must conform to Official Form 9G if the debtor is an individual or if a joint petition is filed. The notice of commencement of case must conform to Official Form 9H if the debtor is a corporation or partnership.

The filing and payment of claims. The procedures, requirements, and priorities for the filing and payment of claims in a chapter 12 case are the same as in a chapter 13 case. See section 3.16, supra, for further reading. Postpetition claims are handled under 11 U.S.C. 364 in chapter 12 cases and are generally treated as administrative expenses. See section 4.07, infra, for further reading.

4.04 Gathering Information and Preparing the Case

A typical chapter 12 case is more complex than most chapter 13 cases. Because of the larger debt limitations under chapter 12, because of the unique eligibility requirements of chapter 12, and because a corporation or partnership may be a debtor under chapter 12, information not needed in chapter 13 cases will usually be required to properly prepare and handle a chapter 12 case. It is important, therefore, that every person involved in the management of either the operational or the financial aspect of the debtor's farming operation be interviewed, and that all relevant documents relating to the debts, assets, taxes, and other legal or financial aspects of the farming operation be personally examined by the debtor's attorney. The attorney should confirm all important financial data.

When gathering information and preparing a chapter 12 case, the following matters should be specifically addressed:

(1) The eligibility of the debtor for relief under chapter 12. The chapter 12 eligibility requirements are set forth in section 4.02, supra. The first item to address is the debtor's form of legal entity. Under chapter 12 the debtor may be an individual, an individual and spouse (i.e., a joint case), a corporation, or a partnership. Of course, if the debtor is an individual no legal documents are needed to verify his or her existence. If the debtor is an individual and spouse, they must be husband and wife. See In re Malone, 50 B.R. 2. If significant farm assets or debts are owned or owed jointly by both spouses, a joint case should be filed.

If the debtor is a corporation, its books and records should be examined to ensure that shares of stock have been issued and that the corporation has been lawfully formed. Also, the corporation's standing with the Secretary of State or other state licensing authority should be checked, for it has been held that a corporation whose charter has been revoked by the state for nonpayment of fees or failure to file reports is not eligible for relief under chapter 11. See In re Vermont Fiberglass, Inc., 38 B.R. 151. Presumably, the same rule would apply in a chapter 12 case.

If the debtor is a partnership, the partnership agreement should be examined and it should be ascertained whether the provisions of the agreement have actually been carried out, especially those calling for the contribution of capital and capital assets to the partnership. If the debtor is operated as an informal partnership with no written agreement, the best practice is to draft a partnership agreement before filing the case. Otherwise, it may later be difficult to establish or verify the asset and aggregate debt requirements of chapter 12, especially if disagreements should later arise among the partners. Also, the court may be reluctant to confirm a plan if the debtor in possession, who under chapter 12 is essentially a trustee, is only an informal partnership.

meeting of
creditors

claims,
procedures and
requirements

gathering data
chapter 12 case

debtor, form of
legal entity

joint debtors,
definition

corporate
debtor, matters
to check

partnership
debtor, matters
to check

If the farming operation is run as a trust, it may qualify as a debtor under chapter 12 if it is a business trust, but not if it is a nonbusiness trust. A business trust is treated as a corporation under the Bankruptcy Code. See 11 U.S.C. 101(9)(A)(v). That a nonbusiness trust does not constitute a person for purposes of title 11, see In re Dalton Lodge Trust No. 35188, 22 B.R. 918. A testamentary trust is usually a nonbusiness trust. That a probate estate is not eligible for chapter 12 relief, see In Re Estate of Grassman, 91 B.R. 928.

trust,
eligibility
under chapter 12

Regardless of the debtor's form of legal entity, the total aggregate dollar amount of the debtor's debts of any nature must be computed to ensure that such total does not exceed $1,500,000 in amount. If the debtor is an individual and spouse, the total aggregate debts of each must be combined. It is important to realistically value each debt, especially contingent or unliquidated debts. Next, a list of all of the debtor's noncontingent, liquidated debts should be compiled for the purpose of determining whether 80 percent or more of such debts arose out of a farming operation owned or operated by the debtor. In compiling this list, it is important to exclude contingent or unliquidated debts (such debts are included for purposes of the $1,500,000 limitation, but excluded for purposes of the 80 percent farm debt limitation). A debt is contingent if the debtor's liability is determined by the happening or nonhappening of a future event. A debt is unliquidated if the amount of the debt has not been established. See In re All Media Properties, Inc., 5 B.R. 126.

aggregate debt
limitation

80% farm debt
requirement

The debt for the debtor's principal residence (or the principal residence of a shareholder or partner, if the debtor is a corporation or partnership) should be examined for includability in the list of noncontingent liquidated debts. The debt is includable only if it arose out of a farming operation. The background of the incurrence of the debt should be examined in this regard, especially the use of the funds for which the debt was incurred. If the debt was incurred solely to purchase the residence, then it clearly did not arise out of a farming operation. If the debt was incurred solely to provide funds or credit for the farming operation, then it clearly arose out of a farming operation and should be included in the list of noncontingent liquidated debts. Obviously, there are many instances where the funds from the incurrence of the debt were used for both purposes, or where the debt for the residence was included in a larger transaction that included debts for the farming operation. In such instances, if the general purpose of the transaction was to finance the farming operation, then the entire debt should be included on the list. It should be noted that the debt for the debtor's principal residence is always includable in the $1,500,000 aggregate debt limitation.

debt for
principal
residence, when
includable

If the debtor is an individual or an individual and spouse, the sources of the debtor's gross income for the taxable year preceding the year of the filing of the case should be examined to ascertain whether more than 50 percent of the debtor's gross income for that taxable year was received from the farming operation. The Bankruptcy Code gives no guidance as to what constitutes "gross income." If the Internal Revenue Code definition is used, certain income (e.g., social security income, municipal bond interest, etc.) would not be includable as income. Probably, however, gross income means income from every source, without exception.

50% farm income
requirement

gross income,
what constitutes

If the debtor is a corporation, the number of shares held by each shareholder should be ascertained and confirmed to ensure that more than 50 percent of the outstanding stock is held by the family (including relatives) that conducts the farming operation. If the debtor is a partnership, the exact partnership interest of each general and limited partner should be ascertained and confirmed to ensure that more than 50 percent of the total partnership interest is held by the family (including relatives) that conducts the farming operation.

corporate or
partnership
debtor, 50%
ownership
requirement

If the debtor is either a corporation or a partnership, all of the debtor's assets should be ascertained, listed separately, and evaluated, to determine whether more than 80 percent of the value of such assets are assets related to the farming operation. If a shareholder or partner of the debtor individually owns land, equipment, or other farm-related assets that are used in the farming operation, it may be necessary to transfer such assets to the debtor (in exchange for stock or a partnership interest) to enable the debtor to meet the 80 percent farm-asset requirement.

corporate or
partnership
debtor, 80%
farm asset
requirement

(2) Whether the debtor is in need of immediate bankruptcy relief. The key factor here is the immediacy of the threat to the debtor's business or property posed by hostile or threatening creditors. If foreclosures, attachments, impoundment of funds, repossessions, or other creditor action that may curtail the debtor's farming operation or deprive the debtor of important assets are pending or likely to be carried out in the immediate future, then the debtor is probably in need of immediate bankruptcy relief. The bankruptcy relief referred to, of course, is the relief provided by the automatic stay, which immediately upon the filing of the petition stays virtually all creditor action against the debtor. See section 4.06, infra, for further reading on the effect and extent of the automatic stay.

If the debtor is in need of immediate bankruptcy relief, three preliminary matters should be addressed before filing the petition. These matters are: (1) the eligibility of the debtor for relief under chapter 12, (2) the appropriateness of chapter 12 as a remedy for the debtor's financial problems, and (3) obtaining the information needed to file the case. The chapter 12 eligibility matters are discussed above in this section and in section 4.02, supra.

Most family farmer debtors are eligible to file under chapter 7 and chapter 11 of the Bankruptcy Code, as well as chapter 12. If the debtor is an individual or an individual and spouse and can meet the debt limitations of chapter 13, then chapter 13 is also an alternative. Generally, if the debtor wishes to liquidate rather than reorganize or rehabilitate the farming operation, then chapter 7 is the best alternative. It should be noted, however, that a debtor may carry out an orderly, debtor-controlled liquidation under chapter 12. See 11 U.S.C. 1222(b)(8). A debtor with substantial assets may find it preferable to sell its farming operation as a going concern under a chapter 12 liquidation plan rather than through a liquidating trustee under chapter 7.

A chapter 12 case is generally less expensive for the debtor and less time consuming than a chapter 11 case. The legislative history of chapter 12 indicates that chapter 12 was adopted because " many family farmers found chapter 11 needlessly complicated, unduly time-consuming, inordinately expensive, and, in many cases, unworkable." Also, adequate protection is more debtor oriented under chapter 12 and it is easier to sell encumbered farmland and farm equipment without the consent of creditors under chapter 12. In nearly every case, chapter 12 will be preferable to chapter 11 for qualifying family farmers.

If a debtor qualifies under chapter 13, chapter 13 will usually be preferable to chapter 12 for most family farmers. See section 3.04, supra, for the chapter 13 eligibility requirements. Because of the chapter 13 debt limitations, most family farmers do not qualify thereunder. The principal advantage of chapter 13 for qualifying debtors is that a chapter 13 case is simpler and less expensive for the debtor than a chapter 12 case. However, chapter 13 does not provide the advantages of debtor-oriented adequate protection or the ability to sell encumbered farmland and farm equipment without creditor consent.

If emergency bankruptcy relief is needed, the petition may be filed accompanied only by a list of creditors and such other documents as may be required by the local rules. If the debtor is a corporation or a partnership, the local rules may require the filing of a resolution authorizing the commencement of the case. The local rules may also require the filing of address cards or an address matrix with the petition. The information needed, then, will be the names and addresses of all of the debtor's creditors and the information necessary to prepare the petition and, if required locally, a resolution authorizing the commencement of the case. The preparation of these documents is covered in section 4.05, infra.

(3) Informing the debtor of the chapter 12 process and of the rights, duties, and functions of a debtor under chapter 12. For a case to proceed smoothly, the debtor must understand the fundamentals of the chapter 12 process and the role of a debtor under chapter 12. The following aspects of a chapter 12 case should be explained to the debtor, in writing if necessary:

[Margin notes:]
immediate bankruptcy relief, when needed

immediate bankruptcy relief, matters to check

chapter 12 vs. chapter 7

liquidating under chapter 12, when preferable

chapter 12 vs. chapter 11

chapter 12 vs. chapter 13

emergency bankruptcy relief, how to obtain

(a) The effect of the automatic stay (see section 4.06, infra).

(b) The functions of the chapter 12 trustee (see section 4.03, supra).

(c) The restrictions on the debtor's use of cash collateral during the case (see section 4.07, infra).

(d) The obtaining of credit during the course of the case (see section 4.07, infra).

(e) The responsibilities of a debtor in possession under chapter 12 (see section 4.07, infra).

(f) The confirmation requirements of a plan and the necessity of complying with the terms of a confirmed plan (see section 4.08, infra).

(g) The anticipated legal and administrative expenses of the case (see below, this section).

(h) The requirements for amending a plan, either before or after confirmation (see section 4.08, infra).

(i) The effect of a chapter 12 discharge (see section 4.09, infra).

The legal and administrative expenses of a chapter 12 case include the following:

(a) the filing fee of $200,

(b) the fee charged by the debtor's attorney,

(c) the fee of the chapter 12 trustee, which is 10 percent of the first $450,000 paid to the trustee by the debtor under the plan, and 3 percent of the balance of such payments,

(d) allowed postpetition debts or credit obligations which are paid as administrative expenses (see section 4.07, infra).

(4) Checking for avoidable preferential or fraudulent transfers. It is important to discover any significant avoidable preferential or fraudulent transfers early in the case for two reasons: (1) to determine the personal liability of the transferees (who are usually insiders or associates thereof) for the funds or property transferred, and (2) to prevent such transfers from later becoming grounds for the removal of the debtor as a debtor in possession.

An avoidable preferential transfer is any transfer of an interest by the debtor in property to or for the benefit of a creditor for payment of a debt owed by the debtor prior to the transfer, made while the debtor was insolvent, made on or within 90 days before the date of filing of the petition or within one year before the date of filing if the creditor was an insider, and that enables the creditor to receive more than he would have received in a chapter 7 liquidation of the debtor's estate. See 11 U.S.C. 547(b). See 11 U.S.C. 101(31) for a definition of insider.

An avoidable fraudulent transfer is a transfer of an interest of the debtor in property or an obligation incurred by the debtor if the debtor made the transfer or incurred the obligation with actual intent to hinder, delay, or defraud its present or future creditors, or received less than a reasonably equivalent value in exchange for the transfer or obligation, and was insolvent at the time of the transaction or became insolvent, undercapitalized, or unable to pay its debts as a result of the transaction. See 11 U.S.C. 548(a).

All significant transfers of funds or property to insiders of the debtor made within the previous 12 months should be checked for avoidability. If it appears that a significant transfer to an insider may be avoidable in bankruptcy, both the debtor and the transferee should be advised. The debtor's attorney should be wary of a possible conflict of interest when dealing with avoidable transfers to insiders because in many instances the interest of the debtor is opposed to that of the insider.

chapter 12
process,
informing debtor

chapter 12
expenses

avoidable
transfers,
necessity of
discovering

preferential
transfer, what
constitutes

fraudulent
transfer, what
constitutes

avoidable
transfers,
conflicts of
interest

avoidable
transfers,
matters to check
All significant transfers of funds or property to persons other than insiders during the 90-day period prior to filing should also be examined for avoidability. Payments or transfers to entities to whom insiders are personally liable should be closely scrutinized. All significant transfers made or obligations incurred by the debtor since the debtor became insolvent should be checked for avoidability as fraudulent transfers. In this regard, it is important to realistically evaluate the consideration received by the debtor for any such transfer or obligation, especially if the transferee or obligee is an insider.

avoiding liens
under sec.
522(f)
(5) Avoiding liens and security interests. Under 11 U.S.C. 522(f), the debtor may avoid judicial liens against exempt property and nonpurchase-money, nonpossessory security interests in certain exempt personal property of the debtor. See section 2.12, supra, for further reading and a full description of the property covered. If the debtor is an individual or an individual and spouse, and has property that is subject to a lien or security interest that may be avoidable under 11 U.S.C. 522(f), the avoidability of such lien or security interest should, of course, be checked. It is usually necessary to test the avoidability of such liens and security interests before the filing of a plan, and the local rules often require the filing of motions to avoid such liens and security interests with the petition or shortly thereafter. The procedure for avoiding such liens and security interests is normally the same in chapter 12 cases as in chapter 7 cases, and the reader is referred to section 2.12, supra, for further reading.

preliminary
plan, necessity
of
(6) Devising a preliminary plan. Under chapter 12, it is not necessary to file a plan until 90 days after the commencement of the case. See 11 U.S.C. 1221. However, to ascertain whether chapter 12 is feasible for the debtor, for purposes of cash flow projections, budgeting, and employee confidence, and to give guidance to the debtor, it is a good practice to devise at least a preliminary plan early in the case: before the case is filed, if possible. It is important that the preliminary plan not be a farce and that it be at least reasonably similar to the plan ultimately proposed by the debtor. While it will usually be necessary to base a preliminary plan on estimates of both income and claims, such estimates should be realistic and made in good faith. See section 4.08, infra, for further reading on the preparation of a plan.

filing fee,
payment of

attorney's fee,
payment of
(7) Making arrangements for payment of the filing fee, the attorney's fee, and any required deposit. If the debtor is an individual or an individual and spouse, the $200 filing fee may be paid in installments, if necessary. See Bankruptcy Rule 1006(b), and section 3.11, supra. If the debtor is a corporation or a partnership, the entire filing fee must be paid when the petition is filed. See Bankruptcy Rule 1006(a). In either instance, appropriate arrangements should be made for the payment of the filing fee. For the protection of both the debtor and the attorney, there should be a clear understanding as to both the amount of compensation to be paid to the attorney for handling the case (or the rate of compensation if it is not feasible to establish a set fee at the outset), and the method and source of payment. If desired, the debtor's plan may provide for the chapter 12 trustee to pay the debtor's attorney out of the payments made by the debtor under the plan. The disadvantage of such an arrangement is that the trustee will assess a 10 percent fee on the payments made by the debtor under the plan to pay the attorney's fee. If either the plan or the local rules require the debtor to make a deposit prior to confirmation, arrangements should be made for its deposit with the trustee.

chapter 12
forms, obtaining
data for
(8) Collecting the information needed to prepare the chapter 12 forms for filing. The forms needed in a chapter 12 case are listed in section 4.05, infra. The best method of gathering the information and data needed in a chapter 12 case is to use work sheets or similar documents that call for all of the required information without repetition or omission. An attorney without work sheets will find the Bankruptcy Work Sheets set forth in Exhibit 2-B at the end of chapter two, supra, useful. Simply photocopy the work sheets and follow the directions contained therein and all of the information required in the petition, schedules, and statement of financial affairs will be assembled in the proper order. The data needed to establish the debtor's eligibility under chapter 12 may be found in the debtor's tax returns for the previous year, in the debtor's corporate or partnership records, and in recent appraisals of the debtor's assets. See (1) above in this section and section 4.02, supra, for further reading on the chapter 12 eligibility requirements.

4.05 Preparing and Filing the Chapter 12 Forms

official chapter
12 forms

Bankruptcy Rule 1001 provides that the Bankruptcy Rules and Forms shall govern the procedure in chapter 12 cases. Bankruptcy Rule 9009 provides that the Official Forms shall be observed and used with alterations as may be appropriate. Bankruptcy Rule 1007(b)(1) requires the debtor in a chapter 12 case, unless the court orders otherwise, to file schedules of assets and liabilities, a schedule of current income expenditures, a schedule of executory contracts and unexpired leases, and a statement of financial affairs prepared as prescribed by the appropriate Official Forms. Bankruptcy Rule 3015(a) provides that the debtor may file a chapter 12 plan with the petition and that if the plan is not filed with the petition it must be filed within the time prescribed in 11 U.S.C. 1221, which is 90 days after the order for relief, unless additional time is granted by the court. There is no official form for a chapter 12 plan, but some districts have adopted a local form for the plan.

The following forms and documents may be needed to prepare a typical chapter 12 case for filing:

chapter 12 forms
and documents

Voluntary Petition (Official Form 1)

Schedules A through J (Official Form 6)

Statement of Financial Affairs (Official Form 7)

Application to Pay Filing Fees in Installments and Order, if needed (Official Form 3)

Disclosure of Compensation of Attorney for Debtor (Bankruptcy Form B 203)

List of Creditors, if needed

Debtor's Resolution Authorizing Commencement of Case, if needed

Application to Employ Attorney, if needed

Address Cards or Address Matrix, if required locally

chapter 12
forms,
where to obtain

In some districts the local rules may require the filing of additional forms or documents in chapter 12 cases. The local rules should be checked in this regard. The required official forms may be purchased from a commercial supplier of legal forms and the required local forms, if not supplied with the official forms, are usually supplied by the clerk of the local bankruptcy court. Samples of required local forms are often contained in the local rules.

chapter 12
forms,
preparation

The petition, schedules, and statement of financial affairs required in a chapter 12 case are the same as those required in a chapter 13 case, and the preparation of all of the forms and documents listed above, except the List of Creditors, the Debtor's Resolution Authorizing Commencement of Case, and the Application to Employ Attorney, is covered in sections 2.07 and 3.09, supra. The reader is referred to those sections for instructions on the preparation of the petition, schedules and statements and for completed samples of each document. It should be noted that a chapter 12 debtor is required to attach a detailed statement to Schedules I and J showing the debtor's income and expenses from the farming operation. If the debtor is a corporation or partnership, the declaration accompanying any petition, list, schedule, statement, or amendment thereto must conform to Official Form 2.

list of
creditors, when
needed

The List of Creditors is needed only if the petition is being filed in advance of the schedules of liabilities. See Bankruptcy Rule 1007(a) and section 4.03, supra. The List of Creditors must contain the name and address of each of the debtor's creditors; secured, unsecured, and priority. No particular form or format is normally required for the list of creditors, although the creditors should be listed in alphabetical order, if feasible.

resolution
authorizing
filing of case

The Debtor's Resolution Authorizing Commencement of Case is required by the local rules in many districts if the debtor is a corporation or partnership. The local rules should be checked in this regard. If the debtor is an individual or individual and spouse, this document is not required. If the debtor is a partnership and all of the general partners sign the petition, this document should not be required. See Bankruptcy Rule 1004(a). If the debtor is a partnership and one or more of the general partners does not sign the petition, this document should be prepared and signed by each general partner, even if the local rules do not so require because Bankruptcy Rule 1004(a) requires the consent of all general partners to the filing of a partnership petition.

same, execution
of

If the debtor is a corporation, the board of directors should normally execute the Debtor's Resolution Authorizing Commencement of Case, unless the corporation's articles of incorporation or bylaws, or a valid shareholders' agreement, provide otherwise. See Williamson, The Attorney's Handbook on Small Business Reorganization Under Chapter 11, sec. 3.05 for further reading. Exhibit 4-B at the end of this chapter may be used as a guide in preparing this document.

application to
employ attorney

motion to avoid
lien

The necessity of filing an Application to Employ Attorney on behalf of the debtor in possession is discussed in section 4.03, supra. Use Exhibit 4-A at the end of this chapter as a guide in preparing this document. In some districts it may be necessary to file motions to avoid liens or security interests in exempt property when the petition is filed or shortly thereafter. This matter is discussed in sections 4.04 and 2.12, supra. Exhibit 2-U at the end of chapter 2, supra, may be used as a guide in preparing such a motion.

chapter 12 case,
filing fee

chapter 12
forms, number of
copies to file

A chapter 12 case is filed in the same manner as a chapter 13 case, and the reader is referred to section 3.10, supra, for further reading. The filing fee for a chapter 12 case is $200. The number of copies of a particular document to be filed is governed by local rule, and the local rules should be checked in this regard. If the local rules are silent on the number of copies of a particular document to be filed, the original and two copies of most documents will suffice. See section 3.10, supra, for further reading.

4.06 The Automatic Stay - Adequate Protection

The filing of a petition under chapter 12 operates as an automatic stay of acts, claims, and proceedings against the debtor and the debtor's property to the same extent as the filing of a petition under chapter 7. See 11 U.S.C. 362. The reader is referred to section 2.10, supra, for further reading on the effect, extent, and duration of the automatic stay. *(automatic stay, extent of)*

Chapter 12 contains a provision dealing with stays of actions against certain codebtors. This provision is identical to the codebtor stay provision in chapter 13, and the reader is referred to section 3.11, supra, for further reading. *(stay of acts against codebtors)*

The bankruptcy court may grant relief from the automatic stay to a party in interest by terminating, annulling, modifying, or conditioning the stay on either of two grounds: (1) for cause, including a lack of adequate protection of an interest of such party in property, or (2) with respect to the stay of acts against property, upon a showing that the debtor has no equity in the property and that the property is not necessary for an effective reorganization. See 11 U.S.C. 362(d). Secured creditors whose claims are not dealt with under the plan are permitted to reclaim or foreclose upon their collateral to the same extent under chapter 12 as under chapter 13. See section 3.11, supra, for further reading. *(relief from automatic stay)* *(secured creditors, repossessions by)*

Secured creditors whose claims are dealt with in the plan are the parties who normally seek relief from the automatic stay. While cause for lifting the stay may include other grounds, the lack of adequate protection of an interest of the creditor in property is the cause most commonly used. Because of the provisions of 11 U.S.C. 1206 (Sales free of interests) and the nature of family farming operations, the second ground for relief listed above (no equity in property not needed for reorganization) is seldom used in chapter 12 cases. A $60 fee is charged for filing a motion for relief from the automatic stay, regardless of the grounds for relief. *(secured creditor, validity of lien)*

A secured creditor seeking relief from the automatic stay on the grounds of lack of adequate protection has the burden of proving the validity of its lien or security interest. See In re Sports Enterprises, 38 B.R. 282. The purpose of adequate protection is to enable a secured creditor to maintain during the course of the case the position it held when the case was filed. See In re Alyucan Interstate Corp., 12 B.R. 803. It should be noted that a secured creditor is entitled to adequate protection of only its interest in the property, not for the full value of the property. See In re George Rugglere Chrysler-Plymouth, Inc., 727 F. 2nd 1017. *(adequate protection, purpose, extent)*

An over-secured creditor is normally not entitled to adequate protection, even if the overall value of its collateral is declining. The "equity cushion" between the amount of the secured claim and the value of the collateral may itself constitute adequate protection of the creditor's interest in the property. See In re Mallas Enterprise, Inc., 37 B.R. 964. However, an over-secured creditor may be entitled to adequate protection if the equity cushion threatens to disappear. See In re Carson, 34 B.R. 502. In determining whether an equity cushion exists, only the lien of the creditor seeking relief and senior liens against the property are considered. Junior liens are not considered. See In re Mellor, 734 F. 2nd 1396. *(equity cushion theory, definition)*

The equity cushion theory, of course, does not apply to partially-secured creditors. A partially-secured creditor is almost always entitled to adequate protection (or a lifting of the stay in the absence thereof) upon a showing that the value of its secured claim is declining. See In re Houston, 32 B.R. 584. The decline in value of a secured claim may be caused by a depreciation in the overall value of the secured property or by an increase in the amount of senior liens against the property. *(partially-secured creditor, adequate protection)*

adequate
protection, when
granted
Upon a finding that the interest of a secured or partially-secured creditor is not adequately protected, the court may either grant relief from the stay and permit the creditor to proceed against the property or require the debtor to adequately protect the interest of the creditor in the property. If the property is of value to the debtor and necessary in the farming operation, the court will normally permit the debtor to provide adequate protection for the creditor. However, it is the burden of the debtor to affirmatively pro-
adequate
protection,
burden of proof
pose the form and extent of the protection to be provided, as the burden of proof on the issue of adequate protection is on the party opposing relief from the stay. See 11 U.S.C. 362(g) and In re St. Peter's School, 16 B.R. 404.

When adequate protection of an interest of an entity in property is required in a chapter 12 case, such protection may be provided by:

adequate
protection,
methods of
providing
(1)   requiring the trustee to make a cash payment or periodic cash payments to such entity, to the extent that the stay under 11 U.S.C. 362, the use, sale, or lease of property under 11 U.S.C. 363, or any grant of a lien under 11 U.S.C. 364 results in a decrease in the value of property securing a claim or of an entity's ownership interest in property;

(2)   providing to such entity an additional or replacement lien to the extent that such stay, use, sale, lease, or grant results in a decrease in the value of property securing a claim or of an entity's ownership interest in property;

(3)   paying to such entity for the use of farmland the reasonable rent customary in the community where the property is located, based upon the rental value, net income, and earning capacity of the property; or

(4)   granting such other relief, other than entitling such entity to compensation allowable under 11 U.S.C. 503(b) as an administrative expense, as will adequately protect the value of property securing a claim or of such entity's ownership interest in property. See 11 U.S.C. 1205(b).

lost opportunity
costs
The above definition of "adequate protection" differs from the definition found in 11 U.S.C. 361, which applies to chapter 11 and chapter 13 cases, but not to chapter 12 cases. See 11 U.S.C. 1205(a). The stated purpose of the above language in 11 U.S.C. 1205(b) is to eliminate the necessity of compensating chapter 12 creditors for "lost opportunity costs," as required in certain chapter 11 cases. See In re American Mariner Industries, Inc., 734 F. 2nd 426. "Lost opportunity costs" are the losses that a creditor incurs by being precluded from foreclosing on the debtor's property and investing the proceeds more profitably elsewhere. Under 11 U.S.C. 1205(b) it is the value of property, not the value of a creditor's investment, that is to be adequately protected.

adequate
protection,
extent of
There are many ways of providing adequate protection. 11 U.S.C. 1205(b) makes it clear that a cash payment, periodic cash payments, providing a replacement or additional lien, and paying a reasonable rent for the use of farmland are methods of providing adequate protection. In addition, adequate protection may be in the form of meaningful guarantees by third parties, the providing of insurance on property or on a loan, and by the payment of accrued taxes on real property. See In re Greenwood Building Supply, Inc., 23 B.R. 720, and In re Roane, 8 B.R. 997. The form of adequate protection that may suffice in a given case usually depends on the type of protection that the creditor needs.

relief from
stay, procedure
The procedure for seeking relief from the automatic stay is set forth in 11 U.S.C. 362(e),(f) and (g) and in Bankruptcy Rules 4001, 9013 and 9014. Relief from the automatic stay is a contested matter and is sought by filing a motion under Bankruptcy Rule 4001(a). Such motions are core proceedings and are handled by the bankruptcy judge. See 28 U.S.C. 157(b)(2)(G). No fee is charged for the filing of such motions, and unless the court orders otherwise, no response to the motion is required. See Bankruptcy
relief from
stay, time
limitations
Rule 9014. The local rules should be checked for requirements pertaining to motions for relief from the automatic stay.

4.07 The Debtor in Possession - Running the Farming Operation

Immediately upon the entry of an order for relief under chapter 12 (which occurs upon the filing of a chapter 12 petition), an entity called a "debtor in possession" comes into existence. In a chapter 12 case, the debtor remains in possession of all property of the estate except as provided in a confirmed plan or in an order confirming a plan, unless the debtor is removed as a debtor in possession. See 11 U.S.C. 1207(b). For practical purposes, then, the debtor in possession is the debtor during the course of a chapter 12 case, unless the court orders otherwise. Unless the court orders otherwise, a chapter 12 debtor in possession has all of the rights, powers, and duties of a trustee in bankruptcy except the right to compensation and the duty to independently investigate and report on the affairs of the debtor. See 11 U.S.C. 1203.

debtor in possession, what constitutes

debtor in possession, rights, powers and duties

The statutory duties of a chapter 12 debtor in possession include the following:

debtor in possession, duties under chapter 12

(1) File a complete inventory of property of the debtor within 30 days after the date of filing, if the court so directs.

(2) Keep a record of receipts and of the disposition of money and property received.

(3) Make periodic reports to any appropriate taxing authority.

(4) Give notice of the case as soon as possible to every person not previously notified of the case who is known to be holding money or property subject to the withdrawal or order of the debtor, including banks, landlords, and insurance companies.

(5) File with the court any required statements and schedules that have not previously been filed.

(6) Account for all property of the estate.

(7) Examine proofs of claim and object to improper claims.

(8) Furnish such information about the estate as may be requested by parties in interest.

(9) File reports with the court, the United States trustee, and appropriate taxing authorities, including a statement of receipts and disbursements and such other information as the court may require.

(10) Make a final report and final account of the administration of the estate.

(11) File a plan.

(12) Furnish information to taxing authorities regarding the debtor's delinquent tax returns, if any.

(13) After confirmation of a plan, file such reports as are necessary or as the court may order.

(14) Operate the debtor's farm. See Bankruptcy Rule 2015(b) and 11 U.S.C. 1203, 1106(a), 704.

It should be noted that the duties described in (6), (7), (8) and (10) above are also required of the chapter 12 trustee. See 11 U.S.C. 1202(b)(1).

On the request of a party in interest and after notice and a hearing, the court, for cause, may order that the debtor shall not be a debtor in possession. Cause may include fraud, dishonesty, incompetence, or gross mismanagement of the debtor's affairs, either before or after the commencement of the case. See 11 U.S.C. 1204(a). If the debtor is removed as a debtor in possession, the duties of the debtor in possession, including the operation of the debtor's farm, are performed by the chapter 12 trustee or its designee. See 11 U.S.C. 1202(b)(5). On the request of a party in interest, and after notice and a hearing, the court may reinstate the debtor in possession. See 11 U.S.C. 1204(b).

removal of debtor as debtor in possession

The property of the debtor's estate under chapter 12 includes:

(1) all legal or equitable interests of the debtor in property as of the commencement of the case, except as provided in 11 U.S.C. 541(b) and 541(c)(2);

(2) all interests of the debtor and the debtor's spouse in community property as of the commencement of the case that is under the sole, equal, or joint management and control of the debtor or that is liable for an allowable claim against the debtor or against the debtor and the debtor's spouse, to the extent of such liability;

(3) any interest in property recovered under 11 U.S.C. 329(b), 363(n), 543, 550, 553 or 723;

(4) any interest in property preserved for the benefit of or transferred to the estate under 11 U.S.C. 510(c) or 551;

(5) any interest in property that would have been property of the estate if held by the debtor on the date the petition was filed if the debtor acquires or becomes entitled to acquire such property within 180 days after the date of filing by bequest, devise, or inheritance, as a result of a property settlement agreement with the debtor's spouse or a divorce decree, or as a beneficiary of a life insurance policy or death benefit plan;

(6) proceeds, product, offspring, rents, or profits of or from property of the estate;

(7) any interest in property that the estate acquires after the commencement of the case;

(8) all property of the kind specified above that the debtor acquires after the commencement of the case but before the case is closed, dismissed, or converted to a case under chapter 7, whichever occurs first; and

(9) earnings from services performed by the debtor after the commencement of the case but before the case is closed, dismissed, or converted to a case under chapter 7, whichever occurs first. See 11 U.S.C. 1207(a), 541(a).

Property of the debtor's estate does not include any power that the debtor may exercise solely for the benefit of another entity or any interest of the debtor as a lessee of nonresidential real property under a lease whose term has expired prior to the commencement of the case, and ceases to include such interest under such a lease that terminates during the case. See 11 U.S.C. 541(b). As a practical matter, in most chapter 12 cases all property of the debtor becomes property of the estate except property lawfully claimed as exempt by a debtor who is an individual or an individual and spouse.

As soon as possible after the filing of a chapter 12 case, certain housekeeping functions should be performed by the debtor in possession in order to comply with the general provisions of the Bankruptcy Code and the local rules. First of all, the debtor in possession should open one or more new bank accounts in order to segregate pre-filing from post-filing funds and receipts. Second, because the debtor in possession, as the representative of the estate, is the "owner" of the debtor's assets, insurance policies, utilities, accounts with suppliers, and similar items should be changed to show the debtor in possession as the owner or customer. Third, arrangements should be made for the payment of employees and necessary farm and personal expenses (see below in this section for further reading). Fourth, arrangements should be made for the preparation and periodic filing of any operating or financial reports required of chapter 12 debtors in possession by the local bankruptcy court or by the local office of the United States trustee.

If practicable, the best practice is to pay the debtor's employees their prefiling wages prior to the commencement of the case. Prefiling payment should be by cash, cashiers check, or other means that do not involve checks written on the debtor's bank accounts, since the accounts will be effectively frozen as of the moment the petition is filed. If prefiling wages are not paid prior to the commencement of the case, the debtor in possession, through its attorney, should apply to the bankruptcy court shortly after the case is filed for an order authorizing the payment of prefiling wages. Because most employees are entitled to a $2,000 priority claim for wages and benefits (11 U.S.C. 507(a)(3),(4)), most courts will authorize the postfiling payment of prefiling wages of up to $2,000 per employee, if there are funds available for the payment of such.

debtor in possession, payment of employees

To obtain funds to meet the debtor's payroll or to pay other necessary farm or personal expenses, it may be necessary for the debtor in possession to use cash collateral. Cash collateral is defined as cash, negotiable instruments, documents of title, securities, deposit accounts, or other cash equivalents, whenever acquired, in which both the estate and another entity have an interest, and includes the proceeds, products, offspring, rents, or profits of property subject to a security interest, whether existing before or after the commencement of the case. See 11 U.S.C. 363(a). A debtor in possession is required to segregate and account for any cash collateral in its possession, custody, or control. See 11 U.S.C. 363(c)(4). Most importantly, a debtor in possession may not use, sell, or lease cash collateral unless each entity that has an interest in the cash collateral consents or the court, after notice and a hearing, authorizes such use, sale, or lease. See 11 U.S.C. 363(c)(2).

debtor in possession, use of cash collateral

cash collateral, definition

Cash collateral normally exists when a secured creditor has a security interest in cash or the equivalent of cash. The creditor's lien may have been originally on the property constituting the cash collateral or the cash collateral may have resulted from a lien on the proceeds of other collateral. For example, cash collateral is often created when the debtor collects accounts receivable that have been pledged as collateral.

cash collateral, example of

If a creditor with an interest in cash collateral will not consent to the use thereof by the debtor, it will be necessary to file a motion for authority to use cash collateral under Bankruptcy Rule 4001(b). The motion and notice of the hearing must be served upon the parties specified in Bankruptcy Rule 4001(b)(1). See Bankruptcy Rule 4001(b)(3). A final hearing on the motion may not be held earlier than 15 days after service of the motion, but a preliminary hearing may be held earlier if requested in the motion. See Bankruptcy Rule 4001(b)(2). The hearing must be scheduled in accordance with the needs of the debtor. See 11 U.S.C. 363(c)(3). A copy of the motion must be transmitted to the United States trustee and a certificate of service filed with the court. See Bankruptcy Rules 9034 and 5005(b)(2).

use of cash collateral, procedure

A motion for authority to use cash collateral should include the following: (1) the amount of cash collateral sought to be used, (2) the name and address of each entity having an interest in the cash collateral, (3) the name and address of the entity in control or having possession of the cash collateral, (4) the facts demonstrating the need to use the cash collateral, (5) the nature of the protection to be provided those having an interest in the cash collateral, and (6) a request for a preliminary hearing, if desired, and the amount of cash collateral sought to be used pending the final hearing and the protection to be provided. A sample Motion For Authority to Use Cash Collateral is set forth in Exhibit 4-C at the end of this chapter.

motion to use cash collateral

It is common for secured creditors to demand adequate protection as a prerequisite to the debtor's use of cash collateral. See 11 U.S.C. 1205. Adequate protection is discussed in section 4.06, supra. The burden of proof on the issue of adequate protection is on the debtor, and the debtor's attorney should be prepared to provide adequate protection to any creditor who opposes a motion by the debtor to use cash collateral.

use of cash collateral

Unless the court orders otherwise, a debtor in possession may enter into transactions, including the sale or lease of property of the estate (other than cash collateral) in the ordinary course of business without notice or a hearing, and may use property of the estate (other than cash collateral) in the ordinary course of business without notice or a hearing. See 11 U.S.C. 363(c)(1). Generally, however, inventory and little else is customarily sold in the ordinary course of business.

Sales not in the ordinary course of business are governed by 11 U.S.C. 363(b), which provides that only after notice and a hearing may the debtor in possession use, sell, or lease property of the estate outside the ordinary course of business. Thus, if the debtor wishes to sell, use, or lease property of the estate other than in the ordinary course of business, a court order authorizing such sale, use, or lease must be first obtained. Notice of a proposed use, sale, or lease of property of the estate outside the ordinary course of business must be filed under Bankruptcy Rule 6004, which governs the procedure in the matter. Bankruptcy Rule 2002(a) requires 20 days notice of any such proposed use, sale, or lease, unless the court orders otherwise. At any hearing under 11 U.S.C. 363, the debtor in possession has the burden of proof on the issue of adequate protection and the creditor has the burden of proof on the issue of the validity of its interest in the property. See 11 U.S.C. 363(o).

After notice and a hearing, the trustee in a chapter 12 case may sell farmland or farm equipment of the estate free and clear of the interest in such property of any entity other than the estate. See 11 U.S.C. 1206. The proceeds of the sale, however, are subject to the creditor's interest. Other property of the estate may be sold free and clear of liens only if the conditions of 11 U.S.C. 363(f) are met. The procedural requirements of implementing 11 U.S.C. 1206 are not clear, but presumably they would be similar to those governing sales outside the ordinary course of business under 11 U.S.C. 363(b), except that the trustee would be the seller instead of the debtor in possession.

If the estate owns property that is burdensome, of inconsequential value, or in which the estate has no equity, it may be advantageous for the debtor in possession to abandon such property. The abandonment of property of the estate is governed by 11 U.S.C. 554 and Bankruptcy Rule 6007.

It is likely that the debtor in possession will need to obtain or incur new credit at some point during the course of a chapter 12 case. The Bankruptcy Code distinguishes credit obtained by the debtor in possession during the course of a chapter 12 case into two categories: credit obtained in the ordinary course of business and credit obtained outside the ordinary course of business. The Bankruptcy Code also distinguishes secured credit from unsecured credit, and different rules are applied to the obtaining of each category and type of credit

Unless the court orders otherwise, a chapter 12 debtor in possession may obtain unsecured credit and incur unsecured debt in the ordinary course of business, and any claim therefor is allowable as an administrative expense under 11 U.S.C. 503(b)(1). See 11 U.S.C. 364(a). Because unsecured debts incurred in the ordinary course of business after the commencement of the case are allowable as administrative expenses while unsecured debts incurred prior to filing are allowable only as general claims under 11 U.S.C. 502, it is important to segregate the debtor's prefiling and postfiling activities and obligations.

The court, after notice and a hearing, may authorize a debtor in possession to obtain unsecured credit or incur unsecured debt outside the ordinary course of business, and any claim therefor is allowable as an administrative expense. See 11 U.S.C. 364(b). If a debtor in possession is unable to obtain unsecured credit allowable as an administrative expense, the court, after notice and a hearing, may authorize the obtaining of credit or the incurring of debt that: (1) has priority over any or all other administrative expenses, (2) is secured by a lien on unencumbered property of the estate, or (3) is secured by a junior lien on encumbered property of the estate. See 11 U.S.C. 364(c).

Finally, the court, after notice and a hearing, may authorize the obtaining of credit or the incurring of debt secured by a senior or equal lien on encumbered property of the estate, but only if the debtor in possession is unable to obtain credit otherwise and there is adequate protection of the interest of the holder of the lien on the encumbered property. See 11 U.S.C. 364(d)(1). At any hearing on the obtaining of such credit, the debtor in possession has the burden of proof on the issue of adequate protection. See 11 U.S.C. 364(d)(2). Adequate protection is discussed in section 4.06, supra.

debtor in possession, obtaining secured credit

If the debtor in possession wishes to obtain credit other than unsecured credit in the ordinary course of business, a motion for authority to obtain credit must be filed under Bankruptcy Rule 9014 and served as provided in Bankruptcy Rule 4001(c). The motion should include the amount and type of credit to be extended, the name and address of the lender, the terms of the credit agreement, the need for the credit, the efforts made to obtain credit from other sources, and, if appropriate, a description of the collateral for the credit and the protection to be accorded to any existing lienholder on the collateral. A copy of any proposed credit agreement must accompany the motion. See Bankruptcy Rule 4001(c)(1).

motion to obtain credit

A final hearing on a motion for authority to obtain credit may not be held earlier than 15 days after service of the motion, but an earlier preliminary hearing may be held if the motion so requests. See Bankruptcy Rule 4001(c)(2). Notice of the hearing must be given in accordance with Bankruptcy Rule 4001(c)(3). A sample Motion for Authority to Obtain Credit is set forth in Exhibit 4-D at the end of this chapter.

motion to obtain credit, hearing requirements

An agreement between the debtor and a creditor relating to the use, sale or lease of property, the use of cash collateral, the obtaining of credit, relief from the automatic stay, or the providing of adequate protection must be approved by the court to be effective. A motion for the approval of such an agreement must comply with Bankruptcy Rule 4001(d). Agreements in settlement of motions may be handled under Bankruptcy Rule 4001(d)(4).

agreements, requirement of court approval

4.08 The Chapter 12 Plan - Preparation and Confirmation

The required and permissible provisions of chapter 12 plans are set forth in 11 U.S.C. 1222, and the confirmation requirements for such plans are found in 11 U.S.C. 1225. Under 11 U.S.C. 1222(a), a chapter 12 plan must:

chapter 12 plan,
required
provisions

    (1) provide for the submission of all or such portion of the debtor's future earnings or income to the supervision and control of the trustee as is necessary for the execution of the plan;

    (2) provide for the full payment, in deferred cash, of all claims entitled to priority under 11 U.S.C. 507, unless the holder of such a claim agrees otherwise; and

    (3) if the plan classifies claims and interests, provide the same treatment for each claim or interest within a particular class unless the holder of such a claim or interest agrees to less favorable treatment.

The above mandatory provisions are identical to those required of chapter 13 plans except that in chapter 12 subsection (3) refers to "claims and interests" and permits the holder of a claim in a particular class to agree to less favorable treatment. The chapter 13 provision refers only to "claims" and does not provide that the holder of a claim may agree to treatment less favorable than other claims in the class.

Under 11 U.S.C. 1222(b), a chapter 12 plan may:

chapter 12 plan,
permitted
provisions

    (1) designate one or more classes of unsecured claims, provided that all claims within a particular class are substantially similar and no class of claims is unfairly discriminated against, except that claims for a consumer debt of the debtor upon which another individual is also liable may be treated differently;

    (2) modify the rights of holders of secured or unsecured claims, or leave unaffected the rights of holders of any class of claims;

    (3) provide for the curing or waiving of any default;

    (4) provide for concurrent payments to be made on any claims, secured or unsecured;

    (5) provide for the curing of any default within a reasonable time and maintenance of payments while the case is pending on any secured or unsecured claim on which the last payment is due after the date on which the final payment under the plan is due;

    (6) provide for the assumption, rejection, or assignment of any executory contract or unexpired lease not previously rejected under 11 U.S.C. 365;

    (7) provide for the payment of all or part of a claim against the debtor from property of the estate or from property of the debtor;

    (8) provide for the sale of all or any part of the property of the estate or the distribution of all or any part of such property among those having an interest in such property;

    (9) provide for payment of allowed secured claims, consistent with 11 U.S.C. 1225(a)(5), over a period exceeding the maximum length of a plan;

    (10) provide for the vesting of property of the estate, on confirmation of the plan or at a later time, in the debtor or in any other entity; and

    (11) include any other appropriate provision not inconsistent with title 11.

The permissive plan provisions listed above are generally similar to those found in chapter 13. The major differences are that subsections (8) and (9) above are not found in chapter 13, and, unlike chapter 13, subsection (2) above makes no exception for the holder of a security interest on the debtor's principal residence and there is no separate provision dealing with postpetition claims. In a chapter 12 case, the debtor may make payments directly to impaired secured creditors and not through the chapter 12 trustee, as long as the payments do not unfairly discriminate among creditors and are made in good faith. See In Re Crum, 85 B.R. 878. The chapter 12 trustee may not collect a fee on payments made directly to creditors by the debtor. See In Re Land, 82 B.R. 572.

direct payments
to creditor,
when permitted

Except as provided in 11 U.S.C. 1222(b)(5) and (9) (i.e., subsections (5) and (9) immediately above), a chapter 12 plan may not provide for payments over a period exceeding three years unless the court, for cause, approves a longer period, which may not exceed five years. See 11 U.S.C. 1222(c). If a plan is later modified so as to extend the period for making payments, the period may not be extended to a date more than five years after the date when the first payment under the original confirmed plan was due. See 11 U.S.C. 1229(c). These time limitations are the same as those in chapter 13.

chapter 12 plan,
maximum length

The confirmation requirements for a chapter 12 plan, which are found in 11 U.S.C. 1225, are identical to those for a chapter 13 plan. The reader is referred to sections 3.08 and 3.13, supra, for further reading.

chapter 12 plan,
confirmation
requirements

With the exceptions noted below, the preparation of a chapter 12 plan is substantially the same as the preparation of a chapter 13 plan, and the reader is referred to section 3.08, supra, for further reading. The local rules should be checked for requirements relating to chapter 12 plans. The significant differences between a chapter 12 plan and a chapter 13 plan are:

chapter 12 plan,
preparation of

(1) a chapter 12 plan may modify the rights of the holder of any claim, including a claim secured by a security interest in the debtor's principal residence;

(2) a chapter 12 plan may not provide for the payment of taxes and necessary consumer debts as postpetition claims under 11 U.S.C. 502;

(3) a chapter 12 plan may provide for the sale of all or any part of the property of the estate or for the distribution of all or any part of such property among those having an interest in such property;

(4) a chapter 12 plan may extend the period for the payment of allowed secured claims beyond the maximum permissible period of the plan;

(5) a chapter 12 plan may provide for the sale of farmland or farm equipment free and clear of the interest of any entity other than the estate under 11 U.S.C. 1206; and

(6) the debtor is not required to commence making payments under a chapter 12 plan until the date specified in the plan.

In some districts local forms are provided for chapter 12 plans. In other districts the forms provided for chapter 13 plans are used for chapter 12 plans. Still other districts provide no forms whatsoever. The local rules should be checked in this regard. If no forms are provided, use Exhibit 3-B at the end of chapter three, supra, as a guide in preparing a chapter 12 plan. The local rules may also require the preparation of documents related to the plan. A summary of the plan, a statement of the debtor, or similar documents may be required. It will be necessary to send a copy of the plan, or a summary thereof, to each creditor with notice of the confirmation hearing, so a sufficient number of copies should be made. See Bankruptcy Rule 3015(d).

chapter 12 plan,
form of

chapter 12 plan,
related
documents

The debtor may file a chapter 12 plan with the petition or not later than 90 days after the order for relief under chapter 12, unless the court extends the period for filing the plan. See 11 U.S.C. 1221 and Bankruptcy Rule 3015(a). The debtor may modify a filed plan at any time before confirmation, but the modified plan must meet the requirements of 11 U.S.C. 1222, which are listed above in this section. See 11 U.S.C. 1223(a). When the debtor files a modification to a plan, the modified plan becomes the plan. See 11 U.S.C. 1223(b). Any holder of a secured claim that has accepted or rejected the plan is deemed to have accepted or rejected the plan as modified, unless the modification changes the rights of such holder and the holder changes its previous acceptance or rejection. See 11 U.S.C. 1223(c). However, the court, upon notice to the trustee and the creditor, may find that a modification does not change the treatment of a creditor's claim. See Bankruptcy Rule 3019. Every proposed plan and any modification thereof must be dated. See Bankruptcy Rule 3015(c).

The clerk, or some other party as the court may direct, must give the debtor, the trustee, all creditors, and all equity security holders notice by mail of the time fixed for filing objections to confirmation of the plan and of time fixed for the hearing to consider confirmation of the plan. Unless the court fixes a shorter period, notice of the hearing must be given not less than 15 days before the hearing. A copy of the plan, or a court-approved summary of the plan, must accompany the notice. See Bankruptcy Rule 3015(d).

A party in interest, the trustee, or the United States trustee may object to confirmation of a plan. See 11 U.S.C. 1224. Objections to confirmation must be filed with the court and served on the debtor, the trustee, and on any other entity designated by the court, within a time fixed by the court. The procedure on an objection to confirmation is governed by Bankruptcy Rule 9014. See Bankruptcy Rule 3020(b)(1).

After notice as provided in Bankruptcy Rule 2002, the court must conduct and conclude a confirmation hearing within the time prescribed by 11 U.S.C. 1224 and rule on confirmation of the plan. See Bankruptcy Rule 3020(b)(2). The confirmation hearing must be concluded not later than 45 days after the plan is filed, unless the court, for cause, extends the time. See 11 U.S.C. 1224. If no objection is timely filed, the court may determine that the plan has been proposed in good faith and not by any means forbidden by law without receiving evidence on those issues. See Bankruptcy Rule 3020(b)(2).

An order of confirmation must conform to Official Form 15, and notice of entry of the order shall be promptly mailed by the clerk, or some other party as the court may direct, to the debtor, the trustee, all creditors and equity security holders, the United States trustee, and other parties in interest. See Bankruptcy Rule 3020(c). Except as noted in the above paragraphs, the chapter 12 confirmation procedures are similar to those for chapter 13, and the reader is referred to section 3.13, supra, for further reading.

The requirements and procedures for modifying a plan after confirmation are the same in a chapter 12 case as in a chapter 13 case. See 11 U.S.C. 1229. The reader is referred to section 3.15, supra, for further reading. Similarly, the requirements and procedures for revoking an order of confirmation are the same in chapter 12 cases as in chapter 13 cases. See 11 U.S.C. 1230. The reader is referred to section 3.13, supra, for further reading.

4.09 Concluding a Chapter 12 Case

A successful chapter 12 case continues until such time as the debtor completes all payments and performs all functions required of the debtor under the plan, at which time the case is closed and the debtor receives a discharge. An unsuccessful chapter 12 case may either be dismissed or converted to a case under chapter 7, and the dismissal or conversion may be at the request of the debtor or upon the motion of a party in interest. See 11 U.S.C. 1208.

chapter 12 case, how concluded

The debtor, without cause, may convert a chapter 12 case to a case under chapter 7 at any time, and any waiver of this conversion right is unenforceable. See 11 U.S.C. 1208(a). On the request of the debtor at any time, if the case has not been converted to chapter 12 from chapter 7 or chapter 11, the court must dismiss a chapter 12 case, and any waiver of this right of dismissal is unenforceable. See 11 U.S.C. 1208(b). It should be noted that there are no notice or hearing requirements for voluntary dismissals or conversions under 11 U.S.C. 1208. See Bankruptcy Rule 1017. A sample notice to convert a case to chapter 7 and a sample motion to dismiss a case are set forth in Exhibits 3-H and 3-I at the end of chapter three, supra.

voluntary conversion or dismissal of case

On the request of a party in interest, and after notice and a hearing, the court may dismiss a chapter 12 case or convert the case to a case under chapter 7 upon a showing that the debtor has committed fraud in connection with the case. See 11 U.S.C. 1208(d). Also, on the request of a party in interest, and after notice and a hearing, the court may dismiss a chapter 12 case for cause, which may include:

dismissal or conversion for fraud

(1) unreasonable delay, or gross mismanagement, by the debtor that is prejudicial to creditors;

(2) nonpayment of any fees and charges required under chapter 123 of title 28 (i.e., filing fees);

(3) failure to file a plan timely under 11 U.S.C. 1221;

(4) failure to commence making timely payments required by a confirmed plan;

(5) denial of confirmation of a plan under 11 U.S.C. 1225 and denial of a request made for additional time for filing another plan or a modification of a plan;

(6) material default by the debtor with respect to a term of a confirmed plan;

(7) revocation of the order of confirmation under 11 U.S.C. 1230, and denial of confirmation of a modified plan under 11 U.S.C. 1229;

(8) termination of a confirmed plan by reason of the occurrence of a condition specified in the plan; or

(9) continuing loss to or diminution of the estate and absence of a reasonable likelihood of rehabilitation. See 11 U.S.C. 1208(c).

involuntary dismissal of case, grounds

While the above-described grounds for the involuntary dismissal or conversion of a chapter 12 case differ somewhat from those in chapter 13, the procedures for involuntary dismissal or conversion of a chapter 12 case are the same as for a chapter 13 case. See Bankruptcy Rule 1017. The reader is referred to handbook section 3.17, supra, for further reading.

involuntary dismissal of case, procedure

As soon as practicable after the completion by the debtor of all payments under the plan, other than payments on claims which extend beyond the period of the plan, the court must grant the debtor a discharge, unless the court approves a written waiver of discharge executed by the debtor after the order for relief under chapter 12. The discharge so granted discharges the debtor from all debts provided for by the plan, allowed under 11 U.S.C. 503 (i.e., administrative expenses), or disallowed under 11 U.S.C. 502, except any debt whose last payment was due after the date on which the final payment was due under the plan under 11 U.S.C. 1222(5), which is to be paid over a period exceeding the period of the plan under 11 U.S.C. 1222(9), or is of a kind specified in 11 U.S.C. 523(a), which are debts that are not dischargeable under chapter 7 (see section 2.17, supra, for a list). See 11 U.S.C. 1228(a). Thus, a successful-plan discharge under chapter 12 is similar to a chapter 7 discharge and is not as broad as the successful-plan discharge under chapter 13. However, unpaid claims for administrative expenses are dischargeable under chapter 12, but not under chapter 13. It should be noted that, unlike chapter 7, a corporate or partnership debtor may receive a discharge under chapter 12.

If a chapter 12 debtor is unable to complete payments under the plan due to circumstances for which the debtor should not justly be held accountable, the debtor may be granted a discharge under 11 U.S.C. 1228(b). The grounds for, the effect of, the procedures for obtaining an unsuccessful-plan discharge under chapter 12 are the same as for an unsuccessful-plan discharge under chapter 13. The reader is referred to section 3.18, supra, for further reading.

The procedures for closing a chapter 12 case are substantially the same as for a chapter 13 case, and the reader is referred to section 3.19, supra, for further reading. It should be noted that under chapter 12 the debtor in possession may have to prepare and file a final report and final accounting of the administration of the estate. See 11 U.S.C. 1203 and Bankruptcy Rule 2015(b).

EXHIBIT 4-A   203

UNITED STATES BANKRUPTCY COURT
FOR THE DISTRICT OF KANSAS

IN RE   Smith Land and Cattle Co.,   )
       a Kansas Corporation   )   Case No. 92-01210
)
                  Debtor   )   Chapter 12

APPLICATION TO EMPLOY ATTORNEYS

The applicant, as debtor in possession, respectfully states and represents as follows:

1. The debtor has filed a petition herein seeking relief under Chapter 12 of the Bankruptcy Code.

2. The debtor is engaged in a farming operation in Lincoln county, Kansas.

3. The debtor, as debtor in possession, wishes to employ John J. Jones and the law firm of Jones and Jones as attorneys under a general retainer to provide legal advice and assistance to the debtor with respect to its powers and duties as a debtor in possession in the operation of the debtor's farming operation and to perform any legal services for the debtor in possession which may become necessary in the case.

4. The applicant has selected John J. Jones and the law firm of Jones and Jones for the reasons that they have filed the petition and initial pleadings in this case on behalf of the debtor, they are knowledgeable as to the debtor's business and property, and are otherwise well qualified to represent the debtor as debtor in possession in this case.

5. To the best of the applicant's knowledge and belief, John J. Jones and the law firm of Jones and Jones have no connection with the debtor, creditors, any other party in interest, their respective attorneys and accountants, the United States trustee, or any person employed in the office of the United States trustee, other than previously representing the debtor and its shareholders generally and preparing and filing the petition and initial pleadings in this case.

WHEREFORE, the applicant respectfully requests this honorable court to authorize the debtor to employ John J. Jones and the law firm of Jones and Jones to represent the debtor as a debtor in possession under a general retainer in this proceeding.

Date: January 10, 1992

Attest: Smith Land and Cattle Co.,
                                        a Kansas Corporation, the Applicant

                                          by _____

_____   _____
Mary R. Smith, Secretary   Henry R. Smith, President

DECLARATION OF PROPOSED ATTORNEY

John J. Jones declares, under penalty of perjury, that he is an attorney duly admitted to practice law in the state of Kansas and before the federal courts in the district of Kansas; that he maintains a practice of law with, and is a partner in, the law firm of Jones and Jones at 554 North Street, Prairie View, Kansas; that said attorney and said law firm have no connection with the Smith Land and Cattle Co., the debtor, it's creditors, any other party in interest in this proceeding, or their respective attorneys and accountants, the United States trustee, or any person employed in the office of the United States trustee, except that said attorneys have represented the debtor and its shareholders generally and in the filing of the Chapter 12 petition in this proceeding; and that the said attorneys represent no interest adverse to the debtor, the debtor in possession, or the estate in this case.

Date: January 10, 1992   _____
                                         John J. Jones,
                                         Attorney at Law

CERTIFICATE OF TRANSMITTAL BY MAIL

The undersigned certifies under penalty of perjury that he or she has on the date shown below, by first class mail addressed to their respective addresses of record, transmitted a true copy of this document to the United States trustee and the Chapter 12 trustee.

Date: _____   _____

CORPORATE RESOLUTION AUTHORIZING COMMENCEMENT OF CASE

I, Mary R. Smith, as Secretary of the SMITH LAND AND CATTLE CO., a Kansas corporation, hereby certify that the following is a true and correct excerpt from the official minutes of said corporation, truly and correctly reflecting the resolutions unanimously adopted by the board of directors of said corporation at a meeting duly called and held on January 5, 1992; to wit:

WHEREAS, it appeared from the information presented to the board of directors that the corporation is no longer able to meet its debts and obligations as they become due and that the corporation qualifies as a debtor under Chapter 12 of the United States Bankruptcy Code, and that it is in the best interest of the corporation to file a petition under Chapter 12 of the Bankruptcy Code; therefore

IT WAS UNANIMOUSLY RESOLVED by the board of directors that the SMITH LAND AND CATTLE CO., a Kansas corporation, should file a petition under Chapter 12 of the Bankruptcy Code and should reorganize thereunder so as to better continue its farming operation.

IT WAS FURTHER RESOLVED that John J. Jones, Attorney at Law, and the law firm of Jones and Jones be retained to represent the corporation on all matters relating to the Chapter 12 proceeding, including the filing of the petition and initial pleadings in the case, and that the said attorney be compensated by the corporation in an equitable manner, subject to the approval of the bankruptcy court.

IT WAS FURTHER RESOLVED that Henry R. Smith, as President of the corporation, be authorized and directed to execute any and all petitions, schedules, statements, and other necessary documents for and on behalf of the corporation in connection with the Chapter 12 case.

Dated: January 5, 1992

_____
Mary R. Smith, Secretary

PARTNERSHIP RESOLUTION AUTHORIZING COMMENCEMENT OF CASE

WHEREAS, it appeared to the general partners of the JONES RANCHING PARTNERSHIP, a general partnership engaged in the business of farming and ranching in the State of Iowa, that the partnership is no longer able to meet its debts and obligations as they become due, that the partnership qualifies as a debtor under Chapter 12 of the United States Bankruptcy Code, and that the best interest of the partnership would be served by reorganizing under Chapter 12; therefore

IT WAS UNANIMOUSLY RESOLVED by the general partners of the JONES RANCHING PARTNERSHIP that the partnership file a petition for relief under Chapter 12 of the Bankruptcy Code and seek to reorganize under Chapter 12.

IT WAS FURTHER RESOLVED that James S. Berry, Attorney at Law, be retained to represent the partnership on all matters relating to the Chapter 12 case, including the filing of the petition and initial pleadings in the case, said attorney to be compensated by the partnership in an equitable manner, subject to the approval of the bankruptcy court.

IT WAS FURTHER RESOLVED that Paul J. Jones, as a general partner of the partnership, be authorized and directed to execute any and all petitions, schedules, statements, and other necessary documents for and on behalf of the partnership in connection with the Chapter 12 case.

Dated: January 12, 1992

_____	_____	_____
Paul J. Jones	Ronald S. Jones	Joseph R. Jones
General Partner	General Partner	General Partner

I, Ronald S. Jones, as a general partner of the JONES RANCHING PARTNERSHIP certify that the foregoing resolution is a true and correct copy of an official resolution duly and lawfully adopted by the partnership on January 12, 1992 at a meeting of all of the general partners of the partnership duly and lawfully called and held.

_____
Ronald S. Jones,
General Partner

EXHIBIT 4-C 205

UNITED STATES BANKRUPTCY COURT
FOR THE DISTRICT OF KANSAS

IN RE   Smith Land and Cattle Co.,   )
         a Kansas Corporation   )   Case No. 92-01210
)
                Debtor   )   Chapter 12

MOTION FOR AUTHORITY TO USE CASH COLLATERAL

The debtor in possession, by its attorney, represents as follows:

1. The debtor filed a voluntary petition under Chapter 12 of The Bankruptcy Code on January 5, 1992. The debtor is now conducting its farming operation in Lincoln County, Kansas as a debtor in possession.

2. The amount of cash collateral sought to be used by the debtor in possession is $4,000.

3. The name and address of each entity having an interest in the cash collateral sought to be used by the debtor in possession is: The First National Bank of Topeka, 700 5th Street, Topeka, Kansas 66604.

4. The name and address of the entity having possession or custody of the cash collateral is: The Apex Grain Company, 200 Main Street, Kansas City, Kansas 66102.

5. The debtor expects to receive cash collateral in the form of checks totalling $4,000 from The Apex Grain Company on or about January 20, 1992 for the payment of grain received by Apex in November, 1991. The debtor proposes to use the cash collateral to meet current living expenses and to pay the expenses of operating the debtor's farm, including the payment of wages to the debtor's employees. The debtor has no other source of current income and payment of such expenses will be in the best interest of the estate and the debtor's reorganization.

6. The protection to be provided to the entity having an interest in the cash collateral is to permit the entity to maintain its lien on other property of the estate, the value of which exceeds the amount of the entity's lien.

7. The debtor hereby requests a preliminary hearing on this motion. The amount of cash collateral sought to be used pending the final hearing is $2,000, and the protection to be provided pending the final hearing is the protection described in paragraph 6 above.

WHEREFORE, the debtor moves this honorable court for an order authorizing the debtor in possession to use the cash collateral in the amounts and in the manner described above in this motion and for such other relief as may be just.

Jones and Jones

by _____
John J. Jones
Attorneys for Debtor in Possession
554 North Street
Prairie View, KS 67111
Telephone: 913-431-7151

CERTIFICATE OF TRANSMITTAL AND SERVICE BY MAIL

The undersigned certifies under penalty of perjury that he or she has, on the date shown below, by first class mail addressed to their respective addresses of record in this case, transmitted and served a true copy of this document to the United States trustee, the Chapter 12 trustee, the creditors listed in the above document, and their respective attorneys of record.

Date: _____   _____

UNITED STATES BANKRUPTCY COURT
FOR THE DISTRICT OF KANSAS

IN RE   Smith Land and Cattle Co.,   )
         a Kansas Corporation   )   Case No. 92-01210
)
                              Debtors   )   Chapter 12

MOTION FOR AUTHORITY TO OBTAIN CREDIT

The debtor in possession, by its attorney, states and represents as follows:

1. The debtor filed a petition seeking relief under Chapter 12 of the Bankruptcy Code on January 5, 1992 and is currently operating its farming operation as a debtor in possession.

2. The debtor in possession is in need of unsecured credit outside the ordinary course of business under 11 U.S.C. 364(b) in the amount of $7,500 for the purpose of paying for the harvesting of the debtor's wheat crop, which must be harvested within the next ten days. The debtor does not have the equipment with which to harvest its wheat crop and proposes to hire Bob Evans Wheat Cutters, Inc., of Wichita, Kansas to harvest the wheat crop at an estimated cost of $7,500, which must be paid to the harvester immediately upon completion of the harvesting.

3. The debtor in possession proposes to borrow the funds with which to pay for the harvesting from Mortimer M. Smith of Smith Center, Kansas at an interest rate of 10 percent per annum. The debtor in possession proposes that Mortimer M. Smith be granted a priority administrative expense allowable under 11 U.S.C. 503(b)(1) in the amount of the principal balance of the loan plus accrued interest. The debtor anticipates receiving payment from the sale of the wheat crop within 30 days after harvesting and proposes to pay the claim of Mortimer M. Smith from such funds. Mortimer M. Smith is the father of Henry R. Smith, the principal shareholder of the debtor.

WHEREFORE, the debtor moves this honorable court for an order authorizing the debtor to obtain unsecured credit outside the ordinary course of business in the manner and in the amount described above in this motion.

Dated: July 17, 1992   Jones and Jones

                                              by _____
                                                 John J. Jones
                                                 Attorneys for Debtor in Possession
                                                 554 North Street
                                                 Prairie View, KS 67111
                                                 Telephone: 913-431-7151

CERTIFICATE OF TRANSMITTAL AND SERVICE BY MAIL

The undersigned certifies under penalty of perjury that he or she has, on the date shown below, by first class mail addressed to their respective addresses of record in this case, transmitted and served a true copy of this document to the United States trustee, the Chapter 12 trustee, and Mortimer M. Smith.

Date: _____   _____

APPENDIX I

UNITED STATES BANKRUPTCY CODE
(TITLE 11 UNITED STATES CODE)
(Current to January 1, 1993)

CONTENTS

Note: Chapter 9 and Chapter 11 of the Bankruptcy Code are omitted because they do not pertain to chapter 7 consumer cases, chapter 12 cases, or chapter 13 cases.

CHAPTER 1 - GENERAL PROVISIONS

Sec.
101. Definitions
102. Rules of construction
103. Applicability of chapters
104. Adjustment of dollar amounts
105. Power of court
106. Waiver of sovereign immunity
107. Public access to papers
108. Extension of time
109. Who may be a debtor

101. Definitions

In this title –

(1) "accountant" means accountant authorized under applicable law to practice public accounting, and includes professional accounting association, corporation, or partnership, if so authorized;

(2) "affiliate" means –

(A) entity that directly or indirectly owns, controls, or holds with power to vote, 20 percent or more of the outstanding voting securities of the debtor, other than an entity that holds such securities –

(i) in a fiduciary or agency capacity without sole discretionary power to vote such securities; or

(ii) solely to secure a debt, if such entity has not in fact exercised such power to vote;

(B) corporation 20 percent or more of whose outstanding voting securities are directly or indirectly owned, controlled, or held with power to vote, by the debtor, or by an entity that directly or indirectly owns, controls, or holds with power to vote, 20 percent or more of the outstanding voting securities of the debtor, other than an entity that holds such securities –

(i) in a fiduciary or agency capacity without sole discretionary power to vote such securities; or

(ii) solely to secure a debt, if such entity has not in fact exercised such power to vote;

(C) person whose business is operated under a lease or operating agreement by a debtor, or person substantially all of whose property is operated under an operating agreement with the debtor; or

(D) entity that operates the business or substantially all of the property of the debtor under a lease or operating agreement;

(3) "Federal depository institutions regulatory agency" means–

(A) with respect to an insured depository institution (as defined in section 3(c)(2) of the Federal Deposit Insurance Act) for which no conservator or receiver has been appointed, the appropriate Federal banking agency (as defined in section 3(q) of such Act);

(B) with respect to an insured credit union (including an insured credit union for which the National Credit Union Administration has been appointed conservator or liquidating agent), the National Credit Union Administration;

(C) with respect to any insured depository institution for which the Resolution Trust Corporation has been appointed conservator or receiver, the Resolution Trust Corporation; and

(D) with respect to any insured depository institution for which the Federal Deposit Insurance Corporation has been appointed conservator or receiver, the Federal Deposit Insurance Corporation.

(4) "attorney" means attorney, professional law association, corporation, or partnership, authorized under applicable law to practice law;

(5) "claim" means –

(A) right to payment, whether or not such right is reduced to judgment, liquidated, unliquidated, fixed, contingent, matured, unmatured, disputed, undisputed, legal, equitable, secured, or unsecured; or

(B) right to an equitable remedy for breach of performance if such breach gives rise to a right to payment, whether or not such right to an equitable remedy is reduced to judgment, fixed, contingent, matured, unmatured, disputed, undisputed, secured, or unsecured;

(6) "commodity broker" means futures commission merchant, foreign futures commission merchant, clearing organization, leverage transaction merchant, or commodity options dealer, as defined in section 761 of this title, with respect to which there is a customer, as defined in section 761(9) of this title;

(7) "community claim" means claim that arose before the commencement of the case concerning the debtor for which property of the kind specified in section 541(a)(2) of this title is liable, whether or not there is any such property at the time of the commencement of the case;

(8) "consumer debt" means debt incurred by an individual primarily for a personal, family, or household purpose;

(9) "corporation"–

(A) includes –

(i) association having a power or privilege that a private corporation, but not an individual or a partnership, possesses;

(ii) partnership association organized under a law that makes only the capital subscribed responsible for the debts of such association;

(iii) joint-stock company;

(iv) unincorporated company or association; or

(v) business trust; but

(B) does not include limited partnership;

(10) "creditor" means –

(A) entity that has a claim against the debtor that arose at the time of or before the order for relief concerning the debtor;

(B) entity that has a claim against the estate of a kind specified in section 348(d), 502(f), 502(g), 502(h), or 502(i) of this title; or

(C) entity that has a community claim;

(11) "custodian" means –

(A) receiver or trustee of any of the property of the debtor, appointed in a case or proceeding not under this title;

(B) assignee under a general assignment for the benefit of the debtor's creditors; or

(C) trustee, receiver, or agent under applicable law, or under a contract, that is appointed or authorized to take charge of property of the debtor for the purpose of enforcing a lien against such property, or for the purpose of general administration of such property for the benefit of the debtor's creditors;

(12) "debt" means liability on a claim;

(13) "debtor" means person or municipality concerning which a case under this title has been commenced;

(14) "disinterested person" means person that –

(A) is not a creditor, an equity security holder, or an insider;

(B) is not and was not an investment banker for any outstanding security of the debtor;

(C) has not been, within three years before the date of the filing of the petition, an investment banker for a security of the debtor, or an attorney for such an investment banker in connection with the offer, sale, or issuance of a security of the debtor;

(D) is not and was not, within two years before the date of the filing of the petition, a director, officer, or employee of the debtor or of an investment banker specified in subparagraph (B) or (C) of this paragraph; and

(E) does not have an interest materially adverse to the interest of the estate or of any class of creditors or equity security holders, by reason of any direct or indirect relationship to, connection with, or interest in, the debtor or an investment banker specified in subparagraph (B) or (C) of this paragraph, or for any other reason;

(15) "entity" includes person, estate, trust, governmental unit, and United States trustee;

(16) "equity security" means –

(A) share in a corporation, whether or not transferable or denominated "stock", or similar security;

(B) interest of a limited partner in a limited partnership; or

(C) warrant or right, other than a right to convert, to purchase, sell, or subscribe to a share, security, or interest of a kind specified in subparagraph (A) or (B) of this paragraph;

(17) "equity security holder" means holder of an equity security of the debtor;

(18) "family farmer" means –

(A) individual or individual and spouse engaged in a farming operation whose aggregate debts do not exceed $1,500,000 and not less than 80 percent of whose aggregate noncontingent, liquidated debts (excluding a debt for the principal residence of such individual or such individual and spouse unless such debt arises out of a farming operation), on the date the case is filed, arise out a farming operation owned or operated by such individual or such individual and spouse, and such individual or such individual and spouse receive from such farming operation more than 50 percent of such individual's or such individual and spouse's gross income for the taxable year preceding the taxable year in which the case concerning such individual or such individual and spouse was filed; or

(B) corporation or partnership in which more than 50 percent of the outstanding stock or equity is held by one family, or by one family and the relatives of the members of such family, and such family or such relatives conduct the farming operation, and

(i) more than 80 percent of the value of its assets consists of assets related to the farming operation;

(ii) its aggregate debts do not exceed $1,500,000 and not less than 80 percent of its aggregate noncontingent, liquidated debts (excluding a debt for one dwelling which is owned by such corporation or partnership and which a shareholder or partner maintains as a principal residence, unless such debt arises out of a farming operation), on the date the case is filed, arise out of the farming operation owned or operated by such corporation or such partnership; and

(iii) if such corporation issues stock, such stock is not publicly traded;

(19) "family farmer with regular annual income" means family farmer whose annual income is sufficiently stable and regular to enable such family farmer to make payments under a plan under chapter 12 of this title;

(20) "farmer" means (except when such term appears in the term "family farmer") person that received more than 80 percent of such person's gross income during the taxable year of such person immediately preceding the taxable year of such person during which the case under this title concerning such person was commenced from a farming operation owned or operated by such person;

(21) "farming operation" includes farming, tillage of the soil, dairy farming, ranching, production or raising of crops, poultry, or livestock, and production of poultry or livestock products in an unmanufactured state;

(21A) "farmout agreement" means a written agreement in which–

(A) the owner of a right to drill, produce, or operate liquid or gaseous hydrocarbons on property agrees or has agreed to transfer or assign all or a part of such right to another entity; and

(B) such other entity (either directly or through its agents or its assigns), as consideration, agrees to perform drilling, reworking, recompleting, testing, or similar or related operations, to develop or produce liquid or gaseous hydrocarbons on the property;

(22) "financial institution" means a person that is a commercial or savings bank, industrial savings bank, savings and loan association, or trust company and, when any such person is acting as agent or custodian for a customer in connection with a securities contract, as defined in section 741(7) of this title, such customer;

(23) "foreign proceeding" means proceeding, whether judicial or administrative and whether or not under bankruptcy law, in a foreign country in which the debtor's domicile, residence, principal place of business, or principal assets were located at the commencement of such proceeding, for the purpose of liquidating an estate, adjusting debts by composition, extension, or discharge, or effecting a reorganization;

(24) "foreign representative" means duly selected trustee, administrator, or other representative of an estate in a foreign proceeding;

(25) "forward contract" means a contract (other than a commodity contract) for the purchase, sale, or transfer of a commodity, as defined in section 761(8) of this title, or any similar good, article, service, right, or interest which is presently or in the future becomes the subject of dealing in the forward contract trade, or product or byproduct thereof, with a maturity date more than two days after the date the contract is entered into, including, but not limited to, a repurchase transaction, reverse repurchase transaction, consignment, lease, swap, hedge transaction, deposit, loan, option, allocated transaction, unallocated transaction, or any combination thereof or option thereon;

(26) "forward contract merchant" means a person whose business consists in whole or in part of entering into forward contracts as or with merchants in a commodity, as defined in section 761(8) of this title, or any similar good, article, service, right, or interest which is presently or in the future becomes the subject of dealing in the forward contract trade;

(27) "governmental unit" means United States; State; Commonwealth; District; Territory; municipality; foreign state; department, agency, or instrumentality of the United States (but not a United States trustee while serving as a trustee in a case under this title), a State, a Commonwealth, a District, a Territory, a municipality, or a foreign state; or other foreign or domestic government;

(28) "indenture" means mortgage, deed of trust, or indenture, under which there is outstanding a security, other than a voting-trust certificate, constituting a claim against the debtor, a claim secured by a lien on any of the debtor's property, or an equity security of the debtor;

(29) "indenture trustee" means trustee under an indenture;

(30) "individual with regular income" means individual whose income is sufficiently stable and regular to enable such individual to make payments under a plan under chapter 13 of this title, other than a stockbroker or a commodity broker;

(31) "insider" includes –

(A) if the debtor is an individual –

(i) relative of the debtor or a general partner of the debtor;

(ii) partnership in which the debtor is a general partner;

(iii) general partner of the debtor; or

(iv) corporation of which the debtor is a director, officer, or person in control;

(B) if the debtor is a corporation –

(i) director of the debtor;

(ii) officer of the debtor;

(iii) person in control of the debtor;

(iv) partnership in which the debtor is a general partner;

(v) general partner of the debtor; or

(vi) relative of a general partner, director, officer, or person in control of the debtor;

(C) if the debtor is a partnership –

(i) general partner in the debtor;

(ii) relative of a general partner in, general partner of, or person in control of the debtor;

(iii) partnership in which the debtor is a general partner;

(iv) general partner of the debtor; or

(v) person in control of the debtor;

(D) if the debtor is a municipality, elected official of the debtor or relative of an elected official of the debtor;

(E) affiliate, or insider of an affiliate as if such affiliate were the debtor; and

(F) managing agent of the debtor

(32) "insolvent" means –

(A) with reference to an entity other than a partnership and a municipality, financial condition such that the sum of such entity's debts is greater than all of such entity's property, at a fair valuation, exclusive of –

(i) property transferred, concealed, or removed with intent to hinder, delay, or defraud such entity's creditors; and

(ii) property that may be exempted from property of the estate under section 522 of this title;

(B) with reference to a partnership, financial condition such that the sum of such partnership's debts is greater than the aggregate of, at fair valuation –

(i) all of such partnership's property, exclusive of property of the kind specified in subparagraph (A)(i) of this paragraph; and

(ii) the sum of the excess of the value of each general partner's nonpartnership property, exclusive of property of the kind specified in subparagraph (A) of this paragraph, over such partner's nonpartnership debts; and

(C) with reference to a municipality, financial condition such that the municipality is –

(i) generally not paying its debts as they become due unless such debts are the subject of a bona fide dispute; or

(ii) unable to pay its debts as they become due

(33) "institution–affiliated party"–

(A) with respect to an insured depository institution (as defined in section 3(c)(2) of the Federal Deposit Insurance Act), has the meaning given it in section 3(u) of the Federal Deposit Insurance Act (12 U.S.C. 1813(u)); and

(B) with respect to an insured credit union, has the meaning given it in section 206(r) of the Federal Credit Union Act (12 U.S.C. 1786(r));

(34) "insured credit union" has the meaning given it in section 101(7) of the Federal Credit Union Act (12 U.S.C. 1752(7));

(35) "insured depository institution"–

(A) has the meaning given it in section 3(c)(2) of the Federal Deposit Insurance Act (12 U.S.C. 1813(c)(2)); and

(B) includes an insured credit union (except in the case of paragraphs (3) and (33)(A) of this subsection);

(36) "judicial lien" means lien obtained by judgment, levy, sequestration, or other legal or equitable process or proceeding;

(37) "lien" means charge against or interest in property to secure payment of a debt or performance of an obligation;

(38) "margin payment" means, for purposes of the forward contract provisions of this title, payment or deposit of cash, a security or other property, that is commonly known in the forward contract trade as original margin, initial margin, maintenance margin, or variation margin, including mark–to–market payments, or variation payments;

(39) "settlement payment" means, for purposes of the forward contract provisions of this title, a preliminary settlement payment, a partial settlement payment, an interim settlement payment, a settlement payment on account, a final settlement payment, a net settlement payment, or any other similar payment commonly used in the forward contract trade;

(40) "municipality" means political subdivision or public agency or instrumentality of a State;

(41) "person" includes individual, partnership, and corporation, but does not include governmental unit, Provided, however, That any governmental unit that acquires an asset from a person as a result of operation of a loan guarantee agreement, or as receiver or liquidating agent of a person, will be considered a person for purposes of section 1102 of this title;

(42) "petition" means petition filed under section 301, 302, 303, or 304 of this title, as the case may be, commencing a case under this title;

(43) "purchaser" means transferee of a voluntary transfer, and includes immediate or mediate transferee of such a transferee;

(44) "railroad" means common carrier by railroad engaged in the transportation of individuals or property or owner of trackage facilities leased by such a common carrier;

(45) "relative" means individual related by affinity or consanguinity within the third degree as determined by the common law, or individual in a step or adoptive relationship within such third degree;

(46) "repo participant" means an entity that, on any day during the period beginning 90 days before the date of the filing of the petition, has an outstanding repurchase agreement with the debtor;

(47) "repurchase agreement" (which definition also applies to a reverse repurchase agreement) means an agreement, including related terms, which provides for the transfer of certificates of deposit, eligible bankers' acceptances, or securities that are direct obligations of, or that are fully guaranteed as to principal and interest by, the United States or any agency of the United States against the transfer of funds by the transferee of such certificates of deposit, eligible bankers' acceptances, or securities with a simultaneous agreement by such transferee to transfer to the transferor thereof certificates of deposit, eligible bankers' acceptances, or securities as described above, at a date certain not later than one year after such transfers or on demand, against the transfer of funds;

(48) "securities clearing agency" means person that is registered as a clearing agency under section 17A of the Securities Exchange Act of 1934 (15 U.S.C. 78q-1) or whose business is confined to the performance of functions of a clearing agency with respect to exempted securities, as defined in section 3 (a)(12) of such Act (15 U.S.C. 78c(12)) for the purposes of such section 17A;

(49) "security" –
    (A) includes –
        (i) note;
        (ii) stock;
        (iii) treasury stock;
        (iv) bond;
        (v) debenture;
        (vi) collateral trust certificate;
        (vii) pre-organization certificate or subscription;
        (viii) transferable share;
        (ix) voting-trust certificate;
        (x) certificate of deposit;
        (xi) certificate of deposit for security;
        (xii) investment contract or certificate of interest or participation in a profit-sharing agreement or in an oil, gas, or mineral royalty or lease, if such contract or interest is required to be the subject of a registration statement filed with the Securities and Exchange Commission under the provisions of the Securities Act of 1933 (15 U.S.C. 77a, et seq.), or is exempt under section 3(b) of such Act (15 U.S.C. 77c(b)) from the requirement to file such a statement;
        (xiii) interest of a limited partner in a limited partnership;
        (xiv) other claim or interest commonly known as "security"; and
        (xv) certificate of interest or participation in, temporary or interim certificate for, receipt for, or warrant or right to subscribe to or purchase or sell, a security; but
    (B) does not include –
        (i) currency, check, draft, bill of exchange, or bank letter of credit;
        (ii) leverage transaction, as defined in section 761(13) of this title;
        (iii) commodity futures contract or forward contract;
        (iv) option, warrant, or right to subscribe to or purchase or sell a commodity futures contract;
        (v) option to purchase or sell a commodity;
        (vi) contract or certificate of a kind specified in subparagraph (A)(xii) of this paragraph that is not required to be the subject of a registration statement filed with the Securities and Exchange Commission and is not exempt under section 3(b) of the Securities Act of 1933 (15 U.S.C. 77c(b)) from the requirement to file such a statement; or
        (vii) debt or evidence of indebtedness for goods sold and delivered or services rendered;

(50) "security agreement" means agreement that creates or provides for a security interest;

(51) "security interest" means lien created by an agreement;

(52) "State" includes the District of Columbia and Puerto Rico, except for the purpose of defining who may be a debtor under chapter 9 of this title;

(53) "statutory lien" means lien arising solely by force of a statute on specified circumstances or conditions, or lien of distress for rent, whether or not statutory, but does not include security interest or judicial lien, whether or not such interest or lien is provided by or is dependent on a statute and whether or not such interest or lien is made fully effective by statute;

(54) "stockbroker" means person –
    (A) with respect to which there is a customer, as defined in section 741(2) of this title; and
    (B) that is engaged in the business of effecting transactions in securities –
        (i) for the account of others; or
        (ii) with members of the general public, from or for such person's own account;

(55) "swap agreement" means –
    (A) an agreement (including terms and conditions incorporated by reference therein) which is a rate swap agreement, basis swap, forward rate agreement, commodity swap, interest rate option, forward foreign exchange agreement, rate cap agreement, rate floor agreement, rate collar agreement, currency swap agreement, cross-currency rate swap agreement, currency option, any other similar agreement (including any option to enter into any of the foregoing);

    (B) any combination of the foregoing; or
    (C) a master agreement for any of the foregoing together with all supplements;

(56) "swap participant" means an entity that, at any time before the filing of the petition, has an outstanding swap agreement with the debtor;

(57) "timeshare plan" means and shall include that interest purchased in any arrangement, plan, scheme, or similar device, but not including exchange programs, whether by membership, agreement, tenancy in common, sale, lease, deed, rental agreement, license, right to use agreement, or by any other means, whereby a purchaser, in exchange for consideration, receives a right to use accommodations, facilities, or recreational sites, whether improved or unimproved, for a specific period of time less than a full year during any given year, but not necessarily for consecutive years, and which extends for a period of more than three years. A "timeshare interest" is that interest purchased in a timeshare plan which grants the purchaser the right to use and occupy accommodations, facilities, or recreational sites, whether improved or unimproved, pursuant to a timeshare plan;

(58) "transfer" means every mode, direct or indirect, absolute or conditional, voluntary or involuntary, of disposing of or parting with property or with an interest in property, including retention of title as a security interest and foreclosure of the debtor's equity of redemption;

(59) "United States", when used in a geographical sense, includes all locations where the judicial jurisdiction of the United States extends, including territories and possessions of the United States;

(60) "intellectual property" means –
    (A) trade secret;
    (B) invention, process, design, or plant protected under title 35;
    (C) patent application;
    (D) plant variety;
    (E) work of authorship protected under title 17; or
    (F) mask work protected under chapter 9 of title 17; to the extent protected by applicable nonbankruptcy law; and

(61) "mask work" has the meaning given it in section 901(a)(2) of title 17.

102. Rules of construction

In this title –

(1) "after notice and a hearing", or a similar phrase –
    (A) means after such notice as is appropriate in the particular circumstances, and such opportunity for a hearing as is appropriate in the particular circumstances; but
    (B) authorizes an act without an actual hearing if such notice is given properly and if –
        (i) such a hearing is not requested timely by a party in interest; or
        (ii) there is insufficient time for a hearing to be commenced before such act must be done, and the court authorizes such act;

(2) "claim against the debtor" includes claim against property of the debtor;

(3) "includes" and "including" are not limiting;

(4) "may not" is prohibitive, and not permissive;

(5) "or" is not exclusive;

(6) "order for relief" means entry of an order for relief;

(7) the singular includes the plural;

(8) a definition, contained in a section of this title that refers to another section of this title, does not, for the purpose of such reference, affect the meaning of a term used in such other section; and

(9) "United States trustee" includes a designee of the United States trustee.

103. Applicability of chapters

(a) Except as provided in section 1161 of this title, chapters 1, 3, and 5 of this title apply in a case under chapter 7, 11, 12, or 13 of this title.

(b) Subchapters I and II of chapter 7 of this title apply only in a case under such chapter.

(c) Subchapter III of chapter 7 of this title applies only in a case under such chapter concerning a stockbroker.

(d) Subchapter IV of chapter 7 of this title applies only in a case under such chapter concerning a commodity broker.

(e) Except as provided in section 901 of this title, only chapters 1 and 9 of this title apply in a case under such chapter 9.

(f) Except as provided in section 901 of this title, subchapters I, II, and III of chapter 11 of this title apply only in a case under such chapter.

(g) Subchapter IV of chapter 11 of this title applies only in a case under such chapter concerning a railroad.

(h) Chapter 13 of this title applies only in a case under such chapter.

(i) Chapter 12 of this title applies only in a case under such chapter.

104. Adjustment of dollar amounts

The Judicial Conference of the United States shall transmit to the Congress and to the President before May 1, 1985, and before May 1 of every sixth year after May 1, 1985, a recommendation for the uniform percentage adjustment of each dollar amount in this title and in section 1930 of title 28.

105. Power of court

(a) The court may issue any order, process, or judgment that is necessary or appropriate to carry out the provisions of this title. No provision of this title providing for the raising of an issue by a party in interest shall be construed to preclude the court from, sua sponte, taking any action or making any determination necessary or appropriate to enforce or implement court orders or rules, or to prevent an abuse of process.

(b) Notwithstanding subsection (a) of this section, a court may not appoint a receiver in a case under this title.

(c) The ability of any district judge or other officer or employee of a district court to exercise any of the authority or responsibilities conferred upon the court under this title shall be determined by reference to the provisions relating to such judge, officer, or employee set forth in title 28. This subsection shall not be interpreted to exclude bankruptcy judges and other officers or employees appointed pursuant to chapter 6 of title 28 from its operation.

106. Waiver of sovereign immunity

(a) A governmental unit is deemed to have waived sovereign immunity with respect to any claim against such governmental unit that is property of the estate and that arose out of the same transaction or occurrence out of which such governmental unit's claim arose.

(b) There shall be offset against an allowed claim or interest of a governmental unit any claim against such governmental unit that is property of the estate.

(c) Except as provided in subsections (a) and (b) of this section and notwithstanding any assertion of sovereign immunity –

(1) a provision of this title that contains "creditor", "entity", or "governmental unit" applies to governmental units; and

(2) a determination by the court of an issue arising under such a provision binds governmental units.

107. Public access to papers

(a) Except as provided in subsection (b) of this section, a paper filed in a case under this title and the dockets of a bankruptcy court are public records and open to examination by an entity at reasonable times without charge.

(b) On request of a party in interest, the bankruptcy court shall, and on the bankruptcy court's own motion, the bankruptcy court may –

(1) protect an entity with respect to a trade secret or confidential research, development, or commercial information; or

(2) protect a person with respect to scandalous or defamatory matter contained in a paper filed in a case under this title.

108. Extension of time

(a) If applicable nonbankruptcy law, an order entered in a nonbankruptcy proceeding, or an agreement fixes a period within which the debtor may commence an action, and such period has not expired before the date of the filing of the petition, the trustee may commence such action only before the later of –

(1) the end of such period, including any suspension of such period occurring on or after the commencement of the case; or

(2) two years after the order for relief.

(b) Except as provided in subsection (a) of this section, if applicable nonbankruptcy law, an order entered in a nonbankruptcy proceeding, or an agreement fixes a period within which the debtor or an individual protected under section 1201 or 1301 of this title may file any pleading, demand, notice, or proof of claim or loss, cure a default, or perform any other similar act, and such period has not expired before the date of the filing of the petition, the trustee may only file, cure, or perform, as the case may be, before the later of –

(1) the end of such period, including any suspension of such period occurring on or after the commencement of the case; or

(2) 60 days after the order for relief.

(c) Except as provided in section 524 of this title, if applicable nonbankruptcy law, an order entered in a nonbankruptcy proceeding, or an agreement fixes a period for commencing or continuing a civil action in a court other than a bankruptcy court on a claim against the debtor, or against an individual with respect to which such individual is protected under section 1201 or 1301 of this title, and such period has not expired before the date of the filing of the petition, then such period does not expire until the later of –

(1) the end of such period, including any suspension of such period occurring on or after the commencement of the case; or

(2) 30 days after notice of the termination or expiration of the stay under section 362, 922, 1201, or 1301 of this title, as the case may be, with respect to such claim.

109. Who may be a debtor

(a) Notwithstanding any other provision of this section, only a person that resides or has a domicile, a place of business, or property in the United States, or a municipality, may be a debtor under this title.

(b) A person may be a debtor under chapter 7 of this title only if such person is not –

(1) a railroad;

(2) a domestic insurance company, bank, savings bank, cooperative bank, savings and loan association, building and loan association, homestead association, credit union, or industrial bank or similar institution which is an insured bank as defined in section 3(h) of the Federal Deposit Insurance Act (12 U.S.C. 1813(h)); or

(3) a foreign insurance company, bank, savings bank, cooperative bank, savings and loan association, building and loan association, homestead association, or credit union, engaged in such business in the United States.

(c) An entity may be a debtor under chapter 9 of this title if and only if such entity –

(1) is a municipality;

(2) is generally authorized to be a debtor under such chapter by State law, or by a governmental officer or organization empowered by State law to authorize such entity to be a debtor under such chapter;

(3) is insolvent;

(4) desires to effect a plan to adjust such debts; and

(5)(A) has obtained the agreement of creditors holding at least a majority in amount of the claims of each class that such entity intends to impair under a plan in a case under such chapter;

(B) has negotiated in good faith with creditors and has failed to obtain the agreement of creditors holding at least a majority in amount of the claims of each class that such entity intends to impair under a plan in a case under such chapter;

(C) is unable to negotiate with creditors because such negotiation is impractical; or

(D) reasonably believes that a creditor may attempt to obtain a transfer that is avoidable under section 547 of this title.

(d) Only a person that may be a debtor under chapter 7 of this title, except a stockbroker or a commodity broker, and a railroad may be a debtor under chapter 11 of this title.

(e) Only an individual with regular income that owes, on the date of the filing of the petition, noncontingent, liquidated, unsecured debts of less than $100,000 and noncontingent, liquidated, secured debts of less than $350,000, or an individual with regular income and such individual's spouse, except a stockbroker or a commodity broker, that owe, on the date of the filing of the petition, noncontingent, liquidated, unsecured debts that aggregate less than $100,000 and noncontingent, liquidated, secured debts of less than $350,000 may a debtor under chapter 13 of this title.

(f) Only a family farmer with regular annual income may be a debtor under chapter 12 of this title.

(g) Notwithstanding any other provision of this section, no individual or family farmer may be a debtor under this title who has been a debtor in a case pending under this title at any time in the preceding 180 days if –

(1) the case was dismissed by the court for willful failure of the debtor to abide by orders of the court, or to appear before the court in proper prosecution of the case; or

(2) the debtor requested and obtained the voluntary dismissal of the case following the filing of a request for relief from the automatic stay provided by section 362 of this title.

CHAPTER 3 – CASE ADMINISTRATION

SUBCHAPTER I – COMMENCEMENT OF A CASE

SUBCHAPTER II – OFFICERS

SUBCHAPTER III – ADMINISTRATION

SUBCHAPTER IV – ADMINISTRATIVE POWERS

SUBCHAPTER I – COMMENCEMENT OF A CASE

301. Voluntary cases

A voluntary case under a chapter of this title is commenced by the filing with the bankruptcy court of a petition under such chapter by an entity that may be a debtor under such chapter. The commencement of a voluntary case under a chapter of this title constitutes an order for relief under such chapter.

302. Joint cases

(a) A joint case under a chapter of this title is commenced by the filing with the bankruptcy court of a single petition under such chapter by an individual that may be a debtor under such chapter and such individual's spouse. The commencement of a joint case under a chapter of this title constitutes an order for relief under such chapter.

(b) After the commencement of a joint case, the court shall determine the extent, if any, to which the debtors' estates shall be consolidated.

303. Involuntary cases

(a) An involuntary case may be commenced only under chapter 7 or 11 of this title, and only against a person, except a farmer, family farmer, or a corporation that is not a moneyed, business, or commercial corporation, that may be a debtor under the chapter under which such case is commenced.

(b) An involuntary case against a person is commenced by the filing with the bankruptcy court of a petition under chapter 7 or 11 of this title—

(1) by three or more entities, each of which is either a holder of a claim against such person that is not contingent as to liability or the subject of a bona fide dispute, or an indenture trustee representing such a holder, if such claims aggregate at least $5,000 more than the value of any lien on property of the debtor securing such claims held by the holders of such claims;

(2) if there are fewer than 12 such holders, excluding any employee or insider of such person and any transferee of a transfer that is voidable under section 544, 545, 547, 548, 549, or 724(a) of this title, by one or more of such holders that hold in the aggregate at least $5,000 of such claims;

(3) if such person is a partnership—

(A) by fewer than all of the general partners in such partnership; or

(B) if relief has been ordered under this title with respect to all of the general partners in such partnership, by a general partner in such partnership, the trustee of such a general partner, or a holder of a claim against such partnership; or

(4) by a foreign representative of the estate in a foreign proceeding concerning such person.

(c) After the filing of a petition under this section but before the case is dismissed or relief is ordered, a creditor holding an unsecured claim that is not contingent, other than a creditor filing under subsection (b) of this section, may join in the petition with the same effect as if such joining creditor were a petitioning creditor under subsection (b) of this section.

(d) The debtor, or a general partner in a partnership debtor that did not join in the petition, may file an answer to a petition under this section.

(e) After notice and a hearing, and for cause, the court may require the petitioners under this section to file a bond to indemnify the debtor for such amounts as the court may later allow under subsection (i) of this section.

(f) Notwithstanding section 363 of this title, except to the extent that the court orders otherwise, and until an order for relief in the case, any business of the debtor may continue to operate, and the debtor may continue to use, acquire, or dispose of property as if an involuntary case concerning the debtor had not been commenced.

(g) At any time after the commencement of an involuntary case under chapter 7 of this title but before an order for relief in the case, the court, on request of a party in interest, after notice to the debtor and a hearing, and if necessary to preserve the property of the estate or to prevent loss to the estate, may order the United States trustee to appoint an interim trustee under section 701 of this title to take possession of the property of the estate and to operate any business of the debtor. Before an order for relief, the debtor may regain possession of property in the possession of a trustee ordered appointed under this subsection if the debtor files such bond as the court requires, conditioned on the debtor's accounting for and delivering to the trustee, if there is an order for relief in the case, such property, or the value, as of the date the debtor regains possession, of such property.

(h) If the petition is not timely controverted, the court shall order relief against the debtor in an involuntary case under the chapter under which the petition was filed. Otherwise, after trial, the court shall order relief against the debtor in an involuntary case under the chapter under which the petition was filed, only if—

(1) the debtor is generally not paying such debtor's debts as such debts become due unless such debts are the subject of a bona fide dispute; or

(2) within 120 days before the date of the filing of the petition, a custodian, other than a trustee, receiver, or agent appointed or authorized to take charge of less than substantially all of the property of the debtor for the purpose of enforcing a lien against such property, was appointed or took possession.

(i) If the court dismisses a petition under this section other than on consent of all petitioners and the debtor, and if the debtor does not waive the right to judgment under this subsection, the court may grant judgment—

(1) against the petitioners and in favor of the debtor for—

(A) costs; or

(B) a reasonable attorney's fee; or

(C) any damages proximately caused by the taking of possession of the debtor's property by a trustee appointed under subsection (g) of this section or section 1104 of this title; or

(2) against any petitioner that filed the petition in bad faith, for—

(A) any damages proximately caused by such filing; or

(B) punitive damages.

(j) Only after notice to all creditors and a hearing may the court dismiss a petition filed under this section—

(1) on the motion of a petitioner;

(2) on consent of all petitioners and the debtor; or

(3) for want of prosecution.

(k) Notwithstanding subsection (a) of this section, an involuntary case may be commenced against a foreign bank that is not engaged in such business in the United States only under chapter 7 of this title and only if a foreign proceeding concerning such bank is pending.

304. Cases ancillary to foreign proceedings

(a) A case ancillary to a foreign proceeding is commenced by the filing with the bankruptcy court of a petition under this section by a foreign representative.

(b) Subject to the provisions of subsection (c) of this section, if a party in interest does not timely controvert the petition, or after trial, the court may—

(1) enjoin the commencement or continuation of—

(A) any action against—

(i) a debtor with respect to property involved in such foreign proceeding; or

(ii) such property; or

(B) the enforcement of any judgment against the debtor with respect to such property, or any act or the commencement or continuation of any judicial proceeding to create or enforce a lien against the property of such estate;

(2) order turnover of the property of such estate, or the proceeds of such property, to such foreign representative; or

(3) order other appropriate relief.

(c) In determining whether to grant relief under subsection (b) of this section, the court shall be guided by what will best assure an economical and expeditious administration of such estate, consistent with—

(1) just treatment of all holders of claims against or interests in such estate;

(2) protection of claim holders in the United States against prejudice and inconvenience in the processing of claims in such foreign proceeding;

(3) prevention of preferential or fraudulent dispositions of property of such estate;

(4) distribution of proceeds of such estate substantially in accordance with the order prescribed by this title;

(5) comity; and

(6) if appropriate, the provision of an opportunity for a fresh start for the individual that such foreign proceeding concerns.

305. Abstention

(a) The court, after notice and a hearing, may dismiss a case under this title, or may suspend all proceedings in a case under this title, at any time if –

(1) the interests of creditors and the debtor would be better served by such dismissal or suspension; or

(2)(A) there is pending a foreign proceeding; and

(B) the factors specified in section 304(c) of this title warrant such dismissal or suspension.

(b) A foreign representative may seek dismissal or suspension under subsection(a)(2) of this section.

(c) An order under subsection (a) of this section dismissing a case or suspending all proceedings in a case, or a decision not so to dismiss or suspend, is not reviewable by appeal or otherwise by the court of appeals under section 158(d), 1291, or 1292 of title 28 or by the Supreme Court of the United States under section 1254 of title 28.

306. Limited appearance

An appearance in a bankruptcy court by a foreign representative in connection with a petition or request under section 303, 304, or 305 of this title does not submit such foreign representative to the jurisdiction of any court in the United States for any other purpose, but the bankruptcy court may condition any order under section 303, 304, or 305 of this title on compliance by such foreign representative with the orders of such bankruptcy court.

307. United States trustee

The United States trustee may raise and may appear and be heard on any issue in any case or proceeding under this title but may not file a plan pursuant to section 1121(c) of this title.

SUBCHAPTER II - OFFICERS

321. Eligibility to serve as trustee

(a) A person may serve as trustee in a case under this title only if such person is–

(1) an individual that is competent to perform the duties of trustee and, in a case under chapter 7, 12, or 13 of this title, resides or has an office in the judicial district within which the case is pending, or in any judicial district adjacent to such district; or

(2) a corporation authorized by such corporation's charter or bylaws to act as trustee, and, in a case under chapter 7, 12, or 13 of this title, having an office in at least one of such districts.

(b) A person that has served as an examiner in the case may not serve as trustee in the case.

(c) The United States trustee for the judicial district in which the case is pending is eligible to serve as trustee in the case if necessary.

322. Qualification of trustee

(a) Except as provided in subsection (b)(1), a person selected under section 701, 702, 703, 1104, 1163, 1302, or 1202 of this title to serve as trustee in a case under this title qualifies if before five days after such selection, and before beginning official duties, such person has filed with the court a bond in favor of the United States conditioned on the faithful performance of such official duties.

(b)(1) The United States trustee qualifies wherever such trustee serves as trustee in a case under this title.

(2) The United States trustee shall determine –

(A) the amount of a bond required to be filed under subsection (a) of this section; and

(B) the sufficiency of the surety on such bond.

(c) A trustee is not liable personally or on such trustee's bond in favor of the United States for any penalty or forfeiture incurred by the debtor.

(d) A proceeding on a trustee's bond may not be commenced after two years after the date on which such trustee was discharged.

323. Role and capacity of trustee

(a) The trustee in a case under this title is the representative of the estate.

(b) The trustee in a case under this title has capacity to sue and be sued.

324. Removal of trustee or examiner

(a) The court, after notice and a hearing, may remove a trustee, other than the United States trustee, or an examiner, for cause.

(b) Whenever the court removes a trustee or examiner under subsection (a) in a case under this title, such trustee or examiner shall thereby be removed in all other cases under this title in which such trustee or examiner is then serving unless the court orders otherwise.

325. Effect of vacancy

A vacancy in the office of trustee during a case does not abate any pending action or proceeding, and the successor trustee shall be substituted as a party in such action or proceeding.

326. Limitation on compensation of trustee

(a) In a case under chapter 7 or 11, the court may allow reasonable compensation under section 330 of this title of the trustee for the trustee's services, payable after the trustee renders such services, not to exceed fifteen percent on the first $1,000 or less, six percent on any amount in excess of $1,000 but not in excess of $3,000, and three percent on any amount in excess of $3,000, upon all moneys disbursed or turned over in the case by the trustee to parties in interest, excluding the debtor, but including holders of secured claims.

(b) In a case under chapter 12 or 13 of this title, the court may not allow compensation for services or reimbursement of expenses of the United States trustee or of a standing trustee appointed under section 586(b) of title 28, but may allow reasonable compensation under section 330 of this title of a trustee appointed under section 1202(a) or 1302(a) of this title for the trustee's services, payable after the trustee renders such services, not to exceed five percent upon all payments under the plan.

(c) If more than one person serves as trustee in the case, the aggregate compensation of such persons for such service may not exceed the maximum compensation prescribed for a single trustee by subsection (a) or (b) of this section, as the case may be.

(d) The court may deny allowance of compensation for services or reimbursement of expenses of the trustee if the trustee failed to make diligent inquiry into facts that would permit denial of allowance under section 328(c) of this title or, with knowledge of such facts, employed a professional person under section 327 of this title.

327. Employment of professional persons

(a) Except as otherwise provided in this section, the trustee, with the court's approval, may employ one or more attorneys, accountants, appraisers, auctioneers, or other professional persons, that do not hold or represent an interest adverse to the estate, and that are disinterested persons, to represent or assist the trustee in carrying out the trustee's duties under this title.

(b) If the trustee is authorized to operate the business of the debtor under section 721, 1202, or 1108 of this title, and if the debtor has regularly employed attorneys, accountants, or other professional persons on salary, the trustee may retain or replace such professional persons if necessary in the operation of such business.

(c) In a case under chapter 7, 12, or 11 of this title, a person is not disqualified for employment under this section solely because of such person's employment by or representation of a creditor, unless there is objection by another creditor or the United States trustee, in which case the court shall disapprove such employment if there is an actual conflict of interest.

(d) The court may authorize the trustee to act as attorney or accountant for the estate if such authorization is in the best interest of the estate.

(e) The trustee, with the court's approval, may employ, for a specified specific purpose, other that to represent the trustee in conducting the case, an attorney that has represented the debtor, if in the best interest of the estate, and if such attorney does not represent or hold any interest adverse to the debtor or to the estate with respect to the matter on which such attorney is to be employed.

(f) The trustee may not employ a person that has served as an examiner in the case.

328. Limitation on compensation of professional persons

(a) The trustee, or a committee appointed under section 1102 of this title, with the court's approval, may employ or authorize the employment of a professional person under section 327 or 1103 of this title, as the case may be, on any reasonable terms and conditions of employment, including on a retainer, on an hourly basis, or on a contingent fee basis. Notwithstanding such terms and conditions, the court may allow compensation different from the compensation provided under such terms and conditions after the conclusion of such employment, if such terms and conditions prove to have been improvident in light of developments not capable of being anticipated at the time of the fixing of such terms and conditions.

(b) If the court has authorized a trustee to serve as an attorney or accountant for the estate under section 327(d) of this title, the court may allow compensation for the trustee's services as such attorney or accountant only to the extent that the trustee performed services as attorney or accountant for the estate and not for performance of any of the trustee's duties that are generally performed by a trustee without the assistance of an attorney or accountant for the estate.

(c) Except as provided in section 327(c), 327(e), or 1107(b) of this title, the court may deny allowance of compensation for services and reimbursement of expenses of a professional person employed under section 327 or 1103 of this title if, at any time during such professional person's employment under section 327 or 1103 of this title, such professional person is not a disinterested person, or represents or holds an interest adverse to the interest of the estate with respect to the matter on which such professional person is employed.

329. Debtor's transactions with attorneys

(a) Any attorney representing a debtor in a case under this title, or in connection with such a case, whether or not such attorney applies for compensation under this title, shall file with the court a statement of the compensation paid or agreed to be paid, if such payment or agreement was made after one year before the date of the filing of the petition, for services rendered or to be rendered in contemplation of or in connection with the case by such attorney, and the source of such compensation.

(b) If such compensation exceeds the reasonable value of any such services, the court may cancel any such agreement, or order the return of any such payment, to the extent excessive, to –

(1) the estate, if the property transferred –

(A) would have been property of the estate; or

(B) was to be paid by or on behalf of the debtor under a plan under chapter 11, 12, or 13 of this title; or

(2) the entity that made such payment.

330. Compensation of officers

(a) After notice to any parties in interest and to the United States trustee and a hearing, and subject to sections 326, 328, and 329 of this title, the court may award to a trustee, to an examiner, to a professional person employed under section 327 or 1103 of this title, or to the debtor's attorney –

(1) reasonable compensation for actual, necessary services rendered by such trustee, examiner, professional person, or attorney, as the case may be, and by any paraprofessional persons employed by such trustee, professional person, or attorney, as the case may be, based on the nature, the extent, and the value of such services, the time spent on such services, and the cost of comparable services other than in a case under this title; and

(2) reimbursement for actual, necessary expenses.

(b) There shall be paid from the filing fee in a case under chapter 7 of this title $45 to the trustee serving in such case, after such trustee's services are rendered.

(c) Unless the court orders otherwise, in a case under chapter 12 or 13 of this title the compensation paid to the trustee serving in the case shall not be less than $5 per month from any distribution under the plan during the administration of the plan.

(d) In a case in which the United States trustee serves as trustee, the compensation of the trustee under this section shall be paid to the clerk of the bankruptcy court and deposited by the clerk into the United States Trustee System Fund established by section 589a of title 28.

331. Interim compensation

A trustee, an examiner, a debtor's attorney, or any professional person employed under section 327 or 1103 of this title may apply to the court not more than once every 120 days after an order for relief in a case under this title, or more often if the court permits, for such compensation for services rendered before the date of such an application or reimbursement for expenses incurred before such date as is provided under section 330 of this title. After notice and a hearing, the court may allow and disburse to such applicant such compensation or reimbursement.

SUBCHAPTER III - ADMINISTRATION

341. Meetings of creditors and equity security holders

(a) Within a reasonable time after the order for relief in a case under this title, the United States trustee shall convene and preside at a meeting of creditors.

(b) The United States trustee may convene a meeting of any equity security holders.

(c) The court may not preside at, and may not attend, any meeting under this section including any final meeting of creditors.

342. Notice

(a) There shall be given such notice as is appropriate, including notice to any holder of a community claim, of an order for relief in a case under this title.

(b) Prior to the commencement of a case under this title by an individual whose debts are primarily consumer debts, the clerk shall give written notice to such individual that indicates each chapter of this title under which such individual may proceed.

343. Examination of the debtor

The debtor shall appear and submit to examination under oath at the meeting of creditors under section 341(a) of this title. Creditors, any indenture trustee, any trustee or examiner in the case, or the United States trustee may examine the debtor. The United States trustee may administer the oath required under this section.

344. Self-incrimination; immunity

Immunity for persons required to submit to examination, to testify, or to provide information in a case under this title may be granted under part V of title 18.

345. Money of estates

(a) A trustee in a case under this title may make such deposit or investment of the money of the estate for which such trustee serves as will yield the maximum reasonable net return on such money, taking into account the safety of such deposit or investment.

(b) Except with respect to a deposit or investment that is insured or guaranteed by the United States or by a department, agency, or instrumentality of the United States or backed by the full faith and credit of the United States, the trustee shall require from an entity with which such money is deposited or invested –

(1) a bond–

(A) in favor of the United States;

(B) secured by the undertaking of a corporate surety approved by the United States trustee for the district in which the case is pending; and

(C) conditioned on –

(i) a proper accounting for all money so deposited or invested and for any return on such money;

(ii) prompt repayment of such money and return; and

(iii) faithful performance of duties as a depository; or

(2) the deposit of securities of the kind specified in section 9303 of title 31.

(c) An entity with which such moneys are deposited or invested is authorized to deposit or invest such moneys as may be required under this section.

346. Special tax provisions

(a) Except to the extent otherwise provided in this section, subsections (b), (c), (d), (e), (g), (h), (i), and (j) of this section apply notwithstanding any State or local law imposing a tax, but subject to the Internal Revenue Code of 1954.

(b)(1) In a case under chapter 7, 12, or 11 of this title concerning an individual, any income of the estate may be taxed under a State or local law imposing a tax on or measured by income only to the estate, and may not be taxed to such individual. Except as provided in section 728 of this title, if such individual is a partner in a partnership, any gain or loss resulting from a distribution of property from such partnership, or any distributive share of income, gain, loss, deduction, or credit of such individual that is distributed, or considered distributed, from such partnership, after the commencement of the case is gain, loss, income, deduction, or credit, as the case may be, of the estate.

(2) Except as otherwise provided in this section and in section 728 of this title, any income of the estate in such a case, and any State or local tax on or measured by such income, shall be computed in the same manner as the income and the tax of an estate.

(3) The estate in such a case shall use the same accounting method as the debtor used immediately before the commencement of the case.

(c)(1) The commencement of a case under this title concerning a corporation or a partnership does not effect a change in the status of such corporation or partnership for the purposes of any State or local law imposing a tax on or measured by income. Except as otherwise provided in this section and in section 728 of this title, any income of the estate in such case may be taxed only as though such case had not been commenced.

(2) In such a case, except as provided in section 728 of this title the trustee shall make any tax return otherwise required by State or local law to be filed by or on behalf of such corporation or partnership in the same manner and form as such corporation or partnership, as the case may be, is required to make such return.

(d) In a case under chapter 13 of this title, any income of the estate or the debtor may be taxed under a State or local law imposing a tax on or measured by income only to the debtor, and may not be taxed to the estate.

(e) A claim allowed under section 502(f) or 503 of this title, other than a claim for a tax that is not otherwise deductible or a capital expenditure that is not otherwise deductible, is deductible by the entity to which income of the estate is taxed unless such claim was deducted by another entity, and a deduction for such claim is deemed to be a deduction attributable to a business.

(f) The trustee shall withhold from any payment of claims for wages, salaries, commissions, dividends, interest, or other payments, or collect, any amount required to be withheld or collected under applicable State or local tax law, and shall pay such withheld or collected amount to the appropriate governmental unit at the time and in the manner required by such tax law, and with the same priority as the claim from which such amount was withheld was paid.

(g)(1) Neither gain nor loss shall be recognized on a transfer–

(A) by operation of law, of property to the estate;

(B) other than a sale, of property from the estate to the debtor; or

(C) in a case under chapter 11 or 12 of this title concerning a corporation, of property from the estate to a corporation that is an affiliate participating in a joint plan with the debtor, or that is a successor to the debtor under the plan, except that gain or loss may be recognized to the same extent that such transfer results in the recognition of gain or loss under section 371 of the Internal Revenue Code of 1954.

(2) The transferee of a transfer of a kind specified in this subsection shall take the property transferred with the same character, and with the transferor's basis, as adjusted under subsection (j)(5) of this section, and holding period.

(h) Notwithstanding sections 728(a) and 1146(a) of this title, for the purpose of determining the number of taxable periods during which the debtor or the estate may use a loss carryover or a loss carryback, the taxable period of the debtor during which the case is commenced is deemed not to have been terminated by such commencement.

(i)(1) In a case under chapter 7, 12, or 11 of this title concerning an individual, the estate shall succeed to the debtor's tax attributes, including–

(A) any investment credit carryover;
(B) any recovery exclusion;
(C) any loss carryover;
(D) any foreign tax credit carryover;
(E) any capital loss carryover; and
(F) any claim of right.

(2) After such a case is closed or dismissed, the debtor shall succeed to any tax attribute to which the estate succeeded under paragraph (1) of this subsection but that was not utilized by the estate. The debtor may utilize such tax attributes as though any applicable time limitations on such utilization by the debtor were suspended during the time during which the case was pending.

(3) In such a case, the estate may carry back any loss of the estate to a taxable period of the debtor that ended before the order for relief under such chapter the same as the debtor could have carried back such loss had the debtor incurred such loss and the case under this title had not been commenced, but the debtor may not carry back any loss of the debtor from a taxable period that ends after such order to any taxable period of the debtor that ended before such order until after the case is closed.

(j)(1) Except as otherwise provided in this subsection, income is not realized by the estate, the debtor, or a successor to the debtor by reason of forgiveness or discharge of indebtedness in a case under this title.

(2) For the purposes of any State or local law imposing a tax on or measured by income, a deduction with respect to a liability may not be allowed for any taxable period during or after which such liability is forgiven or discharged under this title. In this paragraph, "a deduction with respect to a liability" includes a capital loss incurred on the disposition of a capital asset with respect to a liability that was incurred in connection with the acquisition of such asset.

(3) Except as provided in paragraph (4) of this subsection, for the purpose of any State or local law imposing a tax on or measured by income, any net operating loss of an individual or corporate debtor, including a net operating loss carryover to such debtor, shall be reduced by the amount of indebtedness forgiven or discharged in a case under this title, except to the extent that such forgiveness or discharge resulted in a disallowance under paragraph (2) of this subsection.

(4) A reduction of a net operating loss or a net operating loss carryover under paragraph (3) of this subsection or of basis under paragraph (5) of this subsection is not required to the extent that the indebtedness of an individual or corporate debtor forgiven or discharged—
(A) consisted of items of a deductible nature that were not deducted by such debtor; or
(B) resulted in an expired net operating loss carryover or other deduction that—
(i) did not offset income for any taxable period; and
(ii) did not contribute to a net operating loss in or a net operating loss carryover to the taxable period during or after which such indebtedness was discharged.

(5) For the purposes of a State or local law imposing a tax on or measured by income, the basis of the debtor's property or of property transferred to an entity required to use the debtor's basis in whole or in part shall be reduced by the lesser of—
(A)(i) the amount by which the indebtedness of the debtor has been forgiven or discharged in a case under this title; minus
(ii) the total amount of adjustments made under paragraphs (2) and (3) of this subsection; and
(B) the amount by which the total basis of the debtor's assets that were property of the estate before such forgiveness or discharge exceeds the debtor's total liabilities that were liabilities both before and after such forgiveness or discharge.

(6) Notwithstanding paragraph (5) of this subsection, basis is not required to be reduced to the extent that the debtor elects to treat as taxable income, of the taxable period in which indebtedness is forgiven or discharged, the amount of indebtedness forgiven or discharged that otherwise would be applied in reduction of basis under paragraph (5) of this subsection.

(7) For the purposes of this subsection, indebtedness with respect to which an equity security, other than an interest of a limited partner in a limited partnership, is issued to the creditor to whom such indebtedness was owed, or that is forgiven as a contribution to capital by an equity security holder other than a limited partner in the debtor, is not forgiven or discharged in a case under this title—
(A) to any extent that such indebtedness did not consist of items of a deductible nature; or
(B) if the issuance of such equity security has the same consequences under a law imposing a tax on or measured by income to such creditor as a payment in cash to such creditor in an amount equal to the fair market value of such equity security, then to the lesser of—
(i) the extent that such issuance has the same such consequences; and
(ii) the extent of such fair market value.

347. Unclaimed property

(a) Ninety days after the final distribution under section 726, 1226, or 1326 of this title in a case under chapter 7, 12, or 13 of this title, as the case may be, the trustee shall stop payment on any check remaining unpaid, and any remaining property of the estate shall be paid into the court and disposed of under chapter 129 of title 28.

(b) Any security, money, or other property remaining unclaimed at the expiration of the time allowed in a case under chapter 9, 11, or 12 of this title for the presentation of a security or the performance of any other act as a condition to participation in the distribution under any plan confirmed under section 943(b), 1129, 1173, or 1225 of this title, as the case may be, becomes the property of the debtor or of the entity acquiring the assets of the debtor under the plan, as the case may be.

348. Effect of conversion

(a) Conversion of a case from a case under one chapter of this title to a case under another chapter of this title constitutes an order for relief under the chapter to which the case is converted, but, except as provided in subsections (b) and (c) of this section, does not effect a change in the date of the filing of the petition, the commencement of the case, or the order for relief.

(b) Unless the court for cause orders otherwise, in sections 701(a), 727(a)(10), 727(b), 728(a), 728(b), 1102(a), 1110(a)(1), 1121(b), 1121(c), 1141(d)(4), 1146(a), 1146(b), 1301(a), 1305(a), 1201(a), 1221, and 1228(a) of this title, "the order for relief under this chapter" in a chapter to which a case has been converted under section 706, 1112, 1307, or 1208 of this title means the conversion of such case to such chapter.

(c) Sections 342 and 365(d) of this title apply in a case that has been converted under section 706, 1112, 1307, or 1208 of this title, as if the conversion order were the order for relief.

(d) A claim against the estate or the debtor that arises after the order for relief but before conversion in a case that is converted under section 1112, 1307, or 1208 of this title, other than a claim specified in section 503(b) of this title, shall be treated for all purposes as if such claim had arisen immediately before the date of the filing of the petition.

(e) Conversion of a case under section 706, 1112, 1307, or 1208 of this title terminates the service of any trustee or examiner that is serving in the case before such conversion.

349. Effect of dismissal

(a) Unless the court, for cause, orders otherwise, the dismissal of a case under this title does not bar the discharge, in a later case under this title, of debts that were dischargeable in the case dismissed; nor does the dismissal of a case under this title prejudice the debtor with regard to the filing of a subsequent petition under this title, except as provided in section 109(f) of this title.

(b) Unless the court, for cause, orders otherwise, a dismissal of a case other than under section 742 of this title –
(1) reinstates –
(A) any proceeding or custodianship superseded under section 543 of this title;
(B) any transfer avoided under section 522, 544, 545, 547, 548, 549, or 724(a) of this title, or preserved under section 510(c)(2), 522(i)(2), or 551 of this title; and
(C) any lien voided under section 506(d) of this title;
(2) vacates any order, judgment, or transfer ordered, under section 522(i)(1), 542, 550, or 553 of this title; and
(3) revests the property of the estate in the entity in which such property was vested immediately before the commencement of the case under this title.

350. Closing and reopening cases

(a) After an estate is fully administered and the court has discharged the trustee, the court shall close the case.

(b) A case may be reopened in the court in which such case was closed to administer assets, to accord relief to the debtor, or for other cause.

SUBCHAPTER IV - ADMINISTRATIVE POWERS

361. Adequate protection

When adequate protection is required under section 362, 363, or 364 of this title of an interest of an entity in property, such adequate protection may be provided by –
(1) requiring the trustee to make a cash payment or periodic cash payments to such entity, to the extent that the stay under section 362 of this title, use, sale, or lease under section 363 of this title, or any grant of a lien under section 364 of this title results in a decrease in the value of such entity's interest in such property;
(2) providing to such entity an additional or replacement lien to the extent that such stay, use, sale, lease, or grant results in a decrease in the value of such entity's interest in such property; or
(3) granting such other relief, other than entitling such entity to compensation allowable under section 503(b)(1) of this title as an administrative expense, as will result in the realization by such entity of the indubitable equivalent of such entity's interest in such property.

362. Automatic stay

(a) Except as provided in subsection (b) of this section, a petition filed under section 301, 302, or 303 of this title, or an application filed under section 5(a)(3) of the Securities Investor Protection Act of 1970 (15 U.S.C. 78eee(a)(3)), operates as a stay, applicable to all entities, of –
(1) the commencement or continuation, including the issuance or employment of process, of a judicial, administrative, or other action or proceeding against the debtor that was or could have been commenced before the commencement of the case under this title, or to recover a claim against the debtor that arose before the commencement of the case under this title;
(2) the enforcement, against the debtor or against property of the estate, of a judgment obtained before the commencement of the case under this title;
(3) any act to obtain possession of property of the estate or of property from the estate or to exercise control over property of the estate;

(4) any act to create, perfect, or enforce any lien against property of the estate;

(5) any act to create, perfect, or enforce against property of the debtor any lien to the extent that such lien secures a claim that arose before the commencement of the case under this title;

(6) any act to collect, assess, or recover a claim against the debtor that arose before the commencement of the case under this title;

(7) the setoff of any debt owing to the debtor that arose before the commencement of the case under this title against any claim against the debtor; and

(8) the commencement or continuation of a proceeding before the United States Tax Court concerning the debtor.

(b) The filing of a petition under section 301, 302, or 303 of this title, or of an application under section 5(a)(3) of the Securities Investor Protection Act of 1970 (15 U.S.C. 78eee(a)(3)), does not operate as a stay –

(1) under subsection (a) of this section, of the commencement or continuation of a criminal action or proceeding against the debtor;

(2) under subsection (a) of this section, of the collection of alimony, maintenance, or support from property that is not property of the estate;

(3) under subsection (a) of this section, of any act to perfect an interest in property to the extent that the trustee's rights and powers are subject to such perfection under section 546(b) of this title or to the extent that such act is accomplished within the period provided under section 547(e)(2)(A) of this title;

(4) under subsection (a)(1) of this section, of the commencement or continuation of an action or proceeding by a governmental unit to enforce such governmental unit's police or regulatory power;

(5) under subsection (a)(2) of this section, of the enforcement of a judgment, other than a money judgment, obtained in an action or proceeding by a governmental unit to enforce such governmental unit's police or regulatory power;

(6) under subsection (a) of this section, of the setoff by a commodity broker, forward contract merchant, stockbroker, financial institutions, or securities clearing agency of any mutual debt and claim under or in connection with commodity contracts, as defined in section 761(4) of this title, forward contracts, or securities contracts, as defined in section 741(7) of this title, that constitutes the setoff of a claim against the debtor for a margin payment, as defined in section 101(34), 741(5) or 761(15) of this title, or settlement payment, as defined in section 101(35) or 741(8) of this title, arising out of commodity contracts, forward contracts, or securities contracts against cash, securities, or other property held by or due from such commodity broker, forward contract merchant, stockbroker, financial institutions, or securities clearing agency to margin, guarantee, or secure, or settle commodity contracts, forward contracts, or securities contracts;

(7) under subsection (a) of this section, of the setoff by a repo participant, of any mutual debt and claim under or in connection with repurchase agreements that constitutes the setoff of a claim against the debtor for a margin payment, as defined in section 741(5) or 761(15) of this title, or settlement payment, as defined in section 741(8) of this title, arising out of repurchase agreements against cash, securities, or other property held by or due from such repo participant to margin, guarantee, secure or settle repurchase agreements;

(8) under subsection (a) of this section, of the commencement of any action by the Secretary of Housing and Urban Development to foreclose a mortgage or deed of trust in any case in which the mortgage or deed of trust held by the Secretary is insured or was formerly insured under the National Housing Act and covers property, or combinations of property, consisting of five or more living units;

(9) under subsection (a) of this section, of the issuance to the debtor by a governmental unit of a notice of tax deficiency;

(10) under subsection (a) of this section, of any act by a lessor to the debtor under a lease of nonresidential real property that has terminated by the expiration of the stated term of the lease before the commencement of or during a case under this title to obtain possession of such property; or

(11) under subsection (a) of this section, of the presentment of a negotiable instrument and the giving of notice of and protesting dishonor of such an instrument;

(12) under subsection (a) of this section, after the date which is 90 days after the filing of such petition, of the commencement or continuation, and conclusion to the entry of final judgment, of an action which involves a debtor subject to reorganization pursuant to chapter 11 of this title and which was brought by the Secretary of Transportation under the Ship Mortgage Act, 1920 (46 App. U.S.C. 911 et seq.) (including distribution of any proceeds of sale) to foreclose a preferred ship or fleet mortgage, or a security interest in or relating to a vessel under construction, held by the Secretary of Transportation under section 207 or title XI of the Merchant Marine Act, 1936 (46 App. U.S.C. 1117 and 1271 et seq., respectively), or under applicable State law;

(13) under subsection (a) of this section, after the date which is 90 days after the filing of such petition, of the commencement or continuation, and conclusion to the entry of final judgment, of an action which involves a debtor subject to reorganization pursuant to chapter 11 of this title and which was brought by the Secretary of Commerce under the Ship Mortgage Act, 1920 (46 App. U.S.C. 911 et seq.) (including distribution of any proceeds of sale) to foreclose a preferred ship or fleet mortgage in a vessel or a mortgage, deed of trust, or other security interest in a fishing facility held by the Secretary of Commerce under section 207 or title XI of the Merchant Marine Act, 1936 (46 App. U.S.C. 1117 and 1271 et seq., respectively);

(14) under subsection (a) of this section, of the setoff by a swap participant, of any mutual debt and claim under or in connection with any swap agreement that constitutes the setoff of a claim against the debtor for any payment due from the debtor under or in connection with any swap agreement against any payment due to the debtor from the swap participant under or in connection with any swap agreement or against cash, securities, or other property of the debtor held by or due from such swap participant to guarantee, secure or settle any swap agreement;

(15) under subsection (a) of this section, of any action by an accrediting agency regarding the accreditation status of the debtor as an educational institution;

(16) under subsection (a) of this section, of any action by a State licensing body regarding the licensure of the debtor as an educational institution; or

(17) under subsection (a) of this section, of any action by a guaranty agency, as defined in section 435(j) of the Higher Education Act of 1965 (20 U.S.C. 1001 et seq.) or the Secretary of Education regarding the eligibility of the debtor to participate in programs authorized under such Act.

The provisions of paragraphs (12) and (13) of this subsection shall apply with respect to any such petition filed on or before December 31, 1989.

(c) Except as provided in subsections (d), (e), and (f) of this section –

(1) the stay of an act against property of the estate under subsection (a) of this section continues until such property is no longer property of the estate; and

(2) the stay of any other act under subsection (a) of this section continues until the earliest of –

(A) the time the case is closed;

(B) the time the case is dismissed; or

(C) if the case is a case under chapter 7 of this title concerning an individual or a case under chapter 9, 11, 12, or 13 of this title, the time a discharge is granted or denied.

(d) On request of a party in interest and after notice and a hearing, the court shall grant relief from the stay provided under subsection (a) of this section, such as by terminating, annulling, modifying, or conditioning such stay –

(1) for cause, including the lack of adequate protection of an interest in property of such party in interest; or

(2) with respect to a stay of an act against property under subsection (a) of this section, if –

(A) the debtor does not have an equity in such property; and

(B) such property is not necessary to an effective reorganization.

(e) Thirty days after a request under subsection (d) of this section for relief from the stay of any act against property of the estate under subsection (a) of this section, such stay is terminated with respect to the party in interest making such request, unless the court, after notice and a hearing, orders such stay continued in effect pending the conclusion of, or as a result of, a final hearing and determination under subsection (d) of this section. A hearing under this subsection may be a preliminary hearing, or may be consolidated with the final hearing under subsection (d) of this section. The court shall order such stay continued in effect pending the conclusion of the final hearing under subsection (d) of this section if there is a reasonable likelihood that the party opposing relief from such stay will prevail at the conclusion of such final hearing. If the hearing under this subsection is a preliminary hearing, then such final hearing shall be commenced not later than thirty days after the conclusion of such preliminary hearing.

(f) Upon request of a party in interest, the court, with or without a hearing, shall grant such relief from the stay provided under subsection (a) of this section as is necessary to prevent irreparable damage to the interest of an entity in property, if such interest will suffer such damage before there is an opportunity for notice and a hearing under subsection (d) or (e) of this section.

(g) In any hearing under subsection (d) or (e) of this section concerning relief from the stay of any act under subsection (a) of this section –

(1) the party requesting such relief has the burden of proof on the issue of the debtor's equity in property; and

(2) the party opposing such relief has the burden of proof on all other issues.

(h) An individual injured by any willful violation of a stay provided by this section shall recover actual damages, including costs and attorneys' fees, and, in appropriate circumstances, may recover punitive damages.

363. Use, sale, or lease of property

(a) In this section, "cash collateral" means cash, negotiable instruments, documents of title, securities, deposit accounts, or other cash equivalents whenever acquired in which the estate and an entity other than the estate have an interest and includes the proceeds, products, offspring, rents, or profits of property subject to a security interest as provided in section 552(b) of this title, whether existing before or after the commencement of a case under this title.

(b)(1) The trustee, after notice and a hearing, may use, sell, or lease, other than in the ordinary course of business, property of the estate.

(2) If notification is required under subsection (a) of section 7A of the Clayton Act (15 U.S.C. 18a) in the case of a transaction under this subsection, then –

(A) notwithstanding subsection (a) of such section, such notification shall be given by the trustee; and

(B) notwithstanding subsection (b) of such section, the required waiting period shall end on the tenth day after the date of the receipt of such notification, unless the court, after notice and hearing, orders otherwise.

(c)(1) If the business of the debtor is authorized to be operated under section 721, 1108, 1304, 1203, or 1204 of this title and unless the court orders otherwise, the trustee may enter into transactions, including the sale or lease of property of the estate, in the ordinary course of business, without notice or a hearing, and may use property of the estate in the ordinary course of business without notice or a hearing.

(2) The trustee may not use, sell, or lease cash collateral under paragraph (1) of this subsection unless –

(A) each entity that has an interest in such cash collateral consents; or

(B) the court, after notice and a hearing, authorizes such use, sale, or lease in accordance with the provisions of this section.

(3) Any hearing under paragraph (2)(B) of this subsection may be a preliminary hearing or may be consolidated with a hearing under subsection (e) of this section, but shall be scheduled in accordance with the needs of the debtor. If the hearing under paragraph (2)(B) of this subsection is a preliminary hearing, the court may authorize such use, sale, or lease only if there is a reasonable likelihood that the trustee will prevail at the final hearing under subsection (e) of this section. The court shall act promptly on any request for authorization under paragraph (2)(B) of this subsection.

(4) Except as provided in paragraph (2) of this subsection, the trustee shall segregate and account for any cash collateral in the trustee's possession, custody, or control.

(d) The trustee may use, sell, or lease property under subsection (b) or (c) of this section only to the extent not inconsistent with any relief granted under section 362(c), 362(d), 362(e), or 362(f) of this title.

(e) Notwithstanding any other provision of this section, at any time, on request of an entity that has an interest in property used, sold, or leased, or proposed to be used, sold, or leased, by the trustee, the court, with or without a hearing, shall prohibit or condition such use, sale, or lease as is necessary to provide adequate protection of such interest.

(f) The trustee may sell property under subsection (b) or (c) of this section free and clear of any interest in such property of an entity other than the estate, only if –

(1) applicable nonbankruptcy law permits sale of such property free and clear of such interest;

(2) such entity consents;

(3) such interest is a lien and the price at which such property is to be sold is greater than the aggregate value of all liens on such property;

(4) such interest is in bona fide dispute; or

(5) such entity could be compelled, in a legal or equitable proceeding, to accept a money satisfaction of such interest.

(g) Notwithstanding subsection (f) of this section, the trustee may sell property under subsection (b) or (c) of this section free and clear of any vested or contingent right in the nature of dower or courtesy.

(h) Notwithstanding subsection (f) of this section, the trustee may sell both the estate's interest, under subsection (b) or (c) of this section, and the interest of any co-owner in property in which the debtor had, at the time of the commencement of the case, an undivided interest as a tenant in common, joint tenant, or tenant by the entirety, only if –

(1) partition in kind of such property among the estate and such co-owners is impracticable;

(2) sale of the estate's undivided interest in such property would realize significantly less for the estate than sale of such property free of the interests of such co-owners;

(3) the benefit to the estate of a sale of such property free of the interests of co-owners outweighs the detriment, if any, to such co-owners; and

(4) such property is not used in the production, transmission, or distribution, for sale, of electric energy or of natural or synthetic gas for heat, light, or power.

(i) Before the consummation of a sale of property to which subsection (g) or (h) of this section applies, or of property of the estate that is community property of the debtor and debtor's spouse immediately before the commencement of the case, the debtor's spouse, or a co-owner of such property, as the case may be, may purchase such property at the price at which such sale is to be consummated.

(j) After a sale of property to which subsection (g) or (h) of this section applies, the trustee shall distribute to the debtor's spouse or the co-owners of such property, as the case may be, and to the estate, the proceeds of such sale, less the costs and expenses, not including any compensation of the trustee, of such sale, according to the interests of such spouse or co-owners, and of the estate.

(k) At a sale under subsection (b) of this section of property that is subject to a lien that secures an allowed claim, unless the court for cause orders otherwise the holder of such claim may bid at such sale, and, if the holder of such claim purchases such property, such holder may offset such claim against the purchase price of such property.

(l) Subject to the provisions of section 365, the trustee may use, sell, or lease property under subsection (b) or (c) of this section, or a plan under chapter 11, 12, or 13 of this title may provide for the use, sale, or lease of property, notwithstanding any provision in a contract, a lease, or applicable law that is conditioned on the insolvency or financial condition of the debtor, on the commencement of a case under this title concerning the debtor, or on the appointment of or the taking possession by a trustee in a case under this title or a custodian, and that effects, or gives an option to effect, a forfeiture, modification, or termination of the debtor's interest in such property.

(m) The reversal or modification on appeal of an authorization under subsection (b) or (c) of this section of a sale or lease of property does not affect the validity of a sale or lease under such authorization to an entity that purchased or leased such property in good faith, whether or not such entity knew of the pendency of the appeal, unless such authorization and such sale or lease were stayed pending appeal.

(n) The trustee may avoid a sale under this section if the sales price was controlled by an agreement among potential bidders at such sale, or may recover from a party to such agreement any amount by which the value of the property sold exceeds the price at which such sale was consummated, and may recover any costs, attorneys' fees, or expenses incurred in avoiding such sale or recovering such amount. In addition to any recovery under the preceding sentence, the court may grant judgment for punitive damages in favor of the estate and against any such party that entered into such an agreement in willful disregard of this subsection.

(o) In any hearing under this section –

(1) the trustee has the burden of proof on the issue of adequate protection; and

(2) the entity asserting an interest in property has the burden of proof on the issue of the validity, priority, or extent of such interest.

364. Obtaining credit

(a) If the trustee is authorized to operate the business of the debtor under section 721, 1108, 1304, 1203, or 1204 of this title, unless the court orders otherwise, the trustee may obtain unsecured credit and incur unsecured debt in the ordinary course of business allowable under section 503(b)(1) of this title as an administrative expense.

(b) The court, after notice and a hearing, may authorize the trustee to obtain unsecured credit or to incur unsecured debt other than under subsection (a) of this section, allowable under section 503(b)(1) of this title as an administrative expense.

(c) If the trustee is unable to obtain unsecured credit allowable under section 503(b)(1) of this title as an administrative expense, the court, after notice and a hearing, may authorize the obtaining of credit or the incurring of debt –

(1) with priority over any or all administrative expenses of the kind specified in section 503(b) or 507(b) of this title;

(2) secured by a lien on property of the estate that is not otherwise subject to a lien; or

(3) secured by a junior lien on property of the estate that is subject to a lien.

(d)(1) The court, after notice and a hearing, may authorize the obtaining of credit or the incurring of debt secured by a senior or equal lien on property of the estate that is subject to a lien only if –

(A) the trustee is unable to obtain such credit otherwise; and

(B) there is adequate protection of the interest of the holder of the lien on the property of the estate on which such senior or equal lien is proposed to be granted.

(2) In any hearing under this subsection, the trustee has the burden of proof on the issue of adequate protection.

(e) The reversal or modification on appeal of an authorization under this section to obtain credit or incur debt, or of a grant under this section of a priority or a lien, does not affect the validity of any debt so incurred, or any priority or lien so granted, to an entity that extended such credit in good faith, whether or not such entity knew of the pendency of the appeal, unless such authorization and the incurring of such debt, or the granting of such priority or lien, were stayed pending appeal.

(f) Except with respect to an entity that is an underwriter as defined in section 1145(b) of this title, section 5 of the Securities Act of 1933 (15 U.S.C. 77e), the Trust Indenture Act of 1939 (15 U.S.C. 77aaa et seq.), and any State or local law requiring registration for offer or sale of a security or registration or licensing of an issuer of, underwriter of, or broker or dealer in, a security does not apply to the offer or sale under this section of a security that is not an equity security.

365. Executory contracts and unexpired leases

(a) Except as provided in sections 765 and 766 of this title and in subsections (b), (c), and (d) of this section, the trustee, subject to the court's approval, may assume or reject any executory contract or unexpired lease of the debtor.

(b)(1) If there has been a default in an executory contract or unexpired lease of the debtor, the trustee may not assume such contract or lease unless, at the time of assumption of such contract or lease, the trustee –

(A) cures, or provides adequate assurance that the trustee will promptly cure, such default;

(B) compensates, or provides adequate assurance that the trustee will promptly compensate, a party other than the debtor to such contract or lease, for any actual pecuniary loss to such party resulting from such default; and

(C) provides adequate assurance of future performance under such contract or lease.

(2) Paragraph (1) of this subsection does not apply to a default that is a breach of a provision relating to –

(A) the insolvency or financial condition of the debtor at any time before the closing of the case;

(B) the commencement of a case under this title; or

(C) the appointment of or taking possession by a trustee in a case under this title or a custodian before such commencement.

(3) For the purposes of paragraph (1) of this subsection and paragraph (2)(B) of subsection (f), adequate assurance of future performance of a lease of real property in a shopping center includes adequate assurance –

(A) of the source of rent and other consideration due under such lease, and in the case of an assignment, that the financial condition and operating performance of the proposed assignee and its guarantors, if any, shall be similar to the financial condition and operating performance of the debtor and its guarantors, if any, as of the time the debtor became the lessee under the lease;

(B) that any percentage rent due under such lease will not decline substantially;

(C) that assumption or assignment of such lease is subject to all the provisions thereof, including (but not limited to) provisions such as a radius, location, use, or exclusivity provision, and will not breach any such provision contained in any other lease, financing agreement, or master agreement relating to such shopping center; and

(D) that assumption or assignment of such lease will not disrupt any tenant mix or balance in such shopping center.

(4) Notwithstanding any other provision of this section, if there has been a default in an unexpired lease of the debtor, other than a default of a kind specified in paragraph (2) of this subsection, the trustee may not require a lessor to provide services or supplies incidental to such lease before assumption of such lease unless the lessor is compensated under the terms of such lease for any services and supplies provided under such lease before assumption of such lease.

(c) The trustee may not assume or assign any executory contract or unexpired lease of the debtor, whether or not such contract or lease prohibits or restricts assignment of rights or delegation of duties, if –

(1)(A) applicable law excuses a party, other than the debtor, to such contract or lease from accepting performance from or rendering performance to an entity other than the debtor or the debtor in possession whether or not such contract or lease prohibits or restricts assignment of rights or delegation of duties; and

(B) such party does not consent to such assumption or assignment; or

(2) such contract is a contract to make a loan, or extend other debt financing or financial accommodations, to or for the benefit of the debtor, or to issue a security of the debtor;

(3) such lease is of nonresidential real property and has been terminated under applicable nonbankruptcy law prior to the order for relief; or

(4) (This paragraph is excluded because it deals only with air carrier debtors who are lessees of aircraft terminals or gates. These provisions expire on September 3, 1993 unless extended by act of Congress.)

(d)(1) In a case under chapter 7 of this title, if the trustee does not assume or reject an executory contract or unexpired lease of residential real property or of personal property of the debtor within 60 days after the order for relief, or within such additional time as the court, for cause, within such 60–day period, fixes, then such contract or lease is deemed rejected.

(2) In a case under chapter 9, 11, 12, or 13 of this title, the trustee may assume or reject an executory contract or unexpired lease of residential real property or of personal property of the debtor at any time before the confirmation of a plan but the court, on the request of any party to such contract or lease, may order the trustee to determine within a specified period of time whether to assume or reject such contract or lease.

(3) The trustee shall timely perform all the obligations of the debtor, except those specified in section 365(b)(2), arising from and after the order for relief under any unexpired lease of nonresidential real property, until such lease is assumed or rejected, notwithstanding section 503(b)(1) of this title. The court may extend, for cause, the time for performance of any such obligation that arises within 60 days after the date of the order for relief, but the time for performance shall not be extended beyond such 60–day period. This subsection shall not be deemed to affect the trustee's obligations under the provisions of subsection (b) or (f) of this section. Acceptance of any such performance does not constitute waiver or relinquishment of the lessor's rights under such lease or under this title.

(4) Notwithstanding paragraphs (1) and (2), in a case under any chapter of this title, if the trustee does not assume or reject an unexpired lease of nonresidential real property under which the debtor is the lessee within 60 days after the date of the order for relief, or within such additional time as the court, for cause, within such 60–day period, fixes, then such lease is deemed rejected, and the trustee shall immediately surrender such nonresidential real property to the lessor.

(5),(6),(7),(8),(9) These paragraphs are excluded for the reasons set forth in paragraph (c)(4) above.

(e)(1) Notwithstanding a provision in an executory contract or unexpired lease, or in applicable law, an executory contract or unexpired lease of the debtor may not be terminated or modified, and any right or obligation under such contract or lease may not be terminated or modified, at any time after the commencement of the case solely because of a provision in such contract or lease that is conditioned on –

(A) the insolvency or financial condition of the debtor at any time before the closing of the case;

(B) the commencement of a case under this title; or

(C) the appointment of or taking possession by a trustee in a case under this title or a custodian before such commencement.

(2) Paragraph (1) of this subsection does not apply to an executory contract or unexpired lease of the debtor, whether or not such contract or lease prohibits or restricts assignment of rights or delegation of duties, if –

(A)(i) applicable law excuses a party, other than the debtor, to such contract or lease from accepting performance from or rendering performance to the trustee or to an assignee of such contract or lease, whether or not such contract or lease prohibits or restricts assignment of rights or delegation of duties; and

(ii) such party does not consent to such assumption or assignment; or

(B) such contract is a contract to make a loan, or extend other debt financing or financial accommodations, to or for the benefit of the debtor, or to issue a security of the debtor.

(f)(1) Except as provided in subsection (c) of this section, notwithstanding a provision in an executory contract or unexpired lease of the debtor, or in applicable law, that prohibits, restricts, or conditions the assignment of such contract or lease, the trustee may assign such contract or lease under paragraph (2) of this subsection; except that the trustee may not assign an unexpired lease of nonresidential real property under which the debtor is an affected air carrier that is the lessee of an aircraft terminal or aircraft gate if there has occurred a termination event.

(2) The trustee may assign an executory contract or unexpired lease of the debtor only if –

(A) the trustee assumes such contract or lease in accordance with the provisions of this section; and

(B) adequate assurance of future performance by the assignee of such contract or lease is provided, whether or not there has been a default in such contract or lease.

(3) Notwithstanding a provision in an executory contract or unexpired lease of the debtor, or in applicable law that terminates or modifies, or permits a party other than the debtor to terminate or modify, such contract or lease or a right or obligation under such contract or lease on account of an assignment of such contract or lease, such contract, lease, right, or obligation may not be terminated or modified under such provision because of the assumption or assignment of such contract or lease by the trustee.

(g) Except as provided in subsections (h)(2) and (i)(2) of this section, the rejection of an executory contract or unexpired lease of the debtor constitutes a breach of such contract or lease –

(1) if such contract or lease has not been assumed under this section or under a plan confirmed under chapter 9, 11, 12, or 13 of this title, immediately before the date of the filing of the petition; or

(2) if such contract or lease has been assumed under this section or under a plan confirmed under chapter 9, 11, 12, or 13 of this title –

(A) if before such rejection the case has not been converted under section 1112, 1307, or 1208 of this title, at the time of such rejection; or

(B) if before such rejection the case has been converted under section 1112, 1307, or 1208 of this title –

(i) immediately before the date of such conversion, if such contract or lease was assumed before such conversion; or

(ii) at the time of such rejection, if such contract or lease was assumed after such conversion.

(h)(1) If the trustee rejects an unexpired lease of real property of the debtor under which the debtor is the lessor, or a timeshare interest under a timeshare plan under which the debtor is the timeshare interest seller, the lessee or timeshare interest purchaser under such lease or timeshare plan may treat such lease or timeshare plan as terminated by such rejection, where the disaffirmance by the trustee amounts to such a breach as would entitle the lessee or timeshare interest purchaser to treat such lease or timeshare plan as terminated by virtue of its own terms, applicable nonbankruptcy law, or other agreements the lessee or timeshare interest purchaser has made with other parties; or, in the alternative, the lessee or timeshare interest purchaser may remain in possession of the leasehold or timeshare interest under any lease or timeshare plan the term of which has commenced for the balance of such term and for any renewal or extension of such term that is enforceable by such lessee or timeshare interest purchaser under applicable nonbankruptcy law.

(2) If such lessee or timeshare interest purchaser remains in possession as provided in paragraph (1) of this subsection, such lessee or timeshare interest purchaser may offset against the rent reserved under such lease or moneys due for such timeshare interest for the balance of the term after the date of the rejection of such lease or timeshare interest, and any such renewal or extension thereof, any damages occurring after such date caused by the nonperformance of any obligation of the debtor under such lease or timeshare plan after such date, but such lessee or timeshare interest purchaser does not have any rights against the estate on account of any damages arising after such date from such rejection, other than such offset.

(i)(1) If the trustee rejects an executory contract of the debtor for the sale of real property or for the sale of a timeshare interest under a timeshare plan, under which the purchaser is in possession, such purchaser may treat such contract as terminated, or, in the alternative, may remain in possession of such real property or timeshare interest.

(2) If such purchaser remains in possession –

(A) such purchaser shall continue to make all payments due under such contract, but may, offset against such payments any damages occurring after the date of the rejection of such contract caused by the nonperformance of any obligation of the debtor after such date, but such purchaser does not have any rights against the estate on account of any damages arising after such date from such rejection, other than such offset; and

(B) the trustee shall deliver title to such purchaser in accordance with the provisions of such contract, but is relieved of all other obligations to perform under such contract.

(j) A purchaser that treats an executory contract as terminated under subsection (i) of this section, or a party whose executory contract to purchase real property from the debtor is rejected and under which such party is not in possession, has a lien on the interest of the debtor in such property for the recovery of any portion of the purchase price that such purchaser or party has paid.

(k) Assignment by the trustee to an entity of a contract or lease assumed under this section relieves the trustee and the estate from any liability for any breach of such contract or lease occurring after such assignment.

(l) If an unexpired lease under which the debtor is the lessee is assigned pursuant to this section, the lessor of the property may require a deposit or other security for the performance of the debtor's obligations under the lease substantially the same as would have been required by the landlord upon the initial leasing to a similar tenant.

(m) For purposes of this section 365 and sections 541(b)(2) and 362(b)(10), leases of real property shall include any rental agreement to use real property.

(n)(1) If the trustee rejects an executory contract under which the debtor is a licensor of a right to intellectual property, the licensee under such contract may elect –

(A) to treat such contract as terminated by such rejection if such rejection by the trustee amounts to such a breach as would entitle the licensee to treat such contract as terminated by virtue of its own terms, applicable nonbankruptcy law, or an agreement made by the licensee with another entity; or

(B) to retain its rights (including a right to enforce any exclusivity provision of such contract, but excluding any other right under applicable nonbankruptcy law to specific performance of such contract) under such contract and under any agreement supplementary to such contract, to such intellectual property (including any embodiment of such intellectual property to the extent protected by applicable nonbankruptcy law), as such rights existed immediately before the case commenced, for –

(i) the duration of such contract; and

(ii) any period for which such contract may be extended by the licensee as of right under applicable nonbankruptcy law.

(2) If the licensee elects to retain its rights, as described in paragraph (1)(B) of this subsection, under such contract –

(A) the trustee shall allow the licensee to exercise such rights;

(B) the licensee shall make all royalty payments due under such contract for the duration of such contract and for any period described in paragraph (1)(B) of this subsection for which the licensee extends such contract; and

(C) the licensee shall be deemed to waive –

(i) any right of setoff it may have with respect to such contract under this title or applicable nonbankruptcy law; and

(ii) any claim allowable under section 503(b) of this title arising from the performance of such contract.

(3) If the licensee elects to retain its rights, as described in paragraph (1)(B) of this subsection, then on the written request of the licensee the trustee shall –

(A) to the extent provided in such contract, or any agreement supplementary to such contract, provide to the licensee any intellectual property (including such embodiment) held by the trustee; and

(B) not interfere with the rights of the licensee as provided in such contract, or any agreement supplementary to such contract, to such intellectual property (including such embodiment) including any right to obtain such intellectual property (or such embodiment) from another entity.

(4) Unless and until the trustee rejects such contract, on the written request of the licensee the trustee shall –

(A) to the extent provided in such contract or any agreement supplementary to such contract –

(i) perform such contract; or

(ii) provide to the licensee such intellectual property (including any embodiment of such intellectual property to the extent protected by applicable nonbankruptcy law) held by the trustee; and

(B) not interfere with the rights of the licensee as provided in such contract, or any agreement supplementary to such contract, to such intellectual property (including such embodiment), including any right to obtain such intellectual property (or such embodiment) from another entity.

(o) In a case under chapter 11 of this title, the trustee shall be deemed to have assumed (consistent with the debtor's other obligations under section 507), and shall immediately cure any deficit under, any commitment by the debtor to the Federal Deposit Insurance Corporation, the Resolution Trust Corporation, the Director of the Office of Thrift Supervision, the Comptroller of the Currency, or the Board of Governors of the Federal Reserve System, or its predecessors or successors, to maintain the capital of an insured depository institution, and any claim for a subsequent breach of the obligations thereunder shall be entitled to priority under section 507. This subsection shall not extend any commitment that would otherwise be terminated by any act of such an agency.

(p) (This subsection is omitted for the reasons set forth in paragraph (c)(4) above.)

366. Utility service

(a) Except as provided in subsection (b) of this section, a utility may not alter, refuse, or discontinue service to, or discriminate against, the trustee or the debtor solely on the basis of the commencement of a case under this title or that a debt owed by the debtor to such utility for service rendered before the order for relief was not paid when due.

(b) Such utility may alter, refuse, or discontinue service if neither the trustee nor the debtor, within 20 days after the date of the order for relief, furnishes adequate assurance of payment, in the form of a deposit or other security, for service after such date. On request of a party in interest and after notice and a hearing, the court may order reasonable modification of the amount of the deposit or other security necessary to provide adequate assurance of payment.

CHAPTER 5 – CREDITORS, THE DEBTOR, AND THE ESTATE

SUBCHAPTER I - CREDITORS AND CLAIMS

SUBCHAPTER I - CREDITORS AND CLAIMS

501. Filing of proofs of claims or interests

(a) A creditor or an indenture trustee may file a proof of claim. An equity security holder may file a proof of interest.

(b) If a creditor does not timely file a proof of such creditor's claim, an entity that is liable to such creditor with the debtor, or that has secured such creditor, may file a proof of such claim.

(c) If a creditor does not timely file a proof of such creditor's claim, the debtor or the trustee may file a proof of such claim.

(d) A claim of a kind specified in section 502(e)(2), 502(f), 502(g), 502(h) or 502(i) of this title may be filed under subsection (a), (b), or (c) of this section the same as if such claim were a claim against the debtor and had arisen before the date of the filing of the petition.

502. Allowance of claims or interests

(a) A claim or interest, proof of which is filed under section 501 of this title, is deemed allowed, unless a party in interest, including a creditor of a general partner in a partnership that is a debtor in a case under chapter 7 of this title, objects.

(b) Except as provided in subsections (e)(2), (f), (g), (h) and (i) of this section, if such objection to a claim is made, the court, after notice and a hearing, shall determine the amount of such claim in lawful currency of the United States as of the date of the filing of the petition, and shall allow such claim in such amount, except to the extent that –

(1) such claim is unenforceable against the debtor and property of the debtor, under any agreement or applicable law for a reason other than because such claim is contingent or unmatured;

(2) such claim is for unmatured interest;

(3) if such claim is for a tax assessed against property of the estate, such claim exceeds the value of the interest of the estate in such property;

(4) if such claim is for services of an insider or attorney of the debtor, such claim exceeds the reasonable value of such services;

(5) such claim is for a debt that is unmatured on the date of the filing of the petition and that is excepted from discharge under section 523(a)(5) of this title;

(6) if such claim is the claim of a lessor for damages resulting from the termination of a lease of real property, such claim exceeds –

(A) the rent reserved by such lease, without acceleration, for the greater of one year, or 15 percent, not to exceed three years, of the remaining term of such lease, following the earlier of –
(i) the date of the filing of the petition; and
(ii) the date on which such lessor repossessed, or the lessee surrendered, the leased property; plus
(B) any unpaid rent due under such lease, without acceleration, on the earlier of such dates;
(7) if such claim is the claim of an employee for damages resulting from the termination of an employment contract, such claim exceeds –
(A) the compensation provided by such contract, without acceleration, for one year following the earlier of –
(i) the date of the filing of the petition; or
(ii) the date on which the employer directed the employee to terminate, or such employee terminated, performance under such contract; plus
(B) any unpaid compensation due under such contract, without acceleration, on the earlier of such dates; or
(8) such claim results from a reduction, due to late payment, in the amount of an otherwise applicable credit available to the debtor in connection with an employment tax on wages, salaries, or commissions earned from the debtor.
(c) There shall be estimated for purpose of allowance under this section –
(1) any contingent or unliquidated claim, the fixing or liquidation of which, as the case may be, would unduly delay the administration of the case; or
(2) any right to payment arising from a right to an equitable remedy for breach of performance.
(d) Notwithstanding subsections (a) and (b) of this section, the court shall disallow any claim of any entity from which property is recoverable under section 542, 543, 550, or 553 of this title or that is a transferee of a transfer avoidable under section 522(f), 522(h), 544, 545, 547, 548, 549, or 724(a) of this title, unless such entity or transferee has paid the amount, or turned over any such property, for which such entity or transferee is liable under section 522(i), 542, 543, 550, or 553 of this title.
(e)(1) Notwithstanding subsections (a), (b), and (c) of this section and paragraph (2) of this subsection, the court shall disallow any claim for reimbursement or contribution of an entity that is liable with the debtor on or has secured the claim of a creditor, to the extent that –
(A) such creditor's claim against the estate is disallowed;
(B) such claim for reimbursement or contribution is contingent as of the time of allowance or disallowance of such claim for reimbursement or contribution; or
(C) such entity asserts a right of subrogation to the rights of such creditor under section 509 of this title.
(2) A claim for reimbursement or contribution of such an entity that becomes fixed after the commencement of the case shall be determined, and shall be allowed under subsection (a), (b), or (c) of this section, or disallowed under subsection (d) of this section, the same as if such claim had become fixed before the date of the filing of the petition.
(f) In an involuntary case, a claim arising in the ordinary course of the debtor's business or financial affairs after the commencement of the case but before the earlier of the appointment of a trustee and the order for relief shall be determined as of the date such claim arises, and shall be allowed under subsection (a), (b), or (c) of this section or disallowed under subsection (d) or (e) of this section, the same as if such claim had arisen before the date of the filing of the petition.
(g) A claim arising from the rejection, under section 365 of this title or under a plan under chapter 9, 11, 12, or 13 of this title, of an executory contract or unexpired lease of the debtor that has not been assumed shall be determined, and shall be allowed under subsection (a), (b), or (c) of this section or disallowed under subsection (d) or (e) of this section, the same as if such claim has arisen before the date of the filing of the petition.
(h) A claim arising from the recovery of property under section 522, 550, or 553 of this title shall be determined, and shall be allowed under subsection (a), (b), or (c) of this section, or disallowed under subsection (d) or (e) of this section, the same as if such claim had arisen before the date of the filing of the petition.
(i) A claim that does not arise until after the commencement of the case for a tax entitled to priority under section 507(a)(7) of this title shall be determined, and shall be allowed under subsection (a), (b), or (c) of this section, or disallowed under subsection (d) or (e) of this section, the same as if such claim had arisen before the date of the filing of the petition.
(j) A claim that has been allowed or disallowed may be reconsidered for cause. A reconsidered claim may be allowed or disallowed according to the equities of the case. Reconsideration of a claim under this subsection does not affect the validity of any payment or transfer from the estate made to a holder of an allowed claim on account of such allowed claim that is not reconsidered, but if a reconsidered claim is allowed and is of the same class as such holder's claim, such holder may not receive any additional payment or transfer from the estate on account of such holder's allowed claim until the holder of such reconsidered and allowed claim receives payment on account of such claim proportionate in value to that already received by such other holder. This subsection does not alter or modify the trustee's right to recover from a creditor any excess payment or transfer made to such creditor.

503. Allowance of administrative expenses

(a) An entity may file a request for payment of an administrative expense.
(b) After notice and a hearing, there shall be allowed administrative expenses, other than claims allowed under section 502(f) of this title, including –

(1)(A) the actual, necessary costs and expenses of preserving the estate, including wages, salaries, or commissions for services rendered after the commencement of the case;
(B) any tax –
(i) incurred by the estate, except a tax of the kind specified in section 507(a)(7) of this title; or
(ii) attributable to an excessive allowance of a tentative carryback adjustment that the estate received, whether the taxable year to which such adjustment relates ended before or after the commencement of the case; and
(C) any fine, penalty, or reduction in credit relating to a tax of a kind specified in subparagraph (B) of this paragraph;
(2) compensation and reimbursement awarded under section 330(a) of this title;
(3) the actual, necessary expenses, other than compensation and reimbursement specified in paragraph (4) of this subsection, incurred by –
(A) a creditor that files a petition under section 303 of this title;
(B) a creditor that recovers, after the court's approval, for the benefit of the estate any property transferred or concealed by the debtor;
(C) a creditor in connection with the prosecution of a criminal offense relating to the case or to the business or property of the debtor;
(D) a creditor, an indenture trustee, an equity security holder, or a committee representing creditors or equity security holders other than a committee appointed under section 1102 of this title, in making a substantial contribution in a case under chapter 9 or 11 of this title; or
(E) a custodian superseded under section 543 of this title, and compensation for the services of such custodian;
(4) reasonable compensation for professional services rendered by an attorney or an accountant of an entity whose expense is allowable under paragraph (3) of this subsection, based on the time, the nature, the extent, and the value of such services, and the cost of comparable services other than in a case under this title, and reimbursement for actual, necessary expenses incurred by such attorney or accountant;
(5) reasonable compensation for services rendered by an indenture trustee in making a substantial contribution in a case under chapter 9 or 11 of this title, based on the time, the nature, the extent, and the value of such services, and the cost of comparable services other than in a case under this title; and
(6) the fees and mileage payable under chapter 119 of title 28.

504. Sharing of compensation

(a) Except as provided in subsection (b) of this section, a person receiving compensation or reimbursement under section 503(b)(2) or 503(b)(4) of this title may not share or agree to share –
(1) any such compensation or reimbursement with another person; or
(2) any compensation or reimbursement received by another person under such sections.
(b)(1) A member, partner, or regular associate in a professional association, corporation, or partnership may share compensation or reimbursement received under section 503(b)(2) or 503(b)(4) of this title with another member, partner, or regular associate in such association, corporation, or partnership, and may share in any compensation or reimbursement received under such sections by another member, partner, or regular associate in such association, corporation, or partnership.
(2) An attorney for a creditor that files a petition under section 303 of this title may share compensation and reimbursement received under section 503(b)(4) of this title with any other attorney contributing to the services rendered or expenses incurred by such creditor's attorney.

505. Determination of tax liability

(a)(1) Except as provided in paragraph (2) of this subsection, the court may determine the amount or legality of any tax, any fine or penalty relating to a tax, or any addition to tax, whether or not previously assessed, whether of not paid, and whether or not contested before and adjudicated by a judicial or administrative tribunal of competent jurisdiction.
(2) The court may not so determine–
(A) the amount or legality of a tax, fine, penalty, or addition to tax if such amount or legality was contested before and adjudicated by a judicial or administrative tribunal of competent jurisdiction before the commencement of the case under this title; or
(B) any right of the estate to a tax refund, before the earlier of –
(i) 120 days after the trustee properly requests such refund from the governmental unit from which such refund is claimed; or
(ii) a determination by such governmental unit of such request.
(b) A trustee may request a determination of any unpaid liability of the estate for any tax incurred during the administration of the case by submitting a tax return for such tax and a request for such a determination to the governmental unit charged with responsibility for collection or determination of such tax. Unless such return is fraudulent, or contains a material misrepresentation, the trustee, the debtor, and any successor to the debtor are discharged from any liability for such tax–
(1) upon payment of the tax shown on such return, if–

(A) such governmental unit does not notify the trustee, within 60 days after such request, that such return has been selected for examination; or

(B) such governmental unit does not complete such an examination and notify the trustee of any tax due, within 180 days after such request or within such additional time as the court, for cause, permits;

(2) upon payment of the tax determined by the court, after notice and a hearing, after completion by such governmental unit of such examination; or

(3) upon payment of the tax determined by such governmental unit to be due.

(c) Notwithstanding section 362 of this title, after determination by the court of a tax under this section, the governmental unit charged with responsibility for collection of such tax may assess such tax against the estate, the debtor, or a successor to the debtor, as the case may be, subject to any otherwise applicable law.

506. Determination of secured status

(a) An allowed claim of a creditor secured by a lien on property in which the estate has an interest, or that is subject to setoff under section 553 of this title, is a secured claim to the extent of the value of such creditor's interest in the estate's interest in such property, or to the extent of the amount subject to setoff, as the case may be, and is an unsecured claim to the extent that the value of such creditor's interest or the amount so subject to setoff is less than the amount of such allowed claim. Such value shall be determined in light of the purpose of the valuation and of the proposed disposition or use of such property, and in conjunction with any hearing on such disposition or use or on a plan affecting such creditor's interest.

(b) To the extent that an allowed secured claim is secured by property the value of which, after any recovery under subsection (c) of this section, is greater than the amount of such claim, there shall be allowed to the holder of such claim, interest on such claim, and any reasonable fees, costs, or charges provided for under the agreement under which such claim arose.

(c) The trustee may recover from property securing an allowed secured claim the reasonable, necessary costs and expenses of preserving, or disposing of, such property to the extent of any benefit to the holder of such claim.

(d) To the extent that a lien secures a claim against the debtor that is not an allowed secured claim, such lien is void, unless -

(1) such claim was disallowed only under section 502(b)(5) or 502(e) of this title; or

(2) such claim is not an allowed secured claim due only to the failure of any entity to file a proof of such claim under section 501 of this title.

507. Priorities

(a) The following expenses and claims have priority in the following order:

(1) First, administrative expenses allowed under section 503(b) of this title, and any fees and charges assessed against the estate under chapter 123 of title 28.

(2) Second, unsecured claims allowed under section 502(f) of this title.

(3) Third, allowed unsecured claims for wages, salaries, or commissions, including vacation, severance, and sick leave pay -

(A) earned by an individual within 90 days before the date of the filing of the petition or the date of the cessation of the debtor's business, whichever occurs first; but only

(B) to the extent of $2,000 for each such individual.

(4) Fourth, allowed unsecured claims for contributions to an employee benefit plan -

(A) arising from services rendered within 180 days before the date of the filing of the petition or the date of the cessation of the debtor's business, whichever occurs first; but only

(B) for each such plan, to the extent of -

(i) the number of employees covered by each such plan multiplied by $2,000; less

(ii) the aggregate amount paid to such employees under paragraph (3) of this subsection, plus the aggregate amount paid by the estate on behalf of such employees to any other employee benefit plan.

(5) Fifth, allowed unsecured claims of persons -

(A) engaged in the production or raising of grain, as defined in section 557(b)(1) of this title, against a debtor who owns or operates a grain storage facility, as defined in section 557(b)(2) of this title, for grain or the proceeds of grain, or

(B) engaged as a United States fisherman against a debtor who has acquired fish or fish produce from a fisherman through a sale or conversion, and who is engaged in operating a fish produce storage or processing facility -

but only to the extent of $2,000 for each such individual.

(6) Sixth, allowed unsecured claims of individuals, to the extent of $900 for each such individual, arising from the deposit, before the commencement of the case, of money in connection with the purchase, lease, or rental of property, or the purchase of services, for the personal, family, or household use of such individuals, that were not delivered or provided.

(7) Seventh, allowed unsecured claims of governmental units, only to the extent that such claims are for -

(A) a tax on or measured by income or gross receipts -

(i) for a taxable year ending on or before the date of the filing of the petition for which a return, if required, is last due, including extensions, after three years before the date of the filing of the petition;

(ii) assessed within 240 days, plus any time plus 30 days during which an offer in compromise with respect to such tax that was made within the 240 days after such assessment was pending, before the date of the filing of the petition; or

(iii) other than a tax of a kind specified in section 523(a)(1)(B) or 523(a)(1)(C) of this title, not assessed before, but assessable, under applicable law or by agreement, after, the commencement of the case;

(B) a property tax assessed before the commencement of the case and last payable without penalty after one year before the date of the filing of the petition;

(C) a tax required to be collected or withheld and for which the debtor is liable in whatever capacity;

(D) an employment tax on a wage, salary, or commission of a kind specified in paragraph (3) of this subsection earned from the debtor before the date of the filing of the petition, whether or not actually paid before such date, for which a return is last due, under applicable law or under any extension, after three years before the date of the filing of the petition;

(E) an excise tax on -

(i) a transaction occurring before the date of the filing of the petition for which a return, if required, is last due, under applicable law or under any extension, after three years before the date of the filing of the petition; or

(ii) if a return is not required, a transaction occurring during the three years immediately preceding the date of the filing of the petition;

(F) a customs duty arising out of the importation of merchandise-

(i) entered for consumption within one year before the date of the filing of the petition;

(ii) covered by an entry liquidated or reliquidated within one year before the date of the filing of the petition; or

(iii) entered for consumption within four years before the date of the filing of the petition but unliquidated on such date, if the Secretary of the Treasury certifies than failure to liquidate such entry was due to an investigation pending on such date into assessment of antidumping or countervailing duties or fraud, or if information needed for the proper appraisement or classification of such merchandise was not available to the appropriate customs officer before such date;

or

(G) a penalty related to a claim of a kind specified in this paragraph and in compensation for actual pecuniary loss.

(8) Eighth, allowed unsecured claims based upon any commitment by the debtor to the Federal Deposit Insurance Corporation, the Resolution Trust Corporation, the Director of the Office of Thrift Supervision, the Comptroller of the Currency, or the Board of Governors of the Federal Reserve System, or their predecessors or successors, to maintain the capital of an insured depository institution.

(b) If the trustee, under section 362, 363, or 364 of this title, provides adequate protection of the interest of a holder of a claim secured by a lien on property of the debtor and if, notwithstanding such protection, such creditor has a claim allowable under subsection (a)(1) of this section arising from the stay of action against such property under section 362 of this title, from the use, sale, or lease of such property under section 363 of this title, or from the granting of a lien under section 364(d) of this title, then such creditor's claim under such subsection shall have priority over every other claim allowable under such subsection.

(c) For the purpose of subsection (a) of this section, a claim of a governmental unit arising from an erroneous refund or credit of a tax has the same priority as a claim for the tax to which such refund or credit relates.

(d) An entity that is subrogated to the rights of a holder of a claim of a kind specified in subsection (a)(3), (a)(4), (a)(5), or (a)(6) of this section is not subrogated to the right of the holder of such claim to priority under such subsection.

508. Effect of distribution other than under this title

(a) If a creditor receives, in a foreign proceeding, payment of, or a transfer of property on account of, a claim that is allowed under this title, such creditor may not receive any payment under this title on account of such claim until each of the other holders of claims on account of which such holders are entitled to share equally with such creditor under this title has received payment under this title equal in value to the consideration received by such creditor in such foreign proceeding.

(b) If a creditor of a partnership debtor receives, from a general partner that is not a debtor in a case under chapter 7 of this title, payment of, or a transfer of property on account of, a claim that is allowed under this title and that is not secured by a lien on property of such partner, such creditor may not receive any payment under this title on account of such claim until each of the other holders of claims on account of which such holders are entitled to share equally with such creditor under this title has received payment under this title equal in value to the consideration received by such creditor from such general partner.

509. Claims of codebtors

(a) Except as provided in subsection (b) or (c) of this section, an entity that is liable with the debtor on, or that has secured, a claim of a creditor against the debtor, and that pays such claim, is subrogated to the rights of such creditor to the extent of such payment.

(b) Such entity is not subrogated to the rights of such creditor to the extent that -

(1) a claim of such entity for reimbursement or contribution on account of such payment of such creditor's claim is –

    (A) allowed under section 502 of this title;

    (B) disallowed other than under section 502(e) of this title; or

    (C) subordinated under section 510 of this title; or

(2) as between the debtor and such entity, such entity received the consideration for the claim held by such creditor.

(c) The court shall subordinate to the claim of a creditor and for the benefit of such creditor an allowed claim, by way of subrogation under this section, or for reimbursement or contribution, of an entity that is liable with the debtor on, or that has secured, such creditor's claim, until such creditor's claim is paid in full, either through payments under this title or otherwise.

510. Subordination

(a) A subordination agreement is enforceable in a case under this title to the same extent that such agreement is enforceable under applicable nonbankruptcy law.

(b) For the purpose of distribution under this title, a claim arising from rescission of a purchase or sale of a security of the debtor or of an affiliate of the debtor, for damages arising from the purchase or sale of such a security, or for reimbursement or contribution allowed under section 502 on account of such a claim, shall be subordinated to all claims or interests that are senior to or equal the claim or interest represented by such security, except that if such security is common stock, such claim has the same priority as common stock.

(c) Notwithstanding subsections (a) and (b) of this section, after notice and a hearing, the court may –

(1) under principles of equitable subordination, subordinate for purposes of distribution all or part of an allowed claim to all or part of another allowed claim or all or part of an allowed interest to all or part of another allowed interest; or

(2) order that any lien securing such a subordinated claim be transferred to the estate.

SUBCHAPTER II - DEBTOR'S DUTIES AND BENEFITS

521. Debtor's duties

The debtor shall –

(1) file a list of creditors, and unless the court orders otherwise, a schedule of assets and liabilities, a schedule of current income and current expenditures, and a statement of the debtor's financial affairs;

(2) if an individual debtor's schedule of assets and liabilities includes consumer debts which are secured by property of the estate –

    (A) within thirty days after the date of the filing of a petition under chapter 7 of this title or on or before the date of the meeting of creditors, whichever is earlier, or within such additional time as the court, for cause, within such period fixes, the debtor shall file with the clerk a statement of his intention with respect to the retention or surrender of such property and, if applicable, specifying that such property is claimed as exempt, that the debtor intends to redeem such property, or that the debtor intends to reaffirm debts secured by such property;

    (B) within forty-five days after the filing of a notice of intent under this section, or within such additional time as the court, for cause, within such forty-five day period fixes, the debtor shall perform his intention with respect to such property, as specified by subparagraph (A) of this paragraph; and

    (C) nothing in subparagraphs (A) and (B) of this paragraph shall alter the debtor's or the trustee's rights with regard to such property under this title;

(3) if a trustee is serving in the case, cooperate with the trustee as necessary to enable the trustee to perform the trustee's duties under this title;

(4) if a trustee is serving in the case, surrender to the trustee all property of the estate and any recorded information, including books, documents, records, and papers, relating to property of the estate, whether or not immunity is granted under section 344 of this title; and

(5) appear at the hearing required under section 524(d) of this title.

522. Exemptions

(a) In this title –

(1) "dependent" includes spouse, whether or not actually dependent; and

(2) "value" means fair market value as of the date of the filing of the petition or, with respect to property that becomes property of the estate after such date, as of the date such property becomes property of the estate.

(b) Notwithstanding section 541 of this title, an individual debtor may exempt from property of the estate the property listed in either paragraph (1) or, in the alternative, paragraph (2) of this subsection. In joint cases filed under section 302 of this title and individual cases filed under section 301 or 303 of this title by or against debtors who are husband and wife, and whose estates are ordered to be jointly administered under Rule 1015(b) of the Bankruptcy Rules, one debtor may not elect to exempt property listed in paragraph (1) and the other debtor elect to exempt property listed in paragraph (2) of this subsection. If the parties cannot agree on the alternative to be elected, they shall be deemed to elect paragraph (1), where such election is permitted under the law of the jurisdiction where the case is filed. Such property is –

(1) property that is specified under subsection (d) of this section, unless the State law that is applicable to the debtor under paragraph (2)(A) of this subsection specifically does not so authorize; or, in the alternative,

(2)(A) any property that is exempt under Federal law, other than subsection (d) of this section, or State or local law that is applicable on the date of the filing of the petition at the place in which the debtor's domicile has been located for the 180 days immediately preceding the date of the filing of the petition, or for a longer portion of such 180-day period than in any other place; and

    (B) any interest in property in which the debtor had, immediately before the commencement of the case, an interest as a tenant by the entirety or joint tenant to the extent that such interest as a tenant by the entirety or joint tenant is exempt from process under applicable nonbankruptcy law.

(c) Unless the case is dismissed, property exempted under this section is not liable during or after the case for any debt of the debtor that arose, or that is determined under section 502 of this title as if such debt had arisen, before the commencement of the case, except –

(1) a debt of a kind specified in section 523(a)(1) or 523(a)(5) of this title;

(2) a debt secured by a lien that is –

    (A)(i) not avoided under subsection (f) or (g) of this section or under section 544, 545, 547, 548, 549, or 724(a) of this title; and

      (ii) not void under section 506(d) of this title; or

    (B) a tax lien, notice of which is properly filed; or

(3) a debt of a kind specified in section 523(a)(4) or 523(a)(6) of this title owed by an institution-affiliated party of an insured depository institution to a Federal depository institutions regulatory agency acting in its capacity as conservator, receiver, or liquidating agent for such institution.

(d) The following property may be exempted under subsection (b)(1) of this section:

(1) The debtor's aggregate interest, not to $7,500 in value, in real property or personal property that the debtor or a dependent of the debtor uses as a residence, in a cooperative that owns a property that the debtor or a dependent of the debtor uses as a residence, or in a burial plot for the debtor or a dependent of the debtor.

(2) The debtor's interest, not to exceed $1,200 in value, in one motor vehicle.

(3) The debtor's interest, not to exceed $200 in value in any particular item or $4,000 in aggregate value, in household furnishings, household goods, wearing apparel, appliances, books, animals, crops, or musical instruments, that are held primarily for the personal, family, or household use of the debtor or a dependent of the debtor.

(4) The debtor's aggregate interest, not to exceed $500 in value, in jewelry held primarily for the personal, family, or household use of the debtor or a dependent of the debtor.

(5) The debtor's aggregate interest in any property, not to exceed in value $400 plus up to $3,750 of any unused amount of the exemption provided under paragraph (1) of this subsection.

(6) The debtor's aggregate interest, not to exceed $750 in value, in any implements, professional books, or tools, of the trade of the debtor or the trade of a dependent of the debtor.

(7) Any unmatured life insurance contract owned by the debtor, other than a credit life insurance contract.

(8) The debtor's aggregate interest, not to exceed in value $4,000 less any amount of property of the estate transferred in the manner specified in section 542(d) of this title, in any accrued dividend or interest under, or loan value of, any unmatured life insurance contract owned by the debtor under which the insured is the debtor or an individual of whom the debtor is a dependent.

(9) Professionally prescribed health aids for the debtor or a dependent of the debtor.

(10) The debtor's right to receive –

    (A) a social security benefit, unemployment compensation, or a local public assistance benefit;

    (B) a veterans' benefit;

    (C) a disability, illness, or unemployment benefit;

    (D) alimony, support, or separate maintenance, to the extent reasonably necessary for the support of the debtor and any dependent of the debtor;

    (E) a payment under a stock bonus, pension, profitsharing, annuity, or similar plan or contract on account of illness, disability, death, age, or length of service, to the extent reasonably necessary for the support of the debtor and any dependent of the debtor, unless –

      (i) such plan or contract was established by or under the auspices of an insider that employed the debtor at the time the debtor's rights under such plan or contract arose;

      (ii) such payment is on account of age or length of service; and

      (iii) such plan or contract does not qualify under section 401(a), 403(a), 403(b), 408, or 409 of the Internal Revenue Code of 1954 (26 U.S.C. 401(a), 403(a), 403(b), 408, or 409).

(11) The debtor's right to receive, or property that is traceable to –

    (A) an award under a crime victim's reparation law;

    (B) a payment on account of the wrongful death of an individual of whom the debtor was a dependent, to the extent reasonably necessary for the support of the debtor and any dependent of the debtor;

(C) a payment under a life insurance contract that insured the life of an individual of whom the debtor was a dependent on the date of such individual's death, to the extent reasonably necessary for the support of the debtor and any dependent of the debtor;

(D) a payment, not to exceed $7,500, on account of personal bodily injury, not including pain and suffering or compensation for actual pecuniary loss, of the debtor or an individual of whom the debtor is a dependent; or

(E) a payment in compensation of loss of future earnings of the debtor or an individual of whom the debtor is or was a dependent, to the extent reasonably necessary for the support of the debtor and any dependent of the debtor.

(e) A waiver of an exemption executed in favor of a creditor that holds an unsecured claim against the debtor is unenforceable in a case under this title with respect to such claim against property that the debtor may exempt under subsection (b) of this section. A waiver by the debtor of a power under subsection (f) or (h) of this section to avoid a transfer, under subsection (g) or (i) of this section to exempt property, or under subsection (i) of this section to recover property or to preserve a transfer, is unenforceable in a case under this title.

(f) Notwithstanding any waiver of exemptions, the debtor may avoid the fixing of a lien on an interest of the debtor in property to the extent that such lien impairs an exemption to which the debtor would have been entitled under subsection (b) of this section, if such lien is –

(1) a judicial lien; or

(2) a nonpossessory, nonpurchase–money security interest in any –

(A) household furnishings, household goods, wearing apparel, appliances, books, animals, crops, musical instruments, or jewelry that are held primarily for the personal, family, or household use of the debtor or a dependent of the debtor;

(B) implements, professional books, or tools, of the trade of the debtor or the trade of a dependent of the debtor; or

(C) professionally prescribed health aids for the debtor or a dependent of the debtor.

(g) Notwithstanding sections 550 and 551 of this title, the debtor may exempt under subsection (b) of this section property that the trustee recovers under section 510(c)(2), 542, 543, 550, 551, or 553 of this title, to the extent that the debtor could have exempted such property under subsection (b) of this section if such property had not been transferred, if –

(1)(A) such transfer was not a voluntary transfer of such property by the debtor; and

(B) the debtor did not conceal such property ; or

(2) the debtor could have avoided such transfer under subsection (f)(2) of this section.

(h) The debtor may avoid a transfer of property of the debtor or recover a setoff to the extent that the debtor could have exempted such property under subsection (g)(1) of this section if the trustee had avoided such transfer, if –

(1) such transfer is avoidable by the trustee under section 544, 545, 547, 548, 549, or 724(a) of this title or recoverable by the trustee under section 553 of this title; and

(2) the trustee does not attempt to avoid such transfer.

(i)(1) If the debtor avoids a transfer or recovers a setoff under subsection (f) or (h) of this section, the debtor may recover in the manner prescribed by, and subject to the limitations of, section 550 of this title, the same as if the trustee had avoided such transfer, and may exempt any property so recovered under subsection (b) of this section.

(2) Notwithstanding section 551 of this title, a transfer avoided under section 544, 545, 547, 548, 549, or 724(a) of this title, under subsection (f) or (h) of this section, or property recovered under section 553 of this title, may be preserved for the benefit of the debtor to the extent that the debtor may exempt such property under subsection (g) of this section or paragraph (1) of this subsection.

(j) Notwithstanding subsections (g) and (i) of this section, the debtor may exempt a particular kind of property under subsections (g) and (i) of this section only to the extent that the debtor has exempted less property in value of such kind than that to which the debtor is entitled under subsection (b) of this section.

(k) Property that the debtor exempts under this section is not liable for payment of any administrative expense except –

(1) the aliquot share of the costs and expenses of avoiding a transfer of property that the debtor exempts under subsection (g) of this section, or of recovery of such property, that is attributable to the value of the portion of such property exempted in relation to the value of the property recovered; and

(2) any costs and expenses of avoiding a transfer under subsection (f) or (h) of this section, or of recovery of property under subsection (i)(1) of this section, that the debtor has not paid.

(l) The debtor shall file a list of property that the debtor claims as exempt under subsection (b) of this section. If the debtor does not file such a list, a dependent of the debtor may file such a list, or may claim property as exempt from property of the estate on behalf of the debtor. Unless a party in interest objects, the property claimed as exempt on such list is exempt.

(m) Subject to the limitation in subsection (b), this section shall apply separately with respect to each debtor in a joint case.

523. Exceptions to discharge

(a) A discharge under section 727, 1141, 1228(a), 1228(b), or 1328(b) of this title does not discharge an individual debtor from any debt –

(1) for a tax or a customs duty –

(A) of the kind and for the periods specified in section 507(a)(2) or 507(a)(7) of this title, whether or not a claim for such tax was filed or allowed;

(B) with respect to which a return, if required –

(i) was not filed; or

(ii) was filed after the date on which such return was last due, under applicable law or under any extension, and after two years before the date of the filing of the petition; or

(C) with respect to which the debtor made a fraudulent return or willfully attempted in any manner to evade or defeat such tax;

(2) for money, property, services, or an extension, renewal, or refinancing of credit, to the extent obtained by –

(A) false pretenses, a false representation, or actual fraud, other than a statement respecting the debtor's or an insider's financial condition;

(B) use of a statement in writing –

(i) that is materially false;

(ii) respecting the debtor's or an insider's financial condition;

(iii) on which the creditor to whom the debtor is liable for such money, property, services, or credit reasonably relied; and

(iv) that the debtor caused to be made or published with intent to deceive; or

(C) for purposes of subparagraph (A) of this paragraph, consumer debts owed to a single creditor and aggregating more than $500 for "luxury goods or services" incurred by an individual debtor on or within forty days before the order for relief under this title, or cash advances aggregating more than $1,000 that are extensions of consumer credit under an open end credit plan obtained by an individual debtor on or within twenty days before the order for relief under this title, are presumed to be nondischargeable; "luxury goods or services" do not include goods or services reasonably acquired for the support or maintenance of the debtor or a dependent of the debtor; an extension of consumer credit under an open end credit plan is to be defined for purposes of this subparagraph as it is defined in the Consumer Credit Protection Act (15 U.S.C. 1601 et seq.);

(3) neither listed nor scheduled under section 521(1) of this title, with the name, if known to the debtor, of the creditor to whom such debt is owed, in time to permit –

(A) if such debt is not of a kind specified in paragraph (2), (4), or (6) of this subsection, timely filing of a proof of claim, unless such creditor had notice or actual knowledge of the case in time for such timely filing; or

(B) if such debt is of a kind specified in paragraph (2), (4), or (6) of this subsection, timely filing of a proof of claim and timely request for a determination of dischargeability of such debt under one of such paragraphs, unless such creditor had notice or actual knowledge of the case in time for such timely filing and request;

(4) for fraud or defalcation while acting in a fiduciary capacity, embezzlement, or larceny;

(5) to a spouse, former spouse, or child of the debtor, for alimony to, maintenance for, or support of such spouse or child, in connection with a separation agreement, divorce decree or other order of a court of record, determination made in accordance with State or territorial law by a governmental unit, or property settlement agreement, but not to the extent that –

(A) such debt is assigned to another entity, voluntarily, by operation of law, or otherwise (other than debts assigned pursuant to section 402(a)(26) of the Social Security Act, or any such debt which has been assigned to the Federal Government or to a State or any political subdivision of such State); or

(B) such debt includes a liability designated as alimony, maintenance, or support, unless such liability is actually in the nature of alimony, maintenance, or support;

(6) for willful and malicious injury by the debtor to another entity or to the property of another entity;

(7) to the extent such debt is for a fine, penalty, or forfeiture payable to and for the benefit of a governmental unit, and is not compensation for actual pecuniary loss, other than a tax penalty –

(A) relating to a tax of a kind not specified in paragraph (1) of this subsection; or

(B) imposed with respect to a transaction or event that occurred before three years before the date of the filing of the petition;

(8) for an educational benefit overpayment or loan made, insured or guaranteed by a governmental unit, or made under any program funded in whole or in part by a governmental unit or nonprofit institution, or for an obligation to repay funds received as an educational benefit, scholarship or stipend, unless –

(A) such loan, benefit, scholarship, or stipend overpayment first became due more than 7 years (exclusive of any applicable suspension of the repayment period) before the date of the filing of the petition; or

(B) excepting such debt from discharge under this paragraph will impose an undue hardship on the debtor and the debtor's dependents;

(9) for death or personal injury caused by the debtor's operation of a motor vehicle if such operation was unlawful because the debtor was intoxicated from using alcohol, a drug, or another substance;

(10) that was or could have been listed or scheduled by the debtor in a prior case concerning the debtor under this title or under the Bankruptcy Act in which the debtor waived discharge, or was denied a discharge under section 727(a)(2), (3), (4), (5), (6), or (7) of this title, or under section 14c(1), (2), (3), (4), (6), or (7) of such Act;

(11) provided in any final judgment, unreviewable order, or consent order or decree entered in any court of the United States or of any State, issued by a Federal depository institutions regulatory agency, or contained in any settlement agreement entered into by the debtor, arising from any act of fraud or defalcation while acting in a fiduciary capacity committed with respect to any depository institution or insured credit union; or

(12) for malicious or reckless failure to fulfill any commitment by the debtor to a Federal depository institutions regulatory agency to maintain the capital of an insured depository institution, except that this paragraph shall not extend any such commitment which would otherwise be terminated due to any act of such agency.

(b) Notwithstanding subsection (a) of this section, a debt that was excepted from discharge under subsection (a)(1), (a)(3), or (a)(8) of this section, under section 17a(1), 17a(3), or 17a(5) of the Bankruptcy Act, under section 439A of the Higher Education Act of 1965 (20 U.S.C. 1087-3), or under section 733(g) of the Public Health Service Act (42 U.S.C. 294f) in a prior case concerning the debtor under this title, or under the Bankruptcy Act, is dischargeable in a case under this title unless, by the terms of subsection (a) of this section, such debt is not dischargeable in the case under this title.

(c)(1) Except as provided in subsection (a)(3)(B) of this section, the debtor shall be discharged from a debt of a kind specified in paragraph (2), (4), or (6) of subsection (a) of this section, unless, on request of the creditor to whom such debt is owed, and after notice and a hearing, the court determines such debt to be excepted from discharge under paragraph (2), (4), or (6), as the case may be, of subsection (a) of this section.

(2) Paragraph (1) shall not apply in the case of a Federal depository institutions regulatory agency seeking, in its capacity as conservator, receiver, or liquidating agent for an insured depository institution, to recover a debt described in subsection (a)(2), (a)(4), (a)(6), or (a)(11) owed to such institution by an institution–affiliated party unless the receiver, conservator, or liquidating agent was appointed in time to reasonably comply, or for a Federal depository institutions regulatory agency acting in its corporate capacity as a successor to such receiver, conservator, or liquidating agent to reasonably comply, with subsection (a)(3)(B) as a creditor of such institution–affiliated party with respect to such debt.

(d) If a creditor requests a determination of dischargeability of a consumer debt under subsection (a)(2) of this section, and such debt is discharged, the court shall grant judgment in favor of the debtor for the costs of, and a reasonable attorney's fee for, the proceeding if the court finds that the position of the creditor was not substantially justified, except that the court shall not award such costs and fees if special circumstances would make the award unjust.

(e) Any institution–affiliated party of a depository institution or insured credit union shall be considered to be acting in a fiduciary capacity with respect to the purposes of subsection (a) (4) or (11).

524. Effect of discharge

(a) A discharge in a case under this title –

(1) voids any judgment at any time obtained, to the extent that such judgment is a determination of the personal liability of the debtor with respect to any debt discharged under section 727, 944, 1141, 1228 or 1328 of this title, whether or not discharge of such debt is waived;

(2) operates as an injunction against the commencement or continuation of an action, the employment of process, or an act, to collect, recover or offset any such debt as a personal liability of the debtor, whether or not discharge of such debt is waived; and

(3) operates an injunction against the commencement or continuation of an action, the employment of process, or an act, to collect or recover from, or offset against, property of the debtor of the kind specified in section 541(a)(2) of this title that is acquired after the commencement of the case, on account of any allowable community claim, except a community claim that is excepted from discharge under section 523, 1228(a)(1), or 1328(a)(1) of this title, or that would be so excepted, determined in accordance with the provisions of sections 523(c) and 523(d) of this title, in a case concerning the debtor's spouse commenced on the date of the filing of the petition in the case concerning the debtor, whether or not discharge of the debt based on such community claim is waived.

(b) Subsection (a)(3) of this section does not apply if –

(1)(A) the debtor's spouse is a debtor in a case under this title, or a bankrupt or a debtor in a case under the Bankruptcy Act, commenced within six years of the date of the filing of the petition in the case concerning the debtor; and

(B) the court does not grant the debtor's spouse a discharge in such case concerning the debtor's spouse; or

(2)(A) the court would not grant the debtor's spouse a discharge in a case under chapter 7 of this title concerning such spouse commenced on the date of the filing of the petition in the case concerning the debtor; and

(B) a determination that the court would not so grant such discharge is made by the bankruptcy court within the time and in the manner provided for a determination under section 727 of this title of whether a debtor is granted a discharge.

(c) An agreement between a holder of a claim and the debtor, the consideration for which, in whole or in part, is based on a debt that is dischargeable in a case under this title is enforceable only to any extent enforceable under applicable nonbankruptcy law, whether or not discharge of such debt is waived, only if –

(1) such agreement was made before the granting of the discharge under section 727, 1141, 1228, or 1328 of this title;

(2) such agreement contains a clear and conspicuous statement which advises the debtor that the agreement may be rescinded at any time prior to discharge or within sixty days after such agreement is filed with the court, whichever occurs later, by giving notice of rescission to the holder of such claim;

(3) such agreement has been filed with the court and, if applicable, accompanied by a declaration or an affidavit of the attorney that represented the debtor during the course of negotiating an agreement under this subsection, which states that such agreement –

(A) represents a fully informed and voluntary agreement by the debtor; and

(B) does not impose an undue hardship on the debtor or a dependent of the debtor;

(4) the debtor has not rescinded such agreement at any time prior to discharge or within sixty days after such agreement is filed with the court, whichever occurs later, by giving notice of recission to the holder of such claim;

(5) the provisions of subsection (d) of this section have been complied with; and

(6)(A) in a case concerning an individual who was not represented by an attorney during the course of negotiating an agreement under this subsection, the court approves such agreement as –

(i) not imposing an undue hardship on the debtor or a dependent of the debtor; and

(ii) in the best interest of the debtor.

(B) Subparagraph (A) shall not apply to the extent that such debt is a consumer debt secured by real property.

(d) In a case concerning an individual, when the court has determined whether to grant or not to grant a discharge under section 727, 1141, 1228, or 1328 of this title, the court may hold a hearing at which the debtor shall appear in person. At any such hearing, the court shall inform the debtor that a discharge has been granted or the reason why a discharge has not been granted. If a discharge has been granted and if the debtor desires to make an agreement of the kind specified in subsection (c) of this section, then the court shall hold a hearing at which the debtor shall appear in person and at such hearing the court shall –

(1) inform the debtor –

(A) that such an agreement is not required under this title, under nonbankruptcy law, or under any agreement not made in accordance with the provisions of subsection (c) of this section; and

(B) of the legal effect and consequences of –

(i) an agreement of the kind specified in subsection (c) of this section; and

(ii) a default under such an agreement;

(2) determine whether the agreement that the debtor desires to make complies with the requirements of subsection (c)(6) of this section, if the consideration for such agreement is based in whole or in part on a consumer debt that is not secured by real property of the debtor.

(e) Except as provided in subsection (a)(3) of this section, discharge of a debt of the debtor does not affect the liability of any other entity on, or the property of any other entity for, such debt.

(f) Nothing contained in subsection (c) or (d) of this section prevents a debtor from voluntarily repaying any debt.

525. Protection against discriminatory treatment

(a) Except as provided in the Perishable Agricultural Commodities Act, 1930 (7 U.S.C. 499a–499s), the Packers and Stockyards Act, 1921 (7 U.S.C. 181–229), and section 1 of the Act entitled "An Act making appropriations for the Department of Agriculture for the fiscal year ending June 30, 1944, and for other purposes," approved July 12, 1943 (57 Stat. 422; 7 U.S.C. 204), a governmental unit may not deny, revoke, suspend, or refuse to renew a license, permit, charter, franchise, or other similar grant to, condition such a grant to, discriminate with respect to such a grant against, deny employment to, terminate the employment of, or discriminate with respect to employment against, a person that is or has been a debtor under this title or a bankrupt or a debtor under the Bankruptcy Act, or another person with whom such bankrupt or debtor has been associated, solely because such bankrupt or debtor is or has been a debtor under this title or a bankrupt or debtor under the Bankruptcy Act, has been insolvent before the commencement of the case under this title, or during the case but before the debtor is granted or denied a discharge, or has not paid a debt that is dischargeable in the case under this title or that was discharged under the Bankruptcy Act.

(b) No private employer may terminate the employment of, or discriminate with respect to employment against, an individual who is or has been a debtor under this title, a debtor or bankrupt under the Bankruptcy Act, or an individual associated with such debtor or bankrupt, solely because such debtor or bankrupt –

(1) is or has been a debtor under this title or a debtor or bankrupt under the Bankruptcy Act;

(2) has been insolvent before the commencement of a case under this title or during the case but before the grant or denial of a discharge; or

(3) has not paid a debt that is dischargeable in a case under this title or that was discharged under the Bankruptcy Act.

SUBCHAPTER III - THE ESTATE

541. Property of the estate

(a) The commencement of a case under section 301, 302, or 303 of this title creates an estate. Such estate is comprised of all the following property, wherever located and by whomever held:

(1) Except as provided in subsections (b) and (c)(2) of this section, all legal or equitable interests of the debtor in property as of the commencement of the case.

(2) All interests of the debtor and the debtor's spouse in community property as of the commencement of the case that is –

(A) under the sole, equal, or joint management and control of the debtor; or

(B) liable for an allowable claim against the debtor, or for both an allowable claim against the debtor and an allowable claim against the debtor's spouse, to the extent that such interest is so liable.

(3) Any interest in property that the trustee recovers under section 329(b), 363(n), 543, 550, 553, or 723 of this title.

(4) Any interest in property preserved for the benefit of or ordered transferred to the estate under section 510(c) or 551 of this title.

(5) Any interest in property that would have been property of the estate if such interest had been an interest of the debtor on the date of the filing of the petition, and that the debtor acquires or becomes entitled to acquire within 180 days after such date –

(A) by bequest, devise, or inheritance;

(B) as a result of a property settlement agreement with the debtor's spouse, or of an interlocutory or final divorce decree; or

(C) as a beneficiary of a life insurance policy or of a death benefit plan.

(6) Proceeds, product, offspring, rents, or profits of or from property of the estate, except such as are earnings from services performed by an individual debtor after the commencement of the case.

(7) Any interest in property that the estate acquires after the commencement of the case.

(b) Property of the estate does not include –

(1) any power that the debtor may exercise solely for the benefit of an entity other than the debtor;

(2) any interest of the debtor as a lessee under a lease of nonresidential real property that has terminated at the expiration of the stated term of such lease before the commencement of the case under this title, and ceases to include any interest of the debtor as a lessee under a lease of nonresidential real property that has terminated at the expiration of the stated term of such lease during the case;

(3) any eligibility of the debtor to participate in programs authorized under the Higher Education Act of 1965 (20 U.S.C. 1001 et seq.; 42 U.S.C. 2751 et seq.), or any accreditation status or State licensure of the debtor as an educational institution; or

(4) any interest of the debtor in liquid or gaseous hydrocarbons to the extent that –

(A) the debtor has transferred or has agreed to transfer such interest pursuant to a farmout agreement or any written agreement directly related to a farmout agreement; and

(B) but for the operation of this paragraph, the estate could include such interest only by virtue of section 365 or 544(a)(3) of this title.

(c)(1) Except as provided in paragraph (2) of this subsection, an interest of the debtor in property becomes property of the estate under subsection (a)(1), (a)(2), or (a)(5) of this section notwithstanding any provision in an agreement, transfer instrument, or applicable nonbankruptcy law –

(A) that restricts or conditions transfer of such interest by the debtor; or

(B) that is conditioned on the insolvency or financial condition of the debtor, on the commencement of a case under this title, or on the appointment of or taking possession by a trustee in a case under this title or a custodian before such commencement, and that effects or gives an option to effect a forfeiture, modification, or termination of the debtor's interest in property.

(2) A restriction on the transfer of a beneficial interest of the debtor in a trust that is enforceable under applicable nonbankruptcy law is enforceable in a case under this title.

(d) Property in which the debtor holds, as of the commencement of the case, only legal title and not an equitable interest, such as a mortgage secured by real property, or an interest in such a mortgage, sold by the debtor but as to which the debtor retains legal title to service or supervise the servicing of such mortgage or interest, becomes property of the estate under subsection (a)(1) or (2) of this section only to the extent of the debtor's legal title to such property, but not to the extent of any equitable interest in such property that the debtor does not hold.

542. Turnover of property to the estate

(a) Except as provided in subsection (c) or (d) of this section, an entity, other than a custodian, in possession, custody, or control, during the case, of property that the trustee may use, sell, or lease under section 363 of this title, or that the debtor may exempt under section 522 of this title, shall deliver to the trustee, and account for, such property or the value of such property, unless such property is of inconsequential value or benefit to the estate.

(b) Except as provided in subsection (c) or (d) of this section, an entity that owes a debt that is property of the estate and that is matured, payable on demand, or payable on order, shall pay such debt to, or on the order of, the trustee, except to the extent that such debt may be offset under section 553 of this title against a claim against the debtor.

(c) Except as provided in section 362(a)(7) of this title, an entity that has neither actual notice nor actual knowledge of the commencement of the case concerning the debtor may transfer property of the estate, or pay a debt owing to the debtor, in good faith and other than in the manner specified in subsection (d) of this section, to an entity other than the trustee, with the same effect as to the entity making such transfer or payment as if the case under this title concerning the debtor had not been commenced.

(d) A life insurance company may transfer property of the estate or property of the debtor to such company in good faith, with the same effect with respect to such company as if the case under this title concerning the debtor had not been commenced, if such transfer is to pay a premium or to carry out a nonforfeiture insurance option, and is required to be made automatically, under a life insurance contract with such company that was entered into before the date of the filing of the petition and that is property of the estate.

(e) Subject to any applicable privilege, after notice and a hearing, the court may order an attorney, accountant, or other person that holds recorded information, including books, documents, records, and papers, relating to the debtor's property or financial affairs, to turn over or disclose such recorded information to the trustee.

543. Turnover of property by a custodian

(a) A custodian with knowledge of the commencement of a case under this title concerning the debtor may not make any disbursement from, or take any action in the administration of, property of the debtor, proceeds, product, offspring, rents, or profits of such property, or property of the estate, in the possession, custody, or control of such custodian, except such action as is necessary to preserve such property.

(b) A custodian shall –

(1) deliver to the trustee any property of the debtor held by or transferred to such custodian, or proceeds, product, offspring, rents, or profits of such property, that is in such custodian's possession, custody, or control on the date that such custodian acquires knowledge of the commencement of the case; and

(2) file an accounting of any property of the debtor, or proceeds, product, offspring, rents, or profits of such property, that, at any time, came into the possession, custody, or control of such custodian.

(c) The court, after notice and a hearing, shall –

(1) protect all entities to which a custodian has become obligated with respect to such property or proceeds, product, offspring, rents, or profits of such property;

(2) provide for the payment of reasonable compensation for services rendered and costs and expenses incurred by such custodian; and

(3) surcharge such custodian, other than an assignee for the benefit of the debtor's creditors that was appointed or took possession more than 120 days before the date of the filing of the petition, for any improper or excessive disbursement, other than a disbursement that has been made in accordance with applicable law or that has been approved, after notice and a hearing, by a court of competent jurisdiction before the commencement of the case under this title.

(d) After notice and hearing, the bankruptcy court –

(1) may excuse compliance with subsection (a), (b), or (c) of this section, if the interests of creditors and, if the debtor is not insolvent, of equity security holders would be better served by permitting a custodian to continue in possession, custody, or control of such property, and

(2) shall excuse compliance with subsections (a) and (b)(1) of this section if the custodian is an assignee for the benefit of the debtor's creditors that was appointed or took possession more than 120 days before the date of the filing of the petition, unless compliance with such subsections is necessary to prevent fraud or injustice.

544. Trustee as lien creditor and as successor to certain creditors and purchasers

(a) The trustee shall have, as of the commencement of the case, and without regard to any knowledge of the trustee or of any creditor, the rights and powers of, or may avoid any transfer of property of the debtor or any obligation incurred by the debtor that is voidable by –

(1) a creditor that extends credit to the debtor at the time of the commencement of the case, and that obtains, at such time and with respect to such credit, a judicial lien on all property on which a creditor on a simple contract could have obtained such a judicial lien, whether or not such a creditor exists;

(2) a creditor that extends credit to the debtor at the time of the commencement of the case, and obtains, at such time and with respect to such credit, an execution against the debtor that is returned unsatisfied at such time, whether or not such a creditor exists; or

(3) a bona fide purchaser of real property, other than fixtures, from the debtor, against whom applicable law permits such transfer to be perfected, that obtains the status of a bona fide purchaser and has perfected such transfer at the time of the commencement of the case, whether or not such a purchaser exists.

(b) The trustee may avoid any transfer of an interest of the debtor in property or any obligation incurred by the debtor that is voidable under applicable law by a creditor holding an unsecured claim that is allowable under section 502 of this title or that is not allowable only section 502(e) of this title.

545. Statutory liens

The trustee may avoid the fixing of a statutory lien on property of the debtor to the extent that such lien –

(1) first becomes effective against the debtor –

(A) when a case under this title concerning the debtor is commenced;

(B) when an insolvency proceeding other than under this title concerning the debtor is commenced;

(C) when a custodian is appointed or authorized to take or takes possession;

(D) when the debtor becomes insolvent;

(E) when the debtor's financial condition fails to meet a specified standard; or

(F) at the time of an execution against property of the debtor levied at the instance of an entity other than the holder of such statutory lien;

(2) is not perfected or enforceable at the time of the commencement of the case against a bona fide purchaser that purchases such property, whether or not such a purchaser exists;

(3) is for rent; or

(4) is a lien of distress for rent.

546. Limitations on avoiding powers

(a) An action or proceeding under section 544, 545, 547, 548, or 553 of this title may not be commenced after the earlier of –

(1) two years after the appointment of a trustee under section 702, 1104, 1163, 1302, or 1202 of this title; or

(2) the time the case is closed or dismissed.

(b) The rights and powers of a trustee under sections 544, 545, and 549 of this title are subject to any generally applicable law that permits perfection of an interest in property to be effective against an entity that acquires rights in such property before the date of such perfection. If such law requires seizure of such property or commencement of an action to accomplish such perfection, and such property has not been seized or such action has not been commenced before the date of the filing of the petition, such interest in such property shall be perfected by notice within the time fixed by such law for such seizure or commencement.

(c) Except as provided in subsection (d) of this section, the rights and powers of a trustee under sections 544(a), 545, 547, and 549 of this title are subject to any statutory or common-law right of a seller of goods that has sold goods to the debtor, in the ordinary course of such seller's business, to reclaim such goods if the debtor has received such goods while insolvent, but –

(1) such a seller may not reclaim any such goods unless such seller demands in writing reclamation of such goods before ten days after receipt of such goods by the debtor; and

(2) the court may deny reclamation to a seller with such a right of reclamation that has made such a demand only if the court –

(A) grants the claim of such a seller priority as a claim of a kind specified in section 503(b) of this title; or

(B) secures such claim by a lien.

(d) In the case of a seller who is a producer of grain sold to a grain storage facility, owned or operated by the debtor, in the ordinary course of such seller's business (as such terms are defined in section 557 of this title) or in the case of a United States fisherman who has caught fish sold to a fish processing facility owned or operated by the debtor in the ordinary course of such fisherman's business, the rights and powers of the trustee under sections 544(a), 545, 547, and 549 of this title are subject to any statutory or common law right of such producer or fisherman to reclaim such grain or fish if the debtor has received such grain or fish while insolvent, but –

(1) such producer or fisherman may not reclaim any grain or fish unless such producer or fisherman demands, in writing, reclamation of such grain or fish before ten days after receipt thereof by the debtor; and

(2) the court may deny reclamation to such a producer or fisherman with a right of reclamation that has made such a demand only if the court secures such claim by a lien.

(e) Notwithstanding sections 544, 545, 547, 548(a)(2), and 548(b) of this title, the trustee may not avoid a transfer that is a margin payment, as defined in section 101(34), 741(5) or 761(15) of this title, or settlement payment, as defined in section 101(35) or 741(8) of this title, made by or to a commodity broker, forward contract merchant, stockbroker, financial institution, or securities clearing agency, that is made before the commencement of the case, except under section 548(a)(1) of this title.

(f) Notwithstanding sections 544, 545, 547, 548(a)(2), and 548(b) of this title, the trustee may not avoid a transfer that is a margin payment, as defined in section 741(5) or 761(15) of this title, or settlement payment, as defined in section 741(8) of this title, made by or to a repo participant, in connection with a repurchase agreement and that is made before the commencement of the case, except under section 548(a)(1) of this title.

(g) Notwithstanding sections 544, 545, 547, 548(a)(2) and 548(b) of this title, the trustee may not avoid a transfer under a swap agreement, made by or to a swap participant, in connection with a swap agreement and that is made before the commencement of the case, except under section 548(a)(1) of this title.

547. Preferences

(a) In this section –

(1) "inventory" means personal property leased or furnished, held for sale or lease, or to be furnished under a contract for service, raw materials, work in process, or materials used or consumed in a business, including farm products such a crops or livestock, held for sale or lease;

(2) "new value" means money or money's worth in goods, services, or new credit, or release by a transferee of property previously transferred to such transferee in a transaction that is neither void nor voidable by the debtor or the trustee under any applicable law, including proceeds of such property, but does not include an obligation substituted for an existing obligation;

(3) "receivable" means right to payment, whether or not such right has been earned by performance; and

(4) a debt for a tax is incurred on the day when such tax is last payable without penalty, including any extension.

(b) Except as provided in subsection (c) of this section, the trustee may avoid any transfer of an interest of the debtor in property –

(1) to or for the benefit of a creditor;

(2) for or on account of an antecedent debt owed by the debtor before such transfer was made;

(3) made while the debtor was insolvent;

(4) made –

(A) on or within 90 days before the date of the filing of the petition; or

(B) between ninety days and one year before the date of the filing of the petition, if such creditor at the time of such transfer was an insider; and

(5) that enables such creditor to receive more than such creditor would receive if –

(A) the case were a case under chapter 7 of this title;

(B) the transfer had not been made; and

(C) such creditor received payment of such debt to the extent provided by the provisions of this title.

(c) The trustee may not avoid under this section a transfer –

(1) to the extent that such transfer was –

(A) intended by the debtor and the creditor to or for whose benefit such transfer was made to be a contemporaneous exchange for new value given to the debtor; and

(B) in fact a substantially contemporaneous exchange;

(2) to the extent that such transfer was –

(A) in payment of a debt incurred by the debtor in the ordinary course of business or financial affairs of the debtor and the transferee;

(B) made in the ordinary course of business or financial affairs of the debtor and the transferee; and

(C) made according to ordinary business terms;

(3) that creates a security interest in property acquired by the debtor –

(A) to the extent such security interest secures new value that was –

(i) given at or after the signing of a security agreement that contains a description of such property as collateral;

(ii) given by or on behalf of the secured party under such agreement;

(iii) given to enable the debtor to acquire such property; and

(iv) in fact used by the debtor to acquire such property; and

(B) that is perfected on or before 10 days after the debtor receives possession of such property;

(4) to or for the benefit of a creditor, to the extent that, after such transfer, such creditor gave new value to or for the benefit of the debtor –

(A) not secured by an otherwise unavoidable security interest; and

(B) on account of which new value the debtor did not make an otherwise unavoidable transfer to or for the benefit of such creditor;

(5) that creates a perfected security interest in inventory or a receivable or the proceeds of either, except to the extent that the aggregate of all such transfers to the transferee caused a reduction, as of the date of the filing of the petition and to the prejudice of other creditors holding unsecured claims, of any amount by which the debt secured by such security interest exceeded the value of all security interests for such debt on the later of –

(A)(i) with respect to a transfer to which subsection (b)(4)(A) of this section applies, 90 days before the date of the filing of the petition; or

(ii) with respect to a transfer to which subsection (b)(4)(B) of this section applies, one year before the date of the filing of the petition; or

(B) the date on which new value was first given under the security agreement creating such security interest;

(6) that is the fixing of a statutory lien that is not avoidable under section 545 of this title; or

(7) if, in a case filed by an individual debtor whose debts are primarily consumer debts, the aggregate value of all property that constitutes or is affected by such transfer is less than $600.

(d) The trustee may avoid a transfer of an interest in property of the debtor transferred to or for the benefit of a surety to secure reimbursement of such a surety that furnished a bond or other obligation to dissolve a judicial lien that would have been avoidable by the trustee under subsection (b) of this section. The liability of such surety under such bond or obligation shall be discharged to the extent of the value of such property recovered by the trustee or the amount paid to the trustee.

(e)(1) For the purposes of this section –

(A) a transfer of real property other than fixtures, but including the interest of a seller or purchaser under a contract for the sale of real property, is perfected when a bona fide purchaser of such property from the debtor against whom applicable law permits such transfer to be perfected cannot acquire an interest that is superior to the interest of the transferee; and

(B) a transfer of a fixture or property other than real property is perfected when a creditor on a simple contract cannot acquire a judicial lien that is superior to the interest of the transferee.

(2) For the purposes of this section, except as provided in paragraph (3) of this subsection, a transfer is made –

(A) at the time such transfer take effect between the transferor and the transferee, if such transfer is perfected at, or within 10 days after, such time;

(B) at the time such transfer is perfected, if such transfer is perfected after such 10 days; or

(C) immediately before the date of the filing of the petition, if such transfer is not perfected at the later of –

(i) the commencement of the case; or

(ii) 10 days after such transfer takes effect between the transferor and the transferee.

(3) For the purposes of this section, a transfer is not made until the debtor has acquired rights in the property transferred.

(f) For the purposes of this section, the debtor is presumed to have been insolvent on and during the 90 days immediately preceding the date of the filing of the petition.

(g) For the purposes of this section, the trustee has the burden of proving the avoidability of a transfer under subsection (b) of this section, and the creditor or party in interest against whom recovery or avoidance is sought has the burden of proving the nonavoidability of a transfer under subsection (c) of this section.

548. Fraudulent transfers and obligations

(a) The trustee may avoid any transfer of an interest of the debtor in property, or any obligation incurred by the debtor, that was made or incurred on or within one year before the date of the filing of the petition, if the debtor voluntarily or involuntarily –

(1) made such transfer or incurred such obligation with actual intent to hinder, delay, or defraud any entity to which the debtor was or became, on or after the date that such transfer was made or such obligation was incurred, indebted; or

(2)(A) received less than a reasonably equivalent value in exchange for such transfer or obligation; and

(B)(i) was insolvent on the date that such transfer was made or such obligation was incurred, or became insolvent as a result of such transfer or obligation;

(ii) was engaged in business or a transaction, or was about to engage in business or a transaction, for which any property remaining with the debtor was an unreasonably small capital; or

(iii) intended to incur, or believed that the debtor would incur, debts that would be beyond the debtor's ability to pay as such debts matured.

(b) The trustee of a partnership debtor may avoid any transfer of an interest of the debtor in property, or any obligation incurred by the debtor, that was made or incurred on or within one year before the date of the filing of the petition, to a general partner in the debtor, if the debtor was insolvent on the date such transfer was made or such obligation was incurred, or became insolvent as a result of such transfer or obligation.

(c) Except to the extent that a transfer or obligation voidable under this section is voidable under section 544, 545, or 547 of this title, a transferee or obligee of such a transfer or obligation that takes for value and in good faith has a lien on or may retain any interest transferred or may enforce any obligation incurred, as the case may be, to the extent that such transferee or obligee gave value to the debtor in exchange for such transfer or obligation.

(d)(1) For the purposes of this section, a transfer is made when such transfer is so perfected that a bona fide purchaser from the debtor against whom applicable law permits such transfer to be perfected cannot acquire an interest in the property transferred that is superior to the interest in such property of the transferee, but if such transfer is not so perfected before the commencement of the case, such transfer is made immediately before the date of the filing of the petition.

(2) In this section –

(A) "value" means property, or satisfaction or securing of a present or antecedent debt of the debtor, but does not include an unperformed promise to furnish support to the debtor or to a relative of the debtor;

(B) a commodity broker, forward contract merchant, stockbroker, financial institution or securities clearing agency that receives a margin payment, as defined in section 101(34), 741(5) or 761(15) of this title, or settlement payment, as defined in section 101(35) or 741(8) of this title, takes for value to the extent of such payment;

(C) a repo participant that receives a margin payment, as defined in section 741(5) or 761(15) of this title, or settlement payment, as defined in section 741(8) of this title, in connection with a repurchase agreement, takes for value to the extent of such payment; and

(D) a swap participant that receives a transfer in connection with a swap agreement takes for value to the extent of such transfer.

549. Postpetition transactions

(a) Except as provided in subsection (b) or (c) of this section, the trustee may avoid a transfer of property of the estate –

(1) that occurs after the commencement of the case; and

(2)(A) that is authorized only under section 303(f) or 542(c) of this title; or

(B) that is not authorized under this title or by the court.

(b) In an involuntary case, a transfer made after the commencement of such case but before the order for relief to the extent of any value, including services, but not including satisfaction or securing of a debt that arose before the commencement of the case, is given after the commencement of the case in exchange for such transfer, notwithstanding any notice or knowledge of the case that the transferee has.

(c) The trustee may not avoid under subsection (a) of this section a transfer of real property to a good faith purchaser without knowledge of the commencement of the case and for present fair equivalent value unless a copy or notice of the petition was filed, where a transfer of such real property may be recorded to perfect such transfer, before such transfer is so perfected that a bona fide purchaser of such property, against whom applicable law permits such transfer to be perfected, could not acquire an interest that is superior to the interest of such good faith purchaser. A good faith purchaser without knowledge of the commencement of the case and for less than present fair equivalent value has a lien on the property transferred to the extent of any present value given, unless a copy or notice of the petition was so filed before such transfer was so perfected.

(d) An action or proceeding under this section may not be commenced after the earlier of –

(1) two years after the date of the transfer sought to be avoided; or

(2) the time the case is closed or dismissed.

550. Liability of transferee of avoided transfer

(a) Except as otherwise provided in this section, to the extent that a transfer is avoided under section 544, 545, 547, 548, 549, 553(b), or 724(a) of this title, the trustee may recover, for the benefit of the estate, the property transferred, or, if the court so orders, the value of such property, from –

(1) the initial transferee of such transfer or the entity for whose benefit such transfer was made; or

(2) any immediate or mediate transferee of such initial transferee.

(b) The trustee may not recover under section (a)(2) of this section from –

(1) a transferee that takes for value, including satisfaction or securing of a present or antecedent debt, in good faith, and without knowledge of the voidability of the transfer avoided; or

(2) any immediate or mediate good faith transferee of such transferee.

(c) The trustee is entitled to only a single satisfaction under subsection (a) of this section.

(d)(1) A good faith transferee from whom the trustee may recover under subsection (a) of this section has a lien on the property recovered to secure the lesser of –

(A) the cost, to such transferee, of any improvement made after the transfer, less the amount of any profit realized by or accruing to such transferee from such property; and

(B) any increase in the value of such property as a result of such improvement, of the property transferred.

(2) In this subsection, "improvement" includes –

(A) physical additions or changes to the property transferred;

(B) repairs to such property;

(C) payment of any tax on such property;

(D) payment of any debt secured by a lien on such property that is superior or equal to the rights of the trustee; and

(E) preservation of such property.

(e) An action or proceeding under this section may not be commenced after the earlier of –

(1) one year after the avoidance of the transfer on account of which recovery under this section is sought; or

(2) the time the case is closed or dismissed.

551. Automatic preservation of avoided transfer

Any transfer avoided under section 522, 544, 545, 547, 548, 549, or 724(a) of this title, or any lien void under section 506(d) of this title, is preserved for the benefit of the estate but only with respect to property of the estate.

552. Postpetition effect of security interest

(a) Except as provided in subsection (b) of this section, property acquired by the estate or by the debtor after the commencement of the case is not subject to any lien resulting from any security agreement entered into by the debtor before the commencement of the case.

(b) Except as provided in sections 363, 506(c), 522, 544, 545, 547, and 548 of this title, if the debtor and an entity entered into a security agreement before the commencement of the case and if the security interest created by such security agreement extends to property of the debtor acquired before the commencement of the case and to proceeds, product, offspring, rents, or profits of such property, then such security interest extends to such proceeds, product, offspring, rents, or profits acquired by the estate after the commencement of the case to the extent provided by such security agreement and by applicable nonbankruptcy law, except to any extent that the court, after notice and a hearing and based on the equities of the case, orders otherwise.

553. Setoff

(a) Except as otherwise provided in this section and in sections 362 and 363 of this title, this title does not affect any right of a creditor to offset a mutual debt owing by such creditor to the debtor that arose before the commencement of the case under this title against a claim of such creditor against the debtor that arose before the commencement of the case, except to the extent that –

(1) the claim of such creditor against the debtor is disallowed other than under section 502(b)(3) of this title;

(2) such claim was transferred, by an entity other than the debtor, to such creditor –

(A) after the commencement of the case; or

(B)(i) after 90 days before the date of the filing of the petition; and

(ii) while the debtor was insolvent; or

(3) the debt owed to the debtor by such creditor was incurred by such creditor –

(A) after 90 days before the date of the filing of the petition;

(B) while the debtor was insolvent; and

(C) for the purpose of obtaining a right of setoff against the debtor.

(b)(1) Except with respect to a setoff of a kind described in section 362(b)(6), 362(b)(7), 362(b)(14), 365(h)(2), or 365(i)(2) of this title, if a creditor offsets a mutual debt owing to the debtor against a claim against the debtor on or within 90 days before the date of the filing of the petition, then the trustee may recover from such creditor the amount so offset to the extent that any insufficiency on the date of such setoff is less than the insufficiency on the later of –

(A) 90 days before the date of the filing of the petition; and

(B) the first date during the 90 days immediately preceding the date of the filing of the petition on which there is an insufficiency.

(2) In this subsection, "insufficiency" means amount, if any, by which a claim against the debtor exceeds a mutual debt owing to the debtor by the holder of such claim.

(c) For the purposes of this section, the debtor is presumed to have been insolvent on and during the 90 days immediately preceding the date of the filing of the petition.

554. Abandonment of property of the estate

(a) After notice and a hearing, the trustee may abandon any property of the estate that is burdensome to the estate or that is of inconsequential value and benefit to the estate.

(b) On request of a party in interest and after notice and a hearing, the court may order the trustee to abandon any property of the estate that is burdensome to the estate or that is of inconsequential value and benefit to the estate.

(c) Unless the court orders otherwise, any property scheduled under section 521(1) of this title not otherwise administered at time of the closing of a case is abandoned to the debtor and administered for purposes of section 350 of this title.

(d) Unless the court orders otherwise, property of the estate that is not abandoned under this section and that is not administered in the case remains property of the estate.

555. Contractual right to liquidate a securities contract

The exercise of a contractual right of a stockbroker, financial institution, or securities clearing agency to cause the liquidation of a securities contract, as defined in section 741(7), because of a condition of the kind specified in section 365(e)(1) of this title shall not be stayed, avoided, or otherwise limited by operation of any provision of this title or by order of a court or administrative agency in any proceeding under this title unless such order is authorized under the provisions of the Securities Investor Protection Act of 1970 (15 U.S.C. 78aaa et seq.) or any statute administered by the Securities and Exchange Commission. As used in this section, the term "contractual right" includes a right set forth in a rule or bylaw of a national securities exchange, a national securities association, or a securities clearing agency.

556. Contractual right to liquidate a commodities contract or forward contract

The contractual right of a commodity broker or forward contract merchant to cause the liquidation of a commodity contract, as defined in section 761(4), or forward contract because of a condition of the kind specified in section 365(e)(1) of this title, and the right to a variation or maintenance margin payment received from a trustee with respect to open commodity contracts or forward contracts, shall not be stayed, avoided, or otherwise limited by operation of any provision of this title or by the order of a court in any proceeding under this title. As used in this section, the term "contractual right" includes a right set forth in a rule or bylaw of a clearing organization or contract market or in a resolution of the governing board thereof and a right, whether or not evidenced in writing, arising under common law, under law merchant or by reason of normal business practice.

557. Expedited determination of interests in, and abandonment or other disposition of grain assets

(a) This section applies only in a case concerning a debtor that owns or operates a grain storage facility and only with respect to grain and the proceeds of grain. This section does not affect the application of any other section of this title to property other than grain and proceeds of grain.

(b) In this section–

(1) "grain" means wheat, corn, flaxseed, grain sorghum, barley, oats, rye, soybeans, other edible beans, or rice;

(2) "grain storage facility" means a site or physical structure regularly used to store grain for producers, or to store grain acquired from producers for resale; and

(3) "producer" means an entity which engages in the growing of grain.

(c)(1) Notwithstanding sections 362, 363, 365, and 554 of this title, on the court's own motion the court may, and on the request of the trustee or an entity that claims an interest in grain or the proceeds of grain the court shall, expedite the procedures for the determination of interests in and the disposition of grain and the proceeds of grain, by shortening to the greatest extent feasible such time periods as are otherwise applicable for such procedures and by establishing, by order, a timetable having a duration of not to exceed 120 days for the completion of the applicable procedure specified in subsection (d) of this section. Such time periods and such timetable may be modified by the court, for cause, in accordance with subsection (f) of this section.

(2) The court shall determine the extent to which such time periods shall be shortened, based upon–

(A) any need of an entity claiming an interest in such grain or the proceeds of grain for a prompt determination of such interest;

(B) any need of such entity for a prompt disposition of such grain;

(C) the market for such grain;

(D) the conditions under which such grain is stored;

(E) the costs of continued storage or disposition of such grain;

(F) the orderly administration of the estate;

(G) the appropriate opportunity for an entity to assert an interest in such grain; and

(H) such other considerations as are relevant to the need to expedite such procedures in the case.

(d) The procedures that may be expedited under subsection (c) of this section include–

(1) the filing of and response to–

(A) a claim of ownership;

(B) a proof of claim;

(C) a request for abandonment;

(D) a request for relief from the stay of action against property under section 362(a) of this title;

(E) a request for determination of secured status;

(F) a request for determination of whether such grain or the proceeds of grain–

(i) is property of the estate;

(ii) must be turned over to the estate; or

(iii) may be used, sold, or leased; and

(G) any other request for determination of an interest in such grain or the proceeds of grain;

(2) the disposition of such grain or the proceeds of grain, before or after determination of interests in such grain or the proceeds of grain, by way of–

(A) sale of such grain;

(B) abandonment;

(C) distribution; or

(D) such other method as is equitable in the case;

(3) subject to sections 701, 702, 703, 1104, 1202, and 1302 of this title; the appointment of a trustee or examiner and the retention and compensation of any professional person required to assist with respect to matters relevant to the determination of interests in or disposition of such grain or the proceeds of grain; and

(4) the determination of any dispute concerning a matter specified in paragraph (1), (2), or (3) of this subsection.

(e)(1) Any governmental unit that has regulatory jurisdiction over the operation or liquidation of the debtor or the debtor's business shall be given notice of any request made or ordered entered under subsection (c) of this section.

(2) Any such governmental unit may raise, and may appear and be heard on, any issue relating to grain or the proceeds of grain in a case in which a request is made, or an order is entered, under subsection (c) of this section.

(3) The trustee shall consult with such governmental unit before taking any action relating to the disposition of grain in the possession, custody, or control of the debtor or the estate.

(f) The court may extend the period for final disposition of grain or the proceeds of grain under this section beyond 120 days if the court finds that-

(1) the interests of justice so require in light of the complexity of the case; and

(2) the interests of those claimants entitled to distribution of grain or the proceeds of grain will not be materially injured by such additional delay.

(g) Unless an order establishing an expedited procedure under subsection (c) of this section, or determining any interest in or approving any disposition of grain or the proceeds of grain, is stayed pending appeal-

(1) the reversal or modification of such order on appeal does not affect the validity of any procedure, determination, or disposition that occurs before such reversal or modification, whether or not any entity knew of the pendency of the appeal; and

(2) neither the court nor the trustee may delay, due to the appeal of such order, any proceeding in the case in which such order is issued.

(h)(1) The trustee may recover from grain and the proceeds of grain the reasonable and necessary costs and expenses allowable under section 503(b) of this title attributable to preserving or disposing of grain or the proceeds of grain, but may not recover from such grain or the proceeds of grain any other costs or expenses.

(2) Notwithstanding section 326(a) of this title, the dollar amounts of money specified in such section include the value, as of the date of disposition, of any grain that the trustee distributes in kind.

(i) In all cases where the quantity of a specific type of grain held by a debtor operating a grain storage facility exceeds ten thousand bushels, such grain shall be sold by the trustee and the assets thereof distributed in accordance with the provisions of this section.

558. Defenses of the estate

The estate shall have the benefit of any defense available to the debtor as against any entity other than the estate, including statutes of limitation, statutes of frauds, usury, and other personal defenses. A waiver of any such defense by the debtor after the commencement of the case does not bind the estate.

559. Contractual right to liquidate a repurchase agreement

The exercise of a contractual right of a repo participant to cause the liquidation of a repurchase agreement because of a condition of the kind specified in section 365(e)(1) of this title shall not be stayed, avoided, or otherwise limited by operation of any provision of this title or by order of a court or administrative agency in any proceeding under this title, unless, where the debtor is a stockbroker or securities clearing agency, such order is authorized under the provisions of the Securities Investor Protection Act of 1970 (15 U.S.C. 78aaa et seq.) or any statute administered by the Securities and Exchange Commission. In the event that a repo participant liquidates one or more repurchase agreements with a debtor and under the terms of one or more such agreements has agreed to deliver assets subject to repurchase agreements to the debtor, any excess of the market prices received on liquidation of such assets (or if any such assets are not disposed of on the date of liquidation of such repurchase agreements, at the prices available at the time of liquidation of such repurchase agreements from a generally recognized source or the most recent closing bid quotation from such a source) over the sum of the stated repurchase prices and all expenses in connection with the liquidation of such repurchase agreements shall be deemed property of the estate, subject to the available rights of setoff. As used in this section, the term "contractual right" includes a right set forth in a rule or bylaw, applicable to each party to the repurchase agreement, of a national securities exchange, a national securities association, or a securities clearing agency, and a right, whether or not evidenced in writing, arising under common law, under law merchant or by reason of normal business practice.

560. Contractual right to terminate a swap agreement

The exercise of any contractual right of any swap participant to cause the termination of a swap agreement because of a condition of the kind specified in section 365(e)(1) of this title or to offset or net out any termination values or payment amounts arising under or in connection with any swap agreement shall not be stayed, avoided, or otherwise limited by operation of any provision of this title or by order of a court or administrative agency in any proceeding under this title. As used in this section, the term "contractual right" includes a right, whether or not evidenced in writing, arising under common law, under law merchant, or by reason of normal business practice.

CHAPTER 7 – LIQUIDATION

SUBCHAPTER I - OFFICERS AND ADMINISTRATION

SUBCHAPTER III - STOCKBROKER LIQUIDATION
(omitted)*

SUBCHAPTER IV - COMMODITY BROKER LIQUIDATION
(omitted)*

* Indicated subchapter does not pertain to chapter 7 consumer cases and is not included below.

SUBCHAPTER I - OFFICERS AND ADMINISTRATION

701. Interim trustee

(a)(1) Promptly after the order for relief under this chapter, the United States trustee shall appoint one disinterested person that is a member of the panel of private trustees established under section 586(a)(1) of title 28 or that is serving as trustee in the case immediately before the order for relief under this chapter to serve as interim trustee in the case.

(2) If none of the members of such panel is willing to serve as interim trustee in the case, then the United States trustee may serve as interim trustee in the case.

(b) The service of an interim trustee under this section terminates when a trustee elected or designated under section 702 of this title to serve as trustee in the case qualifies under section 322 of this title.

(c) An interim trustee serving under this section is a trustee in a case under this title.

702. Election of trustee

(a) A creditor may vote for a candidate for trustee only if such creditor –
        (1) holds an allowable, undisputed, fixed, liquidated, unsecured claim of a kind entitled to distribution under section 726(a)(2), 726(a)(3), 726(a)(4), 752(a), 766(h), or 766(i) of this title;
        (2) does not have an interest materially adverse, other than an equity interest that is not substantial in relation to such creditor's interest as a creditor, to the interest of creditors entitled to such distribution; and
            (3) is not an insider.

(b) At the meeting of creditors held under section 341 of this title, creditors may elect one person to serve as trustee in the case if election of a trustee is requested by creditors that may vote under subsection (a) of this section, and that hold at least 20 percent in amount of the claims specified in subsection (a)(1) of this section that are held by creditors that may vote under subsection (a) of this section.

(c) A candidate for trustee is elected trustee if –
        (1) creditors holding at least 20 percent in amount of the claims of a kind specified in subsection (a)(1) of this section that are held by creditors that may vote under subsection (a) of this section vote; and
        (2) such candidate receives the votes of creditors holding a majority in amount of claims specified in subsection (a)(1) of this section that are held by creditors that vote for a trustee.

(d) If a trustee is not elected under this section, then the interim trustee shall serve as trustee in the case.

703. Successor trustee

(a) If a trustee dies or resigns during a case, fails to qualify under section 322 of this title, or is removed under section 324 of this title, creditors may elect, in the manner specified in section 702 of this title, a person to fill the vacancy in the office of trustee.

(b) Pending election of a trustee under subsection (a) of this section, if necessary to preserve or prevent loss to the estate, the United States trustee may appoint an interim trustee in the manner specified in section 701(a).

(c) If creditors do not elect a successor trustee under subsection (a) of this section or if a trustee is needed in a case reopened under section 350 of this title, then the United States trustee –

(1) shall appoint one disinterested person that is a member of the panel of private trustees established under section 586(a)(1) of title 28 to serve as trustee in the case; or

(2) may, if none of the disinterested members of such panel is willing to serve as trustee, serve as trustee in the case.

704. Duties of trustee

The trustee shall –

(1) collect and reduce to money the property of the estate for which such trustee serves, and close such estate as expeditiously as is compatible with the best interests of parties in interest;

(2) be accountable for all property received;

(3) ensure that the debtor shall perform his intention as specified in section 521(2)(B) of this title;

(4) investigate the financial affairs of the debtor;

(5) if a purpose would be served, examine proofs of claims and object to the allowance of any claim that is improper;

(6) if advisable, oppose the discharge of the debtor;

(7) unless the court orders otherwise, furnish such information concerning the estate and the estate's administration as is requested by a party in interest;

(8) if the business of the debtor is authorized to be operated, file with the court, with the United States trustee, and with any governmental unit charged with responsibility for collection or determination of any tax arising out of such operation, periodic reports and summaries of the operation of such business, including a statement of receipts and disbursements, and such other information as the United States trustee or the court requires; and

(9) make a final report and file a final account of the administration of the estate with the court and with the United States trustee.

705. Creditors' committee

(a) At the meeting under section 341(a) of this title, creditors that may vote for a trustee under section 702(a) of this title may elect a committee of not fewer than three, and not more than eleven, creditors, each of whom holds an allowable unsecured claim of a kind entitled to distribution under section 726(a)(2) of this title.

(b) A committee elected under subsection (a) of this section may consult with the trustee or the United States trustee in connection with the administration of the estate, make recommendations to the trustee or the United States trustee respecting the performance of the trustee's duties, and submit to the court or the United States trustee any question affecting the administration of the estate.

706. Conversion

(a) The debtor may convert a case under this chapter to a case under chapter 11, 12, or 13 of this title at any time, if the case has not been converted under section 1112, 1307, or 1208 of this title. Any waiver of the right to convert a case under this subsection is unenforceable.

(b) On request of a party in interest and after notice and a hearing, the court may convert a case under this chapter to a case under chapter 11 of this title at any time.

(c) The court may not convert a case under this chapter to a case under chapter 12 or 13 of this title unless the debtor requests such conversion.

(d) Notwithstanding any other provision of this section, a case may not be converted to a case under another chapter of this title unless the debtor may be a debtor under such chapter.

707. Dismissal

(a) The court may dismiss a case under this chapter only after notice and a hearing and only for cause, including –

(1) unreasonable delay by the debtor that is prejudicial to creditors;

(2) nonpayment of any fees and charges required under chapter 123 of title 28; and

(3) failure of the debtor in a voluntary case to file, within fifteen days or such additional time as the court may allow after the filing of the petition commencing such case, the information required by paragraph (1) of section 521, but only on a motion by the United States trustee.

(b) After notice and a hearing, the court, on its own motion or on a motion by the United States trustee, but not at the request or suggestion of any party in interest, may dismiss a case filed by an individual debtor under this chapter whose debts are primarily consumer debts if it finds that the granting of relief would be a substantial abuse of the provisions of this chapter. There shall be a presumption in favor of granting the relief requested by the debtor.

SUBCHAPTER II - COLLECTION, LIQUIDATION, AND DISTRIBUTION OF THE ESTATE

721. Authorization to operate business

The court may authorize the trustee to operate the business of the debtor for a limited period, if such operation is in the best interest of the estate and consistent with the orderly liquidation of the estate.

722. Redemption

An individual debtor may, whether or not the debtor has waived the right to redeem under this section, redeem tangible personal property intended primarily for personal, family, or household use, from a lien securing a dischargeable consumer debt, if such property is exempted under section 522 of this title or has been abandoned under section 554 of this title, by paying the holder of such lien the amount of the allowed secured claim of such holder that is secured by such lien.

723. Rights of partnership trustee against general partners

(a) If there is a deficiency of property of the estate to pay in full all claims which are allowed in a case under this chapter concerning a partnership and with respect to which a general partner of the partnership is personally liable, the trustee shall have a claim against such general partner for the full amount of the deficiency.

(b) To the extent practicable, the trustee shall first seek recovery of such deficiency from any general partner in such partnership that is not a debtor in a case under this title. Pending determination of such deficiency, the court may order any such partner to provide the estate with indemnity for, or assurance of payment of, any deficiency recoverable from such partner, or not to dispose of property.

(c) Notwithstanding section 728(c) of this title, the trustee has a claim against the estate of each general partner in such partnership that is a debtor in a case under this title for the full amount of all claims of creditors allowed in the case concerning such partnership. Notwithstanding section 502 of this title, there shall not be allowed in such partner's case a claim against such partner on which both such partner and such partnership are liable, except to any extent that such claim is secured only by property of such partner and not by property of such partnership. The claim of the trustee under this subsection is entitled to distribution in such partner's case under section 726(a) of this title the same as any other claim of a kind specified in such section.

(d) If the aggregate that the trustee recovers from the estates of general partners under subsection (c) of this section is greater than any deficiency not recovered under subsection (b) of this section, the court, after notice and a hearing, shall determine an equitable distribution of the surplus so recovered, and the trustee shall distribute such surplus to the estates of the general partners in such partnership according to such determination.

724. Treatment of certain liens

(a) The trustee may avoid a lien that secures a claim of a kind specified in section 726(a)(4) of this title.

(b) Property in which the estate has an interest and that is subject to a lien that is not avoidable under this title and that secures an allowed claim for a tax, or proceeds of such property, shall be distributed –

(1) first, to any holder of an allowed claim secured by a lien on such property that is not avoidable under this title and that is senior to such tax lien;

(2) second, to any holder of a claim of a kind specified in section 507(a)(1), 507(a)(2), 507(a)(3), 507(a)(4), 507(a)(5), or 507(a)(6) of this title, to the extent of the amount of such allowed tax claim that is secured by such tax lien;

(3) third, to the holder of such tax lien, to any extent that such holder's allowed tax claim that is secured by such tax lien exceeds any amount distributed under paragraph (2) of this subsection;

(4) fourth, to any holder of an allowed claim secured by a lien on such property that is not avoidable under this title and that is junior to such tax lien;

(5) fifth, to the holder of such tax lien, to the extent that such holder's allowed claim secured by such tax lien is not paid under paragraph (3) of this subsection; and

(6) sixth, to the estate.

(c) If more than one holder of a claim is entitled to distribution under a particular paragraph of subsection (b) of this section, distribution to such holders under such paragraph shall be in the same order as distribution to such holders would have been other than under this section.

(d) A statutory lien the priority of which is determined in the same manner as the priority of a tax lien under section 6323 of the Internal Revenue Code of 1954 (26 U.S.C. 6323) shall be treated under subsection (b) of this section the same as if such lien were a tax lien.

725. Disposition of certain property

After the commencement of a case under this chapter, but before final distribution of property of the estate under section 726 of this title, the trustee, after notice and a hearing, shall dispose of any property in which an entity other than the estate has an interest, such as a lien, and that has not been disposed of under another section of this title.

726. Distribution of property of the estate

(a) Except as provided in section 510 of this title, property of the estate shall be distributed –

(1) first, in payment of claims of the kind specified in, and in the order specified in, section 507 of this title;

(2) second, in payment of any allowed unsecured claim, other than a claim of a kind specified in paragraph (1), (3), or (4) of this subsection, proof of which is –

    (A) timely filed under section 501(a) of this title;

    (B) timely filed under section 501(b) or 501(c) of this title; or

    (C) tardily filed under section 501(a) of this title, if –

        (i) the creditor that holds such claim did not have notice or actual knowledge of the case in time for timely filing of a proof of such claim under section 501(a) of this title; and

        (ii) proof of such claim is filed in time to permit payment of such claim;

(3) third, in payment of any allowed unsecured claim proof of which is tardily filed under section 501(a) of this title, other than a claim of the kind specified in paragraph (2)(C) of this subsection;

(4) fourth, in payment of any allowed claim, whether secured or unsecured, for any fine, penalty, or forfeiture, or for multiple, exemplary, or punitive damages, arising before the earlier of the order for relief or the appointment of a trustee, to the extent that such fine, penalty, forfeiture, or damages are not compensation for actual pecuniary loss suffered by the holder of such claim;

(5) fifth, in payment of interest at the legal rate from the date of the filing of the petition, on any claim paid under paragraph (1), (2), (3), or (4) of this subsection; and

(6) sixth, to the debtor.

(b) Payment on claims of a kind specified in paragraph (1), (2), (3), (4), (5), (6) or (7) of section 507(a) of this title, or in paragraph (2), (3), (4), or (5) of subsection (a) of this section, shall be made pro rata among claims of the kind specified in each such particular paragraph, except that in a case that has been converted to this chapter under section 1112, 1208, or 1307 of this title, a claim allowed under section 503(b) of this title incurred under this chapter after such conversion has priority over a claim allowed under section 503(b) of this title incurred under any other chapter of this title or under this chapter before such conversion and over any expenses of a custodian superseded under section 543 of this title.

(c) Notwithstanding subsections (a) and (b) of this section, if there is property of the kind specified in section 541(a)(2) of this title, or proceeds of such property, in the estate, such property or proceeds shall be segregated from other property of the estate, and such property or proceeds and other property of the estate shall be distributed as follows:

(1) Claims allowed under section 503 of this title shall be paid either from property of the kind specified in section 541(a)(2) of this title, or from other property of the estate, as the interest of justice requires.

(2) Allowed claims, other than claims allowed under section 503 of this title, shall be paid in the order specified in subsection (a) of this section, and, with respect to claims of a kind specified in a particular paragraph of section 507 of this title or subsection (a) of this section, in the following order and manner:

    (A) First, community claims against the debtor or the debtor's spouse shall be paid from property of the kind specified in section 541(a)(2) of this title, except to the extent that such property is solely liable for debts of the debtor.

    (B) Second, to the extent that community claims against the debtor are not paid under subparagraph (A) of this paragraph, such community claims shall be paid form property of the kind specified in section 541(a)(2) of this title that is solely liable for debts of the debtor.

    (C) Third, to the extent that all claims against the debtor including community claims against the debtor are not paid under subparagraph (A) or (B) of this paragraph such claims shall be paid from property of the estate other than property of the kind specified in section 541(a)(2) of this title.

    (D) Fourth, to the extent that community claims against the debtor or the debtor's spouse are not paid under subparagraph (A), (B), or (C) of this paragraph, such claims shall be paid from all remaining property of the estate.

727. Discharge

(a) The court shall grant the debtor a discharge unless –

(1) the debtor is not an individual;

(2) the debtor, with intent to hinder, delay, or defraud a creditor or an officer of the estate charged with custody of property under this title, has transferred, removed, destroyed, mutilated, or concealed, or has permitted to be transferred, removed, destroyed, mutilated, or concealed –

    (A) property of the debtor, within one year before the date of the filing of the petition; or

    (B) property of the estate, after the date of the filing of the petition;

(3) the debtor has concealed, destroyed, mutilated, falsified, or failed to keep or preserve any recorded information, including books, documents, records, and papers, from which the debtor's financial condition or business transactions might be ascertained, unless such act or failure to act was justified under all of the circumstances of the case;

(4) the debtor knowingly and fraudulently, in or in connection with the case –

    (A) made a false oath or account;

    (B) presented or used a false claim;

    (C) gave, offered, received, or attempted to obtain money, property, or advantage, or a promise of money, property, or advantage, for acting or forbearing to act; or

    (D) withheld from an officer of the estate entitled to possession under this title, any recorded information, including books, documents, records, and papers, relating to the debtor's property or financial affairs;

(5) the debtor has failed to explain satisfactorily, before determination of denial of discharge under this paragraph, any loss of assets or deficiency of assets to meet the debtor's liabilities;

(6) the debtor has refused, in the case –

    (A) to obey any lawful order of the court, other than an order to respond to a material question or to testify;

    (B) on the ground of privilege against self-incrimination, to respond to a material question approved by the court or to testify, after the debtor has been granted immunity with respect to the matter concerning which such privilege was invoked; or

    (C) on a ground other than the properly invoked privilege against self-incrimination, to respond to a material question approved by the court or to testify;

(7) the debtor has committed any act specified in paragraph (2), (3), (4), (5), or (6) of this subsection, on or within one year before the date of the filing of the petition, or during the case, in connection with another case, under this title or under the Bankruptcy Act, concerning an insider;

(8) the debtor has been granted a discharge under this section, under section 1141 of this title, or under section 14, 371, or 476 of the Bankruptcy Act, in a case commenced within six years before the date of the filing of the petition;

(9) the debtor has been granted a discharge under section 1228 or 1328 of this title, or under section 660 or 661 of the Bankruptcy Act, in a case commenced with six years before the date of the filing of the petition, unless payments under the plan in such case totaled at least –

    (A) 100 percent of the allowed unsecured claims in such case; or

    (B)(i) 70 percent of such claims; and

        (ii) the plan was proposed by the debtor in good faith, and was the debtor's best effort; or

(10) the court approves a written waiver of discharge executed by the debtor after the order for relief under this chapter.

(b) Except as provided in section 523 of this title, a discharge under subsection (a) of this section discharges the debtor from all debts that arose before the date of the order for relief under this chapter, and any liability on a claim that is determined under section 502 of this title as if such claim had arisen before the commencement of the case, whether or not a proof of claim based on any such debt or liability is filed under section 501 of this title, and whether or not a claim based on any such debt or liability is allowed under section 502 of this title.

(c)(1) The trustee, a creditor, or the United States trustee may object to the granting of a discharge under subsection (a) of this section.

(2) On request of a party in interest, the court may order the trustee to examine the acts and conduct of the debtor to determine whether a ground exists for denial of discharge.

(d) On request of the trustee, a creditor, or the United States trustee, and after notice and a hearing, the court shall revoke a discharge granted under subsection (a) of this section if –

(1) such discharge was obtained through the fraud of the debtor, and the requesting party did not know of such fraud until after the granting of such discharge;

(2) the debtor acquired property that is property of the estate, or became entitled to acquire property that would be property of the estate, and knowingly and fraudulently failed to report the acquisition of or entitlement to such property, or to deliver or surrender such property to the trustee; or

(3) the debtor committed an act specified in subsection (a)(6) of this section.

(e) The trustee, a creditor, or the United States trustee may request a revocation of discharge –

(1) under subsection (d)(1) of this section within one year after such discharge was granted; or

(2) under subsection (d)(2) or (d)(3) of this section before the later of –

    (A) one year after the granting of such discharge; and

    (B) the date the case is closed.

728. Special tax provisions

(a) For the purposes of any State or local law imposing a tax on or measured by income, the taxable period of a debtor that is an individual shall terminate on the date of the order for relief under this chapter, unless the case was converted under section 1112 or 1208 of this title.

(b) Notwithstanding any State or local law imposing a tax on or measured by income, the trustee shall make tax returns of income for the estate of an individual debtor in a case under this chapter or for a debtor that is a corporation in a case under this chapter only if such estate or corporation has net taxable income for the entire period after the order for relief under this chapter during which the case is pending. If such entity has such income, or if the debtor is a partnership, then the trustee shall make and file a return of income for each taxable period during which the case was pending after the order for relief under this chapter.

(c) If there are pending a case under this chapter concerning a partnership and a case under this chapter concerning a partner in such partnership, a governmental unit's claim for any unpaid liability of such partner for a State or local tax on or measured by income, to the extent that such liability arose from the inclusion in such partner's taxable income of earnings of such partnership that were not withdrawn by such partner, is a claim only against such partnership.

(d) Notwithstanding section 541 of this title, if there are pending a case under this chapter concerning a partnership and a case under this chapter concerning a partner in such partnership, then any State or local tax refund or reduction of tax of such partner that would have otherwise been property of the estate of such partner under section 541 of this title—

(1) is property of the estate of such partnership to the extent that such tax refund or reduction of tax is fairly apportionable to losses sustained by such partnership and not reimbursed by such partner; and

(2) is otherwise property of the estate of such partner.

CHAPTER 12 – ADJUSTMENT OF DEBTS OF A FAMILY FARMER WITH REGULAR ANNUAL INCOME

SUBCHAPTER I - OFFICERS, ADMINISTRATION, AND THE ESTATE

SUBCHAPTER I - OFFICERS, ADMINISTRATION, AND THE ESTATE

1201. Stay of action against codebtor

(a) Except as provided in subsections (b) and (c) of this section, after the order for relief under this chapter, a creditor may not act, or commence or continue any civil action, to collect all of any part of a consumer debt of the debtor from any individual that is liable on such debt with the debtor, or that secured such debt, unless –

(1) such individual became liable on or secured such debt in the ordinary course of such individual's business; or

(2) the case is closed, dismissed, or converted to a case under chapter 7 of this title.

(b) A creditor may present a negotiable instrument, and may give notice of dishonor of such an instrument.

(c) On request of a party in interest and after notice and a hearing, the court shall grant relief from the stay provided by subsection (a) of this section with respect to a creditor, to the extent that –

(1) as between the debtor and the individual protected under subsection (a) of this section, such individual received the consideration for the claim held by such creditor;

(2) the plan filed by the debtor proposes not to pay such claim; or

(3) such creditor's interest would be irreparably harmed by continuation of such stay.

(d) Twenty days after the filing of a request under subsection (c)(2) of this section for relief from the stay provided by subsection (a) of this section, such stay is terminated with respect to the party in interest making such request, unless the debtor or any individual that is liable on such debt with the debtor files and serves upon such party in interest a written objection to the taking of the proposed action.

1202. Trustee

(a) If the United States trustee has appointed an individual under section 586(b) of title 28 to serve as standing trustee in cases under this chapter and if such individual qualifies as a trustee under section 322 of this title, then such individual shall serve as trustee in any case filed under this chapter. Otherwise, the United States trustee shall appoint one disinterested person to serve as trustee in the case or the United States trustee may serve as trustee in the case if necessary.

(b) The trustee shall –

(1) perform the duties specified in sections 704(2), 704(3), 704(5), 704(6), 704(7), and 704(9) of this title;

(2) perform the duties specified in section 1106(a)(3) and 1106(a)(4) of this title if the court, for cause and on request of a party in interest, the trustee, or the United States trustee, so orders;

(3) appear and be heard at any hearing that concerns –

(A) the value of property subject to a lien;

(B) confirmation of a plan;

(C) modification of the plan after confirmation; or

(D) the sale of property of the estate;

(4) ensure that the debtor commences making timely payments required by a confirmed plan; and

(5) if the debtor ceases to be a debtor in possession, perform the duties specified in sections 704(8), 1106(a)(1), 1106(a)(2), 1106(a)(6), 1106(a)(7), and 1203.

1203. Rights and powers of debtor

Subject to such limitations as the court may prescribe, a debtor in possession shall have all the rights, other than the right to compensation under section 330, and powers, and shall perform all the functions and duties, except the duties specified in paragraphs (3) and (4) of section 1106(a), of a trustee serving in a case under chapter 11, including operating the debtor's farm.

1204. Removal of debtor as debtor in possession

(a) On request of a party in interest, and after notice and a hearing, the court shall order that the debtor shall not be a debtor in possession for cause, including fraud, dishonesty, incompetence, or gross mismanagement of the affairs of the debtor, either before or after the commencement of the case.

(b) On request of a party in interest, and after notice and a hearing, the court may reinstate the debtor in possession.

1205. Adequate protection

(a) Section 361 does not apply in a case under this chapter.

(b) In a case under this chapter, when adequate protection is required under section 362, 363, or 364 of this title of an interest of an entity in property, such adequate protection may be provided by –

(1) requiring the trustee to make a cash payment or periodic cash payments to such entity, to the extent that the stay under section 362 of this title, use, sale, or lease under section 363 of this title, or any grant of a lien under section 364 of this title results in a decrease in the value of property securing a claim or of an entity's ownership interest in property;

(2) providing to such entity an additional or replacement lien to the extent that such stay, use, sale, lease, or grant results in a decrease in the value of property securing a claim or of an entity's ownership interest in property;

(3) paying to such entity for the use of farmland the reasonable rent customary in the community where the property is located, based upon the rental value, net income, and earning capacity of the property; or

(4) granting such other relief, other than entitling such entity to compensation allowable under section 503(b)(1) of this title as an administrative expense, as will adequately protect the value of property securing a claim or of such entity's ownership interest in property.

1206. Sales free of interests

After notice and a hearing, in addition to the authorization contained in section 363(f), the trustee in a case under this chapter may sell property under section 363(b) and (c) free and clear of any interest in such property of an entity other than the estate if the property is farmland or farm equipment, except that the proceeds of such sale shall be subject to such interest.

1207. Property of the estate

(a) Property of the estate includes, in addition to the property specified in section 541 of this title –

(1) all property of the kind specified in such section that the debtor acquires after the commencement of the case but before the case is closed, dismissed, or converted to a case under chapter 7 of this title, whichever occurs first; and

(2) earnings from services performed by the debtor after the commencement of the case but before the case is closed, dismissed, or converted to a case under chapter 7 of this title, whichever occurs first.

(b) Except as provided in section 1204, a confirmed plan, or an order confirming a plan, the debtor shall remain in possession of all property of the estate.

1208. Conversion or dismissal

(a) The debtor may convert a case under this chapter to a case under chapter 7 of this title at any time. Any waiver of the right to convert under this subsection is unenforceable.

(b) On request of the debtor at any time, if the case has not been converted under section 706 or 1112 of this title, the court shall dismiss a case under this chapter. Any waiver of the right to dismiss under this subsection is unenforceable.

(c) On request of a party in interest, and after notice and a hearing, the court may dismiss a case under this chapter for cause, including –

(1) unreasonable delay, or gross mismanagement, by the debtor that is prejudicial to creditors;

(2) nonpayment of any fees and charges required under chapter 123 of title 28;

(3) failure to file a plan timely under section 1221 of this title;

(4) failure to commence making timely payments required by a confirmed plan;

(5) denial of confirmation of a plan under section 1225 of this title and denial of a request made for additional time for filing another plan or a modification of a plan;

(6) material default by the debtor with respect to a term of a confirmed plan;

(7) revocation of the order of confirmation under section 1230 of this title, and denial of confirmation of a modified plan under section 1229 of this title;

(8) termination of a confirmed plan by reason of the occurrence of a condition specified in the plan; or

(9) continuing loss to or diminution of the estate and absence of a reasonable likelihood of rehabilitation.

(d) On request of a party in interest, and after notice and a hearing, the court may dismiss a case under this chapter or convert a case under this chapter to a case under chapter 7 of this title upon a showing that the debtor has committed fraud in connection with the case.

(e) Notwithstanding any other provision of this section, a case may not be converted to a case under another chapter of this title unless the debtor may be a debtor under such chapter.

1221. Filing of plan

The debtor shall file a plan not later than 90 days after the order for relief under this chapter, except that the court may extend such period if an extension is substantially justified.

1222. Contents of plan

(a) The plan shall –

(1) provide for the submission of all or such portion of future earnings or other future income of the debtor to the supervision and control of the trustee as is necessary for the execution of the plan;

(2) provide for the full payment, in deferred cash payments, of all claims entitled to priority under section 507 of this title, unless the holder of a particular claim agrees to a different treatment of such claim; and

(3) if the plan classifies claims and interests, provide the same treatment for each claim or interest within a particular class unless the holder of a particular claim or interest agrees to less favorable treatment.

(b) Subject to subsections (a) and (c) of this section, the plan may –

(1) designate a class or classes of unsecured claims, as provided in section 1122 of this title, but may not discriminate unfairly against any class so designated; however, such plan may treat claims for a consumer debt of the debtor if an individual is liable on such consumer debt with the debtor differently than other unsecured claims;

(2) modify the rights of holders of secured claims, or of holders of unsecured claims, or leave unaffected the rights of holders of any class of claims;

(3) provide for the curing or waiving of any default;

(4) provide for payments on any unsecured claim to be made concurrently with payments on any secured claim or any other unsecured claim;

(5) provide for the curing of any default within a reasonable time and maintenance of payments while the case is pending on any unsecured claim or secured claim on which the last payment is due after the date on which the final payment under the plan is due;

(6) subject to section 365 of this title, provide for the assumption, rejection, or assignment of any executory contract or unexpired lease of the debtor not previously rejected under such section;

(7) provide for the payment of all or part of a claim against the debtor from property of the estate or property of the debtor;

(8) provide for the sale of all or any part of the property of the estate or the distribution of all or any part of the property of the estate among those having an interest in such property;

(9) provide for payment of allowed secured claims consistent with section 1225(a)(5) of this title, over a period exceeding the period permitted under section 1222(c);

(10) provide for the vesting of property of the estate, on confirmation of the plan or at a later time, in the debtor or in any other entity; and

(11) include any other appropriate provision not inconsistent with this title.

(c) Except as provided in subsections (b)(5) and (b)(9), the plan may not provide for payments over a period that is longer than three years unless the court for cause approves a longer period, but the court may not approve a period that is longer than five years.

1223. Modification of plan before confirmation

(a) The debtor may modify the plan at any time before confirmation, but may not modify the plan so that the plan as modified fails to meet the requirements of section 1222 of this title.

(b) After the debtor files a modification under this section, the plan as modified becomes the plan.

(c) Any holder of a secured claim that has accepted or rejected the plan is deemed to have accepted or rejected, as the case may be, the plan as modified, unless the modification provides for a change in the rights of such holder from what such rights were under the plan before modification, and such holder changes such holder's previous acceptance or rejection.

1224. Confirmation hearing

After expedited notice, the court shall hold a hearing on confirmation of the plan. A party in interest, the trustee, or the United States trustee may object to the confirmation of the plan. Except for cause, the hearing shall be concluded not later than 45 days after the filing of the plan.

1225. Confirmation of plan

(a) Except as provided in subsection (b), the court shall confirm a plan if –

(1) the plan complies with the provisions of this chapter and with the other applicable provisions of this title;

(2) any fee, charge, or amount required under chapter 123 of title 28, or by the plan, to be paid before confirmation, has been paid;

(3) the plan has been proposed in good faith and not by any means forbidden by law;

(4) the value, as of the effective date of the plan, of property to be distributed under the plan on account of each allowed unsecured claim is not less than the amount that would be paid on such claim if the estate of the debtor were liquidated under chapter 7 of this title on such date;

(5) with respect to each allowed secured claim provided for by the plan –

    (A) the holder of such claim has accepted the plan;

    (B)(i) the plan provides that the holder of such claim retain the lien securing such claim; and

      (ii) the value, as of the effective date of the plan, of property to be distributed by the trustee or the debtor under the plan on account of such claim is not less than the allowed amount of such claim; or

    (C) the debtor surrenders the property securing such claim to such holder; and

(6) the debtor will be able to make all payments under the plan and to comply with the plan.

(b)(1) If the trustee or the holder of an allowed unsecured claim objects to the confirmation of the plan, then the court may not approve the plan unless, as of the effective date of the plan –

    (A) the value of the property to be distributed under the plan on account of such claim is not less than the amount of such claim; or

    (B) the plan provides that all of the debtor's projected disposable income to be received in the three-year period, or such longer period as the court may approve under section 1222(c), beginning on the date that the first payment is due under the plan will be applied to make payments under the plan.

(2) For purposes of this subsection, "disposable income" means income which is received by the debtor and which is not reasonably necessary to be expended –

    (A) for the maintenance or support of the debtor or a dependent of the debtor; or

    (B) for the payment of expenditures necessary for the continuation, preservation, and operation of the debtor's business.

(c) After confirmation of a plan, the court may order any entity from whom the debtor receives income to pay all or any part of such income to the trustee.

1226. Payments

(a) Payments and funds received by the trustee shall be retained by the trustee until confirmation or denial of confirmation of a plan. If a plan is confirmed, the trustee shall distribute any such payment in accordance with the plan. If a plan is not confirmed, the trustee shall return any such payments to the debtor, after deducting –

    (1) any unpaid claim allowed under section 503(b) of this title; and

    (2) if a standing trustee is serving in the case, the percentage fee fixed for such standing trustee.

(b) Before or at the time of each payment to creditors under the plan, there shall be paid –

    (1) any unpaid claim of the kind specified in section 507(a)(1) of this title; and

    (2) if a standing trustee appointed under section 1202(d) of this title is serving in the case, the percentage fee fixed for such standing trustee under section 1202(e) of this title.

(c) Except as otherwise provided in the plan or in the order confirming the plan, the trustee shall make payments to creditors under the plan.

1227. Effect of confirmation

(a) Except as provided in section 1228(a) of this title, the provisions of a confirmed plan bind the debtor, each creditor, each equity security holder, and each general partner in the debtor, whether or not the claim of such creditor, such equity security holder, or such general partner in the debtor is provided for by the plan, and whether or not such creditor, such equity security holder, or such general partner in the debtor has objected to, has accepted, or has rejected the plan.

(b) Except as otherwise provided in the plan or the order confirming the plan, the confirmation of a plan vests all of the property of the estate in the debtor.

(c) Except as provided in section 1228(a) of this title and except as otherwise provided in the plan or in the order confirming the plan, the property vesting in the debtor under subsection (b) of this section is free and clear of any claim or interest of any creditor provided for by the plan.

1228. Discharge

(a) As soon as practicable after completion by the debtor of all payments under the plan, other than payments to holders of allowed claims provided for under section 1222(b)(5) or 1222(b)(10) of this title, unless the court approves a written waiver of discharge executed by the debtor after the order for relief under this chapter, the court shall grant the debtor a discharge of all debts provided for by the plan allowed under section 503 of this title or disallowed under section 502 of this title, except any debt –

    (1) provided for under section 1222(b)(5) or 1222(b)(10) of this title; or

    (2) of the kind specified in section 523(a) of this title.

(b) At any time after the confirmation of the plan and after notice and a hearing, the court may grant a discharge to a debtor that has not completed payments under the plan only if –

    (1) the debtor's failure to complete such payments is due to circumstances for which the debtor should not justly be held accountable;

    (2) the value, as of the effective date of the plan, of property actually distributed under the plan on account of each allowed unsecured claim is not less than the amount that would have been paid on such claim if the estate of the debtor had been liquidated under chapter 7 of this title on such date; and

    (3) modification of the plan under section 1229 of this title is not practicable.

(c) A discharge granted under subsection (b) of this section discharges the debtor from all unsecured debts provided for by the plan or disallowed under section 502 of this title, except any debt –

    (1) provided for under section 1222(b)(5) or 1222(b)(10) of this title; or

    (2) of a kind specified in section 523(a) of this title.

(d) On request of a party in interest before one year after a discharge under this section is granted, and after notice and a hearing, the court may revoke such discharge only if –

    (1) such discharge was obtained by the debtor through fraud; and

    (2) the requesting party did not know of such fraud until after such discharge was granted.

(e) After the debtor is granted a discharge, the court shall terminate the services of any trustee serving in the case.

1229. Modification of plan after confirmation

(a) At any time after confirmation of the plan but before the completion of payments under such plan, the plan may be modified, on request of the debtor, the trustee, or the holder of an allowed unsecured claim, to –

    (1) increase or reduce the amount of payments on claims of a particular class provided for by the plan;

    (2) extend or reduce the time for such payments; or

    (3) alter the amount of the distribution to a creditor whose claim is provided for by the plan to the extent necessary to take account of any payment of such claim other than under the plan.

(b)(1) Sections 1222(a), 1222(b), and 1223(c) of this title and the requirements of section 1225(a) of this title apply to any modification under subsection (a) of this section.

(2) The plan as modified becomes the plan unless, after notice and a hearing, such modification is disapproved.

(c) A plan modified under this section may not provide for payments over a period that expires after three years after the time that the first payment under the original confirmed plan was due, unless the court, for cause, approves a longer period, but the court may not approve a period that expires after five years after such time.

1230. Revocation of an order of confirmation

(a) On request of a party in interest at any time within 180 days after the date of the entry of an order of confirmation under section 1225 of this title, and after notice and a hearing, the court may revoke such order if such order was procured by fraud.

(b) If the court revokes an order of confirmation under subsection (a) of this section, the court shall dispose of the case under section 1207 of this title, unless, within the time fixed by the court, the debtor proposes and the court confirms a modification of the plan under section 1229 of this title.

1231. Special tax provisions

(a) For the purpose of any State or local law imposing a tax on or measured by income, the taxable period of a debtor that is an individual shall terminate on the date of the order for relief under this chapter, unless the case was converted under section 706 of this title.

(b) The trustee shall make a State or local tax return of income for the estate of an individual debtor in a case under this chapter for each taxable period after the order for relief under this chapter during which the case is pending.

(c) The issuance, transfer, or exchange of a security, or the making or delivery of an instrument of transfer under a plan confirmed under section 1225 of this title, may not be taxed under any law imposing a stamp tax or similar tax.

(d) The court may authorize the proponent of a plan to request a determination, limited to questions of law, by a State or local governmental unit charged with responsibility for collection or determination of a tax on or measured by income, of the tax effects, under section 346 of this title and under the law imposing such tax, of the plan. In the event of an actual controversy, the court may declare such effects after the earlier of –

    (1) the date on which such governmental unit responds to the request under this subsection; or

    (2) 270 days after such request.

CHAPTER 13 – ADJUSTMENT OF DEBTS OF AN INDIVIDUAL WITH REGULAR INCOME

SUBCHAPTER I - OFFICERS, ADMINISTRATION, AND THE ESTATE

SUBCHAPTER I - OFFICERS, ADMINISTRATION, AND THE ESTATE

1301. Stay of action against codebtor

(a) Except as provided in subsections (b) and (c) of this section, after the order for relief under this chapter, a creditor may not act, or commence or continue any civil action, to collect all or any part of a consumer debt of the debtor from any individual that is liable on such debt with the debtor, or that secured such debt, unless –

(1) such individual became liable on or secured such debt in the ordinary course of such individual's business; or

(2) the case is closed, dismissed, or converted to a case under chapter 7 or 11 of this title.

(b) A creditor may present a negotiable instrument, and may give notice of dishonor of such an instrument.

(c) On request of a party in interest and after notice and a hearing, the court shall grant relief from the stay provided by subsection (a) of this section with respect to a creditor, to the extent that –

(1) as between the debtor and the individual protected under subsection (a) of this section, such individual received the consideration for the claim held by such creditor;

(2) the plan filed by the debtor proposes not to pay such claim; or

(3) such creditor's interest would be irreparably harmed by continuation of such stay.

(d) Twenty days after the filing of a request under subsection (c)(2) of this section for relief from the stay provided by subsection (a) of this section, such stay is terminated with respect to the party in interest making such request, unless the debtor or any individual that is liable on such debt with the debtor files and serves upon such party in interest a written objection to the taking of the proposed action.

1302. Trustee

(a) If the United States trustee appoints an individual under section 586(b) of title 28 to serve as standing trustee in cases under this chapter and if such individual qualifies under section 322 of this title, then such individual shall serve as trustee in the case. Otherwise, the United States trustee shall appoint one disinterested person to serve as trustee in the case or the United States trustee may serve as a trustee in the case.

(b) The trustee shall –

(1) perform the duties specified in sections 704(2), 704(3), 704(4), 704(5), 704(6), 704(7), and 704(9) of this title;

(2) appear and be heard at any hearing that concerns –

(A) the value of property subject to a lien;

(B) confirmation of a plan; or

(C) modification of the plan after confirmation;

(3) dispose of, under regulations issued by the Director of the Administrative Office of the United States Courts, moneys received or to be received in a case under chapter XIII of the Bankruptcy Act;

(4) advise, other than on legal matters, and assist the debtor in performance under the plan; and

(5) ensure that the debtor commences making timely payments under section 1326 of this title.

(c) If the debtor is engaged in business, then in addition to the duties specified in subsection (b) of this section, the trustee shall perform the duties specified in sections 1106(a)(3) and 1106(a)(4) of this title.

1303. Rights and powers of debtor

Subject to any limitations on a trustee under this chapter, the debtor shall have, exclusive of the trustee, the rights and powers of a trustee under sections 363(b), 363(d), 363(e), 363(f), and 363(l), of this title.

1304. Debtor engaged in business

(a) A debtor that is self-employed and incurs trade credit in the production of income from such employment is engaged in business.

(b) Unless the court orders otherwise, a debtor engaged in business may operate the business of the debtor and, subject to any limitations on a trustee under sections 363(c) and 364 of this title and to such limitations or conditions as the court prescribes, shall have, exclusive of the trustee, the rights and powers of the trustee under such sections.

(c) A debtor engaged in business shall perform the duties of the trustee specified in section 704(8) of this title.

1305. Filing and allowance of postpetition claims

(a) A proof of claim may be filed by any entity that holds a claim against the debtor –

(1) for taxes that become payable to a governmental unit while the case is pending; or

(2) that is a consumer debt, that arises after the date of the order for relief under this chapter, and that is for property or services necessary for the debtor's performance under the plan.

(b) Except as provided in subsection (c) of this section, a claim filed under subsection (a) of this section shall be allowed or disallowed under section 502 of this title, but shall be determined as of the date such claim arises, and shall be allowed under section 502(a), 502(b), or 502(c) of this title, or disallowed under section 502(d) or 502(e) of this title, the same as if such claim had arisen before the date of the filing of the petition.

(c) A claim filed under subsection (a)(2) of this section shall be disallowed if the holder of such claim knew or should have known that prior approval by the trustee of the debtor's incurring the obligation was practicable and was not obtained.

1306. Property of the estate

(a) Property of the estate includes, in addition to the property specified in section 541 of this title –

(1) all property of the kind specified in such section that the debtor acquires after the commencement of the case but before the case is closed, dismissed, or converted to a case under chapter 7, 11, or 12 of this title, whichever occurs first; and

(2) earnings from services performed by the debtor after the commencement of the case but before the case is closed, dismissed, or converted to a case under chapter 7, 11, or 12 of this title, whichever occurs first.

(b) Except as provided in a confirmed plan or order confirming a plan, the debtor shall remain in possession of all property of the estate.

1307. Conversion or dismissal

(a) The debtor may convert a case under this chapter to a case under chapter 7 of this title at any time. Any waiver of the right to convert under this subsection is unenforceable.

(b) On request of the debtor at any time, if the case has not been converted under section 706, 1112, or 1208 of this title, the court shall dismiss a case under this chapter. Any waiver of the right to dismiss under this subsection is unenforceable.

(c) Except as provided in subsection (e) of this section, on request of a party in interest or the United States trustee and after notice and a hearing, the court may convert a case under this chapter to a case under chapter 7 of this title, or may dismiss a case under this chapter, whichever is in the best interests of creditors and the estate, for cause, including –

(1) unreasonable delay by the debtor that is prejudicial to creditors;

(2) nonpayment of any fees and charges required under chapter 123 of title 28;

(3) failure to file a plan timely under section 1321 of this title;

(4) failure to commence making timely payments under section 1326 of this title;

(5) denial of confirmation of a plan under section 1325 of this title and denial of a request made for additional time for filing another plan or a modification of a plan;

(6) material default by the debtor with respect to a term of a confirmed plan;

(7) revocation of the order of confirmation under section 1330 of this title, and denial of confirmation of a modified plan under section 1329 of this title;

(8) termination of a confirmed plan by reason of the occurrence of a condition specified in the plan other than completion of payments under the plan;

(9) only on request of the United States trustee, failure of the debtor to file, within fifteen days, or such additional time as the court may allow, after the filing of the petition commencing such case, the information required by paragraph (1) of section 521; or

(10) only on request of the United States trustee, failure to timely file the information required by paragraph (2) of section 521.

(d) Except as provided in subsection (e) of this section, at any time before the confirmation of a plan under section 1325 of this title, on request of a party in interest or the United States trustee and after notice and a hearing, the court may convert a case under this chapter to a case under chapter 11 or 12 of this title.

(e) The court may not convert a case under this chapter to a case under chapter 7, 11, or 12 of this title if the debtor is a farmer, unless the debtor requests such conversion.

(f) Notwithstanding any other provision of this section, a case may not be converted to a case under another chapter of this title unless the debtor may be a debtor under such chapter.

SUBCHAPTER II - THE PLAN

1321. Filing of plan

The debtor shall file a plan.

1322. Contents of plan

(a) The plan shall –

(1) provide for the submission of all or such portion of future earnings or other future income of the debtor to the supervision and control of the trustee as is necessary for the execution of the plan;

(2) provide for the full payment, in deferred cash payments, of all claims entitled to priority under section 507 of this title, unless the holder of a particular claim agrees to a different treatment of such claim; and

(3) if the plan classifies claims, provide the same treatment for each claim within a particular class.

(b) Subject to subsections (a) and (c) of this section, the plan may –

(1) designate a class or classes of unsecured claims, as provided in section 1122 of this title, but may not discriminate unfairly against any class so designated; however, such plan may treat claims for a consumer debt of the debtor if an individual is liable on such consumer debt with the debtor differently than other unsecured claims;

(2) modify the rights of holders of secured claims, other than a claim secured only by a security interest in real property that is the debtor's principal residence, or of holders of unsecured claims, or leave unaffected the rights of holders of any class of claims;

(3) provide for the curing or waiving of any default;

(4) provide for payments on any unsecured claim to be made concurrently with payments on any secured claim or any other unsecured claim;

(5) notwithstanding paragraph (2) of this subsection, provide for the curing of any default within a reasonable time and maintenance of payments while the case is pending on any unsecured claim or secured claim on which the last payment is due after the date on which the final payment under the plan is due;

(6) provide for the payment of all or any part of any claim allowed under section 1305 of this title;

(7) subject to section 365 of this title, provide for the assumption, rejection, or assignment of any executory contract or unexpired lease of the debtor not previously rejected under such section;

(8) provide for the payment of all or part of a claim against the debtor from property of the estate or property of the debtor;

(9) provide for the vesting of property of the estate, on confirmation of the plan or at a later time, in the debtor or in any other entity; and

(10) include any other appropriate provision not inconsistent with this title.

(c) The plan may not provide for payments over a period that is longer than three years, unless the court, for cause, approves a longer period, but the court may not approve a period that is longer than five years.

1323. Modification of plan before confirmation

(a) The debtor may modify the plan at any time before confirmation, but may not modify the plan so that the plan as modified fails to meet the requirements of section 1322 of this title.

(b) After the debtor files a modification under this section, the plan as modified becomes the plan.

(c) Any holder of a secured claim that has accepted or rejected the plan is deemed to have accepted or rejected, as the case may be, the plan as modified, unless the modification provides for a change in the rights of such holder from what such rights were under the plan before modification, and such holder changes such holder's previous acceptance or rejection.

1324. Confirmation hearing

After notice, the court shall hold a hearing on confirmation of the plan. A party in interest may object to confirmation of the plan.

1325. Confirmation of plan

(a) Except as provided in subsection (b), the court shall confirm a plan if –

(1) the plan complies with the provisions of this chapter and with the other applicable provisions of this title;

(2) any fee, charge, or amount required under chapter 123 of title 28, or by the plan, to be paid before confirmation, has been paid;

(3) the plan has been proposed in good faith and not by any means forbidden by law;

(4) the value, as of the effective date of the plan, of property to be distributed under the plan on account of each allowed unsecured claim is not less than the amount that would be paid on such claim if the estate of the debtor were liquidated under chapter 7 of this title on such date;

(5) with respect to each allowed secured claim provided for by the plan–

(A) the holder of such claim has accepted the plan;

(B)(i) the plan provides that the holder of such claim retain the lien securing such claim; and

(ii) the value, as of the effective date of the plan, of property to be distributed under the plan on account of such claim is not less than the allowed amount of such claim; or

(C) the debtor surrenders the property securing such claim to such holder; and

(6) the debtor will be able to make all payments under the plan and to comply with the plan.

(b)(1) If the trustee or the holder of an allowed unsecured claim objects to the confirmation of the plan, then the court may not approve the plan unless, as of the effective date of the plan –

(A) the value of the property to be distributed under the plan on account of such claim is not less than the amount of such claim; or

(B) the plan provides that all of the debtor's projected disposable income to be received in the three–year period beginning on the date that the first payment is due under the plan will be applied to make payments under the plan.

(2) For purposes of this subsection, "disposable income" means income which is received by the debtor and which is not reasonably necessary to be expended –

(A) for the maintenance or support of the debtor or a dependent of the debtor; and

(B) if the debtor is engaged in business, for the payment of expenditures necessary for the continuation, preservation, and operation of such business.

(c) After confirmation of a plan, the court may order any entity from whom the debtor receives income to pay all or any part of such income to the trustee.

1326. Payments

(a)(1) Unless the court orders otherwise, the debtor shall commence making the payments proposed by a plan within 30 days after the plan is filed.

(2) A payment made under this subsection shall be retained by the trustee until confirmation or denial of confirmation of a plan. If a plan is confirmed, the trustee shall distribute any such payment in accordance with the plan. If a plan is not confirmed, the trustee shall return any such payment to the debtor, after deducting any unpaid claim allowed under section 503(b) of this title.

(b) Before or at the time of each payment to creditors under the plan, there shall be paid –

(1) any unpaid claim of the kind specified in section 507(a)(1) of this title; and

(2) if a standing trustee appointed under section 586(b) of title 28 is serving in the case, the percentage fee fixed for such standing trustee under section 586(e)(1)(B) of title 28.

(c) Except as otherwise provided in the plan or in the order confirming the plan, the trustee shall make payments to creditors under the plan.

1327. Effect of confirmation

(a) The provisions of a confirmed plan bind the debtor and each creditor, whether or not the claim of such creditor is provided for by the plan, and whether or not such creditor has objected to, has accepted, or has rejected the plan.

(b) Except as otherwise provided in the plan or the order confirming the plan, the confirmation of a plan vests all of the property of the estate in the debtor.

(c) Except as otherwise provided in the plan or in the order confirming the plan, the property vesting in the debtor under subsection (b) of this section is free and clear of any claim or interest of any creditor provided for by the plan.

1328. Discharge

(a) As soon as practicable after completion by the debtor of all payments under the plan, unless the court approves a written waiver of discharge executed by the debtor after the order for relief under this chapter, the court shall grant the debtor a discharge of all debts provided for by the plan or disallowed under section 502 of this title, except any debt –

(1) provided for under section 1322(b)(5) of this title;

(2) of the kind specified in paragraph (5) or (8) of section 523(a) or 523(a)(9) of this title; or

(3) for restitution included in a sentence on the debtor's conviction of a crime.

(b) At any time after confirmation of the plan and after notice and a hearing, the court may grant a discharge to a debtor that has not completed payments under the plan only if –

(1) the debtor's failure to complete such payments is due to circumstances for which the debtor should not justly be held accountable;

(2) the value, as of the effective date of the plan, of property actually distributed under the plan on account of each allowed unsecured claim is not less than the amount that would have been paid on such claim if the estate of the debtor had been liquidated under chapter 7 of this title on such date; and

(3) modification of the plan under section 1329 of this title is not practicable.

(c) A discharge granted under subsection (b) of this section discharges the debtor from all unsecured debts provided for by the plan or disallowed under section 502 of this title, except any debt –

(1) provided for under section 1322(b)(5) of this title; or

(2) of a kind specified in section 523(a) of this title.

(d) Notwithstanding any other provision of this section, a discharge granted under this section does not discharge the debtor from any debt based on an allowed claim filed under section 1305(a)(2) of this title if prior approval by the trustee of the debtor's incurring such debt was practicable and was not obtained.

(e) On request of a party in interest before one year after a discharge under this section is granted, and after notice and a hearing, the court may revoke such discharge only if –

(1) such discharge was obtained by the debtor through fraud; and

(2) the requesting party did not know of such fraud until after such discharge was granted.

1329. Modification of plan after confirmation

(a) At any time after confirmation of the plan but before the completion of payments under such plan, the plan may be modified, upon request of the debtor, the trustee, or the holder of an allowed unsecured claim, to –

(1) increase or reduce the amount of payments on claims of a particular class provided for by the plan;

(2) extend or reduce the time for such payments; or

(3) alter the amount of the distribution to a creditor whose claim is provided for by the plan to the extent necessary to take account of any payment of such claim other than under the plan.

(b)(1) Sections 1322(a), 1322(b), and 1323(c) of this title and the requirements of section 1325(a) of this title apply to any modification under subsection (a) of this section.

(2) The plan as modified becomes the plan unless, after notice and a hearing, such modification is disapproved.

(c) A plan modified under this section may not provide for payments over a period that expires after three years after the time that the first payment under the original confirmed plan was due, unless the court, for cause, approves a longer period, but the court may not approve a period that expires after five years after such time.

1330. Revocation of an order of confirmation

(a) On request of a party in interest at any time within 180 days after the date of the entry of an order of confirmation under section 1325 of this title, and after notice and a hearing, the court may revoke such order if such order was procured by fraud.

(b) If the court revokes an order of confirmation under subsection (a) of this section, the court shall dispose of the case under section 1307 of this title, unless, within the time fixed by the court, the debtor proposes and the court confirms a modification of the plan under section 1329 of this title.

MISCELLANEOUS STATUTES

11 U.S.C. 1106. Duties of trustee and examiner

(a) A trustee shall –

(1) perform the duties of a trustee specified in sections 704(2), 704(5), 704(7), 704(8), and 704(9) of this title;

(2) if the debtor has not done so, file the list, schedule, and statement required under section 521(1) of this title;

(3) except to the extent that the court orders otherwise, investigate the acts, conduct, assets, liabilities, and financial condition of the debtor, the operation of the debtor's business and the desirability of the continuance of such business, and any other matter relevant to the case or to the formulation of a plan;

(4) as soon as practicable –

(A) file a statement of any investigation conducted under paragraph (3) of this subsection, including any fact ascertained pertaining to fraud, dishonesty, incompetence, misconduct, mismanagement, or irregularity in the management of the affairs of the debtor, or to a cause of action available to the estate; and

(B) transmit a copy or a summary of any such statement to any creditors' committee or equity security holders' committee, to any indenture trustee, and to such other entity as the court designates;

(5) as soon as practicable, file a plan under section 1121 of this title, file a report of why the trustee will not file a plan, or recommend conversion of the case to a case under chapter 7, 12, or 13 of this title or dismissal of the case;

(6) for any year for which the debtor has not filed a tax return required by law, furnish, without personal liability, such information as may be required by the governmental unit with which such tax return was to be filed, in light of the condition of the debtor's books and records and the availability of such information; and

(7) after confirmation of a plan, file such reports as are necessary or as the court orders.

(b) An examiner appointed under section 1104(c) of this title shall perform the duties specified in paragraphs (3) and (4) of subsection (a) of this section, and, except to the extent that the court orders otherwise, any other duties of the trustee that the court orders the debtor in possession not to perform.

11 U.S.C. 1122. Classification of claims or interests

(a) Except as provided in subsection (b) of this section, a plan may place a claim or an interest in a particular class only if such claim or interest is substantially similar to the other claims or interests of such class.

(b) A plan may designate a separate class of claims consisting only of every unsecured claim that is less than or reduced to an amount that the court approves as reasonable and necessary for administrative convenience.

28 U.S.C. 157. Procedures

(a) Each district court may provide that any or all cases under title 11 and any or all proceedings arising under title 11 or arising in or related to a case under title 11 shall be referred to the bankruptcy judges for the district.

(b)(1) Bankruptcy judges may hear and determine all cases under title 11 and all core proceedings arising under title 11, or arising in a case under title 11, referred under subsection (a) of this section, and may enter appropriate orders and judgments, subject to review under section 158 of this title.

(2) Core proceedings include, but are not limited to –

(A) matters concerning the administration of the estate;

(B) allowance or disallowance of claims against the estate or exemptions from property of the estate, and estimation of claims or interests for the purposes of confirming a plan under chapter 11, 12, or 13 of title 11 but not the liquidation or estimation of contingent or unliquidated personal injury tort or wrongful death claims against the estate for purposes of distribution in a case under title 11;

(C) counterclaims by the estate against persons filing claims against the estate;

(D) orders in respect to obtaining credit;

(E) orders to turn over property of the estate;

(F) proceedings to determine, avoid, or recover preferences;

(G) motions to terminate, annul, or modify the automatic stay;

(H) proceedings to determine, avoid, or recover fraudulent conveyances;

(I) determinations as to the dischargeability of particular debts;

(J) objections to discharges;

(K) determinations of the validity, extent, or priority of liens;

(L) confirmations of plans;

(M) orders approving the use or lease of property, including the use of cash collateral;

(N) orders approving the sale of property other than property resulting from claims brought by the estate against persons who have not filed claims against the estate; and

(O) other proceedings affecting the liquidation of the assets of the estate or the adjustment of the debtor-creditor or the equity security holder relationship, except personal injury tort or wrongful death claims.

(3) The bankruptcy judge shall determine, on the judge's own motion or on timely motion of a party, whether a proceeding is a core proceeding under this subsection or is a proceeding that is otherwise related to a case under title 11. A determination that a proceeding is not a core proceeding shall not be made solely on the basis that its resolution may be affected by State law.

(4) Non-core proceedings under section 157(b)(2)(B) of title 28, United States Code, shall not be subject to the mandatory abstention provisions of section 1334(c)(2).

(5) The district court shall order that personal injury tort and wrongful death claims shall be tried in the district court in which the bankruptcy case is pending, or in the district court in the district in which the claim arose, as determined by the district court in which the bankruptcy case is pending.

(c)(1) A bankruptcy judge may hear a proceeding that is not a core proceeding but that is otherwise related to a case under title 11. In such proceeding, the bankruptcy judge shall submit proposed findings of fact and conclusions of law to the district court, and any final order or judgment shall be entered by the district judge after considering the bankruptcy judge's proposed findings and conclusions and after reviewing de novo those matters to which any party has timely and specifically objected.

(2) Notwithstanding the provisions of paragraph (1) of this subsection, the district court, with the consent of all the parties to the proceeding, may refer a proceeding related to a case under title 11 to a bankruptcy judge to hear and determine and to enter appropriate orders and judgments, subject to review under section 158 of this title.

(d) The district court may withdraw, in whole or in part, any case or proceeding referred under this section, on its own motion or on timely motion of any party, for cause shown. The district court shall, on timely motion of a party, so withdraw a proceeding if the court determines that resolution of the proceeding requires consideration of both title 11 and other laws of the United States regulating organizations or activities affecting interstate commerce.

28 U.S.C. 158. Appeals

(a) The district courts of the United States shall have jurisdiction to hear appeals from final judgments, orders, and decrees, and, with leave of the court, from interlocutory orders and decrees, of bankruptcy judges entered in cases and proceedings referred to the bankruptcy judges under section 157 of this title. An appeal under this subsection shall be taken only to the district court for the judicial district in which the bankruptcy judge is serving.

(b)(1) The judicial council of a circuit may establish a bankruptcy appellate panel, comprised of bankruptcy judges from districts within the circuit, to hear and determine, upon the consent of all the parties, appeals under subsection (a) of this section.

(2) If authorized by the Judicial Conference of the United States, the judicial councils of 2 or more circuits may establish a joint bankruptcy appellate panel comprised of bankruptcy judges from the districts within the circuits for which such panel is established, to hear and determine, upon the consent of all the parties, appeals under subsection (a) of this section.

(3) No appeal may be referred to a panel under this subsection unless the district judges for the district, by majority vote, authorize such referral of appeals originating within the district.

(4) A panel established under this section shall consist of three bankruptcy judges, provided a bankruptcy judge may not hear an appeal originating within a district for which the judge is appointed or designated under section 152 of this title.

(c) An appeal under subsections (a) and (b) of this section shall be taken in the same manner as appeals in civil proceedings generally are taken to the courts of appeals from the district courts and in the time provided by Rule 8002 of the Bankruptcy Rules.

(d) The courts of appeals shall have jurisdiction of appeals from all final decisions, judgments, orders, and decrees entered under subsections (a) and (b) of this section.

APPENDIX II

RULES OF PRACTICE AND PROCEDURE IN BANKRUPTCY
(THE FEDERAL RULES OF BANKRUPTCY PROCEDURE)
(Current to January 1, 1993)

CONTENTS

RULES OF PRACTICE AND PROCEDURE IN BANKRUPTCY

Rule 1001. Scope of Rules and Forms; Short Title

The Bankruptcy Rules and Forms govern procedure in cases under title 11 of the United States Code. The rules shall be cited as the Federal Rules of Bankruptcy Procedure and the forms as the Official Bankruptcy Forms. These rules shall be construed to secure the just, speedy, and inexpensive determination of every case and proceeding.

PART I

COMMENCEMENT OF CASE; PROCEEDINGS RELATING TO PETITION AND ORDER FOR RELIEF

Rule 1002. Commencement of Case

(a) PETITION. A petition commencing a case under the Code shall be filed with the clerk.

(b) TRANSMISSION TO UNITED STATES TRUSTEE. The clerk shall forthwith transmit to the United States trustee a copy of the petition filed pursuant to subdivision (a) of this rule.

Rule 1003. Involuntary Petition

(a) TRANSFEROR OR TRANSFEREE OF CLAIM. A transferor or transferee of a claim shall annex to the original and each copy of the petition a copy of all documents evidencing the transfer, whether transferred unconditionally, for security, or otherwise, and a signed statement that the claim was not transferred for the purpose of commencing the case and setting forth the consideration for and terms of the transfer. An entity that has transferred or acquired a claim for the purpose of commencing a case for liquidation under chapter 7 or for reorganization under chapter 11 shall not be a qualified petitioner.

(b) JOINDER OF PETITIONERS AFTER FILING. If the answer to an involuntary petition filed by fewer than three creditors avers the existence of 12 or more creditors, the debtor shall file with the answer a list of all creditors with their addresses, a brief statement of the nature of their claims, and the amounts thereof. If it appears that there are 12 or more creditors as provided in Section 303(b) of the Code, the court shall afford a reasonable opportunity for other creditors to join in the petition before a hearing is held thereon.

Rule 1004. Partnership Petition

(a) VOLUNTARY PETITION. A voluntary petition may be filed on behalf of the partnership by one or more general partners if all general partners consent to the petition.

(b) INVOLUNTARY PETITION; NOTICE AND SUMMONS. After filing of an involuntary petition under Section 303(b)(3) of the Code, (1) the petitioning partners or other petitioners shall cause forthwith a copy of the petition to be sent to or served on each general partner who is not a petitioner; and (2) the clerk shall issue forthwith a summons for service on each general partner who is not a petitioner. Rule 1010 applies to the form and service of the summons.

Rule 1005. Caption of Petition

The caption of a petition commencing a case under the Code shall contain the name of the court, the title of the case, and the docket number. The title of the case shall include the name, social security number and employer's tax identification number of the debtor and all other names used by the debtor within six years before filing the petition. If the petition is not filed by the debtor, it shall include all names used by the debtor which are known to petitioners.

Rule 1006. Filing Fee

(a) GENERAL REQUIREMENT. Every petition shall be accompanied by the prescribed filing fee except as provided in subdivision (b) of this rule.

(b) PAYMENT OF FILING FEE IN INSTALLMENTS.

(1) *Application for Permission to Pay Filing Fee in Installments.* A voluntary petition by an individual shall be accepted for filing if accompanied by the debtor's signed application stating that the debtor is unable to pay the filing fee except in installments. The application shall state the proposed terms of the installment payments and that the applicant has neither paid any money nor transferred any property to an attorney for services in connection with the case.

(2) *Action on Application.* Prior to the meeting of creditors, the court may order the filing fee paid to the clerk or grant leave to pay in installments and fix the number, amount and dates of payment. The number of installments shall not exceed four, and the final installment shall be payable not later than 120 days after filing the petition. For cause shown, the court may extend the time of any installment, provided the last installment is paid not later than 180 days after filing the petition.

(3) *Postponement of Attorney's Fees.* The filing fee must be paid in full before the debtor or chapter 13 trustee may pay an attorney or any other person who renders services to the debtor in connection with the case.

Rule 1007. Lists, Schedules, and Statements; Time Limits

(a) LIST OF CREDITORS AND EQUITY SECURITY HOLDERS.

(1) *Voluntary Case.* In a voluntary case, the debtor shall file with the petition a list containing the name and address of each creditor unless the petition is accompanied by a schedule of liabilities.

(2) *Involuntary Case.* In an involuntary case, the debtor shall file within 15 days after entry of the order for relief, a list containing the name and address of each creditor unless a schedule of liabilities has been filed.

(3) *Equity Security Holders.* In a chapter 11 reorganization case, unless the court orders otherwise, the debtor shall file within 15 days after entry of the order for relief a list of the debtor's equity security holders of each class showing the number and kind of interests registered in the name of each holder, and the last known address or place of business of each holder.

(4) *Extension of Time.* Any extension of time for the filing of the lists required by this subdivision may be granted only on motion for cause shown and on notice to the United States trustee and to any trustee, committee elected pursuant to Section 705 or appointed pursuant to Section 1102 of the Code, or other party as the court may direct.

(b) SCHEDULES AND STATEMENTS REQUIRED.

(1) Except in a chapter 9 municipality case, the debtor, unless the court orders otherwise, shall file schedules of assets and liabilities, a schedule of current income and expenditures, a statement of executory contracts and unexpired leases, and a statement of financial affairs, prepared as prescribed by the appropriate Official Forms.

(2) An individual debtor in a chapter 7 case shall file a statement of intention as required by Section 521(2) of the Code, prepared as prescribed by the appropriate Official Form. A copy of the statement of intention shall be served on the trustee and the creditors named in the statement on or before the filing of the statement.

(c) TIME LIMITS. The schedules and statements, other than the statement of intention, shall be filed with the petition in a voluntary case, or if the petition is accompanied by a list of all the debtor's creditors and their addresses, within 15 days thereafter, except as otherwise provided in subdivisions (d), (e), and (h) of this rule. In an involuntary case the schedules and statements, other than the statement of intention, shall be filed by the debtor within 15 days after entry of the order for relief. Schedules and statements previously filed in a pending chapter 7 case shall be deemed filed in a superseding case unless the court directs otherwise. Any extension of time for the filing of the schedules and statements may be granted only on motion for cause shown and on notice to the United States trustee and to any committee elected pursuant to Section 705 or appointed pursuant to Section 1102 of the Code, trustee, examiner, or other party as the court may direct. Notice of an extension shall be given to the United States trustee and to any committee, trustee, or other party as the court may direct.

(d) LIST OF 20 LARGEST CREDITORS IN CHAPTER 9 MUNICIPALITY CASE OR CHAPTER 11 REORGANIZATION CASE. In addition to the list required by subdivision (a) of this rule, a debtor in a chapter 9 municipality case or a debtor in a voluntary chapter 11 reorganization case shall file with the petition a list containing the name, address and claim of the creditors that hold the 20 largest unsecured claims, excluding insiders, as prescribed by the appropriate Official Form. In an involuntary chapter 11 reorganization case, such list shall be filed by the debtor within 2 days after entry of the order for relief under Section 303(h) of the Code.

(e) LIST IN CHAPTER 9 MUNICIPALITY CASES. The list required by subdivision (a) of this rule shall be filed by the debtor in a chapter 9 municipality case within such time as the court shall fix. If a proposed plan requires a revision of assessments so that the proportion of special assessments or special taxes to be assessed against some real property will be different from the proportion in effect as the date the petition is filed, the debtor shall also file a list showing the name and address of each known holder of title, legal or equitable, to real property adversely affected. On motion for cause shown, the court may modify the requirements of this subdivision and subdivision (a) of this rule.

(f) [Abrogated]

(g) PARTNERSHIP AND PARTNERS. The general partners of a debtor partnership shall prepare and file the schedules of the assets and liabilities, schedule of current income and expenditures, schedule of executory contracts and unexpired leases, and statement of financial affairs of the partnership. The court may order any general partner to file a statement of personal assets and liabilities within such time as the court may fix.

(h) INTERESTS ACQUIRED OR ARISING AFTER PETITION. If, as provided by Section 541(a)(5) of the Code, the debtor acquires or becomes entitled to acquire any interest in property, the debtor shall within 10 days after the information comes to the debtor's knowledge or within such further time the court may allow, file a supplemental schedule in the chapter 7 liquidation case, chapter 11 reorganization case, chapter 12 family farmer's debt adjustment case, or chapter 13 individual debt adjustment case. If any of the property required to be reported under this subdivision is claimed by the debtor as exempt, the debtor shall claim the exemptions in the supplemental schedule. The duty to file a supplemental schedule in accordance with this subdivision continues notwithstanding the closing of the case, except that the schedule need not be filed in a chapter 11, chapter 12, or chapter 13 case with respect to property acquired after entry of the order confirming a chapter 11 plan or discharging the debtor in a chapter 12 or chapter 13 case.

(i) DISCLOSURE OF LIST OF SECURITY HOLDERS. After notice and hearing and for cause shown, the court may direct an entity other than the debtor or trustee to disclose any list of security holders of the debtor in its possession or under its control, indicating the name, address and security held by any of them. The entity possessing this list may be required either to produce the list or a true copy thereof, or permit inspection or copying, or otherwise disclose the information contained on the list.

(j) IMPOUNDING OF LISTS. On motion of a party in interest and for cause shown the court may direct the impounding of the lists filed under this rule, and may refuse to permit inspection by any entity. The court may permit inspection or use of the lists, however, by any party in interest on terms prescribed by the court.

(k) PREPARATION OF LIST, SCHEDULES, OR STATEMENTS ON DEFAULT OF DEBTOR. If a list, schedule, or statement, other than a statement of intention, is not prepared and filed as required by this rule, the court may order the trustee, a petitioning creditor, committee, or other party to prepare and file any of these papers within a time fixed by the court. The court may approve reimbursement of the cost incurred in complying with such an order as an administrative expense.

(l) TRANSMISSION TO UNITED STATES TRUSTEE. The clerk shall forthwith transmit to the United States trustee a copy of every list, schedule, and statement filed pursuant to subdivision (a)(1), (a)(2), (b), (d), or (h) of this rule.

Rule 1008. Verification of Petitions and Accompanying Papers

All petitions, lists, schedules, statements and amendments thereto shall be verified or contain an unsworn declaration as provided in 28 U.S.C. Section 1746.

Rule 1009. Amendments of Voluntary Petitions, Lists, Schedules and Statements

(a) GENERAL RIGHT TO AMEND. A voluntary petition, list, schedule, or statement may be amended by the debtor as a matter of course at any time before the case is closed. The debtor shall give notice of the amendment to the trustee and to any entity affected thereby. On motion of a party in interest, after notice and a hearing, the court may order any voluntary petition, list, schedule, or statement to be amended and the clerk shall give notice of the amendment to entities designated by the court.

(b) STATEMENT OF INTENTION. The statement of intention may be amended by the debtor at any time before the expiration of the period provided in Section 521(2)(B) of the Code. The debtor shall give notice of the amendment to the trustee and to any entity affected thereby.

(c) TRANSMISSION TO UNITED STATES TRUSTEE. The clerk shall forthwith transmit to the United States trustee a copy of every amendment filed pursuant to subdivision (a) or (b) of this rule.

Rule 1010. Service of Involuntary Petition and Summons; Petition Commencing Ancillary Case

On the filing of an involuntary petition or a petition commencing a case ancillary to a foreign proceeding the clerk shall forthwith issue a summons for service. When an involuntary petition is filed, service shall be made on the debtor. When a petition commencing an ancillary case is filed, service shall be made on the parties against whom relief is sought pursuant to Section 304(b) of the Code and on such other parties as the court may direct. The summons shall conform to the appropriate Official Form and a copy shall be served with a copy of the petition in the manner provided for service of a summons and complaint by Rule 7004(a) or (b). If service cannot be so made, the court may order the summons and petition to be served by mailing copies to the party's last known address, and by not less than one publication in a manner and form directed by the court. The summons and petition may be served on the party anywhere. Rule 7004(f) and Rule 4(g) and (h) F. R. Civ. P. apply when service is made or attempted under this rule.

Rule 1011. Responsive Pleading or Motion in Involuntary and Ancillary Cases

(a) WHO MAY CONTEST PETITION. The debtor named in an involuntary petition or a party in interest to a petition commencing a case ancillary to a foreign proceeding may contest the petition. In the case of a petition against a partnership under Rule 1004(b), a nonpetitioning general partner, or a person who is alleged to be a general partner but denies the allegation, may contest the petition.

(b) DEFENSES AND OBJECTIONS; WHEN PRESENTED. Defenses and objections to the petition shall be presented in the manner prescribed by Rule 12 F. R. Civ. P. and shall be filed and served within 20 days after service of the summons, except that if service is made by publication on a party or partner not residing or found within the state in which the court sits, the court shall prescribe the time for filing and serving the response.

(c) EFFECT OF MOTION. Service of a motion under Rule 12(b) F. R. Civ. P. shall extend the time for filing and serving a responsive pleading as permitted by Rule 12(a) F. R. Civ. P.

(d) CLAIMS AGAINST PETITIONERS. A claim against a petitioning creditor may not be asserted in the answer except for the purpose of defeating the petition.

(e) OTHER PLEADINGS. No other pleadings shall be permitted, except that the court may order a reply to an answer and prescribe the time for filing and service.

Rule 1012. [Abrogated]

Rule 1013. Hearing and Disposition of Petition in Involuntary Cases

(a) CONTESTED PETITION. The court shall determine the issues of a contested petition at the earliest practicable time and forthwith enter an order for relief, dismiss the petition, or enter other appropriate orders.

(b) DEFAULT. If no pleading or other defense to a petition is filed within the time provided by Rule 1011, the court, on the next day, or as soon thereafter as practicable, shall enter an order for the relief prayed for in the petition.

(c) ORDER FOR RELIEF. An order for relief shall conform substantially to the appropriate Official Form.

Rule 1014. Dismissal and Change of Venue

(a) DISMISSAL AND TRANSFER OF CASES.

(1) Cases Filed in Proper District. If a petition is filed in a proper district, on timely motion of a party in interest, and after hearing on notice to the petitioners, the United States trustee, and other entities as directed by the court, the case may be transferred to any other district if the court determines that the transfer is in the interest of justice or for the convenience of the parties.

(2) Cases Filed in Improper District. If a petition is filed in an improper district, on timely motion of a party in interest and after hearing on notice to the petitioners, the United States trustee, and other entities as directed by the court, the case may be dismissed or transferred to any other district if the court determines that transfer is in the interest of justice or for the convenience of the parties.

(b) PROCEDURE WHEN PETITIONS INVOLVING THE SAME DEBTOR OR RELATED DEBTORS ARE FILED IN DIFFERENT COURTS. If petitions commencing cases under the Code are filed in different districts by or against (1) the same debtor, or (2) a partnership and one or more of its general partners, or (3) two or more general partners, or (4) a debtor and an affiliate, on motion filed in the district in which the petition filed first is pending and after hearing on notice to the petitioners, the United States trustee, and other entities as directed by the court, the court may determine, in the interest of justice or for the convenience of the parties, the district or districts in which the case or cases should proceed. Except as otherwise ordered by the court in the district in which the petition filed first is pending, the proceedings on the other petitions shall be stayed by the courts in which they have been filed until the determination is made.

Rule 1015. Consolidation or Joint Administration of Cases Pending in Same Court

(a) CASES INVOLVING SAME DEBTOR. If two or more petitions are pending in the same court by or against the same debtor, the court may order consolidation of the cases.

(b) CASES INVOLVING TWO OR MORE RELATED DEBTORS. If a joint petition or two or more petitions are pending in the same court by or against (1) a husband and wife, or (2) a partnership and one or more of its general partners, or (3) two or more general partners, or (4) a debtor and an affiliate, the court may order a joint administration of the estates. Prior to entering an order the court shall give consideration to protecting creditors of different estates against potential conflicts of interest. An order directing joint administration of individual cases of a husband and wife shall, if one spouse has elected the exemptions under Section 522(b)(1) of the Code and the other has elected the exemptions under Section 522(b)(2), fix a reasonable time within which either may amend the election so that both shall have elected the same exemptions. The order shall notify the debtors that unless they elect the same exemptions within the time fixed by the court, they will be deemed to have elected the exemptions provided by Section 522(b)(1).

(c) EXPEDITING AND PROTECTIVE ORDERS. When an order for consolidation or joint administration of a joint case or two or more cases is entered pursuant to this rule, while protecting the rights of the parties under the Code, the court may enter orders as may tend to avoid unnecessary costs and delay.

Rule 1016. Death or Incompetency of Debtor

Death or incompetency of the debtor shall not abate a liquidation case under chapter 7 of the Code. In such event the estate shall be administered and the case concluded in the same manner, so far as possible, as though the death or incompetency had not occurred. If a reorganization, family farmer's debt adjustment, or individual's debt adjustment case is pending under chapter 11, chapter 12, or chapter 13, the case may be dismissed; or if further administration is possible and in the best interest of the parties, the case may proceed and be concluded in the same manner, so far as possible, as though the death or incompetency had not occurred.

Rule 1017. Dismissal or Conversion of Case; Suspension

(a) VOLUNTARY DISMISSAL; DISMISSAL FOR WANT OF PROSECUTION OR OTHER CAUSE. Except as provided in Sections 707(b), 1208(b), and 1307(b) of the Code, a case shall not be dismissed on motion of the petitioner or for want of prosecution or other cause or by consent of the parties prior to a hearing on notice as provided in Rule 2002. For such notice the debtor shall file a list of all creditors with their addresses within the time fixed by the court unless the list was previously filed. If the debtor fails to file the list, the court may order the preparing and filing by the debtor or other entity.

(b) DISMISSAL FOR FAILURE TO PAY FILING FEE.

(1) For failure to pay any installment of the filing fee, the court may after hearing on notice to the debtor and the trustee dismiss the case.

(2) If the case is dismissed or the case closed without full payment of the filing fee, the installments collected shall be distributed in the same manner and proportions as if the filing fee had been paid in full.

(3) Notice of dismissal for failure to pay the filing fee shall be given within 30 days after the dismissal to creditors appearing on the list of creditors and to those who have filed claims, in the manner provided in Rule 2002.

(c) SUSPENSION. A case shall not be dismissed or proceedings suspended pursuant to Section 305 of the Code prior to a hearing on notice as provided in Rule 2002(a).

(d) PROCEDURE FOR DISMISSAL OR CONVERSION. A proceeding to dismiss a case or convert a case to another chapter, except pursuant to Sections 706(a), 707(b), 1112(a), 1208(a) or (b), or 1307(a) or (b), is governed by Rule 9014. Conversion or dismissal pursuant to Sections 706(a), 1112(a), 1208(b), or 1307(b) shall be on motion filed and served as required by Rule 9013. A chapter 12 or chapter 13 case shall be converted without court order on the filing by the debtor of a notice of conversion pursuant to Sections 1208(a) or 1307(a), and the date of the filing of the notice shall be deemed the date of the conversion order for the purpose of applying Section 348(c) of the Code. The clerk shall forthwith transmit to the United States trustee a copy of such notice.

(e) DISMISSAL OF INDIVIDUAL DEBTOR'S CHAPTER 7 CASE FOR SUBSTANTIAL ABUSE. An individual debtor's case may be dismissed for substantial abuse pursuant to Section 707(b) only on motion by the United States trustee or on the court's own motion and after a hearing on notice to the debtor, the trustee, the United States trustee, and such other parties in interest as the court directs.

(1) A motion by the United States trustee shall be filed not later than 60 days following the first date set for the meeting of creditors held pursuant to Section 341(a), unless, before such time has expired, the court for cause extends the time for filing the motion. The motion shall advise the debtor of all matters to be submitted to the court for its consideration at the hearing.

(2) If the hearing is on the court's own motion, notice thereof shall be served on the debtor not later than 60 days following the first date set for the meeting of creditors pursuant to Section 341(a). The notice shall advise the debtor of all matters to be considered by the court at the hearing.

Rule 1018. Contested Involuntary Petitions; Contested Petitions Commencing Ancillary Cases; Proceedings to Vacate Order for Relief; Applicability of Rules in Part VII Governing Adversary Proceedings

The following rules in Part VII apply to all proceedings relating to a contested involuntary petition, to proceedings relating to a contested petition commencing a case ancillary to a foreign proceeding, and to all proceedings to vacate an order for relief: Rules 7005, 7008-7010, 7015, 7016, 7024-7026, 7028-7037, 7052, 7054, 7056, and 7062, except as otherwise provided in Part I of these rules and unless the court otherwise directs. The court may direct that other rules in Part VII shall also apply. For the purposes of this rule a reference in the Part VII rules to adversary proceedings shall be read as a reference to proceedings relating to a contested involuntary petition, or contested ancillary petition, or proceedings to vacate an order for relief. Reference in the Federal Rules of Civil Procedure to the complaint shall be read as a reference to the petition.

Rule 1019. Conversion of Chapter 11 Reorganization Case, Chapter 12 Family Farmer's Debt Adjustment Case, or Chapter 13 Individual's Debt Adjustment Case to Chapter 7 Liquidation Case

When a chapter 11, chapter 12, or chapter 13 case has been converted or reconverted to a chapter 7 case:

(1) Filing of Lists, Inventories, Schedules, Statements.

(A) Lists, inventories, schedules, and statements of financial affairs theretofore filed shall be deemed to be filed in the chapter 7 case, unless the court directs otherwise. If they have not been previously filed, the debtor shall comply with Rule 1007 as if an order for relief had been entered on an involuntary petition on the date of the entry of the order directing that the case continue under chapter 7.

(B) The statement of intention, if required, shall be filed within 30 days following entry of the order of conversion or before the first date set for the meeting of creditors, whichever is earlier. An extension of time may be granted for cause only on motion made before the time has expired. Notice of an extension shall be given to the United States trustee and to any committee, trustee, or other party as the court may direct.

(2) New Filing Periods. A new time period for filing claims, a complaint objecting to discharge, or a complaint to obtain a determination of dischargeability of any debt shall commence pursuant to Rules 3002, 4004, or 4007, provided that a new time period shall not commence if a chapter 7 case had been converted to a chapter 11, 12, or 13 case and thereafter reconverted to a chapter 7 case and the time for filing claims, a complaint objecting to discharge, or a complaint to obtain a determination of the dischargeability of any debt, or any extension thereof, expired in the original chapter 7 case.

(3) Claims Filed in Superseded Case. All claims actually filed by a creditor in the superseded case shall be deemed filed in the chapter 7 case.

(4) Turnover of Records And Property. After qualification of, or assumption of duties by the chapter 7 trustee, any debtor in possession or trustee previously acting in the chapter 11, 12, or 13 case shall, forthwith, unless otherwise ordered, turn over to the chapter 7 trustee all records and property of the estate in the possession or control of the debtor in possession or trustee.

(5) Filing Final Report and Schedule of Postpetition Debts. Unless the court directs otherwise, each debtor in possession or trustee in the superseded case shall: (A) within 15 days following the entry of the order of conversion of a chapter 11 case, file a schedule of unpaid debts incurred after commencement of the superseded case including the name and address of each creditor; and (B) within 30 days following the entry of the order of conversion of a chapter 11, chapter 12, or chapter 13 case, file and transmit to the United States trustee a final report and account. Within 15 days following the entry of the order of conversion, unless the court directs otherwise, a chapter 13 debtor shall file a schedule of unpaid debts incurred after the commencement of a chapter 13 case, and a chapter 12 debtor in possession or, if the chapter 12 debtor is not in possession, the trustee shall file a schedule of unpaid debts incurred after the commencement of a chapter 12 case. If the conversion order is entered after confirmation of a plan, the debtor shall file (A) a schedule of property not listed in the final report and account acquired after the filing of the original petition but before entry of the conversion order; (B) a schedule of unpaid debts not listed in the final report and account incurred after confirmation but before entry of the conversion order; and (C) a schedule of executory contracts and unexpired leases entered into or assumed after the filing of the original petition but before entry of the conversion order. The clerk shall forthwith transmit to the United States trustee a copy of every schedule filed pursuant to this paragraph.

(6) Filing of Postpetition Claims; Notice. On the filing of the schedule of unpaid debts, the clerk, or some other person as the court may direct, shall give notice to those entities, including the United States, any state, or any subdivision thereof, that their claims may be filed pursuant to Rules 3001(a)–(d) and 3002. Unless a notice of insufficient assets to pay a dividend is mailed pursuant to Rule 2002(e), the court shall fix the time for filing claims arising from the rejection of executory contracts or unexpired leases under Sections 348(c) and 365(d) of the Code.

(7) Extension of Time to File Claims Against Surplus. Any extension of time for the filing of claims against a surplus granted pursuant to Rule 3002(c)(6), shall apply to holders of claims who failed to file their claims within the time prescribed, or fixed by the court pursuant to paragraph (6) of this rule, and notice shall be given as provided in Rule 2002.

PART II

OFFICERS AND ADMINISTRATION; NOTICES; MEETINGS; EXAMINATIONS; ELECTIONS; ATTORNEYS AND ACCOUNTANTS

Rule 2001. Appointment of Interim Trustee Before Order for Relief in a Chapter 7 Liquidation Case

(a) APPOINTMENT. At any time following the commencement of an involuntary liquidation case and before an order for relief, the court on written motion of a party in interest may order the appointment of an interim trustee under Section 303(g) of the Code. The motion shall set forth the necessity for the appointment and may be granted only after hearing on notice to the debtor, the petitioning creditors, the United States trustee, and other parties in interest as the court may designate.

(b) BOND OF MOVANT. An interim trustee may not be appointed under this rule unless the movant furnishes a bond in an amount approved by the court, conditioned to indemnify the debtor for costs, attorney's fee, expenses, and damages allowable under Section 303(i) of the Code.

(c) ORDER OF APPOINTMENT. The order directing the appointment of an interim trustee shall state the reason the appointment is necessary and shall specify the trustee's duties.

(d) TURNOVER AND REPORT. Following qualification of the trustee selected under Section 702 of the Code, the interim trustee, unless otherwise ordered, shall (1) forthwith deliver to the trustee all the records and property of the estate in possession or subject to control of the interim trustee and, (2) within 30 days thereafter file a final report and account.

Rule 2002. Notices to Creditors, Equity Security Holders, United States, and United States Trustee

(a) TWENTY–DAY NOTICES TO PARTIES IN INTEREST. Except as provided in subdivisions (h), (i) and (l) of this rule, the clerk, or some other person as the court may direct, shall give the debtor, the trustee, all creditors and indenture trustees not less than 20 days notice by mail of (1) the meeting of creditors pursuant to Section 341 of the Code; (2) a proposed use, sale, or lease of property of the estate other than in the ordinary course of business, unless the court for cause shown shortens the time or directs another method of giving notice; (3) the hearing on approval of a compromise or settlement of a controversy other than approval of an agreement pursuant to Rule 4001(d), unless the court for cause shown directs that notice not be sent; (4) the date fixed for the filing of claims against a surplus in an estate as provided in Rule 3002(c)(6); (5) in a chapter 7 liquidation, a chapter 11 reorganization case, and a chapter 12 family farmer debt adjustment case, the hearing on the dismissal of the case, unless the hearing is pursuant to Section 707(b) of the Code, or the conversion of the case to another chapter; (6) the time fixed to accept or reject a proposed modification of a plan; (7) hearings on all applications for compensation or reimbursement of expenses totalling in excess of $500; (8) the time fixed for filing proofs of claims pursuant to Rule 3003(c); and (9) the time fixed for filing objections and the hearing to consider confirmation of a chapter 12 plan.

(b) TWENTY–FIVE–DAY NOTICES TO PARTIES IN INTEREST. Except as provided in subdivision (l) of this rule, the clerk, or some other person as the court may direct, shall give the debtor, the trustee, all creditors and indenture trustees not less than 25 days notice by mail of (1) the time fixed for filing objections and the hearing to consider approval of a disclosure statement; and (2) the time fixed for filing objections and the hearing to consider confirmation of a chapter 9, chapter 11, or chapter 13 plan.

(c) CONTENT OF NOTICE.

(1) Proposed Use, Sale, or Lease of Property. Subject to Rule 6004 the notice of a proposed use, sale, or lease of property required by subdivision (a)(2) of this rule shall include the time and place of any public sale, the terms and conditions of any private sale and the time fixed for filing objections. The notice of a proposed use, sale, or lease of property, including real estate, is sufficient if it generally describes the property.

(2) Notice of Hearing on Compensation. The notice of a hearing on an application for compensation or reimbursement of expenses required by subdivision (a)(7) of this rule shall identify the applicant and the amounts requested.

(d) NOTICE TO EQUITY SECURITY HOLDERS. In a chapter 11 reorganization case, unless otherwise ordered by the court, the clerk, or some other person as the court may direct, shall in the manner and form directed by the court give notice to all equity security holders of (1) the order for relief; (2) any meeting of equity security holders held pursuant to Section 341 of the Code; (3) the hearing on the proposed sale of all or substantially all of the debtor's assets; (4) the hearing on the dismissal or conversion of a case to another chapter; (5) the time fixed for filing objections to and the hearing to consider approval of a disclosure statement; (6) the time fixed for filing objections to and the hearing to consider confirmation of a plan; and (7) the time fixed to accept or reject a proposed modification of a plan.

(e) NOTICE OF NO DIVIDEND. In a chapter 7 liquidation case, if it appears from the schedules that there are no assets from which a dividend can be paid, the notice of the meeting of creditors may include a statement to that effect; that it is unnecessary to file claims; and that if sufficient assets become available for the payment of a dividend, further notice will be given for the filing of claims.

(f) OTHER NOTICES. Except as provided in subdivision (l) of this rule, the clerk, or some other person as the court may direct, shall give the debtor, all creditors, and indenture trustees notice by mail of (1) the order for relief; (2) the dismissal or the conversion of the case to another chapter; (3) the time allowed for filing claims pursuant to Rule 3002; (4) the time fixed for filing a complaint objecting to the debtor's discharge pursuant to Section 727 of the Code as provided in Rule 4004; (5) the time fixed for filing a complaint to determine the dischargeability of a debt pursuant to Section 523 of the Code as provided in Rule 4007; (6) the waiver, denial, or revocation of a discharge as provided in Rule 4006; (7) entry of an order confirming a chapter 9, 11, or 12 plan; and (8) a summary of the trustee's final report and account in a chapter 7 case if the net proceeds realized exceed $1500. Notice of the time fixed for accepting or rejecting a plan pursuant to Rule 3017(c) shall be given in accordance with Rule 3017(d).

(g) ADDRESSES OF NOTICES. All notices required to be mailed under this rule to a creditor, equity security holder, or indenture trustee shall be addressed as such entity or an authorized agent may direct in a filed request; otherwise, to the address shown in the list of creditors or the schedule whichever is filed later. If a different address is stated in a proof of claim duly filed, that address shall be used unless a notice of no dividend has been given.

(h) NOTICES TO CREDITORS WHOSE CLAIMS ARE FILED. In a chapter 7 case, the court may, after 90 days following the first date set for the meeting of creditors pursuant to Section 341 of the Code, direct that all notices required by subdivision (a) of this rule, except clause (4) thereof, be mailed only to creditors whose claims have been filed and creditors, if any, who are still permitted to file claims by reason of an extension granted under Rule 3002(c)(6).

(i) NOTICES TO COMMITTEES. Copies of all notices required to be mailed under this rule shall be mailed to the committees elected pursuant to Section 705 or appointed pursuant to Section 1102 of the Code or to their authorized agents. Notwithstanding the foregoing subdivisions, the court may order that notices required by subdivision (a)(2), (3) and (7) of this rule be transmitted to the United States trustee and be mailed only to the committees elected pursuant to Section 705 or appointed pursuant to Section 1102 of the Code or to their authorized agents and to the creditors and equity security holders who serve on the trustee or debtor in possession and file a request that all notices be mailed to them. A committee appointed pursuant to Section 1114 shall receive copies of all notices required by subdivisions (a)(1), (a)(6), (b), (f)(2), and (f)(7), and such other notices as the court may direct.

(j) NOTICES TO THE UNITED STATES. Copies of notices required to be mailed to all creditors under this rule shall be mailed (1) in a chapter 11 reorganization case to the Securities and Exchange Commission at Washington, D.C., and at any other place the Commission designates in a filed writing if the Commission has filed a notice of appearance in the case or has made a request in a filed writing; (2) in a commodity broker case, to the Commodity Futures Trading Commission at Washington, D.C.; (3) in a chapter 11 case to the District Director of Internal Revenue for the district in which the case is pending; (4) if the papers in the case disclose a debt to the United States other than for taxes, to the United States attorney for the district in which the case is pending and to the department, agency, or instrumentality of the United States through which the debtor became indebted; or if the filed papers disclose a stock interest of the United States, to the Secretary of the Treasury at Washington, D.C.

(k) NOTICES TO UNITED STATES TRUSTEE. Unless the case is a chapter 9 municipality case or unless the United States trustee otherwise requests, the clerk, or some other person as the court may direct, shall transmit to the United States trustee notice of the matters described in subdivisions (a)(2), (a)(3), (a)(5), (a)(9), (b), (f)(1), (f)(2), (f)(4), (f)(6), (f)(7), and (f)(8) of this rule and notice of hearings on all applications for compensation or reimbursement of expenses. Notices to the United States trustee shall be transmitted within the time prescribed in subdivision (a) or (b) of this rule. The United States trustee shall also receive notice of any other matter if such notice is requested by the United States trustee or ordered by the court. Nothing in these rules shall require the clerk or any other person to transmit to the United States trustee any notice, schedule, report, application or other document in a case under the Securities Investor Protection Act, 15 U.S.C. Section 78aaa et seq.

(l) NOTICE BY PUBLICATION. The court may order notice by publication if it finds that notice by mail is impracticable or that it is desirable to supplement the notice.

(m) ORDERS DESIGNATING MATTER OF NOTICES. The court may from time to time enter orders designating the matters in respect to which, the entity to whom, and the form and manner in which notices shall be sent except as otherwise provided by these rules.

(n) CAPTION. The caption of every notice given under this rule shall comply with Rule 1005.

(o) NOTICE OF ORDER FOR RELIEF IN CONSUMER CASE. In a voluntary case commenced by an individual debtor whose debts are primarily consumer debts, the clerk or some other person as the court may direct shall give the trustee and all creditors notice by mail of the order for relief within 20 days from the date thereof.

Rule 2003. Meeting of Creditors or Equity Security Holders

(a) DATE AND PLACE. Unless the case is a chapter 9 municipality case or a chapter 12 family farmer's debt adjustment case, the United States trustee shall call a meeting of creditors to be held not less than 20 nor more than 40 days after the order for relief. In a chapter 12 case, the United States trustee shall call a meeting of creditors to be held not less than 20 nor more than 35 days after the order for relief. If there is an appeal from or a motion to vacate the order for relief, or if there is a motion to dismiss the case, the United States trustee may set a later time for the meeting. The meeting may be held at a regular place for holding court or at any other place designated by the United States trustee within the district convenient for the parties in interest. If the United States trustee designates a place for the meeting which is not regularly staffed by the United States trustee or an assistant who may preside at the meeting, the meeting may be held not more than 60 days after the order for relief.

(b) ORDER OF MEETING.

(1) Meeting of Creditors. The United States trustee shall preside at the meeting of creditors. The business of the meeting shall include the examination of the debtor under oath and, in a chapter 7 liquidation case, may include the election of a trustee or of a creditors' committee. The presiding officer shall have the authority to administer oaths.

(2) Meeting of Equity Security Holders. If the United States trustee convenes a meeting of equity security holders pursuant to Section 341(b) of the Code, the United States trustee shall fix a date for the meeting and shall preside.

(3) Right to Vote. In a chapter 7 liquidation case, a creditor is entitled to vote at a meeting if, at or before the meeting, the creditor has filed a proof of claim or a writing setting forth facts evidencing a right to vote pursuant to Section 702(a) of the Code unless objection is made to the claim or the proof of claim is insufficient on its face. A creditor of a partnership may file a proof of claim or writing evidencing a right to vote for the trustee for the estate of a general partner notwithstanding that a trustee for the estate of the partnership has previously qualified. In the event of an objection to the amount or allowability of a claim for the purpose of voting, unless the court orders otherwise, the United States trustee shall tabulate the votes for each alternative presented by the dispute and, if resolution of such dispute is necessary to determine the result of the election, the tabulations for each alternative shall be reported to the court.

(c) RECORD OF MEETING. Any examination under oath at the meeting of creditors held pursuant to Section 341(a) of the Code shall be recorded verbatim by the United States trustee using electronic sound recording equipment or other means of recording, and such record shall be preserved by the United States trustee and available for public access until two years after the conclusion of the meeting of creditors. Upon request of any entity, the United States trustee shall certify and provide a copy or transcript of such recording at the entity's expense.

(d) REPORT TO THE COURT. The presiding officer shall transmit to the court the name and address of any person elected trustee or entity elected a member of a creditors' committee. If an election is disputed, the presiding officer shall promptly inform the court in writing that a dispute exists. Pending disposition by the court of a disputed election for trustee, the interim trustee shall continue in office. If no motion for the resolution of such election dispute is made to the court within 10 days after the date of the creditors' meeting, the interim trustee shall serve as trustee in the case.

(e) ADJOURNMENT. The meeting may be adjourned from time to time by announcement at the meeting of the adjourned date and time without further written notice.

(f) SPECIAL MEETINGS. The United States trustee may call a special meeting of creditors on request of a party in interest or on the United States trustee's own initiative.

(g) FINAL MEETING. If the United States trustee calls a final meeting of creditors in a case in which the net proceeds realized exceed $1,500, the clerk shall mail a summary of the trustee's final account to the creditors with a notice of the meeting, together with a statement of the amount of the claims allowed. The trustee shall attend the final meeting and shall, if requested, report on the administration of the estate.

Rule 2004. Examination

(a) EXAMINATION ON MOTION. On motion of any party in interest, the court may order the examination of any entity.

(b) SCOPE OF EXAMINATION. The examination of an entity under this rule or of the debtor under Section 343 of the Code may relate only to the acts, conduct, or property or to the liabilities and financial condition of the debtor, or to any matter which may affect the administration of the debtor's estate, or to the debtor's right to a discharge. In a family farmer's debt adjustment case under chapter 12, an individual's debt adjustment case under chapter 13, or a reorganization case under chapter 11 of the Code, other than for the reorganization of a railroad, the examination may also relate to the operation of any business and the desirability of its continuance, the source of any money or property acquired or to be acquired by the debtor for purposes of consummating a plan and the consideration given or offered therefor, and any other matter relevant to the case or to the formulation of a plan.

(c) COMPELLING ATTENDANCE AND PRODUCTION OF DOCUMENTARY EVIDENCE. The attendance of an entity for examination and the production of documentary evidence may be compelled in the manner provided in Rule 9016 for the attendance of witnesses at a hearing or trial.

(d) TIME AND PLACE OF EXAMINATION OF DEBTOR. The court may for cause shown and on terms as it may impose order the debtor to be examined under this rule at any time or place it designates, whether within or without the district wherein the case is pending.

(e) MILEAGE. An entity other than a debtor shall not be required to attend as a witness unless lawful mileage and witness fee for one day's attendance shall be first tendered. If the debtor resides more than 100 miles from the place of examination when required to appear for an examination under this rule, the mileage allowed by law to a witness shall be tendered for any distance more than 100 miles from the debtor's residence at the date of the filing of the first petition commencing a case under the Code or the residence at the time the debtor is required to appear for the examination, whichever is the lesser.

Rule 2005. Apprehension and Removal of Debtor to Compel Attendance for Examination

(a) ORDER TO COMPEL ATTENDANCE FOR EXAMINATION. On motion of any party in interest supported by an affidavit alleging (1) that the examination of the debtor is necessary for the proper administration of the estate and that there is reasonable cause to believe that the debtor is about to leave or has left the debtor's residence or principal place of business to avoid examination, or (2) that the debtor has evaded service of a subpoena or of an order to attend for examination, or (3) that the debtor has willfully disobeyed a subpoena or order to attend for examination, duly served, the court may issue to the marshal, or some other officer authorized by law, an order directing the officer to bring the debtor before the court without unnecessary delay. If, after hearing, the court finds the allegations to be true, the court shall thereupon cause the debtor to be examined forthwith. If necessary, the court shall fix conditions for further examination and for the debtor's obedience to all orders made in reference thereto.

(b) REMOVAL. Whenever any order to bring the debtor before the court is issued under this rule and the debtor is found in a district other than that of the court issuing the order, the debtor may be taken into custody under the order and removed in accordance with the following rules:

(1) If taken at a place less than 100 miles from the place of issue of the order, the debtor shall be brought forthwith before the court that issued the order.

(2) If taken at a place 100 miles or more from the place of issue of the order, the debtor shall be brought without unnecessary delay before the nearest United States magistrate, bankruptcy judge, or district judge. If, after hearing, the magistrate, bankruptcy judge, or district judge finds that an order has issued under this rule and that the person in custody is the debtor, or if the person in custody waives a hearing, the magistrate, bankruptcy judge, or district judge shall issue an order of removal and the person in custody shall be released on conditions assuring prompt appearance before the court which issued the order to compel the attendance.

(c) CONDITIONS OF RELEASE. In determining what conditions will reasonably assure attendance or obedience under subdivision (a) of this rule or appearance under subdivision (b) of this rule, the court shall be governed by the provisions and policies of title 18, U. S. C., Section 3146(a) and (b).

Rule 2006. Solicitation and Voting of Proxies in Chapter 7 Liquidation Cases

(a) APPLICABILITY. This rule applies only in a liquidation case pending under chapter 7 of the Code.

(b) DEFINITIONS.

(1) Proxy. A proxy is a written power of attorney authorizing any entity to vote the claim or otherwise act as the owner's attorney in fact in connection with the administration of the estate.

(2) Solicitation of Proxy. The solicitation of a proxy is any communication, other than one from an attorney to a regular client who owns a claim or from an attorney to the owner of a claim who has requested the attorney to represent the owner, by which a creditor is asked, directly or indirectly, to give a proxy after or in contemplation of the filing of a petition by or against the debtor.

(c) AUTHORIZED SOLICITATION.

(1) A proxy may be solicited only by (A) a creditor owning an allowable unsecured claim against the estate on the date of the filing of the petition; (B) a committee elected pursuant to Section 705 of the Code; (C) a committee of creditors selected by a majority in number and amount of claims of creditors (i) whose claims are not contingent or unliquidated, (ii) who are not disqualified from voting under Section 702(a) of the Code and (iii) who were present or represented at a meeting of which all creditors having claims of over $500 or the 100 creditors having the largest claims had at least five days notice in writing and of which meeting written minutes were kept and are available reporting the names of the creditors present or represented and voting and the amounts of their claims; or (D) a bona fide trade or credit association, but such association may solicit only creditors who were its members or subscribers in good standing and had allowable unsecured claims on the date of the filing of the petition.

(2) A proxy may be solicited only in writing.

(d) SOLICITATION NOT AUTHORIZED. This rule does not permit solicitation (1) in any interest other than that of general creditors; (2) by or on behalf of any custodian; (3) by the interim trustee or by or on behalf of any entity not qualified to vote under Section 702(a) of the Code; (4) by or on behalf of an attorney at law; or (5) by or on behalf of a transferee of a claim for collection only.

(e) DATA REQUIRED FROM HOLDERS OF MULTIPLE PROXIES. At any time before the voting commences at any meeting of creditors pursuant to Section 341(a) of the Code, or at any other time as the court may direct, a holder of two or more proxies shall file and transmit to the United States trustee a verified list of the proxies to be voted and a verified statement of the pertinent facts and circumstances in connection with the execution and delivery of each proxy, including:

(1) a copy of the solicitation;

(2) identification of the solicitor, the forwarder, if the forwarder is neither the solicitor nor the owner of the claim, and the proxyholder, including their connections with the debtor and with each other. If the solicitor, forwarder, or proxyholder is an association, there shall also be included a statement that the creditors whose claims have been solicited and the creditors whose claims are to be voted were members or subscribers in good standing and had allowable unsecured claims on the date of the filing of the petition. If the solicitor, forwarder, or proxyholder is a committee of creditors, the statement shall also set forth the date and place the committee was organized, that the committee was organized in accordance with clause (B) or (C) of paragraph (c)(1) of this rule, the members of the committee, the amounts of their claims, when the claims were acquired, the amounts paid therefor, and the extent to which the claims of the committee members are secured or entitled to priority;

(3) a statement that no consideration has been paid or promised by the proxyholder for the proxy;

(4) a statement as to whether there is any agreement and, if so, the particulars thereof, between the proxyholder and any other entity for the payment of any consideration in connection with voting the proxy, or for the sharing of compensation with any entity, other than a member or regular associate of the proxyholder's law firm, which may be allowed the trustee or any entity for services rendered in the case, or for the employment of any person as attorney, accountant, appraiser, auctioneer, or other employee for the estate;

(5) if the proxy was solicited by an entity other than the proxyholder, or forwarded to the holder by an entity who is neither a solicitor of the proxy nor the owner of the claim, a statement signed and verified by the solicitor or forwarder that no consideration has been paid or promised for the proxy, and whether there is any agreement, and, if so, the particulars thereof, between the solicitor or forwarder and any other entity for the payment of any consideration in connection with voting the proxy, or for sharing compensation with any entity other than a member or regular associate of the solicitor's or forwarder's law firm which may be allowed the trustee or any entity for services rendered in the case, or for the employment of any person as attorney, accountant, appraiser, auctioneer, or other employee for the estate;

(6) if the solicitor, forwarder, or proxyholder is a committee, a statement signed and verified by each member as to the amount and source of any consideration paid or to be paid to such member in connection with the case other than by way of dividend on the member's claim.

(f) ENFORCEMENT OF RESTRICTIONS ON SOLICITATION. On motion of any party in interest or on its own initiative, the court may determine whether there has been a failure to comply with the provisions of this rule or any other impropriety in connection with the solicitation or voting of a proxy. After notice and a hearing the court may reject any proxy for cause, vacate any order entered in consequence of the voting of any proxy which should have been rejected, or take any other appropriate action.

Rule 2007. Review of Appointment of Creditors' Committee Organized Before Commencement of the Case

(a) MOTION TO REVIEW APPOINTMENT. If a committee appointed by the United States trustee pursuant to Section 1102(a) of the Code consists of the members of a committee organized by creditors before the commencement of a chapter 9 or chapter 11 case, on motion of a party in interest and after a hearing on notice to the United States trustee and other entities as the court may direct, the court may determine whether the appointment of the committee satisfies the requirements of Section 1102(b)(1) of the Code.

(b) SELECTION OF MEMBERS OF COMMITTEE. The court may find that a committee organized by unsecured creditors before the commencement of a chapter 9 or chapter 11 case was fairly chosen if:

(1) it was selected by a majority in number and amount of claims of unsecured creditors who may vote under Section 702(a) of the Code and were present in person or represented at a meeting of which all creditors having unsecured claims of over $1,000 or the 100 unsecured creditors having the largest claims had at least five days notice in writing, and of which meeting written minutes reporting the names of the creditors present or represented and voting and the amounts of their claims were kept and are available for inspection;

(2) all proxies voted at the meeting for the elected committee were solicited pursuant to Rule 2006 and the lists and statements required by subdivision (e) thereof have been transmitted to the United States trustee; and

(3) the organization of the committee was in all other respects fair and proper.

(c) FAILURE TO COMPLY WITH REQUIREMENTS FOR APPOINTMENT. After a hearing on notice pursuant to subdivision (a) of this rule, the court shall direct the United States trustee to vacate the appointment of the committee and may order other appropriate action if the court finds that such appointment failed to satisfy the requirements of Section 1102(b)(1) of the Code.

Rule 2007.1. Appointment of Trustee or Examiner in a Chapter 11 Reorganization Case

(a) ORDER TO APPOINT TRUSTEE OR EXAMINER. In a chapter 11 reorganization case, a motion for an order to appoint a trustee or an examiner pursuant to Section 1104(a) or Section 1104(b) of the Code shall be made in accordance with Rule 9014.

(b) APPROVAL OF APPOINTMENT. An order approving the appointment of a trustee or examiner pursuant to Section 1104(c) of the Code shall be made only on application of the United States trustee, stating the name of the person appointed, the names of the parties in interest with whom the United States trustee consulted regarding the appointment, and, to the best of the applicant's knowledge, all the person's connections with the debtor, creditors, any other parties in interest, their respective attorneys and accountants, the United States trustee, and persons employed in the office of the United States trustee. The application shall be accompanied by a verified statement of the person appointed setting forth the person's connections with the debtor, creditors, any other party in interest, their respective attorneys and accountants, the United States trustee, and any person employed in the office of the United States trustee.

Rule 2008. Notice to Trustee of Selection

The United States trustee shall immediately notify the person selected as trustee how to qualify and, if applicable, the amount of the trustee's bond. A trustee that has filed a blanket bond pursuant to Rule 2010 and has been selected as trustee in a chapter 7, chapter 12, or chapter 13 case that does not notify the court and the United States trustee in writing of rejection of the office within five days after receipt of notice of selection shall be deemed to have accepted the office. Any other person selected as trustee shall notify the court and the United States trustee in writing of acceptance of the office within five days after receipt of notice of selection or shall be deemed to have rejected the office.

Rule 2009. Trustee for Estates When Joint Administration Ordered

(a) ELECTION OF SINGLE TRUSTEE FOR ESTATES BEING JOINTLY ADMINISTERED. If the court orders a joint administration of two or more estates pursuant to Rule 1015(b), creditors may elect a single trustee for the estates being jointly administered.

(b) RIGHT OF CREDITORS TO ELECT SEPARATE TRUSTEE. Notwithstanding entry of an order for joint administration pursuant to Rule 1015(b) the creditors of any debtor may elect a separate trustee for the estate of the debtor as provided in Section 702 of the Code.

(c) APPOINTMENT OF TRUSTEES FOR ESTATES BEING JOINTLY ADMINISTERED.

(1) Chapter 7 Liquidation Cases. The United States trustee may appoint one or more interim trustees for estates being jointly administered in chapter 7 cases.

(2) Chapter 11 Reorganization Cases. If the appointment of a trustee is ordered, the United States trustee may appoint one or more trustees for estates being jointly administered in chapter 11 cases.

(3) Chapter 12 Family Farmer's Debt Adjustment Cases. The United States trustee may appoint one or more trustees for estates being jointly administered in chapter 12 cases.

(4) Chapter 13 Individual's Debt Adjustment Cases. The United States trustee may appoint one or more trustees for estates being jointly administered in chapter 13 cases.

(d) POTENTIAL CONFLICTS OF INTEREST. On a showing that creditors or equity security holders of the different estates will be prejudiced by conflicts of interest of a common trustee who has been elected or appointed, the court shall order the selection of separate trustees for estates being jointly administered.

(e) SEPARATE ACCOUNTS. The trustee or trustees of estates being jointly administered shall keep separate accounts of the property and distribution of each estate.

Rule 2010. Qualification by Trustee; Proceeding on Bond

(a) BLANKET BOND. The United States trustee may authorize a blanket bond in favor of the United States conditioned on the faithful performance of official duties by the trustee or trustees to cover (1) a person who qualifies as trustee in a number of cases, and (2) a number of trustees each of whom qualifies in a different case.

(b) PROCEEDING ON BOND. A proceeding on the trustee's bond may be brought by any party in interest in the name of the United States for the use of the entity injured by the breach of the condition.

Rule 2011. Evidence of Debtor in Possession or Qualification of Trustee

(a) Whenever evidence is required that a debtor is a debtor in possession or that a trustee has qualified, the clerk may so certify and the certificate shall constitute conclusive evidence of that fact.

(b) If a person elected or appointed as trustee does not qualify within the time prescribed by Section 322(a) of the Code, the clerk shall so notify the court and the United States trustee.

Rule 2012. Substitution of Trustee or Successor Trustee; Accounting

(a) TRUSTEE. If a trustee is appointed in a chapter 11 case or the debtor is removed as debtor in possession in a chapter 12 case, the trustee is substituted automatically for the debtor in possession as a party in any pending action, proceeding, or matter.

(b) SUCCESSOR TRUSTEE. When a trustee dies, resigns, is removed, or otherwise ceases to hold office during the pendency of a case under the Code (1) the successor is automatically substituted as a party in any pending action, proceeding, or matter; and (2) the successor trustee shall prepare, file, and transmit to the United States trustee an accounting of the prior administration of the estate.

Rule 2013. Public Record of Compensation Awarded to Trustees, Examiners, and Professionals

(a) RECORD TO BE KEPT. The clerk shall maintain a public record listing fees awarded by the court (1) to trustees and attorneys, accountants, appraisers, auctioneers and other professionals employed by trustees, and (2) to examiners. The record shall include the name and docket number of the case, the name of the individual or firm receiving the fee and the amount of the fee awarded. The record shall be maintained chronologically and shall be kept current and open to examination by the public without charge. "Trustees," as used in this rule, does not include debtors in possession.

(b) SUMMARY OF RECORD. At the close of each annual period, the clerk shall prepare a summary of the public record by individual or firm name, to reflect total fees awarded during the preceding year. The summary shall be open to examination by the public without charge. The clerk shall transmit a copy of the summary to the United States trustee.

Rule 2014. Employment of Professional Persons

(a) APPLICATION FOR AN ORDER OF EMPLOYMENT. An order approving the employment of attorneys, accountants, appraisers, auctioneers, agents, or other professionals pursuant to Section 327, Section 1103, or Section 1114 of the Code shall be made only on application of the trustee or committee. The application shall be filed and, unless the case is a chapter 9 municipality case, a copy of the application shall be transmitted by the applicant to the United States trustee. The application shall state the specific facts showing the necessity for the employment, the name of the person to be employed, the reasons for the selection, the professional services to be rendered, any proposed arrangement for compensation, and, to the best of the applicant's knowledge, all of the person's connections with the debtor, creditors, any other party in interest, their respective attorneys and accountants, the United States trustee, or any person employed in the office of the United States trustee. The application shall be accompanied by a verified statement of the person to be employed setting forth the person's connections with the debtor, creditors, any other party in interest, their respective attorneys and accountants, the United States trustee, or any person employed in the office of the United States trustee.

(b) SERVICES RENDERED BY MEMBER OR ASSOCIATE OF FIRM OF ATTORNEYS OR ACCOUNTANTS. If, under the Code and this rule, a law partnership or corporation is employed as an attorney, or an accounting partnership or corporation is employed as an accountant, or if a named attorney or accountant is employed, any partner, member, or regular associate of the partnership, corporation or individual may act as attorney or accountant so employed, without further order of the court.

Rule 2015. Duty to Keep Records, Make Reports, and Give Notice of Case

(a) TRUSTEE OR DEBTOR IN POSSESSION. A trustee or debtor in possession shall (1) in a chapter 7 liquidation case and, if the court directs, in a chapter 11 reorganization case file and transmit to the United States trustee a complete inventory of the property of the debtor within 30 days after qualifying as a trustee or debtor in possession, unless such an inventory has already been filed; (2) keep a record of receipts and the disposition of money and property received; (3) file the reports and summaries required by Section 704(8) of the Code which shall include a statement, if payments are made to employees, of the amounts of deductions for all taxes required to be withheld or paid for and in behalf of employees and the place where these amounts are deposited; (4) as soon as possible after the commencement of the case, give notice of the case to every entity known to be holding money or property subject to withdrawal or order of the debtor, including every bank, savings or building and loan association, public utility company, and landlord with whom the debtor has a deposit, and to every insurance company which has issued a policy having a cash surrender value payable to the debtor, except that notice need not be given to any entity who has knowledge or has previously been notified of the case; (5) in a chapter 11 reorganization case, on or before the last day of the month after each calendar quarter until a plan is confirmed or the case is converted or dismissed, file and transmit to the United States trustee a statement of disbursements made during such calendar quarter and a statement of the amount of the fee required pursuant to 28 U.S.C. Section 1930(a)(6) that has been paid for such calendar quarter.

(b) CHAPTER 12 TRUSTEE AND DEBTOR AND DEBTOR IN POSSESSION. In a chapter 12 family farmer's debt adjustment case, the debtor in possession shall perform the duties prescribed in clauses (1)–(4) of subdivision (a) of this rule. If the debtor is removed as debtor in possession, the trustee shall perform the duties of the debtor in possession prescribed in this paragraph.

(c) CHAPTER 13 TRUSTEE AND DEBTOR.

(1) Business Cases. In a chapter 13 individual's debt adjustment case, when the debtor is engaged in business, the debtor shall perform the duties prescribed by clauses (1)–(4) of subdivision (a) of this rule.

(2) Nonbusiness Cases. In a chapter 13 individual's debt adjustment case, when the debtor is not engaged in business, the trustee shall perform the duties prescribed by clause (2) of subdivision (a) of this rule.

(d) TRANSMISSION OF REPORTS. In a chapter 11 case the court may direct that copies or summaries of annual reports and copies or summaries of other reports shall be mailed to the creditors, equity security holders, and indenture trustees. The court may also direct the publication of summaries of any such reports. A copy of every report or summary mailed or published pursuant to this subdivision shall be transmitted to the United States trustee.

Rule 2016. Compensation for Services Rendered and Reimbursement of Expenses

(a) APPLICATION FOR COMPENSATION OR REIMBURSEMENT. An entity seeking interim or final compensation for services, or reimbursement of necessary expenses, from the estate shall file an application setting forth a detailed statement of (1) the services rendered, time expended and expenses incurred, and (2) the amounts requested. An application for compensation shall include a statement as to what payments have theretofore been made or promised to the applicant for services rendered or to be rendered in any capacity whatsoever in connection with the case, the source of the compensation so paid or promised, whether any compensation previously received has been shared and whether an agreement or understanding exists between the applicant and any other entity for the sharing of compensation received or to be received for services rendered in or in connection with the case, and the particulars of any sharing of compensation or agreement or understanding thereof, except that details of any agreement by the applicant for the sharing of compensation as a member or regular associate of a firm of lawyers or accountants shall not be required. The requirements of this subdivision shall apply to an application for compensation for services rendered by an attorney or accountant even though the application is filed by a creditor or other entity. Unless the case is a chapter 9 municipality case, the applicant shall transmit to the United States trustee a copy of the application.

(b) DISCLOSURE OF COMPENSATION PAID OR PROMISED TO ATTORNEY FOR DEBTOR. Every attorney for a debtor, whether or not the attorney applies for compensation, shall file and transmit to the United States trustee within 15 days after the order for relief, or at another time as the court may direct, the statement required by Section 329 of the Code including whether the attorney has shared or agreed to share the compensation with any other entity. The statement shall include the particulars of any such sharing or agreement to share by the attorney, but the details of any agreement for the sharing of the compensation with a member or regular associate of the attorney's law firm shall not be required. A supplemental statement shall be filed and transmitted to the United States trustee within 15 days after any payment or agreement not previously disclosed.

Rule 2017. Examination of Debtor's Transactions with Debtor's Attorney

(a) PAYMENT OR TRANSFER TO ATTORNEY BEFORE ORDER FOR RELIEF. On motion by any party in interest or on the court's own initiative, the court after notice and a hearing may determine whether any payment of money or any transfer of property by the debtor, made directly or indirectly and in contemplation of the filing of a petition under the Code by or against the debtor or before entry of the order for relief in an involuntary case, to an attorney for services rendered or to be rendered is excessive.

(b) PAYMENT OR TRANSFER TO ATTORNEY AFTER ORDER FOR RELIEF. On motion by the debtor, the United States trustee, or on the court's own initiative, the court after notice and a hearing may determine whether any payment of money or any transfer of property, or any agreement therefor, by the debtor to an attorney after entry of an order for relief in a case under the Code is excessive, whether the payment or transfer is made or is to be made directly or indirectly, if the payment, transfer, or agreement therefor is for services in any way related to the case.

Rule 2018. Intervention; Right to be Heard

(a) PERMISSIVE INTERVENTION. In a case under the Code, after hearing on such notice as the court directs and for cause shown, the court may permit any interested entity to intervene generally or with respect to any specified matter.

(b) INTERVENTION BY ATTORNEY GENERAL OF A STATE. In a chapter 7, 11, 12, or 13 case, the Attorney General of a State may appear and be heard on behalf of consumer creditors if the court determines the appearance is in the public interest, but the Attorney General may not appeal from any judgment, order, or decree in the case.

(c) CHAPTER 9 MUNICIPALITY CASE. The Secretary of the Treasury of the United States may, or if requested by the court shall, intervene in a chapter 9 case. Representatives of the state in which the debtor is located may intervene in a chapter 9 case with respect to matters specified by the court.

(d) LABOR UNIONS. In a chapter 9, 11, or 12 case, a labor union or employees' association, representative of employees of the debtor, shall have the right to be heard on the economic soundness of a plan affecting the interests of the employees. A labor union or employees' association which exercises its right to be heard under this subdivision shall not be entitled to appeal any judgment, order, or decree relating to the plan, unless otherwise permitted by law.

(e) SERVICE ON ENTITIES COVERED BY THIS RULE. The court may enter orders governing the service of notice and papers on entities permitted to intervene or be heard pursuant to this rule.

Rule 2019. Representation of Creditors and Equity Security Holders in Chapter 9 Municipality and Chapter 11 Reorganization Cases

(a) DATA REQUIRED. In a chapter 9 municipality or chapter 11 reorganization case, except with respect to a committee appointed pursuant to Section 1102 or 1114 of the Code, every entity or committee representing more than one creditor or equity security holder and, unless otherwise directed by the court, every indenture trustee, shall file a verified statement setting forth (1) the name and address of the creditor or equity security holder; (2) the nature and amount of the claim or interest and the time of acquisition thereof unless it is alleged to have been acquired more than one year prior to the filing of the petition; (3) a recital of the pertinent facts and circumstances in connection with the employment of the entity or indenture trustee, and, in the case of a committee, the name or names of the entity or entities at whose instance, directly or indirectly, the employment was arranged or the committee was organized or agreed to act; and (4) with reference to the time of the employment of the entity, the organization or formation of the committee, or the appearance in the case of any indenture trustee, the amounts of claims or interests owned by the entity, the members of the committee or the indenture trustee, the times when acquired, the amounts paid therefor, and any sales or other disposition thereof. The statement shall include a copy of the instrument, if any, whereby the entity, committee, or indenture trustee is empowered to act on behalf of creditors or equity security holders. A supplemental statement shall be filed promptly, setting forth any material changes in the facts contained in the statement filed pursuant to this subdivision.

(b) FAILURE TO COMPLY; EFFECT. On motion of any party in interest or on its own initiative, the court may (1) determine whether there has been a failure to comply with the provisions of subdivision (a) of this rule or with any other applicable law regulating the activities and personnel of any entity, committee, or indenture trustee or any other impropriety in connection with any solicitation and, if it so determines, the court may refuse to permit that entity, committee, or indenture trustee to be heard further or to intervene in the case; (2) examine any representation provision of a deposit agreement, proxy, trust agreement, trust indenture, or deed of trust, or committee or other authorization, and any claim or interest acquired by any entity or committee in contemplation or in the course of a case under the Code and grant appropriate relief; and (3) hold invalid any authority, acceptance, rejection, or objection given, procured, or received by an entity or committee who has not complied with this rule or with Section 1125(b) of the Code.

Rule 2020. Review of Acts by United States Trustee

A proceeding to contest any act of failure to act by the United States trustee is governed by Rule 9014.

PART III

CLAIMS AND DISTRIBUTION TO CREDITORS AND EQUITY INTEREST HOLDERS; PLANS

Rule 3001. Proof of Claim.

(a) FORM AND CONTENT. A proof of claim is a written statement setting forth a creditor's claim. A proof of claim shall conform substantially to the appropriate Official Form.

(b) WHO MAY EXECUTE. A proof of claim shall be executed by the creditor or the creditor's authorized agent except as provided in Rules 3004 and 3005.

(c) CLAIM BASED ON A WRITING. When a claim, or an interest in property of the debtor securing the claim, is based on a writing, the original or a duplicate shall be filed with the proof of claim. If the writing has been lost or destroyed, a statement of the circumstances of the loss or destruction shall be filed with the claim.

(d) EVIDENCE OF PERFECTION OF SECURITY INTEREST. If a security interest in property of the debtor is claimed, the proof of claim shall be accompanied by evidence that the security interest has been perfected.

(e) TRANSFERRED CLAIM.

(1) Transfer of Claim Other Than for Security Before Proof Filed. If a claim has been transferred other than for security before proof of the claim has been filed, the proof of claim may be filed only by the transferee or an indenture trustee.

(2) Transfer of Claim Other Than for Security After Proof Filed. If a claim other than one based on a publicly traded note, bond, or debenture has been transferred other than for security after the proof of claim has been filed, evidence of the transfer shall be filed by the transferee. The clerk shall immediately notify the alleged transferor by mail of the filing of the evidence of transfer and that objection thereto, if any, must be filed within 20 days of the mailing of the notice or within any additional time allowed by the court. If the alleged transferor files a timely objection and the court finds, after notice and a hearing, that the claim has been transferred other than for security, it shall enter an order substituting the transferee for the transferor. If a timely objection is not filed by the alleged transferor, the transferee shall be substituted for the transferor.

(3) Transfer of Claim for Security Before Proof Filed. If a claim other than one based on a publicly traded note, bond, or debenture has been transferred for security before proof of the claim has been filed, the transferor or transferee or both may file a proof of claim for the full amount. The proof shall be supported by a statement setting forth the terms of the transfer. If either the transferor or the transferee files a proof of claim, the clerk shall immediately notify the other by mail of the right to join in the filed claim. If both transferor and transferee file proofs of the same claim, the proofs shall be consolidated. If the transferor or transferee does not file an agreement regarding its relative rights respecting voting of the claim, payment of dividends thereon, or participation in the administration of the estate, on motion by a party in interest and after notice and a hearing, the court shall enter such orders respecting these matters as may be appropriate.

(4) Transfer of Claim for Security After Proof Filed. If a claim other than one based on a publicly traded note, bond, or debenture has been transferred for security after the proof of claim has been filed, evidence of the terms of the transfer shall be filed by the transferee. The clerk shall immediately notify the alleged transferor by mail of the filing of the evidence of transfer and that objection thereto, if any, must be filed within 20 days of the mailing of the notice or within any additional time allowed by the court. If a timely objection is filed by the alleged transferor, the court, after notice and a hearing, shall determine whether the claim has been transferred for security. If the transferor or transferee does not file an agreement regarding its relative rights respecting voting of the claim, payment of dividends thereon, or participation in the administration of the estate, on motion by a party in interest and after notice and a hearing, the court shall enter such orders respecting these matters as may be appropriate.

(5) Service of Objection or Motion; Notice of Hearing. A copy of an objection filed pursuant to paragraph (2) or (4) or a motion filed pursuant to paragraph (3) or (4) of this subdivision together with a notice of a hearing shall be mailed or otherwise delivered to the transferor or transferee, whichever is appropriate, at least 30 days prior to the hearing.

(f) EVIDENTIARY EFFECT. A proof of claim executed and filed in accordance with these rules shall constitute prima facie evidence of the validity and amount of the claim.

(g) To the extent not inconsistent with the United States Warehouse Act or applicable State law, a warehouse receipt, scale ticket, or similar document of the type routinely issued as evidence of title by a grain storage facility, as defined in Section 557 of title 11, shall constitute prima facie evidence of the validity and amount of a claim of ownership of a quantity of grain.

Rule 3002. Filing Proof of Claim or Interest

(a) NECESSITY FOR FILING. An unsecured creditor or an equity security holder must file a proof of claim or interest in accordance with this rule for the claim or interest to be allowed, except as provided in Rules 1019(3), 3003, 3004 and 3005.

(b) PLACE OF FILING. A proof of claim or interest shall be filed in accordance with Rule 5005.

(c) TIME FOR FILING. In a chapter 7 liquidation, chapter 12 family farmer's debt adjustment, or chapter 13 individual's debt adjustment case, a proof of claim shall be filed within 90 days after the first date set for the meeting of creditors called pursuant to Section 341(a) of the Code, except as follows:

(1) On motion of the United States, a state, or subdivision thereof before the expiration of such period and for cause shown, the court may extend the time for filing of a claim by the United States, a state, or subdivision thereof.

(2) In the interest of justice and if it will not unduly delay the administration of the case, the court may extend the time for filing a proof of claim by an infant or incompetent person or the representative of either.

(3) An unsecured claim which arises in favor of an entity or becomes allowable as a result of a judgment may be filed within 30 days after the judgment becomes final if the judgment is for the recovery of money or property from that entity or denies or avoids the entity's interest in property. If the judgment imposes a liability which is not satisfied, or a duty which is not performed within such period or such further time as the court may permit, the claim shall not be allowed.

(4) A claim arising from the rejection of an executory contract or unexpired lease of the debtor may be filed within such time as the court may direct.

(5) If notice of insufficient assets to pay a dividend was given to creditors pursuant to Rule 2002(e), and subsequently the trustee notifies the court that payment of a dividend appears possible, the clerk shall notify the creditors of that fact and that they may file proofs of claim within 90 days after the mailing of the notice.

(6) In a chapter 7 liquidation case, if a surplus remains after all claims allowed have been paid in full, the court may grant an extension of time for the filing of claims against the surplus not filed within the time herein above prescribed.

Rule 3003. Filing Proof of Claim or Equity Security Interest in Chapter 9 Municipality or Chapter 11 Reorganization Cases

(a) APPLICABILITY OF RULE. This rule applies in chapter 9 and 11 cases.

(b) SCHEDULE OF LIABILITIES AND LIST OF EQUITY SECURITY HOLDERS.

(1) Schedule of Liabilities. The schedule of liabilities filed pursuant to Section 521(1) of the Code shall constitute prima facie evidence of the validity and amount of the claims of creditors, unless they are scheduled as disputed, contingent, or unliquidated. It shall not be necessary for a creditor or equity security holder to file a proof of claim or interest except as provided in subdivision (c)(2) of this rule.

(2) List of Equity Security Holders. The list of equity security holders filed pursuant to Rule 1007(a)(3) shall constitute prima facie evidence of the validity and amount of the equity security interests and it shall not be necessary for the holders of such interests to file a proof of interest.

(c) FILING PROOF OF CLAIM.

(1) Who May File. Any creditor or indenture trustee may file a proof of claim within the time prescribed by subdivision (c)(3) of this rule.

(2) Who Must File. Any creditor or equity security holder whose claim or interest is not scheduled or scheduled as disputed, contingent, or unliquidated shall file a proof of claim or interest within the time prescribed by subdivision (c)(3) of this rule; any creditor who fails to do so shall not be treated as a creditor with respect to such claim for the purposes of voting and distribution.

(3) Time for Filing. The court shall fix and for cause shown may extend the time within which proofs of claim or interest may be filed. Notwithstanding the expiration of such time, a proof of claim may be filed to the extent and under the conditions stated in Rule 3002(c)(2), (c)(3), and (c)(4).

(4) Effect of Filing Claim or Interest. A proof of claim or interest executed and filed in accordance with this subdivision shall supersede any scheduling of that claim or interest pursuant to Section 521(1) of the Code.

(5) Filing by Indenture Trustee. An indenture trustee may file a claim on behalf of all known or unknown holders of securities issued pursuant to the trust instrument under which it is trustee.

(d) PROOF OF RIGHT TO RECORD STATUS. For the purposes of Rules 3017, 3018 and 3021 and for receiving notices, an entity who is not the record holder of a security may file a statement setting forth facts which entitle that entity to be treated as the record holder. An objection to the statement may be filed by any party in interest.

Rule 3004. Filing of Claims by Debtor or Trustee

If a creditor fails to file a proof of claim on or before the first date set for the meeting of creditors called pursuant to Section 341(a) of the Code, the debtor or trustee may do so in the name of the creditor, within 30 days after expiration of the time for filing claims prescribed by Rule 3002(c) or 3003(c), whichever is applicable. The clerk shall forthwith mail notice of the filing to the creditor, the debtor and the trustee. A proof of claim filed by a creditor pursuant to Rule 3002 or Rule 3003(c), shall supersede the proof filed by the debtor or trustee.

Rule 3005. Filing of Claim, Acceptance, or Rejection by Guarantor, Surety, Indorser, or Other Codebtor

(a) FILING OF CLAIM. If a creditor has not filed a proof of claim pursuant to Rule 3002 or 3003(c), an entity that is or may be liable with the debtor to that creditor, or who has secured that creditor, may, within 30 days after the expiration of the time for filing claims prescribed by Rule 3002(c) or 3003(c) whichever is applicable, execute and file a proof of claim in the name of the creditor, if known, or if unknown, in the entity's own name. No distribution shall be made on the claim except on satisfactory proof that the original debt will be diminished by the amount of distribution. A proof of claim filed by a creditor pursuant to Rule 3002 or 3003(c) shall supersede the proof of claim filed pursuant to the first sentence of this subdivision.

(b) FILING OF ACCEPTANCE OR REJECTION; SUBSTITUTION OF CREDITOR. An entity which has filed a claim pursuant to the first sentence of subdivision (a) of this rule may file an acceptance or rejection of a plan in the name of the creditor, if known, or if unknown, in the entity's own name but if the creditor files a proof of claim within the time permitted by Rule 3003(c) or files a notice prior to confirmation of a plan of the creditor's intention to act in the creditor's own behalf, the creditor shall be substituted for the obligor with respect to that claim.

Rule 3006. Withdrawal of Claim; Effect on Acceptance or Rejection of Plan

A creditor may withdraw a claim as of right by filing a notice of withdrawal, except as provided in this rule. If after a creditor has filed a proof of claim an objection is filed thereto or a complaint is filed against that creditor in an adversary proceeding, or the creditor has accepted or rejected the plan or otherwise has participated significantly in the case, the creditor may not withdraw the claim except on order of the court after a hearing on notice to the trustee or debtor in possession, and any creditors' committee elected pursuant to Section 705(a) or appointed pursuant to Section 1102 of the Code. The order of the court shall contain such terms and conditions as the court deems proper. Unless the court orders otherwise, an authorized withdrawal of a claim shall constitute withdrawal of any related acceptance or rejection of a plan.

Rule 3007. Objections to Claims

An objection to the allowance of a claim shall be in writing and filed. A copy of the objection with notice of the hearing thereon shall be mailed or otherwise delivered to the claimant, the debtor or debtor in possession and the trustee at least 30 days prior to the hearing. If an objection to a claim is joined with a demand for relief of the kind specified in Rule 7001, it becomes an adversary proceeding.

Rule 3008. Reconsideration of Claims

A party in interest may move for reconsideration of an order allowing or disallowing a claim against the estate. The court after a hearing on notice shall enter an appropriate order.

Rule 3009. Declaration and Payment of Dividends in Chapter 7 Liquidation Cases

In chapter 7 cases, dividends to creditors shall be paid as promptly as practicable in the amounts and at times as ordered by the court. Dividend checks shall be made payable and mailed to each creditor whose claim has been allowed, unless a power of attorney authorizing another entity to receive dividends has been executed and filed in accordance with Rule 9010. In that event, dividend checks shall be made payable to the creditor and to the other entity and shall be mailed to the other entity.

Rule 3010. Small Dividends and Payments in Chapter 7 Liquidation, Chapter 12 Family Farmer's Debt Adjustment, and Chapter 13 Individual's Debt Adjustment Cases

(a) CHAPTER 7 CASES. In a chapter 7 case no dividend in an amount less than $5 shall be distributed by the trustee to any creditor unless authorized by local rule or order of the court. Any dividend not distributed to a creditor shall be treated in the same manner as unclaimed funds as provided in Section 347 of the Code.

(b) CHAPTER 12 AND CHAPTER 13 CASES. In a chapter 12 or chapter 13 case no payment in an amount less than $15 shall be distributed by the trustee to any creditor unless authorized by local rule or order of the court. Funds not distributed because of this subdivision shall accumulate and shall be paid whenever the accumulation aggregates $15. Any funds remaining shall be distributed with the final payment.

Rule 3011. Unclaimed Funds in Chapter 7 Liquidation, Chapter 12 Family Farmer's Debt Adjustment, and Chapter 13 Individual's Debt Adjustment Cases

The trustee shall file a list of all known names and addresses of the entities and the amounts which they are entitled to be paid from remaining property of the estate that is paid into court pursuant to Section 347(a) of the Code.

Rule 3012. Valuation of Security

The court may determine the value of a claim secured by a lien on property in which the estate has an interest on motion of any party in interest and after a hearing on notice to the holder of the secured claim and any other entity as the court may direct.

Rule 3013. Classification of Claims and Interests

For the purposes of the plan and its acceptance, the court may, on motion after hearing on notice as the court may direct, determine classes of creditors and equity security holders pursuant to Sections 1122, 1222(b)(1), and 1322(b)(1) of the Code.

Rule 3014. Election Pursuant to Section 1111(b) by Secured Creditor in Chapter 9 Municipality and Chapter 11 Reorganization Cases

An election of application of Section 1111(b)(2) of the Code by a class of secured creditors in a chapter 9 or 11 case may be made at any time prior to the conclusion of the hearing on the disclosure statement or within such later time as the court may fix. The election shall be in writing and signed unless made at the hearing on the disclosure statement. The election, if made by the majorities required by Section 1111(b)(1)(A)(i), shall be binding on all members of the class with respect to the plan.

Rule 3015. Filing of Plan in Chapter 12 Family Farmer's Debt Adjustment and Chapter 13 Individual's Debt Adjustment Cases

(a) CHAPTER 12 PLAN. The debtor may file a chapter 12 plan with the petition. If a plan is not filed with the petition, it shall be filed within the time prescribed by Section 1221 of the Code.

(b) CHAPTER 13 PLAN. The debtor may file a chapter 13 plan with the petition. If a plan is not filed with the petition, it shall be filed within 15 days thereafter, and such time shall not be further extended except for cause shown and on notice as the court may direct.

(c) DATING. Every proposed plan and any modification thereof shall be dated.

(d) NOTICE AND COPIES. The plan or a summary of the plan shall be included with each notice of the hearing on confirmation mailed pursuant to Rule 2002(b). If required by the court, the debtor shall furnish a sufficient number of copies to enable the clerk to include a copy of the plan with the notice of the hearing.

(e) TRANSMISSION TO UNITED STATES TRUSTEE. The clerk shall forthwith transmit to the United States trustee a copy of the plan and any modification thereof filed pursuant to subdivision (a) or (b) of this rule.

Rule 3016. Filing of Plan and Disclosure Statement in Chapter 9 Municipality and Chapter 11 Reorganization Cases

(a) TIME FOR FILING PLAN. A party in interest, other than the debtor, who is authorized to file a plan under Section 1121(c) of the Code may not file a plan after entry of an order approving a disclosure statement unless confirmation of the plan relating to the disclosure statement has been denied or the court otherwise directs.

(b) IDENTIFICATION OF PLAN. Every proposed plan and any modification thereof shall be dated and, in a chapter 11 case, identified with the name of the entity or entities submitting or filing it.

(c) DISCLOSURE STATEMENT. In a chapter 9 or 11 case, a disclosure statement pursuant to Section 1125 or evidence showing compliance with Section 1126(b) of the Code shall be filed with the plan or within a time fixed by the court.

Rule 3017. Court Consideration of Disclosure Statement in Chapter 9 Municipality and Chapter 11 Reorganization Cases

(a) HEARING ON DISCLOSURE STATEMENT AND OBJECTIONS THERETO. Following the filing of a disclosure statement as provided in Rule 3016(c), the court shall hold a hearing on not less than 25 days notice to the debtor, creditors, equity security holders and other parties in interest as provided in Rule 2002 to consider such statement and any objections or modifications thereto. The plan and the disclosure statement shall be mailed with the notice of the hearing only to the debtor, any trustee or committee appointed under the Code, the Securities and Exchange Commission and any party in interest who requests in writing a copy of the statement or plan. Objections to the disclosure statement shall be filed and served on the debtor, the trustee, any committee appointed under the Code and such other entity as may be designated by the court, at any time prior to approval of the disclosure statement or by such earlier date as the court may fix. In a chapter 11 reorganization case, every notice, plan, disclosure statement, and objection required to be served or mailed pursuant to this subdivision shall be transmitted to the United States trustee within the time provided in this subdivision.

(b) DETERMINATION ON DISCLOSURE STATEMENT. Following the hearing the court shall determine whether the disclosure statement should be approved.

(c) DATES FIXED FOR VOTING ON PLAN AND CONFIRMATION. On or before approval of the disclosure statement, the court shall fix a time within which the holders of claims and interests may accept or reject the plan and may fix a date for the hearing on confirmation.

(d) TRANSMISSION AND NOTICE TO UNITED STATES TRUSTEE, CREDITORS AND EQUITY SECURITY HOLDERS. On approval of a disclosure statement, unless the court orders otherwise with respect to one or more unimpaired classes of creditors or equity security holders, the debtor in possession, trustee, proponent of the plan, or clerk as ordered by the court shall mail to all creditors and equity security holders, and in a chapter 11 reorganization case shall transmit to the United States trustee, (1) the plan, or a court approved summary of the plan; (2) the disclosure statement approved by the court; (3) notice of the time within which acceptances and rejections of such plan may be filed; and (4) such other information as the court may direct including any opinion of the court approving the disclosure statement or a court approved summary of the opinion. In addition, notice of the time fixed for filing objections and the hearing on confirmation shall be mailed to all creditors and equity security holders pursuant to Rule 2002(b), and a form of ballot conforming to the appropriate Official Form shall be mailed to creditors and equity security holders entitled to vote on the plan. In the event the opinion of the court is not transmitted or only a summary of the plan is transmitted, the opinion of the court or the plan shall be provided on request of a party in interest at the expense of the proponent of the plan. If the court orders that the disclosure statement and the plan or a summary of the plan shall not be mailed to any unimpaired class, notice that the class is designated in the plan as unimpaired and notice of the name and address of the person from whom the plan or summary of the plan and disclosure statement may be obtained upon request and at the expense of the proponent of the plan, shall be mailed to members of the unimpaired class together with the notice of the time fixed for filing objections to and the hearing on confirmation. For the purposes of this subdivision, creditors and equity security holders shall include holders of stock, bonds, debentures, notes, and other securities of record at the date the order approving the disclosure statement was entered.

(e) TRANSMISSION TO BENEFICIAL HOLDERS OF SECURITIES. At the hearing held pursuant to subdivision (a) of this rule the court shall consider the procedures for transmitting the documents and information required by subdivision (d) of this rule to beneficial holders of stock, bonds, debentures, notes, and other securities and determine the adequacy of such procedures and enter such orders as the court deems appropriate.

Rule 3018. Acceptance or Rejection of Plans

(a) ENTITIES ENTITLED TO ACCEPT OR REJECT PLAN; TIME FOR ACCEPTANCE OR REJECTION. A plan may be accepted or rejected in accordance with Section 1126 of the Code within the time fixed by the court pursuant to Rule 3017. Subject to subdivision (b) of this rule, an equity security holder or creditor whose claim is based on a security of record shall not be entitled to accept or reject a plan unless the equity security holder or creditor is the holder of record of the security on the date the order approving the disclosure statement is entered. For cause shown, the court after notice and hearing may permit a creditor or equity security holder to change or withdraw an acceptance or rejection. Notwithstanding objection to a claim or interest, the court after notice and hearing may temporarily allow the claim or interest in an amount which the court deems proper for the purpose of accepting or rejecting a plan.

(b) ACCEPTANCES OR REJECTIONS OBTAINED BEFORE PETITION. An equity security holder or creditor whose claim is based on a security of record who accepted or rejected the plan before the commencement of the case shall not be deemed to have accepted or rejected the plan pursuant to Section 1126(b) of the Code unless the equity security holder or creditor was the holder of record of the security on the date specified in the solicitation of such acceptance or rejection for the purposes of such solicitation. A holder of a claim or interest who has accepted or rejected a plan before the commencement of the case under the Code shall not be deemed to have accepted or rejected the plan if the court finds after notice and hearing that the plan was not transmitted to substantially all creditors and equity security holders of the same class, that an unreasonably short time was prescribed for such creditors and equity security holders to accept or reject the plan, or that the solicitation was not in compliance with Section 1126(b) of the Code.

(c) FORM OF ACCEPTANCE OR REJECTION. An acceptance or rejection shall be in writing, identify the plan or plans accepted or rejected, be signed by the creditor or equity security holder or an authorized agent, and conform to the appropriate Official Form. If more than one plan is transmitted pursuant to Rule 3017, an acceptance or rejection may be filed by each creditor or equity security holder for any number of plans transmitted and if acceptances are filed for more than one plan, the creditor or equity security holder may indicate a preference or preferences among the plans so accepted.

(d) ACCEPTANCE OR REJECTION BY PARTIALLY SECURED CREDITOR. A creditor whose claim has been allowed in part as a secured claim and in part as an unsecured claim shall be entitled to accept or reject a plan in both capacities.

Rule 3019. Modification of Accepted Plan Before Confirmation

After a plan has been accepted and before its confirmation, the proponent may file a modification of the plan. If the court finds after hearing on notice to the trustee, any committee appointed under the Code and any other entity designated by the court that the proposed modification does not adversely change the treatment of the claim of any creditor or the interest of any equity security holder who has not accepted in writing the modification, it shall be deemed accepted by all creditors and equity security holders who have previously accepted the plan.

Rule 3020. Deposit; Confirmation of Plan

(a) DEPOSIT. In a chapter 11 case, prior to entry of the order confirming the plan, the court may order the deposit with the trustee or debtor in possession of the consideration required by the plan to be distributed on confirmation. Any money deposited shall be kept in a special account established for the exclusive purpose of making the distribution.

(b) OBJECTIONS TO AND HEARING ON CONFIRMATION.

(1) Objections. Objections to confirmation of the plan shall be filed and served on the debtor, the trustee, the proponent of the plan, any committee appointed under the Code and on any other entity designated by the court, within a time fixed by the court. Unless the case is a chapter 9 municipality case, a copy of every objection to confirmation shall be transmitted by the objecting party to the United States trustee within the time fixed for the filing of objections. An objection to confirmation is governed by Rule 9014.

(2) Hearing. The court shall rule on confirmation of the plan after notice and hearing as provided in Rule 2002. If no objection is timely filed, the court may determine that the plan has been proposed in good faith and not by any means forbidden by law without receiving evidence on such issues.

(c) ORDER OF CONFIRMATION. The order of confirmation shall conform to the appropriate Official Form and notice of entry thereof shall be mailed promptly as provided in Rule 2002(f) to the debtor, the trustee, creditors, equity security holders and other parties in interest. Except in a chapter 9 municipality case, notice of entry of the order of confirmation shall be transmitted to the United States trustee as provided in Rule 2002(k).

(d) RETAINED POWER. Notwithstanding the entry of the order of confirmation, the court may enter all orders necessary to administer the estate.

Rule 3021. Distribution Under Plan

After confirmation of a plan, distribution shall be made to creditors whose claims have been allowed, to holders of stock, bonds, debentures, notes, and other securities of record at the time of commencement of distribution whose claims or equity security interests have not been disallowed and to indenture trustees who have filed claims pursuant to Rule 3003(c)(5) and which have been allowed.

Rule 3022. Final Decree in Chapter 11 Reorganization Case

After an estate is fully administered in a chapter 11 reorganization case, the court, on its own motion or on motion of a party in interest, shall enter a final decree closing the case.

PART IV

THE DEBTOR: DUTIES AND BENEFITS

Rule 4001. Relief from Automatic Stay; Prohibiting or Conditioning the Use, Sale, or Lease of Property; Use of Cash Collateral; Obtaining Credit; Agreements

(a) RELIEF FROM STAY; PROHIBITING OR CONDITIONING THE USE, SALE, OR LEASE OF PROPERTY.

(1) Motion. A motion for relief from an automatic stay provided by the Code or a motion to prohibit or condition the use, sale, or lease of property pursuant to Section 363(e) shall be made in accordance with Rule 9014 and shall be served on any committee elected pursuant to Section 705 or appointed pursuant to Section 1102 of the Code or its authorized agent, or, if the case in a chapter 9 municipality case or a chapter 11 reorganization case and no committee of unsecured creditors has been appointed pursuant to Section 1102, on the creditors included on the list filed pursuant to Rule 1007(d), and on such other entities as the court may direct.

(2) Ex Parte Relief. Relief from a stay under Section 362(a) or a request to prohibit or condition the use, sale, or lease of property pursuant to Section 363(e) may be granted without prior notice only if (A) it clearly appears from specific facts shown by affidavit or by a verified motion that immediate and irreparable injury, loss, or damage will result to the movant before the adverse party or the attorney for the adverse party can be heard in opposition, and (B) the movant's attorney certifies to the court in writing the efforts, if any, which have been made to give notice and the reasons why notice should not be required. The party obtaining relief under this subdivision and Section 362(f) or Section 363(e) shall immediately give oral notice thereof to the trustee or debtor in possession and to the debtor and forthwith mail or otherwise transmit to such adverse party or parties a copy of the order granting relief. On two days notice to the party who obtained relief from the stay without notice or on shorter notice to that party as the court may prescribe, the adverse party may appear and move reinstatement of the stay or reconsideration of the order prohibiting or conditioning the use, sale, or lease of property. In that event, the court shall proceed expeditiously to hear and determine the motion.

(b) USE OF CASH COLLATERAL.

(1) Motion; Service. A motion for authorization to use cash collateral shall be made in accordance with Rule 9014 and shall be served on any entity which has an interest in the cash collateral, on any committee elected pursuant to Section 705 or appointed pursuant to Section 1102 of the Code or its authorized agent, or, if the case is a chapter 9 municipality case or a chapter 11 reorganization case and no committee of unsecured creditors has been appointed pursuant to Section 1102, on the creditors included on the list filed pursuant to Rule 1007(d), and on such other entities as the court may direct.

(2) Hearing. The court may commence a final hearing on a motion for authorization to use cash collateral no earlier than 15 days after service of the motion. If the motion so requests, the court may conduct a preliminary hearing before such 15 day period expires, but the court may authorize the use of only that amount of cash collateral as is necessary to avoid immediate and irreparable harm to the estate pending a final hearing.

(3) Notice. Notice of hearing pursuant to this subdivision shall be given to the parties on whom service of the motion is required by paragraph (1) of this subdivision and to such other entities as the court may direct.

(c) OBTAINING CREDIT.

(1) Motion; Service. A motion for authority to obtain credit shall be made in accordance with Rule 9014 and shall be served on any committee elected pursuant to Section 705 or appointed pursuant to Section 1102 of the Code or its authorized agent, or, if the case is a chapter 9 municipality case or a chapter 11 reorganization case and no committee of unsecured creditors has been appointed pursuant to Section 1102, on the creditors included on the list filed pursuant to Rule 1007(d), and on such other entities as the court may direct. The motion shall be accompanied by a copy of the agreement.

(2) Hearing. The court may commence a final hearing on a motion for authority to obtain credit no earlier than 15 days after service of the motion. If the motion so requests, the court may conduct a hearing before such 15 day period expires, but the court may authorize the obtaining of credit only to the extent necessary to avoid immediate and irreparable harm to the estate pending a final hearing.

(3) Notice. Notice of hearing pursuant to this subdivision shall be given to the parties on whom service of the motion is required by paragraph (1) of this subdivision and to such other entities as the court may direct.

(d) AGREEMENT RELATING TO RELIEF FROM THE AUTOMATIC STAY, PROHIBITING OR CONDITIONING THE USE, SALE, OR LEASE OF PROPERTY, PROVIDING ADEQUATE PROTECTION, USE OF CASH COLLATERAL, AND OBTAINING CREDIT.

(1) Motion; Service. A motion for approval of an agreement (A) to provide adequate protection, (B) to prohibit or condition the use, sale, or lease of property, (C) to modify or terminate the stay provided for in Section 362, (D) to use cash collateral, or (E) between the debtor and an entity that has a lien or interest in property of the estate pursuant to which the entity consents to the creation of a lien senior or equal to the entity's lien or interest in such property shall be served on any committee elected pursuant to Section 705 or appointed pursuant to Section 1102 of the Code or its authorized agent, or, if the case is a chapter 9 municipality case or a chapter 11 reorganization case and no committee of unsecured creditors has been appointed pursuant to Section 1102, on the creditors included on the list filed pursuant to Rule 1007(d), and on such other entities as the court may direct. The motion shall be accompanied by a copy of the agreement.

(2) Objection. Notice of the motion and the time within which objections may be filed and served on the debtor in possession or trustee shall be mailed to the parties on whom service is required by paragraph (1) of this subdivision and to such other entities as the court may direct. Unless the court fixes a different time, objections may be filed within 15 days of the mailing of notice.

(3) Disposition; Hearing. If no objection is filed, the court may enter an order approving or disapproving the agreement without conducting a hearing. If an objection is filed or if the court determines a hearing is appropriate, the court shall hold a hearing on no less than five days' notice to the objector, the movant, the parties on whom service is required by paragraph (1) of this subdivision and such other entities as the court may direct.

(4) Agreement in Settlement of Motion. The court may direct that the procedures prescribed in paragraphs (1), (2), and (3) of this subdivision shall not apply and the agreement may be approved without further notice if the court determines that a motion made pursuant to subdivisions (a), (b), or (c) of this rule was sufficient to afford reasonable notice of the material provisions of the agreement and opportunity for a hearing.

Rule 4002. Duties of Debtor

In addition to performing other duties prescribed by the Code and rules, the debtor shall (1) attend and submit to an examination at the times ordered by the court; (2) attend the hearing on a complaint objecting to discharge and testify, if called as a witness; (3) inform the trustee immediately in writing as to the location of real property in which the debtor has an interest and the name and address of every person holding money or property subject to the debtor's withdrawal or order if a schedule of property has not yet been filed pursuant to Rule 1007; (4) cooperate with the trustee in the preparation of an inventory, the examination of proofs of claim, and the administration of the estate, and (5) file a statement of any change of the debtor's address.

Rule 4003. Exemptions

(a) CLAIM OF EXEMPTIONS. A debtor shall list the property claimed as exempt under Section 522 of the Code on the schedule of assets required to be filed by Rule 1007. If the debtor fails to claim exemptions or file the schedule within the time specified in Rule 1007, a dependent of the debtor may file the list within 30 days thereafter.

(b) OBJECTIONS TO CLAIM OF EXEMPTIONS. The trustee or any creditor may file objections to the list of property claimed as exempt within 30 days after the conclusion of the meeting of creditors held pursuant to Rule 2003(a) or the filing of any amendment to the list or supplemental schedules unless, within such period, further time is granted by the court. Copies of the objections shall be delivered or mailed to the trustee and to the person filing the list and the attorney for such person.

(c) BURDEN OF PROOF. In any hearing under this rule, the objecting party has the burden of proving that the exemptions are not properly claimed. After hearing on notice, the court shall determine the issues presented by the objections.

(d) AVOIDANCE BY DEBTOR OF TRANSFERS OF EXEMPT PROPERTY. A proceeding by the debtor to avoid a lien or other transfer of property exempt under Section 522(f) of the Code shall be by motion in accordance with Rule 9014.

Rule 4004. Grant Or Denial of Discharge

(a) TIME FOR FILING COMPLAINT OBJECTING TO DISCHARGE; NOTICE OF TIME FIXED. In a chapter 7 liquidation case a complaint objecting to the debtor's discharge under Section 727(a) of the Code shall be filed not later than 60 days following the first date set for the meeting of creditors held pursuant to Section 341(a). In a chapter 11 reorganization case, such complaint shall be filed not later than the first date set for the hearing on confirmation. Not less than 25 days notice of the time so fixed shall be given to the United States trustee and all creditors as provided in Rule 2002(f) and (k) and to the trustee and the trustee's attorney.

(b) EXTENSION OF TIME. On motion of any party in interest, after hearing on notice, the court may extend for cause the time for filing a complaint objecting to discharge. The motion shall be made before such time has expired.

(c) GRANT OF DISCHARGE. In a chapter 7 case, on expiration of the time fixed for filing a complaint objecting to discharge and the time fixed for filing a motion to dismiss the case pursuant to Rule 1017(e), the court shall forthwith grant the discharge unless (1) the debtor is not an individual, (2) a complaint objecting to the discharge has been filed, (3) the debtor has filed a waiver under Section 727(a)(10), or (4) a motion to dismiss the case under Rule 1017(e) is pending. Notwithstanding the foregoing, on motion of the debtor, the court may defer the entry of an order granting a discharge for 30 days and, on motion within such period, the court may defer entry of the order to a date certain.

(d) APPLICABILITY OF RULES IN PART VII. A proceeding commenced by a complaint objecting to discharge is governed by Part VII of these rules.

(e) ORDER OF DISCHARGE. An order of discharge shall conform to the appropriate Official Form.

(f) REGISTRATION IN OTHER DISTRICTS. An order of discharge that has become final may be registered in any other district by filing a certified copy of the order in the office of the clerk of that district. When so registered the order of discharge shall have the same effect as an order of the court of the district where registered.

(g) NOTICE OF DISCHARGE. The clerk shall promptly mail a copy of the final order of discharge to those specified in subdivision (a) of this rule.

Rule 4005. Burden of Proof in Objecting to Discharge

At the trial on a complaint objecting to a discharge, the plaintiff has the burden of proving the objection.

Rule 4006. Notice of No Discharge

If an order is entered denying or revoking a discharge or if a waiver of discharge is filed, the clerk, after the order becomes final or the waiver is filed, shall promptly give notice thereof to all creditors in the manner provided in Rule 2002.

Rule 4007. Determination of Dischargeability of a Debt

(a) PERSONS ENTITLED TO FILE COMPLAINT. A debtor or any creditor may file a complaint to obtain a determination of the dischargeability of any debt.

(b) TIME FOR COMMENCING PROCEEDING OTHER THAN UNDER SECTION 523(c) OF THE CODE. A complaint other than under Section 523(c) may be filed at any time. A case may be reopened without payment of any additional filing fee for the purpose of filing a complaint to obtain a determination under this rule.

(c) TIME FOR FILING COMPLAINT UNDER SECTION 523(c) IN CHAPTER 7 LIQUIDATION, CHAPTER 11 REORGANIZATION, AND CHAPTER 12 FAMILY FARMER'S DEBT ADJUSTMENT CASES; NOTICE OF TIME FIXED. A complaint to determine the dischargeability of any debt pursuant to Section 523(c) of the Code shall be filed not later than 60 days following the first date set for the meeting of creditors held pursuant to Section 341(a). The court shall give all creditors not less than 30 days notice of the time so fixed in the manner provided in Rule 2002. On motion of any party in interest, after hearing on notice, the court may for cause extend the time fixed under this subdivision. The motion shall be made before the time has expired.

(d) TIME FOR FILING COMPLAINT UNDER SECTION 523(c) IN CHAPTER 13 INDIVIDUAL'S DEBT ADJUSTMENT CASES; NOTICE OF TIME FIXED. On motion by a debtor for a discharge under Section 1328(b), the court shall enter an order fixing a time for the filing of a complaint to determine the dischargeability of any debt pursuant to Section 523(c) and shall give not less than 30 days notice of the time fixed to all creditors in the manner provided in Rule 2002. On motion of any party in interest after hearing on notice the court may for cause extend the time fixed under this subdivision. The motion shall be made before the time has expired.

(e) APPLICABILITY OF RULES IN PART VII. A proceeding commenced by a complaint filed under this rule is governed by Part VII of these rules.

Rule 4008. Discharge and Reaffirmation Hearing

Not more than 30 days following the entry of an order granting or denying a discharge, or confirming a plan in a chapter 11 reorganization case concerning an individual debtor and on not less than 10 days notice to the debtor and the trustee, the court may hold a hearing as provided in Section 524(d) of the Code. A motion by the debtor for approval of a reaffirmation agreement shall be filed before or at the hearing.

PART V

COURTS AND CLERKS

Rule 5001. Courts and Clerks' Offices

(a) COURTS ALWAYS OPEN. The courts shall be deemed always open for the purpose of filing any pleading or other proper paper, issuing and returning process, and filing, making, or entering motions, orders and rules.

(b) TRIALS AND HEARINGS; ORDERS IN CHAMBERS. All trials and hearings shall be conducted in open court and so far as convenient in a regular court room. All other acts or proceedings may be done or conducted by a judge in chambers and at any place either within or without the district; but no hearing, other than one ex parte, shall be conducted outside the district without the consent of all parties affected thereby.

(c) CLERK'S OFFICE. The clerk's office with the clerk or a deputy in attendance shall be open during business hours on all days except Saturdays, Sundays and the legal holidays listed in Rule 9006(a).

Rule 5002. Restrictions on Approval of Appointments

(a) APPROVAL OF APPOINTMENT OF RELATIVES PROHIBITED. The appointment of an individual as a trustee or examiner pursuant to Section 1104 of the Code shall not be approved by the court if the individual is a relative of the bankruptcy judge approving the appointment or the United States trustee in the region in which the case is pending. The employment of an individual as an attorney, accountant, appraiser, auctioneer, or other professional person pursuant to Sections 327, 1103, or 1114 shall not be approved by the court if the individual is a relative of the bankruptcy judge approving the employment. The employment of an individual as attorney, accountant, appraiser, auctioneer, or other professional person pursuant to Sections 327, 1103, or 1114 may be approved by the court if the individual is a relative of the United States trustee in the region in which the case is pending, unless the court finds that the relationship with the United States trustee renders the employment improper under the circumstances of the case. Whenever under this subdivision an individual may not be approved for appointment or employment, the individual's firm, partnership, corporation, or any other form of business association or relationship, and all members, associates and professional employees thereof also may not be approved for appointment or employment.

(b) JUDICIAL DETERMINATION THAT APPROVAL OF APPOINTMENT OR EMPLOYMENT IS IMPROPER. A bankruptcy judge may not approve the appointment of a person as a trustee or examiner pursuant to Section 1104 of the Code or approve the employment of a person as an attorney, accountant, appraiser, auctioneer, or other professional person pursuant to Sections 327, 1103, or 1114 of the Code if that person is or has been so connected with such judge or the United States trustee as to render the appointment or employment improper.

Rule 5003. Records Kept By the Clerk

(a) BANKRUPTCY DOCKETS. The clerk shall keep a docket in each case under the Code and shall enter thereon each judgment, order, and activity in that case as prescribed by the Director of the Administrative Office of the United States Courts. The entry of a judgment or order in a docket shall show the date the entry is made.

(b) CLAIMS REGISTER. The clerk shall keep in a claims register a list of claims filed in a case when it appears that there will be a distribution to unsecured creditors.

(c) JUDGMENTS AND ORDERS. The clerk shall keep, in the form and manner as the Director of the Administrative Office of the United States Courts may prescribe, a correct copy of every final judgment or order affecting title to or lien on real property or for the recovery of money or property, and any other order which the court may direct to be kept. On request of the prevailing party, a correct copy of every judgment or order affecting title to or lien upon real or personal property or for the recovery of money or property shall be kept and indexed with the civil judgments of the district court.

(d) INDEX OF CASES; CERTIFICATE OF SEARCH. The clerk shall keep indices of all cases and adversary proceedings as prescribed by the Director of the Administrative Office of the United States Courts. On request, the clerk shall make a search of any index and papers in the clerk's custody and certify whether a case or proceeding has been filed in or transferred to the court or if a discharge has been entered in its records.

(e) OTHER BOOKS AND RECORDS OF THE CLERK. The clerk shall also keep such other books and records as may be required by the Director of the Administrative Office of the United States Courts.

Rule 5004. Disqualification

(a) DISQUALIFICATION OF JUDGE. A bankruptcy judge shall be governed by 28 U. S. C. Section 455, and disqualified from presiding over the proceeding or contested matter in which the disqualifying circumstance arises or, if appropriate, shall be disqualified from presiding over the case.

(b) DISQUALIFICATION OF JUDGE FROM ALLOWING COMPENSATION. A bankruptcy judge shall be disqualified from allowing compensation to a person who is a relative of the bankruptcy judge or with whom the judge is so connected as to render it improper for the judge to authorize such compensation.

Rule 5005. Filing and Transmittal of Papers

(a) FILING. The lists, schedules, statements, proofs of claim or interest, complaints, motions, applications, objections and other papers required to be filed by these rules, except as provided in 28 U. S. C. Section 1409, shall be filed with the clerk in the district where the case under the Code is pending. The judge of that court may permit the papers to be filed with the judge, in which event the filing date shall be noted thereon, and they shall be forthwith transmitted to the clerk.

(b) TRANSMITTAL TO THE UNITED STATES TRUSTEE.

(1) The complaints, motions, applications, objections and other papers required to be transmitted to the United States trustee by these rules shall be mailed or delivered to an office of the United States trustee, or to another place designated by the United States trustee, in the district where the case under the Code is pending.

(2) The entity, other than the clerk, transmitting a paper to the United States trustee shall promptly file as proof of such transmittal a verified statement identifying the paper and stating the date on which it was transmitted to the United States trustee.

(3) Nothing in these rules shall require the clerk to transmit any paper to the United States trustee if the United States trustee requests in writing that the paper not be transmitted.

(c) ERROR IN FILING OR TRANSMITTAL. A paper intended to be filed with the clerk but erroneously delivered to the United States trustee, the trustee, the attorney for the trustee, a bankruptcy judge, a district judge, or the clerk of the district court shall, after the date of its receipt has been noted thereon, be transmitted forthwith to the clerk of the bankruptcy court. A paper intended to be transmitted to the United States trustee but erroneously delivered to the clerk, the trustee, the attorney for the trustee, a bankruptcy judge, or the clerk of the district court shall, after the date of its receipt has been noted thereon, be transmitted forthwith to the United States trustee. In the interest of justice, the court may order that a paper erroneously delivered shall be deemed filed with the clerk or transmitted to the United States trustee as of the date of its original delivery.

Rule 5006. Certification of Copies of Papers

The clerk shall issue a certified copy of the record of any proceeding in a case under the Code or of any paper filed with the clerk on payment of any prescribed fee.

Rule 5007. Record of Proceedings and Transcripts

(a) FILING OF RECORD OR TRANSCRIPT. The reporter or operator of a recording device shall certify the original notes of testimony, tape recording, or other original record of the proceeding and promptly file them with the clerk. The person preparing any transcript shall promptly file a certified copy.

(b) TRANSCRIPT FEES. The fees for copies of transcripts shall be charged at rates prescribed by the Judicial Conference of the United States. No fee may be charged for the certified copy filed with the clerk.

(c) ADMISSIBILITY OF RECORD IN EVIDENCE. A certified sound recording or a transcript of a proceeding shall be admissible as prima facie evidence to establish the record.

Rule 5008. [Abrogated]

Rule 5009. Closing Chapter 7 Liquidation, Chapter 12 Family Farmer's Debt Adjustment, and Chapter 13 Individual's Debt Adjustment Cases

If in a chapter 7, chapter 12, or chapter 13 case the trustee has filed a final report and final account and has certified that the estate has been fully administered, and if within 30 days no objection has been filed by the United States trustee or a party in interest, there shall be a presumption that the estate has been fully administered.

Rule 5010. Reopening Cases

A case may be reopened on motion of the debtor or other party in interest pursuant to Section 350(b) of the Code. In a chapter 7, 12, or 13 case a trustee shall not be appointed by the United States trustee unless the court determines that a trustee is necessary to protect the interests of creditors and the debtor or to insure efficient administration of the case.

Rule 5011. Withdrawal and Abstention from Hearing a Proceeding

(a) WITHDRAWAL. A motion for withdrawal of a case or proceeding shall be heard by a district judge.

(b) ABSTENTION FROM HEARING A PROCEEDING. A motion for abstention pursuant to 28 U. S. C. Section 1334(c) shall be governed by Rule 9014 and shall be served on the parties to the proceeding.

(c) EFFECT OF FILING OF MOTION FOR WITHDRAWAL OR ABSTENTION. The filing of a motion for withdrawal of a case or proceeding or for abstention pursuant to 28 U. S. C. Section 1334(c) shall not stay the administration of the case or any proceeding therein before the bankruptcy judge except that the bankruptcy judge may stay, on such terms and conditions as are proper, proceedings pending disposition of the motion. A motion for a stay ordinarily shall be presented first to the bankruptcy judge. A motion for a stay or relief from a stay filed in the district court shall state why it has not been presented to or obtained from the bankruptcy judge. Relief granted by the district judge shall be on such terms and conditions as the judge deems proper.

PART VI

COLLECTION AND LIQUIDATION OF THE ESTATE

Rule 6001. Burden of Proof As to Validity of Postpetition Transfer

Any entity asserting the validity of a transfer under Section 549 of the Code shall have the burden of proof.

Rule 6002. Accounting by Prior Custodian of Property of the Estate

(a) ACCOUNTING REQUIRED. Any custodian required by the Code to deliver property in the custodian's possession or control to the trustee shall promptly file and transmit to the United States trustee a report and account with respect to the property of the estate and the administration thereof.

(b) EXAMINATION OF ADMINISTRATION. On the filing and transmittal of the report and account required by subdivision (a) of this rule and after an examination has been made into the superseded administration, after hearing on notice the court shall determine the propriety of the administration, including the reasonableness of all disbursements.

Rule 6003. [Abrogated]

Rule 6004. Use, Sale, or Lease of Property

(a) NOTICE OF PROPOSED USE, SALE, OR LEASE OF PROPERTY. Notice of a proposed use, sale, or lease of property, other than cash collateral, not in the ordinary course of business shall be given pursuant to Rule 2002(a)(2), (c)(1), (i), and (k) and, if applicable, in accordance with Section 363(b)(2) of the Code.

(b) OBJECTION TO PROPOSAL. Except as provided in subdivisions (c) and (d) of this rule, an objection to a proposed use, sale, or lease of property shall be filed and served not less than five days before the date set for the proposed action or within the time fixed by the court. An objection to the proposed use, sale, or lease of property is governed by Rule 9014.

(c) SALE FREE AND CLEAR OF LIENS AND OTHER INTERESTS. A motion for authority to sell property free and clear of liens or other interests shall be made in accordance with Rule 9014 and shall be served on the parties who have liens or other interests in the property to be sold. The notice required by subdivision (a) of this rule shall include the date of the hearing on the motion and the time within which objections may be filed and served on the debtor in possession or trustee.

(d) SALE OF PROPERTY UNDER $2,500. Notwithstanding subdivision (a) of this rule, when all of the nonexempt property of the estate has an aggregate gross value less than $2,500, it shall be sufficient to give a general notice of intent to sell such property other than in the ordinary course of business to all creditors, indenture trustees, committees appointed or elected pursuant to the Code, the United States trustee and other persons as the court may direct. An objection to any such sale may be filed and served by a party in interest within 15 days of the mailing of the notice, or within the time fixed by the court. An objection is governed by Rule 9014.

(e) HEARING. If a timely objection is made pursuant to subdivision (b) or (d) of this rule, the date of the hearing thereon may be set in the notice given pursuant to subdivision (a) of this rule.

(f) CONDUCT OF SALE NOT IN THE ORDINARY COURSE OF BUSINESS.

(1) Public or Private Sale. All sales not in the ordinary course of business may be by private sale or by public auction. Unless it is impracticable, an itemized statement of the property sold, the name of each purchaser, and the price received for each item or lot or for the property as a whole if sold in bulk shall be filed on completion of a sale. If the property is sold by an auctioneer, the auctioneer shall file the statement, transmit a copy thereof to the United States trustee, and furnish a copy to the trustee, debtor in possession, or chapter 13 debtor. If the property is not sold by an auctioneer, the trustee, debtor in possession, or chapter 13 debtor shall file the statement and transmit a copy thereof to the United States trustee.

(2) Execution of Instruments. After a sale in accordance with this rule the debtor, the trustee, or debtor in possession, as the case may be, shall execute any instrument necessary or ordered by the court to effectuate the transfer to the purchaser.

Rule 6005. Appraisers and Auctioneers

The order of the court approving the employment of an appraiser or auctioneer shall fix the amount or rate of compensation. No officer or employee of the Judicial Branch of the United States or the United States Department of Justice shall be eligible to act as appraiser or auctioneer. No residence or licensing requirement shall disqualify an appraiser or auctioneer from employment.

Rule 6006. Assumption, Rejection and Assignment of Executory Contracts and Unexpired Leases

(a) PROCEEDING TO ASSUME, REJECT OR ASSIGN. A proceeding to assume, reject, or assign an executory contract or unexpired lease, other than as part of a plan, is governed by Rule 9014.

(b) PROCEEDING TO REQUIRE TRUSTEE TO ACT. A proceeding by a party to an executory contract or unexpired lease in a chapter 9 municipality case, chapter 11 reorganization case, chapter 12 family farmer's debt adjustment case, or chapter 13 individual's debt adjustment case, to require the trustee, debtor in possession, or debtor to determine whether to assume or reject the contract or lease is governed by Rule 9014.

(c) HEARING. When a motion is made pursuant to subdivision (a) or (b) of this rule, the court shall set a hearing on notice to the other party to the contract or lease, to other parties in interest as the court may direct, and, except in a chapter 9 municipality case, to the United States trustee.

Rule 6007. Abandonment or Disposition of Property

(a) NOTICE OF PROPOSED ABANDONMENT OR DISPOSITION; OBJECTIONS. Unless otherwise directed by the court, the trustee or debtor in possession shall give notice of a proposed abandonment or disposition of property to the United States trustee, all creditors, indenture trustees and committees elected pursuant to Section 705 or appointed pursuant to Section 1102 of the Code. An objection may be filed and served by a party in interest within 15 days of the mailing of the notice, or within the time fixed by the court.

(b) MOTION BY PARTY IN INTEREST. A party in interest may file and serve a motion requiring the trustee or debtor in possession to abandon property of the estate.

(c) HEARING. If a timely objection is made as prescribed by subdivision (a) of this rule, or if a motion is made as prescribed by subdivision (b), the court shall set a hearing on notice to the United States trustee and to other entities as the court may direct.

Rule 6008. Redemption of Property from Lien or Sale

On motion by the debtor, trustee, or debtor in possession and after hearing on notice as the court may direct, the court may authorize the redemption of property from a lien or from a sale to enforce a lien in accordance with applicable law.

Rule 6009. Prosecution and Defense of Proceedings by Trustee or Debtor in Possession

With or without court approval, the trustee or debtor in possession may prosecute or may enter an appearance and defend any pending action or proceeding by or against the debtor, or commence and prosecute any action or proceeding in behalf of the estate before any tribunal.

Rule 6010. Proceeding to Avoid Indemnifying Lien or Transfer to Surety

If a lien voidable under Section 547 of the Code has been dissolved by the furnishing of a bond or other obligation and the surety thereon has been indemnified by the transfer of, or the creation of a lien upon, nonexempt property of the debtor, the surety shall be joined as a defendant in any proceeding to avoid the indemnifying transfer or lien. Such proceeding is governed by the rules in Part VII.

PART VII

ADVERSARY PROCEEDINGS

Rule 7001. Scope of Rules of Part VII

An adversary proceeding is governed by the rules of this Part VII. It is a proceeding (1) to recover money or property, except a proceeding to compel the debtor to deliver property to the trustee, or a proceeding under Section 554(b) or Section 725 of the Code, Rule 2017, or Rule 6002, (2) to determine the validity, priority, or extent of a lien or other interest in property, other than a proceeding under Rule 4003(d), (3) to obtain approval pursuant to Section 363(h) for the sale of both the interest of the estate and of a co-owner in property, (4) to object to or revoke a discharge, (5) to revoke an order of confirmation of a chapter 11, chapter 12, or chapter 13 plan, (6) to determine the dischargeability of a debt, (7) to obtain an injunction or other equitable relief, (8) to subordinate any allowed claim or interest, except when subordination is provided in a chapter 9, 11, 12, or 13 plan, (9) to obtain a declaratory judgment relating to any of the foregoing, or (10) to determine a claim or cause of action removed pursuant to 28 U. S. C. Section 1452.

Rule 7002. References to Federal Rules of Civil Procedure

Whenever a Federal Rule of Civil Procedure applicable to adversary proceedings makes reference to another Federal Rule of Civil Procedure, the reference shall be read as a reference to the Federal Rule of Civil Procedure as modified in this Part VII.

Rule 7003. Commencement of Adversary Proceeding

Rule 3 F. R. Civ. P. applies in adversary proceedings.

Rule 7004. Process; Service of Summons, Complaint

(a) SUMMONS; SERVICE; PROOF OF SERVICE. Rule 4(a), (b), (c)(2)(C)(i), (d), (e) and (g)–(j) F. R. Civ. P. applies in adversary proceedings. Personal service pursuant to Rule 4(d) F. R. Civ. P. may be made by any person not less than 18 years of age who is not a party and the summons may be delivered by the clerk to any such person.

(b) SERVICE BY FIRST CLASS MAIL. In addition to the methods of service authorized by Rule 4(c)(2)(C)(i) and (d) F. R. Civ. P., service may be made within the United States by first class mail postage prepaid as follows:

(1) Upon an individual other than an infant or incompetent, by mailing a copy of the summons and complaint to the individual's dwelling house or usual place of abode or to the place where the individual regularly conducts a business or profession.

(2) Upon an infant or an incompetent person, by mailing a copy of the summons and complaint to the person upon whom process is prescribed to be served by the law of the state in which service is made when an action is brought against such defendant in the courts of general jurisdiction of that state. The summons and complaint in such case shall be addressed to the person required to be served at that person's dwelling house or usual place of abode or at the place where the person regularly conducts a business or profession.

(3) Upon a domestic or foreign corporation or upon a partnership or other unincorporated association, by mailing a copy of the summons and complaint to the attention of an officer, a managing or general agent, or to any other agent authorized by appointment or by law to receive service of process and, if the agent is one authorized by statute to receive service and the statute so requires, by also mailing a copy to the defendant.

(4) Upon the United States, by mailing a copy of the summons and complaint to the United States attorney for the district in which the action is brought and also the Attorney General of the United States at Washington, District of Columbia, and in any action attacking the validity of an order of an officer or an agency of the United States not made a party, by also mailing a copy of the summons and complaint to such officer or agency.

(5) Upon any officer or agency of the United States, by mailing a copy of the summons and complaint to the United States as prescribed in paragraph (4) of this subdivision and also to the officer or agency. If the agency is a corporation, the mailing shall be as prescribed in paragraph (3) of this subdivision of this rule. If the United States trustee is the trustee in the case and service is made upon the United States trustee solely as trustee, service may be made as prescribed in paragraph (10) of this subdivision of this rule.

(6) Upon a state or municipal corporation or other governmental organization thereof subject to suit, by mailing a copy of the summons and complaint to the person or office upon whom process is prescribed to be served by the law of the state in which service is made when an action is brought against such defendant in the courts of general jurisdiction of that state, or in the absence of the designation of any such person or office by state law, then to the chief executive officer thereof.

(7) Upon a defendant of any class referred to in paragraph (1) or (3) of this subdivision of this rule, it is also sufficient if a copy of the summons and complaint is mailed to the entity upon whom service is prescribed to be served by any statute of the United States or by the law of the state in which service is made when an action is brought against such defendant in the court of general jurisdiction of that state.

(8) Upon any defendant, it is also sufficient if a copy of the summons and complaint is mailed to an agent of such defendant authorized by appointment or by law to receive service of process, at the agent's dwelling house or usual place of abode or at the place where the agent regularly carries on a business or profession and, if the authorization so requires, by mailing also a copy of the summons and complaint to the defendant as provided in this subdivision.

(9) Upon the debtor, after a petition has been filed by or served upon the debtor and until the case is dismissed or closed, by mailing copies of the summons and complaint to the debtor at the address shown in the petition or statement of affairs or to such other address as the debtor may designate in a filed writing and, if the debtor is represented by an attorney, to the attorney at the attorney's post-office address.

(10) Upon the United States trustee, when the United States trustee is the trustee in the case and service is made upon the United States trustee solely as trustee, by mailing a copy of the summons and complaint to an office of the United States trustee or another place designated by the United States trustee in the district where the case under the Code is pending.

(c) SERVICE BY PUBLICATION. If a party to an adversary proceeding to determine or protect rights in property in the custody of the court cannot be served as provided in Rule 4(d) or (i) F. R. Civ. P. or subdivision (b) of this rule, the court may order the summons and complaint to be served by mailing copies thereof by first class mail postage prepaid, to the party's last known address and by at least one publication in such manner and form as the court may direct.

(d) NATIONWIDE SERVICE OF PROCESS. The summons and complaint and all other process except a subpoena may be served anywhere in the United States.

(e) SERVICE ON DEBTOR AND OTHERS IN FOREIGN COUNTRY. The summons and complaint and all other process except a subpoena may be served as provided in Rule 4(d)(1) and (d)(3) F. R. Civ. P. in a foreign country (A) on the debtor, any person required to perform the duties of a debtor, any general partner of a partnership debtor, or any attorney who is a party to a transaction subject to examination under Rule 2017; or (B) on any party to an adversary proceeding to determine or protect rights in property in the custody of the court; or (C) on any person whenever such service is authorized by a federal or state law referred to in Rule 4(c)(2)(C)(i) or (e) F. R. Civ. P.

(f) SUMMONS: TIME LIMIT FOR SERVICE. If service is made pursuant to Rule 4(d)(1)–(6) F. R. Civ. P. it shall be made by delivery of the summons and complaint within 10 days following issuance of the summons. If service is made by any authorized form of mail, the summons and complaint shall be deposited in the mail within 10 days following issuance of the summons. If a summons is not timely delivered or mailed, another summons shall be issued and served.

(g) EFFECT OF AMENDMENT TO RULE 4 F. R. CIV. P. The subdivisions of Rule 4 F. R. Civ. P. made applicable by these rules shall be the subdivisions of Rule 4 F. R. Civ. P. in effect on January 1, 1990, notwithstanding any amendment to Rule 4 F. R. Civ. P. subsequent thereto.

Rule 7005. Service and Filing of Pleadings and Other Papers

Rule 5 F. R. Civ. P. applies in adversary proceedings.

Rule 7007. Pleadings Allowed

Rule 7 F. R. Civ. P. applies in adversary proceedings.

Rule 7008. General Rules of Pleading

(a) APPLICABILITY OF RULE 8 F. R. CIV. P. Rule 8 F. R. Civ. P. applies in adversary proceedings. The allegation of jurisdiction required by Rule 8(a) shall also contain a reference to the name, number, and chapter of the case under the Code to which the adversary proceeding relates and to the district and division where the case under the Code is pending. In an adversary proceeding before a bankruptcy judge, the complaint, counterclaim, cross-claim, or third-party complaint shall contain a statement that the proceeding is core or non-core and, if non-core, that the pleader does or does not consent to entry of final orders or judgment by the bankruptcy judge.

(b) ATTORNEY'S FEES. A request for an award of attorney's fees shall be pleaded as a claim in a complaint, cross-claim, third-party complaint, answer, or reply as may be appropriate.

Rule 7009. Pleading Special Matters

Rule 9 F. R. Civ. P. applies in adversary proceedings.

Rule 7010. Form of Pleadings

Rule 10 F. R. Civ. P. applies in adversary proceedings, except that the caption of each pleading in such a proceeding shall conform substantially to the appropriate Official Form.

Rule 7012. Defenses and Objections- When and How Presented- By Pleading or Motion- Motion for Judgment on the Pleadings

(a) WHEN PRESENTED. If a complaint is duly served, the defendant shall serve an answer within 30 days after the issuance of the summons, except when a different time is prescribed by the court. The court shall prescribe the time for service of the answer when service of a complaint is made by publication or upon a party in a foreign country. A party served with a pleading stating a cross-claim shall serve an answer thereto within 20 days after service. The plaintiff shall serve a reply to a counterclaim in the answer within 20 days after service of the answer or, if a reply is ordered by the court, within 20 days after service of the order, unless the order otherwise directs. The United States or an officer or agency thereof shall serve an answer to a complaint within 35 days after the issuance of the summons, and shall serve an answer to a cross-claim, or a reply to a counterclaim, within 35 days after service upon the United States attorney of the pleading in which the claim is asserted. The service of a motion permitted under this rule alters these periods of time as follows, unless a different time is fixed by order of the court: (1) if the court denies the motion or postpones its disposition until the trial on the merits, the responsive pleading shall be served within 10 days after notice of the court's action; (2) if the court grants a motion for a more definite statement, the responsive pleading shall be served within 10 days after the service of a more definite statement.

(b) APPLICABILITY OF RULE 12(b)–(h) F. R. CIV. P. Rule 12(b)–(h) F. R. Civ. P. applies in adversary proceedings. A responsive pleading shall admit or deny an allegation that the proceeding is core or non-core. If the response is that the proceeding is non-core, it shall include a statement that the party does or does not consent to entry of final orders or judgment by the bankruptcy judge. In non-core proceedings final orders and judgments shall not be entered on the bankruptcy judge's orders except with the express consent of the parties.

Rule 7013. Counterclaim and Cross-Claim

Rule 13 F. R. Civ. P. applies in adversary proceedings, except that a party sued by a trustee or debtor in possession need not state as a counterclaim any claim that the party has against the debtor, the debtor's property, or the estate, unless the claim arose after the entry of an order for relief. A trustee or debtor in possession who fails to plead a counterclaim through oversight, inadvertence, or excusable neglect, or when justice so requires, may by leave of court amend the pleading, or commence a new adversary proceeding or separate action.

Rule 7014. Third-Party Practice

Rule 14 F. R. Civ. P. applies in adversary proceedings.

Rule 7015. Amended and Supplemental Pleadings

Rule 15 F. R. Civ. P. applies in adversary proceedings.

Rule 7016. Pre-Trial Procedure; Formulating Issues

Rule 16 F. R. Civ. P. applies in adversary proceedings.

Rule 7017. Parties Plaintiff and Defendant; Capacity

Rule 17 F. R. Civ. P. applies in adversary proceedings, except as provided in Rule 2010(b).

Rule 7018. Joinder of Claims and Remedies

Rule 18 F. R. Civ. P. applies in adversary proceedings.

Rule 7019. Joinder of Persons Needed for Just Determination

Rule 19 F. R. Civ. P. applies in adversary proceedings, except that (1) if an entity joined as a party raises the defense that the court lacks jurisdiction over the subject matter and the defense is sustained, the court shall dismiss such entity from the adversary proceeding and (2) if an entity joined as a party properly and timely raises the defense of improper venue, the court shall determine, as provided in 28 U. S. C. Section 1412, whether that part of the proceeding involving the joined party shall be transferred to another district, or whether the entire adversary proceeding shall be transferred to another district.

Rule 7020. Permissive Joinder of Parties

Rule 20 F. R. Civ. P. applies in adversary proceedings.

Rule 7021. Misjoinder and Non-Joinder of Parties

Rule 21 F. R. Civ. P. applies in adversary proceedings.

Rule 7022. Interpleader

Rule 22(1) F. R. Civ. P. applies in adversary proceedings.

Rule 7023. Class Proceedings

Rule 23 F. R. Civ. P. applies in adversary proceedings.

Rule 7023.1. Derivative Proceedings by Shareholders

Rule 23.1 F. R. Civ. P. applies in adversary proceedings.

Rule 7023.2. Adversary Proceedings Relating to Unincorporated Associations

Rule 23.2 F. R. Civ. P. applies in adversary proceedings.

Rule 7024. Intervention

Rule 24 F. R. Civ. P. applies in adversary proceedings.

Rule 7025. Substitution of Parties

Subject to the provisions of Rule 2012, Rule 25 F. R. Civ. P. applies in adversary proceedings.

Rule 7026. General Provisions Governing Discovery

Rule 26 F. R. Civ. P. applies in adversary proceedings.

Rule 7027. Depositions Before Adversary Proceedings or Pending Appeal

Rule 27 F. R. Civ. P. applies in adversary proceedings.

Rule 7028. Persons Before Whom Depositions May Be Taken

Rule 28 F. R. Civ. P. applies in adversary proceedings.

Rule 7029. Stipulations Regarding Discovery Procedure

Rule 29 F. R. Civ. P. applies in adversary proceedings.

Rule 7030. Depositions Upon Oral Examination

Rule 30 F. R. Civ. P. applies in adversary proceedings.

Rule 7031. Deposition Upon Written Questions

Rule 31 F. R. Civ. P. applies in adversary proceedings.

Rule 7032. Use of Depositions in Adversary Proceedings

Rule 32 F. R. Civ. P. applies in adversary proceedings.

Rule 7033. Interrogatories to Parties

Rule 33 F. R. Civ. P. applies in adversary proceedings.

Rule 7034. Production of Documents and Things and Entry Upon Land for Inspection and Other Purposes

Rule 34 F. R. Civ. P. applies in adversary proceedings.

Rule 7035. Physical and Mental Examination of Persons

Rule 35 F. R. Civ. P. applies in adversary proceedings.

Rule 7036. Requests for Admission

Rule 36 F. R. Civ. P. applies in adversary proceedings.

Rule 7037. Failure to Make Discovery: Sanctions

Rule 37 F. R. Civ. P. applies in adversary proceedings.

Rule 7040. Assignment of Cases for Trial

Rule 40 F. R. Civ. P. applies in adversary proceedings.

Rule 7041. Dismissal of Adversary Proceedings

Rule 41 F. R. Civ. P. applies in adversary proceedings, except that a complaint objecting to the debtor's discharge shall not be dismissed at the plaintiff's instance without notice to the trustee, the United States trustee, and such other persons as the court may direct, and only on order of the court containing terms and conditions which the court deems proper.

Rule 7042. Consolidation of Adversary Proceedings; Separate Trials

Rule 42 F. R. Civ. P. applies in adversary proceedings.

Rule 7052. Findings by the Court

Rule 52 F. R. Civ. P. applies in adversary proceedings.

Rule 7054. Judgments; Costs

(a) JUDGMENTS. Rule 54(a)–(c) F. R. Civ. P. applies in adversary proceedings.
(b) COSTS. The court may allow costs to the prevailing party except when a statute of the United States or these rules otherwise provides. Costs against the United States, its officers and agencies shall be imposed only to the extent permitted by law. Costs may be taxed by the clerk on one day's notice; on motion served within five days thereafter, the action of the clerk may be reviewed by the court.

Rule 7055. Default

Rule 55 F. R. Civ. P. applies in adversary proceedings.

Rule 7056. Summary Judgment

Rule 56 F. R. Civ. P. applies in adversary proceedings.

Rule 7062. Stay of Proceedings to Enforce a Judgment

Rule 62 F. R. Civ. P. applies in adversary proceedings. An order granting relief from an automatic stay provided by Section 362, Section 922, Section 1201, or Section 1301 of the Code, an order authorizing or prohibiting the use of cash collateral or the use, sale or lease of property of the estate under Section 363, an order authorizing the trustee to obtain credit pursuant to Section 364, and an order authorizing the assumption or assignment of an executory contract or unexpired lease pursuant to Section 365 shall be additional exceptions to Rule 62(a).

Rule 7064. Seizure of Person or Property

Rule 64 F. R. Civ. P. applies in adversary proceedings.

Rule 7065. Injunctions

Rule 65 F. R. Civ. P. applies in adversary proceedings, except that a temporary restraining order or preliminary injunction may be issued on application of a debtor, trustee, or debtor in possession without compliance with Rule 65(c).

Rule 7067. Deposit in Court

Rule 67 F. R. Civ. P. applies in adversary proceedings.

Rule 7068. Offer of Judgment

Rule 68 F. R. Civ. P. applies in adversary proceedings.

Rule 7069. Execution

Rule 69 F. R. Civ. P. applies in adversary proceedings.

Rule 7070. Judgment for Specific Acts; Vesting Title

Rule 70 F. R. Civ. P. applies in adversary proceedings and the court may enter a judgment divesting the title of any party and vesting title in others whenever the real or personal property involved is within the jurisdiction of the court.

Rule 7071. Process in Behalf of and Against Persons Not Parties

Rule 71 F. R. Civ. P. applies in adversary proceedings.

Rule 7087. Transfer of Adversary Proceeding

On motion and after a hearing, the court may transfer an adversary proceeding or any part thereof to another district pursuant to 28 U. S. C. Section 1412, except as provided in Rule 7019(2).

PART VIII

APPEALS TO DISTRICT COURT OR BANKRUPTCY APPELLATE PANEL

Rule 8001. Manner of Taking Appeal; Voluntary Dismissal

(a) APPEAL AS OF RIGHT; HOW TAKEN. An appeal from a final judgment, order, or decree of a bankruptcy judge to a district court or bankruptcy appellate panel shall be taken by filing a notice of appeal with the clerk within the time allowed by Rule 8002. Failure of an appellant to take any step other than the timely filing of a notice of appeal does not affect the validity of the appeal, but is ground only for such action as the district court or bankruptcy appellate panel deems appropriate, which may include dismissal of the appeal. The notice of appeal shall conform substantially to the appropriate Official Form, shall contain the names of all parties to the judgment, order, or decree appealed from and the names, addresses and telephone numbers of their respective attorneys, and be accompanied by the prescribed fee. Each appellant shall file a sufficient number of copies of the notice of appeal to enable the clerk to comply promptly with Rule 8004.

(b) APPEAL BY LEAVE; HOW TAKEN. An appeal from an interlocutory judgment, order or decree of a bankruptcy judge as permitted by 28 U. S. C. Section 158(a) shall be taken by filing a notice of appeal, as prescribed in subdivision (a) of this rule, accompanied by a motion for leave to appeal prepared in accordance with Rule 8003 and with proof of service in accordance with Rule 8008.

(c) VOLUNTARY DISMISSAL.

(1) Before Docketing. If an appeal has not been docketed, the appeal may be dismissed by the bankruptcy judge on the filing of a stipulation for dismissal signed by all parties, or on motion and notice by the appellant.

(2) After Docketing. If an appeal has been docketed and the parties to the appeal sign and file with the clerk of the district court or the clerk of the bankruptcy appellate panel an agreement that the appeal be dismissed and pay any court costs or fees that may be due, the clerk of the district court or the clerk of the bankruptcy appellate panel shall enter an order dismissing the appeal. An appeal may also be dismissed on motion of the appellant on terms and conditions fixed by the district court or bankruptcy appellate panel.

(d) [Abrogated]

(e) CONSENT TO APPEAL TO BANKRUPTCY APPELLATE PANEL. Unless otherwise provided by a rule promulgated pursuant to Rule 8018, consent to have an appeal heard by a bankruptcy appellate panel may be given in a separate statement of consent executed by a party or contained in the notice of appeal or cross appeal. The statement of consent shall be filed before the transmittal of the record pursuant to Rule 8007(b) or within 30 days of the filing of the notice of appeal, whichever is later.

Rule 8002. Time for Filing Notice of Appeal

(a) TEN-DAY PERIOD. The notice of appeal shall be filed with the clerk within 10 days of the date of the entry of the judgment, order, or decree appealed from. If a timely notice of appeal is filed by a party, any other party may file a notice of appeal within 10 days of the date on which the first notice of appeal was filed, or within the time otherwise prescribed by this rule, whichever period last expires. A notice of appeal filed after the announcement of a decision or order but before entry of the judgment, order, or decree shall be treated as filed after such entry and on the day thereof. If a notice of appeal is mistakenly filed with the district court or the bankruptcy appellate panel, the clerk of the district court or the clerk of the bankruptcy appellate panel shall note thereon the date on which it was received and transmit it to the clerk and it shall be deemed filed with the clerk on the date so noted.

(b) EFFECT OF MOTION ON TIME FOR APPEAL. If a timely motion is filed by any party: (1) under Rule 7052(b) to amend or make additional findings of fact, whether or not an alteration of the judgment would be required if the motion is granted; (2) under Rule 9023 to alter or amend the judgment; or (3) under Rule 9023 for a new trial, the time for appeal for all parties shall run from the entry of the order denying a new trial or granting or denying any other such motion. A notice of appeal filed before the disposition of any of the above motions shall have no effect; a new notice of appeal must be filed. No additional fees shall be required for such filing.

(c) EXTENSION OF TIME FOR APPEAL. The bankruptcy judge may extend the time for filing the notice of appeal by any party for a period not to exceed 20 days from the expiration of the time otherwise prescribed by this rule. A request to extend the time for filing a notice of appeal must be made before the time for filing a notice of appeal has expired, except that a request may be made no more than 20 days after the expiration of the time for filing a notice of appeal may be granted upon a showing of excusable neglect if the judgment or order appealed from does not authorize the sale of any property or the obtaining of credit or the incurring of debt under Section 364 of the Code, or is not a judgment or order approving a disclosure statement, confirming a plan, dismissing a case, or converting a case to a case under another chapter of the Code.

Rule 8003. Leave to Appeal

(a) CONTENT OF MOTION; ANSWER. A motion for leave to appeal under 28 U. S. C. Section 158(a) shall contain: (1) a statement of the facts necessary to an understanding of the questions to be presented by the appeal; (2) a statement of those questions and of the relief sought; (3) a statement of the reasons why an appeal should be granted; and (4) a copy of the judgment, order, or decree complained of and of any opinion or memorandum relating thereto. Within 10 days after service of the motion, an adverse party may file with the clerk an answer in opposition.

(b) TRANSMITTAL; DETERMINATION OF MOTION. The clerk shall transmit the notice of appeal, the motion for leave to appeal and any answer thereto to the clerk of the district court or the clerk of the bankruptcy appellate panel as soon as all parties have filed answers or the time for filing an answer has expired. The motion and answer shall be submitted without oral argument unless otherwise ordered.

(c) APPEAL IMPROPERLY TAKEN REGARDED AS A MOTION FOR LEAVE TO APPEAL. If a required motion for leave to appeal is not filed, but a notice of appeal is timely filed, the district court or bankruptcy appellate panel may grant leave to appeal or direct that a motion for leave to appeal be filed. The district court or the bankruptcy appellate panel may also deny leave to appeal but in so doing shall consider the notice of appeal as a motion for leave to appeal. Unless an order directing that a motion for leave to appeal be filed provides otherwise, the motion shall be filed within 10 days of entry of the order.

Rule 8004. Service of the Notice of Appeal

The clerk shall serve notice of the filing of a notice of appeal by mailing a copy thereof to counsel of record of each party other than the appellant or, if a party is not represented by counsel, to the party's last known address. Failure to serve notice shall not affect the validity of the appeal. The clerk shall note on each copy served the date of the filing of the notice of appeal and shall note in the docket the names of the parties to whom copies are mailed and the date of the mailing. The clerk shall forthwith transmit to the United States trustee a copy of the notice of appeal, but failure to transmit such notice shall not affect the validity of the appeal.

Rule 8005. Stay Pending Appeal

A motion for a stay of the judgment, order, or decree of a bankruptcy judge, for approval of a supersedeas bond, or for other relief pending appeal must ordinarily be presented to the bankruptcy judge in the first instance. Notwithstanding Rule 7062 but subject to the power of the district court and the bankruptcy appellate panel reserved hereinafter, the bankruptcy judge may suspend or order the continuation of other proceedings in the case under the Code or make any other appropriate order during the pendency of an appeal on such terms as will protect the rights of all parties in interest. A motion for such relief, or for modification or termination of relief granted by a bankruptcy judge, may be made to the district court or the bankruptcy appellate panel, but the motion shall show why the relief, modification, or termination was not obtained from the bankruptcy judge. The district court or the bankruptcy appellate panel may condition the relief it grants under this rule on the filing of a bond or other appropriate security with the bankruptcy court. When an appeal is taken by a trustee, a bond or other appropriate security may be required, but when an appeal is taken by the United States or an officer or agency thereof or by direction of any department of the Government of the United States a bond or other security shall not be required.

Rule 8006. Record and Issues on Appeal

Within 10 days after filing the notice of appeal as provided by Rule 8001(a) or entry of an order granting leave to appeal the appellant shall file with the clerk and serve on the appellee a designation of the items to be included in the record on appeal and a statement of the issues to be presented. Within 10 days after the service of the statement of the appellant the appellee may file and serve on the appellant a designation of additional items to be included in the record on appeal and, if the appellee has filed a cross appeal, the appellee as cross appellant shall file and serve a statement of the issues to be presented on the cross appeal and a designation of additional items to be included in the record. A cross appellee may, within 10 days of service of the statement of the cross appellant, file and serve on the cross appellant a designation of additional items to be included in the record. The record on appeal shall include the items so designated by the parties, the notice of appeal, the judgment, order, or decree appealed from, and any opinion, findings of fact, and conclusions of law of the court. Any party filing a designation of the items to be included in the record shall provide to the clerk a copy of the items designated or, if the party fails to provide the copy, the clerk shall prepare the copy at the expense of the party. If the record designated by any party includes a transcript of any proceeding or a part thereof, the party shall immediately after filing the designation deliver to the reporter and file with the clerk a written request for the transcript and make satisfactory arrangements for payment of its cost. All parties shall take any other action necessary to enable the clerk to assemble and transmit the record.

Rule 8007. Completion and Transmission of the Record; Docketing of the Appeal

(a) DUTY OF REPORTER TO PREPARE AND FILE TRANSCRIPT. On receipt of a request for a transcript, the reporter shall acknowledge on the request the date it was received and the date on which the reporter expects to have the transcript completed and shall transmit the request, so endorsed, to the clerk or the clerk of the bankruptcy appellate panel. On completion of the transcript the reporter shall file it with the clerk and, if appropriate, notify the clerk of the bankruptcy appellate panel. If the transcript cannot be completed within 30 days of receipt of the request the reporter shall seek an extension of time from the clerk or the clerk of the bankruptcy appellate panel and the action of the clerk shall be entered in the docket and the parties notified. If the reporter does not file the transcript within the time allowed, the clerk or the clerk of the bankruptcy appellate panel shall notify the bankruptcy judge.

(b) DUTY OF CLERK TO TRANSMIT COPY OF RECORD; DOCKETING OF APPEAL. When the record is complete for purposes of appeal, the clerk shall transmit a copy thereof forthwith to the clerk of the district court or the clerk of the bankruptcy appellate panel. On receipt of the transmission the clerk of the district court or the clerk of the bankruptcy appellate panel shall enter the appeal in the docket and give notice promptly to all parties to the judgment, order, or decree appealed from of the date on which the appeal was docketed. If the bankruptcy appellate panel directs that additional copies of the record be furnished, the clerk of the bankruptcy appellate panel shall notify the appellant and, if the appellant fails to provide the copies, the clerk shall prepare the copies at the expense of the appellant.

(c) RECORD FOR PRELIMINARY HEARING. If prior to the time the record is transmitted a party moves in the district court or before the bankruptcy appellate panel for dismissal, for a stay pending appeal, for additional security on the bond on appeal or on a supersedeas bond, or for any intermediate order, the clerk at the request of any party to the appeal shall transmit to the clerk of the district court or the clerk of the bankruptcy appellate panel a copy of the parts of the record as any party to the appeal shall designate.

Rule 8008. Filing and Service

(a) FILING. Papers required or permitted to be filed with the clerk of the district court or the clerk of the bankruptcy appellate panel may be filed by mail addressed to the clerk, but filing shall not be timely unless the papers are received by the clerk within the time fixed for filing, except that briefs shall be deemed filed on the day of mailing. An original and one copy of all papers shall be filed when an appeal is to the district court; an original and three copies shall be filed when an appeal is to a bankruptcy appellate panel. The district court or bankruptcy appellate panel may require that additional copies be furnished.

(b) SERVICE OF ALL PAPERS REQUIRED. Copies of all papers filed by any party and not required by these rules to be served by the clerk of the district court or the clerk of the bankruptcy appellate panel shall, at or before the time of filing, be served by the party or a person acting for the party on all other parties to the appeal. Service on a party represented by counsel shall be made on counsel.

(c) MANNER OF SERVICE. Service may be personal or by mail. Personal service includes delivery of the copy to a clerk or other responsible person at the office of counsel. Service by mail is complete on mailing.

(d) PROOF OF SERVICE. Papers presented for filing shall contain an acknowledgement of service by the person served or proof of service in the form of a statement of the date and manner of service and of the names of the persons served, certified by the person who made service. The clerk of the district court or the clerk of the bankruptcy appellate panel may permit papers to be filed without acknowledgement or proof of service but shall require the acknowledgement or proof of service to be filed promptly thereafter.

Rule 8009. Briefs and Appendix; Filing and Service

(a) BRIEFS. Unless the district court or the bankruptcy appellate panel by local rule or by order excuses the filing of briefs or specifies different time limits:

(1) The appellant shall serve and file a brief within 15 days after entry of the appeal on the docket pursuant to Rule 8007.

(2) The appellee shall serve and file a brief within 15 days after service of the brief of appellant. If the appellee has filed a cross appeal, the brief of the appellee shall contain the issues and argument pertinent to the cross appeal, denominated as such, and the response to the brief of the appellant.

(3) The appellant may serve and file a reply brief within 10 days after service of the brief of the appellee, and if the appellee has cross-appealed, the appellee may file and serve a reply brief to the response of the appellant to the issues presented in the cross appeal within 10 days after service of the reply brief of the appellant. No further briefs may be filed except with leave of the district court or the bankruptcy appellate panel.

(b) APPENDIX TO BRIEF. If the appeal is to a bankruptcy appellate panel, the appellant shall serve and file with the appellant's brief excerpts of the record as an appendix, which shall include the following:

(1) The complaint and answer or other equivalent pleadings;
(2) Any pretrial order;
(3) The judgment, order, or decree from which the appeal is taken;
(4) Any other orders relevant to the appeal;
(5) The opinion, findings of fact, or conclusions of law filed or delivered orally by the court and citations of the opinion if published;
(6) Any motion and response on which the court rendered decision;
(7) The notice of appeal;
(8) The relevant entries in the bankruptcy docket; and
(9) The transcript or portion thereof, if so required by a rule of the bankruptcy appellate panel.

An appellee may also serve and file an appendix which contains material required to be included by the appellant but omitted by appellant.

Rule 8010. Form of Briefs; Length

(a) FORM OF BRIEFS. Unless the district court or the bankruptcy appellate panel by local rule otherwise provides, the form of brief shall be as follows:

(1) Brief of the Appellant. The brief of the appellant shall contain under appropriate headings and in the order here indicated:

(A) A table of contents, with page references, and a table of cases alphabetically arranged, statutes and other authorities cited, with references to the pages of the brief where they are cited.

(B) A statement of the basis of appellate jurisdiction.

(C) A statement of the issues presented and the applicable standard of appellate review.

(D) A statement of the case. The statement shall first indicate briefly the nature of the case, the course of the proceedings, and the disposition in the court below. There shall follow a statement of the facts relevant to the issues presented for review, with appropriate references to the record.

(E) An argument. The argument may be preceded by a summary. The argument shall contain the contentions of the appellant with respect to the issues presented, and the reasons therefor, with citations to the authorities, statutes and parts of the record relied on.

(F) A short conclusion stating the precise relief sought.

(2) Brief of the Appellee. The brief of the appellee shall conform to the requirements of paragraph (1) (A)–(E) of this subdivision, except that a statement of the basis of appellate jurisdiction, of the issues, or of the case need not be made unless the appellee is dissatisfied with the statement of the appellant.

(b) REPRODUCTION OF STATUTES, RULES, REGULATIONS, OR SIMILAR MATERIAL. If determination of the issues presented requires reference to the Code or other statutes, rules, regulations, or similar material, relevant parts thereof shall be reproduced in the brief or in an addendum or they may be supplied to the court in pamphlet form.

(c) LENGTH OF BRIEFS. Unless the district court or the bankruptcy appellate panel by local rule or order otherwise provides, principal briefs shall not exceed 50 pages, and reply briefs shall not exceed 25 pages, exclusive of pages containing the table of contents, tables of citations and any addendum containing statutes, rules, regulations, or similar material.

Rule 8011. Motions

(a) CONTENT OF MOTIONS; RESPONSE; REPLY. A request for an order or other relief shall be made by filing with the clerk of the district court or the clerk of the bankruptcy appellate panel a motion for such order or relief with proof of service on all other parties to the appeal. The motion shall contain or be accompanied by any matter required by a specific provision of these rules governing such a motion, shall state with particularity the grounds on which it is based, and shall set forth the order or relief sought. If a motion is supported by briefs, affidavits or other papers, they shall be served and filed with the motion. Any party may file a response in opposition to a motion other than one for a procedural order within seven days after service of the motion, but the district court or the bankruptcy appellate panel may shorten or extend the time for responding to any motion.

(b) DETERMINATION OF MOTIONS FOR PROCEDURAL ORDERS. Notwithstanding subdivision (a) of this rule, motions for procedural orders, including any motion under Rule 9006, may be acted on at any time, without awaiting a response thereto and without hearing. Any party adversely affected by such action may move for reconsideration, vacation, or modification of the action.

(c) DETERMINATION OF ALL MOTIONS. All motions will be decided without oral argument unless the court orders otherwise. A motion for a stay, or for other emergency relief may be denied if not presented promptly.

(d) EMERGENCY MOTIONS. Whenever a movant requests expedited action on a motion on the ground that, to avoid irreparable harm, relief is needed in less time than would normally be required for the district court or bankruptcy appellate panel to receive and consider a response, the word "Emergency" shall precede the title of the motion. The motion shall be accompanied by an affidavit setting forth the nature of the emergency. The motion shall state whether all grounds advanced in support thereof were submitted to the bankruptcy judge and, if any grounds relied on were not submitted, why the motion should not be remanded to the bankruptcy judge for reconsideration. The motion shall include the office addresses and telephone numbers of moving and opposing counsel and shall be served pursuant to Rule 8008. Prior to filing the motion, the movant shall make every practicable effort to notify opposing counsel in time for counsel to respond to the motion. The affidavit accompanying the motion shall also state when and how opposing counsel was notified or if opposing counsel was not notified why it was not practicable to do so.

(e) POWER OF A SINGLE JUDGE TO ENTERTAIN MOTIONS. A single judge of a bankruptcy appellate panel may grant or deny any request for relief which under these rules may properly be sought by motion, except that a single judge may not dismiss or otherwise decide an appeal or a motion for leave to appeal. The action of a single judge may be reviewed by the panel.

Rule 8012. Oral Argument

Oral argument shall be allowed in all cases unless the district judge or the judges of the bankruptcy appellate panel unanimously determine after examination of the briefs and record, or appendix to the brief, that oral argument is not needed. Any party shall have an opportunity to file a statement setting forth the reason why oral argument should be allowed.

Oral argument will not be allowed if (1) the appeal is frivolous; (2) the dispositive issue or set of issues has been recently authoritatively decided; or (3) the facts and legal arguments are adequately presented in the briefs and record and the decisional process would not be significantly aided by oral argument.

Rule 8013. Disposition of Appeal; Weight Accorded Bankruptcy Judge's Findings of Fact

On an appeal the district court or bankruptcy appellate panel may affirm, modify, or reverse a bankruptcy judge's judgment, order, or decree or remand with instructions for further proceedings. Findings of fact, whether based on oral or documentary evidence, shall not be set aside unless clearly erroneous, and due regard shall be given to the opportunity of the bankruptcy court to judge the credibility of the witnesses.

Rule 8014. Costs

Except as otherwise provided by law, agreed to by the parties, or ordered by the district court or bankruptcy appellate panel, costs shall be taxed against the losing party on an appeal. If a judgment is affirmed or reversed in part, or is vacated, costs shall be allowed only as ordered by the court. Costs incurred in the production of copies of briefs, the appendices, and the record and in the preparation and transmission of the record, the cost of the reporter's transcript, if necessary for the determination of the appeal, the premiums paid for cost of supersedeas bonds or other bonds to preserve rights pending appeal and the fee for filing the notice of appeal shall be taxed by the clerk as costs of the appeal in favor of the party entitled to costs under this rule.

Rule 8015. Motion for Rehearing

Unless the district court or the bankruptcy appellate panel by local rule or by court order otherwise provides, a motion for rehearing may be filed within 10 days after entry of the judgment of the district court or the bankruptcy appellate panel. If a timely motion for rehearing is filed, the time for appeal to the court of appeals for all parties shall run from the entry of the order denying rehearing or the entry of a subsequent judgment.

Rule 8016. Duties of Clerk of District Court and Bankruptcy Appellate Panel

(a) ENTRY OF JUDGMENT. The clerk of the district court or the clerk of the bankruptcy appellate panel shall prepare, sign and enter the judgment following receipt of the opinion of the court or the appellate panel or, if there is no opinion, following the instruction of the court or the appellate panel. The notation of a judgment in the docket constitutes entry of judgment.

(b) NOTICE OF ORDERS OR JUDGMENTS; RETURN OF RECORD. Immediately on the entry of a judgment or order the clerk of the district court or the clerk of the bankruptcy appellate panel shall transmit a notice of the entry to each party to the appeal, to the United States trustee, and to the clerk, together with a copy of any opinion respecting the judgment or order, and shall make a note of the transmission in the docket. Original papers transmitted as the record on appeal shall be returned to the clerk on disposition of the appeal.

Rule 8017. Stay of Judgment of District Court or Bankruptcy Appellate Panel

(a) AUTOMATIC STAY OF JUDGMENT ON APPEAL. Judgments of the district court or the bankruptcy appellate panel are stayed until the expiration of 10 days after entry, unless otherwise ordered by the district court or the bankruptcy appellate panel.

(b) STAY PENDING APPEAL TO THE COURT OF APPEALS. On motion and notice to the parties to the appeal, the district court or the bankruptcy appellate panel may stay its judgment pending an appeal to the court of appeals. The stay shall not extend beyond 30 days after the entry of the judgment of the district court or the bankruptcy appellate panel unless the period is extended for cause shown. If before the expiration of a stay entered pursuant to this subdivision there is an appeal to the court of appeals by the party who obtained the stay, the stay shall continue until final disposition by the court of appeals. A bond or other security may be required as a condition to the grant or continuation of a stay of the judgment. A bond or other security may be required if a trustee obtains a stay but a bond or security shall not be required if a stay is obtained by the United States or an officer or agency thereof or at the direction of any department of the Government of the United States.

(c) POWER OF COURT OF APPEALS NOT LIMITED. This rule does not limit the power of a court of appeals or any judge thereof to stay proceedings during the pendency of an appeal or to suspend, modify, restore, or grant an injunction during the pendency of an appeal or to make any order appropriate to preserve the status quo or the effectiveness of the judgment subsequently to be entered.

Rule 8018. Rules by Circuit Councils and District Courts

Circuit councils which have authorized bankruptcy appellate panels pursuant to 28 U. S. C. Section 158(b) and the district courts may by action of a majority of the judges of the council or district court make and amend rules governing practice and procedure for appeals from orders or judgments of bankruptcy judges to the respective bankruptcy appellate panel or district court, not inconsistent with the rules of this Part VIII. Rule 83 F. R. Civ. P. governs the procedure for making and amending rules to govern appeals. In all cases not provided for by rule, the district court or the bankruptcy appellate panel may regulate its practice in any manner not inconsistent with these rules.

Rule 8019. Suspension of Rules in Part VIII

In the interest of expediting decision or for other cause, the district court or the bankruptcy appellate panel may suspend the requirements or provisions of the rules in Part VIII, except Rules 8001, 8002, and 8013, and may order proceedings in accordance with the direction.

PART IX

GENERAL PROVISIONS

Rule 9001. General Definitions

The definitions of words and phrases in Section 101, Section 902 and Section 1101 and the rules of construction in Section 102 of the Code govern their use in these rules. In addition, the following words and phrases used in these rules have the meanings indicated:

(1) "Bankruptcy clerk" means a clerk appointed pursuant to 28 U. S. C. Section 156(b).

(2) "Bankruptcy Code" or "Code" means title 11 of the United States Code.

(3) "Clerk" means bankruptcy clerk, if one has been appointed, otherwise clerk of the district court.

(4) "Court" or "judge" means the judicial officer before whom a case or proceeding is pending.

(5) "Debtor." When any act is required by these rules to be performed by a debtor or when it is necessary to compel attendance of a debtor for examination and the debtor is not a natural person: (A) if the debtor is a corporation, "debtor" includes, if designated by the court, any or all of its officers, members of its board of directors or trustees or of a similar controlling body, a controlling stockholder or member, or any other person in control; (B) if the debtor is a partnership, "debtor" includes any or all of its general partners or, if designated by the court, any other person in control.

(6) "Firm" includes a partnership or professional corporation of attorneys or accountants.

(7) "Judgment" means any appealable order.

(8) "Mail" means first class, postage prepaid.

(9) "Regular associate" means any attorney regularly employed by, associated with, or counsel to an individual or firm.

(10) "Trustee" includes a debtor in possession in a chapter 11 case.

(11) "United States trustee" includes an assistant United States trustee and any designee of the United States trustee.

Rule 9002. Meanings of Words in the Federal Rules of Civil Procedure When Applicable to Cases Under The Code

The following words and phrases used in the Federal Rules of Civil Procedure made applicable to cases under the Code by these rules have the meanings indicated unless they are inconsistent with the context:

(1) "Action" or "civil action" means an adversary proceeding or, when appropriate, a contested petition, or proceedings to vacate an order for relief or to determine any other contested matter.

(2) "Appeal" means an appeal as provided by 28 U. S. C. Section 158.

(3) "Clerk" or "clerk of the district court" means the court officer responsible for the bankruptcy records in the district.

(4) "District court," "trial court," "court," or "judge" means bankruptcy judge if the case or proceeding is pending before a bankruptcy judge.

(5) "Judgment" includes any order appealable to an appellate court.

Rule 9003. Prohibition of Ex Parte Contacts

(a) GENERAL PROHIBITION. Except as otherwise permitted by applicable law, any examiner, any party in interest, and any attorney, accountant, or employee of a party in interest shall refrain from ex parte meetings and communications with the court concerning matters affecting a particular case or proceeding.

(b) UNITED STATES TRUSTEE. Except as otherwise permitted by applicable law, the United States trustee and assistants to and employees or agents of the United States trustee shall refrain for ex parte meetings and communications with the court concerning matters affecting a particular case or proceeding. This rule does not preclude communications with the court to discuss general problems of administration and improvement of bankruptcy administration, including the operation of the United States trustee system.

Rule 9004. General Requirements of Form

(a) LEGIBILITY; ABBREVIATIONS. All petitions, pleadings, schedules and other papers shall be clearly legible. Abbreviations in common use in the English language may be used.

(b) CAPTION. Each paper filed shall contain a caption setting forth the name of the court, the title of the case, the bankruptcy docket number, and a brief designation of the character of the paper.

Rule 9005. Harmless Error

Rule 61 F. R. Civ. P. applies in cases under the Code. When appropriate, the court may order the correction of any error or defect or the cure of any omission which does not affect substantial rights.

Rule 9006. Time

(a) COMPUTATION. In computing any period of time prescribed or allowed by these rules or by the Federal Rules of Civil Procedure made applicable by these rules, by the local rules, by order of court, or by any applicable statute, the day of the act, event, or default from which the designated period of time begins to run shall not be included. The last day of the period so computed shall be included, unless it is a Saturday, a Sunday, or a legal holiday, or when the act to be done is the filing of a paper in court, a day on which weather or other conditions have made the clerk's office inaccessible, in which event the period runs until the end of the next day which is not one of the aforementioned days. When the period of time prescribed or allowed is less than 8 days, intermediate Saturdays, Sundays, and legal holidays shall be excluded in the computation. As used in this rule and in Rule 5001(c), "legal holiday" includes New Year's Day, Birthday of Martin Luther King, Jr., Washington's Birthday, Memorial Day, Independence Day, Labor Day, Columbus Day, Veterans Day, Thanksgiving Day, Christmas Day, and any other day appointed as a holiday by the President or the Congress of the United States, or by the state in which the bankruptcy court is held.

(b) ENLARGEMENT.

(1) In General. Except as provided in paragraphs (2) and (3) of this subdivision, when an act is required or allowed to be done at or within a specified period by these rules or by a notice given thereunder or by order of court, the court for cause shown may at any time in its discretion (1) with or without motion or notice order the period enlarged if the request therefor is made before the expiration of the period originally prescribed or as extended by a previous order or (2) on motion made after the expiration of the specified period permit the act to be done where the failure to act was the result of excusable neglect.

(2) Enlargement Not Permitted. The court may not enlarge the time for taking action under Rules 1007(d), 1017(b)(3), 2003(a) and (d), 7052, 9023, and 9024.

(3) Enlargement Limited. The court may enlarge the time for taking action under Rules 1006(b)(2), 1017(e), 3002(c), 4003(b), 4004(a), 4007(c), 8002, and 9033, only to the extent and under the conditions stated in those rules.

(c) REDUCTION.

(1) In General. Except as provided in paragraph (2) of this subdivision, when an act is required or allowed to be done at or within a specified time by these rules or by a notice given thereunder or by order of court, the court for cause shown may in its discretion with or without motion or notice order the period reduced.

(2) Reduction Not Permitted. The court may not reduce the time for taking action under Rules 2002(a)(4) and (a)(8), 2003(a), 3002(c), 3014, 3015, 4001(b)(2), (c)(2), 4003(a), 4004(a), 4007(c), 8002, and 9033(b).

(d) FOR MOTIONS-AFFIDAVITS. A written motion, other than one which may be heard ex parte, and notice of any hearing shall be served not later than five days before the time specified for such hearing, unless a different period is fixed by these rules or by order of the court. Such an order may for cause shown be made on ex parte application. When a motion is supported by affidavit, the affidavit shall be served with the motion; and, except as otherwise provided in Rule 9023, opposing affidavits may be served not later than one day before the hearing, unless the court permits them to be served at some other time.

(e) TIME OF SERVICE. Service of process and service of any paper other than process or of notice by mail is complete on mailing.

(f) ADDITIONAL TIME AFTER SERVICE BY MAIL. When there is a right or requirement to do some act or undertake some proceedings within a prescribed period after service of a notice or other paper and the notice or paper other than process is served by mail, three days shall be added to the prescribed period.

(g) GRAIN STORAGE FACILITY CASES. This rule shall not limit the court's authority under Section 557 of the Code to enter orders governing procedures in cases in which the debtor is an owner or operator of a grain storage facility.

Rule 9007. General Authority to Regulate Notices

When notice is to be given under these rules, the court shall designate, if not otherwise specified herein, the time within which, the entities to whom, and the form and manner in which the notice shall be given. When feasible, the court may order any notices under these rules to be combined.

Rule 9008. Service or Notice by Publication

Whenever these rules require or authorize service or notice by publication, the court shall, to the extent not otherwise specified in these rules, determine the form and manner thereof, including the newspaper or other medium to be used and the number of publications.

Rule 9009. Forms

The Official Forms prescribed by the Judicial Conference of the United States shall be observed and used with alterations as may be appropriate. Forms may be combined and their contents rearranged to permit economies in their use. The Director of the Administrative Office of the United States Courts may issue additional forms for use under the Code. The forms shall be construed to be consistent with these rules and the Code.

Rule 9010. Representation and Appearances; Powers of Attorney

(a) AUTHORITY TO ACT PERSONALLY OR BY ATTORNEY. A debtor, creditor, equity security holder, indenture trustee, committee or other party may (1) appear in a case under the Code and act either in the entity's own behalf or by an attorney authorized to practice in the court, and (2) perform any act not constituting the practice of law, by an authorized agent, attorney in fact, or proxy.

(b) NOTICE OF APPEARANCE. An attorney appearing for a party in a case under the Code shall file a notice of appearance with the attorney's name, office address and telephone number, unless the attorney's appearance is otherwise noted in the record.

(c) POWER OF ATTORNEY. The authority of any agent, attorney in fact, or proxy to represent a creditor for any purpose other than the execution and filing of a proof of claim or the acceptance or rejection of a plan shall be evidenced by a power of attorney conforming substantially to the appropriate Official Form. The execution of any such power of attorney shall be acknowledged before one of the officers enumerated in 28 U. S. C. Section 459, Section 953, Rule 9012, or a person authorized to administer oaths under the laws of the state where the oath is administered.

Rule 9011. Signing and Verification of Papers

(a) SIGNATURE. Every petition, pleading, motion and other paper served or filed in a case under the Code on behalf of a party represented by an attorney, except a list, schedule, or statement, or amendments thereto, shall be signed by at least one attorney of record in the attorney's individual name, whose office address and telephone number shall be stated. A party who is not represented by an attorney shall sign all papers and state the party's address and telephone number. The signature of an attorney or a party constitutes a certificate that the attorney or party has read the document; that to the best of the attorney's or party's knowledge, information, and belief formed after reasonable inquiry it is well grounded in fact and is warranted by existing law or a good faith argument for the extension, modification, or reversal of existing law; and that it is not interposed for any improper purpose, such as to harass or to cause unnecessary delay or needless increase in the cost of litigation or administration of the case. If a document is not signed, it shall be stricken unless it is signed promptly after the omission is called to the attention of the person whose signature is required. If a document is signed in violation of this rule, the court on motion or on its own initiative, shall impose on the person who signed it, the represented party, or both, an appropriate sanction, which may include an order to pay to the other party or parties the amount of the reasonable expenses incurred because of the filing of the document, including a reasonable attorney's fee.

(b) VERIFICATION. Except as otherwise specifically provided by these rules, papers filed in a case under the Code need not be verified. Whenever verification is required by these rules, an unsworn declaration as provided in 28 U. S. C. Section 1746 satisfies the requirement of verification.

(c) COPIES OF SIGNED OR VERIFIED PAPERS. When these rules require copies of a signed or verified paper, it shall suffice if the original is signed or verified and the copies are conformed to the original.

Rule 9012. Oaths and Affirmations

(a) PERSONS AUTHORIZED TO ADMINISTER OATHS. The following persons may administer oaths and affirmations and take acknowledgements: a bankruptcy judge, clerk, deputy clerk, United States trustee, officer authorized to administer oaths in proceedings before the courts of the United States or under the laws of the state where the oath is to be taken, or a diplomatic or consular officer of the United States in any foreign country.

(b) AFFIRMATION IN LIEU OF OATH. When in a case under the Code an oath is required to be taken, a solemn affirmation may be accepted in lieu thereof.

Rule 9013. Motions: Form and Service

A request for an order, except when an application is authorized by these rules, shall be by written motion, unless made during a hearing. The motion shall state with particularity the grounds therefor, and shall set forth the relief or order sought. Every written motion other than one which may be considered ex parte shall be served by the moving party on the trustee or debtor in possession and on those entities specified by these rules or, if service is not required or the entities to be served are not specified by these rules, the moving party shall serve the entities the court directs.

Rule 9014. Contested Matters

In a contested matter in a case under the Code not otherwise governed by these rules, relief shall be requested by motion, and reasonable notice and opportunity for hearing shall be afforded the party against whom relief is sought. No response is required under this rule unless the court orders an answer to a motion. The motion shall be served in the manner provided for service of a summons and complaint by Rule 7004, and, unless the court otherwise directs, the following rules shall apply: 7021, 7025, 7026, 7028-7037, 7041, 7042, 7052, 7054-7056, 7062, 7064, 7069, and 7071. The court may at any stage in a particular matter direct that one or more of the other rules in Part VII shall apply. An entity that desires to perpetuate testimony may proceed in the same manner as provided in Rule 7027 for the taking of a deposition before an adversary proceeding. The clerk shall give notice to the parties of the entry of any order directing that additional rules of Part VII are applicable or that certain of the rules of Part VII are not applicable. The notice shall be given within such time as is necessary to afford the parties a reasonable opportunity to comply with the procedures made applicable by the order.

Rule 9015. [Abrogated]

Rule 9016. Subpoena

Rule 45 F. R. Civ. P. applies in cases under the Code.

Rule 9017. Evidence

The Federal Rules of Evidence and Rules 43, 44, and 44.1 F. R. Civ. P. apply in cases under the Code.

Rule 9018. Secret, Confidential, Scandalous, or Defamatory Matter

On motion or on its own initiative, with or without notice, the court may make any order which justice requires (1) to protect the estate or any entity in respect of a trade secret or other confidential research, development, or commercial information, (2) to protect any entity against scandalous or defamatory matter contained in any paper filed in a case under the Code, or (3) to protect governmental matters that are made confidential by statute or regulation. If an order is entered under this rule without notice, any entity affected thereby may move to vacate or modify the order, and after a hearing on notice the court shall determine the motion.

Rule 9019. Compromise and Arbitration

(a) COMPROMISE. On motion by the trustee and after a hearing on notice to creditors, the United States trustee, the debtor and indenture trustees as provided in Rule 2002 and to such other entities as the court may designate, the court may approve a compromise or settlement.

(b) AUTHORITY TO COMPROMISE OR SETTLE CONTROVERSIES WITHIN CLASSES. After a hearing on such notice as the court may direct, the court may fix a class or classes of controversies and authorize the trustee to compromise or settle controversies within such class or classes without further hearing or notice.

(c) ARBITRATION. On stipulation of the parties to any controversy affecting the estate the court may authorize the matter to be submitted to final and binding arbitration.

Rule 9020. Contempt Proceedings

(a) CONTEMPT COMMITTED IN PRESENCE OF BANKRUPTCY JUDGE. Contempt committed in the presence of a bankruptcy judge may be determined summarily by a bankruptcy judge. The order of contempt shall recite the facts and shall be signed by the bankruptcy judge and entered of record.

(b) OTHER CONTEMPT. Contempt committed in a case or proceeding pending before a bankruptcy judge, except when determined as provided in subdivision (a) of this rule, may be determined by the bankruptcy judge only after a hearing on notice. The notice shall be in writing, shall state the essential facts constituting the contempt charged and describe the contempt as criminal or civil and shall state the time and place of hearing, allowing a reasonable time for the preparation of the defense. The notice may be given on the court's own initiative or on application of the United States attorney or by an attorney appointed by the court for that purpose. If the contempt charged involves disrespect to or criticism of a bankruptcy judge, that judge is disqualified from presiding at the hearing except with the consent of the person charged.

(c) SERVICE AND EFFECTIVE DATE OF ORDER; REVIEW. The clerk shall serve forthwith a copy of the order of contempt on the entity named therein. The order shall be effective 10 days after service of the order and shall have the same force and effect as an order of contempt entered by the district court unless, within the 10 day period, the entity named therein serves and files objections prepared in the manner provided in Rule 9033(b). If timely objections are filed, the order shall be reviewed as provided in Rule 9033.

(d) RIGHT TO JURY TRIAL. Nothing in this rule shall be construed to impair the right to jury trial whenever it otherwise exists.

Rule 9021. Entry of Judgment

Except as otherwise provided herein, Rule 58 F. R. Civ. P. applies in cases under the Code. Every judgment entered in an adversary proceeding or contested matter shall be set forth on a separate document. A judgment is effective when entered as provided in Rule 5003. The reference in Rule 58 F. R. Civ. P. to Rule 79(a) F. R. Civ. P. shall be read as a reference to Rule 5003 of these rules.

Rule 9022. Notice of Judgment or Order

(a) JUDGMENT OR ORDER OF BANKRUPTCY JUDGE. Immediately on the entry of a judgment or order the clerk shall serve a notice of the entry by mail in the manner provided by Rule 7005 on the contesting parties and on other entities as the court directs. Unless the case is a chapter 9 municipality case, the clerk shall forthwith transmit to the United States trustee a copy of the judgment or order. Service of the notice shall be noted in the docket. Lack of notice of the entry does not affect the time to appeal or relieve or authorize the court to relieve a party for failure to appeal within the time allowed, except as permitted in Rule 8002.

(b) JUDGMENT OR ORDER OF DISTRICT JUDGE. Notice of a judgment or order entered by a district judge is governed by Rule 77(d) F. R. Civ. P. Unless the case is a chapter 9 municipality case, the clerk shall forthwith transmit to the United States trustee a copy of a judgment or order entered by a district judge.

Rule 9023. New Trials; Amendment Of Judgments

Rule 59 F. R. Civ. P. applies in cases under the Code, except as provided in Rule 3008.

Rule 9024. Relief from Judgment or Order

Rule 60 F. R. Civ. P. applies in cases under the Code except that (1) a motion to reopen a case under the Code or for the reconsideration of an order allowing or disallowing a claim against the estate entered without a contest is not subject to the one year limitation prescribed in Rule 60(b), (2) a complaint to revoke a discharge in a chapter 7 liquidation case may be filed only within the time allowed by Section 727(e) of the Code, and (3) a complaint to revoke an order confirming a plan may be filed only within the time allowed by Section 1144, Section 1230, or Section 1330.

Rule 9025. Security: Proceedings Against Sureties

Whenever the Code or these rules require or permit the giving of security by a party, and security is given in the form of a bond or stipulation or other undertaking with one or more sureties, each surety submits to the jurisdiction of the court, and liability may be determined in an adversary proceeding governed by the rules in Part VII.

Rule 9026. Exceptions Unnecessary

Rule 46 F. R. Civ. P. applies in cases under the Code.

Rule 9027. Removal

(a) NOTICE OF REMOVAL.

(1) WHERE FILED; FORM AND CONTENT. A notice of removal shall be filed with the clerk for the district and division within which is located the state or federal court where the civil action is pending. The notice shall be signed pursuant to Rule 9011 and contain a short and plain statement of the facts which entitle the party filing the notice to remove, contain a statement that upon removal of the claim or cause of action the proceeding is core or non-core and, if non-core, that the party filing the notice does or does not consent to entry of final orders or judgment by the bankruptcy judge, and be accompanied by a copy of all process and pleadings.

(2) TIME FOR FILING; CIVIL ACTION INITIATED BEFORE COMMENCEMENT OF THE CASE UNDER THE CODE. If the claim or cause of action in a civil action is pending when a case under the Code is commenced, a notice of removal may be filed only within the longest of (A) 90 days after the order for relief in the case under the Code, (B) 30 days after entry of an order terminating a stay, if the claim or cause of action in a civil action has been stayed under Section 362 of the Code, or (C) 30 days after a trustee qualifies in a chapter 11 reorganization case but not later than 180 days after the order for relief.

(3) TIME FOR FILING; CIVIL ACTION INITIATED AFTER COMMENCEMENT OF THE CASE UNDER THE CODE. If a case under the Code is pending when a claim or cause of action is asserted in another court, a notice of removal may be filed with the clerk only within the shorter of (A) 30 days after receipt, through service or otherwise, of a copy of the initial pleading setting forth the claim or cause of action sought to be removed or (B) 30 days after receipt of the summons if the initial pleading has been filed with the court but not served with the summons.

(b) NOTICE. Promptly after filing the notice of removal, the party filing the notice shall serve a copy of it on all parties to the removed claim or cause of action.

(c) FILING IN NON-BANKRUPTCY COURT. Promptly after filing the notice of removal, the party filing the notice shall file a copy of it with the clerk of the court from which the claim or cause of action is removed. Removal of the claim or cause of action is effected on such filing of a copy of the notice of removal. The parties shall proceed no further in that court unless and until the claim or cause of action is remanded.

(d) REMAND. A motion for remand of the removed claim or cause of action shall be governed by Rule 9014 and served on the parties to the removed claim or cause of action.

(e) PROCEDURE AFTER REMOVAL.

(1) After removal of a claim or cause of action to a district court the district court or, if the case under the Code has been referred to a bankruptcy judge of the district, the bankruptcy judge, may issue all necessary orders and process to bring before it all proper parties whether served by process issued by the court from which the claim or cause of action was removed or otherwise.

(2) The district court or, if the case under the Code has been referred to a bankruptcy judge of the district, the bankruptcy judge, may require the party filing the notice of removal to file with the clerk copies of all records and proceedings relating to the claim or cause of action in the court from which the claim or cause of action was removed.

(3) Any party who has filed a pleading in connection with the removed claim or cause of action, other than the party filing the notice of removal, shall file a statement admitting or denying any allegation in the notice of removal that upon removal of the claim or cause of action the proceeding is core or non-core. If the statement alleges that the proceeding is non-core, it shall state that the party does or does not consent to entry of final orders or judgment by the bankruptcy judge. A statement required by this paragraph shall be signed pursuant to Rule 9011 and shall be filed not later than 10 days after the filing of the notice of removal. Any party who files a statement pursuant to this paragraph shall mail a copy to every other party to the removed claim or cause of action.

(f) PROCESS AFTER REMOVAL. If one or more of the defendants has not been served with process, the service has not been perfected prior to removal, or the process served proves to be defective, such process or service may be completed or new process issued pursuant to Part VII of these rules. This subdivision shall not deprive any defendant on whom process is served after removal of the defendant's right to move to remand the case.

(g) APPLICABILITY OF PART VII. The rules of Part VII apply to a claim or cause of action removed to a district court from a federal or state court and govern procedure after removal. Repleading is not necessary unless the court so orders. In a removed action in which the defendant has not answered, the defendant shall answer or present the other defenses or objections available under the rules of Part VII within 20 days following the receipt through service or otherwise of a copy of the initial pleading setting forth the claim for relief on which the action or proceeding is based, or within 20 days following the service of summons on such initial pleading, or within five days following the filing of the notice of removal, whichever period is longest.

(h) RECORD SUPPLIED. When a party is entitled to copies of the records and proceedings in any civil action or proceeding in a federal or state court, to be used in the removed civil action or proceeding, and the clerk of the federal or state court, on demand accompanied by payment or tender of the lawful fees, fails to deliver certified copies, the court may, on affidavit reciting the facts, direct such record to be supplied by affidavit or otherwise. Thereupon the proceedings, trial and judgment may be had in the court, and all process awarded, as if certified copies had been filed .

(i) ATTACHMENT OR SEQUESTRATION; SECURITIES. When a claim or cause of action is removed to a district court, any attachment or sequestration of property in the court from which the claim or cause of action was removed shall hold the property to answer the final judgment or decree in the same manner as the property would have been held to answer final judgment or decree had it been rendered by the court from which the claim or cause of action was removed. All bonds, undertakings, or security given by either party to the claim or cause of action prior to its removal shall remain valid and effectual notwithstanding such removal. All injunctions issued, orders entered and other proceedings had prior to removal shall remain in full force and effect until dissolved or modified by the court.

Rule 9028. Disability of a Judge

Rule 63 F.R. Civ. P. applies in cases under the Code.

Rule 9029. Local Bankruptcy Rules

Each district court by action of a majority of the judges thereof may make and amend rules governing practice and procedure in all cases and proceedings within the district court's bankruptcy jurisdiction which are not inconsistent with these rules and which do not prohibit or limit the use of the Official Forms. Rule 83 F. R. Civ. P. governs the procedure for making local rules. A district court may authorize the bankruptcy judges of the district, subject to any limitation or condition it may prescribe and the requirements of 83 F. R. Civ. P., to make rules of practice and procedure which are not inconsistent with these rules and which do not prohibit or limit the use of the Official Forms. In all cases not provided for by rule, the court may regulate its practice in any manner not inconsistent with the Official Forms or with these rules or those of the district in which the court acts.

Rule 9030. Jurisdiction and Venue Unaffected

These rules shall not be construed to extend or limit the jurisdiction of the courts or the venue of any matters therein.

Rule 9031. Masters Not Authorized

Rule 53 F. R. Civ. P. does not apply in cases under the Code.

Rule 9032. Effect of Amendment of Federal Rules of Civil Procedure

The Federal Rules of Civil Procedure which are incorporated by reference and made applicable by these rules shall be the Federal Rules of Civil Procedure in effect on the effective date of these rules and as thereafter amended, unless otherwise provided by such amendment or by these rules.

Rule 9033. Review of Proposed Findings of Fact and Conclusions of Law in Non-Core Proceedings

(a) SERVICE. In non-core proceedings heard pursuant to 28 U. S. C. Section 157(c)(1), the bankruptcy judge shall file proposed findings of fact and conclusions of law. The clerk shall serve forthwith copies on all parties by mail and note the date of mailing on the docket.

(b) OBJECTIONS: TIME FOR FILING. Within 10 days after being served with a copy of the proposed findings of fact and conclusions of law a party may serve and file with the clerk written objections which identify the specific proposed findings or conclusions objected to and state the grounds for such objection. A party may respond to another party's objections within 10 days after being served with a copy thereof. A party objecting to the bankruptcy judge's proposed findings or conclusions shall arrange promptly for the transcription of the record, or such portions of it as all parties may agree upon or the bankruptcy judge deems sufficient, unless the district judge otherwise directs.

(c) EXTENSION OF TIME. The bankruptcy judge may for cause extend the time for filing objections by any party for a period not to exceed 20 days from the expiration of the time otherwise prescribed by this rule. A request to extend the time for filing objections must be made before the time for filing objections has expired, except that a request made no more than 20 days after the expiration of the time for filing objections may be granted upon a showing of excusable neglect.

(d) STANDARD OF REVIEW. The district judge shall make a de novo review upon the record or, after additional evidence, of any portion of the bankruptcy judge's findings of fact or conclusions of law to which specific written objection has been made in accordance with this rule. The district judge may accept, reject, or modify the proposed findings of fact or conclusions of law, receive further evidence, or recommit the matter to the bankruptcy judge with instructions.

Rule 9034. Transmittal of Pleadings, Motion Papers, Objections, and Other Papers to the United States Trustee

Unless the United States trustee requests otherwise or the case is a chapter 9 municipality case, any entity that files a pleading, motion, objection, or similar paper relating to any of the following matters shall transmit a copy thereof to the United States trustee within the time required by these rules for service of the paper:

(a) a proposed use, sale, or lease of property of the estate other than in the ordinary course of business;

(b) the approval of a compromise or settlement of a controversy;

(c) the dismissal or conversion of a case to another chapter;

(d) the employment of professional persons;

(e) an application for compensation or reimbursement of expenses;

(f) a motion for, or approval of an agreement relating to, the use of cash collateral or authority to obtain credit;

(g) the appointment of a trustee or examiner in a chapter 11 reorganization case;

(h) the approval of a disclosure statement;

(i) the confirmation of a plan;

(j) an objection to, or waiver or revocation of, the debtor's discharge;

(k) any other matter in which the United States trustee requests copies of filed papers or the court orders copies transmitted to the United States trustee.

Rule 9035. Applicability of Rules in Judicial Districts in Alabama and North Carolina

In any case under the Code that is filed in or transferred to a district in the State of Alabama or the State of North Carolina and in which a United States trustee is not authorized to act, these rules apply to the extent that they are not inconsistent with the provisions of title 11 and title 28 of the United States Code effective in the case.

PART X [Abrogated]

APPENDIX III

EXEMPT PROPERTY

CONTENTS

NOTE: Statutes current through January 1, 1993, except as noted.

FEDERAL BANKRUPTCY EXEMPTIONS

Type of Property	Amount of Exemption	Statute Creating Exemption
Debtor's aggregate interest in real or personal property that the debtor or a dependent of the debtor uses as a residence; or in a cooperative that owns property that the debtor or a dependent of the debtor uses as a residence; or in a burial lot for the debtor or a dependent of the debtor	$7,500.00	11 USC § 522(d)(1)
1 motor vehicle	$1,200.00	11 USC § 522(d)(2)
household furnishings, household goods, wearing apparel, appliances, books, animals, crops, or musical instruments held primarily for the personal, family, or household use of the debtor or a dependent of the debtor.	$4,000.00 aggregate value limitations with $200.00 limitation on value of each item.	11 USC § 522(d)(3)
Jewelry held primarily for personal, family, or household use of debtor or a dependent of the debtor	$500.00	11 USC § 522(d)(4)
Any property selected by debtor	Unused portion of § 522(d)(1) exemption plus $400.00, with $3,750.00 aggregate value limitation	11 USC § 522(d)(5)
Implements, professional books, or tools, of the trade of debtor or a dependent of the debtor	$750.00	11 USC § 522(d)(6)
Unmatured life insurance contracts owned by debtor, except credit life insurance contracts	100%	11 USC § 522(d)(7)
Accrued dividends or interest under, or loan value of, any unmatured life insurance contract owned by debtor in which the insured is the debtor or a person of whom the debtor is a dependent	$4,000.00 less any amounts transferred by insurer from cash reserve for payment of premiums	11 USC § 522(d)(8)
Professionally prescribed health aids of debtor and dependents	100%	11 USC § 522 (d)(9)
Social security, unemployment compensation, or public assistance benefits	100%	11 USC § 522(d)(10)(A)
Veterans' benefits	100%	11 USC § 522(d)(10)(B)
Disability, illness, or unemployment benefits	100%	11 USC § 522(d)(10)(C)
Alimony, support, or separate maintenance	100% of amount reasonably necessary for support of debtor and dependents	11 USC § 522(d)(10)(D)
Payments under stock bonus, pension, profitsharing, annuity, or similar plan or contract on account of illness, disability, death, age, or length of service	100% of amount reasonably necessary for support of debtor and dependents	11 USC § 522(d)(10)(E)

NOTE – Exemption does not apply if: plan or contract was established under auspices of insider that employed debtor at time plan or contract arose; such payment is on account of age or length of service; and such plan or contract does not qualify under 26 USC §§ 401(a), 403(a), 403(b), 408, or 409.

Type of Property	Amount of Exemption	Statute Creating Exemption
Crime victim's reparation law benefits or awards	100%	11 USC § 522(d)(11)(A)
Payments on account of the wrongful death of individual of whom debtor was a dependent	100% of amount reasonably necessary for support of debtor and independents	11 USC § 522(d)(11)(B)
Payments under life insurance contract insuring life of an individual of whom debtor was a dependent	100% of amount reasonably necessary for support of debtor and dependents	11 USC § 522(d)(11)(C)
Payments on account of personal bodily injury of debtor or person of whom debtor is a dependent (does not include compensation for pain and suffering or actual pecuniary loss)	$7,500.00	11 USC § 522(d)(11)(D)
Payments in compensation for loss of future earnings of debtor or person of whom debtor is a dependent	100% of amount reasonably necessary for support of debtor and dependents	11 USC § 522(d)(11)(E)

FEDERAL - NONBANKRUPTCY

Type of Property	Amount of Exemption	Statute Creating Exemption
Disposable earnings (earnings after deductions required by law)	75% OR 30 times the federal minimum hourly wage per week.* WHICHEVER IS GREATER	15 USC § 1673
Wages due masters, seamen and apprentices	no limit (does not apply to claims for maintenance and support of spouse and dependent children)	46 USC § 601
Veterans Administration benefits (includes pensions, life insurance and disability benefits)	no limit	38 USC § 3101(a)
Social Security benefits (includes retirement, death and disability benefits)	no limit	42 USC § 407
Longshoremen and harbor workers medical, disability and death benefits	no limit	33 USC § 916
Railroad employees retirement and disability annuities	no limit	45 USC § 231m
Federal civil service disability and death benefits	no limit	5 USC § 8130
Federal civil service retirement benefits	no limit	5 USC § 8346(a)
Military Survivor Benefit Plan annuities	no limit	10 USC § 1450(i)
Annuities paid to widows and dependent children of Federal Justices and Judges	no limit	28 USC § 376(n)
Servicemen's group life insurance benefits	no limit	38 USC § 770(g)
Veteran's group life insurance benefits	no limit	38 USC § 770(g)
Deposits made in U.S. servicemen's savings institutions by servicemen while on permanent duty assignment outside U.S. and its possessions	no limit	10 USC § 1035(a)

*This exemption does not apply to state and federal tax claims and smaller amounts are exempt against support claims. The federal minimum hourly wage is $4.25 per hour. See 29 USC § 206(a)(1).

ALABAMA

Type of Property	Amount of Exemption	Statute Creating Exemption
Homestead of resident (includes mobile home)	$5,000	*CA § 6-10-2
	(cannot exceed 160 acres) NOTE – Homestead and other personal exemptions must be filed with Probate Court to be effective (CA §§ 6-10-20, 21)	
Burial lots and seat or pew in place of public worship	100%	CA § 6-10-5
Personal property of resident, except wages, salaries and compensation	$3,000	CA § 6-10-6
Necessary wearing apparel of resident debtor and family	100%	CA § 6-10-6
Family portraits or pictures and all books used by family	100%	CA § 6-10-6
Wages, salaries and compensation for personal services	75%	CA § 6-10-7
Proceeds and avails of life insurance policies payable to person other than the insured (includes cash surrender value, loan value and dividends)	100%	CA §§ 6-10-8, 27-14-29
Disposable earnings (earnings less deductions required by law and deductions as periodic payments to pension, retirement or disability programs)	75% or 30 times the federal minimum hourly wage per week, whichever is greater	CA § 5-19-15
Growing or ungathered crops	100%	CA § 6-9-41
Public assistance payments	100%	CA § 38-4-8
Workmen's compensation benefits	100%	CA § 25-5-86
Unemployment compensation benefits	100%	CA § 25-4-140
Proceeds and avails of disability insurance contracts	$250 per month	CA § 27-14-31
Fraternal Benefit Society benefits	100%	CA § 27-34-27
Teachers' retirement system benefits	100%	CA § 16-25-23
State employees retirement system benefits	100%	CA § 36-27-28
Peace officers retirement and disability benefits	100%	CA § 36-21-77
Partner's interest in specific partnership property	100%	CA § 10-8-72(b)(3)

*CA stands for Code of Alabama

ALASKA

Use of federal bankruptcy
exemptions in 11 USC § 522(d)
not permitted in this state. See
AS § 9.38.055

Type of Property	Amount of Exemption	Statute Creating Exemption
Property used as principal residence of debtor or dependents	$54,000 (exemption may be claimed pro rata by joint or multiple owners)	AS § 9.38.010
Burial plots, health aids, medical benefits, crime victim's reparation awards, longevity bonuses, benefits exempt under federal law, liquor licenses, limited entry fishing permits, and tuition credits authorized under AS § 14.40.809(a), and permanent fund dividends exempt under AS § 43.23.065(a)	100%	AS § 9.38.015(a)
State disability, unemployment or illness benefits; teachers'; judges'; and public employees' retirement benefits; elected public officials retirement benefits; and state child support collections	100%	AS § 9.38.015(b) AS § 14.25.200 AS § 23.20.405 AS § 22.25.100
Assets and benefits of retirement plans	100%	AS § 9.38.017(a)
Household goods, wearing apparel, personal books and musical instruments, and family portraits and heirlooms	$3,000 aggregate value	AS § 9.38.020(a)
Personal jewelry of debtor and dependents	$1,000	AS § 9.38.020(b)
Implements, professional books and tools of trade	$2,800	AS § 9.38.020(c)
Pets	$1,000	AS § 9.38.020(d)
One motor vehicle not exceeding $20,000 in value	$3,000	AS § 9.38.020(e)
Unmatured life insurance and annuity contracts, including accrued dividends and loan value	100% except $10,000 limit on accrued dividends and loan value	AS § 9.38.025(a)
Periodic earnings of resident debtor	$350 per week or equivalent	AS § 9.38.030(a)
Cash and liquid assets of resident debtor without periodic earnings	$1,400 per month (does not include permanent fund dividends)	AS § 9.38.030(b)
Partner's interest in specific partnership property	100%	AS § 9.38.100(b)
Aid to dependent children and public assistance payments	As provided in § 9.38 above	AS § 47.25.395 AS § 47.25.210 AS § 47.25.550
Workmen's compensation benefits	As provided in § 9.38 above	AS § 23.30.160
Child support installments paid directly by debtor's employer	100%	AS § 9.55.210 (2)
Fraternal Benefit Society benefits	100%	AS § 21.84.240
Materials furnished by mechanics for construction of buildings	100%	AS § 34.35.105
Tenancies by the entireties	100%	AS § 34.15.140

NOTES: AS § 9.38.055 provides that only the exemptions in AS §§ 9.38.010, 9.38.015(a), 9.38.017, 9.38.020, 9.38.025 and 9.38.030 apply in bankruptcy proceedings. AS § 9.38.115 provides that the dollar amounts in AS § 9.38 are to be adjusted in the even numbered years to reflect cost of living changes.

ARIZONA

Use of federal bankruptcy exemptions in 11 USC § 522(d) not permitted in this state. See ARS § 33–1133

Type of Property	Amount of Exemption	Statute Creating Exemption
Homestead, consisting of debtor's equity in real property used as residence, an apartment of horizontal property, or mobile home and land upon which located	$100,000 NOTE – The total exemption claimed by both spouses may not exceed $100,000. The exemption must be recorded with the county recorder to be valid. The exemption applies to identifiable cash proceeds of a homestead sale for 18 months after the sale	ARS § 33–1101
1 kitchen table, 1 dining room table, 4 chairs for each table (plus 1 chair per table for each dependent residing in household exceeding 4), 1 living room couch, 1 living room chair plus 1 per dependent residing in household, 3 living room coffee or end tables, 3 living room lamps, 1 living room carpet or rug, 2 beds plus 1 per dependent residing in household, 1 bed table, dresser and lamp per each allowed bed, bedding for each allowed bed, pictures, oil paintings and drawings made by debtor, family portraits and frames, 1 television set, 1 radio, 1 stove, 1 refrigerator, 1 washing machine, 1 clothes dryer, 1 vacuum cleaner.	$4,000 aggregate value	ARS § 33–1123
Food, fuel and 6 months' provisions	100%*	ARS § 33–1124
Wearing apparel	$500*	ARS § 33–1125(1)
Musical instruments of debtor & family	$250*	ARS § 33–1125(2)
Domestic pets, horses, milk cows, and poultry	$500*	ARS § 33–1125(3)
Engagement and wedding rings	$1,000*	ARS § 33–1125(4)
Library	$250*	ARS § 33–1125(5)
1 typewriter, 1 bicycle, 1 sewing machine, a family bible, a lot in burying ground, 1 rifle, shotgun, or pistol	$500* aggregate value	ARS § 33–1125(7)
1 watch	$100*	ARS § 33–1125(6)
1 motor vehicle	$1,500* ($4,000 if debtor maimed or crippled)	ARS § 33–1125(8)
Wheel chair & prescribed health aids	100%*	ARS § 33–1125(9)
Interest in retirement plan qualified under Internal Revenue Code	100% (does not apply to contributions made within 120 days of filing of petition)	ARS § 33–1126B.
Prepaid rent and security deposits for debtor's residence	Lesser of $1,000 or 1 1/2 months rent (cannot be claimed if homestead exemption is claimed)	ARS § 33–1126C.
Life insurance proceeds paid or payable to surviving spouse or child	$20,000	ARS § 33–1126A.(1)
Earnings of minor child	100%	ARS § 33–1126A.(2)
Health, accident or disability insurance benefits	100% (certain debts excepted)	ARS § 33–1126A.(3)
Insurance proceeds for damage or destruction of exempt property	100% of exemption given for damaged or destroyed property	ARS § 33–1126A.(4)
Cash surrender value of debtor's life insurance policies payable to debtor's spouse, child, parent, siblings or dependent	$25,000 (debtor must own policies for at least 2 years) (excludes cash value increases caused by excessive payments in previous 2 years)	ARS § 33–1126A.(5) ARS §20–1131(D)

(continued on next page)

* must be used primarily for personal, family or household purpose. In case of married persons, each spouse may claim exemption, which may be combined with other spouses' exemption in same property.

270

ARIZONA

Type of Property	Amount of exemption	Statute Creating Exemption
Damages for wrongful levy or execution	100%	ARS § 33–1126A.(6)
One single bank account	$150	ARS § 33–1126A.(7)
Necessary tools, equipment, instruments and books used in business or profession by debtor or spouse	$2,500 (does not include personal motor vehicle)	ARS § 33–1130(1)
Machinery, utensils, feed, grain, seed and animals of farmer	$1,500	ARS § 33–1130(2)
Arms, uniforms and accoutrements required by law to be kept by debtor	100%	ARS § 33–1130(3)
Disposable earnings (earnings less deduction required by law) – includes pension and retirement payments	75% or 30 times the federal minimum hourly wage per week, WHICHEVER IS GREATER	ARS § 33–1131
Fraternal Benefit Society benefits	100%	ARS § 20–881
Unemployment compensation benefits	100%	ARS § 23–783
Workmen's compensation benefits	100%	ARS § 23–1068
Welfare assistance	100%	ARS § 46–208
Firemen's relief and pension benefits	100%	ARS § 9–968
Police pension benefits	100%	ARS § 9–931
Teachers' retirement benefits	100%	ARS § 15–1440
State employees' retirement benefits	100%	ARS § 38–762
Specific Partnership Property	100% of partner's interest	ARS § 29–225

ARKANSAS

Use of federal bankruptcy exemptions in 11 USC § 522(d) not permitted in this state. See ACA § 16–66–217

Type of Property	Amount of Exemption	Statute Creating Exemption
Wearing apparel of debtor and family	100%	Constitution art. 9, §§1 & 2
Personal property of unmarried resident debtor who is not head of family	$200	Constitution art. 9, § 1
Personal property of resident debtor who is married or head of family	$500	Constitution art. 9, § 2
Homestead of resident who is married or head of family (Homestead must be owned and occupied as residence by debtor. Exemption applies to minor children upon death of parents.)	$2,500 (Cannot exceed 160 acres and cannot be reduced to less than 80 acres regardless of value if not in city, town or village. Cannot exceed 1 acre and cannot be reduced to less than 1/4 acre regardless of value if in city, town or village.)	Constitution art. 9, §§3, 4, 5 ACA § 16–66–210
Homestead of deceased homesteader leaving widow or minor children	100% of value of homestead plus rents and profits therefrom for life of widow or children during minority.	Constitution art. 9, § 6
Net earnings for 60 days	$25 per week (may include excess earnings in personal property exemption)	ACA § 16–66–208
Family burial grounds	100%	ACA § 16–66–207
Proceeds of life, sickness, accident, or disability insurance policies	100%	ACA § 16–66–209
Contributions to Individual Retirement Account made more than one year prior to filing of bankruptcy case	$20,000 (limit applies to individual debtor and to husband and wife combined)	ACA § 16–66–218(b)(16)
Assets in and payments from retirement plans qualified under Internal Revenue Code	100% of qualified contributions	ACA § 16–66–220
Proceeds of annuity contracts	amount otherwise exempt under applicable law	ACA § 23–79–134
Public assistance grants	100%	ACA § 20–76–430
Unemployment compensation benefits	100% (support claims excepted)	ACA § 11–10–109
Workmen's compensation benefits	100%	ACA § 11–9–110
Disability insurance benefits	100%	ACA § 23–79–133
Fraternal Benefit Society benefits	100%	ACA § 23–74–119
Stipulated premium insurance benefits	100%	ACA § 23–71–112
Mutual assessment life insurance benefits	$1,000	ACA § 23–72–114
Group life insurance proceeds	100%	ACA § 23–79–132
Teachers' retirement benefits	100%	ACA § 24–7–715
State police retirement benefits	100%	ACA § 24–6–223
Firemen's relief & pension benefits	100%	ACA § 24–11–814
Policemen's pension & relief benefits	100%	ACA § 24–11–417, 515, 611, 713
Local police & fire retirement benefits	100%	ACA § 24–10–616
Specific partnership property	100%	ACA § 4–42–502(c)

NOTE: The following exemptions apply only to bankruptcy proceedings and are in addition to any other applicable exemptions.

Type of Property	Amount of Exemption	Statute Creating Exemption
The debtor's aggregate interest in real or personal property, including an interest in a cooperative, used by the debtor or a dependent of the debtor as a residence or as a burial plot	$800 for unmarried debtor $1,200 for married debtor	ACA § 16–66–218(a)(1)
One motor vehicle	$1,200	ACA § 16–66–218(a)(2)
Wedding bands, including diamonds of 1/2 carat or less	100%	ACA § 16–66–218(a)(3)
Implements, professional books, or tools of trade of debtor or a dependent of the debtor	$750	ACA § 16–66–218(a)(4)

CALIFORNIA

Use of federal bankruptcy exemptions in 11 USC § 522(d) not permitted in this state. See C.C.P. 703.130

Type of Property	Amount of Exemption	Statute Creating Exemption
Homestead exemption. Includes house + outbuildings & land, or mobile home, or boat; and includes proceeds from sale, damage or taking thereof	$75,000 for family unit member living with 1 or more non-owner family unit members. $100,000 for person who is 65 or older, disabled, or over 55 with annual gross income of $15,000 or less if single or $20,000 or less if married. $50,000 for any other person	*C.C.P § 704.730 NOTE– Debtor or spouse must reside in homestead and the exemption must be apportioned between the spouses if both are entitled to the exemption.
Necessary personal household furnishings, provisions, appliances, wearing apparel and personal effects of debtor and family	100%	C.C.P. § 704.020
Equity in motor vehicles, including insurance or execution sale proceeds for 90 days under § 704.010	$1,200	C.C.P. § 704.010
Tools, implements, materials, books and equipment used in trade or business (can include motor vehicle if not claimed under C.C.P. § 704.010)	$2,500 each for debtor & spouse if each is engaged in trade or business	C.C.P. § 704.060
Prosthetic and orthopedic appliances and health aids	100%	C.C.P. § 704.050
Jewelry, heirlooms and works of art	$2,500	C.C.P. § 704.040
Residential building materials	$1,000	C.C.P. § 704.030
Prisoners' funds in inmates' trust accounts	$1,000	C.C.P. § 704.090
Bank accounts used for direct deposit of Social Security funds	$500 for single payee $750 for 2 or more payees (all Social Security funds in account are exempt)	C.C.P. § 704.080
Earnings in deposit accounts or in cash or its equivalent	75%, except that all earnings subject support orders or assignments are exempt	C.C.P. § 704.070
Unmatured life insurance policies	100%	C.C.P. § 704.100(a)
Aggregate loan values of unmatured life insurance policies	$4,000 each for debtor and spouse	C.C.P. § 704.100(b)
Proceeds of matured life insurance policies	Amount reasonably necessary to support debtor and dependents	C.C.P. § 704.100(c)
Retirement funds and benefits held or payable by a public entity	100% (support claims excepted)	C.C.P. § 704.110(b) Government Code § 21201
Public retirement benefits received	100%	C.C.P. § 704.110(d)
State and public employees' vacation credits	100% (lump sum payments subject to federal earnings exemptions)	C.C.P. § 704.113
Funds and benefits of private retirement plans, except benefits of self-employed retirement plans	100% (support claims excepted)	C.C.P. § 704.115(b)
Self employed retirement plan benefits	Amounts necessary to support debtor and dependents (periodic payments subject only to federal earnings exemption)	C.C.P. § 704.115(e)(f)
Health and disability insurance benefits	100% with health care claims excepted	C.C.P. § 704.130
Personal injury and wrongful death claims	100%	C.C.P. §§ 704.140(a), 704.150(a)
Proceeds of personal injury and wrongful death claims	Amount necessary to support debtor and dependents (periodic payments subject only to federal earnings exemption)	C.C.P. §§ 704.140(d), 704.150(c)

(continued on next page)

* C.C.P. stands for Code of Civil Procedure

CALIFORNIA

Type of Property	Amount of Exemption	Statute Creating Exemption
Workmen's compensation benefits	100% (support claims excepted)	C.C.P. § 704.160
Unemployment insurance contributions and benefits	100% (support claims excepted)	C.C.P. § 704.120
Relocation payments	100%	C.C.P. § 704.180
Welfare and Fraternal Benefit Society benefits	$500 until 7-1-83, then 100%	C.C.P. § 704.170
Students' financial aid from institution of higher learnings	100%	C.C.P. § 704.190
Burial plots of debtor and spouse	100%	C.C.P. § 704.200
Specific partnership property	100% of partner's interest	Corp. Code § 15025

NOTE: The exemptions listed below apply only to title 11 cases and may only be used in lieu of the exemptions listed above. The exemptions listed below may be used as follows: (1) if a husband and wife file a joint petition, they must both use either the exemptions listed above or the exemptions listed below, but not both; (2) if a married person files a single petition, the exemptions listed above must be used unless both spouses sign a written waiver waiving the above exemptions for the period in which the case is pending; (3) a single person may use either the exemptions listed above or the exemptions listed below, but not both. See C.C.P. § 703.140(a). The exemptions listed above and below apply jointly to both debtors in a joint case and may not be claimed separately by each debtor in a joint case. See C.C.P. § 703.110 and In Re Talmadge, 832 F. 2d 1120.

Type of Property	Amount of Exemption	Statute Creating Exemption
Debtor's aggregate interest in real or personal property that the debtor or a dependent of the debtor uses as a residence; or in a cooperative that owns property that the debtor or a dependent of the debtor uses as a residence; or in a burial lot for the debtor or a dependent of the debtor	$7,500.00	C.C.P. § 703.140(b)(1)
1 motor vehicle	$1,200.00	C.C.P. § 703.140(b)(2)
Household furnishings, household goods, wearing apparel, appliances, books, animals, crops, or musical instruments held primarily for the personal, family, or household use of the debtor or a dependent of the debtor	$200.00 per item (no aggregate limit)	C.C.P. § 703.140(b)(3)
Jewelry held primarily for personal, family, or household use of debtor or a dependent of the debtor	$500.00	C.C.P. § 703.140(b)(4)
Any property selected by debtor	Unused portion of § 703.140(b)(1) exemption plus $400.00	C.C.P. § 703.140(b)(5)
Implements, professional books, or tools, of the trade of debtor or a dependent of the debtor	$750.00	C.C.P. § 703.140(b)(6)
Unmatured life insurance contracts owned by debtor, except credit life insurance contracts	100%	C.C.P. § 703.140(b)(7)
Accrued dividends or interest under, or loan value of, any unmatured life insurance contract owned by debtor in which the insured is the debtor or a person of whom the debtor is a dependent	$4,000.00	C.C.P. § 703.140(b)(8)
Professionally prescribed health aids of debtor and dependents	100%	C.C.P. § 703.140(b)(9)
Social security, unemployment compensation, or public assistance benefits	100%	C.C.P. § 703.140(b)(10)(A)

(continued on next page)

CALIFORNIA

Type of Property	Amount of Exemption	Statute Creating Exemption
Veterans' benefits	100%	C.C.P. § 703.140(b)(10)(B)
Disability, illness, or unemployment benefits	100%	C.C.P. § 703.140(b)(10)(C)
Alimony, support, or separate maintenance	100% of amount reasonably necessary for support of debtor and dependents	C.C.P. § 703.140(b)(10)(D)
Payments under stock bonus, pension, profitsharing, annuity, or similar plan or contract on account of illness, disability, death, age, or length of service	100% of amount reasonably necessary for support of debtor and dependents	C.C.P. § 703.140(b)(10)(E)

NOTE – Exemption does not apply if: plan or contract was established under auspices of insider that employed debtor at time plan or contract arose; such payment is on account of age or length of service; and such plan or contract does not qualify under 26 USC §§ 401(a), 403(a), 403(b), 408, or 409.

Type of Property	Amount of Exemption	Statute Creating Exemption
Crime victim's reparation law benefits or awards	100%	C.C.P. § 703.140(b)(11)(A)
Payments on account of the wrongful death of individual of whom debtor was a dependent	100% of amount reasonably necessary for support of debtor and independents	C.C.P. § 703.140(b)(11)(B)
Payments under life insurance contract insuring life of an individual of whom debtor was a dependent	100% of amount reasonably necessary for support of debtor and dependents	C.C.P. § 703.140(b)(11)(C)
Payments on account of personal bodily injury of debtor or person of whom debtor is a dependent (does not include compensation for pain and suffering or actual pecuniary loss)	$7,500.00	C.C.P. § 703.140(b)(11)(D)
Payments in compensation for loss of future earnings of debtor or person of whom debtor is a dependent	100% of amount reasonably necessary for support of debtor and dependents	C.C.P. § 703.140(b)(11)(E)

Type of Property	Amount of Exemption	Statute Creating Exemption
Homestead or Mobile Home occupied as home by owner	$30,000	CRS 38-41-201, 202
Necessary wearing apparel	$750	CRS 13-54-102 (1)(a)
Watches, jewelry and articles of adornment	$500	CRS 13-54-102 (1)(b)
Personal library, family pictures and school books	$750	CRS 13-54-102 (1)(c)
Burial sites for family members	100%	CRS 13-54-102 (1)(d)
Household goods	$1,500	CRS 13-54-102 (1)(e)
Provisions and fuel	$300	CRS 13-54-102 (1)(f)
Livestock and poultry of farmer	$3,000	CRS 13-54-102 (1)(g)
Machinery and tools of farmer	$2,000	CRS 13-54-102 (1)(g)
Armed Forces pension	100%	CRS 13-54-102 (1)(h)
Stock in trade, equipment and tools used in occupation	$1,500 **See note below	CRS 13-54-102 (1)(i)
Automobile used in occupation	$1,000	CRS 13-54-102 (1)(j)(I)
1 motor vehicle of disabled or elderly (65 or over) person used to obtain medical care for himself or for disabled or elderly dependent	$3,000	CRS 13-54-102(1)(j)(II)
Library of professional person	$1,500 **See note below	CRS 13-54-102 (1)(k)
Avails of life insurance policies	$5,000	CRS 13-54-102 (1)(l)
Proceeds of claim and avails of insurance policies covering loss or destruction of exempt property	Extent of exemption given for the lost or destroyed property	CRS 13-54-102 (1)(m)
Proceeds of claim for personal injuries	100%	CRS 13-54-102 (1)(n)
House trailer or trailer coach used as residence	$3,500	CRS 13-54-102 (1)(o)(I)
Mobile home used as residence	$6,000	CRS 13-54-102 (1)(o)(II)
Professionally-prescribed health aids	100%	CRS 13-54-102 (1)(p)
Crime victims reparation law awards	100%	CRS 13-54-102 (1)(q)
Security and utility deposits held by third parties	100%	CRS 13-54-102 (1)(r)
Funds in and benefits of any pension, retirement, or deferred compensation plan, including pensions, plans, and IRAs qualified under the I.R.C.	100% (child support claims excepted)	CRS 13-54-102 (1)(s)
Homestead sale proceeds (for 1 year)	$20,000 (cannot be commingled)	CRS 38-41-207
Disposable earnings (net earnings after deductions) – Includes health, accident, or disability insurance benefits	75% of disposable earnings OR 30 times the federal minimum hourly wage per week, WHICHEVER IS GREATER	CRS 5-5-105, 13-54-104 (exemption may be increased for totally disabled debtor)
Insurance proceeds from loss of homestead	Same as homestead exemption	CRS 38-41-209

(continued on next page)

COLORADO

Type of Property	Amount of Exemption	Statute Creating Exemption
Workers' compensation benefits	no limit	CRS 8–52–107(1)
Unemployment compensation benefits	no limit	CRS 8–80–103
Proceeds of group life insurance policies	no limit	CRS 10–7–205
Proceeds of annuity contract or life insurance policy in hands of insurer, if so provided in contract or policy	100%	CRS 10–7–106
Sickness and accident insurance benefits	$200 per month and no limit on lump sum payments	CRS 10–8–114
Fraternal Benefit Society benefits	no limit	CRS 10–14–122
Teacher's retirement benefits	no limit	CRS 22–64–120
Public employee's retirement benefits	no limit	CRS 24–51–212
Public assistance payments	no limit	CRS 26–2–131
Police pension benefits	no limit	CRS 31–30–313, 616
Firemen's pension benefits	no limit	CRS 31–30–412, 518
Public employees' deferred compensation	75% or 30 times the federal minimum hourly wage per week, WHICHEVER IS GREATER	CRS 24–52–102(4)
Specific partnership property	100% of partner's interest	CRS 7–60–125

**Note: may use either the exemption in CRS 13–54–102 (1)(i) or the exemption in CRS 13–54–102 (1)(k), but not both.

CONNECTICUT

Use of federal bankruptcy
exemptions under 11 USC §
522(d) permitted in this state

Type of Property	Amount of Exemption	Statute Creating Exemption
Necessary apparel, bedding, food, household furniture and appliances	100%	GSC § 52–352b(a)
Tools, books, instruments, farm animals and livestock feed necessary for occupation, profession or farming operation	100%	GSC § 52–352b(b)
Family burial plot	100%	GSC § 52–352b(c)
Public assistance payments and wages earned by public assistance recipient under incentive earnings or similar program	100%	GSC § 52–352b(d)
Health and disability insurance payments	100%	GSC § 52–352b(e)
Necessary health aids	100%	GSC § 52–352b(f)
Worker's compensation, social security, veteran's and unemployment benefits	100%	GSC § 52–352b(g)
Court approved child support payments	100%	GSC § 52–352b(h)
Arms, military equipment, uniforms and musical instruments of members of militia or U.S. armed services	100%	GSC § 52–352b(i)
1 motor vehicle	$1,500	GSC § 52–352b(j)
Wedding and engagement rings	100%	GSC § 52–352b(k)
Residential utility deposits and one residential security deposit	100%	GSC § 52–352b(l)
Payments received under profit–sharing, pension, annuity or similar retirement plan that qualifies under §§ 401, 403, 404 or 408 of the I.R.C., if private, or is established by federal or state statute, and assets and benefits in a Keogh or corporate retirement plan qualified under I.R.C.	Extend of earnings exempt under GSC § 52–361 (see below)	GSC § 52–352b(m)
Alimony and support payments other than child support	Extend of earnings exempt under GSC § 52–361 (see below)	GSC § 52–352b(n)
Awards under crime reparations act	100%	GSC § 52–352b(o)
Disposable earnings (earnings less deductions required by law)	75% or 40 times the federal minimum hourly wage per week, WHICHEVER IS GREATER	GSC § 52–361
Benefits payable on account of sickness or infirmity	100%	GSC § 52–352b(p)
Insurance proceeds from policies covering exempt property	Amount of exemption for covered property	GSC § 352b(q)
Liquor permits	100%	GSC § 30–14
Fraternal Benefit Society benefits	100%	GSC § 38–229
Proceeds of life insurance policies not payable to the insured	100%	GSC § 38–161
Teachers', state employees' and city employees retirement benefits	100%	GSC §§ 10–183q, 5–171 7–446
Specific partnership property	100% of partner's interest	GSC § 34–63
No–fault insurance payments	100%	GSC § 38–336

DELAWARE

Use of federal bankruptcy exemptions in 11 USC § 522(d) **not** permitted in this state. See DCA 10 § 4914(a)

Type of Property	Amount of Exemption	Statute Creating Exemption
Wages, salaries & commissions	85%	DCA 10 § 4913
Family Bible, school books, family library, family pictures, seat or pew in place of worship, lot in burial ground, all wearing apparel of debtor and family, sewing machines	100%	DCA 10 § 4902(a), (c)
Tools, implements and fixtures necessary to carry on trade or profession	$75.00 in New Castle and Sussex Counties, $50.00 in Kent County	DCA 10 § 4902(b)
Any property selected by debtor	$5,000 (applies only to bankruptcy proceedings and applies separately to each debtor in a joint case)	DCA 10 § 4914(b)
Pianos and organs leased to debtor	100%	DCA 10 § 4902(d)
Specific partnership property	100% of partner's interest	DCA 6 § 1525
Personal property of any nature	$500 (applies only to head of family)	DCA 10 § 4903
Proceeds and avails of life insurance policies payable to person other than the insured	100% (except transfers made in defraud of creditors)	DCA 18 § 2725
Fraternal Benefit Society benefits	100%	DCA 18 § 6118
Proceeds of health insurance policies	100%	DCA 18 § 2726
Group insurance proceeds	100%	DCA 18 § 2727
Annuity contract proceeds	$350 per month, less amounts paid in defraud of creditors	DCA 18 § 2728
Workmen's compensation benefits	100%	DCA 19 § 2355
Unemployment compensation benefits	100%	DCA 19 § 3374
Aid to blind persons	100%	DCA 31 § 2309
Public assistance payments	100%	DCA 31 § 513
State employees' pension benefits	100%	DCA 29 § 5503
Kent County employees' pension benefits	100%	DCA 9 § 4316
Sussex County employees' pension	100%	DCA 9 § 6415
Tenancies by the entirety	100% (see note below)	11 USC § 522(b) (2) (B)

NOTE: See Citizens Savings Bank v. Astrin, 44 Del. 451, 61 A. 2nd 419.

DISTRICT OF COLUMBIA

Use of federal bankruptcy
exemptions in 11 USC § 522(d)
permitted in this district

Type of Property	Amount of Exemption	Statute Creating Exemption
Wearing apparel of debtor and family	$300.00 per person	DCCE § 15–501(a)(1)
Beds, bedding, household furniture and furnishings, sewing machines, radios, stoves and cooking utensils	$300.00	DCCE § 15–501(a)(2)
Provisions & fuel for 3 months	100%	DCCE § 15–501(a)(3), (4)
Mechanics' tools and implements of debtor's trade or business	$200.00 (also applies to merchants)	DCCE § 15–501(a)(5)
Stock or materials for carrying on debtor's trade or business	$200.00 (also applies to merchants)	DCCE § 15–501(a)(5)
Library, office furniture and implements of professional man or artist	$300.00	DCCE § 15–501(a)(6)
One horse or mule & family pictures	100%	DCCE § 15–501(a)(7), (8)
One cart, wagon or dray and harness or one motor vehicle used principally by the debtor in his trade of business	$500.00	DCCE § 15–501(a)(7)
Family library	$400.00	DCCE § 15–501(a)(8)

NOTE: The above exemptions under DCCE § 15–501(a) apply only to the head of a family or householder who either resides in the District of Columbia or earns the major portion of his livelihood in the District of Columbia regardless of his place of residence, except that § 15–501(a)(5) also applies to merchants.

Type of Property	Amount of Exemption	Statute Creating Exemption
Disposable wages (wages include any compensation for personal services and include periodic payments under pension or retirement plans)	75% or 30 times the federal minimum hourly wage per week, WHICHEVER IS GREATER	DCCE § 16–572
Two–months' earnings (other than wages) and insurance, annuity or pension or retirement payments	$200.00 per month for principal supporter of family; $60.00 per month for any other person	DCCE § 15–503(a), (b)
Wearing apparel of person not principal supporter of family	$300.00	DCCE § 15–503(b)
Specific partnership property	100% of partner's interest	DCCE § 41–124
Residential condominium escrow deposits	100%	DCCE § 45–1869
Mechanics' tools of person not principal supporter of family	$200.00	DCCE § 15–503(b)

NOTE: The above exemptions under DCCE § 15–503 apply to persons who reside in or who earn the major portion of their livelihood in the District of Columbia.

Type of Property	Amount of Exemption	Statute Creating Exemption
Wages of prisoner on work release	100%	DCCE § 24–466
Unemployment compensation benefits	100%	DCCE § 46–318
Workmen's compensation benefits	100%	DCCE § 36–501 (33 USC § 916)
Shares and membership certificates in Cooperative Associations	$50.00	DCCE § 29–828
Seals and documents of Notaries Public	100%	DCCE § 1–507
Disability insurance benefits	100%	DCCE § 35–717
Fraternal Benefit Society benefits	100%	DCCE § 35–911
Group life insurance benefits	100%	DCCE § 35–718
Proceeds and avails of life insurance policies payable to person other than the insured	100% (except for premiums paid in defraud of creditors)	DCCE § 35–716 (see also §§ 30–212 and 30–213)
Public assistance payments	100%	DCCE § 3–215
Teachers' retirement benefits	100%	DCCE § 31–718
Public employees' retirement benefits	100%	DCCE § 1–217 (5 USC § 8346(a))
Wrongful death recoveries	100% less amounts awarded for expenses of last illness and burial	DCCE § 16–2703

NOTE: Tenancies by the entirety may be exempt under 11 USC § 522(b)(2)(B). See Travis v. Benson, 300 A.2nd 506.

FLORIDA

Use of federal bankruptcy exemptions in 11 U.S.C. § 522(d) not permitted in this state. See FSA § 222.20.

Type of Property	Amount of Exemption	Statute Creating Exemption
Homestead of any person (may be recorded by written statement with Circuit Court)	160 acres of contiguous land and improvements if located outside municipality or 1/2 acre of contiguous land and improvements in municipality used as residence by owner or his family	Art. 10, § 4(a)(1) of Constitution, FSA §§ 222.01 and 222.02
Compensation for personal services or labor of resident family head **	100%	FSA § 222.11
Personal property of any nature	$1,000.00	Art. 10, § 4(a)(2) of Constitution, FSA § 222.06
Dwelling house, mobile home used as residence, or modular home, owned and occupied by debtor on the land of another	100%	FSA § 222.05
Proceeds of life insurance policies of resident insured payable to another	100%	FSA § 222.13
Cash surrender value of life insurance policies on lives of state residents	100%	FSA § 222.14
Proceeds of annuity contracts of state residents or citizens	100%	FSA § 222.14
Disability insurance benefits	100%	FSA § 222.18
Pension money of U.S. pensioner	3 months' pension if needed for support of debtor or family	FSA § 222.21(1)
Benefits and contributions to retirement or profit–sharing plan qualified under I.R.C.	100%	FSA § 222.21(2)
Property listed in 11 U.S.C. 522(d)(10) (See Federal Bankruptcy Exemptions, supra, this Appendix, for specific property)	100%	FSA § 222.201
Assets and benefits of Prepaid Postsecondary Education Expense Trust Fund	100%	FSA § 222.22
Workmen's compensation benefits	100%	FSA § 440.22
Unemployment compensation benefits	100%	FSA § 443.17
Fraternal benefit Society benefits	100%	FSA 632.621
Police retirement benefits	100%	FSA § 185.25
Firemen's retirement benefits	100%	FSA § 175.241
Specific partnership property	100% of partner's interest	FSA § 620.68
Teacher's retirement benefits	100%	FSA § 238.15
Public employees' retirement benefits	100%	FSA § 121.131, 121.055 (6)(e) 2.
State and county employees' retirement benefits	100%	FSA § 122.15
Old age assistance benefits	100%	FSA § 400.162
Damages for injuries or death awarded to employees in hazardous occupations	100%	FSA § 769.05
Veterans' benefits	100%	FSA § 744.625 (3)
Government employees deferred compensation benefits	100%	FSA § 112.215(11)
Retired public employees health insurance subsidies	100%	FSA § 112.363(9)

** NOTE: Family head includes unmarried, divorced, legally-separated, or widowed person who provides more than 1/2 of the support of a child or other dependent. This exemption also applies to wages deposited in bank account by debtor if the funds can be traced and identified as wages.

NOTE: Tenancies by the entirety may be exempt under 11 USC § 522(b)(2)(B). See In Re Lunger, 5 C.B.C.2nd 43.

GEORGIA

Type of Property	Amount of Exemption	Statute Creating Exemption
Real or personal property (homestead)	$5,000	*GCA 44-13-1

NOTE: To obtain this exemption the debtor must file an application with the probate court of the county in which he or she resides. See GCA 44-13-4. Spouse or minor children of debtor may apply for exemption if debtor refuses. See GCA 44-13-2. Debtor and spouse cannot both claim exemption. See GCA 44-13-43.

Type of Property	Amount of Exemption	Statute Creating Exemption
Disposable earnings (Includes pension & retirement payments – see GCA 18-4-22)	75% OR 30 times the federal minimum hourly wage per week; WHICHEVER IS GREATER	GCA 18-4-20
Retirement and pension funds and benefits	100% until distribution, then same as GCA 18-4-20	GCA 18-4-22
Funds and benefits of employee benefit plans subject to ERISA	100% (alimony & support claims excepted)	GCA-18-4-22.1
Wages of deceased employee	$2,500	GCA 34-7-4
Proceeds and avails of life insurance policy payable to person other than insured	100%	GCA 33-25-11
Proceeds and avails of accident and sickness insurance policies	100%	GCA 33-29-15 GCA 33-30-10
Fraternal Benefit Society benefits	100%	GCA 33-15-20
Workmen's Compensation benefits	100%	GCA 34-9-84
Unemployment Compensation benefits	100%	GCA 34-8-7
Old age assistance payments	100%	GCA 49-4-35
Blind person's benefits	100%	GCA 49-4-58
Sheriff & Peace Officer's retirement benefits	100%	GCA 47-16-122, 47-17-103
Firemen's pension benefits	100%	GCA 47-7-122
District Attorney's retirement benefits	100%	GCA 47-13-90
Judges & Court employees' retirement benefits	100%	GCA 47-9-91, 47-10-120, 47-11-91, 47-14-91
State, county, and city employees' retirement benefits	100%	GCA 47-2-332 GCA 47-5-71
Teachers' retirement benefits	100%	GCA 47-3-28, 47-4-120
Legislator retirement benefits	100%	GCA 47-6-100

*NOTE: The Code section numbers shown are those of the Georgia Code Annotated, 1981

(continued on next page)

GEORGIA

Use of federal bankruptcy
exemptions under 11 USC § 522(d)
not permitted in this state.
See GCA 44-13-100 (b)

Type of Property	Amount of Exemption	Statute Creating Exemption
NOTE: The following exemptions may only be used in lieu of the exemptions provided in GCA 44-13-1. Debtor must file schedule of exempt property with probate court. See GCA 44-13-101		
Debtor's aggregate interest in real or personal property used by debtor or a dependent as residence, in cooperative owning property used by debtor or dependent as residence, or in burial plot of debtor or dependent	$5,000	GCA 44-13-100(a)(1)
Debtor's right to receive social security benefits, unemployment compensation, veterans' benefits, or disability, illness or unemployment benefits	100%	GCA 44-13-100 (a)(2)(A),(B),(C)
Alimony, support or maintenance payments, and payments under pension, annuity or similar plans or contracts on account of illness, disability, death, age or length of service	Amount reasonably necessary for support of debtor and dependents	GCA 44-13-100 (a)(2)(D)(E)
All motor vehicles	$1,000	GCA 44-13-100 (a)(3)
Household furnishings, household goods, wearing apparel, appliances, books, animals, crops or musical instruments, held primarily for the personal, family or household use of debtor or dependent	$200 per item, with $3,500 aggregate limit	GCA 44-13-100 (a)(4)
Personal jewelry of debtor or dependents	$500	GCA 44-13-100 (a)(5)
Debtor's aggregate interest in any property	$400 plus unused portion of exemption under GCA 51-1301.1 (1) above	GCA 44-13-100 (a)(6)
Implements, professional books or tools of trade of debtor or dependent	$500	GCA 44-13-100 (a)(7)
Any unmatured life insurance contract owned by debtor, except credit life insurance contract	100%	GCA 44-13-100 (a)(8)
Debtor's aggregate interest in accrued dividends or interest or loan value of any unmatured life insurance contract owned by debtor wherein the insured is the debtor or an individual of whom the debtor is a dependent	$2,000 less transfers described in 11 U.S.C. § 542(d)	GCA 44-13-100 (a)(9)
Professionally prescribed health aids of debtor and dependents	100%	GCA 44-13-100 (a)(10)
Awards made under crime reparation laws	100%	GCA 44-13-100 (a)(11)(A)
Payments on account of the wrongful death of an individual of whom the debtor was a dependent	Amount reasonably necessary for the support of debtor and dependents	GCA 44-13-100 (a)(11)(B)
Proceeds of life insurance contract insuring life of individual of whom debtor was a dependent on date of death	Amount reasonably necessary for the support of debtor and dependents	GCA 44-13-100 (a)(11)(C)
Payments on account of personal bodily injury, not including pain and suffering or compensation for actual pecuniary loss, of debtor or individual of whom debtor is a dependent	$7,500	GCA 44-13-100 (a)(11)(D)
Payments in compensation for loss of future earnings of debtor or of an individual of whom debtor is or was a dependent	Amount reasonably necessary for the support of debtor and dependents	GCA 44-13-100 (a)(11)(E)
Debtor's interest in public, nonprofit, or private pension or retirement plan	100% for public or nonprofit plans. private plans subject to limits set forth in federal bankruptcy exemptions.	GCA 44-13-100 (a)(2.1)

Use of federal bankruptcy
exemptions in 11 USC § 522(d)
permitted in this state

Type of Property	Amount of Exemption	Statute Creating Exemption
Real property owned by debtor	$30,000 if family head or if 65 or more years old; $20,000 if any other person	* HRS § 651–92

NOTE: Head of family includes man and woman when married, and every individual residing on the real property who has under his care or maintenance a minor child of his own or of a deceased brother, sister or spouse, a minor or unmarried brother or sister, or a father, mother or grandparent of either himself or a deceased spouse. See HRS § 651–91.

Type of Property	Amount of Exemption	Statute Creating Exemption
Necessary household furnishings and appliances, books and wearing apparel used by debtor and family	100%	HRS § 651–121(1)
Jewelry, watches and items of personal adornment	$1,000	HRS § 651–121(1)
Equity in one motor vehicle	$1,000 (wholesale value)	HRS § 651–121(2)
Tools, implements, instruments, uniforms, furnishings, books, equipment, 1 commercial fishing boat and nets, 1 motor vehicle, and other personal property used in trade, business or profession	100%	HRS § 651–121(3)
Lot in burying ground not exceeding 250 sq. ft., including improvements	100%	HRS § 651–121(4)
Proceeds of insurance on, and proceeds of sale of, exempt property for period of 6 months after receipt	Amount of exemption given for property destroyed or sold	HRS § 651–121(5)
Wages, salaries and commissions for personal services during last 31 days	100%	HRS § 651–121(6)
Wages	95% of first $100 per month 90% of next $100 per month 80% of balance per month	HRS § 652–1
Debtor's rights to pension, annuity, retirement, disability, or death benefits, optional benefits, or any other rights under any retirement plan qualified under Internal Revenue Code.	100%	HRS § 651–124
Proceeds and cash value of life insurance policies, endowment policies, and annuity contracts where beneficiary is spouse, child, parent or dependent of the insured	100%	HRS § 431–440
Disability insurance proceeds	100%	HRS § 431–439
Group life insurance proceeds	100%	HRS § 431–441
Fraternal Benefit Society benefits	100%	HRS § 434–19
Workmens' compensation benefits	100%	HRS § 386–57
Employment security benefits	100%	HRS § 383–163
Public assistance payments	100%	HRS § 346–33
Prisoners' earnings held by state	100%	HRS § 353–30
Specific partnership property	100% of partner's interest	HRS § 425–125
Tenancies by the entirety	100% *	11 USC § 522(b)(2)(B)
Policemen, Firemen and Bandsmen Pension System benefits	100%	HRS § 88–169
Public officers and employees pension and retirement benefits	100%	HRS §§ 88–91, 653–3

* See Sewada v. Endo, 57 Haw. 608, 561 P. 2nd 1291

IDAHO

Use of federal bankruptcy exemptions in 11 USC § 522(d) not permitted in this state. See IC § 11-609

Type of Property	Amount of Exemption	Statute Creating Exemption
Homestead, consisting of dwelling house or mobile home in which debtor resides and the land on which it is located	$30,000	IC § 55-1003

NOTE: The homestead exemption may not be claimed separately by both spouses. See IC § 55-1002. The homestead exemption also covers the proceeds of a homestead sale and insurance proceeds in the event of a loss, both for a period of six months after the event. See IC § 55-1113. Recording is not required.

Type of Property	Amount of Exemption	Statute Creating Exemption
Disposable earnings (earnings less deductions required by law)	75% or 30 times the federal minimum hourly wage per week WHICHEVER IS GREATER	IC § 11-207 different exemptions apply to support claims, see § 11-207 (2)(b)
Burial plot	100%	IC § 11-603(1)
Necessary health aids	100%	IC § 11-603(2)
Federal social security benefits, veterans' benefits and federal, state and local public assistance payments	100%	IC § 11-603(3)
Benefits payable for medical, surgical or hospital care	100%	IC § 11-603(5)
Benefits payable by reason of disability or illness	Amount reasonably necessary for support of debtor and dependents (see note below)	IC § 11-604(1)(a)
Amounts received for alimony, support or separate maintenance	Amount reasonably necessary for support of debtor and dependents (see note below)	IC § 11-604(1)(b)
Proceeds of claims for bodily injury of debtor or for bodily injury or wrongful death of person of whom debtor was or is a dependent	Amount reasonably necessary for support of debtor and dependents (see note below)	IC § 11-604(1)(c)
Proceeds or benefits payable upon death of insured who was spouse of debtor or upon whom the debtor was a dependent	Amount reasonably necessary for support of debtor and dependents (see note below)	IC § 11-604(1)(d)
Assets or benefits payable under stock bonus, pension, profit-sharing, annuity, or similar plan or contract providing benefits by reason of age, illness, disability or length of service	Amount reasonably necessary for support of debtor and dependents (see note below)	IC § 11-604(1)(d)

NOTE: The amount reasonably necessary for the support of the debtor and his dependents is the property required to meet the present and anticipated needs of the debtor and his dependents considering the debtor's responsibilities and all of the present and anticipated property and income of the debtor, including that which is exempt. See IC § 11-604(2). The exemptions allowed under IC § 11-604 are lost immediately upon the commingling of any of the exempt funds with other funds. See IC § 11-604(3).

Type of Property	Amount of Exemption	Statute Creating Exemption
Furnishings and appliances for one household, including one firearm	$500 per item (see note below)	IC § 11-605(1)(a)
Wearing apparel, animals, books and musical instruments held for personal use of debtor or his dependents	$500 per item (see note below)	IC § 11-605(1)(b)
Family portraits and heirlooms	$500 per item (see note below)	IC § 11-605(1)(c)
Personal jewelry	$250	IC § 11-605(2)
Implements, professional books and tools of trade	$1,000	IC § 11-605(3)
One motor vehicle	$1,500	IC § 11-605(3)
Arms, uniforms and accoutrements of peace officer, national guardsman, or member of military service	100%	IC § 11-605(5)
Water rights for irrigation of lands actually cultivated by debtor	160 inches of water	IC § 11-605(6)
Crops growing or grown on 50 acres of land leased, owned or possessed by debtor cultivating same	$1,000	IC § 11-605(6)

NOTE: The total amount of exemption claimed under IC § 605(1) cannot exceed $4,000 per household.

(continued on next page)

IDAHO

Type of Property	Amount of Exemption	Statute Creating Exemption
Proceeds of condemnation, loss, damage or destruction of exempt property for period of 3 months after receipt by debtor	Amount of exemption given for lost, damaged or destroyed property	IC § 11–606
Disability insurance benefits	100%	IC § 41–1834
Group life and disability insurance benefits	100%	IC { 41–1835(1)
Annuity contract proceeds	$350 per month	IC § 41–1836(1)(b)
Proceeds and avails of life insurance policies payable to person other than the insured	100%	IC § 41–1833(1)
Fraternal Benefits Society benefits	100%	IC § 41–3218
Workmens' compensation benefits	100%	IC § 72–802
Unemployment compensation benefits	100% (support claims excepted)	IC § 72–1375 & § 11–603(6)
Public assistance benefits	100%	IC § 56–233 & § 11–603(4)
Public employee's retirement fund benefits	100%	IC § 59–1325
Firemen's retirement benefits	100%	IC § 72–1417
Policemen's retirement and death benefits	100%	IC § 50–1517
Financial responsibility deposits under motor vehicle law	100%	IC § 49–1525
Specific partnership property	100% of partner's interest	IC § 53–325
Assets and benefits of pension, retirement, or profit–sharing plan qualified under Internal Revenue Code	100%	IC § 55–1011

ILLINOIS

Use of federal bankruptcy
exemptions under 11 USC §
522(d) not permitted in this state.
See SHA ch. 110, § 12-1201

Type of Property	Amount of Exemption	Statute Creating Exemption
Residence or homestead of individual. Includes farm, lot + buildings, condominium, personal property or cooperative Can be owned or leased.	$7,500 (includes proceeds of sale for 1 year; ¶12-906)	*SHA ch. 110, ¶12-901
Necessary wearing apparel, bible, school books, family pictures and prescribed health aids of debtor & dependents	100%	SHA ch. 110, ¶12-1001 (a), (e)
Any personal property of debtor	$2,000	SHA ch. 110, ¶12-1001(b)
One motor vehicle	$1,200	SHA ch. 110, ¶12-1001(c)
Implements, books & tools of trade	$750	SHA ch. 110, ¶12-1001(d)
Proceeds and cash value of life insurance policies and annuity contracts payable to dependent of insured	100%	SHA ch. 110, ¶12-1001(f)
Social Security benefits, unemployment compensation benefits, public assistance benefits, veteran's benefits, and disability and illness benefits	100%	SHA ch. 110, ¶12-1001(g) (1), (2), (3)
Alimony, support or separate maintenance	Amount reasonably necessary to support debtor & dependents	SHA ch. 110, ¶12-1001 (g)(4)
Restitution payments made under 50 U.S.C. App. 1989b, 1989c	100%	SHA ch. 110, ¶12-1001 (g)(5)
Debtor's interest in a retirement plan qualified under the Internal Revenue Code or a public employee pension plan	100%	SHA ch. 110, ¶12-1006

(NOTE: Includes stock bonus, pension, profit-sharing, annuity, or similar plans, self-employed or simplified employee pension plans, government or church retirement plans, and individual retirement annuities or accounts.)

Type of Property	Amount of Exemption	Statute Creating Exemption
Crime victim's reparation law awards	100%	SHA ch. 110, ¶12-1001(h)(1)
Wrongful death payments resulting from death of person of whom debtor was a dependent	Amount reasonably necessary to support debtor and dependents	SHA ch. 110, ¶12-1001(h)(2)
Life insurance payments from policy insuring person of whom debtor was a dependent	Amount reasonably necessary to support debtor and dependents	SHA ch. 110, ¶12-1001(h)(3)
Payments on account of bodily injury of debtor or person of whom debtor was a dependent	$7,500	SHA ch. 110, ¶12-1001(h)(4)

NOTE: Proceeds from sale of exempt personal property are also exempt. Nonexempt property converted into exempt property in fraud of creditors is not exempt. Property acquired within 6 months of the filing of bankruptcy is presumed to have been acquired in contemplation of bankruptcy. The exemptions in SHA ch. 110, ¶12-1001(h) extend for 2 years after the debtor's right to receive the payments accrues, and, as to property traceable therefrom, for 5 years after accrual. See SHA ch. 110, ¶12-1001.

Type of Property	Amount of Exemption	Statute Creating Exemption
Specific partnership property	100% of partner's interest	SHA ch. 106 1/2, ¶25
Gross earnings or disposable earnings (disposable earnings are gross earnings less deductions required by law)	85% of gross earnings, OR disposable earnings equal to 45 times the federal minimum hourly wage per week, WHICHEVER IS GREATER	SHA ch. 110, ¶12-803 (includes periodic pension or retirement payments – SHA ch. 48 ¶39.4)
Proceeds & cash value of life or endowment insurance policy or annuity contract payable to insured's spouse or dependent	100% (applies against creditors of insured)	SHA ch. 73, ¶850
Fraternal Benefit Society benefits	100%	SHA ch. 73, ¶925
Workmen's compensation benefits	100%	SHA ch. 48, ¶138.21
Unemployment compensation benefits	100% (support claims excepted)	SHA ch. 48, ¶540
Public welfare benefits	100%	SHA ch. 23, ¶11-3
Property held in trust for debtor	100%	SHA ch. 110, ¶2-1403

*SHA stands for Smith-Hurd Illinois Annotated Statutes

INDIANA

Type of Property	Amount of Exemption	Statute Creating Exemption
Real Estate or personal Property constituting Personal or Family Residence of domiciled debtor	$7,500 (Exemption may be used individually by joint debtors if property is jointly owned)	BIS 34-2-28-1(a)(1)
Other Real Estate and tangible personal property of domiciled debtor	$4,000	BIS 34-2-28-1(a)(2)
Intangible Personal Property of domiciled debtor (includes choses in action but excludes debts and income owing)	$100	BIS 34-2-28-1(a)(3)

LIMITATION -- The aggregate of all of the above exemptions cannot exceed the total sum of $10,000 and apply only to debts growing out of or founded upon express or implied contract or a tort claim. See BIS 34-2-28-1(a), (c).

Type of Property	Amount of Exemption	Statute Creating Exemption
Professionally prescribed health aids of debtor and dependents	100%	BIS 34-2-28-1(a)(4)
Debtor's interest in real estate held as tenant by the entirety on date of filing, unless debtor and spouse file joint petition or their bankruptcy cases are subsequently consolidated	100%	BIS 34-2-28-1(a)(5)
Debtor's interest in pension or retirement fund, annuity plan, individual retirement account, or similar fund, either private or public	100%	BIS 34-2-28-1(a)(6)
Disposable earnings (net earnings after deductions required by law)	30 times the federal minimum hourly wage per week OR 75% of disposable earnings WHICHEVER IS GREATER	BIS 24-4.5-5-105
Public assistance benefits of disabled or blind persons	100%	BIS 12-1-6-12 BIS 12-1-7.1-14
Crime victim's reparation awards	100%	BIS 16-7-3.6-15
Mutual life & accident ins. proceeds	100%	BIS 27-8-3-23
Teachers' pension benefits	no limit	BIS 21-6.1-5-17(a)
Police pension benefits	no limit	BIS 17-3-14-17 BIS 19-1-18-21 BIS 19-1-24-4
Fraternal Benefit Society benefits	no limit	BIS 21-1-14-16
Group life insurance proceeds	no limit	BIS 27-1-12-29
Municipal utility employees' pension benefits	no limit	BIS 19-3-31-5
Firemen's pension benefits	no limit	BIS 19-1-37-22 BIS 18-1-12-11
Workmen's compensation benefits	no limit	BIS 22-3-2-17
Widow's allowance upon death of spouse	$8,500	BIS 34-1-40-9
Specific partnership property	100% of partner's interest	BIS 23-4-1-25
Proceeds and avails of life insurance policies payable to spouse, children, dependent relative or creditor of insured	no limit	BIS 27-1-12-14

IOWA

Use of federal bankruptcy exemptions in 11 USC § 522(d) not permitted in this state. See CI § 627.10.

Type of Property	Amount of Exemption	Statute Creating Exemption
Homestead of any person (persons living together as a single household unit may claim exemption once in the aggregate.)	1/2 acre including dwelling house and appurtenances if within city plat; otherwise, 40 acres including dwelling house and appurtenances (acreage may be enlarged if value is less than $500)	CI §§ 561.2, 561.16
Wearing apparel of debtor and dependents and receptacles containing same	$1,000 (plus wedding or engagement ring received prior to marriage)	CI § 627.6(1)
1 shotgun and either 1 musket or 1 rifle	100%	CI § 627.6(2)
Libraries, family Bibles, portraits, pictures, musical instruments, and paintings not kept for sale	$1,000 aggregate	CI § 627.6(3)
Burying ground or interment space	1 acre	CI § 627.6(4)
Household furnishings, goods & appliances held for personal, family or household use of debtor or dependents	$2,000 aggregate	CI § 627.6(5)
Debtor's interest in life insurance policy payable to spouse, child or dependent of debtor (includes loan or cash surrender value and accrued dividends or interest)	100%	CI § 627.6(6)
Professionally-prescribed health aids	100%	CI § 627.6(7)
Debtor's rights in Social Security unemployment compensation, local public assistance benefits, veterans benefits, or disability or illness benefits	100%	CI § 627.6(8)(a),(b),(c)
Debtor's rights to alimony, support or separate maintenance	Amount reasonably necessary to support debtor & dependents	CI § 627.6(8)(d)
Debtor's right to payments under pension, annuity or similar plan or contract on account of illness, death, age or length of service	100% (payments resulting from excessive personal contributions within previous year are not exempt)	CI § 627.6(8)(e)
Personal musical instruments of debtor or dependents; one motor vehicle; and the debtor's interest in accrued wages and state and federal tax refunds.	$5,000 aggregate (Does not include radios, television sets, or record or tape players and there is a $1,000 limit on accrued wages and tax refunds.	CI § 627.6(9) NOTE: The accrued wages and tax refund exemption applies to bankruptcy cases only and is in addition to the exemption in CI §§ 537.5105 & 624.21.
Implements, professional books, or tools of trade of nonfarmer debtor and dependents	$10,000	CI § 627.6(10)
Implements, equipment, livestock and livestock feed, if reasonably related to normal farming operation	$10,000 (debtor must be engaged in farming)	CI § 627.6(11) NOTE: This exemption is in addition to the motor vehicle exemption in CI § 627.6(9).
Disposable earnings from others	100% for 2 years after entry of deficiency judgment. (Earnings paid to debtor directly or indirectly by debtor are not exempt)	CI § 627.6(12) NOTE: This exemption applies only to deficiency judgments entered in foreclosures actions on agricultural land in which the debtor does not exercise the delay of enforcement provisions of CI § 654.6.
Specific partnership property	100% of partner's interest	CI § 544.25
United States Government pension benefits	100% (includes homestead purchased with pension money)	CI §§ 627.8, 627.9
Worker's Compensation benefits	100% (support claims excepted)	CI § 627.13
Assistance for adopted children	100%	CI § 627.19
Disposable earnings (earnings less deductions required by law)	75% OR 40 times the federal minimum hourly wage per week WHICHEVER IS GREATER. NOTE: only the following amounts may be garnished during a calendar year Debtor's expected annual earnings / Amount that can be garnished in calendar year $12,000 or less — $ 250 $12,000 to $16,000 — 400 $16,000 to $24,000 — 800 $24,000 to $35,000 — 1,500 $35,000 to $50,000 — 2,000 $50,000 or more — 10% of expected earnings	CI § 642.21, CI § 537.5105

(continued on next page)

IOWA

Type of Property	Amount of Exemption	Statute Creating Exemption
Aid to dependent children benefits	100%	CI § 239.13
Group insurance benefits	same as provided in chapter 627	CI §§ 509.12, 509A.9
Benefits or proceeds of accident, health, disability or endowment insurance policy	100% (exemption applies to insured or to spouse and children of deceased insured)	CI § 511.37
Benefit or indemnity paid under accident, health or disability insurance policy	100%	CI § 627.6(6)
Avails of life, accident, health or disability insurance policy payable to spouse, child, or dependent of insured	$15,000 (applies to debts of beneficiary contracted prior to death of insured)	CI § 627.6(6)
Fraternal insurance benefits	same as provided in chapter 627	CI § 512.17
National Guard and State Guard equipment owned by members	no monetary limit	CI §§ 29A.41, 29A.70
Pension benefits of policemen and firemen	100%	CI §§ 411.13, 410.11
Public employees retirement benefits	100%	CI § 97B.39
Unemployment compensation benefits	100%	CI § 96.15
Liquor licenses	100%	CI § 123.38

KANSAS

Type of Property	Amount of Exemption	Statute Creating Exemption
160 acres of farming land, or 1 acre in an incorporated town or city, or a manufactured or mobile home, if occupied as a residence by the owner or the owner's family	100%	KSA § 60-2301
Furnishings, equipment and supplies, including food, fuel and clothing, at principal residence necessary for 1 year	100%	KSA § 60-2304(a)
Jewelry and personal ornaments	$1,000	KSA § 60-2304(b)
One means of conveyance	$20,000 (no limit for the handicapped)	KSA § 60-2304(c)
Burial plot or crypt or cemetery lot exempt under KSA § 17-1302	100%	KSA § 60-2304(d)
Books, documents, furniture, tools, instruments, implements, equipment, breeding stock, seed grain, growing plant stock, or other tangible means of production necessary to carry on trade, profession, business or occupation.	$7,500	KSA § 60-2304(e)
Property listed in 11 U.S.C. § 522(d)(10)	100% (See Federal Bankruptcy Exemption, supra in this Appendix for a list of the exempt property)	KSA § 69-2312
Disposable earnings (net earnings after deductions required by law	75% of disposable earnings or 30 times the federal minimum hourly wage per week, whichever is greater (see note below)	KSA § 60-2310
Proceeds and other interests (including cash value) of life insurance policies	100% of portion issued more than one year prior to filing of bankruptcy case	KSA § 40-414
Crime victim's reparation awards	100%	KSA § 74-7313
Unemployment compensation benefits	100%	KSA § 44-718
Workmen's compensation benefits	100%	KSA § 44-514
Public assistance payments	100%	KSA § 39-717
Liquor license, club license, or malt beverage wholesale or distribution license	100%	KSA §§ 41-326, 41-2629, 41-2714
United States pension benefits for three months if necessary to support family	100%	KSA § 60-2308
Fraternal Benefit Society benefits	100%	KSA § 40-711
Luggage & property detained by innkeeper	100%	KSA § 36-202
Uniforms, arms and equipment of national guardsman	100%	KSA § 48-245
Specific partnership property	100% of partner's interest	KSA § 56-325
Funds in prearranged funeral agreement or plan	100%	1987 Senate Bill No. 11, §2
Pension, annuity, retirement, disability or death benefits of state employees, police, firemen, school employees, and other public employees	100%	KSA §§ 12-111a, 12-5005, 13-1246a, 13-14,102, 13-14a10 14-10a10, 20-2618, 72-1768 72-5526,74-4923, 74-4978g, 74-49,105, 74-49,106
Goods held on approval of sale	100%	KSA § 84-2-326

Note: 100% of a debtor's disposable earnings are exempt for a two-month period after the debtor returns to work if the debtor was unable to work for a period of two weeks or more on account of sickness of the debtor or the debtor's family.

KENTUCKY

Use of federal bankruptcy exemptions in 11 USC § 522(d) not permitted in this state. See KRS § 427.170

Type of Property	Amount of Exemption	Statute Creating Exemption
Land or personal property used by debtor or dependent as permanent residence within state, or burial plot of debtor or dependent	$5,000	KRS § 427.060
Disposable earnings (earnings after deductions required by law)	75% or 30 times the federal minimum hourly wage, whichever is greater NOTE: If wages earned out of state see KRS § 427.050 for exemption	KRS § 427.010(2)
Household furnishing, personal clothing, ornaments and jewelry	$3,000 (applies to residents only)	KRS § 427.010(1)
Tools, equipment and livestock (including poultry) of farmer	$3,000 (applies to residents only)	KRS § 427.101(1)
One motor vehicle and accessories (including 1 spare tire)	$2,500 (applies to residents only)	KRS § 427.010(1)
Professionally prescribed health aids of debtor and dependents	100%	KRS § 427.010(1)
One motor vehicle and accessories (including 1 spare tire) of mechanic or skilled artisan engaged in repair, replacement or servicing of essential equipment	$2,500	KRS § 427.030
One motor vehicle and accessories (including 1 spare tire) of minister, attorney, physician, surgeon, chiropractor, veterinarian or dentist	$2,500	KRS § 427.040
Necessary tools of trade	$300.00	KRS § 427.030
Professional library, office equipment, instruments and furnishings of minister, attorney, physician, surgeon, chiropractor, veterinarian, or dentist	$1,000.00	KRS § 427.040
Proceeds and avails of life insurance policy payable to person other than the insured or person effecting the policy	100%	KRS § 304.14-300
Benefits paid by assessment, cooperative life or casualty insurance company or by a fraternal benefit society	100%	KRS § 427.110
Proceeds and avails of health insurance contracts and disability provisions supplemental to life insurance or annuity contracts	100%	KRS § 304.14-310
Policies of group life insurance and group health insurance and proceeds therefrom	100%	KRS § 304.14-320
Annuity contracts benefits	100%	KRS § 304.14-330
Basic no-fault insurance benefits	100%	KRS § 304.39-206
Workmen's compensation benefits	100%	KRS § 342.180
Unemployment compensation benefits	100%	KRS § 341.470
Police and firemen's pension benefits in cities of first through fourth classes	100%	KRS § 427.120 & 427.125
State employees' retirement benefits	100%	KRS § 61.690
Teachers' retirement benefits	100%	KRS § 161.700
Public assistance payments	100%	KRS § 205.220
Money or property received as alimony, support or maintenance	Amount reasonably necessary for support of debtor and dependents	KRS § 427.150(1)
Debtor's right or interest in individual retirement account or annuity or other pension or retirement plan that qualifies under the I.R.C.	100% NOTE- Contributions made within 120 days prior to filing are not exempt.	KRS § 427.150(2)(f)
Crime victim's reparation law awards	100%	KRS § 427.150(2)(a)
Payments on account of the wrongful death of individual of whom debtor was a dependent	Amount reasonably necessary to support debtor and dependents	KRS § 427.150(2)(b)

(continued on next page)

KENTUCKY

Type of Property	Amount of Exemption	Statute Creating Exemption
Personal bodily injury payment, not including compensation for pain and suffering or actual pecuniary loss, of debtor or individual of whom debtor is a dependent	$7,500	KRS § 427.150(2)(c)
Payment in compensation of loss of future earnings of debtor or individual of whom debtor is a dependent	Amount reasonably necessary to support debtor and dependents	KRS § 427.150(2)(d)
Assets held, payments, and amounts payable under pension and retirement systems for teachers, state employees, policemen and firemen	100%	KRS § 427.150(2)(e)
Property of any nature	$1,000 (this exemption applies only to bankruptcy cases)	KRS § 427.160
Specific partnership property	100% of partner's interest	KRS § 362.270

NOTE: The exceptions granted in KRS chapter 427 are not applicable to property upon which the debtor has voluntarily granted a lien to the extent of the balance due on the debt secured thereby. See KRS § 427.010(4). Grain storage receipts are prima facie evidence in bankruptcy of the claimant's rights to the grain shown therein. See KRS § 427.180.

LOUISIANA

Type of Property	Amount of Exemption	Statute Creating Exemptions
Homestead (must be occupied as homestead and title to property must be in debtor or spouse)	$15,000 (cannot exceed 160 acres)	* LSA–RS 20:1 Constitution Art 12, § 9
Pensions, annuities & tax–exempt contributions to retirement plans qualified under I.R.C. if made more than 1 year prior to filing of case	100% (support claims excepted)	LSA–RS 20–33(1)
Gratuitous payments made by employers to employees or former employers or their survivors	100%	LSA–RS 29:33(2)
Disposable earnings (earnings less deductions required by law)	75% or 30 times the federal minimum hourly wage per week, WHICHEVER IS GREATER (50% for support claims)	LSA–13:3881A(1)
Tools, instruments, books, one utility trailer, and one pickup truck (under 3 tons gross weight) or one motor vehicle, if necessary for earning livelihood	100% (luxury vehicles and vehicles used solely for transportation to and from work are excluded)	LSA–RS 13:3881A(2)
Income from total property and rights of usufruct of estates of minor children	100%	LSA–RS 13:3881A(3)
Clothing, bedding linen, chinaware, non-sterling silverware, glassware, living room, bedroom and dining room furniture, cooking stove, heating and cooling equipment, kitchen utensils, pressing irons, washers, dryers, refrigerators, deep freezers (electric or otherwise) 1 noncommercial sewing machine, required therapy equipment, used by debtor or his family	100%	LSA–RS 13:3881A(4)
Family portraits, arms and military accoutrements, musical instruments of debtor and family, and poultry, fowl and 1 cow kept for family use, and all dogs, cats and other household pets	100%	LSA–RS 13:3881A(4)
Wedding or engagement rings	$5,000	LSA–RS 13:3881(A)(5)
Pensions, annuity payments, individual retirement accounts and other retirement plans that qualify under the I.R.C.	100% of tax–exempt amounts NOTE– Contributions made within 1 year prior to filing are not exempt.	LSA–RS 13–3881 D
Spendthrift trust proceeds	100% – excludes amounts contributed by or subject to voluntary alienation by beneficiary	LSA–RS 9:2004
Proceeds and avails of life insurance policies	100%	LSA–RS 22:647A
Fraternal Benefit Society benefits	100%	LSA–RS 22:564
Annuity contract proceeds and avails	100%	LSA–RS 22:647B
Proceeds of group life insurance policies	100%	LSA–RS 22:649A
Workmen's compensation benefits	100%	LSA–RS 23:1205
Unemployment compensation benefits	100% (support claims excepted)	LSA–RS 23:1693
Public assistance payments	100%	LSA–RS 46–111
Wages earned out of state	100% (applies only against out–of–state debts)	LSA–RS 13:3951
Assessors' retirement fund benefits	100%	LSA–RS 47:1921
Court clerks' retirement benefits	100%	LSA–RS 13:939
District Attorney's retirement benefits	100%	LSA–RS 16:1003
Firemen's relief and pension benefits	100%	LSA–RS 33:2120, 33:2035, 33:2140
Louisiana State University retirement system benefits	100%	LSA–RS 17:1613
Municipal employees retirement benefits	100%	LSA–RS 33:7155
School employees retirement benefits	100%	LSA–RS 17:1013, 17:1233, 17:833

(continued on next page)

* LSA–RS stands for West's Louisiana Statutes Annotated, Revised Statutes

NOTE: Property upon which the debtor has voluntarily granted a lien is not exempt to the extent of the balance due on the debt secured thereby. See LSA–RS 13:3881(B)(2).

LOUISIANA

(continued from previous page)

Type of Property	Amount of Exemption	Statute Creating Exemption
Teachers retirement benefits	100%	LSA–RS 17:573
State employees retirement system benefits	100%	LSA–RS 42:545
Registrars of voters employees retirement benefits	100%	LSA–RS 18:1653
Parochial employees retirement benefits	100%	LSA–RS 33:6103
Sheriff's pension and relief fund benefits	100%	LSA–RS 33:1428
Police pension and relief benefits	100%	LSA–RS 33:2381, 33:2233, 33:2385.7, 33:2302, 33:2363
Judicial retirement benefits	100%	LSA–RS 13:5.7, 13:25.1

MAINE

Type of Property	Amount of Exemption	Statute Creating Exemption
Debtor's interest in real or personal property used by debtor as residence, or a burial plot (includes a cooperative and proceeds of sale for six months)	$12,500 ($25,000 if minor dependents reside there) ($60,000 if debtor or dependent is age 60 or older or disabled)	14 MRSA § 4422(1) (In jointly owned property the exemption is the lesser of $12,500 or the debtor's fractional share times $25,000)
One motor vehicle	$2,500	14 MRSA § 4422(2)
Household furnishings & goods, wearing apparel, appliances, books, animals, crops, or musical instruments	$200 per item (must be held primarily for the personal, family, or household use of the debtor or a dependent)	14 MRSA § 4422(3)
Personal jewelry of debtor or dependent	$750	14 MRSA § 4422(4)
Debtor's wedding band & engagement	100%	14MRSA § 4422(4)
Implements, professional books, or tools of the trade of the debtor or a dependent	$5,000	14 MRSA § 4422(5)
One cooking stove, all furnaces or heating stoves, and fuel not to exceed 10 cords of wood, 5 tons of coal, 1,000 gallons of oil, or its equivalent	100% (must be held primarily for the personal, family, or household use of the debtor or a dependent)	14 MRSA § 4422(6)
6 months' food provisions; seeds, fertilizers, feed, & other materials needed for one growing season: and all tools & equipment needed for raising & harvesting food	100% (must be held primarily for the personal, family, or household use of the debtor or a dependent)	14 MRSA § 4422(7)
One of every type of farm implement reasonably needed for debtor to raise & harvest agricultural products commercially, including personal property incidental thereto	100%	14 MRSA § 4422(8)
One commercial fishing boat not exceeding 5 tons burden	100%	14 MRSA § 4422(9)
Any unmatured life insurance contract owned by debtor, except credit life insurance contract	100%	14 MRSA § 4422(10)
Accrued dividends or interest under, or loan value of, any unmatured life insurance contract owned by debtor under which the insured is the debtor or a person of whom the debtor is a dependent.	$4,000 less transfers made under nonforfeiture provisions of policy	14 MRSA § 4422(11)
Professionally prescribed health aids	100%	14 MRSA § 4422(12)
Social Security benefits, unemployment compensation, local public assistance benefits, veterans' benefits, & disability, illness or unemployment benefits	100%	14 MRSA § 4422(13)(A), (B), (C)
Alimony, support or separate maintenance payments	Amount reasonably necessary to support debtor & dependents	14 MRSA § 4422(13)(D)
Payments under stock bonus, pension, profitsharing, annuity or similar plan or contract on account of illness, disability, death, age or length of service	Amount reasonably necessary to support debtor & dependents	14 MRSA § 4422(13)(E)

NOTE: This exemption does not apply if: The plan or contract was established under the auspices of an insider that employed the debtor at the time the plan or contract arose; such payment is on account of age or length of service; and the plan or contract does not qualify under 26 USC §§ 401(a), 403(a), 403(b), 408, or 409.

Type of Property	Amount of Exemption	Statute Creating Exemption
Crime victims reparation law awards	100%	14 MRSA § 4422(14)(A)
Payments on the account of the wrongful death of an individual of whom the debtor was a dependent	Amount reasonably necessary to support debtor & dependents	14 MRSA § 4422(14)(B)
Payments under life insurance contract insuring the life of an individual of whom the debtor was a dependent on the date of death	Amount reasonably necessary to support debtor & dependents	14 MRSA § 4422(14)(C)
Payments on account of bodily injury, not including pain & suffering or compensation for actual pecuniary loss, of the debtor or an individual of whom the debtor is a dependent	$12,500	14 MRSA § 4422(14)(D)
Payments in compensation of loss of future earnings of the debtor or an individual of whom the debtor is or was a dependent	Amount reasonably necessary to support debtor & dependents	MRSA § 4422(14)(E)
Debtor's interest in any property, whether or not otherwise exempt	$400	14 MRSA 4422(15)
Any property exempt under 14 MRSA § 4422(3), (5) & (14)	Amount equal to any unused portion of the residence exemption under 14 MRSA § 4422(1), but not exceeding $6,000.	14 MRSA § 4422(16)

(continued on next page)

MAINE

(continued from previous page)

Type of Property	Amount of Exemption	Statute Creating Exemption
Proceeds and avails of life, endowment, annuity or accident insurance policies wherein beneficiary is not the insured	100%	24–A MRSA § 2428
Proceeds of health insurance policies and disability insurance supplemental to life insurance or annuity contracts	100%	24–A MRSA § 2429
Group life and health insurance	100%	24–A MRSA § 2430
Individual annuity contract proceeds	$450 per month	24–A MRSA § 2431
Employees' interest in group annuities and pension trusts	100%	24–A MRSA § 2432
Military uniforms, arms and equipment of militiaman or serviceman	100%	37–A MRSA § 1051
Aid to needy persons	100%	22 MRSA § 3180
Aid to dependent children	100%	22 MRSA § 3753
State retirement system benefits	100%	5 MRSA § 1003
Unemployment compensation benefits	100%	26 MRSA § 1044
Workmen's compensation benefits	100%	39 MRSA § 67
Specific partnership property	100% of partner's interest	31 MRSA § 305
Disposal earnings	75% or 30 times the federal minimum hourly rate per week, whichever is greater	14 MRSA § 3127

NOTE: If within 90 days of the date of filing the debtor transfers his nonexempt property and as a result acquires, improves, or increases in value property otherwise exempt under 14 MRSA § 4422, his interest shall not be exempt to the extent that the acquisition, improvement or increase in value exceeds the reasonable needs of the debtor or his dependents. See 14 MRSA § 4423. Also, the exemptions contained in 14 MRSA § 4422 do not apply to property fraudulently conveyed by the debtor. See 14 MRSA § 4422.

MARYLAND

Use of federal bankruptcy exemptions in 11 USC § 522 (d) not permitted in this state. See ACM, C & JP § 11–504(G).

Type of Property	Amount of Exemption	Statute Creating Exemption
Personal wearing apparel, books, tools, instruments, or appliances of trade or profession	$2,500	ACM, C & JP § 11–504(b)(1)
Money payable in the event of sickness, accident, injury or death of any person	100%	ACM, C & JP § 11–504(b)(2)
Professionally prescribed health aids of debtor or dependent	100%	ACM, C & JP § 11–504(b)(3)
Household furnishings & goods, wearing apparel, books, pets, and other items held primarily for the personal, family or household use of the debtor or a dependent	$500	ACM, C & JP § 11–504(b)(4)
Money or property of any kind	$3,000	ACM, C & JP § 11–504(b)(5)
Real or personal property	$2,500 (applies only to bankruptcy cases)	ACM, C & JP § 11–504(f)
Assets and benefits of retirement plan qualified under Internal Revenue Code	100%	ACM, C & JP § 11–504(h)
Disposable earnings (earnings after deductions required by law)	75% or $145 per week (30 times the federal minimum hourly wage in Caroline, Kent, Queen Anne's & Worcester counties) WHICHEVER IS GREATER	ACM, CL § 15–601.1
Proceeds of life insurance policy or annuity contract payable to spouse, children or dependent relations of insured	100% (includes death benefits, cash & loan values, waived premiums and dividends)	ACM, Art. 48A § 385
Fraternal Benefit Society benefits	no limit	ACM, Art. 48A § 328
Old age assistance benefits	no limit	ACM, Art. 88A § 73
Teachers retirement benefits	no limit	ACM, Art 77 § 206
State employees pension benefits	no limit	ACM, Art. 73B § 17
Workmen's compensation	no limit	ACM, Art. 101 § 50
Unemployment insurance benefits	no limit	ACM, Art. 95A § 16
Burial lots	100%	ACM, Art. 23 § 164
Specific partnership property	100% of partner's interest	ACM, C & A § 9–502

NOTE: Tenancies by the entirety may be exempt under 11 USC § 522(b) (2) (B). See In Re Ford, 3 B.R. 559.

Use of federal bankruptcy
exemptions under 11 USC §
522(d) permitted in this state

Type of Property	Amount of Exemption	Statute Creating Exemption
Residence owned or leased by householder with family	$100,000	MGLA c.188 § 1

NOTE: Must designate homestead estate on deed of conveyance or on subsequent declaration for homestead exemption to be effective (c.188 § 2). Can be used by wife and minor children (c.188 § 3.) Continues after death of householder for benefit of widow and minor children (c.188 § 4).

Type of Property	Amount of Exemption	Statute Creating Exemption
Necessary wearing apparel, beds, bedding, and heating unit used by debtor and family plus up to $75/mo. for fuel	no limit except for fuel	MGLA c.235 § 34(1)
Other household furniture	$3,000	MGLA c.235 § 34(2)
Bibles, school books and library	$200	MGLA c.235 § 34(3)
2 cows, 12 sheep, 2 swine and 4 tons of hay	no limit	MGLA c.235 § 34(4)
Tools, implements and fixtures of trade or business	$500	MGLA c.235 § 34(5)
Materials and stock used in trade or business	$500	MGLA c.235 § 34(6)
Provisions for family (or money therefor)	$300	MGLA c.235 § 34(7)
One pew in house of public worship	no limit	MGLA c.235 § 34(8)
Boats, fishing tackle and nets of fisherman	$500	MGLA c.235 § 34(9)
Uniform and required arms and accoutrements of militiaman	no limit	MGLA c. 235 § 34(10)
Tombs and rights of burial	no limit	MGLA c.235 § 34(11)
1 sewing machine	$200	MGLA c.235 § 34(12)
Shares in cooperative associations	$100	MGLA c.235 § 34(13)
Money used to pay rent (in lieu of homestead exemption)	amt. of actual rental not exceeding $200 per month	MGLA c.235 § 34(14)
Cash, savings, deposits in banks, and money owed for wages	$125	MGLA c.235 § 34(15)
Public assistance payments	no limit	MGLA c.235 § 34(15) & c.118 § 10
Automobile	$700	MGLA c.235 § 34(16)
Debtor's interest in annuity, pension, profit–sharing, or other retirement plan that qualifies under the I.R.C., or a similar plan or contract purchased with assets of qualified plan.	100% (individual contributions made during last 5 years in excess of 7% of income excepted) (support & crime reparation claims excepted)	MGLA c.235 § 34A
Wages and salaries assigned	$10 OR 75% of weekly earnings, WHICHEVER IS GREATER	MGLA c.154 §§ 2, 3
Payroll deductions of public employees for repaying loans	no limit	MGLA c.149 § 178B
Disability insurance payments	$35 per week	MGLA c.175 § 110A
Group annuity contract benefits	no limit	MGLA c.175 § 132C
Group insurance policies and proceeds	no limit	MGLA c.175 § 135
Life insurance or annuity contract benefits retained by Co.	no limit	MGLA c.175 § 119A
Relocation payments	no limit	MGLA c.79A § 7, c.79 § 6A
Funds deposited in payroll accounts	no limit	MGLA c.246 § 20
Wages for personal service	$125 per week	MGLA c.246 § 28
Veterans benefits	no limit	MGLA c.115 § 5
Pension payments	$100 per week	MGLA c.246 § 28
Monies in bank accounts	$500	MGLA c.246 § 28A
Wages of seaman	no limit	MGLA c.246 § 32(7)
Public employees retirement benefits	no limit	MGLA c.32 § 19
Workmen's Compensation Benefits	100%	MGLA c.152 § 47
Unemployment Compensation Benefits	100%	MGLA c.151A § 36
Specific partnership property	100% of partner's interest	MGLA c.108A § 25
Real property of persons 65 and over and disabled persons unable to engage in gainful employment	$150,000 (debtor must file elderly or disabled person homestead declaration with registry of deeds)	MGLA c.188 § 1A

NOTE: A wife's interest in tenancies by the entirety may be exempt under 11 USC § 522(b)(2)(B). See Friedman v. Harold, 638 F. 2nd 262.

299

Use of federal bankruptcy
exemptions under 11 USC §
522(d) permitted in this state

Type of Property	Amount of Exemption	Statute Creating Exemption
Family pictures, legally required arms and accoutrements, wearing apparel and 6 months' provisions and fuel	100%	MSA §27A.6023(1)(a)
Household goods, furniture, utensils, books and appliances	$1,000	MSA §27A.6023(1)(b)
Seat, pew or slip in place of worship	100%	MSA §27A.6023(1)(c)
Family burial sites	100%	MSA §27A.6023(1)(c)
10 sheep, 2 cows, 5 swine, 100 hens, 5 roosters, and a six–month supply of feed	100%	MSA §27A.6023(1)(d)
Tools, implements, materials, stock, apparatus, team, horses, harness, etc. and motor vehicle necessary to carry on principal trade, business or profession of debtor	$1,000	MSA §27A.6023(1)(e)
Disability insurance payments	100%	MSA §27A.6023(1)(f)
Building and loan association shares	$1,000 at par value (cannot be claimed if homestead exemption is claimed)	MSA §27A.6023(1)(g)
Homestead (can not exceed 40 acres of rural land and buildings or one lot with building in village, town or city)	$3,500 (can be claimed by any Michigan resident who owns and occupies a house, whether or not he owns the land)	MSA §27A.6023(1)(h)
Equity of redemption	100%	MSA §27A.6023(1)(i)
Family homestead after death of owner and during minority of children	100%	MSA §27A.6023(1)(j)
Homestead of deceased homestead owner if surviving spouse is not a homestead owner	100% of homestead until remarriage of surviving spouse	MSA §27A.6023(3)
Individual retirement account or annuity, or pension plan qualified under I.R.C.	100% of qualified amounts, except contributions made within 120 days of filing	MSA §27A.6023(1)(k), (l)
Judges' retirement benefits	100%	MSA §§27.125(26) & 27.3178(60.27)
Legislative retirement benefits	100%	MSA §2.169(57)
Municipal employees' pension benefits	100%	MSA §5.4064
Public school employees' pension benefits	100%	MSA §15.893(25), (90)
Social welfare benefits	100%	MSA §16.463
State employees' retirement benefits	100%	MSA §3.981(40)
Financial Responsibility deposits	100%	MSA §9.2224
Workmen's compensation benefits	100%	MSA §17.237(821)
Fraternal Benefit Society benefits	100%	MSA §24.18046
Police and Firemen's pension benefits	100%	MSA §5.3375(9)
Employment security benefits	100%	MSA §17.532
Proceeds and avails of life insurance policies payable to spouse or children, if so provided in policy	100%	MSA §24.12207
Proceeds from sale of milk or cream	60% (applies to farmers only)	MSA §27A.4031
WWII & Korean War veterans' benefits	100%	MSA §§4.1093(26) & 4.1094(7)
Specific partnership property	100% of partner's interest	MSA §20.25

NOTE: Tenancies by the entirety may be exempt under 11 USC § 522(b)(2)(B). See In Re Trickett, 5 C.B.C. 2nd 85.

MINNESOTA

Use of federal bankruptcy exemptions in 11 USC § 522(d) permitted in this state with restrictions (see below) *

Type of Property	Amount of Exemption	Statute Creating Exemption
Homestead, consisting of house and land occupied by debtor as dwelling place (title may be in either spouse; includes equitable interests in land and proceeds of sale of exempt homestead for 1 year)	160 acres if not in city or 1/2 acre if in city	MS §§ 510.01, 510.02
Family Bible, library, and musical instruments	100%	MS § 550.37 subd. 2
Seat or pew in place of worship and lot in burying ground	100%	MS § 550.37 subd. 3
All wearing apparel, 1 watch, and food	100%	MS § 550.37 subd. 4(a)
Household furniture, utensils, appliances, phonographs, radio and television receivers, foodstuffs of debtor and family	$4,500	MS § 550.37 subd. 4(b)
Farm machines and implements of farmer used in farming, livestock, farm produce, standing crops	$13,000 (Certain family members may claim family partnership assets as personal assets)	MS § 550.37 subd. 5
Tools, implements, machines, instruments, office furniture, stock in trade, and library, used in trade, business or profession	$5,000.00 NOTE – Total selected by debtor under subd. 5 and 6 cannot exceed $13,000	MS § 550.37 subd. 6
All money arising from any claim on account of destruction of or damage to exempt property	100%	MS § 550.37 subd. 9
Benefits payable to surviving wife or child from insurance on life of deceased husband or father	$20,000 plus $5,000 for each dependent of surviving wife or child	MS § 500.37 subd.10
Benefits payable by police, fire, beneficiary, or fraternal benefit association	100%	MS § 550.37 subd. 11
Mobile home used as home	100%	MS § 550.37 subd. 12
One motor vehicle	$2,000.00	MS § 550.37 subd. 12a.
All relief based upon need and earnings or salary of recipient of such relief for period ending 6 months after relief is terminated	100% NOTE: Includes inmates of correctional institution, and applies to exempt funds deposited in financial Institution for period of 6 months	MS § 550.37 subd. 14
Earnings of minor child of debtor	100%	MS § 550.37 subd. 15
Damages for wrongful levy or execution	100%	MS § 550.37 subd. 16
Personal injury claims of debtor or relative	100%	MS § 550.37 subd.22
Debtor's aggregate interest in dividends, interest, or loan value of unmatured life insurance contract owned by debtor or individual of whom debtor is a dependent	$4,000.00	MS § 550.37 subd.23
Debtor's right to receive payments under stock bonus, profit sharing, annuity, individual retirement account or annuity, simplified employee pension, or similar plan or contract on account of illness, disability, death, age or length of service	100%	MS § 550.37 subd. 24
Veteran's pension benefits	100%	MS § 550.38
Accident or disability insurance benefits	100%	MS § 550.39
Disposable earnings (earnings after deductions required by law)	75% or 40 times federal minimum hourly wage per week, whichever is greater	MS § 571.55

NOTE: Exemption covers exempt earnings deposited in financial institution for period of 20 days

NOTE: The exemption amounts in § 550.37 (except subd. 5 & 7) are adjusted biannually for cost of living changes.

* A husband & wife cannot split the state and federal bankruptcy exemptions in a joint case or in separate cases filed within 3 years of each other. Both spouses must use either the state or the federal bankruptcy exemptions. See MS § 550.371.

(continued on next page)

MINNESOTA

Type of Property	Amount of Exemption	Statute Creating Exemption
Police & Firemen's pension benefits	100%	MS §§ 69.62, 423A.16
Teacher's Retirement Fund Assoc. benefits	100%	MS §§ 354.10 & 354A.11 & 550.40
Public Employees' Retirement Assoc. benefits	100%	MS § 353.15
State Retirement Act benefits	100%	MS § 352.15
Fraternal Benefit Society benefits	100%	MS § 64A.23, §64B.18
Unemployment compensation benefits	100%	MS § 268.17
Workers' compensation benefits	100%	MS § 176.175
Cash bail posted in court	100%	MS § 629.53
Official seal and register of notary public	100%	MS § 359.03
Equipment of National Guard member	100%	MS § 192.25
Specific partnership property	100% of partner's interest	MS § 323.24
Prisoner's earning held by state	100%	MS § 241.26(6)

MISSISSIPPI

Use of federal bankruptcy
exemptions in 11 U.S.C. § 522(d)
not permitted in this state.
See MCA § 85-3-2

Type of Property	Amount of Exemption	Statute Creating Exemption
Homestead of householder (debtor must reside in homestead unless he is over 60 and previously qualified for exemption)	$75,000 (cannot exceed 160 acres)	MCA § 85-3-21
Insurance proceeds from destruction of exempt homestead	$75,000	MCA § 85-3-23
Personal property selected by debtor (except wages, salaries or commissions)	$250.00 or articles specified as exempt if head of family (see below)	MCA § 85-3-23
Tangible personal property of any kind, except wages	$10,000	MCA § 85-3-1(a)
Insurance or sales proceeds from exempt property	amount of exemption applicable to property damaged or sold	MCA § 85-3-1(b)(i)
Income from disability insurance	100%	MCA § 85-3-1(b)(ii)
Property and pension trusts qualified under Internal Revenue Code, except contributions made within one year prior to filing of bankruptcy petition	100% of qualified amounts (includes Keogh plans and IRAs)	MCA § 85-3-1(b)(iii)
Property for the collection or enforcement of any order or judgment for civil or criminal contempt of court	100%	MCA § 85-3-1(c)
Wages, salaries and compensation for personal services	100% of earnings for last 30 days, then 75% or 30 times the federal minimum hourly wage for week, WHICHEVER IS GREATER	MCA § 85-3-4
Proceeds of life insurance policies payable to another (includes cash surrender and loan values)	$50,000	MCA § 85-3-11
Proceeds of life insurance policies payable to estate of insured	$5,000	MCA § 85-3-13
Proceeds of personal injury judgment	$10,000	MCA § 85-3-17
Fraternal Benefit Society benefits	100%	MCA § 83-29-39
Insurance proceeds in hands of insurance company if contract so provides	100%	MCA § 83-7-5
Aid to disabled persons	100%	MCA § 43-29-15
Aid to blind persons	100%	MCA § 43-3-71
Old age assistance payments	100%	MCA § 43-9-19
Employee trust plan benefits	100%	MCA § 71-1-43
Unemployment compensation benefits	100%	MCA § 71-5-539
Workmen's compensation benefits	100%	MCA § 71-3-43
Firemen and policemen retirement and disability benefits	100%	MCA § 21-29-257
Municipal employees' retirement benefits	100%	MCA § 21-29-51
State employees' retirement benefits	100%	MCA § 25-11-129
Teachers' retirement benefits	100%	MCA § 25-11-201
Specific partnership property	100% of partner's interest	MCA § 79-12-49

303

Use of federal bankruptcy exemptions in 11 U.S.C. § 522(d) not permitted in this state. See VAMS § 513.427

Type of Property	Amount of Exemption	Statute Creating Exemption
Personal household furnishings & goods, wearing apparel, books, animals, crops, and musical instruments of debtor and dependents	$1,000	* VAMS 513.430(1)
Personal, family or household jewelry of debtor or dependents	$500	VAMS 513.430(2)
Any property of debtor	$400	VAMS 513.430(3)
Implements, books or tools of trade of debtor or dependent	$2,000	VAMS 513.430(4)
Motor vehicle	$500	VAMS 513.430(5)
Mobile home used as principal residence	$1,000	VAMS 513.430(6)
Unmatured life insurance contracts, except credit life	100%	VAMS 513.430(7)
Dividends, interest, or loan values of unmatured life insurance contracts more than 6 months old insuring debtor or person of whom debtor is a dependent	100% in bankruptcy proceeding, otherwise $5,000 with support claims excepted. (The 6–month age require–ment applies only to bankruptcy)	VAMS 513.430(8)
Health aids of debtor or dependents	100%	VAMS 513.430(9)
Social Security benefits, unemployment, compensation, public assistance benefits, veterans' benefits, and disability, illness or unemployment benefits	100%	VAMS 513.430(10)(a), (b), (c)
Alimony, support or separate maintenance	$500 per month	VAMS 513.430(10)(d)
Payments under stock–bonus, pension, profit–sharing, annuity, or similar plans, unless established by insider and payments are on account of age or length of service and do not qualify under 26 USC §§ 401(a), 403(a) or (b), 408 or 409.	Amount reasonably necessary to support debtor & dependents (Fraudulent contributions are not exempt. See VAMS 513.430(10)(f))	VAMS 513.430(10)(e)
Payments on account of the wrongful death of a person of whom the debtor was a dependent	Amount reasonably necessary to support debtor & dependents	VAMS 513.430(11)
Choice of any other property whatsoever except 10% of any debt, income, salary or wages	$850 plus $250 per dependent minor child (applies only to head of family)	VAMS 513.440
Homestead (consists of house and land used therewith)	$8,000	VAMS 513.475
Net earnings after deduction required by law (includes wages, salary, commissions, bonuses, pensions and retirement payments)	For head of family – 90% OR 30 times the federal minimum hourly wage per week, whichever is greater. For any other person – 75% OR 30 times the federal minimum hourly wage per week, whichever is greater.	VAMS 525.030(2)
Life insurance benefits under assessment or stipulated premium plans	100%	VAMS 377.090, 377.330
Teacher and school employee retirement benefits	no limit	VAMS 169.090, 169.240, 169.380, 169.520 & 169.691
Police relief and pension benefits	no limit	VAMS 86.190, 86.353, 86.493 & 86.563
Firemen's retirement & relief benefits	no limit	VAMS 87.090, 87.365 & 87.485
Highway patrol and employees' retirement benefits	no limit	VAMS 104.250
Local government employees' pension and retirement benefits	no limit	VAMS 70.695
City employees' retirement benefits	no limit	VAMS 71.207
State employees' retirement benefits	no limit	VAMS 104.540
Workmen's compensation benefits	no limit	VAMS 287.260
Police department civilian employees' retirement benefits	no limit	VAMS 86.780
Financial responsibility deposits with state treasurer	no limit	VAMS 303.240
Burial lots	100%	VAMS 214.190
Specific partnership property	100% of partner's interest	VAMS 358.250

* VAMS stands for Vernon's Annotated Missouri Statutes

GENERAL NOTE: there are no exemptions for debts for taxes, for debts of $90 or less owed to laborers and servants, for debts for maintenance and child support, and for persons about to leave the state. Tenancies by the entirety may be exempt under 11 U.S.C. § 522(b)(2)(B). See Miner v. Anderson, 12 B.R. 483.

MONTANA

Use of federal bankruptcy
exemptions in 11 USC § 522(d)
not permitted in this state.
See MCA § 31-2-106

Type of Property	Amount of Exemption	Statute Creating Exemption
Homestead, consisting of mobile home or dwelling in which debtor resides and land on which it is located, if any	$40,000 – A written declaration of homestead must be recorded with county clerk. Includes traceable proceeds for 18 months after sale.	MCA § 70-32-104
Professionally prescribed health aids	100%	MCA § 25-13-608(1)
Social Security benefits and public assistance benefits	100%	MCA § 25-13-608(2)
Veterans' benefits	100%	MCA § 25-13-608(3)
Disability or illness benefits	100%	MCA § 25-13-608(4)
Medical, surgical or hospital care benefits, if used for medical care	100%	MCA § 25-13-608(5)
Maintenance and child support	100%	MCA § 25-13-608(6)
Burial plot of debtor and family	100%	MCA § 25-13-608(7)
Household furnishings and goods, appliances, jewelry, wearing apparel, books, firearms, sporting goods, animals, feed, crops, and musical instruments	$600 per item $4,500 aggregate value	MCA § 25-13-609(1)
Debtor's interest in 1 motor vehicle	$1,200	MCA § 25-13-609(2)
Implements, professional books, or tools of trade of debtor or dependent	$3,000	MCA § 25-13-609(3)
Unmatured life insurance contracts	$4,000	MCA § 25-13-609(4)
Traceable proceeds of lost, damaged, or destroyed exempt property	100% of applicable exemption for a period of 6 months	MCA § 25-13-610(1)
Aggregate net earnings of debtor	75% OR 30 times the federal minimum hourly wage per week, WHICHEVER IS GREATER	MCA § 25-13-614

Note: earnings are exempt for 45 days after receipt if traceable; See MCA § 25-13-610(2)

Type of Property	Amount of Exemption	Statute Creating Exemption
Benefits from qualifying private or governmental retirement, pension or similar plan	100% – except contributions made within 1 year before the petition was filed that exceed 15% of the debtor's gross income for that year are not exempt	MCA § 31-2-106(3)
Required arms, uniforms and accouterments, and one gun	100%	MCA § 25-13-613(1)(c)
Proceeds and avails of life insurance policies where beneficiary is not the insured	100%	MCA § 33-15-511
Group life insurance proceeds	100%	MCA § 33-15-512
Fraternal Benefit Society benefits	100%	MCA § 33-7-522
Disability insurance proceeds	100%	MCA § 33-15-513
Annuity contract benefits	$350 per month	MCA § 33-15-514
Public assistance payments	100%	MCA § 53-2-607
Workers' compensation benefits	100%	MCA § 39-71-743
Unemployment compensation benefits	100%	MCA § 39-51-3105, 31-2-106(2)
Silicosis benefits	100%	MCA § 39-73-110
Shares in cooperative associations	$500 par value	MCA § 35-15-404
Cemetery association lots	100%	MCA § 35-20-217
Plots owned in Mausoleum and Columbarium Authorities	100%	MCA § 35-21-406
Firefighters' retirement benefits	100%	MCA § 19-11-612
Game wardens' retirement benefits	100%	MCA § 19-8-805
Highway patrolmen's retirement benefits	100%	MCA § 19-6-705
Judges' retirement benefits	100%	MCA § 19-5-704
Police retirement benefits	100%	MCA § 19-9-1006, 19-10-504
Public employees' retirement benefits	100%	MCA § 19-3-105
Sheriffs' retirement benefits	100%	MCA § 19-7-705
Teachers' retirement benefits	100%	MCA § 19-4-706
Specific partnership property	100% of partner's interest	MCA § 35-10-502

NEBRASKA

Use of federal bankruptcy exemptions under 11 USC § 522(d) <u>not</u> permitted in this state. See R.R.S., 1943, § 25–15,105

Type of Property	Amount of Exemption	Statute Creating Exemption
Homestead of head of family (exemption also covers related persons residing with & supported by head of family – R.R.S. § 40–115)	$10,000 (cannot exceed 160 acres if not in city or village or 2 lots if in city or village)	* R.R.S., 1943, § 40–101
Proceeds of sale of homestead for 6 months after sale	$4,000	R.R.S., 1943, § 40–116
Personal property of head of family who does not qualify for homestead exemption	$2,500 (Does not apply to wages)	R.R.S., 1943, § 25–1552
Immediate personal possessions of resident debtor & family	100%	R.R.S., 1943, § 25–1556
Necessary wearing apparel of resident debtor & family	100%	R.R.S., 1943, § 25–1556
Kitchen utensils & household furniture of resident debtor	$1,500	R.R.S., 1943, § 25–1556
Equipment or tools used by resident debtor & family for their support	$1,500	R.R.S., 1943, § 25–1556
Provisions of resident debtor & family, whether provided or growing	Amount necessary to support family for 6 months	R.R.S., 1943, § 25–1556
Fuel on hand	6 months' supply	R.R.S., 1943, § 25–1556
Disposable earnings (earnings less deductions required by law)	75% OR 85% for head of family OR 30 times the federal minimum hourly wage per week, WHICHEVER IS GREATER	R.R.S., 1943, § 25–1558
Pensions of resident disabled veterans	100%	R.R.S., 1943, § 25–1559
Property of resident disabled veterans purchased or improved with pension money	$2,000	R.R.S., 1943, § 25–1559
Assistance payments to the blind, the aged or the disabled	100%	R.R.S., 1943, § 68–1013
Unemployment compensation benefits	100%	R.R.S., 1943, § 48–647
Workmen's compensation benefits	100%	R.R.S, 1943, § 48–149
Proceeds, avails, cash values & other benefits of life insurance policies not payable to insured's estate	$5,000 on loan value 100% of proceeds	R.R.S., 1943, § 44–371
Benefits of accident or health insurance policies	100%	R.R.S., 1943, § 44–371
Annuity contract benefits	100%	R.R.S., 1943 § 44–371
Benefits of sickness & accident insurance policies	100% of lump sum payments & $200 per month of periodic payments	R.R.S., 1943, § 44–754
Fraternal insurance benefits	100%	R.R.S., 1943, § 44–1029
Cash deposits under Motor Vehicle Safety Responsibility Act	100%	R.R.S., 1943, § 60–550
Burial lots	100%	R.R.S., 1943, §§ 12–517, 12–520, 12–605
Property subject to Innkeeper's lien	100%	R.R.S., 1943, § 41–124
State employees' retirement benefits	100%	R.R.S., 1943, § 84–1324
County employees' retirement benefits	100%	R.R.S., 1943, § 23–2322
Safety patrolmen's retirement benefits	100%	R.R.S., 1943, § 81–2032
School employees' & teachers' retirement benefits	100%	R.R.S., 1943, §§ 79–1552, 79–1060
Specific partnership property	100% of partner's interest	R.R.S. § 67–325
Interest of debtor or dependent in stock bonus, pension, profit sharing, or similar retirement plan qualified under Internal Revenue Code	100% of qualified amounts NOTE: plans of insiders established or amended within 2 years prior to filing of petition are not exempt	R.R.S., 1943, § 25–1563.01
Proceeds or benefits from structured settlement of personal injury claim	100%	R.R.S., 1943, § 25–1563.02

* R.R.S. stands for Reissue Revised Statutes of Nebraska.

NEVADA

Use of federal bankruptcy exemptions in 11 USC § 522(d) not permitted in this state. See NRS § 21.090(3).

Type of Property	Amount of Exemption	Statute Creating Exemption
Homestead, consisting of land and dwelling house, or mobile home with or without underlying land	$95,000 (written declaration must be filed in county recorder's office for exemption to be valid)	NRS §§ 115.010, 21.090(1)(l)
Dwelling house of debtor occupied as home situated on lands owned by another (i.e., a condominium)	$95,000	NRS § 21.090(1)(m)
Private libraries	$1,500	NRS § 21.090(1)(a)
Family pictures and keepsakes	100%	NRS § 21.090(1)(a)
Necessary household goods, as defined in 16 CFR 444.1(i), and yard equipment	$3,000 (See note below)	NRS § 21.090(1)(b)
Farm truck, stock, tools, equipment, supplies and seed	$4,500	NRS § 21.090(1)(c)
Professional libraries, office equipment and supplies, and tools, instruments and materials used to carry on trade	$4,500	NRS § 21.090(1)(d)
Cabin, dwelling, cars, implements appliances, and mining claim of miner or prospector	$4,500	NRS § 21.090(1)(e)
One vehicle	$1,500 (100% if equipped for disabled debtor)	NRS § 21.090(1)(f), (o)
Disposable earnings (earnings less deductions required by law)	75% OR 30 times the federal Minimum hourly wage per week WHICHEVER IS GREATER	NRS § 21.090(1)(g)
All arms, uniforms and accouterments required by law to be kept, and 1 gun selected by debtor	100%	NRS § 21.090(1)(i)
Money, benefits, privileges and immunities accruing or growing out of life insurance policies	Amount purchased by $1,000 annual premium	NRS § 21.090(1)(k)
Prosthesis or equipment prescribed by physician or dentist	100%	NRS § 21.090(1)(p)
Money held in I.R.C. qualifying IRA, simplified employee pension plan, deferred compensation arrangement, or stock bonus, pension or profit-sharing plan	$100,000	NRS § 21.090(1)(q)
Proceeds and avails of life insurance policies wherein beneficiary is not the insured	100%	NRS § 687B.260
Group life insurance benefits and group health insurance proceeds	100%	NRS § 687B.280
Proceeds of health insurance contracts and of disability insurance supplemental to life insurance or annuity contracts	100%	NRS § 687B.270
Annuity contract proceeds	$350 per month	NRS § 687B.290
Fraternal Benefit Society benefits	100%	NRS § 695A.220
Aid to dependent children	100%	NRS § 425.210
Supplemental security income benefits	100%	NRS § 427.060
Industrial insurance compensation	100%	NRS § 616.550
Unemployment compensation benefits	100%	NRS § 612.710
Legislator's retirement benefits	100%	NRS § 218.2386
Public employees' retirement benefits	100%	NRS § 286.670
Cemetery lots and plats	100%	NRS § 83.110
Escrow funds of escrow agent	100%	NRS § 645A.170
Prepaid funeral service contract trust funds	100%	NRS § 689.335
Property held in spendthrift trust	100%	NRS § 21.080(2)
Mineral collections, art curiosities, and paleontological remains	100%	NRS § 21.100
Public assistance payments	100%	NRS § 422.291, 615.270
Specific partnership property	100% of partner's interest	NRS § 87.250(2c)

NOTE: Household goods include clothing, furniture, appliances, 1 radio, 1 television, linens, china, crockery, kitchenware, and personal effects of debtor and dependents. Household goods do not include works of art, electronic entertainment equipment (except 1 radio and 1 television), items acquired as antiques (i.e., items over 100 years old), and jewelry other than wedding rings. See 16 CFR 444.1(i).

307

NEW HAMPSHIRE

(Current to January 1, 1992)

Use of federal bankruptcy
exemption in 11 USC § 522(d)
not permitted in this state.
See RSA § 511.2a

Type of Property	Amount of Exemption	Statute Creating Exemption
Homestead (includes manufactured housing owned and occupied by debtor)	$5,000	* RSA § 480:1
Necessary wearing apparel, beds, bedsteads and bedding of debtor and family	100%	RSA § 511:2
Household furniture	$2,000	RS § 511:2
One cooking stove and necessary furniture to same, and 1 sewing machine used by debtor	100%	RSA § 511:2
Provisions and fuel	$400	RSA § 511:2
Uniforms, arms and accouterments of militiaman	100%	RSA § 511:2
Bibles, school books and library of debtor and family	$800	RSA § 511:2
Necessary tools of occupation	$1,200	RSA § 511:2
One hog and pig and pork from same, 6 sheep and fleeces from same, 1 cow, 1 yoke of oxen or a horse if used in farming or teaming, and 4 tons of hay	100%	RSA § 511:2
Domestic fowl	$300	RSA § 511:2
One pew in place of worship, and 1 cemetery lot or burial right	100%	RSA § 511:2
Jewelry of debtor and family	$500	RSA § 511:2
Wages	50 times the federal minimum hourly wage per week	RSA § 512:21

NOTE: Wages for personal services of wife and minor children of debtor are 100% exempt against creditors of debtor. If debtor is a married woman her wages are 100% exempt against debts for small loans wherein husband is obligor. In any event, there is a $50 per week exemption applicable to all debtors as against debts for small loans.

Type of Property	Amount of Exemption	Statute Creating Exemption
Pension or bounty money authorized by federal law	100%	RSA § 512:21
Jury and witness fees	100%	RSA § 512:21
Damages recovered for conversion of exempt property	100%	RSA § 512:21
Insurance proceeds from loss or destruction of exempt property	Amount of exemption given for lost or destroyed property, except homestead money is limited to $1,500	RSA § 512.21
Workmen's compensation benefits	100%	RSA § 281.45
Unemployment compensation benefits	100%	RSA § 282.13
Public assistance payments	100%	RSA § 167:26
Fraternal Benefit Society benefits	100%	RSA § 418.24
Firemen's Retirement System benefits	100%	RSA § 102:23
Firemen's Relief Fund benefits	100%	RSA § 402:69
One automobile	$1,000	RSA § 511.2
Specific partnership property	100% of partner's interest	RSA § 304–A:25

* RSA stands for New Hampshire Revised Statutes Annotated

NEW JERSEY

Use of federal bankruptcy exemptions under 11 USC § 522(d) permitted in this state

Type of Property	Amount of Exemption	Statute Creating Exemption
Wearing apparel	no limit	NJSA 2A: 17–19
Household goods & furniture	$1,000	NJSA 2A: 26–4
Goods, chattels, shares of stock & personal property of any kind	$1,000	NJSA 2A: 17–19
Wages, earnings, salary, income & profits	100% if less than $48 per week; 90% if greater than $48 per week & less than $7,500 per year, no specific exemption if greater than $7,500 per year. (Certain support claims excepted)	NJSA 2A: 17–50, 17–56, 17–57
Unemployment compensation benefits	no limit	NJSA 43: 21–15(c), 21–53
Old age assistance payments	no limit	NJSA 44: 7–35
Workmen's compensation benefits	no limit	NJSA 34: 15–29
Military pay, allowances & benefits of members of state militia	no limit	NJSA 38A: 4–8
Health & disability insurance proceeds & avails	no limit	NJSA 17B: 24–8
Fraternal Benefit Society benefits	no limit	NJSA 17: 44A–19
Annuity contract benefits	$500 per month	NJSA 17B: 24–7
Proceeds & avails of life insurance policies payable to persons other than the insured and the person effecting the insurance	no limit	NJSA 17B: 24–6
Group life insurance policies & proceeds	no limit	NJSA 17B: 24–9
Civil defense injury & death benefits	no limit	NJSA App. A: 9–57.6
City Board of Health employees pension benefits	no limit	NJSA 43: 18–12
Street & Water Dept. employees pension benefits	no limit	NJSA 43: 19–17
Prison officers retirement benefits	no limit	NJSA 43: 7–13(e)
Municipal employees retirement & pension benefits	no limit	NJSA 43: 13–9, 13–22.34, 13–22.60, 13–37.5, 13–44
County employees retirement & pension benefits	no limit	NJSA 43: 10–14, 10–18.22, 10–18.71, 10–57
Police & Firemen's retirement & pension benefits	no limit	NJSA 43: 16–7, 16A–17
Alcoholic Beverage Law Enforcement Officers pension fund benefits	no limit	NJSA 43: 8A–20
Judicial Retirement Systems benefits	no limit	NJSA 43: 6A–41
School district employees retirement & pension benefits	no limit	NJSA 18: 5–80 18A: 66–116
Teacher's retirement & pension benefits	no limit	NJSA 18: 13–112.53
State Police retirement & pension benefits	no limit	NJSA 53: 5A–45
Specific partnership property	100% of partner's interest	NJSA 42: 1–25
Crime victim's compensation	100%	NJSA 52: 4B–18

Type of Property	Amount of Exemption	Statute Creating Exemption
Homestead of each spouse, widow, widower, or a person who supports another person	$20,000 (NOTE: joint owners may each claim a full personal exemption)	NMS § 42-10-9

NOTE: A homestead consists of a dwelling house, plus the land upon which it is located, that is owned and personally occupied by the debtor, or a dwelling house that the debtor owns, leases or is purchasing, even though it is located on land owned by another.

Type of Property	Amount of Exemption	Statute Creating Exemption
Exemption in lieu of homestead (may be any real or personal property)	$2,000 (exemption may be claimed only by debtor who does not claim homestead exemption)	NMS § 42-10-10
Personal property of any kind, including money	$500 * applies only to married persons or heads of households	NMS § 42-10-1
Clothing, furniture, books, personally-used medical health equipment and interests in and proceeds from pension or retirement funds	100% *	NMS §§ 42-10-1, 2
Jewelry	$2,500 *	NMS § 42-10-1, 2
Tools of trade	$1,500 *	NMS § 42-10-1, 2
1 motor vehicle	$4,000 *	NMS § 42-10-1, 2
Personal property other than money	$500 * (applies only to debtor who supports only himself)	NMS § 42-10-2
Cash surrender value of life insurance policy, withdrawal value of annuity contract, deposit with life insurance company, proceeds of life, accident or health insurance policies and annuity contracts	100% (applies to citizens and residents of state)	NMS § 42-10-3
Disposable earnings (earnings less deductions required by law)	75% OR 40 times the federal minimum hourly wage per week, WHICHEVER IS GREATER	NMS § 35-12-7
Beneficiary funds of benevolent associations or societies set apart for or paid to family member of deceased person	$5,000	NMS § 42-104 & § 59-26-21
Proceeds of life insurance policies	100%	NMS § 42-10-5
Beneficiaries' interest in spendthrift trusts	100%	NMS § 42-9-4
Property covered by assignment for benefit of creditors	100%	NMS § 56-9-46
Occupational disease disablement compensation benefits	100%	NMS § 52-3-37
Workmen's compensation benefits	100%	NMS § 52-1-52
Unemployment compensation	100% (support claims excepted)	NMS § 51-1-37
Public assistance payments	100%	NMS § 27-2-21
Public employees retirement funds and benefits	100%	NMS § 10-11-36
Educational retirement benefits and contributions	100%	NMS § 22-11-42
State police pension benefits	100%	NMS § 29-4-10
Membership holdings in cooperative associations	Minimum amount required for membership	NMS § 53-4-28
Materials purchased for digging or operating an oil or gas well that are subject to a materialman's lien	100%	NMS § 70-4-12
Crime victim's reparation awards	100%	NMS § 31-22-15
Specific partnership property	100% of partner's interest	NMS § 54-1-21

* Exempt property to be valued at value of used chattels.

NEW YORK

Type of Property	Amount of Exemption	Statute Creating Exemption
All stoves & 60–days' fuel; 1 sewing machine & appurtenances, family bible & pictures; school books, seat in place of worship, 60–days' food, all wearing apparel, household furniture, crockery, tableware, and cooking utensils of debtor & family; 1 refrigerator; 1 radio; 1 television set; 1 wedding ring	100% (See Note 1 below)	* CPLR § 5205(a)(1)
Books in family library	$50 (See Note 1 below)	CPLR § 5205(a)(2)
Domestic animals + 60–days' feed	$450 (See Note 1 below)	CPLR § 5205(a)(4)
One watch	$35 (See Note 1 below)	CPLR § 5205(a)(6)
Necessary tools of trade & professional instruments, furniture & library	$600 (See Note 1 below)	CPLR § 5205(a)(7)
Claim for loss or destruction of exempt property & proceeds of claim for one year	Amount of exemption for lost or destroyed property	CPLR § 5205(b)
Property held under a trust created by another for benefit of debtor **	100%	CPLR § 5205(c)
90% of income from trust exempt under CPLR § 5205(c), 90% of last 60–days' earnings, and 100% of matrimonial payments for support of wife or child	Amount reasonably required by debtor & dependents	CPLR § 5205(d)
Military pay of enlisted men; military rewards, pensions, medals, arms & equipment of state or federal armed forces	100% (support claims excepted)	CPLR § 5205(e)
Milk sales proceeds of farmer	90%	CPLR § 5205(f)
Residential rental, utility, telephone & telegraph money security deposits of debtor & family	100%	CPLR § 5205(g)
Necessary medical & dental accessions to human body, equipment used to provide mobility for disabled person, and guide, service, or hearing dog or similar animals and food therefor	Amount reasonably required by debtor & dependents	CPLR § 5205(h)
Property owned & occupied as principal residence (includes land + dwelling, shares in cooperative, condominium units, and mobile homes)	$10,000	CPLR § 5206(a)
Burial grounds	100% (cannot exceed 1/4 acre)	CPLR § 5206(f)
Proceeds & avails of life insurance policies not payable to insured	100%	Insurance Law § 3212
Disability insurance benefits	100% of lump sum payments $400 per month of periodic payments	Insurance Law § 3212
Annuity contract benefits	Amount reasonably required by debtor & dependents (See Note 1 below)	Insurance Law § 3212
One motor vehicle	$2,400	Debtor & Creditor Law § 282
Social Security benefits, unemployment compensation, public assistance benefits, veterans benefits, and disability, illness or unemployment benefits	100%	Debtor & Creditor Law § 282

(continued on next page)

* CPLR stands for Civil Practice Law and Rules

** includes self employed or corporate retirement plan qualified under Internal Revenue Code

311

NEW YORK

Type of Property	Amount of Exemption	Statute Creating Exemption
Alimony, support or separate maintenance	Amount reasonably necessary to support debtor & dependents	Debtor & Creditor Law § 282
Payments under stock-bonus, pension, profit-sharing or similar plan, unless payments are for age or length of service and plan was created by insider and does not qualify under 26 USC §§ 401(a), 403(a), or (b), 408, 409, or 457.	Amount reasonably necessary to support debtor & dependents	Debtor & Creditor Law § 282
Crime victim's reparation awards	100%	Debtor & Creditor Law § 282
Payments on account of wrongful death of person of whom debtor was a dependent	Amount reasonably necessary to support debtor & dependents	Debtor & Creditor Law § 282
Payments on account of bodily injury of debtor or person of whom debtor was a dependent	$7,500 (does not include damages for pain & suffering or actual pecuniary loss)	Debtor & Creditor Law § 282
Compensation for loss of future earnings of debtor or person of whom debtor is or was a dependent	Amount reasonably necessary to support debtor & dependents	Debtor & Creditor Law § 282
Cash, U.S. savings bonds, and tax refunds of debtor not using homestead exemption under CPLR § 5206	$2,500 or $5,000 less amounts exempted under CPLR § 5205(a) and for certain annuities (see Note 1 below) WHICHEVER IS LESS	Debtor & Creditor Law § 283

NOTE 1: The aggregate amount that a debtor may exempt under CPLR § 5205(a) and under certain annuity contracts cannot exceed $5,000. The annuity contracts subject to this limitation are those initially purchased within 6 months of the filing of the bankruptcy petition, those not described in 26 USC § 805(d) (i.e., pension plan reserves), and those not purchased by the application of proceeds under settlement options of annuity contracts purchased more than 6 months prior to the filing of the bankruptcy petition or under settlement options of life insurance policies.

NOTE 2: Section 282 of the Debtor & Creditor Law specifies that only the exemptions shown above may be claimed in a bankruptcy proceeding by a person domiciled in New York State. Other properties exempt under various other state laws include: police, firemen, teachers, and state employees retirement benefits, earnings of public assistance recipients, international exhibits, employer's liability benefits, workmen's compensation benefits, shares in savings & loan associations and credit unions up to a value of $600, and a partner's interest in specific partnership property.

NORTH CAROLINA

Use of federal bankruptcy exemptions in 11 USC § 522(d) not permitted in this state. See G.S. § 1C-1601(f).

Type of Property	Amount of Exemption	Statute Creating Exemption
Debtor's aggregate interest in real or personal property, including a cooperative, used as residence by debtor or a dependent, or in a burial plot for debtor or dependent	$10,000	G.S. § 1C-1601(a)(1)
Debtor's aggregate interest in any property	$3,500 less any amount claimed under G.S. § 1C-1601(a)(1) above	G.S. § 1C-1601(a)(2)
Debtor's interest in 1 motor vehicle	$1,500	G.S. § 1C-1601(a)(3)
Debtor's aggregate in household furnishings & goods, wearing apparel, appliances, books, animals, crops, or musical instruments held primarily for personal, family or household use of debtor or dependent	$3,500 plus $750 for each dependent, not to exceed $3,000 for dependents	G.S. § 1C-1601(a)(4)
Implements, professional books or tools of the trade of debtor or dependent	$750	G.S. § 1C-1601(a)(5)
Professionally prescribed health aids of debtor or dependent	100%	G.S. § 1C-1601(a)(7)
Compensation for personal injury or death of a person of whom the debtor was a dependent	100% (Exemption does not apply to claims for funeral, legal, medical, dental, hospital & health care charges related to accident or injury giving rise to the compensation)	G.S. § 1C-1601(a)(8)

NOTE: The exemptions provided in G.S. § 1C-1601(a)(2), (3), (4) & (5) do not apply with respect to tangible personal property purchased by the debtor less than 90 days prior to the initiation of judgement collection proceedings or the filing of a bankruptcy petition. The debtor may elect to take the Constitutionally mandated exemptions listed below (Article X, §§ 1 and 2) in lieu of the exemptions in Chapter 1C above, but may not use both sets of exemptions.

Personal property selected by debtor	$500	Art. X, § 1 of Constitution
Homestead (may be claimed by owner or surviving spouse or children of owner)	$1,000.00	Art. X, § 2 of Constitution
Proceeds & cash surrender value of life insurance policies for sole use and benefit of spouse or children of insured	100%	Art. X, § 5 of Constitution. G.S. §§ 1C-1601(a)(6), 58-205, 58-206
Earnings from personal services of debtor	60 days earnings, if needed to support family	G.S. § 1-362
Workmen's compensation benefits	100%	G.S. § 97-21
Employment security benefits	100%	G.S. § 96-17
Aid to families with dependent children	100%	G.S. § 108-47
Aid to aged or disabled persons	100%	G.S. § 108-47
Aid to blind persons	100%	G.S § 111-18
Fraternal benefit society benefits	100%	G.S. § 58-283
Group life insurance benefits	100%	G.S. § 58-213
Firemen's pension fund benefits	100%	G.S. § 118-49
City & county employees' retirement benefits	100%	G.S. § 128-31
Teachers' and state employees' retirement benefits	100%	G.S. § 135-9
Specific partnership property	100% of partner's interest	G.S. § 59-55
Legislative retirement system benefits	100%	G.S. § 120-4-29
Crime victims Compensation awards	100%	G.S. § 15B-17

NOTE: Tenancies by the entirety may be exempt under 11 USC § 522(b)(2)(B). See Grabenhofer v. Garrett, 260 N.C. 118, 131 S.E. 2nd 765.

NORTH DAKOTA

Use of federal bankruptcy
exemptions in 11 USC § 522(d)
not permitted in this state.
See NDCC § 28-22-17.

Type of Property	Amount of Exemption	Statute Creating Exemption
Homestead of any person, consisting of lands & dwelling where debtor resides & appurtenances	$80,000 (proceeds of sale of homestead are exempt)	NDCC § 47-18-01
Earnings for personal services within last 60 days	Amount necessary to support debtor's family (See Note below)	NDCC § 28-25-11
Disposable earnings (earnings less deductions required by law. Includes periodic pension and retirement benefits)	The greater of 75% or 40 times the federal minimum hourly wage per week, plus $20 per week for each dependent family member residing with debtor	NDCC § 32-09.1-03
Family pictures, pew in place of worship, lots in burial ground, family Bible, school books, family library, wearing apparel and clothing of debtor and family, one-year's provisions and fuel for debtor and family, crops and grain grown on 160 acres, benefits from insurance covering absolute exemptions, and house trailer or mobile home occupied as residence	100%, except $100 limit on family library (these are absolute exemptions and are applicable to any debtor, whether or not he is a head of family)	NDCC § 28-22-02
Personal property of any kind	$5,000	NDCC § 28-22-03

NOTE: The debtor may claim either this exemption or the specific exemptions under NDCC § 28-22-04 (see below); he may not claim both. Also, this exemption, and the exemptions in § 28-22-04, may only be claimed by a debtor who is a head of family and who does not claim the crop and grain exemption under NDCC § 28-22-02 (above). Head of family includes husband or wife and debtor who supports children or certain relatives. See NDCC § 28-22-01.1 for definition. A debtor's wages are exempt only to the extent provided in NDCC § 32-09.1-03.

Type of Property	Amount of Exemption	Statute Creating Exemption
Miscellaneous books and musical instruments	$1,500 (see note above)	NDCC § 28-22-04(1)
Household and kitchen furniture	$1,000 (see note above)	NDCC § 28-22-04(2)
Livestock and farm implements	$4,500 (see note above)	NDCC § 28-22-04(3)
Tools and implements of trade of mechanic, plus stock in trade	$1,000 (see note above)	NDCC § 28-22-04(4)
Library and instruments of professional person	$1,000 (see note above)	NDCC § 28-22-04(4)
Personal property of any kind	$2,500 (this exemption applies only to a single person who does not claim the crop and grain exemption under § 28-22-02)	NDCC § 28-22-05
Property of any kind	$500 (applies only against judgments on criminal bond forfeitures)	NDCC § 28-22-16
Exemption in lieu of homestead	$7,500	NDCC § 28-22-03.1(1)
One motor vehicle	$1,200	NDCC § 28-22-03.1(2)
Pension, annuity policy or plan, life insurance policy payable to spouse, children or dependent, individual retirement account, Keogh plan, simplified employee pension plan, or other plan qualified under Internal Revenue Code, and proceeds therefrom	$100,000 limit for each plan, pension or policy, with $200,000 aggregate limit for all plans, pensions or policies; OR amount necessary for support of debtor and dependents, WHICHEVER IS GREATER	NDCC § 28-22-03.1(3)
Cash surrender value of life insurance policies payable to wife, children or dependent relative of debtor	amount specified in NDCC § 28-22-03.1 (see above for limits)	NDCC § 26.1-33-36
Avails of life insurance policy or mutual aid contract of benevolent society	100% (must be payable to deceased or estate)	NDCC § 26.1-33-40
Unemployment compensation benefits	100%	NDCC § 52-06-30
Workmens compensation benefits	100%	NDCC § 65-05-29
Aid to dependent children	100%	NDCC § 28-22-19(3)
Recoveries for wrongful death	100% – applies only to creditors of deceased	NDCC § 32-21-04
Vietnam veteran's bonuses	100%	NDCC § 37-25-07
All pensions or annuities or retirement, disability, death or other benefits paid or payable by a retirement system of the state or a political subdivision thereof, or by a firemen's relief association	100%	NDCC § 28-22-19(1)
Awards to crime victims	100%	NDCC § 28-22-19(2)

(continued on next page)

(continued from previous page)

Type of Property	Amount of Exemption	Statute Creating Exemption
Payments on the account of the wrongful death of an individual of whom the debtor was a dependent	Amount reasonably necessary to support debtor & dependents, not to exceed $7,500	NDCC § 28–22–03.1(4)(a)
Payment on the account of personal bodily injury, not including pain and suffering or compensation for actual pecuniary loss, of the debtor or an individual of whom the debtor is a dependent	$7,500	NDCC § 28–22–03.1(4)(b)
Social Security benefits	100%	NDCC § 28–22–03.1(4)(c)
Veteran's disability pension benefits	100%	NDCC § 28–22–03.1(4)(d)
Specific partnership property	100% of partner's interest	NDCC § 45–08–02

OHIO

Use of federal bankruptcy exemptions under 11 USC § 522(d) is <u>not</u> permitted in this state. See R.C. § 2329.662.

Type of Property	Amount of Exemption	Statute Creating Exemption
Homestead consisting of 1 parcel or item of real or personal property used as residence by debtor or a dependent of the debtor	$5,000	R.C. § 2329.66(A)(1)
1 motor vehicle	$1,000	R.C. § 2329.66(A)(2)
Wearing apparel, beds & bedding	$200 per item (no aggregate limit)	R.C. § 2329.66(A)(3)
1 cooking unit & 1 refrigerator or other food preservation unit	$300 each unit	R.C. § 2329.66(A)(3)
Cash on hand, money due & payable, money due within 90 days, tax refunds, and money on deposit (may include portion of earnings not otherwise exempt)	$400 (this exemption applies only in bankruptcy cases)	R.C. § 2329.66(A)(4)(a)
Household furnishing & goods, appliances, books, animals, crops, musical instruments, firearms, and hunting & fishing equipment held primarily for the personal, family or household use of the debtor	$200 per item, but cannot include items listed in division (A)(3), above. (See Note below for aggregate limit)	R.C. § 2329.66(A)(4)(b)
Items of jewelry	$400 for 1 item and $200 each for other items (See NOTE below for aggregate limit)	R.C. § 2329.66(A)(4)(c)

NOTE – If debtor claims a homestead exemption under division (A)(1) above, the total aggregate exemption allowed under divisions (A)(4)(b) and (A)(4)(c) combined is $1,500.00. If the debtor does not claim a homestead exemption under division (A)(1) above, the total aggregate exemption allowed under divisions (A)(4)(b) and (A)(4)(c) combined is $2,000.00.

Type of Property	Amount of Exemption	Statute Creating Exemption
Implements, professional books, or tools of debtor's profession, trade or business, including agriculture	$750	R.C. § 2329.66(A)(5)
Death benefits paid by benevolent society or association to family of deceased member	$5,000	R.C. §§ 2329.63, 2329.66(A)(6)(a)
Proceeds & avails of life insurance & annuity policies payable to spouse, children, dependent relative, or creditor of insured	100%	R.C. §§ 3911.10, 2329.66(A)(6)(b)
Group life insurance policies & proceeds	100%	R.C. §§ 3917.05, 2329.66(A)(6)(c)
Fraternal Benefit Society benefits	100%	R.C. §§ 3921.18, 2329.66(A)(6)(d)
Sickness & accident insurance benefits	$600 per month	R.C. §§ 3923.19, 2329.66(A)(6)(e)
Medically necessary or professionally prescribed health aids	100%	R.C. § 2329.66(A)(7)
Burial lots	100%	R.C. §§ 1721.10, 517.09, 2329.66(A)(8)
Vocational rehabilitation benefits	100%	R.C. §§ 3304.19, 2329.66(A)(9)(a)
Workmen's compensation benefits	100%	R.C. §§ 4123.67, 2329.66(A)(9)(b)
Unemployment compensation benefits	100%	R.C. §§ 4141.32, 2329.66(A)(9)(c)
Aid to dependent children	100%	R.C. §§ 5107.12, 2329.66(A)(9)(d)
General assistance payments	100%	R.C. § 5113.01, 2329.66(A)(9)(e)
Disability assistance payments	100%	R.C. §§ 2329.66(A)(9)(f), 5115.07
Pension & retirement benefits of public employees, volunteer firemen's dependents, firemen, policemen, teachers, school employees & highway patrolmen	100%	R.C. § 2329.66(A)(10)(a) & § 521.09
The right to payments under certain private pension or annuity plans (see statute for limitations)	Amount reasonably necessary to support debtor & dependents	R.C. § 2329.66(A)(10)(b)
Assets and benefits of individual retirement account, individual retirement annuity, or Keogh or H.R. 10 Plan	Amount reasonably necessary for the support of debtor and dependents	RC § 2329.66(A)(10)(c)
Right to receive alimony, child support, an allowance or maintenance	Amount reasonably necessary to support debtor & dependents	R.C. § 2329.66(A)(11)

NOTE: All Ohio exemptions apply only to persons who have their domicile on Ohio. Tenancies by the entirety may be exempt under 11 USC § 522(b)(2)(B). **See** In Re Thomas, 14 B.R. 423.

* R.C. stands for Page's Ohio Revised Code

(continued on next page)

OHIO

Type of Property	Amount of Exemption	Statute Creating Exemption
**Crime reparations awards	100% (exemption does not apply against creditors furnishing products, services or accommodations included in the award	R.C. §§ 2743.66(d), 2329.66(A)(12)(a)
**Payments on account of the wrongful death of person of whom debtor was a dependent	Amount reasonably necessary to support debtor & dependents	*R.C. § 2329.66(A)(12)(b)
**Personal injury awards to debtor or to a person for whom debtor is a dependent (does not include amounts awarded for pain & suffering or for actual pecuniary loss)	$5,000	R.C. § 2329.66(A)(12)(c)
**Payments in compensation for loss of future earnings of debtor or of a person of whom debtor is or was a dependent	Amount reasonably necessary to support debtor & dependents	R.C. § 2329.66(A)(12)(d)

** These exemptions apply only to money received, or the right to receive same, during the preceding 12 months.

Type of Property	Amount of Exemption	Statute Creating Exemption
Disposable earnings earned in preceding 30 days (disposable earnings are earnings less deductions required by law)	75% OR 30 times the federal minimum hourly wage per week (65 times if paid semimonthly, 130 times if paid monthly) WHICHEVER IS GREATER	R.C. § 2329.66(A)(13)

NOTE: 100% of debtor's earnings are exempt as against debts covered by valid debt scheduling agreement with Consumer Credit Counseling Service. See R.C. § 2715.11.

Type of Property	Amount of Exemption	Statute Creating Exemption
Debtor's interest in specific partnership property	100%	R.C. §§ 1775.24, 2329.66(A)(14)
Seal & register of notary public	100%	R.C. §§ 147.04, 2329.66(A)(15)
Any property exempt under any non-bankruptcy federal statute	100% of federal exemption	R.C. § 2329.66(A)(16)
Any property chosen by debtor	$400 (this exemption applies only in bankruptcy cases)	R.C. § 2329.66(A)(17)

OKLAHOMA

Use of federal bankruptcy exemptions in 11 USC § 522(d) <u>not</u> permitted in this state. See 31 OSA § 1B.

Type of Property	Amount of Exemption	Statute Creating Exemption
Homestead, home or manufactured home constituting principal residence of debtor	160 acres of rural land <u>OR</u> 1 acre of urban land not exceeding $5,000 in value, except that urban homestead may not be reduced to less than 1/4 acre regardless of value	31 OSA §§ 1A1, 2
Household and kitchen furniture	100%	31 OSA § 1A3
Cemetery lots	100%	31 OSA § 1A4
Implements of husbandry used on homestead	$5,000 (combined with § 1A6)	31 OSA § 1A5
Tools, apparatus and books used in trade or profession by debtor or dependents	$5,000 (combined with § 1A5)	31 OSA § 1A6
Armed services pension benefits	100%	31 OSA § 1A7
Personal books, portraits and pictures of debtor or dependents	100%	31 OSA § 1A7
Personal wearing apparel of debtor or dependents	$4,000	31 OSA § 1A8
Professionally prescribed health aid of debtor and dependents	100%	31 OSA § 1A9
5 milk cows & their calves under 6 months old, 100 chickens, 2 horses, 2 bridles, 2 saddles, 10 hogs, 20 sheep, and 1 year's provisions or forage on hand or growing for exempt stock	100% (stock must be held primarily for personal, family or household use of debtor or dependents)	31 OSA §§ 1A10, 11, 12, 15, 16, 17
Debtor's interest in one motor vehicle	$3,000	31 OSA § 1A13
One personal gun	100%	31 OSA § 1A14
Wages or earnings from personal services during last 90 days	75%	31 OSA § 1A18
Alimony, support, or maintenance payments	Amount necessary for support of debtor and dependents	31 OSA § 1A19
Personal or corporate retirement plans and arrangements qualified under Internal Revenue Code	100% of tax exempt portions	31 OSA § 1A20
Claims for personal injury, death, or workers compensation	$50,000	31 OSA § 1A21
Crime victim's reparation awards	100%	21 OSA § 142.13
Group life insurance proceeds	100%	36 OSA § 3632
Proceeds of life insurance policies payable to person other than insured	100%	36 OSA § 3631
Fraternal Benefit Society benefits	100%	36 OSA § 2720
Workmen's compensation benefits	100%	85 OSA § 48
Unemployment compensation benefits	100%	40 OSA § 2-203
Public assistance payments	100%	56 OSA § 173
Interests in retirement, pension, or profit-sharing plans, trusts or contracts	100%, if so provided in plan, trust or contract	60 OSA § 327
War bond payroll savings accounts	100%	51 OSA § 42
Specific partnership property	100% of partner's interest	54 OSA § 225
Firemen's pension benefits	100%	11 OSA § 49-126
Police pension benefits	100%	11 OSA § 50-124
Schoolteachers' retirement benefits	100%	70 OSA § 17-109
Public employees' retirement benefits	100%	74 OSA § 923
Judges' retirement benefits	100%	20 OSA § 1111

OREGON

Use of federal bankruptcy exemptions in 11 USC § 522(d) <u>not</u> permitted in this state. See ORS 23.305

Type of Property	Amount of Exemption	Statute Creating Exemption
Homestead occupied by debtor (exemption applies to proceeds of sale of homestead for 1 year and applies to condominium units under ORS 91.581(3)	15,000 for single debtor $20,000 for combined exemptions of 2 or more debtor–owners (cannot exceed 160 acres or 1 city block)	ORS 23.240
Mobile home & land thereon owned by debtor & used by debtor & family as residence (can also include houseboat)	$15,000 for single debtor ($13,000 if no land) $20,000 for combined exemptions of 2 or more debtor–owners ($18,000 if no land)	ORS 23.164
NOTE – A debtor may only take one of the above exemptions.		
Books, pictures & musical instruments	$300	ORS 23.160(1)(a)
Wearing apparel, jewelry & personal items	$900	ORS 23.160(1)(b)
Tools, implements, apparatus, a team of horses or mules, harness, or library, necessary to carry on trade occupation or profession	$750 plus 60 days supply of food for team	ORS 23.160(1)(c)
1 vehicle or motor vehicle	$1,200	ORS 23.160(1)(d)
Domestic animals & poultry kept for family use	$1,000 plus 60 days supply of food for same	ORS 23.160(1)(e)
Household goods, furniture, radios, a television set, & utensils (must be held primarily for personal, family or household use of debtor)	$1,450	ORS 23.160(1)(f)
Professionally prescribed health aids of debtor & dependents	100%	ORS 23.160(1)(h)
Spousal support, child support & separate maintenance payments	Amount reasonably necessary to support debtor & dependents	ORS 23.160(1)(i)
Crime victim's reparation law awards	100%	ORS 23.160(1)(j)(A)
Payments on account of personal bodily injury, not including pain & suffering or compensation for actual pecuniary loss, of debtor or an individual of whom the debtor was a dependent	$7,500	ORS 23.160(1)(j)(B)
Payments in compensation for the loss of future earnings of the debtor or an individual of whom the debtor was a dependent	Amount reasonably necessary to support debtor & dependents	ORS 23.160(1)(j)(C)
Any personal property	$400 (cannot be used to increase any other exemption)	ORS 23.160 (1)(k)
Provisions & fuel for debtor & family	60 days' supply	ORS 23.160(1)(f)
Pension benefits granted by reason of period of employment or service	100%	ORS 23.170, 239.261, 237.201
Otherwise exempt earnings and benefits when deposited in bank	$7,500 (funds must be identifiable)	ORS 23.166
Disposable earnings (earnings less deductions required by law)	75% or $150 per week WHICHEVER IS GREATER	ORS 23.185
NOTE – Exempt amount increases to $160 on 7-1-92 and $170 on 7-1-93.		
1 rifle or shotgun & 1 pistol	100% (applies only to persons above age 16)	ORS 23.210
Vocational rehabilitation payments	100%	ORS 344.580
Aid to blind persons	100%	ORS 412.115
Aid to disabled persons	100%	ORS 412.610
Homestead or rental assistance tax refunds	100%	ORS 310.637

(continued on next page)

OREGON

Type of Property	Amount of Exemption	Statute Creating Exemption
Old age assistance payments	100%	ORS 413.130
Public assistance grants	100%	ORS 411.760, 414.095
Civil defense & disaster relief benefits	100%	ORS 401.225
Fraternal Benefit Society benefits	100%	ORS 748.225
Proceeds & cash surrender value of life insurance policies of insured where the beneficiary is person with insurable interest in insured's life	100%	ORS 743.099
Group life insurance policy proceeds payable to person other that the insured or his estate	100%	ORS 743.102
Annuity policy benefits	$250 per month	ORS 743.105
Health & disability insurance benefits	100%	ORS 743.108
Unemployment compensation benefits	100%	ORS 657.855
Workmen's compensation benefits	100%	ORS 656.234
Burial lots	100%	ORS 61.770
Benefits to injured trainees & inmates	100%	ORS 655.430, 655.530
State loans to veterans	100%	ORS 407.110
Specific partnership property	100% of partner's interest	ORS 68.420

PENNSYLVANIA

Type of Property	Amount of Exemption	Statute Creating Exemption
Wages & salary in hands of employer	100%	42 Pa.C.S. § 8127
Wearing apparel, bibles & school books	no limit	42 Pa.C.S § 8124(a)
Property of any kind	$300	42 Pa.C.S. § 8123(a)
Sewing machines of seamstresses & private families	no limit	42 Pa.C.S § 8124(a)
Annuities & insurance benefits payable to insured	$100 per month	42 Pa.C.S. § 8124(c)(3)
Annuities or pension benefits paid by private corporation or employer to retired employee residing in Pa. if benefits not assignable under plan or contract	no limit	42 Pa.C.S. § 8124(b)(7)
Proceeds of life insurance policy or annuity contract payable to spouse, children or dependent relative of insured	no limit	42 Pa.C.S § 8124(c)(6)
Proceeds of accident or disability insurance policies	no limit	42 Pa.C.S § 8124(c)(7)
Fraternal Benefit Society benefits	no limit	42 Pa.C.S § 8124(c)(1), 40 Pa.C.S. § 6531, 15 Pa.C.S § 8516
Proceeds of group life insurance policies	no limit	42 Pa.C.S. § 8124(c)(5)
Life insurance and annuity contract proceeds retained by Ins. company if contract provides that proceeds are not assignable	no limit	40 Pa.C.S § 514 42 Pa.C.S. § 8124(c)(4)
Workmen's Compensation benefits	no limit	77 Pa.C.S. § 621 42 Pa.C.S. § 8124(c)(2)
Unemployment Compensation benefits	no limit	43 Pa.C.S. § 863
Veteran's compensation benefits	no limit	51 Pa.C.S. §§ 20012, 20048, 20098, 20127
Tangible personal property at international exhibition under auspices of federal government	no limit	42 Pa.C.S. § 8125
Uniforms, arms, ammunition & accoutrements of National Guardsmen	no limit	51 Pa.C.S. § 4103 42 Pa.C.S. § 8124(a)(4)
Property acquired after court-approved assignment for benefit of creditors	no limit (applies only against creditors prior to assignment)	39 Pa.C.S. § 102
County employees retirement benefits	no limit	16 Pa.C.S. § 4716
Public officers & employees retirement benefits	no limit	53 Pa.C.S. § 13445 42 Pa.C.S. § 8124(b)(4)
City employees retirement & pension benefits	no limit	53 Pa.C.S. § 23572, 39351, 39383 42 Pa.C.S. § 8124(b)(5)
State employees retirement benefits	no limit	71 Pa.C.S. § 5953 42 Pa.C.S. § 8124(b)(2)
Police pension fund benefits	no limit	53 Pa.C.S. § 764 42 Pa.C.S. § 8124(b)(3)
Public school employees retirement benefits	no limit	24 Pa.C.S. § 8533 42 Pa.C.S. § 8124(b)(1)
Municipal employees retirement benefits	no limit	53 Pa.C.S. § 881.115 42 Pa.C.S § 8124(b)(6)
Self-employed person's retirement or annuity funds (to the extent payments thereto made while solvent)	100%	42 Pa.C.S. § 8124(b)(8)
Specific partnership property	100% of partner's interest	59 Pa.C.S. § 342
Crime victim's reparation awards	100%, except injury expenses	71 Pa.C.S. § 180-7.10
Financial Responsibility Act benefits	100%	42 Pa.C.S. § 8124(c)(9)

NOTE: Tenancies by the entirety may be exempt under 11 USC § 522(b)(2)(B). See In Re Barsotti, 3 C.B.C. 2nd 306.

RHODE ISLAND

Use of federal bankruptcy exemptions in 11 USC § 522(d) permitted in this state

Type of Property	Amount of Exemption	Statute Creating Exemption
Necessary wearing apparel	100%	GL § 9–26–4(1)
Working tools used in occupation	$500	GL § 9–26–4(2)
Professional library of professional man in actual practice	100%	GL § 9–26–4(2)
Household furniture and family stores of housekeeper	$1,000	GL § 9–26–4(3)
Bibles, school books and other books	$300	GL § 9–26–4(4)
One lot or right of burial in cemetery	100%	GL § 9–26–4(5)
Wages of seaman	100%	GL § 9–26–4(6)
Debts secured by bills of exchange or negotiable promissory notes	100%	GL § 9–26–4(7)
Salary or wages of debtor due or payable from any welfare director or from any public charity, if the funds are for relief of poor or unemployed	100%	GL § 9–26–4(8)(A)
Wages or salary of debtor who has been on state, federal or local relief during past year	100% (exemption lasts for 1 year after debtor goes off relief)	GL § 9–26–4(8)(B)
Wages or salary of any other debtor	$50	GL § 9–26–4(8)(C)
Wages and salary of wife and minor children of debtor	100%	GL § 9–26–4(9)
Assets and distributions from Individual Retirement Account qualified under IRC	100% of qualified amounts	GL § 9–26–4(11)
Annuity, pension, profit–sharing, or other retirement account or plan qualified under IRC	100% of qualified amounts	GL § 9–26–4(12)
Pay and allowance of militiaman	100%	GL § 30–7–9
Employment security benefits	100%	GL § 28–44–58
Workmen's compensation benefits	100%	GL § 28–33–27
Public assistance payments	100%	GL § 40–6–14
Proceeds and avails of life insurance policies not payable to insured	100%	GL § 27–4–11
Specific partnership property	100% of partner's interest	GL § 7–12–36
Disability insurance benefits	100%	GL § 28–41–32
Assessment plan insurance benefits payable to wife, minor child or dependent of insured	100%	GL § 27–15–10
Proceeds of life or endowment insurance and annuity contracts where contract or policy so provides	100% (exemption applies to beneficiary only)	GL § 27–4–12
Public employee retirement benefits	100%	GL § 36–10–34
Proceeds, avails and benefits of accident and sickness insurance	100%	GL § 27–18–24
Fraternal Benefit Society benefits	100%	GL § 27–28–9
Policeman and firemen pension funds and benefits	100%	GL § 9–26–5
Consumers cooperative membership	$50	GL § 7–8–25

NOTE: Tenancies by the entirety may be exempt under 11 USC § 522(b)(2)(B). See In Re Gibbons, 17 B.R. 373.

(current to January 1, 1992)

Type of Property	Amount of Exemption	Statute Creating Exemption
Real or personal property, including a cooperative, used as residence by debtor or a dependent, OR a burial plot	$5,000 (If multiple owners, exemption cannot exceed $10,000/no. of owners)	CLSC § 15-41-30(1)
One motor vehicle	$1,200	CLSC § 15-41-30(2)
Personal household furnishings & goods, wearing apparel, appliances, books, animals, crops, or musical instruments of debtor or dependent	$2,500	CLSC § 15-41-30(3)
Personal, family, or household jewelry of debtor or dependent	$500	CLSC § 15-41-30(4)
Cash & liquid assets of debtor not claiming homestead exemption	$1,000	CLSC § 15-41-30(5)
Implements, books, or tools of trade of debtor or a dependent	$750	CLSC § 15-41-30(6)
Unmatured life insurance contract other than credit life	100%	CLSC § 15-41-30(7)
Loan value or accrued interest or dividends in unmatured life insurance contract insuring debtor or person of whom debtor is a dependent	$4,000 less nonforfeiture transfers	CLSC § 15-41-30(8)
Prescribed health aids of debtor or dependent	100%	CLSC § 15-41-30(9)
Debtor's right to receive Social Security benefits; unemployment compensation; public assistance benefits; veterans benefits; disability, illness or unemployment benefits; alimony, support or separate maintenance; and certain payments under stock-bonus, pension, profit-sharing, annuity, or similar plans.	100%	CLSC § 15-41-30(10)
Debtor's right to receive or property traceable to a crime victim's reparation award or payments on account of bodily injury of debtor or wrongful death or bodily injury of person of whom debtor was or is a dependent	100%	CLSC § 15-41-30(11)(A),(B)
Debtor's right to receive, or property traceable to, payments under life insurance contracts insuring life of person of whom debtor was a dependent on the date of death	Amount reasonably necessary to support debtor & dependents	CLSC § 15-41-30(11)(C)
Earnings from personal services	100%	CLSC § 15-39-410
Fraternal Benefit Association benefits	100%	CLSC § 38-21-870
Workmen's compensation benefits	100%	CLSC § 42-9-360
State retirement system benefits	100%	CLSC § 9-1-1680
General Assembly retirement benefits	100%	CLSC § 9-9-180
Peace officers' retirement benefits	100%	CLSC § 9-11-270
Firemen's pension benefits	100%	CLSC § 9-13-230
Specific partnership property	100% of partner's interest	CLSC § 33-41-720

NOTE: Section 4 of 1981 Act No. 53 provides that the provisions of 15-41-200 shall prevail over previously-enacted laws dealing with the same matters. Thus, the following statutes appear to be superceded: CLSC §§ 15-41-10, 15-41-310, 21-15-700, 38-9-340, 41-39-20 and 43-5-130.

SOUTH DAKOTA

Use of federal bankruptcy exemptions in 11 USC § 522(d) <u>not</u> permitted in this state. (See SDCL §§ 43-31-30, 43-45-13)

Type of Property	Amount of Exemption	Statute Creating Exemption
Homestead of resident family	100%	SDCL §§ 43-31-1, 43-45-3

NOTES: A family may consist of one person; see Somers v. Somers, 33 S.D. 551, 146 N.W. 716. The homestead may consist of a mobile home if it is so used. However, the mobile home must be registered in the state for 6 months before the exemption applies; see SDCL § 43-31-2. There is no monetary limit to the homestead exemption of a person 70 or more years old or the unremarried surviving spouse of such person. The homestead is limited to one acre if in town or city, 160 acres if in the country, and 40 acres if on mineral land; see SDCL § 43-31-4. The homestead exemption is absolute. $30,000 of sales proceeds exempt for 1 year.

Type of Property	Amount of Exemption	Statute Creating Exemption
Family pictures, pew in place of worship, lots in burial ground, wearing apparel of debtor and family, and one-year's provisions for debtor and family	100% (absolute exemption)	SDCL § 43-45-2
Family Bible, school books and library	$200 (absolute exemption)	SDCL § 43-45-2
Personal property of any kind	$4,000 for head of family $2,000 for any other person	SDCL § 43-45-4
Family books and musical instruments	$200 (see note below)	SDCL § 43-45-5(1)
Household and kitchen furniture	$200 (see note below)	SDCL § 43-45-5(2)
Two cows, 5 swine, 2 yoke of oxen or 1 span of horses or mules, 25 sheep and their lambs under 6 months old and all wool and cloth therefrom, plus 1-year's supply of feed for exempt animals	100% (see note below)	SDCL § 43-45-5(3)
One wagon, 1 sleigh, 2 plows, 1 harrow, and farming equipment and machinery	$1250 (see note below)	SDCL § 43-45-5(3)
Tools and implements of trade of mechanic	100% (see note below)	SDCL § 43-45-5(4)
Stock in trade of mechanic	$200 (see note below)	SDCL § 43-45-5(4)
Library and instruments of professional person	$300 (see note below)	SDCL § 43-45-5(5)

NOTE: The exemptions contained in SDCL § 43-45-5 may only be claimed by a debtor who is a head of family and who does not claim the personal property exemption under § 43-45-4.

Type of Property	Amount of Exemption	Statute Creating Exemption
Proceeds of life insurance policy payable to insured's estate when insured dies leaving surviving widow, husband or children (includes cash surrender value of policy, see Schuler v. Johnson, 61 S.D. 141, 246 N.W. 632)	$10,000	SDCL § 43-45-6
Annuity contract benefits	$250 per month	SDCL §§ 58-12-6, 7, 8
Proceeds of life or health insurance or endowment policy	$20,000	SDCL § 58-12-4
Fraternal Benefit Society benefits	100%	SDCL § 58-37-68
Proceeds of life or health insurance policies (includes cash surrender value, see Magnuson v. Wagner, 1 F. 2d 99)	$20,000	SDCL § 58-12-4
Public Employees Retirement System benefits	100%	SDCL § 3-12-115
Aid to dependent children	100%	SDCL § 28-7-16
Maintenance to the visually impaired	100%	SDCL § 28-10-15
Workmen's compensation benefits	100%	SDCL § 62-4-42
Unemployment compensation benefits	100%	SDCL § 61-6-28
Earnings of prisoners on work release	100%	SDCL § 24-8-10
Specific partnership property	100% of partner's interest	SDCL § 48-4-14
60 days earnings	100% (if needed to support family)	SDCL § 15-20-12
Aggregate disposable earnings	The greater of 80% or 40 times the Federal minimum hourly wage per week, plus $25 per week for each dependent family member residing with the debtor	SDCL § 21-18-51

TENNESSEE

Type of Property	Amount of Exemption	Statute Creating Exemption
Homestead consisting of real property used by debtor, his spouse, or a dependent as principal residence	$5,000.00 for individual debtor $7,500.00 if jointly owned and both debtors are involved in the proceeding (must be divided equally) (exemption also applies to life estates, equitable estates and leasehold estates; see TCA §§ 26-2-302, 26-2-303).	TCA § 26-2-301
Insurance proceeds from destroyed exempt homestead	$5,000.00	TCA § 26-2-304
Personal property of state resident (includes money and bank deposits)	$4,000.00	TCA § 26-2-102
Necessary wearing apparel of debtor and family and receptacles for holding same, family portraits and pictures, family Bible and school books	100%	TCA § 26-2-103
Disposable earnings (earnings after deductions required by law)	75% OR 30 times the federal minimum hourly wage per week, WHICHEVER IS GREATER, (Add $2.50 per week for each dependent child of the debtor under age 16 residing in state; TCA § 26-2-207.	TCA § 26-2-106
Family cemetery or burial lot	100%	TCA § 26-2-102
Accident, health and disability insurance benefits	100%	TCA § 26-2-110(a)
Annuity contracts benefits payable to spouse, children or dependent of insured	100% (includes cash surrender value)	TCA § 56-7-203
Assets and benefits of private retirement plan qualified under Internal Revenue Code	100%	TCA § 26-2-104(b)
Fraternal benefit society payments	100%	TCA § 56-25-208
Workmen's compensation benefits	100%	TCA § 50-1016
Employment security benefits	100%	TCA § 50-1349
Specific partnership property	100% of partner's interest	TCA § 61-1-124
Pension benefits received from state or subdivision or municipality thereof	100%	TCA § 26-2-104(a)
Cooperative scholarship benefits	100%	TCA § 49-4507
Aid to dependent children	100%	TCA § 14-8-121
Aid to the blind	100%	TCA § 14-13-117
Aid to the disabled	100%	TCA § 14-16-112
Old age assistance payments	100%	TCA § 14-2-116
Social security, unemployment, public assistance, veterans, disability or illness benefits	100%	TCA § 26-2-111(1)(A), (B), (C)
Certain payments under stock bonus, pension, profit sharing, annuity or similar plan or contracts (see statute for specifics)	Same as under TCA § 26-2-106 above	TCA § 26-2-111(1)(D)
Alimony due more than 30 days after assertion of claim	100%	TCA § 26-2-111(1)(E)
Crime victim's reparation law awards	$5,000.00 (see note below)	TCA § 26-2-111(2)(A)
Personal injury payments to debtor or individual of whom debtor is a dependent, excluding compensation for pain and suffering and actual pecuniary loss	$7,500.00 (see note below)	TCA § 26-2-111(2)(B)
Payments for the wrongful death of debtor or individual of whom debtor was a dependent	$10,000.00 (see note below)	TCA § 26-2-111(2)(C)

NOTE: The aggregate amounts claimed under TCA § 26-2-111(2) cannot exceed $15,000.00

Type of Property	Amount of Exemption	Statute Creating Exemption
Compensation for loss of future earnings of debtor or individual of whom debtor is a dependent	Amount reasonably necessary for support of debtor and dependents	TCA § 26-2-111(3)
Implements, professional books, or tools of trade of debtor or dependent	$750.00	TCA § 26-2-111(4)
Professionally prescribed health aids of debtor and dependents	100%	TCA § 26-2-111(5)

NOTE: Tenancies by the entirety may be exempt under 11 USC § 522(b)(2)(B). See In Re Dawson, 5 C.B.C. 2nd 404.

Use of federal bankruptcy
exemptions under 11 USC §
522(d) permitted in this state

Type of Property	Amount of Exemption	Statute Creating Exemption
Homestead (must be used as rural or urban home or as a place to exercise a calling or business in urban area)	200 acres for family (100 acres for single adult) of rural land OR one acre of urban land (land may be in one or more parcels and improvements are included; no value limit)	Constitution Art. 16, §§ 50, 51 Property Code §§ 41.001, 41.002
Proceeds of voluntary sale of homestead (good for 6 months after sale)	same as for homestead that was sold	Property Code § 41.001(c)
Lots held as burying grounds	100%	Property Code § 41.001(a)
Current wages for personal services	100% (child support claims excepted)	Property Code § 42.001(b)(1)
Professionally prescribed health aids	100%	Property Code § 42.001(b)(2)
Unpaid commissions for personal services (see note below)	$15,000 for debtor who is a family member $7,500 for single nonfamily–member, adult	Property Code § 42.001(d)
Home furnishings, including family heirlooms	100% (see note below)	Property Code §§ 42.001(a), 42.002(a)(1)
Provisions for consumption	100% (see note below)	Property Code §§ 42.001(a), 42.002(a)(2)
Farming or ranching vehicles and implements	100% (see note below)	Property Code §§ 42.001(a), 42.002(a)(3)
Tools, equipment, books, and apparatus, used in a trade or profession	100% (see note below) (includes boats and motor vehicles)	Property Code §§ 42.001(a), 42.002(a)(4)
Wearing apparel	100% (see note below)	Property Code §§ 42.001(a), 42.002(a)(5)
Jewelry (see note below)	$15,000 for debtor who is a family member 7,500 for single nonfamily–member adult	Property Code §§ 42.001(a), 42.002(a)(6)
Two firearms	100% (see note below)	Property Code §§ 42.001(a), 42.002(a)(7)
Athletic and sporting equipment, including bicycles	100% (see note below)	Property Code §§ 42.001(a), 42.002(a)(8)
One motor vehicle (2,3, or 4 wheeled) for debtor with driver's license or driver	100% (see note below)	Property Code §§ 42.001(a), 42.002(a)(9)
2 horses, mules or donkeys plus a saddle, blanket, and bridle for each, 12 head of cattle, 60 head of other types of livestock, 120 fowl, forage on hand for each animal	100% (see note below)	Property Code §§ 42.001(a), 42.002(a)(10)
Household pets	100% (see note below)	Property Code §§ 42.001(a), 42.002(a)(11)
Present value of life insurance policy payable to family member or dependent	100% (see note below)	Property Code §§ 42.001(a), 42.002(a)(12)

NOTE: The aggregate limitation on the exemptions specified in Property Code §§ 42.001(d) and 42.002(a) are $60,000 for a debtor who is a family member and $30,000 for a single adult who is not a family member. Also, a debtor who uses nonexempt property to obtain, improve, or pay an indebtedness on exempt personal property with the intent to defraud, delay or hinder a creditor may lose the exemption. See Property Code § 42.004.

Type of Property	Amount of Exemption	Statute Creating Exemption
Proceeds and property of I.R.C. qualified personal or corporate retirement plans	100% of qualified amounts	Property Code § 42.0021
Partner's interest in partnership property	100%	VACS art. 6132b, § 25
Employees group life insurance benefits & contributions	100%	Ins. Code art. 3.50–2, § 10, art. 3.50, § 9
Benefits paid under life, health or accident insurance policies	100%	Ins. Code art. 21.22, § 1
Fraternal Benefit Society benefits	100%	Ins. Code art. 10.28
Unemployment compensation benefits	100%	VACS art. 5221b–13(c)
Workmen's compensation benefits	100%	VACS art. 8306, § 3
Public assistance benefits	100%	Texas Humble Residents Code § 31–040
Medical assistance payments to needy	100%	Texas Humble Resident, Code § 32–036
State employees retirement & pension benefits	100%	VACS title 110B, § 21.005
Judicial system retirement benefits	100%	VACS Title 110B, § 41.004
Law enforcement officers' survivors benefits	100%	VACS art. 6228f, § 8
County & district employees pension & retirement benefits	100%	VACS Title 110B, § 51.006
Municipal employees retirement benefits	100%	Title 110B, § 61.006; art. 6243g § 20
Police, firemen & fire alarm operators pension, relief & retirement benefits	100%	VACS arts. 6243a § 16, 6243b § 15, 6243d–1 § 17, 6243e § 13, 6243e.1 § 12, 6243e.2 § 12, 6243f § 18, 6243g–1 § 20, 6243j § 20
Teachers pension & retirement benefits	100%	VACS Title 110B, § 31.005
Crime victim's compensation	100%	VACS art. 8309–1, § 7(f)
Public School employees insurance benefits and contributions	100%	Insurance Code § 3.50–4(11)

* VACS stands for Vernon's Annotated Revised Civil Statutes of the State of Texas

UTAH

Use of federal bankruptcy
exemptions in 11 USC § 522(d)
<u>not</u> permitted in this state.
See UCA § 78-23-15.

Type of Property	Amount of Exemption	Statute Creating Exemption
Homestead consisting of property in the state; may consist of 1 or more parcels of real property with appurtenances, a mobile home in which the claimant resides, or both.	$8,000 for head of family $2,000 for spouse $500 for each other dependent	UCA § 78-23-3(1)

NOTE: Head of family includes a single individual with or without dependents, or a husband or wife if claimant is married, but exemption may only be claimed once. If claimant is married, the homestead may be selected from separate property of husband, or, with her consent, from the wife's separate property. A declaration of homestead must be filed with the county recorder for homestead to be valid. See UCA § 78-23-4.

Type of Property	Amount of Exemption	Statute Creating Exemption
Water rights & interests owned by homestead claimant & necessary for supplying water to homestead	100%	UCA § 78-23-3(4)
Proceeds of sale of homestead for 1 year after sale	same as homestead exemption	UCA § 78-23-3(5)
Burial plot	100%	UCA § 78-23-5(1)(a)
Necessary health aids of debtor or dependents	100%	UCA 78-23-5(1)(b)
Disability, illness or unemployment benefits of debtor or dependent	100%	UCA § 78-23-5(1)(c)
Benefits payable for medical, surgical or hospital care	Extent used by debtor or dependent for such care	UCA § 78-23-5(1)(d)
Veterans benefits	100%	UCA § 78-23-5(1)(e)
Child support payments & the rights thereto	100%	UCA § 78-23-5(1)(f)
1 clothes washer & dryer, 1 refrigerator, 1 freezer, 1 stove, 1 sewing machine, all carpets in use, 3-months' provisions, all wearing apparel (not including jewelry or furs), all beds & bedding, of debtor & dependents	100%	UCA § 78-23-5(1)(g)
Personal works of art depicting debtor & family or produced by debtor & family	100%	UCA § 78-23-5(1)(h)
Proceeds of claims for bodily injury of debtor or proceeds of claims for bodily injury or wrongful death of an individual of whom debtor was or is a dependent	extent that proceeds are compensatory	UCA § 78-23-5(1)(i)
Alimony or separate maintenance payments and the rights thereto	Amount reasonably necessary for support of debtor & dependents	UCA § 78-23-6(1)
Life insurance proceeds paid or payable to spouse or dependent of insured	Amount reasonably necessary for support of debtor & dependents	UCA § 78-23-6(2)
Assets & benefits under stock bonus, pension, profit-sharing, annuity or similar plan providing benefits other than for illness or disability	Amount reasonably necessary for support of debtor & dependents	UCA § 78-23-6(3)
Accrued dividends & loan values of unmatured life insurance policies owned by debtor	$1,500	UCA § 78-23-7
Furnishings & appliances necessary for one household	$500	UCA § 78-23-8(1)(a)
Animals, books & musical instruments held for personal use of debtor or dependents	$500	UCA § 78-23-8(1)(b)
Personal heirlooms	$500	UCA § 78-23-8(1)(c)
Implements, professional books, or tools of trade	$1,500	UCA § 78-23-8(2)
One motor vehicle used in debtor's business or profession, other than for traveling to and from work	$1,500	UCA § 78-23-8(2)

(continued on next page)

Type of Property	Amount of Exemption	Statute Creating Exemption
Proceeds from sale, condemnation, damage or destruction of exempt property	Amount of exemption given for lost or damaged property	UCA § 78–23–9(1)
Military property of National Guardsman	100%	UCA § 39–1–47
Occupational Disease Act compensation	100%	UCA § 35–2–35
Workmen's compensation benefits	100%	UCA § 35–1–80
Unemployment compensation benefits	100%	UCA § 35–4–18
Public assistance payments	100%	UCA § 55–15–32
Public Safety Retirement Act benefits	100%	UCA § 49–11–43
School employees retirement benefits	100%	UCA § 53–29–46, 56
State Retirement Act benefits	100%	UCA § 49–10–48
Firemen's Retirement Act benefits	100%	UCA § 49–6a–36
Judges Retirement Act benefits	100%	UCA § 49–7a–33
Fraternal Benefit Society benefits	100%	UCA § 31–29–25
Partner's interest in specific partner-ship property, except on claim against partnership	100%	UCA § 48–1–22(2)(c)
Assets and benefits in retirement plan qualified under Internal Revenue Code	100% – except contributions made within 180 days of filing	UCA § 78–23–5(1)(j)

VERMONT

Use of federal bankruptcy
exemptions in 11 USC § 522(d)
permitted in this state

Type of Property	Amount of Exemption	Statute Creating Exemption
Homestead, consisting of dwelling house, outbuildings and land used in connection therewith, including rents, issues, profits, and products thereof	$30,000	27 VSA § 101
Motor vehicles	$2,500	12 VSA § 2740(1)
Professional or trade books or tools of debtor or dependent	$5,000	12 VSA § 2740(2)
One wedding ring	100%	12 VSA § 2740(3)
Personal, family, or household jewelry of debtor or dependent	$500	12 VSA § 2740(4)
Personal, family or household furnishings, goods, appliances, books, wearing apparel, animals, crops, or musical instruments of debtor or dependent	$2,500	12 VSA § 2740(5)
Growing crops	$5,000	12 VSA § 2740(6)
Debtor's interest in any property	$400 plus up to $7,000 of any unused exemption provided under 12 VSA § 2740(1), (2), (4), (5) or (6)	12 VSA § 2740(7)
Cook stove, heating appliance, refrigerator freezer, water heater, and sewing machines	100%	12 VSA § 2740(8)
10 cords of firewood or 500 gallons of oil	100%	12 VSA § 2740(9)
500 gallons of bottled gas	100%	12 VSA § 2740(10)
1 cow, 2 goats, 10 sheep, 10 chickens, and one winter's feed for each	100%	12 VSA § 2740(11)
3 swarms of bees with hives & produce	100%	12 VSA § 2740(12)
1 yoke of oxen or steers or 2 team horses	100%	12 VSA § 2740(13)
2 harnesses, 2 halters, 2 chains, 1 plow, and 1 ox yoke	100%	12 VSA § 2740(14)
Bank deposits or deposit accounts	$700	12 VSA § 2740(15)
Self-directed retirement accounts	$10,000	12 VSA § 2740(16)
Professionally prescribed health aids	100%	12 VSA § 2740(17)
Unmatured life insurance contracts	100% (credit life insurance excluded)	12 VSA § 2740(18)
Social security benefits, veteran's benefits, disability or illness benefits, alimony, support, or separate maintenance, and crime victims' reparation awards	Amount reasonably necessary for the support of debtor and dependents	12 VSA § 2740(19)(A)–(E)
Compensation for personal injury, pain & suffering, or actual pecuniary loss, compensation for wrongful death, and compensation for loss of future earnings	Amount reasonably necessary for the support of debtor and dependents	12 VSA § 2740(19)(F),(G),(I)
Life insurance payments and payments under pension, annuity, profit-sharing, stock bonus, or similar plans on account of death, disability, illness or retirement	Amount reasonably necessary for the support of debtor and dependents	12 VSA § 2740(19)(H),(J)
Disposable earnings (earnings less deductions required by law	75% OR 30 times the federal minimum hourly wage per week WHICHEVER IS GREATER	12 VSA § 3170
Personal earnings of minor child or married woman	100% (applies against creditors or parent or husband)	12 VSA § 3020(6)
Fees of jurors and fees and room and board expenses of legislators	100%	12 VSA § 3020(3)(4)
Fire insurance proceeds resulting from loss by fire of exempt property	100%	12 VSA § 3020(1)
Proceeds of life insurance policy	$500	12 VSA § 3020(2)
Proceeds of group life insurance and group disability insurance	100%	8 VSA § 3708
Proceeds and avails of life insurance policies wherein beneficiary is not the insured	100% (less premiums paid in defraud of creditors)	8 VSA § 3706
Beneficial interests in insurance policies or annuity contracts containing spendthrift clauses	100%	8 VSA § 3705

(continued on next page)

VERMONT

(continued from previous page)

Type of Property	Amount of Exemption	Statute Creating Exemption
Annuity contract benefits	$350 per month	8 VSA § 3709
Fraternal Benefit Society benefits	100%	8 VSA § 4478
Disability insurance benefits that are supplemental to life insurance or annuity contracts	100%	8 VSA § 3707
Unemployment compensation benefits	100%	21 VSA § 1367
Workmen's compensation benefits	100%	21 VSA § 681
Public assistance payments	100%	33 VSA § 2575
Vermont Employees Retirement System benefits and funds	100%	3 VSA § 476
Health insurance benefits	$200 per month	8 VSA § 4086
Specific partnership property	100% of partner's interest	11 VSA § 1282
Amounts owing to debtor from sale of exempt property	Same as exemption given for property sold	12 VSA § 3023

NOTE: Tenancies by the entirety may be exempt under 11 USC § 522(b)(2)(B). See Lowell v. Lowell, 138 VT. 514, 419 A. 2nd 321.

VIRGINIA

Use of federal bankruptcy
exemptions in 11 USC § 522(d)
not permitted in this state
See CV § 34-3.1

Type of Property	Amount of Exemption	Statute Creating Exemption
Real & personal property (Includes money & debts owed to debtor)	$5,000 plus $500 for each dependent (applies to householder or resident head of family) (exempt real estate must be claimed by recording written declaration. See CV § 34-6)	CV § 34-4

NOTE: A householder debtor must set apart the property claimed as exempt on or before the 5th day after the first date set for the first meeting of creditors. See CV § 34-17.

Type of Property	Amount of Exemption	Statute Creating Exemption
Real & personal property of disabled veteran (must be rated 40% or more disabled by V.A,)	$2,000	CV § 34-4.1
Rents & profits of exempt property	100%	CV § 34-18
Exempt property of deceased householder leaving spouse or minor children	same as for householder ("householder" includes any person maintaining a separate residence or living quarters)	CV § 64.1-127
Disposable earnings (earnings less deductions required by law)	75% OR 30 times federal minimum hourly wage per week, WHICHEVER IS GREATER	CV § 34-29
Family Bible	100%	CV § 34-26(1)
Wedding & engagement rings	100%	CV § 34-26(1a)
Family portraits and heirlooms	$5,000	CV § 34-26(2)
Burial lot	100%	CV § 34-26(3)
Wearing apparel	$1,000	CV § 34-26(4)
Household furnishings	$5,000	CV § 34-26(4a)
Animals owned as pets	100%	CV § 34-26(5)
Medically prescribed health aids	100%	CV § 34-26(6)
Tools, books, instruments implements, equipment, and machines (including motor vehicles, vessels and aircraft) used in trade or occupation	$10,000 (motor vehicles, vessels and aircraft used only to commute to and from place of work are not covered under this exemption)	CV § 34-26(7)
Motor vehicle	$2,000	CV § 34-26(8)
1 pair of horses or mules with necessary gearing, 1 wagon or cart, 1 tractor, 2 plows, 1 drag, 1 harvest cradle, 1 pitchfork, 1 rake, 2 iron wedges, fertilizer	no limit, except: $3,000 for tractor $1,000 for fertilizer (applies only to householder actually engaged in agriculture)	CV § 34-27
Causes of action for and proceeds of personal injury claims	100%	CV § 34-28.1
Debtor's interest in retirement plan	Amount necessary to provide annual benefit of $17,500 NOTE- Contributions made in currrent and 2 preceding fiscal years and earnings thereon are not exempt. Restrictions also apply to joint debtors.	CV § 34-34
Growing crops	no limit	CV § 8.01-489
Awards to crime victims	no limit	CV § 19.2-368.12
Proceeds & avails of life insurance policies payable to another	no limit	CV § 38.1-448
Cash surrender or loan value of life insurance policies of householder or head of family	policies totaling $10,000 of insurance coverage (100% if right to change beneficiary is reserved)	CV § 38.1-449 CV § 38.1-448
Group life insurance policies & proceeds	no limit	CV §§ 38.1-482 & 51-111.67:8
Life benefit company benefits	no limit	CV § 38.1-510
Fraternal Benefit Society benefits	no limit	CV § 38.1-638.33
Burial society benefits	no limit	CV § 38.1-563
Burial contracts	$200	CV § 11-28

(continued on next page)

VIRGINIA

(continued from previous page)

Type of Property	Amount of Exemption	Statute Creating Exemption
Arms, uniforms & equipment of national guardsman or naval militiaman	no limit	CV § 44-96
Industrial sick benefit insurance benefits	no limit	CV § 38.1-488
Workmen's Compensation benefits	no limit	CV § 65.1-82
Unemployment Compensation benefits	no limit	CV § 60.1-125
Earnings of debtor under court-approved assignment for benefit of creditors	no limit	CV § 55-165
Retirement benefits under Supplemental Retirement Act	no limit	CV § 51-111
Retirement benefits of county, city & town employees	no limit	CV §§ 51-112 & 51-127.7
Public assistance payments	100%	CV § 63.1-88
Specific partnership property	100% of partner's interest	CV § 50-25(2)(c)
Periodic payments under accident & sickness insurance policies	100%	CV § 63.1-88

NOTE: Tenancies by the entirety may be exempt under 11 USC § 522(b)(2)(B). See Ragsdale v. Genesco, inc., 674 F. 2nd 277.

WASHINGTON

Use of federal bankruptcy exemptions in 11 USC § 522(d) permitted in this state.

Type of Property	Amount of Exemption	Statute Creating Exemption
Homestead consisting of house or mobile home in which owner resides, plus appurtenances & land, if any, on which situate	$30,000 (proceeds of sale of homestead exempt for 1 year in same amount)	RCW 6.13.030
NOTE: Homestead declaration must be recorded in county recording office if property is not yet occupied as homestead.		
All wearing apparel	no limit, except value of furs, jewelry & personal ornaments cannot exceed $1000	RCW 6.15.010(1)
Private library of debtor	$1,500	RCW 6.15.010(2)
Family pictures & keepsakes	100%	RCW 6.15.010(2)
Household goods, appliances, furniture & home & yard equipment of debtor & family, including provisions & fuel	$2,700	RCW 6.15.010(3)(a)
Other personal property of debtor and family, except personal earnings	$1000 with $100 limit on cash and $100 limit on bank accounts & securities	RCW 6.15.010(3)(b)
2 motor vehicles used for personal transportation	$2,500 in aggregate value	RCW 6.15.010(3)(c)
Farm trucks, stock, tools, equipment, supplies & seed of farmer	$5,000	RCW 6.15.010(4)(a)
Library & office furniture, equipment & supplies of physician, attorney, clergyman or other professional person	$5,000	RCW 6.15.010(4)(b)
Tools, instruments & materials used to carry on trade for support of debtor & family	$5,000	RCW 6.15.010(4)(c)
Disposable earnings (earnings less deductions required by law)	75% OR 30 times the federal minimum hourly wage per week, WHICHEVER IS GREATER	RCW 6.27.150
Federal pension benefits	100%	RCW 6.15.020(2)
Debtor's right to retirement, disability or death benefits from employee benefit plan qualified under Internal Revenue Code	100% of qualified amounts	RCW 6.15.020(3)
Fire insurance proceeds of policies covering exempt property	100% of exemption for covered property	RCW 6.15.030
Industrial insurance benefits	100%	RCW 51.32.040
Unemployment compensation benefits	100% (support claims excepted)	RCW 50.40.020
Disability insurance benefits	100%	RCW 48.18.400
Proceeds & avails of life insurance policies wherein beneficiary is person other than the insured or the person effecting the policy	100%	RCW 48.18.410
Group life insurance proceeds	100%	RCW 48.18.420
Annuity contract benefits	$250 per month	RCW 48.18.430
Public assistance grants & payments	100%	RCW 74.08.210, 74.13.070
Income or proceeds from trust for benefit of debtor created & funded by another person	100%	RCW 6.32.250
Uniforms, arms & equipment of state militiaman	100%	RCW 38.40.080
Personal or family burying grounds	100%	RCW 68.24.220, 68.20.120
City employees retirement benefits	100%	RCW 41.44.240, 41.28.200, 41.20.180
Police & Firemen's retirement benefits	100%	RCW 41.26.180, 41.20.180, 41.24.240 & 43.43.310
State employees retirement benefits	100%	RCW 41.40.380
Teachers retirement benefits	100%	RCW 41.32.055
Judges retirement benefits	100%	RCW 2.10.180, 2.12.090
Specific partnership property	100% of partner's interest	RCW 25.04.250
Fraternal Benefit Society benefits	100%	RCW 48.36A.180
Crime victims' compensation	100%	RCW 7.68.070, 51.32.040
Earnings from work release	100%	RCW 72.65.060
Property of incompetent	100%	RCW 11.92.060

WEST VIRGINIA

Use of federal bankruptcy exemptions in 11 USC § 522(d) not permitted in this state. See WVC § 38–10–4.

Type of Property	Amount of Exemption	Statute Creating Exemption
Homestead of resident head of household	$5,000	WVC § 38–9–1
Personal property of head of household	$1,000	WVC § 38–8–1
Tools of trade of mechanic, artisan or laborer	$50	WVC § 38–8–1
NOTE – The total exemptions allowed to one person under WVC § 38–8–1 is $1,000.		
Unripe crops	100%	WVC § 38–8–14
Proceeds & avails of life insurance policies wherein the beneficiary is a person other than the insured or the person affecting the policy	100%	WVC § 33–6–27
Group life insurance proceeds	100%	WVC § 33–6–28
Fraternal Benefit Society benefits	100%	WVC § 33–23–21
Workmen's compensation benefits	100%	WVC § 23–4–18
Unemployment compensation benefits	100% (certain claims excepted)	WVC § 21A–10–2
Public welfare assistance payments	100%	WVC § 9–5–1
Judges' retirement benefits	100%	WVC § 51–9–14
Public employees retirement benefits	100%	WVC § 5–10–46
Teachers retirement benefits	100%	WVC § 18–7A–30
NOTE – The following exemptions apply only to bankruptcy proceedings.		
Debtor's interest in real or personal property, including a cooperative, used as a residence by debtor or a dependent, or in a burial plot	$7,500	WVC § 38–10–4(a)
One motor vehicle	$1,200	WVC § 38–10–4(b)
Household furnishings & goods, wearing apparel, appliances, books, animals, crops or musical instruments, that are held primarily for the personal, family or household use of debtor or a dependent	$200 per item $1,000 aggregate	WVC § 38–10–4(c)
Jewelry held primarily for personal, family or household use of debtor or a dependent	$500	WVC § 38–10–4(d)
Any property of debtor	$400 plus any unused portion of the residence exemption under WVC § 30–10–4(a) above	WVC § 38–10–4(e)
Implements, professional books or tools of trade of debtor or a dependent	$750	WVC § 38–10–4(f)
Any unmatured life insurance contract owned by debtor other than credit life insurance	100%	WVC § 38–10–4(g)
Accrued interest or dividends or loan value of unmatured life insurance contract owned by debtor wherein the insured is the debtor or a person of whom the debtor is a dependent	$4,000 less any transfers made under nonforfeiture provisions in policy	WVC § 38–10–4(h)
Professionally prescribed health aids of debtor or dependents	100%	WVC § 38–10–4(i)
Social Security benefits, unemployment compensation, local public assistance benefits, veterans benefits & disability, illness or unemployment benefits	100%	WVC § 38–10–4(j)(1), (2) & (3)

(continued on next page)

WEST VIRGINIA

Type of Property	Amount of Exemption	Statute Creating Exemption
Alimony, support or separate maintenance	amount reasonably necessary for support of debtor & dependents	WVC § 38–10–4(j)(4)
Payments under stock bonus, pension profitsharing, annuity, or similar plan or contract on account of illness, disability, death, or age or length of service	Amount reasonably necessary for support of debtor & dependents	WVC § 38–10–4(j)(5)

NOTE: This exemption does not apply if the plan or contract was established by an insider that employed debtor when the debtor's rights under the plan or contract arose, the payment is on account of age or length of service, and the plan or contract does not qualify under 26 USC §§ 401(a), 403(a), 403(b), 408 or 409.

Type of Property	Amount of Exemption	Statute Creating Exemption
Crime victim's reparation law awards	100%	WVC § 38–10–4(k)(1)
Payments on account of the wrongful death of an individual of whom the debtor was a dependent	Amount reasonably necessary to support debtor & dependents	WVC § 38–10–4(k)(2)
Payments under life insurance contract insuring life of an individual of whom the debtor was a dependent on the date of death	Amount reasonably necessary to support debtor & dependents	WVC § 38–10–4(k)(3)
Payments on account of personal bodily injury, not including pain & suffering or compensation for actual pecuniary loss, of debtor or an individual of whom the debtor is a dependent	$7,500	WVC § 38–10–4(k)(4)
Payments in compensation of loss of future earnings of debtor or an individual of whom the debtor was a dependent	Amount reasonably necessary to support debtor & dependents	WVC § 38–10–4(k)(5)
Specific partnership property	100% of partner's interest	WVC § 47–8A–25

WISCONSIN

Use of federal bankruptcy exemptions in 11 USC § 522(d) permitted in this state

Type of Property	Amount of Exemption	Statute Creating Exemption
Homestead occupied by resident owner (includes proceeds from sale of homestead held with intent to procure another homestead for 2 years)	$40,000.00 NOTE– includes dwelling (including condominium, mobile home, house trailer or coop.) and up to 40 acres of land. See WSA § 990.01(14).	WSA § 815.21
Cemetary lots, tombstones, coffins & other articles of burial intended for burial of debtor or debtor's family	100%	WSA § 815.18(3)(a)
Equipment, inventory, farm products, and professional books used in business of debtor or dependent	$7,500	WSA § 815.18(3)(b)
Alimony, child support, family support, or maintenance payments	Amount reasonably necessary for support of debtor and dependents	WSA § 815.18(3)(c)
Household goods & furnishings, wearing apparel, keepsakes, jewelry & articles of adornment, appliances, books, musical instruments, firearms, sporting goods, animals, and other personalty held primarily for the personal, family or household use of the debtor or a dependent	$5,000	WSA § 815.18(3)(d)
Federal disability insurance benefits	100%	WSA § 815.18(3)(ds)
Fire and casualty insurance proceeds on exempt property for two years after receipt	100%	WSA § 815.18(3)(e)
Fire and police pension fund benefits payable on account of service in Wisconsin city of more than 100,000 population	100%	WSA § 815.18(3)(ef)
Unmatured life insurance contracts insuring and owned by debtor, except credit life contracts	100%	WSA § 815.18(3)(f)
Debtor's aggregate interest in accrued dividends, interest or loan value of all unmatured life insurance contracts owned by debtor and insuring the debtor, a dependent, or an individual of whom the debtor is a dependent	$4,000	WSA § 815.18(3)(f)
Motor vehicles	$1,200 plus unused portion of exemption for household goods, etc.	WSA § 815.18(3)(g)
Net income per week	The greater of 75% or 30 times the greater of the state or federal minimum wage, (limited to amount reasonably necessary to support debtor and dependents)	WSA § 815.18(3)(h)
Life insurance, personal injury and wrongful death claims, and property traceable thereto	100% ($25,000 limit on certain personal injury claims)	WSA § 815.18(3)(i)
Assets and benefits of retirement, pension, disability, death benefits, stock bonus, profit sharing, annuity, individual retirement accounts, or similar plans	100% NOTE– plans must qualify under I.R.C. or meet other qualifications	WSA § 815.18(3)(j)
Depository accounts	$1,000	WSA § 815.18(3)(k)
War pensions	100%	WSA § 815.18(3)(n)
Schoolteachers' retirement benefits	100%	WSA § 42.52
Public employees' retirement benefits	100%	WSA § 41.22(1)(a)
Aid to families with dependent children	100%	WSA § 49.41
Social services payments & benefits, both state & federal	100%	WSA § 49.41
Crime victims awards	100%	WSA § 949.07
Fraternal Benefit Society benefits	100%	WSA § 614.96
Public employee trust fund benefits	100%	WSA § 40.08(1)
City employee retirement benefits	100%	WSA § 66.81
Tenant's interest in housing co-op	100%	WSA § 182.004(6)
Salary used to purchase exempt bonds	100%	WSA § 20.921(1)(e)
Veterans' benefits	100%	WSA § 45.35(8)(b)
Workmen's compensation benefits	100%	WSA § 102.27
Unemployment compensation benefits	100%	WSA § 108.13
Specific partnership property	100% of partner's interest	WSA § 178.21

WYOMING

Type of Property	Amount of Exemption	Statute Creating Exemption
Homestead occupied by resident	$10,000	WSA § 1-20-101

NOTE: The homestead exemption also applies to the survivors of a deceased homesteader; see WSA § 1-20-103. A homestead may consist of a house and lot in a city or town, a farm, or a trailer or other moveable home; see WSA § 1-20-104. Exemption may be claimed by each person if jointly owned and occupied by 2 or more persons; see WSA § 1-20-102(b).

Type of Property	Amount of Exemption	Statute Creating Exemption
Necessary wearing apparel (includes wedding rings, but not other jewelry.	$1,000	WSA § 1-20-105
Family Bible, pictures and school books	100%	WSA § 1-20-106(a)(i)
Lot in burial ground	100%	WSA § 1-20-106(a)(ii)
Furniture, bedding, provisions, and household articles of any kind	$2,000 (if 2 or more persons occupy same residence, each may claim exemption)	WSA § 1-20-106(a)(iii)
One motor vehicle	$2,000	WSA § 1-20-106(a)(iv)
Tools, implements, and stock in trade used to carry on trade or business, OR library, instruments and implements of professional person	$2,000	WSA § 1-20-106(b)
Earnings for personal services rendered within last 60 days (must be necessary to support family)	50%	WSA § 1-17-411
Proceeds and avails of life insurance policies wherein the beneficiary is not the insured	100%	WSA § 26-15-129
Proceeds and avails of disability insurance policies	100%	WSA § 26-15-130
Group life and disability insurance benefits	100%	WSA § 26-15-131
Proceeds of annuity contracts	$350 per month	WSA § 26-15-132
Fraternal Benefit Society benefits	100%	WSA § 26-29-116
Unemployment compensation benefits	100%	WSA § 27-3-319
Worker's compensation benefits	100%	WSA § 27-12-708
Public assistance payments	100%	WSA § 42-1-114
Seal of notary public	100%	WSA § 32-1-106
Wyoming Retirement System benefits	100%	WSA § 9-3-426
Highway patrol and Game & Fish Warden retirement benefits	100%	WSA § 31-3-120
Firemen's pension benefits	100%	WSA § 15-5-209
Liquor licenses & permits	100%	WSA § 12-4-604
Earnings of inmates	100%	WSA § 7-13-724
Specific partnership property	100% of partner's interest	WSA § 17-13-502
Pension or annuity benefits of retired employees	100%	WSA § 1-20-110(a)(i)
Retirement or annuity funds of self employed persons	100% of amounts qualified under Internal Revenue Code	WSA § 1-20-110(a)(ii)

NOTE: Tenancies by the entirety may be exempt under 11 USC § 522(b)(2)(B). See Amick v. Elwood, 77 Wyo. 269, 314 P. 2nd 944.

SUBJECT INDEX

For Chapter Two

(Chapter 7 Cases)

ARGYLE PUBLISHING COMPANY

10395 West Colfax Avenue - Suite 380
Lakewood, Colorado 80215-3925
Toll Free 1-800-955-4569
Local: (303) 237-6467
Fax: (303) 237-2617

March 10, 1993

Dear Instructor:

Enclosed is a complimentary copy of **The Attorney's Handbook on Consumer Bankruptcy and Chapter 13**, 17th edition, 1993, which we publish. We hope that you will consider using this book as a text or course book in the bankruptcy or debtor-creditor course that you teach at your school.

The unique features of this handbook include the following:

(1) It contains a series of questions and answers about Chapter 7 and Chapter 13 that are designed to inform the reader of the basic concepts and terminology of bankruptcy proceedings (see pages 5 and 121 respectively).

(2) The text is easy to read and understand.

(3) It contains bankruptcy worksheets, completed bankruptcy forms, a sample Chapter 13 plan, and samples of commonly used motions, notices, orders, applications and documents (see pages 70-118 and 169-179).

(4) It covers Chapter 12 cases (see page 181-206).

(5) It contains the Bankruptcy Code and the Bankruptcy Rules.

(6) It contains a list of exempt property for each state (see page 265).

(continued on next page)

SUBJECT INDEX

For Chapter Two

(Chapter 7 Cases)

(continued on next page)

SUBJECT INDEX
For Chapter Two
(Chapter 7 Cases)

SUBJECT INDEX
For Chapter Two
(Chapter 7 Cases)

SUBJECT INDEX

For Chapter Three

(Chapter 13 Cases)

SUBJECT INDEX
For Chapter Three
(Chapter 13 Cases)

SUBJECT INDEX

For Chapter Four

(Chapter 12 Cases)